WEB TECHNOLOGIES

TCP/IP, Web/Java Programming, and Cloud Computing

Third Edition

ABOUT THE AUTHORS

Achyut Godbole is currently the Managing Director of Softexcel Consultancy Services advising global companies about strategies of growth and setting up of delivery organizations and processes for offshore centers.

Having been a National Merit Scholar throughout his educational career and with a BTech. in Chemical Engineering from IIT, Mumbai, Godbole has over 30 years of software development experience in India, USA and UK in companies like IBM, Hindustan Unilever (Formerly Hindustan Lever), Systime (UK), Syntel, L&T Infotech, Apar Technologies and Disha Technologies.He has contributed to building of companies such as Patni (as GM), Syntel (as MD), L&T Infotech (as CEO), Apar Technologies (as CEO) and Disha Technologies (as Executive Director). All these companies grew many times in terms of revenue and profitability during his tenure.

Apart from this, Godbole has written technical books like *Operating Systems, Data Communications and Networking*, and *Web Technologies,* all published by McGraw-Hill Education (India). Some of these have been published in Singapore by McGraw-Hill for international distribution and have been translated in different languages including Chinese.

Atul Kahate has over 17 years of experience in Information Technology in India and abroad in various capacities. He currently works as Adjunct Professor in Computer Science in Pune University and Symbiosis International University. His last IT employment was as Consulting Practice Director at Oracle Financial Services Software Limited (earlier known as I-Flex Solutions Limited). He has conducted several training programs/seminars in institutions such as IIT, Symbiosis, Pune University, and many other colleges.

A prolific writer, Kahate is also the author of 38 books on Computer Science, Science, Technology, Medicine, Economics, Cricket, Management, and History. Books such as *Web Technologies, Cryptography and Network Security, Operating Systems, Data Communications and Networks,* and *An Introduction to Database Management Systems* are used as texts in several universities in India and many other countries. Some of these have been translated into Chinese.

Atul Kahate has won prestigious awards such as Computer Society of India's award for contribution to IT literacy, Indradhanu's Yuvonmesh Puraskar, Indira Group's Excellence Award, Maharashtra Sahitya Parishad's "Granthakar Puraskar", and several others.

He has appeared on quite a few programmes on TV channels such as Doordarshan's Sahyadri channel, IBN Lokmat, Star Maaza, and Saam TV related to IT, education, and careers. He has also worked as official cricket scorer and statistician in several international cricket matches.

Besides these achievements, he has written over 4000 articles and various columns on IT, Cricket, Science, Technology, History, Medicine, Economics, Management, careers in popular newspapers/ magazines such as *Loksatta, Sakal, Maharashtra Times, Lokmat, Lokprabha, Saptahik Sakal, Divya Marathi*, among others.

WEB TECHNOLOGIES

TCP/IP, Web/Java Programming, and Cloud Computing

Third Edition

Achyut Godbole

Managing Director

Softexcel Consultancy Services

Atul Kahate

Adjunct Professor

Pune University and Symbiosis International University

Author in Computer Science

McGraw Hill Education (India) Private Limited

NEW DELHI

McGraw Hill Education Offices

New Delhi New York St Louis San Francisco Auckland Bogotá Caracas
Kuala Lumpur Lisbon London Madrid Mexico City Milan Montreal
San Juan Santiago Singapore Sydney Tokyo Toronto

McGraw Hill Education (India) Private Limited

Published by McGraw Hill Education (India) Private Limited
P-24, Green Park Extension, New Delhi 110 016

Web Technologies: TCP/IP, Web/Java Programming, and Cloud Computing, 3/e

ISBN 13: 978-9-38-328657-7

ISBN 10: 9-38-328657-1

Vice President and Managing Director: *Ajay Shukla*

Head—Higher Education (Publishing and Marketing): *Vibha Mahajan*
Publishing Manager (SEM & Tech. Ed.): *Shalini Jha*
Asst. Sponsoring Editor: *Smruti Snigdha*
Editorial Researcher: *Sourabh Maheshwari*
Manager—Production Systems: *Satinder S Baveja*
Copy Editor: *Preyoshi Kundu*
Sr. Production Executive: *Suhaib Ali*
Asst. General Manager (Marketing)—Higher Education: *Vijay Sarathi*
Sr. Product Specialist (SEM & Tech. Ed.): *Tina Jajoriya*
Sr. Graphic Designer—Cover: *Meenu Raghav*

General Manager—Production: *Rajender P Ghansela*
Manager—Production: *Reji Kumar*

Typeset at The Composers, 260, C.A. Apt., Paschim Vihar, New Delhi 110 063, and printed at
India Binding house, A-98, Sector-65, Noida U.P.

Cover: India Binding house

RAZBCRCODRQDL

To

Sulabha and Sharad Pishavikar
Vinayak and Vaishali Godbole
Pushpa Agarkar
For always being there to encourage
and applaud!

Achyut Godbole

To

my parents
Late Dr Meena and Dr Shashikant Kahate
For always giving me the freedom to
carve my own path!

Atul Kahate

CONTENTS

PREFACE

ABOUT THE BOOK

Web technologies are one of the most crucial areas today. It is a very vast subject, ranging from basic concepts in protocols to the latest trends such as cloud computing and web usability. Consequently, these topics are covered in this edition. The main focus of the book is to explain every topic in a very lucid fashion with plenty of diagrams.

The response received from the students, teachers, and IT professionals in the last two editions has been overwhelming. *Web Technologies* is already in use as a textbook or source of reference in several undergraduate and postgraduate course involving computer science/data communications/Web technologies/Internet concepts as a subject. The present edition would not only satisfy the needs of these syllabi, but would also lead to updates to these syllabi.

The book is meant to explain the key concepts in Web technologies to anyone who has basic understanding in computer science and networking concepts.

SALIENT FEATURES OF THE BOOK

- Balanced coverage includes TCP/IP architecture and programming aspects imparting a complete view of Internet and Web technologies
- Lucid explanations with numerous diagrams and illustrations
- Coverage of all the latest and futuristic technologies
- Plenty of hands-on examples for readers to try out on their own
- Focus on practical situations along with relevant theory
- Java programming aspects enhanced through elaboration of the topics viz. Java Servlets, JavaScript, HTML

- Enhanced pedagogy includes
  150 Multiple-Choice Questions
  150 Long Answer-type Questions
  75 Exercises
  621 Illustrations

NEW TO THIS EDITION

- Topical additions such as TCP sockets, Java Servlets, JavaScript
- New chapters on PHP, Cloud Computing and Web Usability
- Latest trends like Struts 2, HTML 5, etc.

CHAPTER ORGANIZATION

Chapter 1 introduces the concept of networking protocols. It then discusses the OSI protocol suite. The organization of the OSI model and the details of the various layers are discussed with relevant examples. **Chapter 2** introduces the idea of internetworking. The concepts of internetworking, what it takes to form an internetwork are discussed. We also discuss the basics of the Internet, its history and architecture.

Chapters 3 to 6 discuss the TCP/IP protocol suite in great depth. All the key aspects of TCP/IP and all the important TCP/IP protocols are discussed. **Chapter 3** discusses the Internet layer protocols, namely IP, ARP, RARP and ICMP. We examine why IP makes the Internet such an exciting proposition, and discuss the other protocols in the context of IP. **Chapter 4** covers the two transport layer protocols in the TCP/IP suite: the reliable TCP and the unreliable UDP. We also study the differences between the two. **Chapter 5** examines some of the key application of TCP/IP, namely the DNS, email, FTP and TFTP. The important email protocols, such as SMTP, POP and IMAP are discussed. We also examine how FTP and TFTP work for file transfer applications. **Chapter 6** introduces the key Web application protocols, HTTP and WWW. For the sake of completeness, we also discuss the older TELNET protocol. In this chapter, we also study what HTML is, and how it is used in the creation of Web pages.

Chapter 7 covers the important technical topics of JavaScript and Ajax. We cover all the important syntaxes of these extremely popular technologies with several examples that can be tried out by the reader easily. **Chapter 8** is a new addition. It covers the widely used PHP-MySQL technology that is used to create powerful Web sites. Starting from the basic syntaxes in these technologies, the chapter covers all the important concepts and examples. **Chapter 9** discusses Microsoft's popular .NET technology with reference to the Internet. Here the ASP.NET is also discussed. It is a very simple and yet powerful way of creating dynamic Web sites with minimal effort.

Chapter 10 moves on to cover Java Web technologies. Starting with simple Java Servlets and JSP, the chapter moves onto other important Java Web technologies such as Struts and JSF. The chapter contains many examples that can be tried out by the reader. **Chapter 11** talks about the various security issues related to the Internet. We study the basics of cryptography here. We study what are digital certificates, digital signatures, how they can be created and used. **Chapter 12** deals with the remaining Internet security aspects. More specifically, here we concentrate on the network security areas instead of the application security areas, which are covered in the earlier chapter.

Chapter 13 discusses the exciting new technology of XML. We take a technical look at the XML world, and also see how it is useful in the design of Web-based solutions. More specifically, we concentrate on the issues that make XML *the modern ASCII*. **Chapter 14** is a new chapter that covers the popular Cloud computing technology. We talk about what we mean by cloud computing, why it is useful and how it can be used in practice. Various conceptual and technical aspects pertaining to Cloud technologies are covered here. **Chapter 15** is a new chapter that covers the aspects pertaining to Web Usability. More specifically, we explain how to ensure that the Web pages and Web sites that we create are easier on the user. Several tips and guidelines in this context are provided.

Each chapter has an introduction that explains the scope of coverage and a chapter summary at the end. There are multiple-choice and detailed questions to verify the students' understanding. Several case studies are included at appropriate places to give a practical flavor to the subject. Every difficult concepts are explained using diagrams. Unnecessary mathematics has been avoided wherever possible.

WEB SUPPLEMENTS

The following web supplements are available at *http://www.mhhe.com/godbole/webtech3:*

- **For Students**
  Extra Reading Material
  Self-Assessment Quiz
  Web References
- **For Instructors**
  Solutions Manual
  PowerPoint Slides
  Sample Tests

ACKNOWLEDGEMENTS

We would like to thank our family members, colleagues, and friends for all their help. Hundreds of students and professors have appreciated the previous editions of the book, which makes the efforts of coming up with a new edition very enjoyable. More specifically, we would like to thank Atul's ex-students Manish Singh, Swapnil Panditrao and Pranav Sorte, who have helped us with the third edition, including writing completely fresh content. Their efforts are highly appreciated.

We would like to thank the editorial team of McGraw-Hill Education for their support in bringing out the present edition.

In addition, we would also like to thank the following reviewers for assessing the script and providing constructive suggestions:

J P Rankhambe	*K.E. Society's Rajarambapu Institute of Technology, Sangli*
Soumadip Ghosh	*Academy of Technology, Adisaptagram*
G P Vishwas	*Indian School of Mines, Dhanbad*
V Senthil Kumaran	*PSG College of Technology, Coimbatore*

Achyut Godbole
Atul Kahate

FEEDBACK

Readers are welcome to send any feedback/comments on our Websites *www.achyutgodbole.com* and *www.atulkahate.com* (in the Testimonials section) or via email at *achyut.godbole@gmail.com* and *akahate@gmail.com*.

Achyut Godbole
Atul Kahate

PUBLISHER'S NOTE

Do you have a feature request or a suggestion? We are always open to new ideas (the best ideas come from you!). You may send your comments to *tmh.csefeedback@gmail.com* (don't forget to mention the title and authors' names in the subject line).

NETWORKING PROTOCOLS AND OSI MODEL 1

INTRODUCTION

Protocol is nothing but a convention. We encounter this term quite often in newspapers when describing the meeting between the leaders of two nations. To signify that "Everything is okay and the train can start" by a green flag is also a protocol. When we write a letter, we follow a certain protocol. The place where we write the address, afix the stamp, write the name of the recipient, and the way we begin with the pleasantries and write "Yours lovingly" or "Yours sincerely", etc., all define a protocol.

Protocols can and normally have layers hidden in them, if we look into them a little carefully. A good example is human conversation, in general, and over the telephone, in particular. Figure 1.1 depicts these layers. We will take this example and describe the exact steps to learn about these layers. An interesting point is that we do this without knowing that we use protocols. While studying this, we will encounter a number of terms, which are also used in the computer networks.

We will assume that two persons *X* and *Y* want to have a conversation over the telephone about the World War and we will also assume that each one is taking down what the other has to say. Thus, we will term this *World War* as an *idea*. Normally, the conversation takes place in terms of several messages from either end, hopefully one after the other. A message is a block of statements or sentences. A message could also consist of only one word such as *okay* or *yes*, denoting a **positive acknowledgement (ACK)** of what has been heard or received. A message could also mean a **negative acknowledgement (NAK)** or request for repeating such as *Come again* or, *Pardon me* or, *Can you repeat please,* etc. Remember that this can happen both ways. For instance, a typical conversation could be as follows.

X: In World War II, the Allied countries should have.... However, they did not do so because of the climatic conditions. In addition, they did not have enough ammunition.

Y: Yeah, I agree.

X: Also, if you consider the factor of the atomic energy....

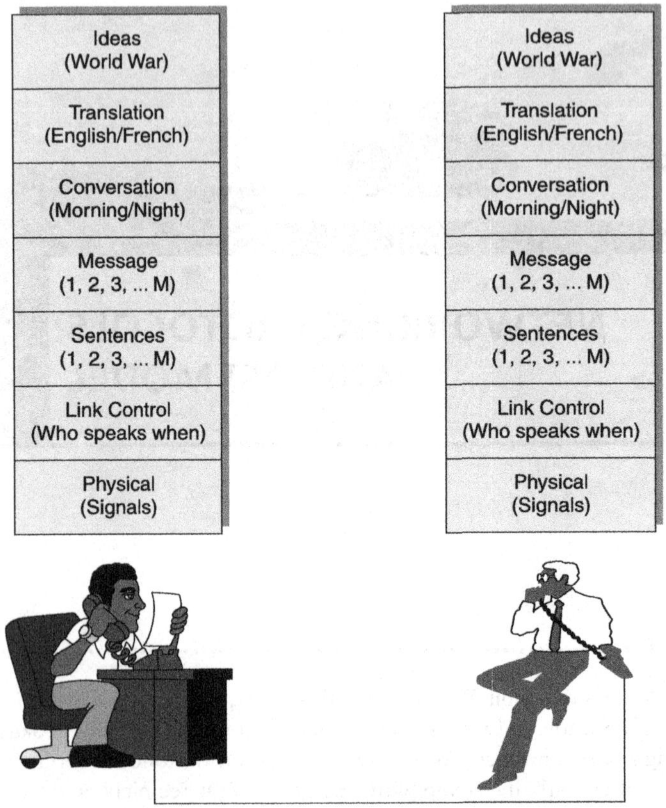

Fig. 1.1 *Layers in human communication*

Y: No, but, I think, there is another angle to it. If you consider the boundary between the two countries, it will be obvious. There is also a great book on the subject.

X: Come again.

Y: No, but I think there is another angle to it.

X: Yeah, but that is not the only factor...

Y: Could you repeat, please?

X: ...

Therefore, at the level of *ideas*, both X and Y feel that they are discussing an idea such as *World War*. However, in reality the conversation consists of a number of messages from both sides, as discussed before. Therefore, at a lower level, the view would be that a number of messages are sent at both ends. The protocol at this level decides what denotes a positive acknowledgement, what denotes a negative acknowledgement, etc., for the entire message.

A message could be too long. In this case, it may not be wise for *X* to speak for half an hour, only to receive a request for repeating the message in the end from *Y*. It is, therefore, prudent to send/receive positive or negative acknowledgements after each sentence in a message by *Yeah*, *Okay* or *Come again*, etc. A *sentence* is like a *packet* in the computer parlance. In this case also, one could decide a protocol to necessarily send a positive or negative acknowledgement after each sentence. If that is the case, the sender (the speaker) *X* will not proceed to the next statement until he hears some form of acknowledgement, or otherwise, and, in fact, repeat the statement if he receives a negative acknowledgement before proceeding. An alternative to this would be a *time-out* strategy. The speaker *X* would speak a sentence and wait for some time to hear any kind of acknowledgement. If he does not hear anything back, he assumes that the previous statement was not received properly, and therefore, repeats the sentence. A form of *sliding window* would mean speaking and acknowledging multiple sentences simultaneously, maybe 3 or 4 at a time. This is via media between acknowledging each sentence or the full message. We are not aware of this, but we actually follow all these protocols in daily conversations.

Apart from this **error control**, we also take care of **flow control**. This refers to the speed mismatch between the speaker and the listener. If the speaker speaks too fast, the listener says *Go slow* or *Please wait* if he is taking down the message. In the world of computers, if the receiving computer is not fast enough, or if its memory buffer is full, which cannot hold any further data, it has to request the sender to wait. This is called *flow control*. Thus, the **data link control layer** is responsible for the error control at the sentences level, and the flow control. This layer also decides who is going to speak, when, by a convention, or in brief, who has a control of the medium (in this case, the telephone line). This is called **media access control**. This function of media access control becomes necessary, because, the telephone line is shared between *X* and *Y*, and both can and usually do speak simultaneously, causing chaos. In fact, it can so happen that after a pause, thinking that the other party is waiting to hear from you, you may start speaking. However, exactly at the same time, the other party also can start speaking, thinking that you want the other party to speak. This results in a **collision**. The conversation gets mixed up normally, and both the parties realize about this collision and stop talking for a while (unless it is a married couple!). Hopefully, the parties will pause for different time intervals, thereby avoiding collision. Otherwise, this process repeats. When to start speaking, how long to wait after the collision before restarting, etc., are typical conventions followed at this layer. These are the unwritten protocols of the media access control that we follow in our everyday conversation.

In actual practice, we know that when we speak, the electrical signals in the telephone wires change. This is a **physical layer**. There must be a protocol here, too! This level signifies how the telephone instruments are constructed, the way the telephone wires are manufactured and laid, the signal levels to denote engaged or busy tone, the signal level to generate a ring, the signal levels required to carry human voice, etc. This is a protocol at a physical layer. Obviously, if a telephone and a refrigerator were connected at two ends of a wire, communication would be impossible!

PROTOCOLS IN COMPUTER COMMUNICATIONS.................................. 1.1

The same concept of protocols applies equally well to the computer communications. Let us see, how. Let us imagine a network of computers, as shown in Fig. 1.2.

Each computer is called a **node**. In distributed processing, different parts of databases/files can and normally do reside on different nodes, as per the need. This necessitates transmitting files or messages from one node to the other as and when needed. Let us assume that node *A* wants to transfer a file *X* to node *D*. Node *A* is not directly connected to node *D*. This is very common, because connecting every node to every other node would mean a huge amount of wiring.

This is the reason that the concept of **store and forward** is used in computer networks. First of all, a path is chosen. Let us say that it is *A-F-G-D*. Using this path, node *A* sends the file to node *F*. The computer at *F* normally has to store this file in its memory buffer or on the disk. This storing is necessary, because the link *F-G* may be busy at this juncture, or node *F* may have received a number of messages/

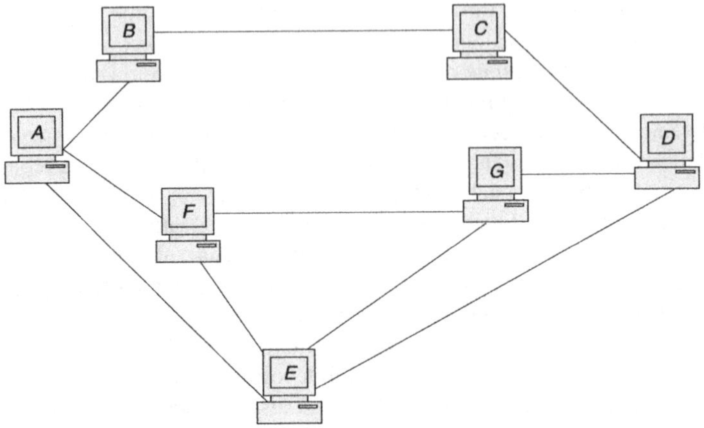

Fig. 1.2 *A typical computer network*

files to be sent to other nodes (*A*, *E* or *G*) already, and those could be waiting in a queue at node *F*. When the link *F-G* is free and ready for transmitting the file from *F* to *G*, node *F* actually transmits it to the node *G*. Thus, the node *F stores and forwards* the file from *A* to *G*. This process repeats until the file reaches the destination node *D*. This procedure demands that each node maintains a memory buffer to store the file, and some software, which controls the queuing of different messages and then transmitting them to the next nodes. This software also will have to take care of error and flow control functions in an error-free manner.

When the file/message is transmitted, both the nodes (source and destination), as well as all the intermediate nodes, have to agree on some basic fundamentals. For example, what is a bit 1 and what is a bit 0? As we know, ultimately, bit 0 and 1 correspond to some physical property (voltage level 0 = bit 0, voltage level 5 = bit 1, etc.). If there is no understanding between the nodes, the bits could be completely misinterpreted. This understanding or protocol at the physical level is called the **physical layer**. It deals with things like bits 0 and 1, the communication modes (serial/parallel, simplex/half-duplex/duplex, synchronous/asynchronous, etc.).

How does the *next* node find out whether the file or the message was received correctly or not? And also, how does that node react if it finds an error? There are several methods to detect an error in transmission. Obviously, we will need to compute the **Cyclic Redundancy Check (CRC)** for the whole file, append it with the data, re-compute the CRC on the received data portion at the destination, and compare the received and computed CRC to ensure that they are the same.

There are many ways in which the positive or negative acknowledgement can be sent by the receiving node to the source node. If no error is detected, the receiving node can send a positive acknowledgement back, meaning that everything is OK. However, if an error is detected, the receiving node can either send a negative acknowledgement or choose not to send anything. The latter is called **time out**. In this method, the source node can wait for some time for the positive acknowledgement and having not received it in a specific time, conclude that the file has not been received OK at the destination and then send it again. This is a good method, except that when the source node starts sending the file again, the **positive acknowledgement** (*OK* message) from the receiving node could have been already traveled half way to the source node. When this acknowledgement is received at the source node, it will be too late for the source node! The file/message would have been already sent twice to the destination node! There is normally a protocol to handle such a situation (e.g., the receiving node discards the second copy of the file). A surer way is to definitely send either *OK* or *NOT OK* message back, and not to use the time out method, i.e., wait until either a positive or **negative acknowledgement** is received. However, this entails long waits because these messages themselves could take long time to travel, due to the network traffic. The overall network efficiency in this case reduces, as the source node has to wait until it receives *some* acknowledgement.

All these functions of error detection, acknowledgements and retransmissions are clubbed under a name *error control*, and constitute an important part of the communications software, i.e., the **data link layer** in the networking terminology, residing at every node, i.e., the source, destination as well as all the intermediate nodes, because the message has to reach correctly to the *next* node first, before it reaches the destination node correctly. The data link layer also takes care of flow control and the speed mismatch between any two adjacent communicating computers. If the sending computer sends data too fast, it can get lost at the destination. The speeds, therefore, have to be continuously adjusted or monitored. This is called as *flow control*.

If an error is detected, the entire file will have to be retransmitted. If the file size is large, the probability of an error is higher, as well as the time that it will take for retransmission. Also, the chances of an error in a retransmission are higher. This is the reason that large messages (such as a file) are broken down in smaller chunks or blocks. These are called **packets**. To avoid error, data is sent in packets also when two pairs of computers want to use a shared transmission line. Imagine that computer *A* wants to send a big file of 10 MB to computer *D* by a route *A-F-G-D*. Also, at the same time, computer *F* wants to send a small file of 2 KB to computer *G*. Further, suppose that the transmission of the big file over the link *F-G* starts momentarily ahead of the smaller file transmission over *F-G*. Assuming that only one pair of computers can use one transmission line exclusively, the smaller transmission will have to wait for a long time before the bigger transmission gets over. Thus, a bigger transmission simply can hold up smaller transmissions, causing great injustice. Thus, it is better that each communication party breaks down their transmission into packets and takes turn to send down packets. Thus, both the files are broken down into packets first. At node *F*, a packet from the big file is followed by a packet from the small file, etc. This is called as *Time Division Multiplexing*, (TDM). At the other end (*G*), the smaller file is reassembled and used, whereas the packets for the bigger file are separated, stored and forwarded to the node *D*.

Obviously, every packet will have to have a header containing **source address**, **destination address**, packet number and CRC. The destination address is used for ***forwarding*** or ***routing*** the packet to the *next* node, and ultimately to the final destination. The packet number helps in reassembling the packets in case they reach the destination out of sequence. The CRC is used for error control.

There are two ways in which the path can be chosen. One is the **virtual circuit** approach, and the other is the **datagram approach**. In a virtual circuit, the path is chosen in the beginning and all the packets belonging to the same message follow the same route. For instance, if a route *A-F-G-D* is chosen to send the file from *A* to *D*, all the packets of that file will traverse by the same route. At *D*, therefore, they will be received in the same order only, thereby avoiding the function of re-sequencing. This is because, even if packet 2 is received erroneously by node *G* from node *F*, node *G* will ask for its retransmission. Node *F* will then retransmit packet 2, and before sending packet 3, wait until making sure that node *G* has received packet 2 without any error. It will send packet 3 only after ensuring this. All this necessitates maintaining many buffers at different nodes for storing and forwarding the packets. As against this, in datagram, the entire circuit is not pre-determined. A packet is sent to the *next* node on the route, which is the *best* at that time, and will take the packet to the ultimate destination.

Choosing a path or *routing* is not a simple task by any stretch of imagination. Remember, each node is receiving many packets from different nodes to be temporarily stored and then forwarded to different nodes. For instance, node *F* in Fig. 1.2 can have packets received from *A* to be forwarded to *E* or *G*, or meant for itself. It can also have packets received from *E* to be forwarded to *A* or to *G*, or to *D* via *G*, or the packets meant for itself. Node *F* can be receiving packets from node *G* meant for nodes *A*, *E* or for itself. In addition, node *F* itself will want to send various packets to different nodes. Therefore, the buffer of node *F* will contain all these packets. The source and destination addresses come handy in keeping track of these packets. We can imagine a buffer memory at node *F*, where all these packets are stored and then a scheduling algorithm picks them up one by one and sends or forwards them based on the destination node and the route chosen.

Now, to send the data from node *A* to node *D*, should it be sent via *A-F-G-D* or *A-B-C-D* or *A-E-D* or *A-F-E-D* or *A-F-G-E-D* or *A-F-E-G-D*? Apparently, *A-E-D* seems to be an obvious answer, as *AED* appears to be the shortest route. However, looks can be deceptive. Node *E*'s buffer may be full at a given moment due to a message to be sent to node *A* from nodes *G* or *D*. If we follow a First Come First Serve (FCFS) method for forwarding the messages, there will be a long wait before our message received from *A* will be forwarded to *D*.

This is an example of **network congestion**. These congestion levels have to be known before the route is chosen. Also, a path may be required to be chosen from one node to any other node. Therefore, this information about congestion or load on all the nodes and all the lines should be available at every node. Each node then has algorithms to choose the best path at that moment. This again is an important part of communications software, the **network layer** in the OSI parlance, residing at every node.

Note that although we have shown the network to be consisting of only the computers called as nodes, in real life, it is not so simple. Since these computers in a network are used for specialized purposes (such as running an application program or serving files on request), the job of routing packets from the sending computer to the receiving computer is handled by dedicated computers called **routers**. A router is a special computer that has the sole job of routing packets between the various computers on a network. It decides which packet to forward to which next node, so that it can ultimately reach the final destination. The necessary routing software runs inside the router to carry out this routing process. Therefore, although we have not shown for the sake of simplicity, in real life, we would have a number of routers connecting the various portions of a network to each other.

In the case of the datagram approach, different packets belonging to a single message can travel by different routes. For a packet, a decision is taken about the *next* node to which it should be sent. For instance, at a given moment, the node *F* as well as the line *A-F* could have the least congestion (as compared to *A-E* and *A-B*). Therefore, the packet is sent via the route *A-F*. It takes a finite time for the packet to reach the node *F*, and then for the node *F* to check the CRC and send back the acknowledgement. Only after this, the node *A* decides to send the next packet. However, during this time interval, a number of packets could have arrived at node *F* from node *E*, to be forwarded to either *A* or *G*, or the ones meant for *F* itself. Therefore, the congestion at node *F* may have increased. Hence, the next packet could be sent by node *A* via the route *A-E* to be ultimately forwarded to *D*.

Therefore, different packets belonging to a message may not travel by a given pre-determined route. In this case, it is possible that packet 3 may arrive before packet 2 at node *D*. This necessitates the function of re-sequencing and making sure that the entire message has been received without error. One could think of a CRC for the entire message level to be recomputed and matched before acknowledging the error-free receipt of the whole message. This packet consisting of the acknowledgement for the entire message will travel from the destination node to the source node. This function of ensuring in sequence and error-free receipt of the entire message and its acknowledgement retransmission is again a part of the communication software, typically the Transport Layer in the networking parlance. It is clear that in case of the virtual circuit approach, there is a guarantee that packets will arrive at the destination in the order that they were sent, because, in this case, a route (also called a **Virtual Circuit Number—VCN)** is chosen in the beginning itself. It is used for all the packets belonging to that message. This is also why the packet in the virtual circuits does not require the full source and destination addresses. It only requires the Virtual Circuit Number (VCN). The routing tables maintained at the various nodes maintain the VCN and the *next node* entries. They are sufficient for routing. The datagram approach demands that the packet carry the source and destination node addresses, which can be utilized for routing, and finding the *next node* each time by using **routing algorithms**.

We will realize that there are two types of protocols. Some protocols are necessary between any two adjacent nodes and generally they operate at a packet level, i.e., they make sure that the next adjacent node receives a packet or frame correctly. In the networking parlance, **physical**, **data link** and **network layers** are the layers, which belong to this category. The other type of protocols is between the end points, i.e., the source node and the destination node (nodes *A* and *D* in this example). They make sure a **connection** is established between these two points, **sessions** started and terminated properly, messages (and not packets) are sent/received and acknowledged properly, and necessary **data encryption/decryption** or **compression/decompression** and code conversions/translations are done before handing the message over to the destination node. These are typically **transport**, **session**, **presentation**, and **application** layers in the networking parlance. Table 1.1 depicts this.

Table 1.1 *OSI layers*

Layer Number	*Layer Name*
1 (Lowest) →	Physical
2	Data Link
3	Network
4	Transport
5	Session
6	Presentation
7 (Highest) →	Application

Actually, communication software dealing with algorithm for error/flow control, routing, data compression, encryption, etc., could have been coded in one single program. However, such a program would have been difficult to code and maintain. It is for this reason that this function is divided into its logical parts or modules called as **layers**. Using this concept, many manufacturers started coding their communication software in different number of layers. Thus, there was chaos.

Finally, the standards body ISO decided that there has to be a standard for this communication so that different computers by different manufacturers could communicate with one another very smoothly. They came up with a seven-layer architecture known as **Open System Interconnection (OSI)**. Regardless of the number of layers, all these functions described above have to be taken care of by any communication software, and this software has to reside at every node. Today, OSI has become a standard with which you can compare, though very few have actually implemented the OSI layers exactly as they are described in the standard. Therefore, OSI is actually a *reference model*. We will study it from this perspective.

THE OSI MODEL 1.2

1.2.1 Introduction

The OSI model is structured on seven layers, described in Table 1.1.

The usual manner in which these seven layers are represented is shown in Fig. 1.3.

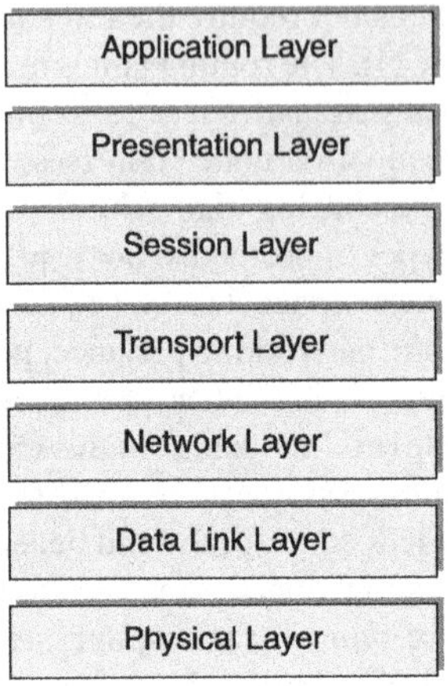

Fig. 1.3 *OSI layers arranged in a hierarchy*

Let us now study Fig. 1.4. Suppose host *X* wants to send a message to another host *Y*. This message would travel via a number of intermediate nodes. These intermediate nodes are concerned with the lowermost three OSI layers, i.e., physical, data link and network, as shown in Fig. 1.4. The other four layers are used by the sender (*X*) and the recipient (*Y*) only. Therefore, they are called *end-to-end layers*.

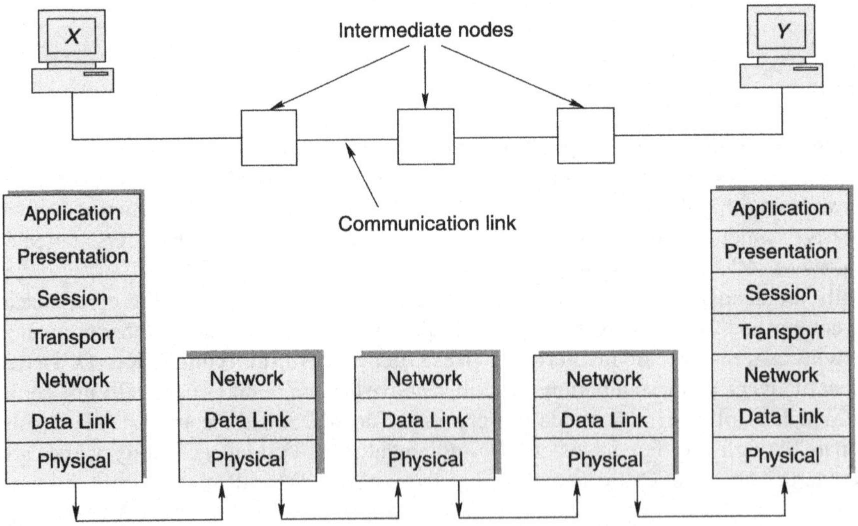

Fig. 1.4 *Communication between hosts X and Y using the OSI layers*

Note that within a host (either *X* or *Y* in this example), each layer calls upon the services of its lower layer. For instance, layer 7 uses the services provided by layer 6. Layer 6 in turn, uses the services of layer 5, and so on. Between X and Y, the communication appears to be taking place between the layers at the same level. This is called **virtual communication** or **virtual path** between X and Y. For instance, layer 7 on host X *thinks* that it is communicating directly with layer 7 on host Y. Similarly, layer 6 on host X and layer 6 on host Y have a *virtual communication* connection between them.

It is pointless keeping all the communication software functions in every node. Therefore, the functions of the bottom-most three layers are contained into a special computer called *router*. You could, now, construct a network of all routers, and imagine that the nodes are attached to the various routers as shown in Fig. 1.5, which is the same as Fig. 1.2, except that we employ routers.

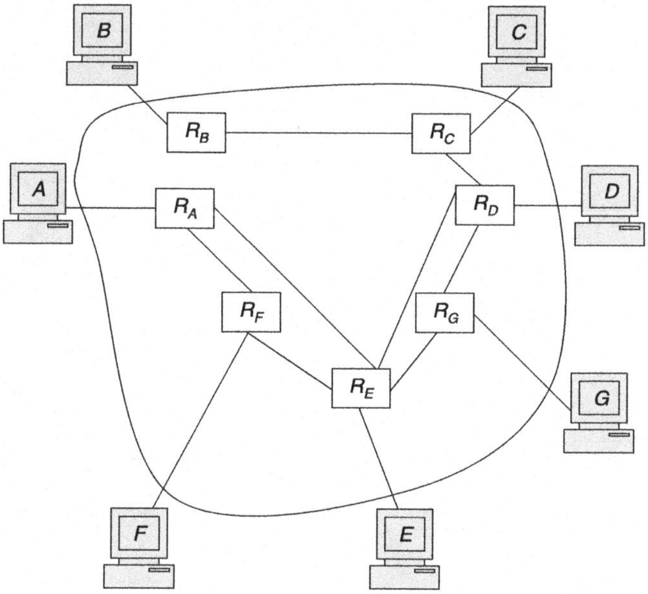

Fig. 1.5 *Routers in a network*

All that we said about data link layer functions, routing, etc., is still valid as we can see. When node A wants to send a message to node F, node A sends it to router R_A. After this, it gets through a specific route to router R_F, and then it reaches the node F.

1.2.2 Layered Organization

The application layer software running at the source node creates the data to be transmitted to the application layer software running at a destination node (remember *virtual path*?). It hands it over to the presentation layer at the source node. Each of the remaining OSI layers from this point onwards adds its own header to the packet as it moves from this layer (presentation layer) to the bottom-most layer (the physical layer) at the source node. At the lowest physical layer, the data is transmitted as voltage pulses across the communication medium, such as coaxial cable.

That means that the application layer (layer 7) hands over the entire data to the presentation layer. Let us call this as *L7 data*, as shown in Fig. 1.6. After the presentation layer receives and processes this data, it adds its own header to the original data and sends it to the next layer in the hierarchy (i.e., the session layer). Therefore, from the sixth (presentation) layer to the fifth (session) layer, the data is sent as *L7 data* + *H6*, as shown in Fig. 1.5, where *H6* is the header added by the sixth (presentation) layer.

Now, for the fifth (session) layer, *L7 data* + *H6* is the input data (see Fig. 1.5). Let us call this together as *L6 data*. When the fifth (session) layer sends this data to the next, i.e., the fourth (transport) layer, it sends the original data (which is *L6 data)* plus its own header *H5* together, i.e., *L6 data* + *H5*, and so on. In the end, the original data (*L7*) and all the headers are sent across the physical medium.

Figure 1.6 illustrates this process.

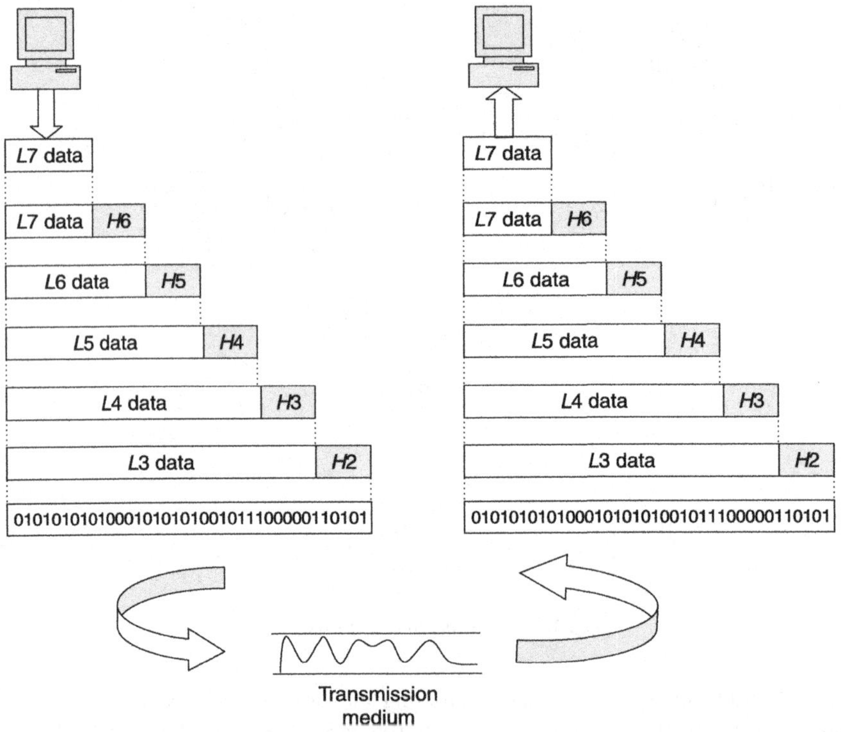

Fig. 1.6 *Data exchange using OSI layers*

OSI LAYER FUNCTIONS 1.3

1.3.1 Physical Layer

The **physical layer** is concerned with sending raw bits between the source and destination nodes, which, in this case, are adjacent nodes. To do this, the source and the destination nodes have to agree on a number of factors such as voltage which constitutes a bit value *0*, voltage which constitutes bit value *1*, what is the bit interval (i.e., the bit rate), whether the communication is in only one or both the directions simultaneously (i.e., **simplex**, **half-duplex** or **full-duplex**), and so on. It also deals with the electrical and mechanical specifications of the cables, connectors, and interfaces such as **RS 232-C**, etc.

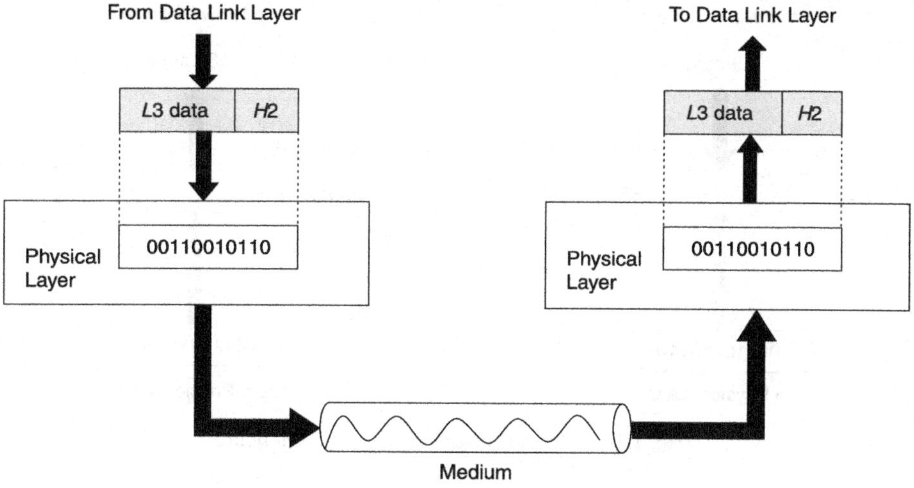

Fig. 1.7 *Physical layer between adjacent nodes*

To summarize, the physical layer has to take into account the following factors:

1. **Signal encoding** How are the bits *0* and *1* to be represented?
2. **Medium** What is the medium used, and what are its properties?
3. **Bit synchronization** Is the transmission asynchronous or synchronous?
4. **Transmission type** Is the transmission serial or parallel?
5. **Transmission mode** Is the transmission simplex, half-duplex, or full-duplex?
6. **Topology** What is the topology (mesh, star, ring, bus or hybrid) used?
7. **Multiplexing** Is multiplexing used, and if so, what is its type (FDM, TDM)?
8. **Interface** How are the two closely linked devices connected?
9. **Bandwidth** Which of baseband or broadband communication is used?
10. **Signal type** Are analog signals used, or digital ones?

1.3.2 Data Link Layer

The **data link layer** is responsible for transmitting a group of bits between the adjacent nodes. The group of bits is generally called as *frame*. The network layer passes a data unit to the data link layer. At this stage, the data link layer adds the header and trailer information to this, as shown in Fig. 1.8. This now becomes a data unit to be passed to the physical layer.

The header (and trailer, which is not shown, but is instead assumed to be present) contains the addresses and other control information. The addresses at this level refer to the physical addresses of the adjacent nodes in the network, between which the frame is being sent. Thus, these addresses change as the frame travels from different nodes on a route from the source node to the destination node. The addresses of the end nodes, i.e., those of the source and destination nodes, are already a part of data unit transferred from the network layer to the data link layer. Therefore, it is not a part of the header and trailer added and deleted at the data link layer. Hence, they remain unchanged as the frame moves through different nodes from the source to the destination.

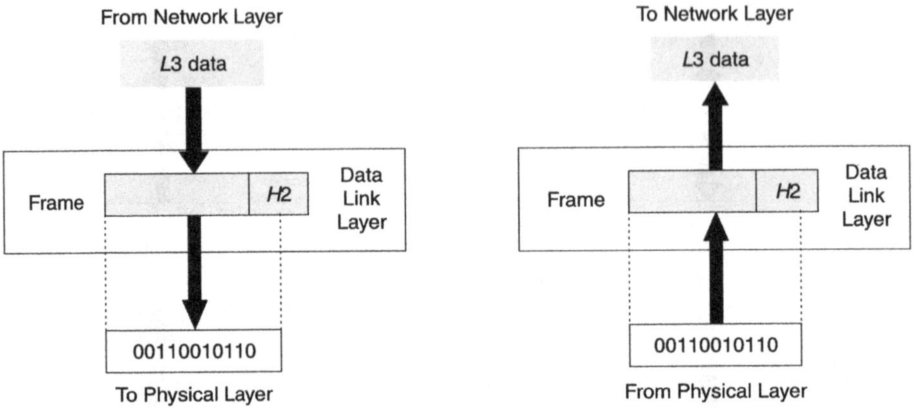

Fig. 1.8 *Data link layer between adjacent nodes*

Let us illustrate this by an example. Let us refer to Fig. 1.2. Let us imagine that node *A* wants to send a packet to node *D*. Let us imagine that we use the datagram approach. In this case, the logical (i.e., IP) addresses of nodes *A* and *D*, say ADDL (A) and ADDL (D) are the source and destination addresses. The data unit passed by the network layer to the data link layer will contain them. The data unit will look as it is shown in Fig. 1.9. Let us call this as D_N.

ADDL (A)	ADDL (D)	Actual Data ...

Fig. 1.9 *Data unit at the network layer (D_N)*

When this data unit (D_N) is passed from the network layer at node *A* to the data link layer at node *A*, the following happens:

1. The routing table is consulted, which mentions the *next node* to which the frame should be sent for a specific destination node, which is node *D* in this case. Let us imagine that the next node is *F*, based on the congestion conditions at that time, i.e., the path *A-F* is selected.
2. At this juncture, the data link layer at node *A* forms a data unit, say D_D, which looks, as shown in Fig. 1.10. We will notice that D_D has encapsulated D_N and added the physical addresses of *A* and *F* (i.e., those of the NICs of *A* and *F*) as ADDP (A) and ADDP (F) to it.
3. Using the physical addresses of adjacent nodes *A* and *F*, the packet moves from node *A* to node *F* after performing the flow control functions, as discussed later (i.e., checking if node *F* is ready to accept a frame from *A* and at what data rate, etc.). Here, the packet is passed on from the data link layer to the network layer of node *F* after performing the error-control function (i.e., verifying that the packet is error-free). Here, ADDP (A) and ADDP (F) are removed and D_N is recovered. Now, this D_N needs to be sent to the next hop to reach node *D*. For this, the final destination address, i.e., ADDL (D), is extracted from D_N. The frame now has to be sent from node *F* to node *D*.

ADDP (A)	ADDP (F)	D_N			Other Info
		ADDL (A)	ADDL (D)	Actual Data	

Fig. 1.10 *Data unit at the data link layer (D_D) at node A*

4. Again, the routing algorithm is performed at node *F* using ADDR (D) as the final destination, and the congestion conditions, etc., and a path is chosen. Let us say that the chosen path is *FG*.
5. The network layer at node *F* passes D_N to the data link layer at node *F*. Here, the physical addresses of *F* and *G* are added to form the data unit at the data link layer at node *F*, as shown in Fig. 1.11.

ADDP (F)	ADDP (G)	D_N			Other Info
		ADDL (A)	ADDL (D)	Actual Data	

Fig. 1.11 *Data unit at data link layer (D_D) at node F*

6. This continues until the data unit at data link layer D_D reaches node *D*. There again, the physical addresses are removed to get the original D_N, which is passed on to the network layer at node *D*. the network layer verifies ADDL (A) and ADDL (D), ensures that the packet is meant for itself, removes these addresses, and sends the actual data to the transport layer at node *D*.

The data link layer also performs the flow control function. Based on the speeds of the CPUs, transmission, buffer size and congestion condition, it is determined whether the frame/packet can be sent to the adjacent node, and if so, at what speed. If it can be sent, the node is ready to send the data. However, we have to make sure that the medium is free to carry the frame/packet.

If the connection is a multipoint type (i.e., the medium is shared), then the problem of who should send how much data at what times, has to be solved. This problem typically arises in **Local Area Networks (LANs)**, and is solved by the **Media Access Control (MAC)** protocol. Therefore, in LANs, the data ink layer is split into two sublayers, as shown in Fig. 1.12. In this case, LLC takes care of normal data link layer functions, such as error control and flow control, etc.

Fig. 1.12 *Data link layer in LANs*

In **Wide Area Networks (WANs)**, where mostly point-to-point connections are used, this problem does not arise.

Thus, the data link layer performs the following functions:

1. **Addressing** Headers and trailers are added, containing the physical addresses of the adjacent nodes, and removed upon a successful delivery.
2. **Flow control** This avoids overwriting the receiver's buffer by regulating the amount of data that can be sent.
3. **Media Access Control (MAC)** In LANs, it decides who can send data, when and how much.
4. **Synchronization** Headers have bits, which tell the receiver when a frame is arriving. It also contains bits to synchronize its timing to know the bit interval to recognize the bit correctly. Trailers mark the end of a frame, apart from containing the error control bits.
5. **Error control** It checks the CRC to ensure the correctness of the frame. If incorrect, it asks for retransmission. Again, here there are multiple schemes (**positive acknowledgement, negative acknowledgement, go-back-n, sliding window**, etc.).
6. **Node-to-node delivery** Finally, it is responsible for error-free delivery of the entire frame to the *next* adjacent node (node-to-node delivery).

1.3.3 Network Layer

The **network layer** is responsible for routing a packet within the subnet, i.e., from the source to the destination nodes across multiple nodes in the same network, or across multiple networks. The "packet" at network layer is usually referred to as a **datagram**. This layer ensures the successful delivery of a packet to the destination node. To perform this, it has to choose a route. As discussed before, a route could be chosen before sending all the packets belonging to the same message (virtual circuit) or it could be chosen for each packet at each node (datagram). This layer is also responsible for tackling the congestion problem at a node, when there are too many packets *stored* at a node to be *forwarded* to the next node. Whenever there is only one small network based on *broadcast* philosophy (e.g., a single Ethernet LAN), this layer is either absent or has very minimal functionality.

There are many private or public subnet operators who provide the hardware links and the software consisting of physical, data link and network layers (e.g., X.25). They guarantee an error-free delivery of a packet to the destination at a charge. This layer has to carry out the **accounting function** to facilitate this billing based on how many packets are routed, when and, etc. When packets are sent across national boundaries, the rates may change, thus making this accounting function complex.

A router can connect two networks with different protocols, packet lengths and formats. The network layer is responsible for the creation of a homogeneous network by helping to overcome these problems.

At this layer, a header is added to a packet, which includes the source and destination addresses (logical addresses). These are not the same as the physical addresses between each pair of adjacent nodes at the data link layer, as seen before. If we refer to Fig. 1.2 where we want to send a packet from A to D, addresses of nodes A and D (i.e., ADDL (A) and ADDL (D)) are these addresses, which are added to the actual data to form a data unit at the network layer (D_N). These addresses and, in fact, the whole of D_N remains unchanged throughout the journey of the packet from A to F to G to D. Only physical addresses of the adjacent nodes keep getting added and removed, as the packet travels from A to F to G to D. Finally, at node D, after verifying the addresses, ADDL (A) and ADDL (D) are removed and the actual data is recovered and sent to the transport layer at node D, as shown in Fig. 1.13.

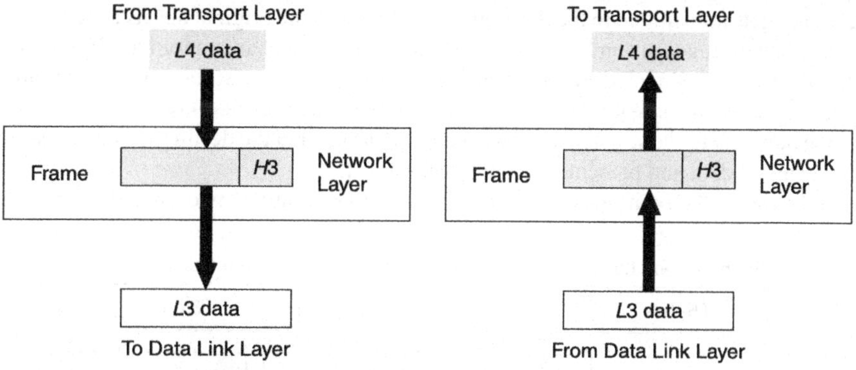

Fig. 1.13 *Network layer between adjacent nodes*

To summarize, the network layer performs the following functions:

1. **Routing** As discussed before.
2. **Congestion control** As discussed before.
3. **Logical addressing** Source and destination logical addresses (e.g., IP addresses).
4. **Address transformations** Interpreting logical addresses to get their physical equivalent (e.g., ARP protocol). We shall discuss this in detail later in the book.
5. **Accounting and billing** As discussed before.
6. **Source-to-Destination error-free delivery** of a packet.

1.3.4 Transport Layer

Transport layer is the first end-to-end layer, as shown in Fig. 1.4. Therefore, a header at the transport layer contains information that helps to send the message to the corresponding layer at the destination node, although the message broken into packets may travel through a number of intermediate nodes. As we know, each end node may be running several processes (maybe for several users through several terminals). The transport layer ensures that the complete message arrives at the destination, and in the proper order and is passed on to the proper application. The transport layer takes care of error control and flow control, both at the source and at the destination for the entire message, rather than only for a packet. Incidentally, a "packet" is either termed as a **segment** or as a **datagram** at the transport layer.

As we know, these days, a computer can run many applications at the same time. All these applications could need communication with the same or different remote computers at the same time. For example, suppose we have two computers *A* and *B*. Let us say *A* hosts a file server, in which *B* is interested. Similarly, suppose another messaging application on *A* wants to send a message to *B*. Since the two different applications want to communicate with their counterparts on remote computers at the same time, it is very essential that a communication channel between not only the two computers must be established, but also between the respective applications on the two computers. This is the job of the transport layer. It enables communication between two applications residing on different computers.

The transport layer receives data from the session layer on the source computer, which needs to be sent across to the other computer. For this, the transport layer on the source computer breaks the data into smaller packets and gives them to the lower layer (network layer), from which it goes to still lower layers and finally gets transmitted to the destination computer. If the original data is to be re-created at the session layer of the destination computer, we would need some mechanism for identifying the sequence in which the data was fragmented into packets by the transport layer at the source computer. For this purpose, when it breaks the session layer data into segments, the transport layer of the source computer adds sequence numbers to the segments. Now, the transport layer at the destination can reassemble them to create the original data and present it to the session layer.

Figure 1.14 shows the relationship between transport layer and its two immediate neighbors.

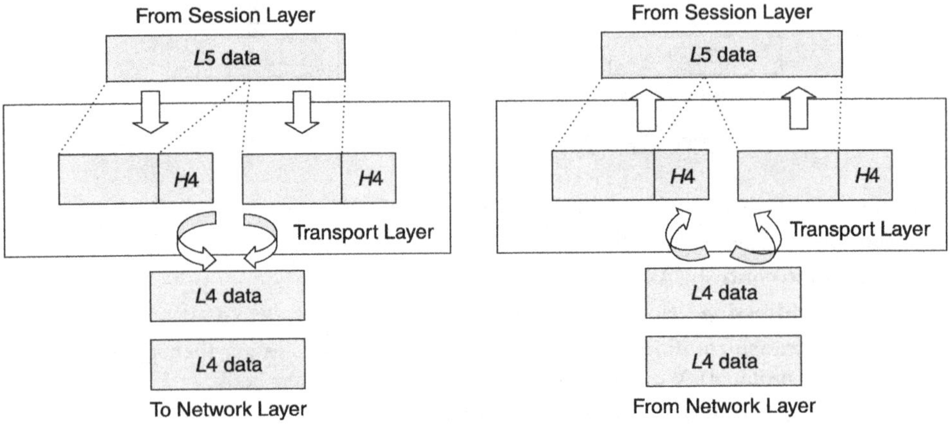

Fig. 1.14 *Transport layer*

The transport layer may also establish a **logical connection** between the source and the destination. A connection is a logical path that is associated with all the packets of a message, between the source and the destination. A connection consists of three phases which are, **establishment**, **data transfer** and **connection release**. By using connections, the transport layer can perform the sequencing, error detection and correction in a better way.

To summarize, the responsibilities of the transport layer are as follows:

1. **Host-to-host message delivery** Ensuring that all the segments of a message sent by a source node arrive at the intended destination.
2. **Application-to-application communication** The transport layer enables communication between two applications running on different computers.
3. **Segmentation and reassembly** The transport layer breaks a message into segments, numbers them by adding sequence numbers at the source, and uses the sequence numbers at the destination to reassemble the original message.
4. **Connection** The transport layer might create a logical connection between the source and the destination for the duration of the complete message transfer for better control over the message transfer.

1.3.5 Session Layer

The main functions of the **session layer** are to establish, maintain and synchronize the interaction between two communicating hosts. It makes sure that a session once established is closed gracefully, and not abruptly. For example, suppose that a user wants to send a very big document consisting of 1000 pages to another user on a different computer. Suppose that after the first 105 pages have been sent, the connection between the two hosts is broken for some reason. The question now is, when the connection between the two hosts is restored after some time, must the transmission start all over again, i.e., from the first page? Or can the user start with the 106th page? These issues are the concerns of the session layer.

The session layer checks and establishes connections between the hosts of two different users. For this, the users might need to enter identification information such as login and password. Besides this, the session layer also decides things such as whether both users can send as well as receive data at the same time, or whether only one host can send and the other can receive, and so on (i.e., whether the communication is simplex, half duplex or full duplex).

Let us reiterate our earlier example of the transmission of a very big document between two hosts. To avoid a complete retransmission from the first page, the session layer between the two hosts could create subsessions. After each subsession is over, a checkpoint can be taken. For instance, the session layers at the two hosts could decide that after a successful transmission of a set of every 10 pages, they would take a checkpoint. This means that if the connection breaks after the first 105 pages have been transmitted, after the connection is restored, the transmission would start at the 101st page. This is because the last checkpoint would have been taken after the 100th page was transmitted. The session layer is shown in Fig. 1.15.

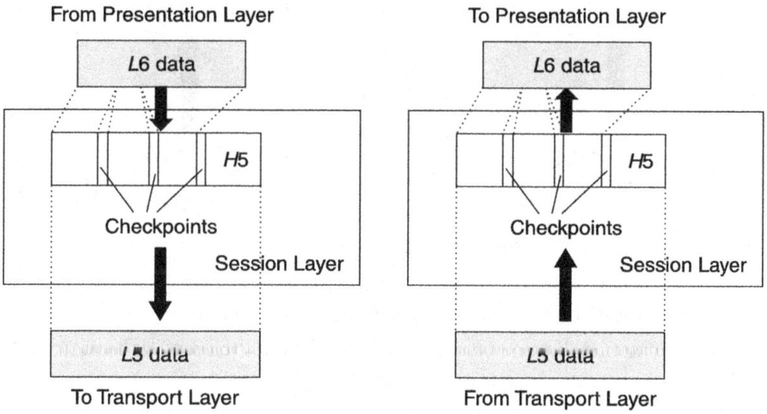

Fig. 1.15 *Session layer*

In some cases, the checkpointing may not be required at all, as the data being transmitted is trivial and small. Regardless of whether it is required or not, when the session layer receives data from the presentation layer, it adds a header to it, which among other things also contains information as to whether there is any checkpointing, and if there is, at what point.

To summarize, the responsibilities of the session layer are as follows:

1. **Sessions and subsessions** The session layer divides a session into subsessions for avoiding retransmission of entire messages by adding the checkpointing feature.
2. **Synchronization** The session layer decides the order in which data needs to be passed to the transport layer.
3. **Dialog control** The session layer also decides which user/application sends data, and at what point of time, and whether the communication is simplex, half duplex or full duplex.

4. **Session closure** The session layer ensures that the session between the hosts is closed gracefully.

1.3.6 Presentation Layer

When two hosts are communicating with each other, they might be using different encoding standards and character sets for representing data internally. For instance, one host could be using **ASCII** code for character representation, whereas the other host could be using **EBCDIC**. The **presentation layer** is responsible for taking care of such differences. It is also responsible for (a) data encryption and decryption for security and (b) data compression and decompression for more efficiency in data transmission. Figure 1.16 shows the responsibilities of the presentation layer.

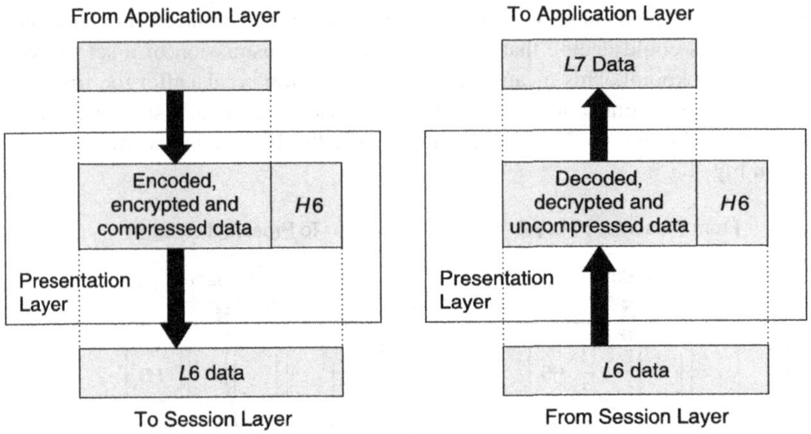

Fig. 1.16 *Presentation layer*

To summarize, the responsibilities of the presentation layer are as follows:

1. **Translation** The translation between the sender's and the receiver's message formats is done by the presentation layer if the two formats are different.
2. **Encryption** The presentation layer performs data encryption and decryption for security.
3. **Compression** For efficient transmission, the presentation layer performs data compression before sending and decompression at the destination.

1.3.7 Application Layer

The **application layer**, the topmost layer in the OSI model, enables a user to access the network. The application programs using the network services also reside at this layer. This layer provides user interface for network applications, such as remote log in (TELNET), World Wide Web (WWW), File Transfer Protocol (FTP), electronic mail (email), remote database access, etc. The users and application programs interact with a physical network at this layer. This should not be confused with the application system like accounting or purchasing, etc. If an accounting application requires an access to a remote database, or wants a file to be transferred, it will invoke the appropriate application layer protocol (e.g., FTP). Thus, this layer can be considered as *consisting of* the *application*, such as FTP, email, WWW, etc., which are the different ways in which one can access the network services. Thus, the application layer provides an abstracted view of the layers underneath, and allows the users and applications to concentrate on their tasks, rather than worrying about lower level network protocols.

The conceptual position of the application layer is shown in Fig. 1.17.

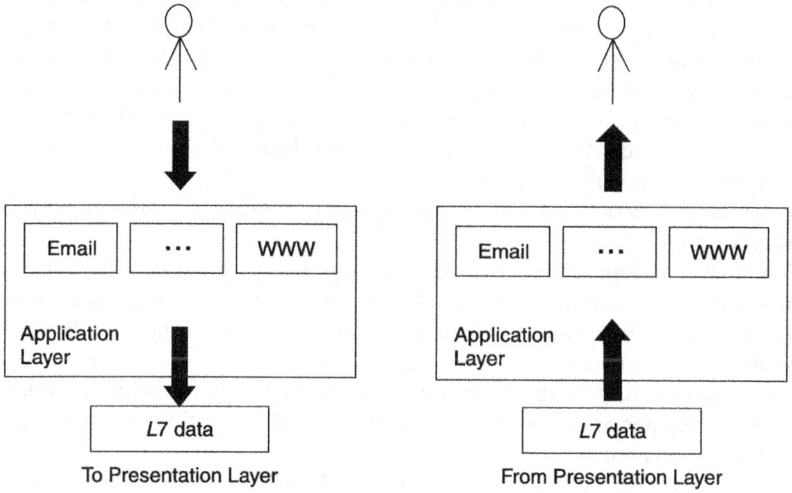

Fig. 1.17 *Application layer*

To summarize, the responsibilities of the application layer are as follows:

1. **Network abstraction** The application layer provides an abstraction of the underlying network to an end user and an application.
2. **File access and transfer** It allows a user to access, download or upload files from/to a remote host.
3. **Mail services** It allows the users to use the mail services.
4. **Remote login** It allows logging in a host, which is remote.
5. **World Wide Web (WWW)** Accessing the Web pages is also a part of this layer.

Key Terms and Concepts

Address transformations • Addressing • Application layer • Application-to-application communication • Bandwidth • Bit synchronization • Collision • Compression • Congestion control • Connection • Data link layer • Datagram • Dialog control • Encryption • Error control • Flow control • Frame • Host-to-host message delivery • Interface • Logical address • Mail services • Media Access Control (MAC) • Multiplexing • Negative acknowledgement (NAK) • Network abstraction • Network layer • Node • Node to node delivery • OSI model • Packets • Physical layer • Positive acknowledgement (ACK) • Presentation layer • Remote login • Routing • Segment • Segmentation and reassembly • Session closure • Session layer • Sessions and subsessions • Signal encoding • Signal type • Store and forward • Synchronization • Time out • Topology • Transmission mode • Transmission type • Transport layer • Virtual Circuit • Virtual Circuit Number • Virtual communication • Virtual path • World Wide Web (WWW)

SUMMARY

- Protocol means convention. When computers need to communicate with each other either to exchange information or for sharing common resources, they use a common protocol.
- There are a number of requirements for data communication, such as data transmission, flow control, error control, routing, data compression, encryption, etc. These features are logically subgrouped and then the subgroups are further grouped into groups called as layers.
- The model of communication protocols defines seven such layers, i.e., physical, data link, network, transport, session, presentation, and application. Each layer has an interface with its adjacent layers, and performs specific functions.
- The physical layer is concerned with sending raw bits between the adjacent nodes, across the communication medium.
- The data link layer is responsible for transmitting a group of bits between the adjacent nodes.
- The data link layer is responsible for Error detection/recovery and Congestion Control.
- The network layer is responsible for routing a packet within the subnet, i.e., from the source to the destination nodes across multiple nodes in the same network, or across multiple networks.
- The transport layer is responsible for host-to-host message delivery, application-to-application communication, segmentation and reassembly, and logical connection management between the source and the destination.
- The main functions of the session layer are to establish, maintain and synchronize the interaction between two communicating hosts.
- When two hosts are communicating with each other, they might be using different encoding standards and character sets for representing data internally. The presentation layer is responsible to take care of such differences.
- The application layer, the topmost layer in the OSI model, enables a user to access the network. The application programs using the network services also reside at this layer.

MULTIPLE-CHOICE QUESTIONS

1. NAK is a __________ acknowledgement.
   (a) positive (b) negative (c) neutral (d) None of these
2. The speed mismatch between the sender and the receiver is called as __________.
   (a) error control (b) speed error
   (c) flow control (d) transmission control
3. In order that a bigger transmission does not overhaul a smaller one, the data is sent in the form of __________.
   (a) boxes (b) baskets (c) groups (d) packets
4. The __________ layer is the lowest layer in the OSI model.
   (a) physical (b) transport (c) session (d) application
5. The __________ layer is the topmost layer in the OSI model.
   (a) physical (b) transport (c) session (d) application
6. The intermediate nodes are concerned with the __________ layers only.
   (a) top 3 (b) middle 3
   (c) bottom 3 (d) topmost, middle and bottommost

7. The __________ layer is responsible for node to node delivery of packets.
   (a) physical (b) transport (c) data link (d) application
8. The __________ layer is responsible for routing packets within or across networks.
   (a) physical (b) network (c) data link (d) application
9. The __________ layer ensures a correct delivery of a complete message.
   (a) data link (b) transport (c) session (d) presentation
10. Encryption is handled by the __________ layer.
    (a) data link (b) transport (c) session (d) presentation

DETAILED QUESTIONS

1. Explain the term *protocol* in general.
2. Explain the different layers and their roles in protocols of computer communications.
3. Explain the different layers in the OSI model.
4. Explain the physical layer in OSI model.
5. How does the data link layer in OSI model work?
6. Discuss the role of network layer in OSI model.
7. How does the transport layer ensure that the complete message arrives at the destination, and in the proper order?
8. Explain how a session layer establishes, maintains and synchronizes the interaction between two communicating hosts.
9. Explain the role played by the presentation layer in handling different data formats.
10. Explain the topmost layer in the OSI model, the application layer.

EXERCISES

1. Find out about network protocols such as SNA and TCP/IP. How similar or different are they from the OSI model?
2. Study the background and need for the OSI model.
3. Investigate which of the OSI layers are considered to be very useful and which ones are not quite in use.
4. Consider an analogy wherein a person who knows only French wants to send a fax message to a person who knows only Urdu. Describe this process with reference to the appropriate OSI model layers.
5. Why has TCP/IP become so popular as compared to the OSI model? Investigate the reasons behind this.

2 INTERNET WORKING CONCEPTS, DEVICES, INTERNET BASICS, HISTORY, AND ARCHITECTURE

INTRODUCTION

In the previous chapter, we have studied the basic principles of protocols. Let us now study another extremely important concept of connecting many such computer networks together. This is called **internet working**. A network of computer networks is called an **internetwork** or simply, **internet** (note the lowercase *i*). The worldwide Internet (note the uppercase I) is an example of the internet working technology. The Internet, as we have seen, is a huge network of computer networks. The following sections describe the motivations behind such a technology, as well as how it actually works.

When two or more devices have to be connected for sharing data or resources or exchanging messages, we call it as networking. When two networks need to be connected for the same purpose, we call it internet working. The main difference between networking and internet working is that whereas in case of networking all the devices are compatible with each other (e.g., hosts in a LAN), it may or may not be the case with internet working. When we want to connect two or more networks to form an internetwork, it is quite possible that the networks are incompatible with each other in many respects. For instance, we might want to connect an Ethernet LAN with a Token Ring LAN and a WAN. All the three types of networks are quite different from each other. They differ in terms of their topologies, signaling, transmission mechanism, as well as wiring, etc. Therefore, the challenge in internet working is more in terms of handling these incompatibilities and bringing all the incompatible networks to a common platform.

In this chapter, we shall discuss various connecting devices that are required to facilitate networking and internet working. These devices form the backbones of any network or internetwork (abbreviated as internet, which is different from the worldwide network of networks, i.e., the Internet: note the case difference).

The Internet has been acknowledged as one of the greatest things to happen during the 20th century. In fact, people talk about the Internet in the same way as the revolutionary inventions such as electricity and the printing press, among others. The Internet is here to stay even if the dotcoms have perished. In this chapter, we shall look at the fundamentals of the Internet technology. More specifically, we shall study how the Internet is organized and how it works. We shall also take a look at the historical perspective of the Internet.

We shall first study the basic concepts behind the Internet. We shall then see how the different components of the Internet work. The Internet is basically the world's largest network of computer networks. Many different kinds of applications run over the Internet. We shall discuss those in detail. The **Transmission Control Protocol/Internet Protocol (TCP/IP)** protocol is the backbone of the Internet. We shall see how it works.

WHY INTERNET WORKING? 2.1

The main reason for having an internet is that each computer network is designed with a specific task in mind. For example, a LAN is typically used to connect computers in a smaller area (such as an office) and it provides fast communication between these computers. On the other hand, WAN technologies are used for communication over longer distances. As a result, networks become specialized entities. Moreover, a large organization having diversifying needs has multiple networks. In many cases, these networks do not use the same technology in terms of the hardware as well as communication protocols.

Consequently, a computer can only communicate with other computers attached to the same network. As more and more organizations had multiple computer networks in the 1970s, this became a major issue. Computer networks became small islands! In many cases, an employee had to physically move for using computers connected to different networks. For example, to print a document, the employee would need to use a computer that is connected to a print server. Similarly, for accessing a file on another network, the employee had to use a computer on that network, and so on. Clearly, this was a nuisance. This affected productivity, as people did not like to move around for performing trivial tasks.

As a result, the concept of **universal service** came into being. In simple terms, it means that there was no dependence on the underlying physical technology, or on the fact that there were many separate physical networks. Like a telephone network, people wanted a single computer network in their organization. A user should be able to print a document or send a message to any other user from his computer, without needing to use a separate computer on another network for each such task. For this to be possible, all computer networks should be connected together. This means that there should be a network of physically separate networks. This forms the basis of internet working.

PROBLEMS IN INTERNET WORKING 2.2

It is fine to think of a network of computer networks or an internet, in theory. However, one must also remember that organizations invest so much when they build computer networks in terms of cost as well as infrastructure (cabling, providing space in the building for it, etc.). Therefore, they would want to reuse their existing infrastructure rather than creating everything from scratch. However, there are problems in this. Electrical as well as software incompatibility makes it impossible to form a network merely by interconnecting wires from two networks. For example, one network could represent a binary 0 by–5 volts, whereas another network could represent it by +5 volts. Similarly, one network could use a packet size of say 128 bytes, whereas another could use 256-byte packets. The method of acknowledgement or error detection/recovery could also be entirely different. There could be many more such differences like routing algorithms, etc.

Thus, any two networks cannot directly communicate with each other by just connecting a wire between them. Since there are many incompatible networking technologies, the problem becomes more acute. An organization could have many networks of different types. This means that there is a large amount of disagreement between the networks in terms of signaling, data representation and error detection/recovery, etc. Therefore, the concept of universal service through internet working is not simple to achieve, although it is highly desirable.

DEALING WITH INCOMPATIBILITY ISSUES 2.3

In spite of the problems mentioned earlier, computer scientists have found out a mechanism by which computer networks can be connected together to form an internet. The incompatibility issues are addressed in two respects.

2.3.1 Hardware Issues

At the hardware level, some additional hardware is used to connect physically distinct computer networks. This hardware component is most commonly a router. A router is a special-purpose computer that is used specifically for internet working purposes. A router has a processor (CPU) and memory like any other computer. However, it has more than one I/O interface that allows it to connect to multiple computer networks. From a network's point of view, connecting to a router is not extraordinary in any way. A network connects to a router in the same way as it connects to any other computer. A router connects two or more computer networks, as shown in Fig. 2.1.

A network has many computers or nodes attached to it. Therefore, an address of a node or a computer could be treated as network id + node id. Each node has a **Network Interface Card (NIC)**, which has this address hardcoded into it. If a router is treated as yet another computer by the network, it means that the router basically has two addresses—one for each network, at points *X* and *Y*, as shown in Fig. 2.1.

The router is a special computer that has two Network Interface Cards (NICs), which connect to these two networks. These two NICs correspond to the two physical addresses of the router.

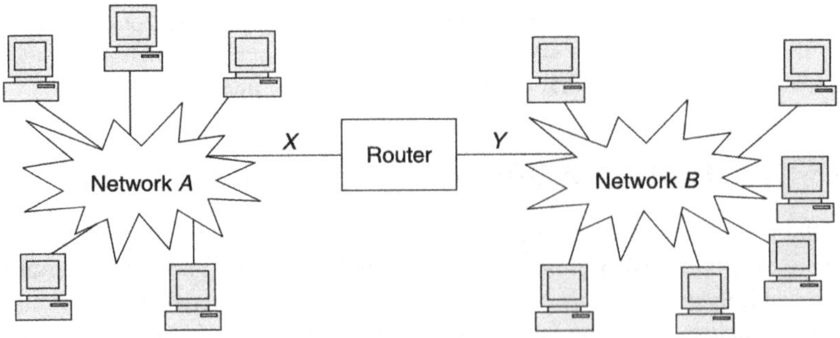

Fig. 2.1 *A router connects two or more computer networks together*

The most important point in this discussion is that a router can connect incompatible networks. That is, networks *A* and *B* in the figure could be both LANs of the same or different types, both WANs of the same or different types, or one of them could be a LAN and the other a WAN, etc. A router has the capability to connect them together. How is this possible? For this, a router has the necessary hardware (NIC for each type of network) as well as software (protocols) that make it possible. Moreover, even if both *A* and *B* in the figure are of the same category—say LANs—they could internally use different technology (one could use Ethernet and another could use FDDI). The router handles all these incompatibilities as well. Again, this is possible because of the hardware and software contained by a router. The point is that *A* and *B* in the figure could be arbitrary networks. However, the router would still be able to interconnect them.

Interestingly, the Internet (note the uppercase I) looks as shown in Fig. 2.2.

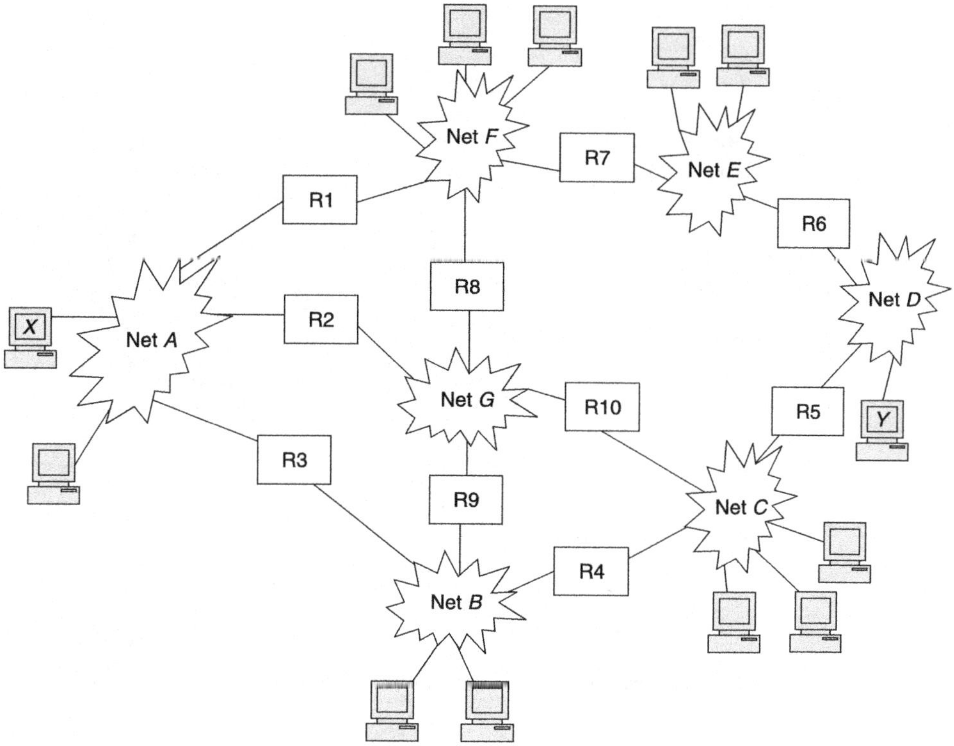

Fig. 2.2 *A portion of the Internet*

Figure 2.2 shows seven networks connected by ten routers. Network *A* could be an Ethernet, network *B* could be an FDDI, and network *C* could be a Token Ring, whereas network *G* could be a WAN! A router connects two networks through two NICs that are contained by each such router.

If computer *X* on network *A* wants to send a message to computer *Y* on network *D*, the message can be sent in different routes or paths given below.

1. *X* – Net *A* – R2 – Net *G* – R10 – Net *C* – R5 – Net *D* – *Y*
2. *X* – Net *A* – R1 – Net *F* – R7 – Net *E* – R6 – Net *D* – *Y*
3. *X* – Net *A* – R3 – Net *B* – R4 – Net *C* – R5 – Net *D* – *Y*

Many more routes also exist.

The router is responsible for routing the packets to the destination. To do this, the software computes the routing algorithm, and based on this, each router stores the routing table, which states for each destination, the next hop, to which the packet is to be sent.

It is for this reason that the router is supposed to act at the network layer of the OSI model. It neither examines the contents of the packet, nor tries to interpret them. Figure 2.3 shows this.

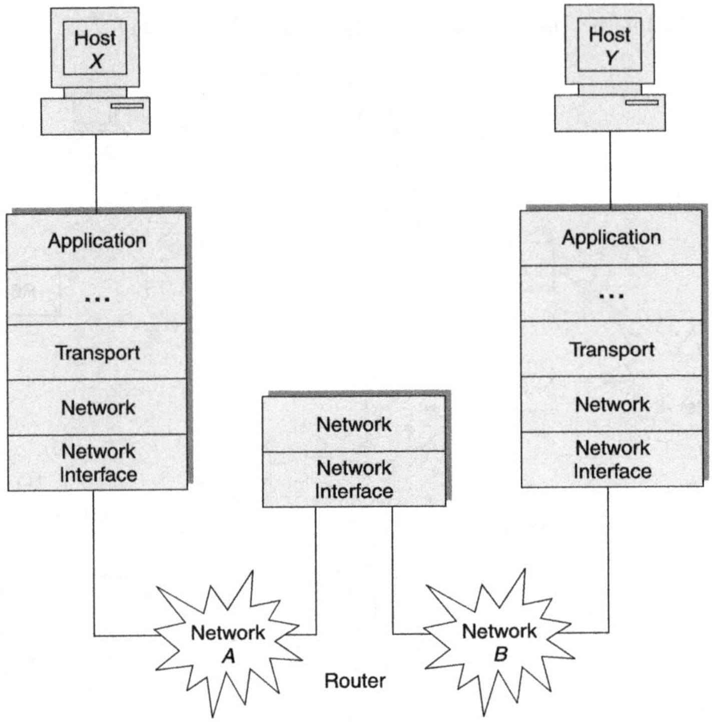

Fig. 2.3 *Router is at the network layer of the OSI model*

2.3.2 Software Issues

At the software level, routers must agree about the way in which information from the source computer on one network would be transmitted to destination computer on a different network. Since this information is likely to travel via one or more routers, there must be a pre-specified standard to which all routers must conform. This task is not easy. Packet formats and addressing mechanisms used by the underlying networks may not be the same. Does the router actually perform the conversion and re-conversion of the packets corresponding to the different network formats? Though not impossible, this approach is very difficult and cumbersome. This is done by defining a standard packet format in which the sender breaks down the original message. We will study this later. Therefore, some networking protocols are required that can standardize communication between incompatible networks. Only then, the concept of universal service can be truly realized. In the case of all Internet communications, the TCP/IP suite of protocols makes this possible.

The basic idea is that TCP/IP defines a packet size, routing algorithms, error control methods, etc., universally. Let us refer to Fig. 2.2 again. If node *X* wants to send some message to node *Y* by route number 1 given above (*X* – Net *A* – R2 – Net *G* – R10 – Net *C* – R5 – Net *D* – *Y*), the following processes happen, imagining that Net *A* is Ethernet and Net *G* is Token Ring.

1. The message is broken down into the packets as per the TCP/IP protocol. Each packet has the source and destination addresses of *X* and *Y*.
2. Each packet is inserted into the Ethernet frame. Ethernet frame can be carried only on the Ethernet network (in this case, Net *A*). The TCP/IP packet along with its final source/destination addresses (of *X* and *Y*) is enclosed within an Ethernet frame, which has additional source and destination addresses, which are physical addresses on the same network (of *X* and R2 as both are on Net *A*). After this, the CRC is computed and appended to the Ethernet frame.
3. Both, node *X* as well as R2 are on Net *A*, which is Ethernet. Thus, the frame travels from *X* to R2 using CSMA/CD, using the Ethernet source/destination addresses of *X* and R2.
4. At R2, the CRC is checked, the Ethernet header dropped, and the original TCP/IP packet recovered. It contains the final source and destination addresses of *X* and *Y*.
5. From the destination address, routing algorithm is used to find out the *next hop*, which is R10, in this case. We know that both R2 and R10 are on the Token Ring network Net *G*.
6. Net *G* is a Token Ring. Therefore, R2, which knows this fact, puts this TCP/IP packet as data in the Token Ring frame format after adding the header, etc. Here also, the TCP/IP packet, which contains the final addresses of *X* and *Y*, is encapsulated in the Token Ring frame, which has additional source and destination addresses of R2 and R10, respectively, for transporting the packet from R2 to R10 on the Token Ring, etc.
7. Like before, R2 as well as R10 are on Token Ring using the Token Ring source/destination addresses of R2 and R10. Thus, the packet reaches R10, etc.
8. This process repeats until the packet reaches *Y*. At *Y*, the header is removed to get the original TCP/IP packet. The destination address is verified and the packet is stored.
9. After all the packets are received at *Y*, the TCP/IP at *Y* ensures the error-free receipt of all packets of the message and then passes it on to the application layer at *Y*.

This is how TCP/IP solves the problem of connecting heterogeneous networks seamlessly.

A VIRTUAL NETWORK 2.4

The Internet software makes it appear that there is a single, seamless system of communication to which many computers are attached. The internal details of many real, actual networks connecting together to form it are hidden, and instead, it appears to be a single, large network. Every computer on the Internet has an address assigned to it. This is like the postal address assigned to a home. Using this address, any user can send packets to any other computer on the Internet. The users of the Internet do not have to be bothered about the internal structure of the physical networks, their interconnection, routing decisions, or the presence of routers themselves. Thus, an illusion of a **virtual network** is created. This is an abstracted view presented to a common user, who is not interested in knowing the internal organization of the communication system. For example, a telephone user simply wants to dial someone's number and talk with that person instead of knowing how the signaling system works or how many telephone exchanges exist in the system and how they function. Similarly, an Internet user is merely interested in communicating with another user of the Internet, using the computer address of the other user, or he is interested in using the services on that computer.

The concept of a virtual network is very important. It ensures that different computer networks cannot only be connected together, but also be looked upon and used as a single network. This forms the basis of the biggest network of networks, the Internet. This concept is illustrated in Fig. 2.4. The figure shows the illusion of a single, large virtual network corresponding to the real network (shown in Fig. 2.2).

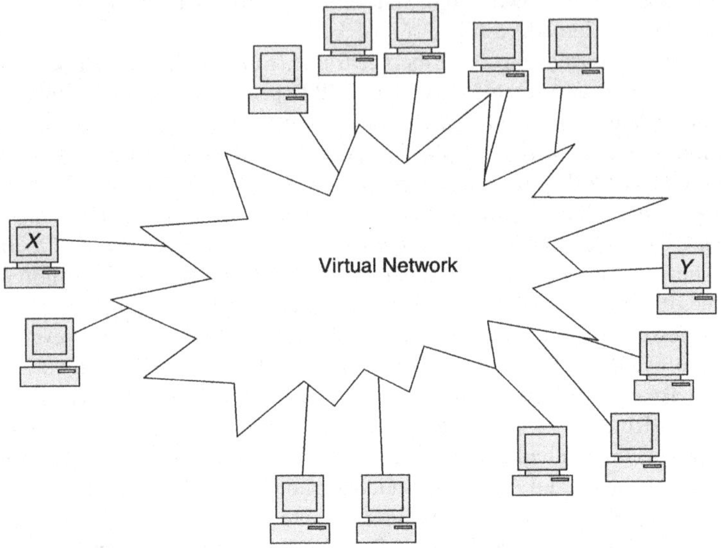

Fig. 2.4 *The Internet is a virtual network of computer networks*

INTERNET WORKING DEVICES 2.5

At a high level, the **connecting devices** can be classified into **networking devices** and **internet working devices**. Each of them has another level of classification, as shown in Fig. 2.5. We have discussed routers in brief in the previous chapter.

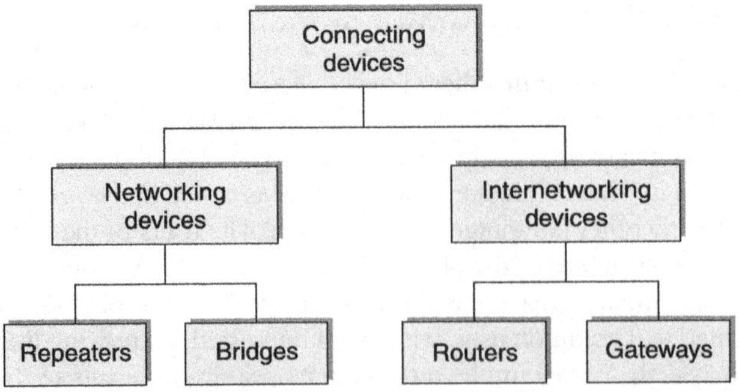

Fig. 2.5 *Connecting devices*

Let us summarize these devices first as shown in Table 2.1, before we take a detailed look at each of them.

Table 2.1 *Summary of networking devices*

Device	*Purpose*	*Present in which OSI layer*
Repeaters	Electrical specifications of a signal	Physical
Bridges	Addressing protocols	Data link
Routers	Internet working between compatible networks	Network
Gateways	Translation services between incompatible networks	All

Note that in each of the last three cases, the device is present in the layer mentioned in the table, as well as one level below it. That is, a bridge is present in the data link layer as well as the physical layer. A repeater is already at the lowest OSI layer (i.e., the physical layer), and therefore, it is present in that layer only.

REPEATERS 2.6

A repeater, also called a **regenerator**, is an electronic device, which simply regenerates a signal. It works at the physical layer of the OSI protocol, as shown in Fig. 2.6. Signals traveling across a physical wire travel some distance before they become weak (in a process called as attenuation), or get corrupted as they get interfered with other signals/noise. This means that the integrity of the data, carried by the signal, is in danger. A repeater receives such a signal, which is likely to become weak or corrupted, and regenerates it. For instance, let us assume that a computer works on a convention that 5 volts represent 1, and 0 volts represent 0. If the signal becomes weak/distorted and the voltage becomes 4.5, the repeater has the *intelligence* to realize that it is still a bit 1 and therefore, it can regenerate the bit (i.e., 5 volts). That is, the repeater simply recreates the bit pattern of the signal, and puts this regenerated signal back on to the transmission medium. In effect, the original signal is *created* once again.

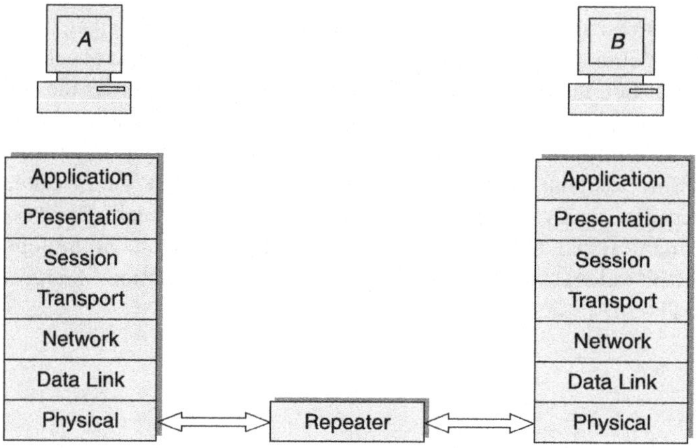

Fig. 2.6 *Repeater at the physical layer*

We would realize that a repeater allows extending a network beyond the physical boundaries, otherwise imposed by the data transmission media. Note that a repeater does not anyway change the data that is being transmitted, or the characteristics of a network. The only responsibility of a repeater is to take a stream of bits, in the form of a signal, regenerate it so that the signal is accurate now, and send it forward. It does not perform any intelligent function.

For instance, in the sample network (LAN) shown in Fig. 2.7, host *A* wants to send a packet containing the bit stream 01100110 to host *D*. Note that the two hosts are on the same LAN, but on different portions of the LAN. By the time the signal sent by host *A* can reach host *D*, it becomes very weak. Therefore, host *D* may not be able to get it in the form of the original signal. Instead, the bits could change to say 01100111 before the signal reaches host *D*. Of course, at a higher level, the error control functions would detect and correct such an anomaly. However, even before this can happen, at the lowest level, the repeater simply prevents it from occurring by taking the input signal corresponding to bits 01100110 sent by host *A*, simply regenerating it to create a signal with the same bit format and the original signal strength, and sending it forward.

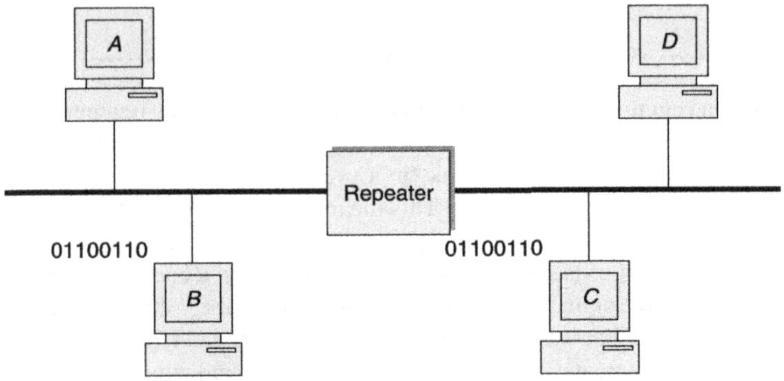

Fig. 2.7 *Repeater regenerating a signal*

People sometimes confuse between repeaters and amplifiers. However, they are different. An amplifier is used for analog signals. In analog signals, it is impossible to separate the original signal and the noise. An amplifier, therefore, amplifies an original signal as well as the noise in the signal, as it cannot differentiate between the two. On the other hand, a repeater knows that the signal has to be identified as either 0 or 1 only. Therefore, it does not amplify the incoming signal—it regenerates it in the original bit pattern. Since a signal must reach a repeater before it becomes too weak to be unidentifiable, the placement of repeaters is an important concern. A signal must reach a repeater before too much noise is introduced in the signal. Otherwise, the noise can change the bits in the signal (i.e., the voltage corresponding to the bit values), and therefore, corrupt it. After corruption, if a repeater regenerates it, incorrect data would be forwarded by the repeater.

BRIDGES 2.7

2.7.1 Introduction

A **bridge** is a computer that has its own processor, memory and two NIC cards to connect to two portions of a network. A bridge does not run application programs, and instead, facilitates host-to-host communication within a network. It operates at the physical as well as data link layers of the OSI protocol hierarchy. This is shown in Fig. 2.8.

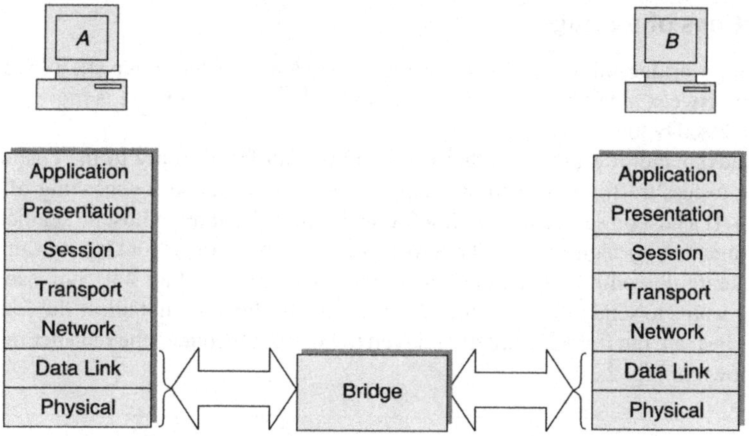

Fig. 2.8 *Bridge at the last two OSI layers*

The main idea of using a bridge is to divide a big network into smaller subnetworks, called **segments**. This is shown in Fig. 2.9. Here, the bridge splits the entire network into two segments, shown with dotted lines. We have also shown two repeaters, which we shall disregard for the current scope of discussion. Due to the bridge, the two segments act as a part of the single network.

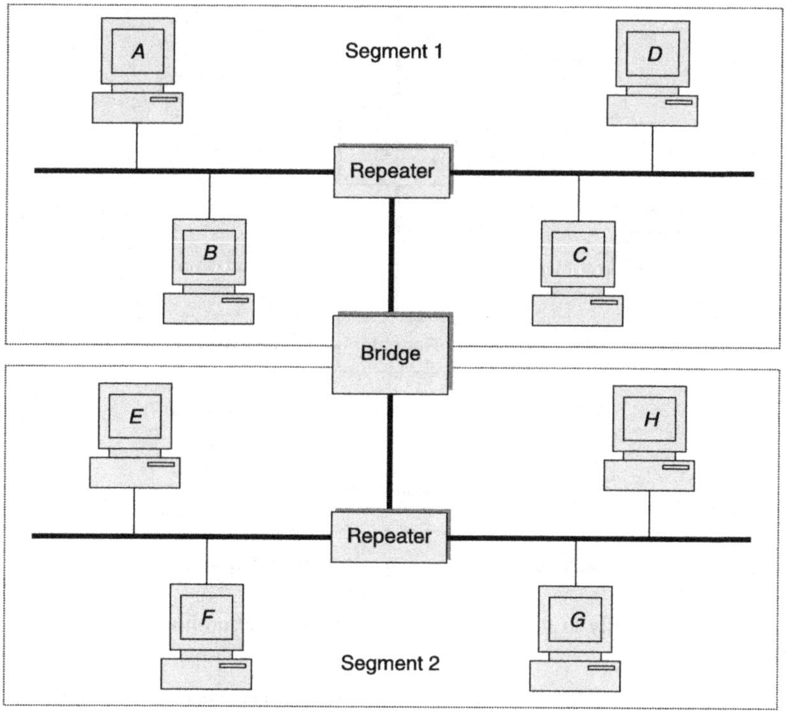

Fig. 2.9 *Bridge connecting two segments*

2.7.2 Functions of a Bridge

At a broad level, a bridge might appear to be the same as a repeater. After all, a bridge enables the communication between smaller segments of a network. However, a bridge is more intelligent than a repeater, as discussed below.

The main advantage of a bridge is that it sends the data frames only to the concerned segment, thus preventing excess traffic. For example, suppose we have a network consisting of four segments numbered 1 to 4. If a host on segment 1 sends a frame destined for another host on segment 3, the bridge forwards the frame only to segment 3, and not to segments 2 and 4, thus blocking unwanted data traffic.

Let us illustrate this with an example network shown earlier in Fig. 2.9. Suppose in our sample network, host *A* wants to send a frame to host *D*. Then, the bridge does not allow the frame to enter the lower segment. Instead, the frame is directly relayed to host *D*. Of course, the repeater might regenerate the frame as shown in Fig. 2.10.

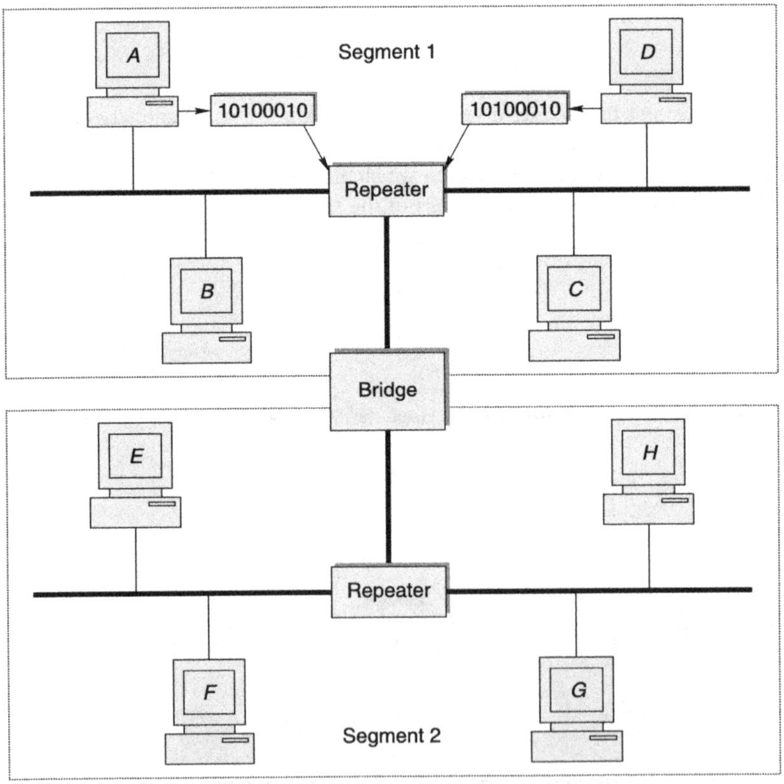

Fig. 2.10 *A bridge minimizes unwanted traffic*

By forwarding frames only to the segment where the destination host resides, a bridge serves the following purposes:

1. Unwanted traffic is minimized, thus network congestion can also be minimized to the maximum extent possible.

2. Busy links or links in error can be identified and isolated, so that the traffic does not go to them.
3. Security features or access controls (e.g., a host on segment can send frames to another host on network *C* but not to a host on network *B*) can be implemented.

Since bridges operate at the data link layer, they know the physical addresses of the different hosts on the network. Bridges can also take on the role of repeaters in addition to network segmenting. Thus, a bridge can not only regenerate an incoming frame, but also forward this regenerated copy of the frame to only the concerned segment, to which the destination host is attached. In such cases, the repeaters can be done away with.

2.7.3 Types of Bridges

As we have learned, a bridge forwards frames to only that segment of a network to which the destination host is attached. However, how does it know to which segment is the destination host attached? For instance, in Fig. 2.9, if node *A* sends data/message to node *D*, the bridge should know that node *D* is not on the lower segment (2) and therefore, block that frame from entering the lower segment (2). On the other hand, if node *A* wants to send data/message to node *G*, it should pass it to the lower segment (2). How does it do this filtering function?

In order to achieve this, a bridge maintains a table of host addresses versus the segment numbers to which they belong. For the sample network and segments shown in Fig. 2.9, we can have a simple table used by the bridge, as shown in Table 2.2. Note that instead of showing the 48-bit physical addresses, we have shown the host ids for ease of reference.

Table 2.2 *Host address to segment mapping*

Host address	*Segment number*
A	1
B	1
C	1
D	1
E	2
F	2
G	2
H	2

Bridges are classified into three categories based on (a) how they create this mapping table between host addresses and their corresponding segment numbers, and (b) how many segments are connected by one bridge. These three types of bridges are shown in Fig. 2.11.

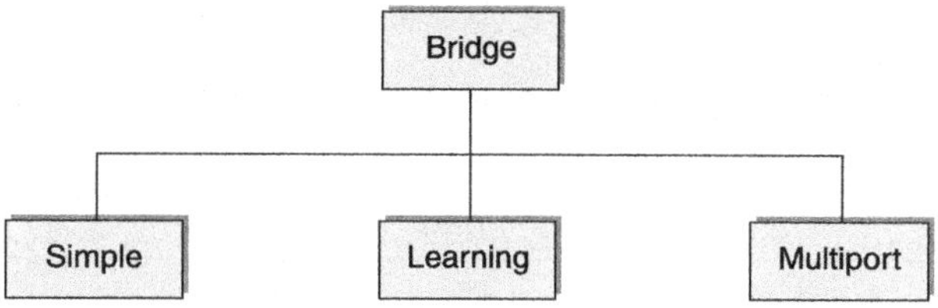

Fig. 2.11 *Types of bridges*

Let us discuss these three types of bridges now.

1. **Simple bridge** This is a very primitive type of bridge. A **simple bridge** connects two segments. Therefore, it maintains a table of host addresses versus segment numbers mapping for the two segments. This table has to be entered by an operator manually by doing data entry of all the host addresses and their segment numbers. Whenever a new host is added, or an existing host is replaced/deleted, the table has to be updated again. For these reasons, simple bridges are the cheapest, but also have a lot of scope for error due to manual intervention.
2. **Learning bridge** A *learning bridge*, also called an *adaptive bridge*, does not have to be programmed manually, unlike a simple bridge. Instead, it performs its own bridging functions. How does it do it? For building the host address to segment number mapping table, a learning bridge examines the source and destination addresses inside the received frames, and uses them to create the table. Therefore, when a bridge receives a frame from a host, it examines its table to check if the address of the sending host is available in the table. If not, it adds it to the table along with its segment number. Then it looks at the destination address to see if it is available in its mapping table. If it is available, the bridge knows on which segment the destination host is located. Therefore, it delivers the frame to that segment. If the destination address, and therefore, the segment number of the destination address is not available in its mapping table, the bridge sends the frame to all the segments to which it is connected.

   Consequently, with the first packet transmitted by each host, the bridge learns the segment number for that host, and therefore, it creates an entry for that host in its mapping table containing the host address and its segment number. Over a period of time, the bridge constructs the complete mapping between the hosts and their segment numbers for the entire network. Since the bridge continues checking and updating its mapping table all the time, even if new hosts are added, existing hosts are removed or their NICs replaced, it does not matter! The bridge *learns* about these changes and adapts to them automatically.

   Let us understand how a learning bridge creates its mapping table, with reference to Fig. 2.9. Suppose that the hosts on the network shown in Fig. 2.9 are just about to start transmissions for the first time. Note how the bridge first builds, and then updates, its mapping table, as shown in Table 2.3, for the sequence of transmission shown.

Table 2.3 *A learning bridge building a mapping table*

Frame sent by host	*Frame sent by host*	*Entry in the host address column of the bridge's mapping table*	*Entry in the segment id column of the bridge's mapping table*
A	D	A	1
D	C	D	1
A	B	–	–
B	C	B	1
H	C	H	2
E	G	E	2
F	E	F	2
G	B	G	2
C	E	C	1

The last two columns of Table 2.3 show the mapping table of the bridge. Each of the rows indicates the updation process of the mapping table. For example, in the very first case, host *A* sends a frame to host *D*. The bridge receives the frame, examines the source address and realizes that it does not have an entry for the source (A) in its mapping table. Therefore, it creates an entry for the host *A* as the last two columns of the first row signify. In the same manner, all the other updates can be easily understood. The third row is different and interesting. Here, host *A* has sent a frame to host *B*. However, since the mapping table of the bridge already has an entry for *A*, the bridge does not add it again to its mapping table.

3. **Multiport bridge** A multiport bridge is a special case of either the simple or the learning bridge. When a simple or learning bridge connects more than two network segments, it is called a *multiport bridge*.

ROUTERS 2.8

2.8.1 Introduction

A **router** operates at the physical, data link and network layer of the OSI model, as shown in Fig. 2.12. A router is termed as an *intelligent device*. Therefore, its capabilities are much more than those of a repeater or a bridge. A router is useful for interconnecting two or more networks. These networks can be heterogeneous, which means that they can differ in their physical characteristics, such as frame size, transmission rates, topologies, addressing, etc. Thus, if a router has to connect such different networks, it has to consider all these issues. A router has to determine the best possible transmission path, among several available.

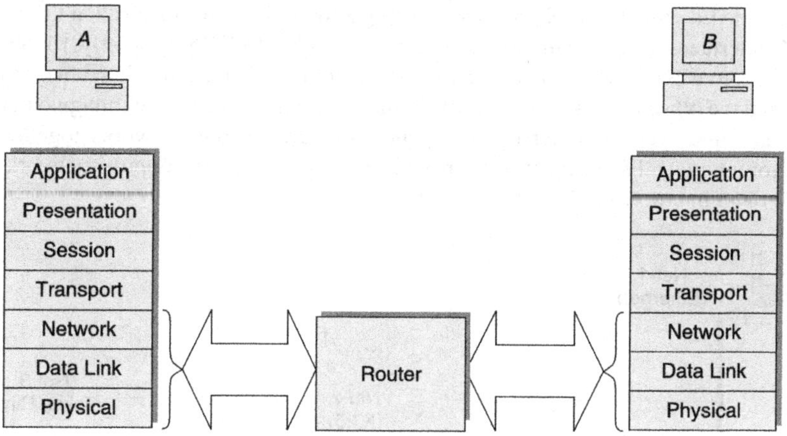

Fig. 2.12 *Router at the last three OSI layers*

2.8.2 How does a Router Work?

The concept of a router can be illustrated with the help of Fig. 2.13. As shown in the figure, there is a Token Ring network *A*, and an Ethernet network *B* based on bus architecture. A router connects to the Token Ring at point *X*, and to the Ethernet network at point *Y*. Since the same router connects to the

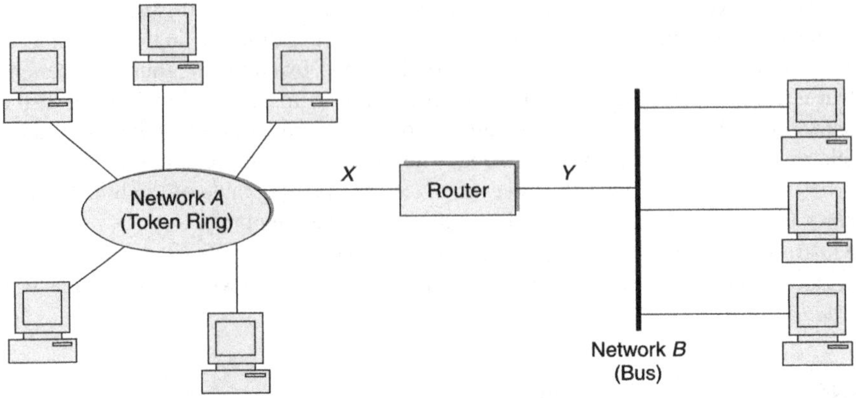

Fig. 2.13 *Router connecting a Token Ring and a bus*

two networks at these points, it means that this router must have two NICs. That is, the router is capable of working as a special host on a Token Ring as well as the Ethernet network, in this case. Similarly, a router can connect other combinations of networks, such as an Ethernet with an FDDI, a Token Ring with an FDDI and with an Ethernet, and so on. The point is that each of the router's NIC is specific to one network type to which it connects. In this example, the NIC at point *X* is a Token Ring NIC, whereas the NIC at point *Y* is an Ethernet NIC.

Going a step further, we can connect multiple networks with the help of more than one router. For example, suppose we have an Ethernet, a X.25 network and a Token Ring as shown in Fig. 2.13. Then we can connect the Ethernet to the X.25 network using a router R1. This means that the router R1 must have two NIC interfaces, one catering to Ethernet and the other to X.25. Similarly, router R2 connects the X.25 network to a Token Ring. This means that the router R2 must also have two NIC interfaces, one for X.25 and the other for Token Ring. This is shown in Fig. 2.14. We can imagine that using more routers, we can connect any number of homogeneous/heterogeneous networks together to form an internetwork (or internet). The Internet (note the upper case), which is the popular network of networks, is an example of an internetwork.

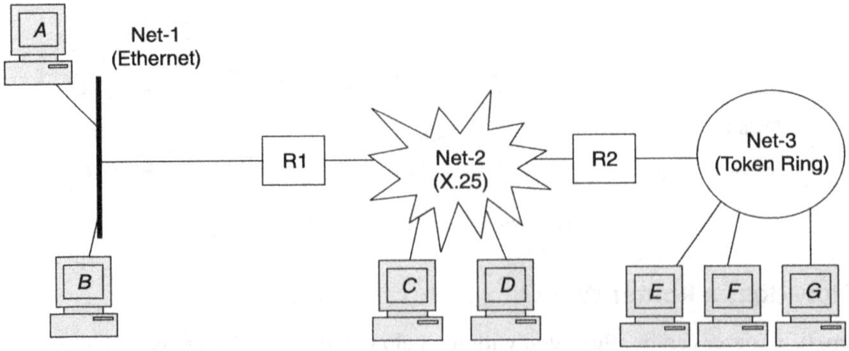

Fig. 2.14 *Two routers connecting three networks together*

2.8.3 Issues Involved in Routing

Having two NIC interfaces is fine. However, two major questions remain unanswered. They are related to the *frame format* and *physical addresses*, as discussed below.

Suppose host *A* on network 1 sends a frame for host *G* on network 3. As we can see from Fig. 2.14, the frame must pass through routers R1 and R2 before it can reach host *G*. However, the *frame format* and the *physical addressing mechanisms* used by network 1 (Ethernet) and network 3 (Token Ring) would be different.

1. What would happen if host *A* attempts to send an Ethernet frame to host *G*? Because the frame would reach router R1 first, which is also connected to network 1 (i.e., Ethernet), it would understand the format of the Ethernet frame, and because it has to now forward the frame to router R2, which is a X.25 network, router R1 would have to reformat the frame to X.25 format and send it to router R2. Router R2 can then transform the frame to the Token Ring frame format, and hand it over to host *G*, which is local to it. However, this reformatting is extremely complex. This is because it not only involves converting the frame from one format to the other but it also involves mimicking the other protocol—including acknowledgement (Token Ring provides for it, Ethernet does not), priorities, etc. Can there be a better solution?
2. Similarly, what would host *A* put in the *destination address* field of the frame that it wants to send to host *G*? Should it put the physical address of host *G* in this field? In this case, it might work correctly, as both Ethernet and Token Ring use 48-bit physical addresses. However, what if host *A* wanted to send a frame to host *D*, instead of *G*? In this case, the address sizes of host *A* (Ethernet) and host *D* (X.25) would differ. Therefore, using physical addresses of hosts on other networks can be dangerous on an internet. How do we resolve this issue?

To resolve such issues, the network layer proposes two solutions as follows:

1. To resolve the issue of different frame formats, we should use a single *logical frame format,* which is independent of the physical networks. That is, we should have a common logical frame format, which does not depend on whether the source or the destination is an Ethernet or Token Ring, or any other network. Similarly, the intermediate networks can also be different from the source and the destination networks (as happens in our case, for example, where the source is Ethernet (network 1), the intermediate network is a X.25 network (network 2) and the destination is a Token Ring (network 3)). We can then use that logical frame format universally, regardless of the underlying network types.

   Therefore, the sender *A* must encapsulate this logical frame into an Ethernet frame and give it to its local router R1. The router R1 must extract the original logical frame from this Ethernet frame, transform it into a X.25 frame format by adding the appropriate X.25 headers, which is compatible with the next network via which it has to move forward, and send it to router R2. Router R2 should then extract the logical frame out from the X.25 frame, transform it into a Token Ring frame by adding the appropriate Token Ring headers, and give it to host *G*. At node *G* again, the original logical frame is extracted. When all such frames (i.e., the entire message) arrive at node *G*, it can be handed over to the upper layers at node *G* for processing.

   We shall examine this process in detail in a separate chapter later, when we discuss TCP/IP.
2. To resolve the issue of different address formats, a **universal address** or **logical address** or **network-layer address** can be used across all networks. This logical address would be independent of all the underlying physical addresses, and their formats. Therefore, when the sender wants to send a frame to host *G*, it would put the logical address of host *G* in the

destination address field. Using this logical destination address and the logical addresses of the intermediate nodes, routing will be done so that the frame can move forward from host *A* to router R1, from router R1 to router R2, and from router R2 to host *G*. At various stages, the logical addresses would need to be translated to their equivalent physical addresses, because physical networks understand physical, and not logical addresses.

We shall examine this process also later.

In both the cases, routers play a very significant role. Of course, apart from these, the routers have to find the most optimal path for routing frames. We have already discussed this concept earlier.

GATEWAYS 2.9

As shown in Fig. 2.15, a **gateway** operates at all the seven layers of the OSI model.

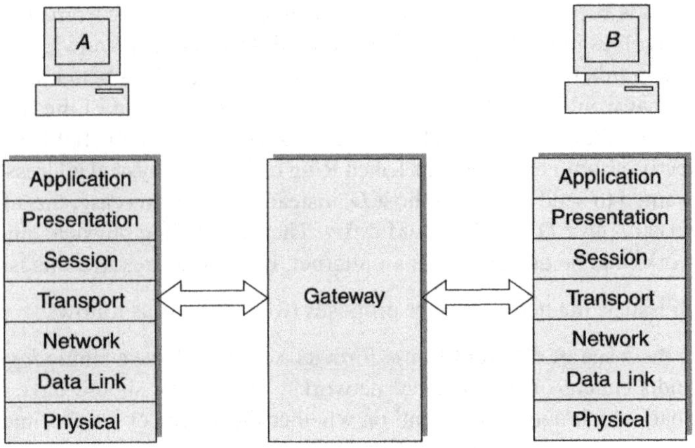

Fig. 2.15 *Gateway at all the OSI layers*

As we know, a router can forward packets across different network types (e.g., Ethernet, Token Ring, X.25, FDDI, etc.). However, all these dissimilar networks must use a common transmission protocol (such as TCP/IP or AppleTalk) for communication. If they are not using the same protocol, a router would not be able to forward packets from one network to another. On the other hand, at a still higher level, a gateway can forward packets across different networks that may also use different protocols. That is, if network *A* is a Token Ring network using TCP/IP and network *B* is a Novell Netware network, a gateway can relay frames between the two.

This means that a gateway has to not only have the ability of translating between different frame formats, but also different protocols. The gateway is aware of, and can work with, the protocols used by each network connected to a router, and therefore, it can translate from one to the other. In certain situations, the only changes required are to the frame header. In other cases, the gateway must take care of differing frame sizes, data rates, formats, acknowledgement schemes, priority schemes, etc. That means that the task of the gateway is very tough.

Clearly, a gateway is a very powerful computer as compared to a bridge or a router. It is typically used to connect huge and incompatible networks.

A BRIEF HISTORY OF THE INTERNET 2.10

2.10.1 Introduction

Although the Internet seems to have become extremely popular over the last decade or so, it has a 40-year long history. The motives behind the creation of the Internet were two-fold.

1. Researchers wanted to communicate with each other and share their research papers and documents.
2. The US military system wanted a strong communications infrastructure to withstand any nuclear attack by the erstwhile Soviet Union. The idea was that even if both the countries were completely destroyed by the World War, important American scientists and diplomats could hide in the underground bunkers and still communicate with each other to reconstruct America ahead of Soviet Union and therefore, win the World War that would follow!

These developments date back to 1960s. This necessitated a large decentralized network of computers within the United States. In 1961, Baran first introduced the concept of **store and forward packet switching**. These concepts were very useful in the development of the Internet.

2.10.2 ARPAnet

Baran's original ideas did not attract publicity for quite some time. Actually, similar ideas were put forward by Zimmerman in France. Baran's ideas were first used by the **Advanced Research Project Agency (ARPA)** of the US Department of Defense. They sponsored a network of computers called as **ARPAnet**, which was developed with the aim of sharing of scattered time-sharing systems. This made sharing of long-distance telephone lines possible, which were quite expensive. ARPAnet was first proposed in 1966 and was actually built by a few researchers in 1969. This was the pioneering effort in actually practicing concepts of wide-area packet switching networks, decentralized routing, flow control and many applications such as **TELNET** (which allows a user to log in to a computer from remote distance) and **FTP (File Transfer Protocol)**, which are used even today.

Once ARPAnet started becoming popular, people thought of connecting other networks to ARPAnet, thus creating a network of computer networks, or the *internetwork*. This led to the ideas of shared packet format, routing and addressing schemes. The important point is, throughout these developments, care was taken to ensure that the network of networks should be kept as decentralized as possible. The concept of a *router* was defined at this stage. As we have discussed, a router is a computer that is mainly used for transferring data packets between computer networks. Also, IP protocol was so designed that no assumptions were made regarding the underlying transmission medium (such as twisted pair) or the frame format used by a specific network (e.g., Ethernet). It was kept independent of the transmission medium and the specific network hardware/software.

Other networks such as CSNET and NEARnet were developed using the same philosophy as of ARPAnet. Soon, many such networks started developing. Because of the inherent design, these networks could all be connected together. By early 1980s, ten such networks had formed what is now called the *Internet.*

2.10.3 The World Wide Web (WWW)

The **World Wide Web (WWW)** is an application that runs on the Internet—and is one of the most popular of all the Internet applications. The WWW was first developed with a very simple intention—to enable document sharing between researchers and scientists that were located at physically different places. In 1989, Tim Berrners-LEE at the Conseil Europeen pour la Recherche Nucleaire (CERN)—now known as the European Laboratory for Particle Physics, started the WWW project. His goals were in two areas, as given below:

1. Developing ways of linking documents that were not stored on the same computer, but were scattered across many different physical locations (i.e., hyperlinks).
2. Enabling users to work together—a process called **collaborative authoring**. After over a decade's growth, the first goal has been successfully met. However, the second is still not complete.

Interestingly, as soon as the basic outline of the WWW was ready, CERN published the software code for the general public. This attracted programmers very much to the WWW. This concept of **open source code** or **freeware** (unlike **proprietary source code**, which is not made available to the general public), meant that people could not only experiment with the WWW software, but also add new functionalities and extend them to new heights. Soon, hundreds of programmers from the National Center for Supercomputing Applications (NCSA) at the University of Illinois started working on the initial WWW software development. Making use of the basic code developed at CERN, NCSA came up with the first **Web browser** with graphical user interface called **Mosaic** in 1993. A browser is simply a program running on a **client computer** that retrieves and allows viewing a document stored on a remote **server computer** (we shall soon study the meaning of client and server computers).

Key members of the teams that developed Mosaic and the original **Web server** software [A Web server is a computer program that waits for requests from remote clients (i.e., Web browsers) for documents stored on the server computer, retrieves them, and sends these back to the clients] at CERN came together to form a company called Netscape Communications. They developed Netscape Navigator, a new browser, in December 1994. This browser was the first commercial Web browser for the WWW that included many new features, most important among them being security, which enabled commercial transactions over the WWW in the years to follow. Over the next few years, the WWW grew from experimentation to a truly commercial project. This can be judged from the value ratings of Netscape Communications. Netscape Communications, a company with two-year-history with almost no revenue, went public in August 1995. It was initially valued at $1.1 billion, a figure that rose almost five times in the next four months!

To avoid proprietary influences, the WWW project shifted from CERN to Massachusetts Institute of Technology (MIT) in 1995, and is now called the **W3 Consortium**. This Consortium coordinates the development of WWW standards and ensures uniformity and minimum duplication of efforts.

GROWTH OF THE INTERNET 2.11

While ARPA was working on the Internet research project, the UNIX operating system was also taking the computing world by storm. A group of computer researchers developed UNIX in the early 1970s at the Bell Labs. Bell Labs allowed universities to have copies of UNIX for teaching and research purposes. To encourage its portability, Bell Labs provided the source code of the UNIX operating system to the students. This meant that the students could try it out in a variety of ways to see if it worked and could also modify it to make it better. A group of students at the University of California at Berkeley wrote application programs and modified the UNIX operating system to have network capabilities (e.g., sending a message to another computer, accessing a file stored on a remote computer, etc.). This version of UNIX, later called as **BSD UNIX** (Berkeley Software Distribution) became very popular.

ARPA noticed that BSD was now a well-known entity. They signed a deal with Berkeley researchers under which the BSD UNIX now incorporated TCP/IP protocol in the operating system itself. Thus, with the next version of BSD UNIX, people got TCP/IP software almost free. Although few universities who bought BSD UNIX had connection to the Internet, they usually had their own **Local Area Networks (LANs)**. They now started using TCP/IP for LANs. Later on, the same concept was applied to the Internet. Thus, TCP/IP first entered the LANs at the universities, and from there, to other networks.

By early 1980s, the Internet had become reliable. The main interconnection at this stage was between academic and research sites. The Internet had demonstrated that the basic internet working principles were quite sound. This convinced the US military. They now connected their computers to the Internet using TCP/IP software. In 1982, the US military decided to use the Internet as its primary computer communication medium. At the start of 1983, ARPANET and the concerned military networks stopped running old communication software and made TCP/IP the de facto standard.

Before the US military started switching its computers to use TCP/IP, there were about 200 computers connected to the Internet. In 1984, this number almost doubled. Other US government agencies, such as Department of Defense (DOD) and National Aeronautics and Space Administration (NASA), also got themselves connected to the Internet. Meanwhile, the Cold War suddenly ended. The Internet came out of the secret world of the military and became open to the general public and businesses. Since then, the number of computers connected to the Internet kept almost doubling every year. In 1990, there were approximately 290,000 computers connected to the Internet. At the time of going to the press, it is estimated that every three seconds a new computer connects to the Internet. Table 2.4 shows the number of computers connected to the Internet from 1995 to 2007. It is indeed quite an explosive growth!

This is shown graphically in Fig. 2.16.

Table 2.4 *Growth of the Internet*

Year	*Number of Users (in Millions)*
1995	16
1996	36
1997	70
1998	147
1999	248
2000	361
2001	513
2002	587
2003	719
2004	817
2005	1018
2006	1093
2007	1133

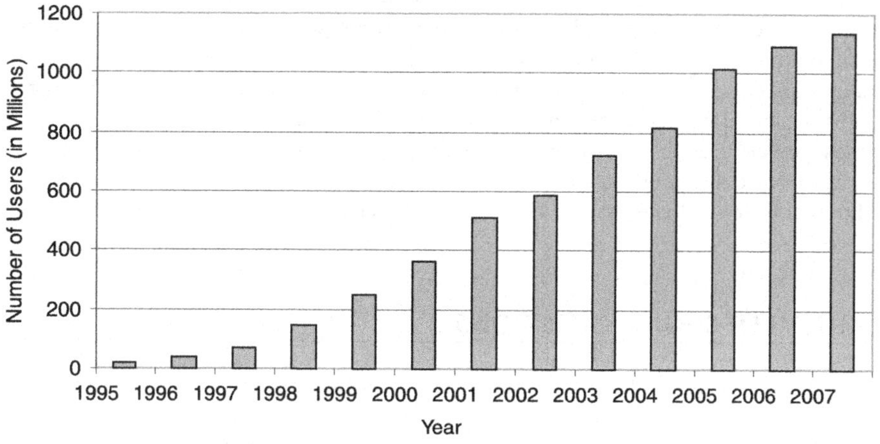

Fig. 2.16 *Graph showing growth of the Internet*

Key Terms and Concepts

Adaptive Bridge • Advanced Research Project Agency (ARPA) • ARPAnet • Bridge • Browsing • Client computer • Collaborative authoring • Connecting devices • Dial-up program • Email • Email id • Email service • File Transfer Protocol (FTP) • Freeware • Gateway • Internet • Internet Service Provider (ISP) • IP addresses • ISP portal • Internet working • Internet working devices • Learning Bridge • Logical address • Modem • Networking devices • Network-layer address • Open source code • Proprietary source code • Regenerator • Repeater • Router • Segment • Server computer • Simple bridge • SMTP server • Store and forward packet switching • TELNET • Transmission Control Protocol/Internet Protocol (TCP/IP) • Universal address • Universal service • Virtual network • Web browser • Web page hosting • Web server • W3 Consortium • World Wide Web (WWW)

SUMMARY

- When multiple computers are connected to each other, a computer network is formed. When multiple computer networks are connected to each other, it becomes an internetwork, or an internet.
- A router is a special-purpose computer that can connect multiple computer networks. For this, a router has an interface (NIC) to each of the networks that it connects to.
- The Internet is a virtual network of computer networks. The term *virtual* arises because it is actually a network of a number of networks, which differ in their hardware and software characteristics, and yet work seamlessly with each other.
- Networking and internet working devices are used respectively for connecting computers and networks together.
- Networking devices include repeaters and bridges. Internet working devices can be classified into routers and gateways.
- A repeater is an electronic device, which simply regenerates a bit stream. It works at the physical layer of the OSI protocol.
- A bridge is a computer that has its own processor, memory and two NIC cards to connect to two portions of a network. A bridge does not run application programs, and instead, facilitates host-to-host communication within a network.
- A router is an *intelligent* device. Its capabilities are much more than those of a repeater or a bridge. A router is useful for interconnecting two or more networks.
- The most powerful device is a gateway. A gateway can forward packets across different networks that may also use different protocols.
- The Internet is one of the most significant developments of the 20th century.

MULTIPLE-CHOICE QUESTIONS

1. In internet working, the two or more networks that connect with each other ________ incompatible with one another.
   (a) have to be (b) may be (c) must not be (d) None of these

2. Usually, a ________ is used for internet working purposes.
   (a) host (b) wire (c) router (d) joiner
3. A router must have at least ________ NICs.
   (a) 2 (b) 3 (c) 4 (d) 5
4. There are ________ incompatibility issues when forming an internet out of networks.
   (a) both hardware and software (b) only hardware
   (c) only software (d) software but not hardware
5. A bridge is a ________ device.
   (a) networking (b) connecting (c) internet working (d) routing
6. A ________ is the simplest of all networking/internet working devices.
   (a) repeater (b) bridge (c) router (d) gateway
7. Generally, a ________ is used to divide a network into segments.
   (a) repeater (b) bridge (c) router (d) gateway
8. A ________ builds its mapping table as and when it gets more information about the network.
   (a) simple bridge (b) repeater (c) adaptive bridge (d) regenerator
9. A logical address is ________ the physical address.
   (a) the same as (b) tightly coupled with
   (c) sometimes related to (d) completely unrelated to
10. A can understand multiple networking protocols.
    (a) repeater (b) bridge (c) router (d) gateway

DETAILED QUESTIONS

1. Discuss the motives for internet working.
2. What is universal service?
3. What are the various broad-level issues in internet working?
4. How does a router facilitate interconnection between two or more networks?
5. Explain the role played by the repeater at the physical layer.
6. What is a bridge? Explain its functions.
7. What are the types of bridges? Explain the simple bridge.
8. What is a router? How does it work?
9. How does a gateway work?
10. Discuss in brief the history of the Internet.

EXERCISES

1. Find out more about the history of the Internet.
2. Investigate what is required to become an ISP.
3. If your background is not in data communications, learn more about the various data communications and networking technologies, such as LAN (Ethernet, Token Ring, FDDI), MAN (SMDS, DQDB) and WAN (X.25, Frame Relay).
4. Assume that you have to build a router on your own. What would be the hardware/software requirements for the same?
5. Find out what sort of router or bridge is being used by your organization, college or university.

3 TCP/IP PART I INTRODUCTION TO TCP/IP, ARP, RARP, ICMP

INTRODUCTION

The **Transmission Control Protocol/Internet Protocol (TCP/IP)** suite of protocols forms the basis of Internetworking (note the uppercase, which means that we are referring to the worldwide network of computer networks). It is TCP/IP that creates an illusion of a virtual network when multiple computer networks are connected together. TCP/IP was developed in early 1970s. Interestingly, the development of Local Area Networks and of course, the Internet, was during the same time. Thus, TCP/IP grew with the Internet and because LANs also became popular soon, connecting LANs was one of the early goals of TCP/IP. In fact, when multiple networks with multiple frame/datagram formats and also multiple other algorithms (routing, error control, compression, etc.) are to be connected, there are two alternatives which are: (a) Protocol conversion, and (b) A universal protocol with its frame/datagram size and other algorithms operating at every node in every network in addition to the existing protocols with algorithms of converting to/from that network's frame/datagram from/to the frame/datagram of the universal protocol. TCP/IP uses the latter philosophy.

We have seen the OSI model of network protocols. TCP/IP was developed before OSI. Therefore, the layers present in TCP/IP do not match exactly with those in OSI. Instead, the TCP/IP suite consists of four layers. It considers the data link layer and physical layer to be made up of a single layer. However, for the sake of understanding, we shall consider it to be made up of five layers, as shown in Fig. 3.1.

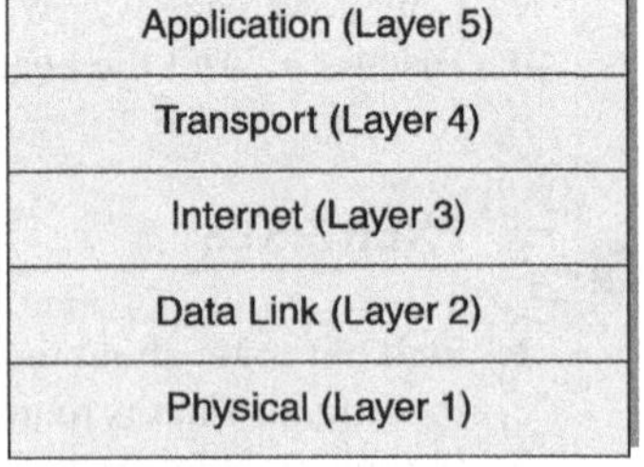

Fig. 3.1 *TCP/IP layers*

Layer 1 Physical Layer The physical layer in TCP/IP is not different in any way to the physical layer of the OSI model. This layer deals with the hardware level, voltages, etc., and there is nothing significantly different here in case of TCP/IP.

Layer 2 Data Link Layer The data link layer is also very similar to other network models. This covers the **Media Access and Control (MAC)** strategies—i.e., who can send data and when, etc. This also deals with the frame formats (e.g., Ethernet, etc.) and so on.

Layer 3 Internet Layer or Network Layer The Internet layer is very important from the context of communication over an internet or the Internet. This layer is concerned with the format of datagrams, as defined in the **Internet Protocol (IP)**, and also about the mechanism of forwarding datagrams from the source computer to the final destination via one or more routers. Thus, this layer is also responsible for actual routing of datagrams. This layer makes internetworking possible, and thus creates an illusion of a virtual network. We shall study this in detail.

The IP portion of the TCP/IP suite deals with this layer. This layer follows a datagram philosophy. That is, it routes and forwards a datagram to the next hop, but is not responsible for the accurate and timely delivery of all the datagrams to the destination in a proper sequence. Other protocols in this layer are **Address Resolution Protocol (ARP), Reverse Address Resolution Protocol (RARP)** and **Internet Control Message Protocol (ICMP)**.

Layer 4 Transport Layer There are two main protocols in this layer—**Transmission Control Protocol (TCP)** and **User Datagram Protocol (UDP)**. TCP ensures that the communication between the sender and the receiver is reliable, error-free and in sequence. The IP layer sends individual datagrams through various routers, choosing a path for each datagram each time. Thus, different datagrams may reach the destination via different routes and may reach out of sequence. In addition, a datagram may not reach the destination correctly. IP does not even check the CRC for the data in each datagram at each router. At the destination, the TCP software is responsible for checking the CRC, detecting any errors, reporting them, and acknowledging the correct delivery of datagrams. Finally, it also sequences all the datagrams that are received correctly, to form the original message. TCP uses a **sliding window** technique, so that multiple datagrams can be sent/acknowledged in one shot, instead of waiting for the acknowledgement of each datagram before sending the next one. As we shall see later, **UDP** is also used in this layer. However, UDP does not offer reliability. It is, therefore, far faster. Whenever we are not bothered about slight variations as much as about speed (i.e., in case of voice or video), we can use UDP. However, it is better to use TCP for sending data such as in banking transactions.

Layer 5 Application Layer Like the OSI model, the application layer allows an end user to run various applications on the Internet and use the Internet in different ways. These applications (and various underlying protocols) are **File Transfer Protocol (FTP)**, **Trivial File Transfer protocol (TFTP)**, **email (SMTP)**, **remote login (TELNET)**, and the **World Wide Web (HTTP)**. The application layer corresponds to layers 6 and 7 in the OSI model. The layer 5 of OSI, i.e., session layer, is not very important in the case of TCP/IP. Therefore, it is almost stripped/ignored.

TCP/IP BASICS 3.1

Before we discuss TCP/IP in detail, let us draw a diagram of the various sub-protocols that together compose the TCP/IP software, as shown in Figs. 3.2 and 3.3. We shall discuss all these protocols in detail subsequently.

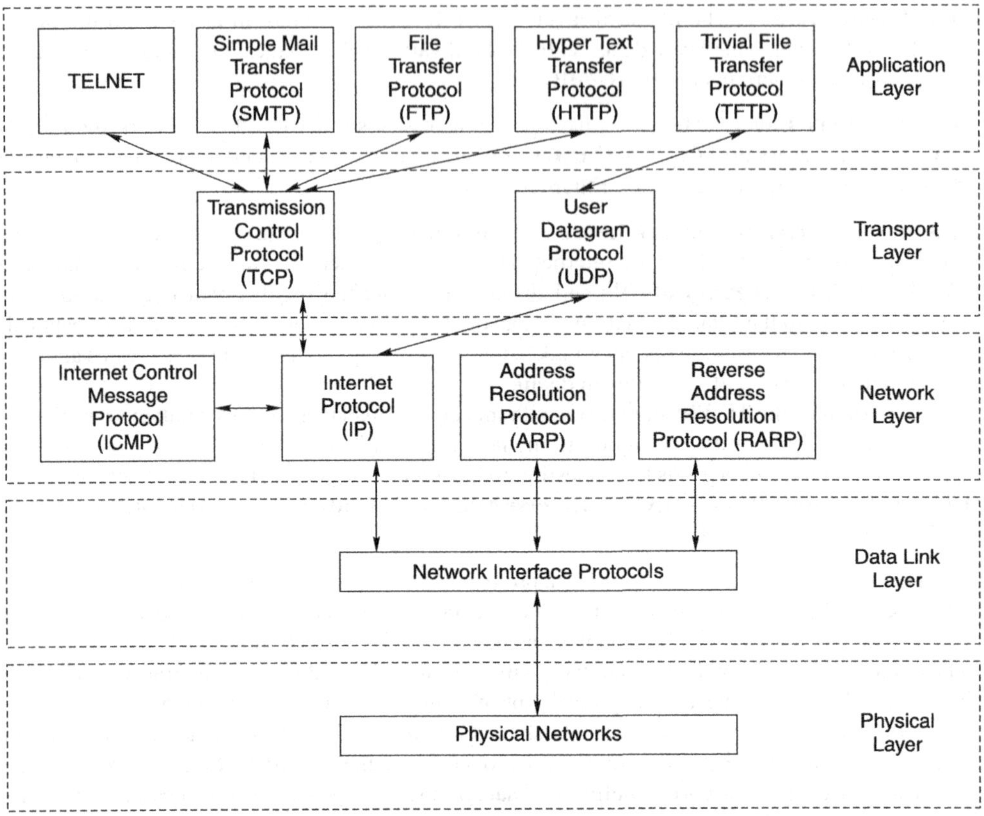

Fig. 3.2 *Protocols in the TCP/IP suite at different layers*

It is important to know the mapping between the OSI model and the TCP/IP model. That gives us a good understanding of where things fit in. Figure 3.3 shows the encapsulation of data units at different layers of the TCP/IP protocol suite in comparison with the OSI model. As the figure shows, the data unit initially created at the application layer is called as a *message*. A message is then broken down into *user datagrams* or segments by TCP or UDP in the transport layer. They are encapsulated by IP and then into *frames* by the data link layer. Remember, if for instance, Ethernet is an underlying network, the entire thing consisting of IP header + TCP header + datagram is treated as the data portion of the Ethernet frame to which Ethernet frame header is attached. This frame header contains the addresses of the source and the destination nodes, which are the physical addresses of the adjacent routers on the chosen path. This is how the datagram travels from router to router using the underlying network. When the frame reaches the next router, the CRC is checked, the frame header dropped, the final source and destination addresses are checked in the IP/TCP headers, the next router is decided, based on the path, and again the datagram is encapsulated in the frame format of the underlying network connecting those routers. When all the datagrams reach the destination node, TCP at that node puts all the datagrams together to form the original message.

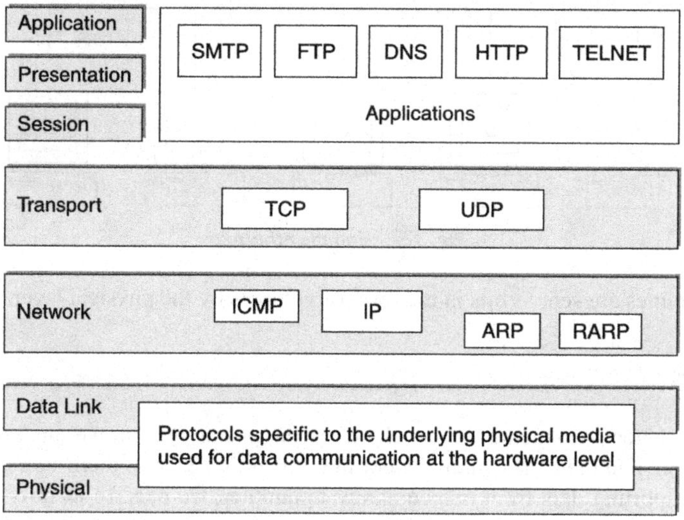

Fig. 3.3 *Mapping of TCP/IP protocols with the OSI model*

At a broad level, each datagram of a message travels from the source to the destination, as shown in the figure. For simplicity, it is assumed that the message is very small and fits in one datagram/frame.

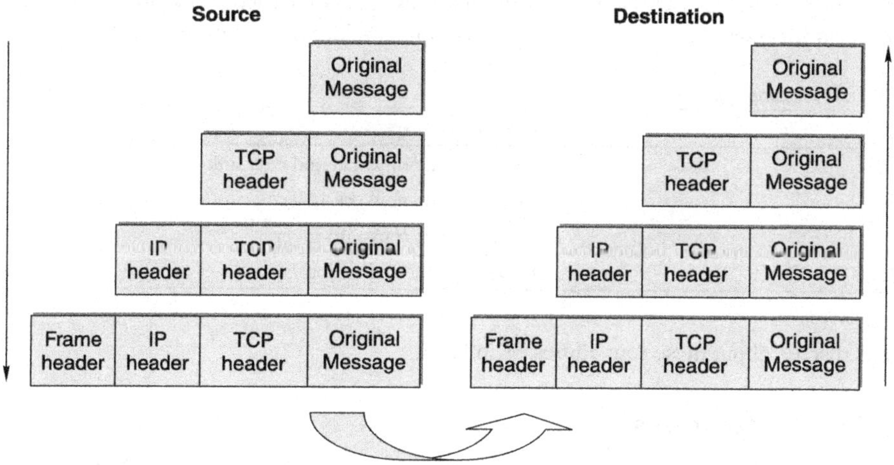

Fig. 3.4 *Message transfer from the source to the destination at different layers*

At the lowest level (physical layer), if a datagram is to be sent from node-*A* to node-*E* over the Ethernet shown in Fig. 3.5, it will ultimately be sent as an Ethernet frame by appending the frame header by node-*A*. At node-*E*, the header will be discarded and the original datagram will be retrieved.

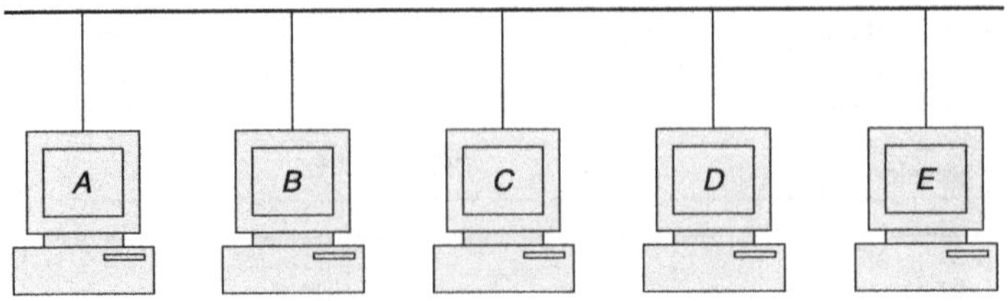

Fig. 3.5 Sample ethernet

Finally, the frames are sent as bits in the form of voltages by the physical layer.

ADDRESSING 3.2

For transporting a letter contained in an envelope via the postal system, we must be able to identify each home/office/shop in the world uniquely. For this, we assign each of them a unique postal address. Similarly, for transporting data from one computer to another, we need to identify each computer in the world uniquely. For this, we use addresses again! Therefore, just as the person who writes the letter puts it in an envelope and mentions the address of the receiver on it, the computer which is sending a message puts the message inside a logical envelope and mentions the address of the receiving computer on the envelope. We know that in the postal system, the intermediate post offices successfully route the letter from the sender to the receiver. Here, we have the routers, who do the same job.

Before we get into the discussion of how this happens in detail, we would like to examine the concept of **computer addresses**. There are four types of computer addresses identified, as shown in Table 3.1.

Table 3.1 *Addressing types*

Address type	*Meaning/Purpose*
Physical	Used by the physical and data link layers
Logical	Used by the network layer
Port	Used by the transport layer
Specific	Used by the application layer

Let us discuss about these four addresses in brief.

3.2.1 Physical Addresses

Physical addresses are defined by the Local Area Network (LAN) or Wide Area Network (WAN), to which the computer belongs. It has authority only within that LAN or WAN. Outside of a LAN or WAN, it can lead to ambiguity. To understand this, *East Street* may be there in hundreds of cities in the world. However, within a city, *East Street* has an authority (i.e., it is well known/understood). Outside of it, it leads to ambiguity. The size and formats of physical addresses vary across technologies. For example, we know that Ethernet uses 48 bits to identify a computer uniquely (i.e., uses 48-bit addresses). On the other hand, Apple LocalTalk uses just 8-bit addresses. Apart from different address sizes, we know that the hardware frame formats themselves differ across various networking technologies.

3.2.2 Logical Addresses

Logical addresses also are called universal addresses. In other words, they are independent of the underlying networking infrastructure (software and hardware). As we shall discuss shortly, they use a universal size (32 bits) so as to be consistent and are called IP addresses.

Each router has more than one physical address and more than one logical address. Although we shall examine this in detail subsequently, the way the routing process works is conceptually simple to understand. The sender only needs to know the logical address of the receiver. It is important to know that when a packet goes from the sender to the destination via one or more routers, the source and destination logical (i.e., IP) addresses in the packet never change. However, the source and destination physical addresses keep changing at every step, as we shall study later.

3.2.3 Port Addresses

Logical and physical addresses help packets to travel from the source to the destination. To understand this, let us consider an example. Suppose that person *A* working in organization *X* wants to make a call to person *B* working in organization *Y*. Like *A* and *B*, there would be several people making several calls to several other people. The telephone infrastructure knows how to route a call from organization *X* to organization *Y*. However, that is not good enough, once the call reaches the telephone network of organization *Y*, we must be able to forward it to the telephone extension of person *B*. This situation is depicted in Fig. 3.6.

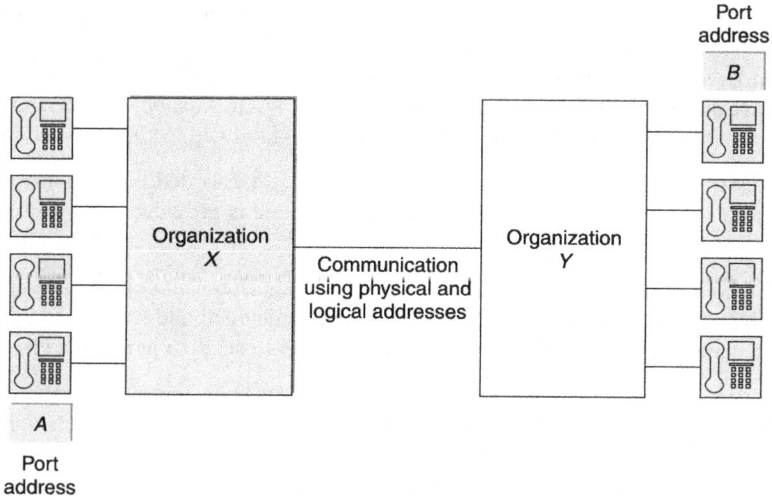

Fig. 3.6 *Port addressing concept*

In a similar fashion, when the sending computer sends packets to the receiving computer, the router infrastructure ensures that packets travel from the sender to the receiver. However, we must also ensure that not only do the packets reach the right receiver, but also that they reach the right application on the receiving computer. In other words, if the sending application has sent an email, the receiving computer must also hand it over to the local email software, and not to, say, the **File Transfer Protocol (FTP)** application.

This is where the port address comes into picture. It uniquely identifies an application on the receiving (destination) computer, so that there is no confusion.

3.2.4 Specific Addresses

Specific addresses are user-friendly versions of addresses. Examples of such addresses are email addresses (e.g., akahate@gmail.com) or Web addresses (e.g., www.google.com). Users (i.e., humans) work with these specific addresses. On the other hand, computers work with logical and port addresses. Therefore, the specific addresses get converted into logical and port addresses, as necessary, for the actual transfer of packets. This allows humans (who like specific addresses) and computers (who like IP and port addresses) to work with what they find more friendly.

WHY IP ADDRESSES? 3.3

How does the Internet Protocol (IP) know where a datagram comes from and where it has to be delivered? Recall our previous discussion of a virtual network. The primary goal of the Internet is to provide an abstracted view of the complexities involved inside it. For a common user, the Internet must appear as a single large network of computers, and the fact that it is internally a network of many incompatible networks must be hidden from him. At the same time, people dealing with the networks that make up the Internet must be free to choose the hardware and networking technologies that suit their requirements, such as Ethernet, Token Ring, SNA, etc. This means that a common interface is required to bind the two views together—that of an end user of the Internet and the other of the people dealing with their own networks.

Consequently, identifying a computer over the Internet is a big challenge. Different networking technologies have different *physical addressing* mechanisms. What is the *physical address* or *hardware address* of a computer? There are three methods to assign the hardware address to a computer:

1. Static addresses In this scheme, the physical address is hardcoded on the **Network Interface Card (NIC)** of the computer. This address does not change, and is provided by the network hardware manufacturer.

2. Configurable addresses In this case, the physical address is configured inside a computer when it is first installed at a site. Unlike a static address, which is decided and hardcoded by the hardware manufacturer, a configurable address allows the end customer to set up a physical address.

3. Dynamic addresses In this scheme, every time a computer boots, a server computer dynamically assigns it a physical address. This also means that the physical address keeps on changing every time a computer is switched off and on. A pool of free physical addresses is used to identify free addresses out of them, and one such free address is assigned to the newly booting computer. Instead of using one of the pool of free addresses, the dynamic address can be generated as a random number at run time, and it is ensured that the same random number is not used as a physical address by any other computer in that network.

We shall not discuss these types further. However, it is essential to remember that static addresses are the simplest of the three, and therefore, are most popular, as they need no manual interventions or dynamic processing. In any case, the point to note is that there is a unique physical address or hardware address for every computer on a network. This address gets stored on the NIC of that computer. The network must use that address for delivery of messages to that computer.

The NIC is simply an I/O interface on a computer that allows communication between the computer and all other computers on a given network. The NIC is a small computer having a small amount of memory, which is responsible for the communication between the computer and the network to which it is attached. This is shown in Fig. 3.7.

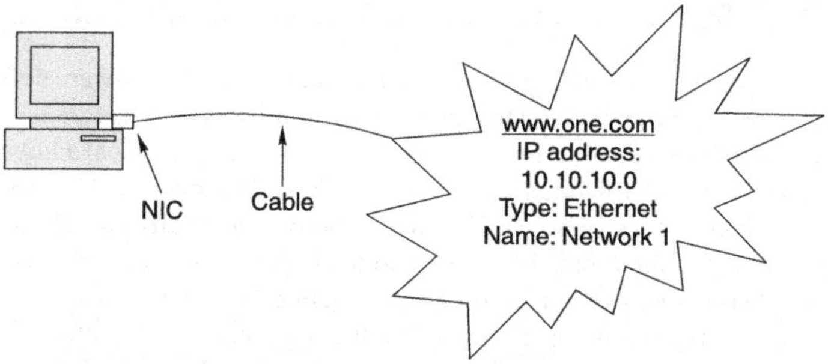

Fig. 3.7 *The Network Interface Card (NIC) is the interface between a host and the network to which it attaches*

Although the NIC is shown separately for ease of understanding, it actually fits in one of the slots of the motherboard of the computer, and therefore, is inside the computer. It is very similar to the way a hard disk fits in one of the slots of the computer's motherboard. The NIC appears like a thick card.

The main point to note is that the NIC is *between* a computer and the network to which it belongs. Thus, it acts as an interface between a computer and its network. When a computer wants to send a message to another computer on the same network, the following things happen:

1. The computer sends a message to its NIC. The NIC is a small computer, as we have noted. Therefore, it also has its own memory. The NIC stores this message in its memory.
2. The NIC now breaks the message into frames as appropriate to the underlying network protocol (e.g., Ethernet, Token Ring, etc.).
3. The NIC inserts the source and destination *physical* addresses into the frame header. It also computes the CRC and inserts it into the appropriate field of the frame header.
4. The NIC waits until it gets control of the network medium (e.g., in Ethernet, when the bus is free, or in Token Ring, when it grabs the token, etc.). When it gets the control, it sends one or more frames on to the network.
5. Each frame then travels over the network and is received by the respective NICs of all the computers on the network. Each NIC compares its own physical address with that of the destination address contained in the frame. If there is a mismatch, it discards the frame. Thus, only the correct recipient's NIC accepts the frame, as its address matches with the destination address of the frame.
6. The correct recipient receives all the frames in the same fashion.
7. The recipient NIC computes the CRC for each frame, and matches it with that in the frame to check for error, and if acceptable, uses all these frames to reconstruct the original message after discarding the header, etc.
8. The NIC of the recipient computer now hands over the entire message to the recipient computer.

The physical address of a computer is pre-decided by the manufacturer and is always unique. However, the trouble is that the physical addressing scheme differs from one manufacturer to another. To give the appearance of a single and uniform Internet, all computers on the Internet must use a uniform addressing mechanism wherein no two addresses are the same. Since physical networks differ in terms of the address sizes and formats, physical addresses cannot be used. Therefore, IP cannot use the physical address of a computer. It must have a layer on top of the physical address.

LOGICAL ADDRESSES 3.4

To guarantee uniform addressing for all computers on the Internet, the IP software defines an addressing mechanism that does not depend on the underlying physical addresses. This is called **logical addressing**. It is very important to understand the difference between the physical and logical addresses of a computer. Whereas the physical address is hardcoded on the NIC inside a computer—and is thus a hardware entity, a logical address is purely an abstraction—and is thus a creation of the software. This abstraction permits computers over the Internet to think only in terms of logical addresses. Thus, there is no dependence on the physical addresses, and therefore, on the underlying networking mechanisms.

When a computer wants to communicate with another computer on the Internet, it uses the logical address of the destination computer. It is not bothered with the physical address of the destination computer, and therefore, the size and format of the physical address. Thus, even if these two computers have totally different physical addressing mechanisms, they can easily communicate using their logical addresses! This makes communication so simple that sometimes people find it hard to believe that these are not the physical addresses of the computers, and are, in fact, purely logical entities! Of course, internally, we have to find out the physical address from the IP address of the node to actually transmit a frame over a network. This is achieved by a protocol called **Address Resolution Protocol (ARP)**. The example in the next section will clarify this.

TCP/IP EXAMPLE 3.5

3.5.1 Introduction

Let us illustrate the working of TCP/IP with the help of an example. Let us assume that there are three networks, an Ethernet, a X.25 WAN and a Token Ring. Each one has a frame format that is recognized within that network. The sizes and the formats of these frames obviously are different. Figure 3.8 shows these networks connected by routers R1 and R2.

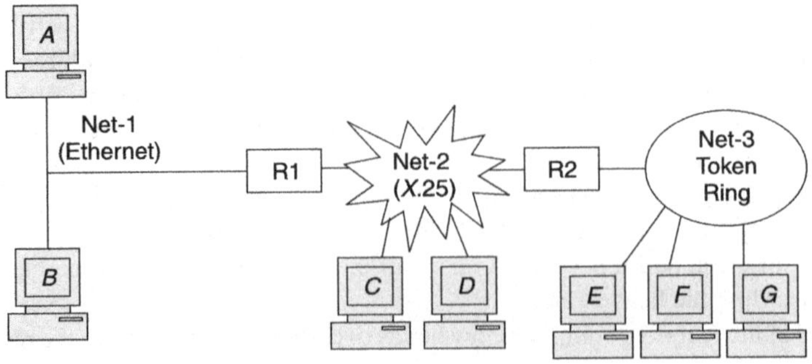

Fig. 3.8 *Different networks in the Internet*

If computer *A* of Net-1 wants to send a message (e.g., an email or a file) to computer *G* of Net-3, how can we achieve this? The networks and their frame formats are different. Ethernet frame, X.25 datagram and Token Ring frame formats are different as shown in Fig. 3.9 (not shown to proportion).

As we can see, there is a vast difference not only between the sizes of the three frame/datagram formats, but also between, the individual field lengths and contents. Now, in which format should the communication take place? This is where IP plays a major role, as we shall see.

Preamble (8 bytes)	Destination Address (6 bytes)	Source Address (6 bytes)	Frame Type (2 bytes)	Data (46–1500 bytes)	CRC (4 bytes)

(a) Ethernet frame format

General Format Identifier (4 bytes)	Logical Channel Identifier (12 bytes)	Receive Number (4 bytes)	Send Number (4 bytes)	Data (Variable length)

(b) X.25 frame format

Preamble (8 bytes)	Access Control Field (8 bytes)	Frame Control (48 bytes)	Destination Address (48 bytes)	Source Address (48 bytes)	Data (Variable length)	Other data (56 bytes)

(c) Token Ring frame format

Fig. 3.9 *Different frame formats*

3.5.2 IP Datagrams

The structure of the standard format, called an **IP datagram**, is shown in Fig. 3.10.

An IP datagram is a variable-length datagram. A message can be broken down into multiple datagrams and a datagram in turn can be fragmented into different fragments, as we shall see. The datagram can contain a maximum of 65,536 bytes. A datagram is made up of two main parts, the **header** and the **data**. The header has a length of 20 to 60 bytes and essentially contains information about the routing and delivery. The data portion contains the actual data to be sent to the recipient. The header is like an envelope, as it contains information *about* the data. The data is analogous to the letter inside the envelope. Let us examine the header.

1. Version This field currently contains a value *4*, which indicates **IP version 4 (IPv4)**. In future, this field would contain a value *6* when **IP version 6 (IPv6)** becomes the standard.

2. Header Length (HLEN) Indicates the size of the header in a multiple of four-byte words. When the header size is 20 bytes as shown in the figure, the value of this field is 5 (because $5 \times 4 = 20$), and when the option field is at the maximum size, the value of HLEN is 15 (because $15 \times 4 = 60$).

3. Service type This field is used to define service parameters, such as the priority of the datagram and the level of reliability desired.

4. Total length This field contains the total length of the IP datagram. Because it is two bytes long, an IP datagram cannot be more than 65,536 bytes ($2^{16} = 65,536$).

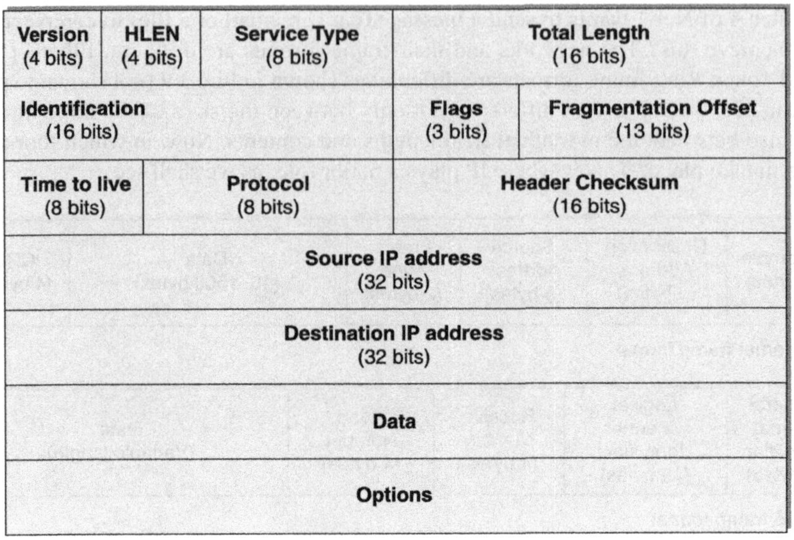

Fig. 3.10 *IP datagram*

5. Identification This field is used in the situations when a datagram is fragmented. As a datagram passes through different networks, it might be fragmented into smaller subdatagrams to match the physical frame size of the underlying network. In these situations, the subdatagrams are sequenced using the identification field, so that the original datagram can be reconstructed from them.

6. Flags This field corresponds to the earlier field (identification). It indicates whether a datagram can be fragmented in the first place—and if it can be fragmented, whether it is the first or the last fragment, or it can be a middle fragment, etc.

7. Fragmentation offset If a datagram is fragmented, this field is useful. It is a pointer that indicates the offset of the data in the original datagram before fragmentation. This is useful when reconstructing a datagram from its fragments.

8. Time to live We know that a datagram travels through one or more routers before reaching its final destination. In case of network problems, some of the routes to the final destination may not be available because of many reasons, such as hardware failure, link failure, or congestion. In that case, the datagram may be sent through a different route. This can continue for a long time if the network problems are not resolved quickly. Soon, there could be many datagrams traveling in different directions through lengthy paths, trying to reach their destinations. This can create congestion and the routers may become too busy, thus bringing at least parts of the Internet to a virtual halt. In some cases, the datagrams can continue to travel in a loop in between, without reaching the final destination and in fact, coming back to the original sender. To avoid this, the datagram sender initializes this field (that is, *Time to live*) to some value. As the datagram travels through routers, this field is decremented each time. If the value in this field becomes zero or negative, it is immediately discarded. No attempt is made to forward it to the next hop. This avoids a datagram travelling for an infinite amount of time through various routers, and therefore, helps avoid network congestion. After all the other datagrams have reached the destination, the TCP protocol operating at the destination will find out this missing datagram and will have to request for its retransmission. Thus, IP is not responsible for the error-free, timely and in-sequence delivery of the entire message—it is done by TCP.

9. Protocol This field identifies the transport protocol running on top of IP. After the datagram is reconstructed from its fragments, it has to be passed on to the upper layer software piece. This could be TCP or UDP. This field specifies which piece of software at the destination node the datagram should be passed on to.

10. Source address This field contains the 32-bit IP address of the sender.

11. Destination address This field contains the 32-bit IP address of the final destination.

12. Options This field contains optional information such as routing details, timing, management, and alignment. For instance, it can store the information about the exact route that the datagram has taken. When it passes through a router, the router puts in its id, and optionally, also the time when it passed through that router, in one of the slots in this field. This helps tracing and fault detection of datagrams. However, most of the time, this space in this field is not sufficient for all these details, and therefore, it is not used very often.

All the computers on the Internet have to run the TCP/IP software stack and therefore, have to understand the IP datagram format. Also, all the routers need to have the IP software running on them. Hence, they have to understand the IP datagram format.

Each computer in the whole Internet has a 32-bit unique **IP address**, which consists of two parts, **network id** and **host id** within that network. It is the network id portion of the IP address of the destination, which is used for routing the datagrams to the destination network through many other routers. To enable this, a routing table is used, which gives the address of the next hop for a specific destination. Each router uses its own routing table. Once the datagram reaches the destination network, the *host id* portion of the destination IP address is used to send the datagram to the destination computer on that network. Also, as we have noted, each computer attached to the network has to have a Network Interface Card (NIC), which understands and transmits frames corresponding to that network.

3.5.3 More on IP

As we have mentioned before, the TCP/IP protocol suite uses the IP protocol for transmission of datagrams between routers. IP has two important properties, which are that it is **unreliable** and it is **connectionless**. Let us understand what it means before we discuss our example in detail.

1. IP is unreliable When we say that IP is unreliable, it means that IP does not provide a guarantee that a datagram sent from a source computer definitely will arrive at the destination. In this sense, it is called a **best-effort delivery** mechanism.

For understanding this, consider what happens when we send a letter to somebody through the post service. We write the letter, put it in a stamped envelope and drop it in a post box. The letter then travels through one or more post offices, depending on the destination (e.g., if it is in the same or different city, state and country) and finally reaches the destination. However, the postal service does not guarantee a delivery, but promises to try their best to deliver the letter at the earliest, to the recipient. The job of each post office is simple. It forwards the letter to the next appropriate destination, which may or may not be the final destination. For instance, if we send a letter from Boston to Houston, the Boston city post office will forward our letter to the Houston city post office along with all other letters destined for Houston. The Houston post office would forward the letter to the concerned area post office within

Houston. This will happen as the letter passes through a number of intermediate post offices, which essentially act as exchanges or routers. Finally, the letter would be forwarded to the ultimate destination. However, at no point of time is any post office checking back to see if the letter is properly received by the next recipient. They all assume in good faith that it is happening that way!

IP works on a very similar principle. In internetworking terms, IP does not have any error-checking or tracking mechanisms. Therefore, IP's job is restricted to forwarding a datagram from its initial source onto the final destination through a series of routers. However, it does not in any way check to see if the datagram reached its next hop. IP assumes that the underlying medium is reliable and makes the best possible effort of delivery. There could be many reasons that cause datagrams to be lost—such as bit errors during transmission, a congested router, disabled links, and so on. IP lets the reliability become the responsibility of the transport layer (i.e., TCP), as we shall see later.

Just as the postal system has a concept of registered letters wherein each post office keeps a track of letters received from the various sources and heading for various destinations, the Internet has this capability in the form of TCP. TCP makes every datagram work like a registered letter to keep its track and ensure error-free delivery. We shall discuss TCP in detail later.

2. IP is connectionless Consider what happens when we make a phone call to someone. After we dial the number and the two of us start speaking, we are the only users of the communication channel. That means, even if neither of us speak for some duration, the communication channel remains unused—it is not allocated to another telephone conversation between two other persons. This concept of *switched circuits* makes telephone communications connection oriented. However, IP, like other networking protocols, does not assume any connection between the sender and the receiver of datagrams. Instead, each datagram sent by IP is considered to be an independent datagram and it does not require any connection to be set up between the sender and the receiver before datagrams can be transmitted. Any computer can send datagrams to any other computer any time, with no regard to other computers on the Internet.

Clearly, if this has to work, a datagram must contain information about the sender and the receiver. Otherwise, the routers would not know where to forward the datagrams. Thus, a datagram has to contain not only data, but also additional information such as where the datagram originated from and where it is heading. Using the analogy from the postal department, a datagram has derived its name. Whereas in the *virtual circuit* philosophy, a circuit, i.e., the entire path from the source to the destination is established before all datagrams in a message are routed, and which remains fixed throughout, this is not the case with datagrams, where for each datagram, the route is decided at routing time. We have discussed this before in packet switching. Therefore, IP is a *packet switching technology*.

3.5.4 Communication using TCP/IP

Now, the actual communication takes place as discussed below. We shall assume the network as shown in Fig. 2.14 for this example. We still assume that a user on node *A* wants to send a message (e.g., an email) to a user on node *G*. The following steps will be executed to accomplish this task:

1. The application layer running on node *A* (e.g., an email program) hands over the message to be transmitted to the TCP layer running on node *A*.
2. The TCP layer breaks the message into smaller segments, and appends the TCP header to each one, as shown in Fig. 3.11. We will talk about this later when we discuss TCP in detail.

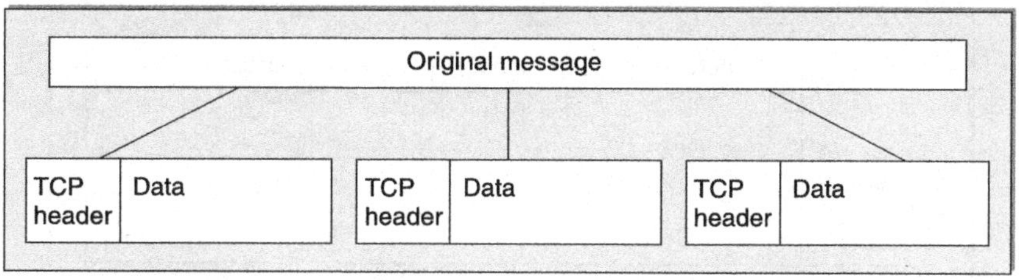

Fig. 3.11 *TCP layer breaks down the original message into segments*

3. The IP layer breaks each segment further into fragments if necessary, and appends the IP header to each one. We will assume for simplicity that the fragmentation is not necessary. At the IP level, the TCP header + datagram is treated together as data. This is the basic process of encapsulation. Thus, in this case, it will just append the IP header to the datagram for IP (i.e., the original datagram plus TCP header). This becomes the datagram for the lower layer (i.e., Ethernet). The datagram now looks as shown in Fig. 3.12.

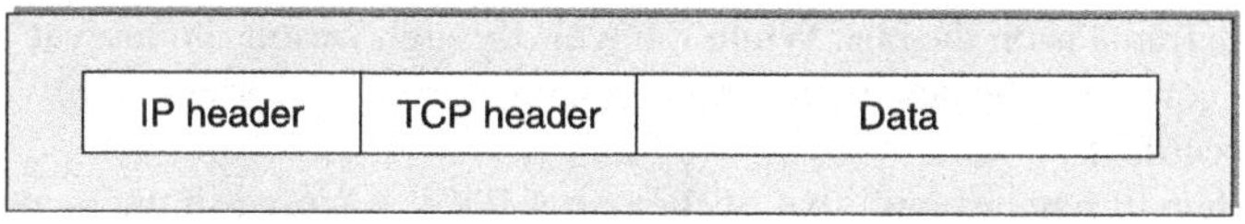

Fig. 3.12 *IP header is added to the TCP segment*

The IP header contains the 32-bit source as well as destination addresses corresponding respectively to the source and destination computers.

4. Now, the whole IP datagram shown earlier is treated as *data* as far as Net-1 (which is an Ethernet) is concerned. The IP software at node *A* realizes from the network id portion of the destination IP address (contained in IP header) that it is not the same as the network id of the IP address of computer *A*. Therefore, it realizes that the destination computer is on a different network. Therefore, it simply has to hand the datagram over to router R1. As a general rule, every node has to hand over all datagrams that have a different network id than their own, in the destination address field, to a router, based on the routing algorithm. In this case, based on this algorithm, node *A* decides that it has to hand over the datagram to R1. Note that both *A* and R1 are on the same Ethernet network, and Ethernet only understands frames of certain format. Here is where encapsulation comes handy.
5. The datagram now reaches the NIC of node *A*. Here, an Ethernet frame is formed as shown in Fig. 3.13. The data portion in the frame is the IP header + TCP header + datagram. The Ethernet header contains the 48-bit source and destination addresses. As we know, these are physical addresses given by the manufacturer to the NICs of the source (i.e., node *A*) and destination (i.e., router R1) computers. The problem is how do we get these physical addresses?

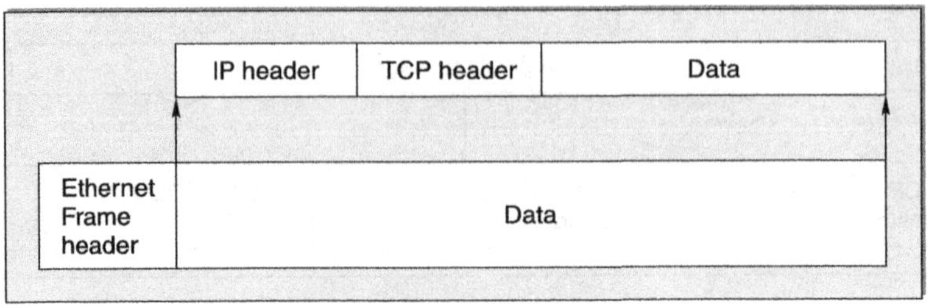

Fig. 3.13 *Ethernet frame*

6. The NIC at node *A* has to move 48-bit physical source and destination addresses into the Ethernet frame as well as compute the CRC. The source address is that of NIC of A itself, which the node *A* knows. The problem is to get the same for the destination, which is the NIC of router R1. To get this, an **Address Resolution Protocol (ARP)** is used. The Ethernet frame now is ready to be transmitted.
7. Now, the usual CSMA/CD protocol is used. The bus is continuously monitored. When it is idle, the frame is sent. If a collision is encountered, it is resent after a random wait and so on. Finally, the frame is on the bus. While it travels through various nodes, each node's NIC reads the frame, compares the destination address in the frame header with its own, and if it does not match, discards it.
8. Finally, when it matches with that of the router R1, it is stored in the memory of the router's NIC. The NIC of the router verifies the CRC and accepts the frame.
9. The NIC of the router removes the Ethernet frame header and obtains back the original IP datagram, as shown in Fig. 3.14, and passes it on to the router.

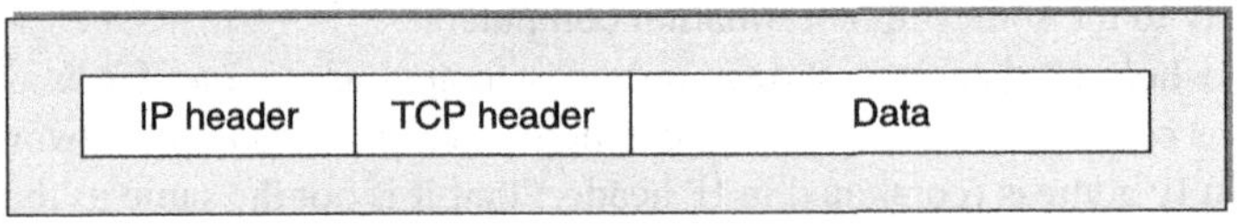

Fig. 3.14 *Original IP datagram*

10. Now, the router checks its routing table to learn that if the final destination is *G*, the next hop for this datagram is router R2. To use the routing table, the destination 32-bit IP address has to be extracted from the IP header, because the routing tables contain the destination IP address and the *next hop* to reach there. In this case, the *next hop* is router R2.The router R1 knows that there is a X.25 WAN connecting it and R2. In fact, R1 and R2 both are on this X.25 WAN (though R1 is also on the Ethernet LAN).
11. At this stage, the IP header + TCP header + data, all put together, is treated as *data* again for X.25, and a header for X.25 is generated and a datagram in the X.25 format is prepared. The datagram header contains the source and destination addresses, which are those of R1 and R2, respectively, as our intention is to transport the datagram from R1 to R2, both on the X.25 network, wherein the datagram also now is in the X.25 format. Router R1 then releases the datagram on to the X.25 network using ARP as before. The frame is shown in Fig. 3.15.

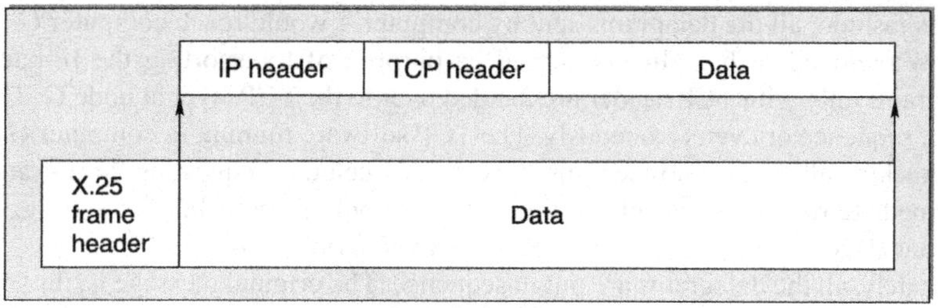

Fig. 3.15 *X.25 frame*

12. The X.25 network has its own ways of acknowledgement between adjacent nodes within the X.25 network, etc. The datagram travels through various nodes and ultimately reaches the R2 router.
13. R2 strips the X.25 datagram of its header to get the original IP datagram, as shown in Fig. 3.16. R2 now extracts the source and destination 32-bit IP addresses from the IP header.

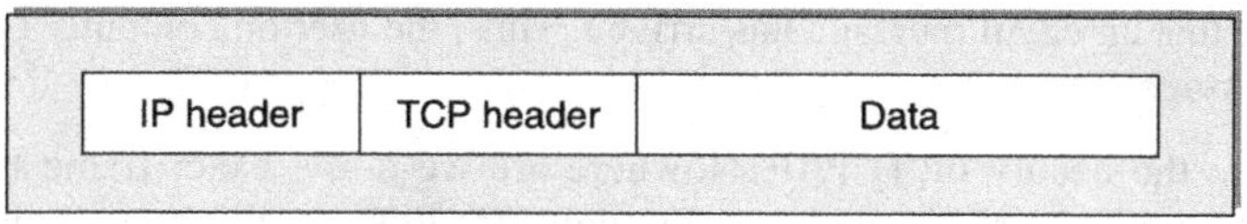

Fig. 3.16 *Original IP datagram*

14. R2 is also connected to the Token Ring network. Now, R2 compares the network id portion of the 32-bit destination IP address in the above datagram with its own and realizes that both are the same. As a consequence, it comes to know that computer *G* is local to it.
15. R2 now constructs a Token Ring frame out of this IP datagram by adding the Token Ring header, as shown in Fig. 3.17. The format shows 48-bit physical source and destination addresses. These are now inserted for those of R2 and *G* respectively, frame control bits are computed and the Token Ring frame is now ready to go. For this, again ARP is used.

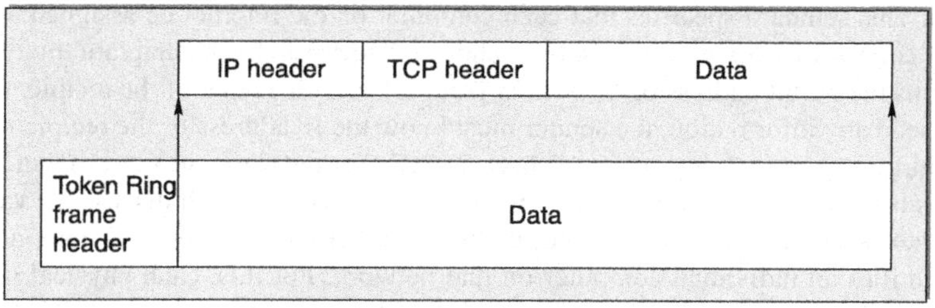

Fig. 3.17 *Token Ring frame*

16. R2 now directly delivers the Token Ring frame to computer *G*. *G* discards the Token Ring frame header to get the original IP datagram.

17. In this fashion, all the datagrams sent by computer *A* would reach computer *G*. The IP header is now removed (it has already served its purpose of transporting the IP packet). And the datagrams only with TCP header are handed over to the TCP layer at node *G*. They may reach out of sequence or even erroneously. The TCP software running in computer *G* is responsible for checking all this, acknowledging the correct receipt, or requesting for re-transmission. The intermediate routers do not check this. They are only responsible for routing. Therefore, we say that *IP is connectionless* but *TCP is connection oriented.*
18. Ultimately, all the datagrams are put in sequence. The original message is, thus, reconstructed.
19. The message is now passed on to the appropriate application program such as email running on computer *G*. The TCP header contains the fields source and destination **socket numbers**. These socket numbers correspond to different application programs—many of them are standardized, which means that given a socket number, its corresponding application program is known. These socket numbers are used to deliver the datagrams to the correct application program on computer *G*. This is important because *G* could be a multi-programming computer that is currently executing more than one application. So, it is essential that the correct application program receives these datagrams.
20. The program on computer *G* can process the message, e.g., it can inform the user of that computer that an email message has arrived. Thus, the user on computer *G* can then read the email message.

We will notice the beauty of TCP/IP. Nowhere are we doing exact frame format or protocol conversion. TCP/IP works on all the nodes and routers, but Ethernet works as it did before. It carries the frame in its usual fashion and follows the usual CSMA/CD protocol. The same is true about X.25 and Token Ring. The point to note is TCP/IP *fools* all these networks and still carries a message (email, file, Web page, etc.) from any node to any other node or any other network in the world!

Therein lies the beauty of TCP/IP.

CONCEPT OF IP ADDRESS 3.6

3.6.1 Introduction

On the Internet, the IP protocol defines the addressing mechanism to which all participating computers must conform. This standard specifies that each computer on the Internet be assigned a unique 32-bit number called **Internet Protocol address**, or in short, **IP address**. Each datagram traveling across the Internet contains the 32-bit address of the sender (source) as well as that of the recipient (destination). Therefore, to send any information, the sender must know the IP address of the recipient.

The IP address consists of three parts, a **class**, a **prefix** (or **network number**) and a **suffix** (or **host number**). This is done to make routing efficient, as we shall see. We shall discuss the various types of classes in the next section. The prefix denotes the physical network to which the computer is attached. The suffix identifies an individual computer on that network. For this, each physical network on the Internet is assigned a unique **network number**—this is the prefix portion of the IP address. Since no two network numbers across the Internet can be the same, assigning network numbers must be done at the global level, to ensure that there is no clash with another network number. The **host number** denotes the suffix, as shown in Fig. 3.18. *Host* is just another name for a computer on the Internet. The assignment of host numbers can be done locally.

Fig. 3.18 *Three parts of IP address*

The network number is analogous to a street name and the host number is similar to a house number. For example, only one house can have number 56 on James Street. There is no confusion if we have a house number 56 on George Street in the neighborhood. Thus, across streets, the same house number can be repeated. But in a given street, it must be unique.

In this case, within a network (identified by network number), no two hosts can have the same host number. However, if their network numbers differ, the host numbers can be the same. For example, suppose the Internet consists of only three networks, each consisting of three computers each. Then, we can number the networks as 1, 2 and 3. Within each network, the hosts could be numbered in the same way, i.e., 1, 2 and 3. Therefore, logically, the address of the second computer on the third network would be 3.2, where 3 is the network number and 2 is the host number. The IP addressing mechanism works in a very similar fashion. Note that conceptually, this is very similar to the two-part WAN addressing that we had discussed earlier.

To summarize, IP addressing scheme ensures the following:

1. Each computer is assigned a unique address on the Internet.
2. Although network addressing is done globally (worldwide), host addressing (suffixing) can be carried out locally without needing to consult the global coordinators.

3.6.2 Who Decides the IP Addresses?

To ensure that no two IP addresses are ever the same, there has to be a central authority that issues the prefix—or network number portion of the IP addresses. Suppose an organization wants to connect its network to the Internet. It has to approach one of the local Internet Service Providers (ISPs) for obtaining a unique IP address prefix. At the global level, the **Internet Assigned Number Authority (IANA)** allocates an IP address prefix to the ISP, which in turn, allocates the host numbers or suffixes to each different customer, one by one. Thus, it is made sure that IP addresses are never duplicated.

Conceptually, we can consider that IANA is a *wholesaler* and an ISP is a *retailer* of IP addresses. The ISPs (retailers) purchase IP addresses from the IANA (*wholesaler*), and sell them to the individual customers.

3.6.3 Classes of IP Addresses

As we know, the designers had decided two things:

1. Use 32 bits for representing an IP address.
2. Divide an IP address into three parts—namely a class, a prefix and a suffix.

The next question was to determine how many bits to reserve for the prefix (i.e., the network number) and how many for the suffix (i.e., the host number). Allocating more bits to one of suffix and prefix would have meant lesser bits to the other. If we allocate a large portion of the IP address to the network number, more networks could be addressed and therefore, accommodated, on the Internet, but then the number of bits allocated for host number would have been less, thus reducing the number of hosts that can be attached to each network. On the other hand, if the host number were allocated more bits, a large number of computers on less number of physical networks each would be allowed.

Since the Internet consists of many networks, some of which contain more hosts than the others, rather than favoring either of the schemes, the designers took a more prudent approach of making everybody happy, as shown in Fig. 3.19, and described thereafter.

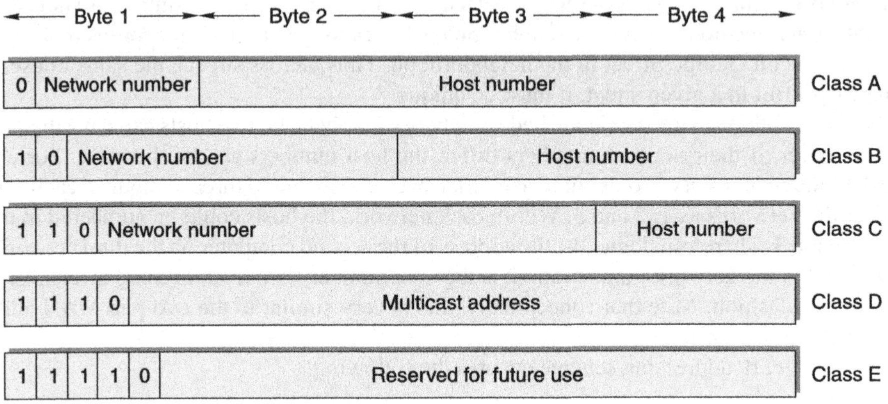

Fig. 3.19 *Classes of IP address*

As shown in the figure, the concept of a class was introduced. The IP address space is divided into three **primary classes** named A, B and C. In each of these classes, a different number of bits are reserved for the network number and the host number portions of an IP address. For example, class A allows 7 bits for the network number and 24 bits for the host number—thus allowing fewer networks to have a large number of hosts, each. Class B is somewhere in-between. On the other hand, class C reserves 21 bits for the network number and just 8 bits for the host number—thus useful for a large number of networks that have smaller number of hosts. This makes sure that a network having a large number of hosts can be accommodated in the IP addressing scheme with the same efficiency as a network that has very few hosts attached to it.

In addition to the three primary classes, there are two more classes named D and E, which serve special purpose. Class D is used for **multicasting**, which is used when a single message is to be sent to a group of computers. For this to be possible, a group of computers must share the common **multicast address**. Class E is not used as of now. It is reserved for future use.

How do we determine, given an IP address, which class it belongs to? The initial few bits in the IP address indicate this. If the first bit in the IP address is a 0, it must be an address belonging to class A. Similarly, if the first two bits are 10, it must be a class B address. If the first three bits are 110, it belongs to class C. Finally, if the first four bits are 1110, the IP address belongs to class D. When class E would come in use, the first five bits would indicate this fact by having a value of 11110. Excepting these bits reserved for the class, the remaining bits contain the IP address itself. These bits are divided into network number and host number using the philosophy described earlier.

This concept can also be illustrated, as shown in Fig. 3.20.

How is this mechanism useful in practice? Simply put, there are two possibilities in case of data transmission in the form of IP datagrams from a source to a destination.

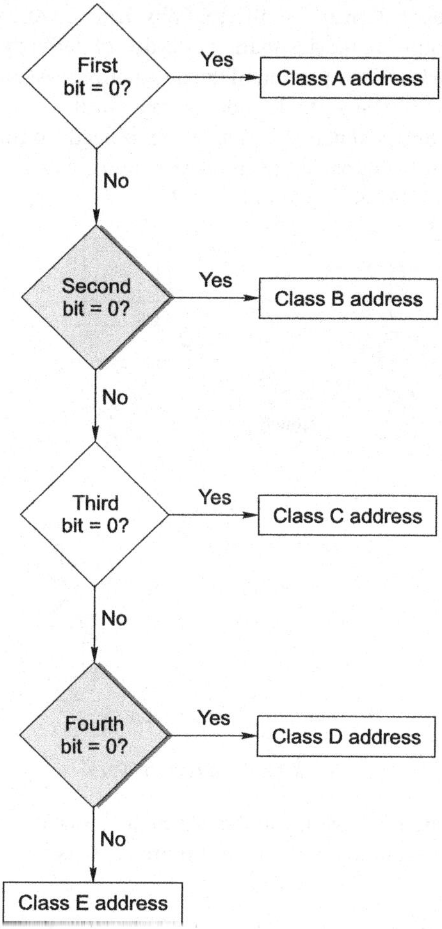

Fig. 3.20 *Determining class of an IP address*

1. The source and the destination are on the same physical network. In this case, we call the flow of packets from the source to the destination as **direct delivery**. To determine this, the source can extract the *network number* portion of the destination host and compare it with the *network number* portion of itself. If the two match, the source knows that the destination host is on the same physical network. Therefore, it need not go to its router for delivery, and instead, can use the local network mechanism to deliver the packet, as shown in Fig. 3.21.

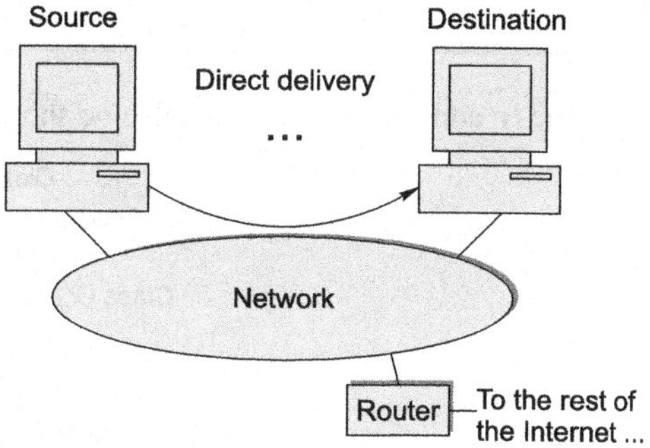

Fig. 3.21 *Direct delivery*

2. The source and the destination are on different physical networks. In this case, we call the flow of packets from the source to the destination as **indirect delivery**. To determine this, the source can extract the *network number* portion of the destination host and compare it with the *network number* portion of itself. Since the two do not match, the source knows that the destination host is on a different physical network. Therefore, it needs to forward the packet to the router, which, in turn, forwards the packet to the destination (via more routers, a possibility, which we shall ignore here). This is shown in Fig. 3.22.

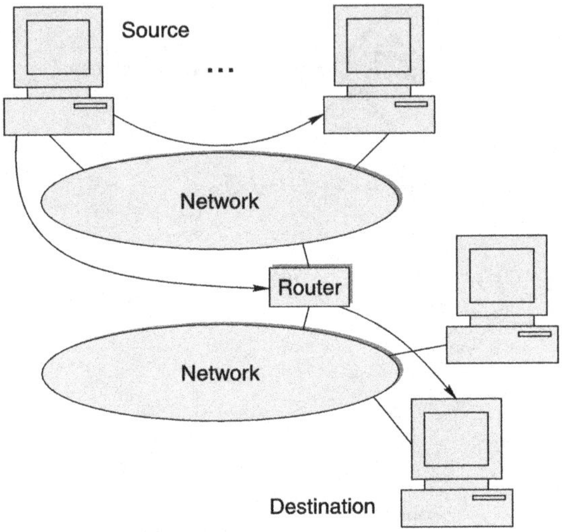

Fig. 3.22 *Indirect delivery*

Now, let us find out how many networks and hosts each class can serve, depending on the number of bits allocated for the network number and the host number. This is shown in Table 3.2.

Table 3.2 *Classes of IP addresses*

Class	*Prefix (in bits)*	*Maximum networks possible*	*Suffix (in bits)*	*Maximum number*
A	7	128	24	16,777,216
B	14	16,384	16	65,536
C	21	2,097,152	8	256

The IP addressing space can also be shown as depicted in Fig. 3.23.

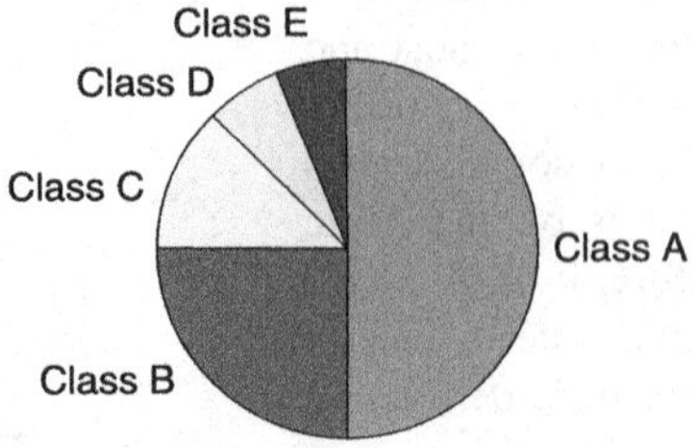

Fig. 3.23 *IP addresses per class*

The tabular explanation of this diagram is provided in Table 3.3.

Table 3.3 *IP address space*

Class	*Number of Addresses*	*Percentage of address space*
A	20 Lakh	50%
B	10 Lakh	25%
C	5 Lakh	12.5%
D	2.5 Lakh	6.25%
E	2.5 Lakh	6.25%

3.6.4 Dotted Decimal Notation

It is very difficult to talk about IP addresses as 32-bit binary numbers in regular communication. For example, an IP address could be:

10000000 10000000 11111111 00000000

Clearly, it is just not possible for humans to remember such addresses. Computers would, of course, work happily with this scheme. Therefore, the **dotted decimal notation** is used for our convenience. In simple terms, the 32 bits are divided into four **octets**. Octets are the same as bytes. Each octet, as the name suggests, contains eight bits. Each octet is then translated into its equivalent decimal value and all the four octets are written one after the other, separated by dots. Thus, the above address becomes:

117.117.255.0

This can be shown diagrammatically in Fig. 3.24.

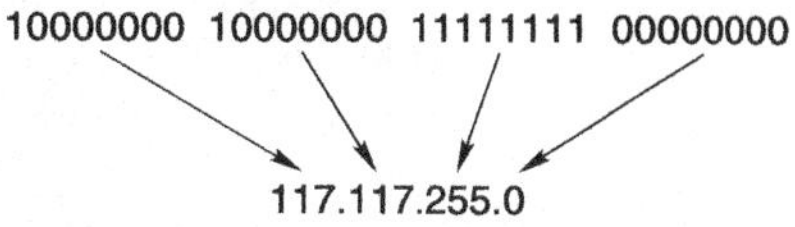

Fig. 3.24 *Equivalence between binary and dotted decimal notation*

Note that the lowest value that an octet can take is 0 in decimal (00000000 in binary) and the highest is decimal 255 (11111111 in binary). Consequently, IP addresses, when written in dotted decimal notation, range from 0.0.0.0 to 255.255.255.255. Thus, any valid IP address must fall in this range.

Another way to represent the classification is as shown in Fig. 3.25.

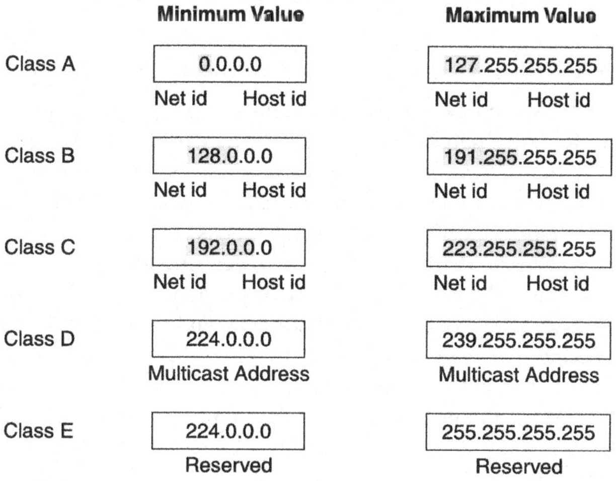

Fig. 3.25 *IP address ranges in decimal notation system*

It should be mentioned that class A and B are already full! No new network can be assigned an address belonging to either of these categories. IP addresses belonging only to class C are still available. Therefore, whenever a company sets up a new LAN, which it wants to get connected to the Internet, it is normally assigned a class C address. We shall discuss this limitation when we discuss **IPv6**.

3.6.5 Routers and IP Addresses

We have seen that a router is a special-purpose computer that is mainly used for forwarding datagrams between computer networks over the Internet. This means that a router connects two or more networks, as we had discussed. As a result, a router needs to have as many IP addresses as the number of networks that it connects, usually at least two. Figure 3.26 shows an example. Here, router R1 connects two networks, an Ethernet (whose IP network number is 130.100.17.0, i.e., the full IP address of any host on that network would be 130.100.17.*, where * is the host number between 0 and 255), and a Token Ring (whose IP network number is 231.200.117.0, i.e., the full IP address of any host on that network would be 231.200.117.*, where * is the host number between 0 and 255). We will note that both of these are class C networks. Similarly, router R2 connects the same Token Ring network to a WAN whose IP address prefix is 87.12.0.0, which is a class A network. Note that the routers are assigned IP addresses for both the interfaces that they connect to. Thus, as Fig. 3.26 shows, router R1 has an IP address 130.100.17.7 on the Ethernet LAN, whereas it has an IP address of 231.200.117.19 on the Token Ring network. The same thing can be observed in R2. In general, if a router connects to *n* networks, it will have *n* IP addresses.

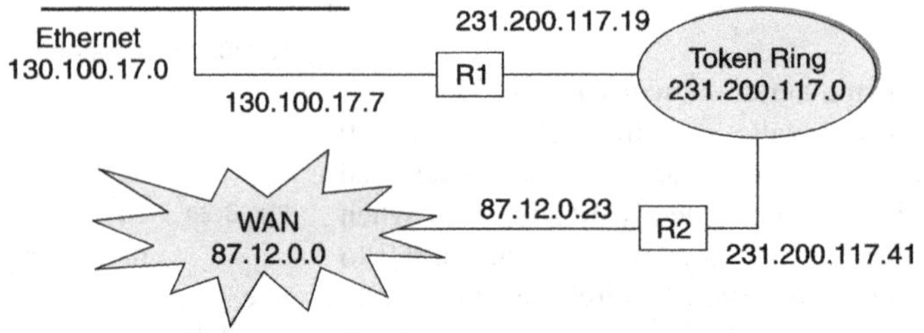

Fig. 3.26 *A router has two or more IP addresses*

3.6.6 IP Version 6 (IPv6)

As we have discussed, IP has been extremely successful in making the Internet a worldwide network that hides the complexities involved in its underlying networks, hardware changes and increases in scale amazingly well. However, there is one major problem with the original design of IP. Like those involved in almost every other invention, the designers IP failed to realize its immense future capabilities and popularity. They decided to use only 32 bits for the IP address.

At that time, it seemed to be a large number. However, due to the mind boggling growth of the Internet over the last few years, the range of IP addresses is appearing to be too less. IP addresses are exhausting too fast, and soon there would simply be not enough IP addresses! We need more addressing space. Secondly, the Internet is being used for applications that few would have dreamt of even a few years ago. Real-time audio-video and collaborative technologies (analogous to virtual meeting among people, over the Internet) are becoming very popular. The current IP version 4 (IPv4) does not deal with these well because it does not know how to handle the complex addressing and routing mechanisms required for such applications.

The new practical version of IP, called **IP version 6 (IPv6)**, also known as **IP Next Generation (IPng)** deals with these issues. It retains all the good features of IPv4 and adds newer ones. Most importantly, it uses a 128 bits IP address. It is assumed (and more importantly, *hoped*) that IP address of this size would be sufficient for many more decades, until the time people realize that IPv6 is actually too small! Apart from this, IPv6 also has support for audio and video. It is expected that IPv4 would be phased out in the next few years and IPv6 would take over from it.

ADDRESS RESOLUTION PROTOCOL (ARP).. 3.7

In the last sections, we have seen the importance of IP addressing. In simple terms, it makes addressing on the Internet uniform. However, having only an IP address of a node is not good enough. There must be a process for obtaining the physical address of a computer based on its IP address, in order to be able to finally actually transmit the frame/datagram over the network, to which the node belongs. This process is called **address resolution**. This is required because at the hardware level, computers identify each other based on the physical addresses hard-coded on their Network Interface Cards (NICs). They neither know the relationship between the IP address prefix and a physical network, nor the relationship between an IP address suffix and a particular computer.

Networking hardware demands that a datagram should contain the physical address of the intended recipient. It has no clue about the IP addresses. To solve this problem, the **Address Resolution Protocol (ARP)** was developed. ARP takes the IP address of a host as input and gives its corresponding physical address as the output. This is shown in Fig. 3.27.

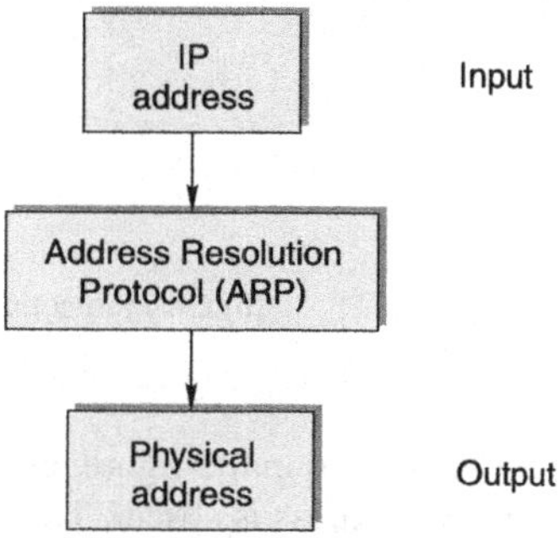

Fig. 3.27 *Address Resolution Protocol (ARP)*

There are three methods for obtaining the physical address based on an IP address. These three methods are as follows:

1. Table lookup Here, the mapping information between IP addresses and their corresponding physical addresses is stored in a table in the computer's memory. The network software uses this table when it needs to find out a physical address, based on the IP address.

2. Closed-form computation Using carefully computed algorithms, the IP addresses can be transformed into their corresponding physical addresses by performing some fundamental arithmetic and Boolean operations on them.

3. Message exchange In this case, a message is broadcasted to all the computers on the network in the form *Are you the one whose IP address is X? If so, please send me your physical address.* The computer whose IP address matches *X* (the broadcasted IP address), sends a reply, and along with it, its physical address to the broadcasting computer. All other computers ignore the broadcast. This method is the simplest one and hence most popular, and we shall discuss it in detail.

3.7.1 ARP using Message Exchange

How message exchange works is simple. We assume that every host knows its IP address as well as physical address. It also knows the IP address of the destination where it wants to send a datagram. However, while sending a frame on a specific network such as Ethernet, the physical addresses of both the source and the destination have to be specified in the frame. Therefore, the sender node has to know the physical address of the destination. All it knows is its IP address.

Anytime a host or a router needs to find the physical address of another host on its network, it creates a special datagram called **ARP query datagram** that includes the IP address of the destination whose physical address is needed. This special datagram is then broadcasted over the network, as shown in Fig. 3.28.

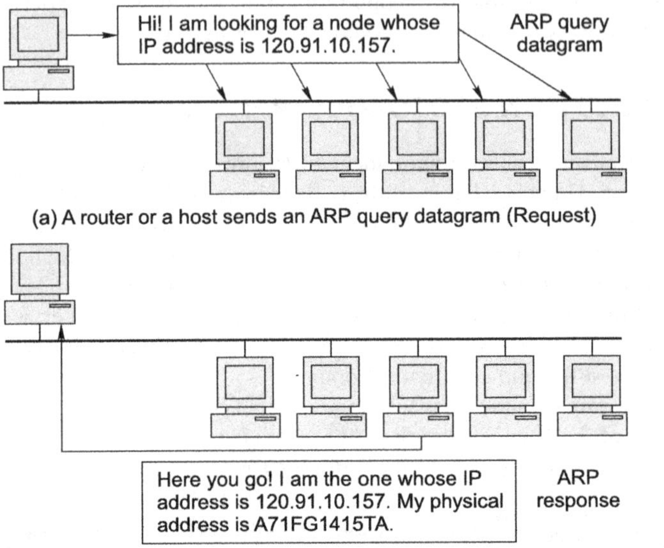

(a) A router or a host sends an ARP query datagram (Request)

(b) Only the concerned host replies back and also sends its physical address

Fig. 3.28 *Example of ARP*

As shown in the figure, every host on the network receives this datagram even if the destination physical address is absent. This is because this is a broadcast request, which means that the datagram should go to all the hosts in the network. Every host then checks the IP address of the destination mentioned in the ARP query datagram with its own. If it does not match, it discards it. However, if it matches, it sends back its physical address to the original node. Thus, only one of the hosts on the network would respond back to the ARP query datagram, as shown in the figure.

This whole process, datagram/response, formats, etc., together constitute the Address Resolution Protocol (ARP).

The ARP packet format is shown in Fig. 3.29.

8 bits	8 bits	16 bits
Hardware type		Protocol type
Hardware length	Protocol length	Operation (Request = 1, Reply = 2)
Sender's physical address		
Sender's 32-bit IP address		
Receiver's physical address (Empty if this is a Request message)		
Receiver's 32-bit IP address		

Fig. 3.29 *ARP packet format*

An ARP packet is encapsulated inside an Ethernet (or the appropriate data link layer) frame, as shown in Fig. 3.30.

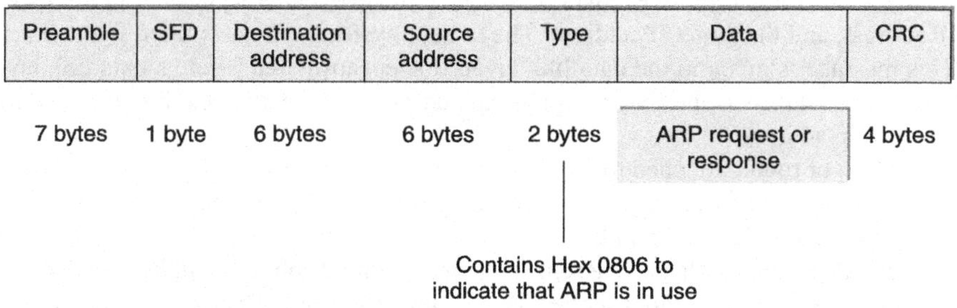

Fig. 3.30 *How ARP is encapsulated inside an Ethernet frame*

Figure 3.31 depicts a sample ARP exchange between two computers.

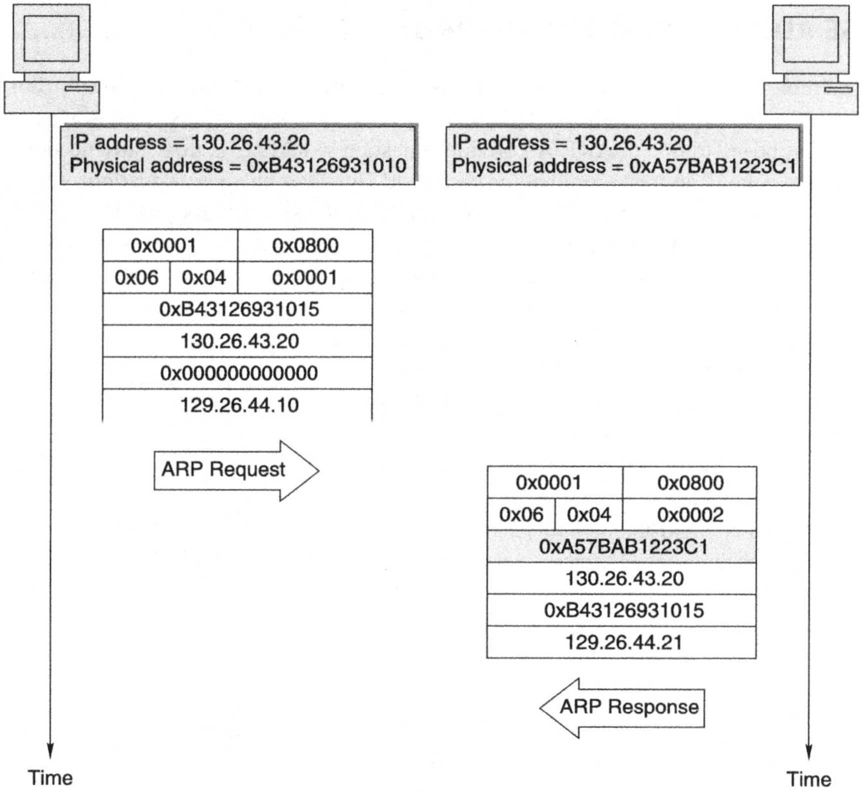

Fig. 3.31 *Sample ARP exchange*

We can summarize as follows:

1. Sender knows the destination IP address. We will call it "target address."
2. IP asks ARP to create an ARP request message. It fills the sender's physical address, the sender's IP address, and the target IP address. The target physical address is filled with all zeros.
3. This message is given to the data link layer. It is encapsulated inside a data link layer frame. The source address is the sender's physical address, and the physical broadcast address is the destination address.
4. Every host or router attached to the network receives the frame. All of them remove the frame header and pass it to the ARP module. All hosts/routers except the actual target drop the packet. The target recognizes its IP address.
5. The target responds with an ARP reply message, filling its physical address in the ARP packet. It sends it only to the original sender. That is, this is not broadcasted.
6. The sender now knows the physical address of the target, and hence can communicate with it. For this, it creates an IP datagram, encapsulates it inside a data link layer frame, and sends it to the target.

REVERSE ADDRESS RESOLUTION PROTOCOL (RARP) 3.8

There is one more protocol in the ARP suite of protocols. The **Reverse Address Resolution Protocol (RARP)** is used to obtain the IP address of a host based on its physical address. That is, it performs a job that is exactly opposite to that of ARP. An obvious question would be, is this really needed? After all, a host should have the IP address stored on its hard disk! However, there are situations when this is not the case. Firstly, a host may not have a hard disk at all (e.g., a diskless workstation). Secondly, when a new host is being connected to a network for the very first time, it does not know its IP address. Finally, a computer may be discarded and replaced by another computer, but the same network card could be re-used. In all these situations, the computer does not know its own IP address.

RARP works in a very similar way to ARP, but in the exactly opposite direction, as shown in Fig. 3.32.

In RARP, the host interested in knowing its IP address broadcasts an **RARP query datagram**. This datagram contains its physical address. Every other computer on the network receives the datagram. All the computers except a centralized computer (the server computer) ignore this datagram. However, the server recognizes this special kind of datagram and returns the broadcasting computer its IP address. The server contains a list of the physical addresses and their corresponding IP addresses for all diskless workstations. This is shown in Fig. 3.33.

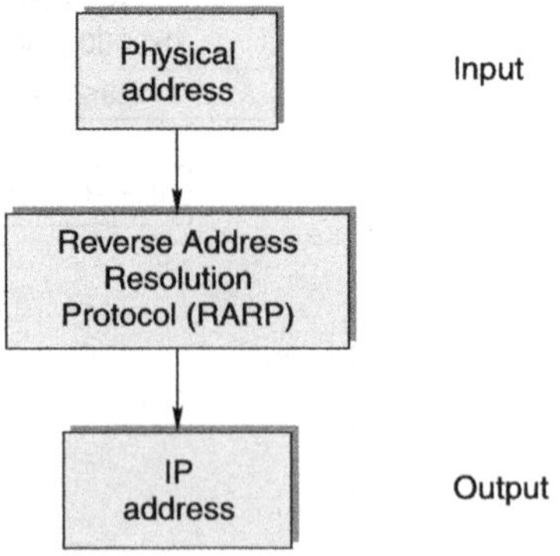

Fig. 3.32 *Reverse Address Resolution Protocol (RARP)*

RARP suffers from the following drawbacks:

1. It operates as a low-level broadcast protocol.
2. It requires adjustments for various hardware types.
3. RARP server needs to be configured on every network.
4. It provides for only IP address, and nothing else.

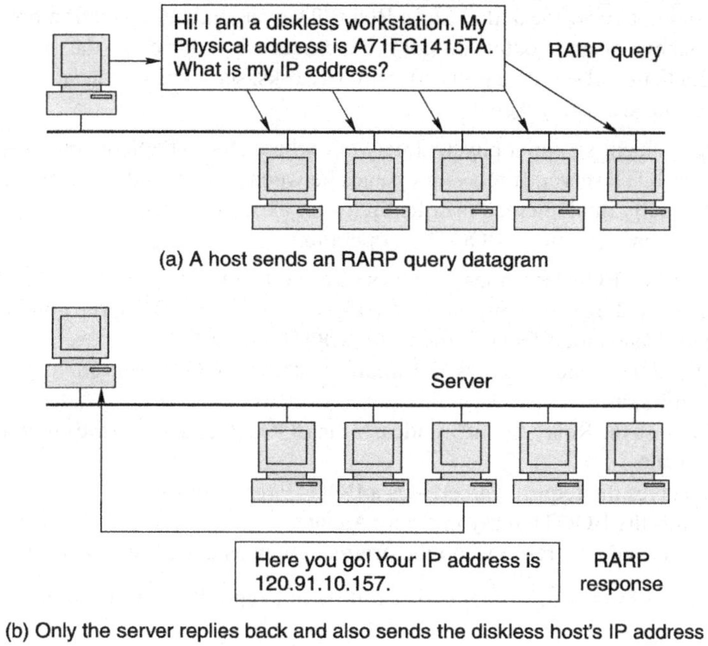

Fig. 3.33 *Example of RARP*

BOOTP 3.9

As a replacement for RARP, a new protocol was designed, called **Bootstrap Protocol (BOOTP)**. BOOTP has the following characteristics:

1. It uses UDP, and is hence independent of hardware.
2. It supports sending additional configuration information to the client, in addition to its IP address.
3. Client and server can be on different networks, thus supports internetworking.

BOOTP works on the following principles.

The BOOTP server maintains mapping between IP and physical addresses. Client sends a request with its physical address, asking for its own IP address. Server looks up physical address of the client in its tables, and returns the IP address. A special well-known port (67) is used for BOOTP UDP requests.

There is a concept of **relay agents** in BOOTP. This can be explained as follows.

BOOTP is designed to allow the BOOTP server and clients to be on different networks. This centralizes the BOOTP server and greatly reduces the amount of work for system administrators. However, this means the protocol is more complex.

1. RARP works at data link layer, so cannot allow clients and server to be on different physical networks.
2. The whole point about BOOTP is to allow use of IP, and if IP is used, we should be able to send packets from one network to another arbitrarily! But BOOTP (like RARP) uses broadcasting.

3. Client does not know the address of a BOOTP server, and hence sends a broadcast request.
4. For efficiency reasons, routers do not route broadcasts—this clogs the network.
5. Hence, if client and server are on different networks, server cannot hear the client's broadcast.
6. Hence, we need a Relay Agent.

A BOOTP relay agent sits on a physical network where BOOTP clients may be located and acts as a proxy for the BOOTP server. It relays messages between a client and a server, and hence is called *Relay Agent*. It is usually implemented in software on an existing router.

The following is an example of BOOTP in operation.

1. Client creates a BOOTP request and broadcasts it to address 255.255.255.255.
2. Relay agent on the client's physical network is listening on UDP port 67 on the server's behalf.
3. Relay agent sends the BOOTP request to BOOTP server.
   (a) If the Relay Agent knows the address of the BOOTP server, it would be a unicast transmission.
   (b) Otherwise the Relay Agent broadcasts the BOOTP requests on the other interface to which it connects.
4. Server receives the request and creates a BOOTP reply message.
5. Server sends the BOOTP reply to Relay Agent.
6. Relay agent sends the response to the original client as unicast or broadcast.

BOOTP has a big limitation, which is that it does not support dynamic addresses. So, we need a better technology.

DHCP 3.10

The **Dynamic Host Configuration Protocol (DHCP)** is even better than BOOTP. Unlike BOOTP, which considers a mapping table, DHCP can also allocate IP addresses dynamically. It is useful when hosts move, etc. It can work in a static allocation mode, like BOOTP. In this case, the address allocation is done manually. However, it can also support dynamic allocation. Here, it maintains another table of *available* IP addresses, from which one can be assigned. This is done automatically. Normally, a DHCP server would check the static database to see if it finds a match on the host so as to return the static address; if not, it returns the dynamic address.

The way DHCP works is as follows:

1. Client creates a *DISCOVER* message, which contains the client's own physical address and a unique transaction ID.
2. Client broadcasts this message.
3. Each DHCP server (there can be several of them) on the local network receives this message. It tries to locate the client's physical address in its mapping tables, and free IP addresses, etc.
4. Servers create DHCPOFFER messages, containing the following:
   (a) The IP address to be assigned to the client.
   (b) The time for which this IP address is being assigned, etc.
   (c) The same transaction ID as was sent by the client.
5. Servers ensure that the same IP address is not in use by sending an ICMP ECHO message (and not getting a response).
6. Servers send the DHCPOFFER messages (unicast/broadcast).
7. Client receives and processes DHCPOFFER messages. Client can decide which one to accept.

8. Client creates DHCPREQUEST message for the selected server. The message contains the following:
   (a) The identifier of the server to indicate which one is chosen.
   (b) The IP address that the server had assigned to this client.
9. Client broadcasts DHCPREQUEST message.
10. Servers receive and process the DHCPREQUEST message. Servers not selected will simply ignore this message.
11. Selected server sends back DHCPACK or DHCPNAK message to indicate whether the offered IP address is still available.
12. Client receives and processes DHCPACK or DHCPNAK message received from the server.
13. Client checks whether the IP address is in use, by sending an ARP request packet.
14. Client finalizes the allocation.

INTERNET CONTROL MESSAGE PROTOCOL (ICMP) 3.11

As we have studied previously, the Internet Protocol (IP) is a *connectionless, best-effort* data transport protocol.

By connectionless, we mean that IP sends each datagram without assuming that there is a connection between the source and the destination. Every datagram is viewed by IP as independent from all other datagrams. Of course, in order to send the datagram to the correct destination, the IP datagram header contains the destination address.

By best effort, we mean that IP makes the best effort of delivering a datagram from a source to a destination. However, it does not guarantee that the datagram would be delivered correctly. As we shall see, the correct delivery is guaranteed by the TCP protocol. It only means that IP itself does not contain any error detection/acknowledgement/retransmission schemes for regular data datagrams. TCP, however, has all these facilities.

However, this does not mean that IP does not have any error control mechanisms at all. Although the issues of connection management between the source and the destination, correct delivery, etc., are handled by TCP, IP includes a protocol for reporting errors that can potentially bring down the Internet, at least temporarily. For example, suppose a router is receiving datagrams for forwarding at a rate that is too fast for it to handle. Or suppose that a host on the Internet is down, and not knowing this, another host is trying to send datagrams to that host repeatedly. When we consider that at the same time thousands of routers or hosts could potentially face these issues, their severe consequences can be grasped easily. Therefore, to avoid such disasters, the designers of the Internet have included the **Internet Control Message Protocol (ICMP)** that serves as an error reporting mechanism in such and similar cases.

There is another purpose for ICMP. Sometimes, a host needs to find out if a particular router is working or if it is down. ICMP facilitates these network management queries as well.

ICMP enables the detection and reporting of problems in the Internet. However it does not play any role in the correction of these problems. That is left to the hosts or routers. For instance, consider a very simple example as shown in Fig. 3.34. Router R connects two hosts *A* and *B*. We have deliberately kept it very simple. As shown, suppose that the wire between R and *B* is accidentally cut. Now, if host *A* sends any datagrams for host *B*, router R cannot transport them, as its connection with host *B* is lost. Therefore, the ICMP software (which is a part of the IP software, anyway) in router R takes over and informs host *A* that the destination (i.e., host *B*) is unreachable. However, it does not prevent *A* from sending more datagrams for *B*. Therefore, ICMP does not involve any error correction mechanisms.

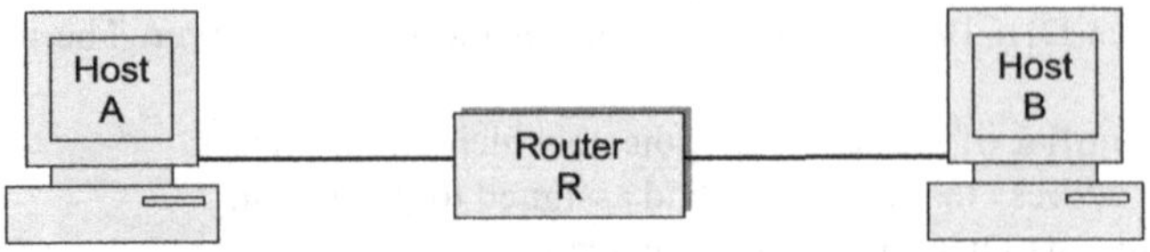

Fig. 3.34 *Connection between a host and a router is lost*

3.11.1 How ICMP Works

ICMP works by sending an error message for a specific reason to the concerned host. For instance, in our example of Fig. 3.35, the ICMP software on router R would send a message *Destination unreachable* to host *A*, when host *A* sends any datagrams destined for host *B*. Similarly, for other kinds of problems, different messages are used.

Let us consider a few examples of ICMP error messages.

1. Destination unreachable We have already discussed this with reference to the figure. Whenever a router realizes that a datagram cannot be delivered to its final destination, it sends a *Destination unreachable* message back to the host, which sent the datagram originally. This message also includes a flag to indicate whether the destination host itself is unreachable, or whether the network containing the end destination is down.

2. Source quench There are occasions when a router receives so many datagrams than it cannot handle them. That is, the number of datagrams arrived at a router could exhaust the size of its memory buffer, where it usually stores these datagrams temporarily before forwarding them to the next router / the final destination. The router cannot simply accept any more datagrams. In such situations, any more datagrams that the router receives must be discarded. However, if the router simply discards them, how would the senders know that there is a problem? The senders would have no clue! And, they could go on sending more datagrams to this router. In order to prevent such a situation, the router sends a *Source quench* message to all the senders who are sending it more datagrams. This signals the hosts sending datagrams to the router, that they should not send any datagrams to that router now. Rather, they should wait for some time before transmitting more datagrams or before re-transmitting the datagrams discarded by the router.

3. Redirect When a host creates a datagram for sending it to a particular destination, it first sends it to the nearest router. The router then forwards it on to another router, or the end destination, if the end destination is directly reachable. However, during the journey of a datagram via one or more routers like this, it could happen that a router incorrectly receives a datagram, which is not on the path of the end destination. The datagram should, instead, go to another router. In such a case, the router that received the datagram incorrectly sends a *Redirect* message to the host or network from where it received that datagram.

Figure 3.35 shows such an example. Here, host *A* wants to send a datagram to host *B*. We realize that the datagram should be first forwarded to the router R2 as both host *A* and router R2 are on the LAN shown in the figure. Thereafter, the router R2 should forward it to the host *B*, as both router R2 and the host *B* are on the WAN shown in the figure. Let us assume that, by mistake, the host *A* first sends the datagram to router R1. However, R1 is not directly on the route of host *B*. Router R1 realizes this, and forwards the datagram to the appropriate router R2 after consulting its routing table, which tells R1 that if you have to send a datagram from R1 to *B*, it will have to be sent to R2. At the same time, R1 sends a *Redirect* message back to host *A* to ensure that host *A* updates its routing table and sends all datagrams destined for host *B* thereafter to router R2.

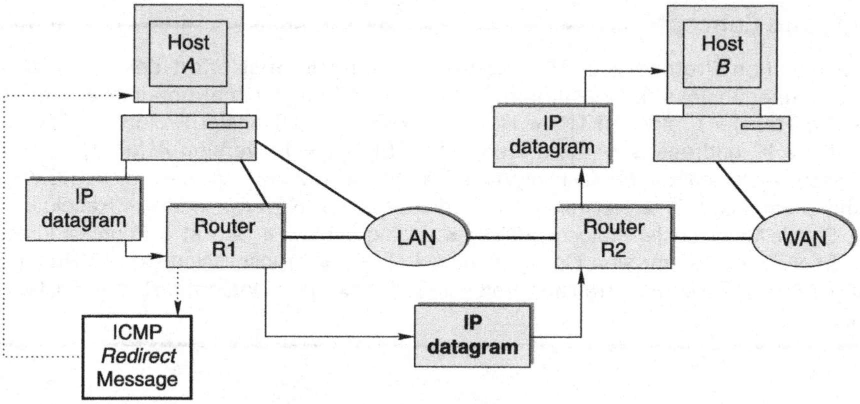

Fig. 3.35 *Example of Redirect ICMP message*

4. Time exceeded We know that every IP datagram contains a field called as *Time to live*. This field is used to determine how long the datagram can live. This helps the Internet infrastructure in preventing datagrams from living and moving on for too long, especially when there are network problems. For instance, suppose that host *A* sends a datagram to host *B* and that the two hosts are separated by a number of intermediate routers. Initially, the host *A* sets this value based on the expected number of routers that the datagram is expected to pass through (may be a little more than that number). Then every time a datagram moves from *A* to *B* via these routers, the router reduces the amount of the field *Time to live* of that datagram by a certain value before forwarding it to the next router. If a router receives this field with the value of *Time to live* being zero, it means that the datagram must be discarded, as it is moving through too many routers. Therefore, the router discards this datagram. It then communicates this fact to the original sending host by a *Time exceeded* ICMP message. The original host can then take an appropriate corrective action, such as choosing another router, or waiting for some time before retransmission.

To avoid sending long text messages such as *Destination unreachable*, ICMP actually maps these messages to error codes, and just sends the error code to the host. For instance, when a router has to send a *Destination unreachable* message to a host, it sends an error code of 3. The number 3 corresponds to the *Destination unreachable* message. This can be done by standardizing all error codes vis-à-vis their corresponding messages, and making that table of codes and messages a part of the ICMP software. A few ICMP error codes and their corresponding messages for the ones discussed earlier are shown in Table 3.4.

Table 3.4 *ICMP error codes and error messages*

Error code	*Error message*
3	Destination unreachable
4	Source quench
5	Redirect
11	Time exceeded

Key Terms and Concepts

Address Resolution Protocol (ARP) • Address binding • Best effort delivery • Class of IP address • Connectionless • Destination address • Dotted decimal notation • Electronic mail (Email) • File Transfer Protocol (FTP) • Host id • Hyper Text Transfer Protocol (HTTP) • Internet Protocol (IP) • IP address • IP Next Generation (IPng) • IP version 4 (IPv4) • IP version 6 (IPv6) • Internet Assigned Number Authority (IANA) • Internet Control Message Protocol (ICMP) • Media Access and Control (MAC) • Network id • Remote login • Reverse Address Resolution Protocol (RARP) • Simple Mail Transfer Protocol (SMTP) • Sliding window • Socket • Source address • Time to live • TELNET • Transmission Control Protocol (TCP) • Transmission Control Protocol/Internet Protocol (TCP/IP) • Trivial File Transfer protocol (TFTP) • User Datagram Protocol (UDP) • World Wide Web

SUMMARY

- Computers within the same network communicate with each other using their physical addresses.
- Different networks have different address lengths as well as addressing formats. Therefore, we cannot use physical addresses to identify computers across different physical networks.
- Logical addressing is used, which is uniform and does not depend on the underlying network. This logical address is called as IP address.
- The Internet is a network of many heterogeneous computer networks.
- The Address Resolution Protocol (ARP) is the mechanism that specifies the IP address of a computer, and gets back its physical address.
- In some situations, the reverse of what ARP does, is required. In such situations, the Reverse Address Resolution Protocol (RARP) is used.
- A router maintains a table to decide which destination addresses are directly reachable, and for which other addresses it has to forward the datagrams to another router.
- The physical address or the hardware address of a computer is hard coded on the Network Interface Card (NIC) of the computer.
- The IP address consists of three parts: class, network number and host number.
- Each network on the Internet is given a unique network number. Within a network, each host is assigned a unique host number.
- IP addresses are made up of 32 bits. Thus, an IP address would contain 32 ON/OFF flags (i.e., 0 or 1).
- Since it is cumbersome to write IP addresses this way, the dotted-decimal notation is used, instead.
- The Transmission Control Protocol / Internet Protocol (TCP/IP) suite of communication protocols makes the Internet a worldwide network of computer networks.
- Technically, TCP/IP consists of four layers, but for the sake of understanding, we can ignore this and consider it to be made up of five of them: Physical, Data Link, Internet, Transport and Application.
- The physical layer is concerned with the physical characteristics of the transmission medium, such as what voltage level signifies a binary 0 or 1, etc.

- The data link layer deals with the issues of media access and control.
- The Internet layer is unique to TCP/IP. The IP protocol at this layer is responsible for uniform host addressing, datagram formats and lengths and routing.
- The transport layer is responsible for end-to-end delivery of IP datagrams, and contains two main and widely differing protocols: Transmission Control Protocol (TCP) and User Datagram Protocol (UDP).
- TCP is a reliable protocol that guarantees delivery of IP datagrams between two hosts.
- UDP does not guarantee a successful delivery of datagrams, and instead, makes the best attempt for delivery.
- The application layer sits on top of the transport layer, and allows the end users to do Web browsing (using HTTP), file transfers (using FTP) and send emails (using SMTP), etc.
- The Internet Control Message Protocol (ICMP) is a error-reporting (but not error-correcting) protocol for error detection and reporting.
- Examples of ICMP messages are *destination unreachable*, *source quench*, *redirect*, *time exceeded*, etc.

MULTIPLE-CHOICE QUESTIONS

1. Layer 4 from bottom in TCP/IP is the ________.
(a) physical layer (b) application layer (c) transport layer (d) internet layer

2. ARP lies in the ________.
(a) physical layer (b) application layer (c) transport layer (d) internet layer

3. ________ does not offer reliable delivery mechanism.
(a) UDP (b) TCP (c) ARP (d) FTP

4. IP address ________ the physical address.
(a) is the same as (b) has no relation with
(c) means (d) None of these

5. Currently, the IP address has a size of ________ bits.
(a) 128 (b) 64 (c) 32 (d) 16

6. The ________ field helps routers in discarding packets that are likely to cause congestion.
(a) time to live (b) options
(c) protocol (d) fragmentation offset

7. IP makes a ________ of datagram delivery.
(a) worst effort (b) guaranteed delivery
(c) best effort (d) All of these

8. In ________ scheme, the physical address is hard coded on the NIC of a computer.
(a) configurable addresses (b) static addresses
(c) dynamic addresses (d) None of these

9. The ________ for all computers on the same physical network is the same.
(a) host id (b) physical address (c) IP address (d) network id

10. If an IP address starts with a bit sequence of 110, it is a class ________ address.
(a) A (b) B (c) C (d) D

DETAILED QUESTIONS

1. What are the different methods of assigning physical address to a computer?
2. Explain the process of message transfer between two computers.
3. Describe the three parts of an IP address.
4. Describe the various fields in the IP datagram header.
5. What is the purpose of the *time to live* field of the IP datagram header?
6. Why is IP called connectionless?
7. How does the Address Resolution Protocol (ARP) work?
8. Why is IP called the *best-effort delivery* protocol?
9. Explain the following ICMP messages: (a) Destination unreachable, (b) Source quench, and (c) Redirect.
10. What is the purpose of the field *time to live* in the IP datagram header?

EXERCISES

1. Observe that when you connect to busy Web sites such as Yahoo or Hotmail, the IP address of that site keeps changing. Investigate why this is the case.
2. Think what could happen if domain names are not unique. Assuming that there are multiple entries in the DNS for a single domain, what problems could come up?
3. If all physical networks in the world were to be replaced by a single, uniform network such as Ethernet or Token ring, would IP addressing be still required? Why?
4. Find out how your computer at work or office obtains an IP address to communicate over the Internet.
5. Many organizations set up a proxy server. Find out more details about the proxy server in your organization, college or university, if there is one.

TCP/IP PART II TCP, UDP 4

INTRODUCTION

The transport layer runs on top of the Internet layer and is mainly concerned with the transport of packets from the source to the ultimate destination (i.e., **end to end delivery**). Unlike IP, which is involved in the routing decisions, the main function of the TCP protocol that runs in the transport layer is to ensure a correct delivery of packets between the end-points. In TCP/IP, the transport layer is represented by two protocols, TCP and UDP. Of the two, UDP is simpler. UDP is useful when speed of the delivery is critical—never mind the loss of a few datagrams such as in the transmission of digitized images, voice or video. TCP is useful when it is essential to make sure that datagrams travel without errors from the source to the destination, even if that makes the overall delivery slightly more time consuming. This is not only useful but also necessary in the transmission of business of scientific data. This is shown in Fig. 4.1.

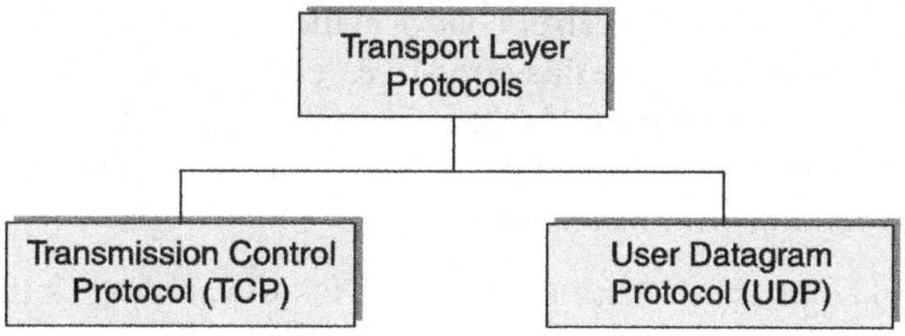

Fig. 4.1 *Transport layer protocols on the Internet*

In this chapter, we shall discuss TCP and UDP.

TCP BASICS 4.1

The Transmission Control Protocol (TCP) works extremely well with IP. Since the Internet uses packet switching technique, there could be congestion at times. TCP takes care of these situations and makes the Internet reliable. For example, if a router has too many packets, it would discard some of them. Consequently, they would not travel to the final destination and would get lost. TCP automatically checks for lost packets and handles this problem. Similarly, because the Internet offers alternate routes (through routers) for data to flow across it, packets may not arrive at the destination in the same order as they were sent. TCP handles this issue as well. It puts the packets (known as **segments**) back in order. Similarly, if some segments are duplicated due to some hardware malfunction, TCP discards duplicates. We shall discuss how TCP deals with these issues later.

FEATURES OF TCP 4.2

Let us list the main features offered by the TCP portion of the TCP/IP protocol suite. These are: *reliability*, *point-to-point communication* and *connection-oriented approach*.

1. Reliability TCP ensures that any data sent by a sender finally arrives at the destination as it was sent. This means, there cannot be any data loss or change in the order of the data. Reliability at the transport layer (TCP) has four important aspects, as shown in Fig. 4.2.

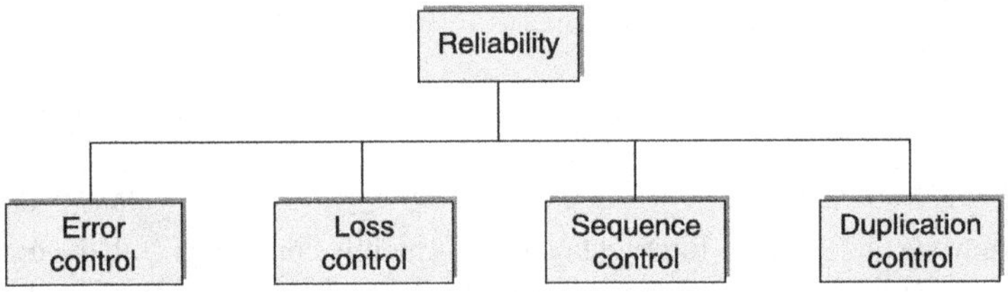

Fig. 4.2 *Four aspects of reliability in transport layer delivery*

Let us examine these four aspects in brief.

(a) Error control Data must reach the destination exactly as it was sent by the sender. We have studied mechanisms such as checksums and CRC that help achieve error control at the lower layer, the data link layer. However, TCP provides its own **error control** at a higher layer, the transport layer. Why is this additional error control at the transport layer necessary when the data link layer already takes care of it? The answer lies in the fact that whereas the error control at the data link layer ensures error-free delivery between two networks, it cannot guarantee this error-free delivery end-to-end (i.e., between the source and the destination). The reason behind this is that if a router that connects two networks introduces some errors, the data link layer does not catch them. This is shown in Fig. 4.3. This is the reason why TCP provides for its own error control mechanism.

(b) Loss control It might so happen that the source TCP software breaks the original message into three segments, and sends the three segments to the destination. As we know, the IP software is connectionless and does not guarantee delivery (*best effort*). It might so happen that one of the three segments (transformed later into IP datagrams) gets lost mid-way, and never reaches the destination. TCP should ensure that the destination knows about this, and requests for a retransmission of the missing datagrams. This is **loss control**.

How can this be achieved? It should be easy to imagine that TCP can number segments as 1, 2 and 3 when breaking the original message into segments, and can check if all the three have arrived correctly at the destination in the form of IP datagrams. This is shown in Fig. 4.4.

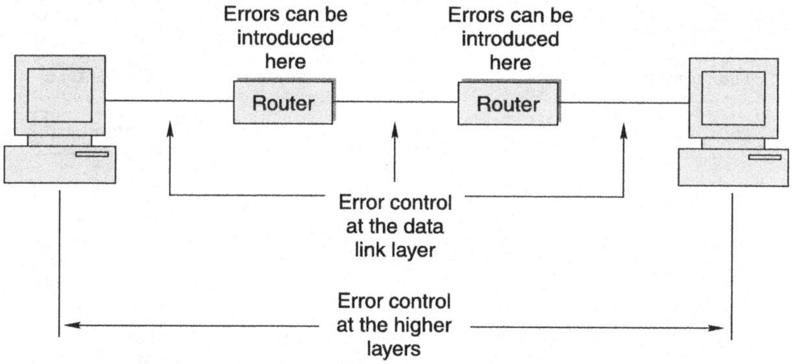

Fig. 4.3 *Transport layer and data link layer error control*

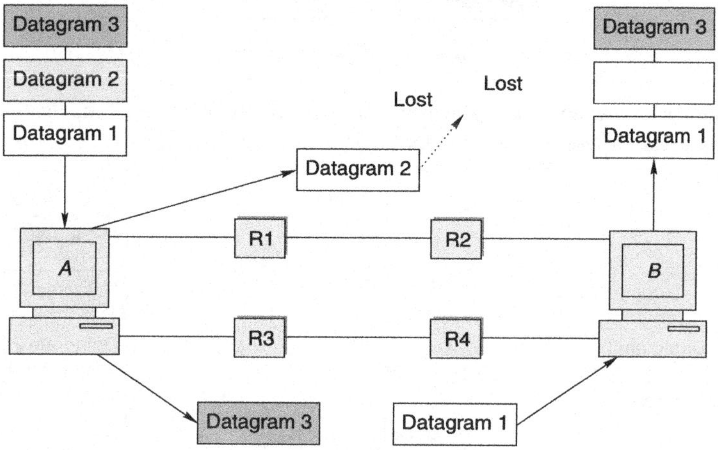

Fig. 4.4 *Loss control*

(c) Sequence control Since different IP datagrams of the same message can take different routes to reach the same destination, they could reach out of sequence.

For instance, suppose the sender host *A* sends three IP datagrams, destined for another host *B*. Suppose that datagram 1 and datagram 3 travel via routers R3 and R4, whereas datagram 2 travels via routers R1 and R2. It might very well happen that the receiver host *B* receives datagrams 1 and 3 first, and then datagram 2 (because there are some congestion conditions on the route *A*-R1-R2-*B*). Thus, the sending sequence from *A* was datagrams 1, 2, and 3. The receiving sequence at host *B* is datagrams 1, 3, and 2. This problem is shown in Fig. 4.5. TCP deals with such a problem with the help of proper **sequence control** mechanisms.

(d) Duplication control *Duplication control* is somewhat opposite to the *loss control*. In case of *loss control*, one or more *lost* datagrams are detected. In *duplication control*, one or more *duplicate* datagrams are detected. Since the same datagram can arrive at the destination twice or more, the destination must have some mechanism to detect this. Thus, it can accept only the first datagram, and reject all its (duplicate) copies.

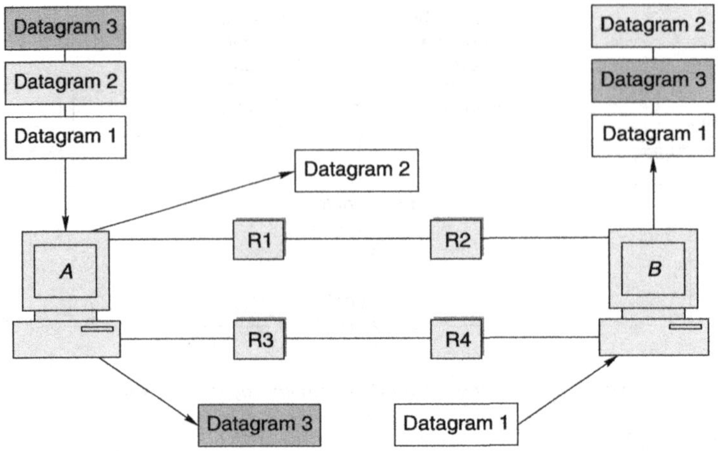

Fig. 4.5 *Sequence control*

Figure 4.6 shows an example of duplication. Here, datagram 3 arrives at the destination host *B* two times. The TCP software at host *B* would detect this, and retain only one of them, discarding the other (redundant) copy.

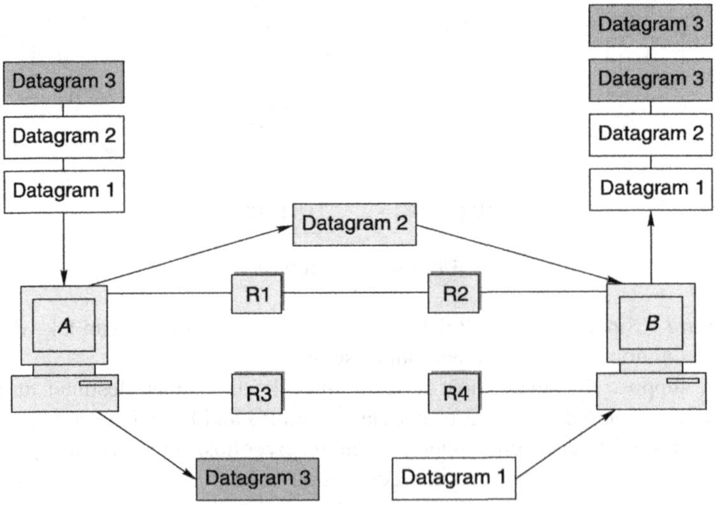

Fig. 4.6 *Duplication control*

2. Point-to-Point communication Also called **port-to-port communication**, each TCP connection has exactly two end points: a source and a destination. Moreover, for the communicating parties, the internal details such as routing are irrelevant. They communicate as if there is a direct connection between them! Also, there is no confusion about who is sending the data or who is receiving it, simply because only two computers are involved in a TCP connection. Also, this communication is *full duplex*, which means that both the participating computers can send messages to the other, simultaneously.

3. Connection-oriented TCP is connection-oriented. The connections provided by TCP are called **virtual connections**. The term *virtual* is used because physically there is no direct connection between the computers—it is achieved in the software, rather than in the hardware. This means that a connection must be established between the two ends of a transmission before either can transmit data. Thus, an application must first request TCP for a connection to a destination and only when that connection is established can it perform the data transmission. It is very important to note that this is different from a *virtual circuit*. In a *virtual circuit*, the sender and the receiver agree upon a specific physical connection (path) to be used among all those possible, before transmission can start. This path defines the physical route of transmission (i.e., which routers the message shall pass through) for every message/packet. Thus, the entire transmission path is aware of a connection. However, in a TCP *virtual connection*, only the sender and the receiver are aware of the connection—the intermediate nodes and routers do not have a clue about this. From their perspective, it is simply a matter of passing the received packets forward via the best route possible—this route itself may (and actually does, many times) vary for every packet.

RELATIONSHIP BETWEEN TCP AND IP.. 4.3

It is interesting to know the relationship between TCP and IP. Each TCP segment gets encapsulated in an IP datagram and then the datagram is sent across the Internet. When IP transports the datagram to the final destination, it informs the TCP software running on the final destination about it and hands the datagram over to TCP. IP does not bother about the contents of the message. It does not read them, and thus, does not attempt to interpret them in any manner. IP acts like the postal service that simply transfers datagrams between two computers. Therefore, from the viewpoint of TCP, IP is simply a communication channel that connects computers at two end points. Thus, TCP views the entire Internet as a communication channel that can accept and deliver messages without altering or interpreting their contents. From the viewpoint of IP, each TCP message is *some* data that needs to be transferred—*what* that data is, is of little consequence. This is shown in Fig. 4.7.

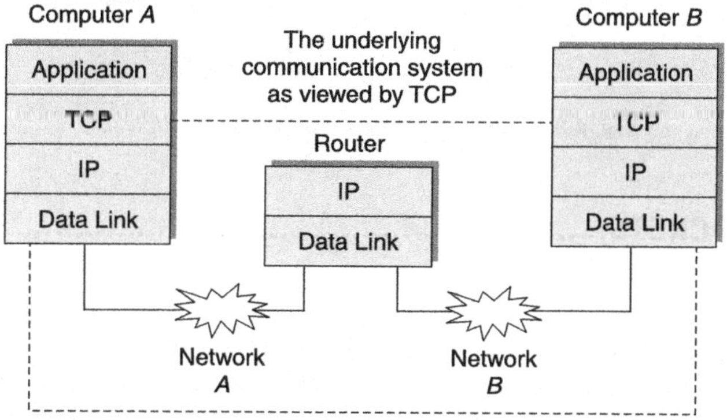

Fig. 4.7 *TCP protocol's view of the Internet communication system*

Conceptually, we can think that many applications (such as File Transfer Protocol—FTP, Remote login—TELNET, Email—SMTP, World Wide Web—HTTP, etc.) keep sending data to the TCP software on a sending computer. The TCP software acts as a data multiplexer at the sender's end. The TCP software receives data from the applications, multiplexes them and gives it to the local IP software. That is, regardless of which application (FTP, TELNET, etc.) is sending data, TCP puts this data into TCP segments and gives it to IP. IP adds its own header to each such TCP segment to create an IP datagram out of it, and from there, it is converted into a hardware frame and sent to the appropriate destination.

At the destination's end, the IP software receives this multiplexed data (i.e., an IP datagram after removing the frame header) from its physical layer, and gives it to the local TCP software. The TCP software at the destination's end then demultiplexes the data (i.e., first removes the IP header to extract the TCP segment, and then removes the TCP header to get the original message) and gives it to the concerned application. This idea of multiplexing and de-multiplexing is shown in Fig. 4.8.

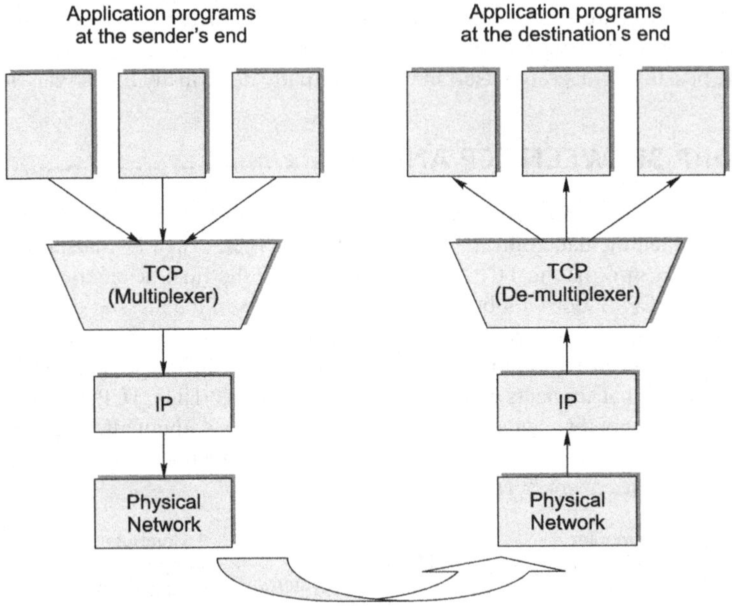

Fig. 4.8 *TCP acts as a multiplexer-de-multiplexer*

PORTS AND SOCKETS.. 4.4

4.4.1 Ports

Applications running on different hosts communicate with TCP with the help of a concept called **ports**. A port is a 16-bit unique number allocated to a particular application. When an application on one computer wants to open a TCP connection with another application on a remote computer, the concept of port comes handy. To understand why, let us use a simple analogy. Suppose a person *A* wants to call another person *B*, working in an office, over phone. First, *A* has to dial the phone number of *B*'s office. After *A* does this, suppose an operator answers the call at the other end. Now, *A* must tell *B*'s extension number (or name) to be able to connect to *B*. The operator would use this information (the extension number or name of *B*) to redirect the call to *B*.

In exactly the same fashion, suppose *A* is an application on a computer *X*, which wants to communicate with another application *B* on a remote computer *Y*. Now, the application *A* must know that it has to first reach computer *Y*, and then reach the application *B* on that computer. Why is just the destination computer's address (*Y*) not enough? This is because, at the same time, another application *C* on computer *X* might want to communicate with yet another application *D* on computer *Y*. If application *A* does not specify that it wants to communicate with application *B*, and instead just specifies that it wants to communicate with *some* application on computer *Y*, clearly, this would lead to chaos. How would computers *X* and *Y* know that application *A* wants to communicate with application *B*, and not *D*, for example?

Figure 4.9 shows an example of using a port number in conjunction with an IP address. As shown in the figure, an application *A* running on computer *X* wants to communicate with another application *B* running on computer *Y*. Application *A* provides the IP address of computer *Y* (i.e., 192.20.10.10) and the port number corresponding to application *B* (i.e., 80) to computer *X*. Using the IP address, computer *X* contacts computer *Y*. At this point, computer *Y* uses the port number to redirect the request to application *B*.

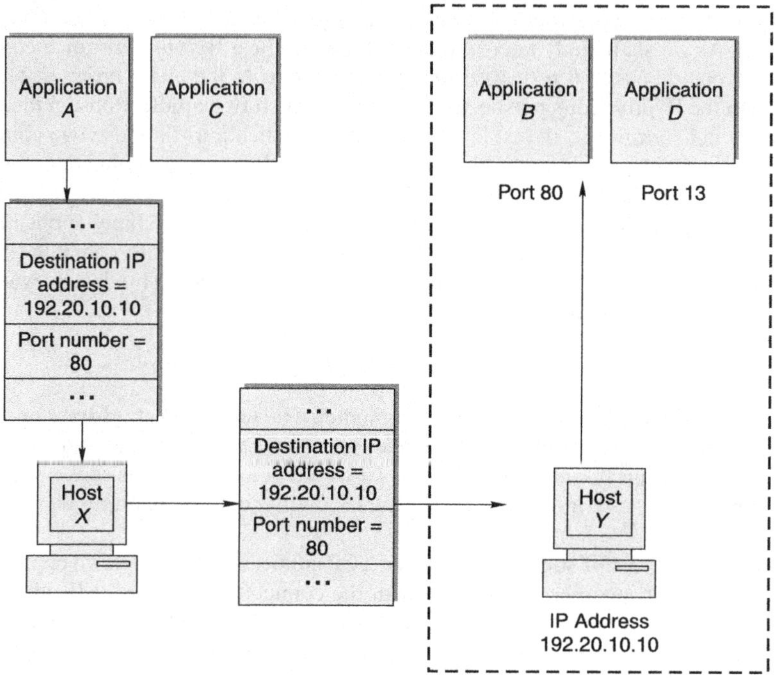

Fig. 4.9 *Use of port numbers*

This is the reason why, when an application wants to communicate with another application on a remote computer, it first opens a TCP connection (discussed in the next section) with the application on the remote computer, using the IP address (like the telephone number) of the remote computer and the port number of the target application (like the extension of the person to speak with). Thus, the IP protocol enables communication between different two computers, whereas TCP enables the communication at a higher level than IP—between two applications on these different computers. This is shown in Fig. 4.10.

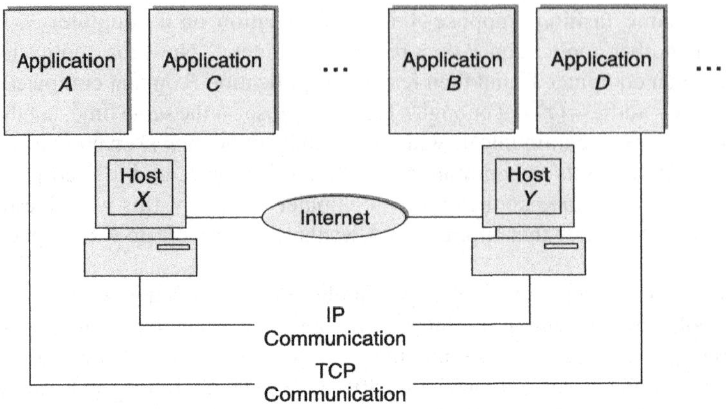

Fig. 4.10 *Levels at which TCP and IP reside*

As shown in the figure, application *A* on host *X* communicates with application *B* on host *Y* using the TCP protocol. As we shall study later, application *A* could be a *Web browser* on a *client computer*, and application *B* could be a *Web server* serving the documents to the client browser. This is the TCP perspective. From the IP protocol's perspective, however, which two applications on the two hosts are communicating is not significant. IP just knows that *some* applications on these two computers *X* and *Y* are communicating with each other. Thus, TCP enables application-to-application communication, whereas IP enables computer-to-computer communication.

However, if many applications on different computers are talking to many applications on other computers, on many links between the two nodes, it may be economical to combine (multiplex) the data between them and separate (demultiplex) at the appropriate nodes. This is achieved by the TCP software running on the various nodes.

4.4.2 Sockets

A port identifies a single application on a single computer. The term **socket address** or simply **socket** is used to identify the IP address and the port number concatenated together, as shown in Fig. 4.11.

For instance, port 80 on a computer 192.20.10.10 would be referred to as socket 192.20.10.10:80. Note that the port number is written after the IP address, with a colon separating them. This is shown in Fig. 4.12.

As we can imagine, **pair of sockets** identifies a TCP connection between two applications on two different hosts, because it specifies the end points of the connection in terms of IP addresses and port numbers, together. Thus, we have a unique combination of (Source IP address + Source port number + Destination IP address + Destination port number) to identify a TCP connection between any two hosts (typically a client and a server).

Fig. 4.11 *Socket*

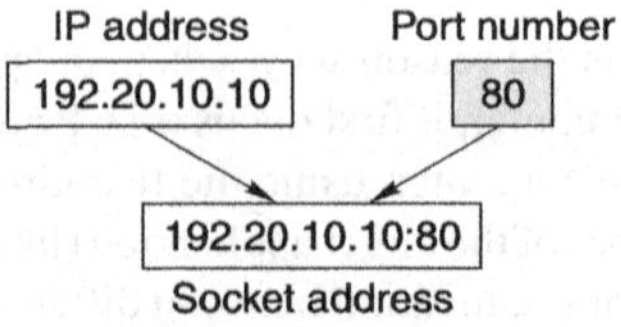

Fig. 4.12 *Socket example*

Normally, the server port numbers are called as **well-known ports**. This is because a client (such as an Internet user) needs to know beforehand where (i.e., *on which port*) a particular application on the server is running. This would enable the client application to send a request to the server application (using the server's IP address and port number) to set up a TCP connection. If the client does not know whether the server is running its email software on port 100 or port 200, how can the client use either of them for requesting a connection?

It is similar to a situation where we have 1000 electrical plugs available (of which only one is working), and we do not know which one to use for plugging in a wire to glow a lamp. In the worst case, we might need to try 1000 times to establish the right connection! How nice it would be, instead, if someone says "Hey, use that plug number (in the case of TCP, *port number*) 723".

For this reason, at least the standard applications on a server are known to execute on specific ports, so that the client has no ambiguity while requesting for a TCP connection with the server. For instance, the HTTP protocol almost always runs on port 80 on the server, waiting to accept TCP connection requests from clients.

This is also the reason why multiple TCP connections between different applications—or even the same applications—on the two hosts are possible. Although the IP addresses of the two hosts would be the same in all the TCP connections, the port numbers would differ. When a client initiates a TCP connection, the TCP software on the client allocates an unused port number as the port number for this connection. Let us assume that this port number is 3000. Further, let us assume that the client is sending an HTTP request (which means that the server's port number will be 80). Thus, from the client's point of view, the source port number is 3000, and the destination port number is 80. When the server wants to send an HTTP response back to the client, the server shall now consider 80 as the source port number and 3000 as the destination port number. This is shown in Fig. 4.13.

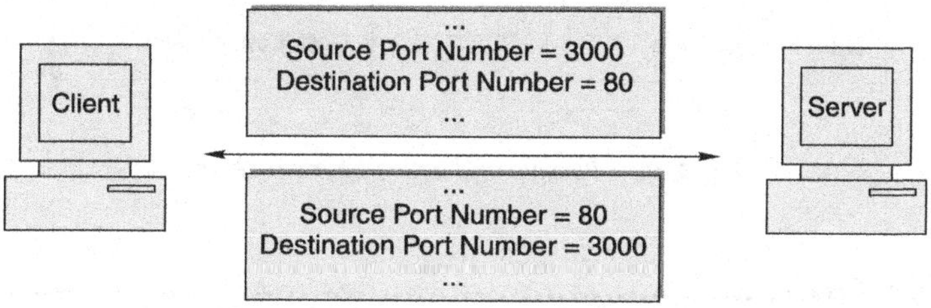

Fig. 4.13 *Source and destination port numbers*

CONNECTIONS—PASSIVE OPEN AND ACTIVE OPEN 4.5

Applications over the Internet communicate with each other using the connection (also called as *virtual connection*) mechanism provided by TCP. We shall subsequently discuss how a TCP connection between two hosts is established and closed. These TCP connections are established and closed as and when required. That is, whenever an application *X* needs to communicate with another application *Y* on a different computer on the Internet, the application *X* requests the TCP software on its computer to establish a connection with the TCP software running on the computer where application *Y* is running. We have already discussed this in detail.

In this interaction model, one computer (called as the *client*) always requests for a TCP connection to be established with the other (called the *server*). However, how does the server accept connections from one or more clients? For this, the TCP software on a server executes a process called as

passive open. In simple terms, this means that a server computer expects one or more clients to request it for establishing TCP connections with them. Therefore, the TCP software on a server waits endlessly for such connection requests from the clients. This is what passive open means. As a result of a passive open, a server computer allows TCP connection requests to be received, but not to be sent. This means that the server is interested only in accepting incoming TCP connection requests, and never in sending outgoing TCP connection requests. In contrast, a client always initiates a TCP connection request by sending such a request to the server. Therefore, the client is said to be in an **active open** mode.

Thus, when a publicly accessible server (e.g., a Web server) starts, it executes a passive open process, which means that it is ready to accept incoming TCP connections. A client (e.g., a Web browser) would then send an active open request for opening a TCP connection with that server. This is shown in Fig. 4.14. As shown in the figure, when a client needs to get a document from a remote server, the client issues an *active open request* to the local TCP software, providing it with the IP address and TCP port of the destination server application. The TCP software on the client then uses this information to open a connection with the remote server.

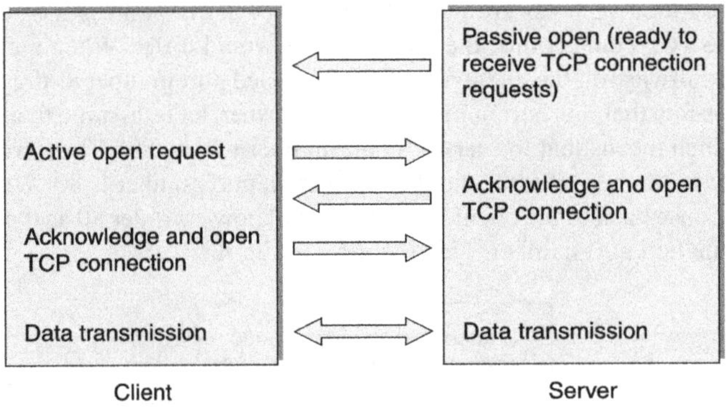

Fig. 4.14 *Passive and active open processes*

TCP CONNECTIONS 4.6

We have been saying that TCP is a connection-oriented protocol. Let us examine this statement in more detail now. To ensure that a connection is established between the two hosts that are interacting for a message transfer, TCP creates a logical connection between them. For this, TCP uses a technique called **three-way handshake**. This means that three messages are exchanged between the sender and the receiver of the message for establishing the connection. Only after this three-way handshake is successful that a connection between them is established. After this, they can exchange messages, assured that TCP would guarantee a reliable delivery of those. It has been proved that a three-way handshake is necessary and sufficient for establishing a successful connection between any two hosts. We shall not go into the details of this proof.

To be able to create a TCP connection between any two hosts, one of them must wait passively to accept active connection requests from the other host. In TCP/IP, it is the server who waits passively for connection requests. The client always initiates a connection request. Thus we can imagine that at a slightly lower level, the server would execute function calls such as *LISTEN* and *ACCEPT*. *LISTEN* would mean that the server is ready to listen to incoming TCP connection requests at a particular port, and *ACCEPT* would be invoked when a server is ready to accept a particular TCP connection request from a client, who has requested for it. On the other hand, the client would invoke a *CONNECT* request, specifying the IP address and port number of the server with which it wants to establish a TCP connection.

Conceptually, this is extremely similar to how telephone conversations between any two persons begin as shown in Fig. 4.15.

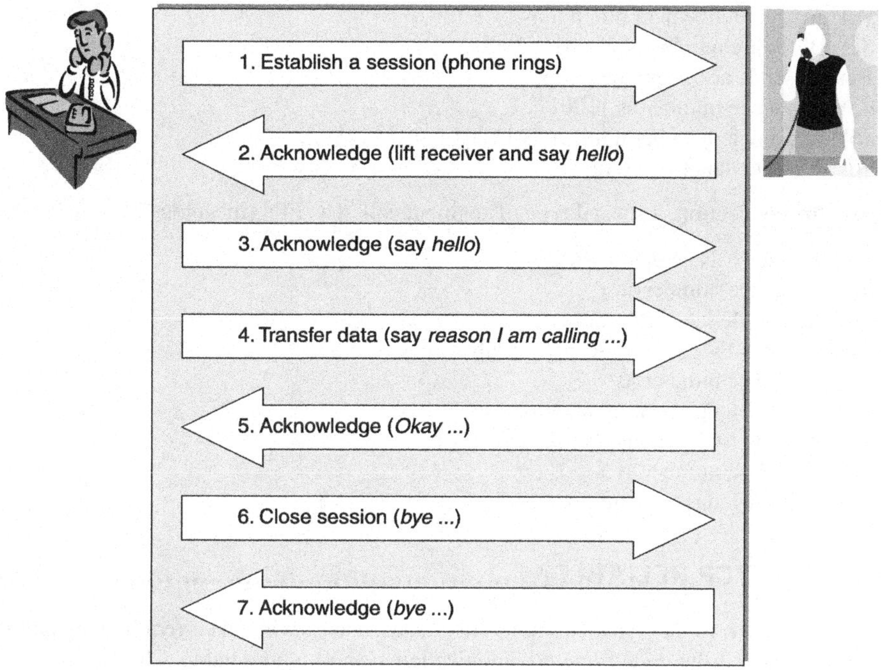

Fig. 4.15 *Concept of a TCP connection with reference to a telephone call*

If we replace the two humans speaking over phone in the diagram with hosts using TCP virtual circuits for communication, we can easily understand the concepts such as *CONNECT*, *LISTEN* and *ACCEPT*.

For connection management, TCP uses special types of segments, called SYN (meaning synchronize), ACK (acknowledge), and their combinations. An example is given below.

1. Sender sends SYN segment with sequence number as 9000.
2. Receiver sends SYN+ACK segment with sequence number as 9001 and acknowledgement number as 12000.
3. Sender sends SYN+ACK segment with sequence number as 9000 and acknowledgement number as 12001.

Once the connection is established, they can perhaps send the following data, as an example:

1. Sender sends data+ACK segment 1 with
   (a) Sequence number as 9001
   (b) Acknowledgement number as 12001
   (c) Bytes are numbered 9001–10000

2. Sender sends data+ACK segment 2 with
   (a) Sequence number as 10001
   (b) Acknowledgement number as 12001
   (c) Bytes are numbered 10001–11000
3. Receiver sends data+ACK segment with
   (a) Sequence number as 15001
   (b) Acknowledgement number as 11001
   (c) Bytes are numbered 15001–17000
4. Sender sends ack segment 3 with
   (a) Sequence number as 11001
   (b) Acknowledgement number as 17001
   (c) With no data to be sent

To close the connection, a special type of segment called as FIN (meaning finish) is used.

1. Client sends FIN segment with
   (a) Sequence number as x
   (b) Acknowledgement number as y
2. Server sends FIN + ACK segment with
   (a) Sequence number as y
   (b) Acknowledgement number as $x + 1$
3. Client sends ACK segment with
   (a) Sequence number as x
   (b) Acknowledgement number as $y + 1$

WHAT MAKES TCP RELIABLE? 4.7

Before we understand how TCP achieves reliability, let us discuss why this is required, in the first place. The main reason is that the underlying communication system is unreliable. This means that there is no guarantee that the IP datagrams sent across the communication system would reach the ultimate destination, unless this is checked at the transport layer. Another problem is that the Internet layer has no means of checking duplicate datagrams and therefore, of rejecting them.

For achieving reliability, the TCP software in the destination computer checks each segment upon arrival and sees if the same segment had arrived before. If so, it simply discards this duplicate segment. For detecting a segment loss, TCP employs the **acknowledgement** mechanism. In simple terms, whenever a segment arrives at the destination, the TCP software in the destination computer sends an acknowledgement back to the sending computer. If the sending computer does not receive this acknowledgement in a pre-specified time interval, it automatically resends the segment, using a process called **retransmission**. For this, the sending computer starts a timer as soon as it first sends a segment (actually a datagram, since the segment would be converted into an IP datagram by the Internet layer). If this timer expires before the acknowledgement for that segment arrives, the sending computer thinks that the receiver has not received it for some reason, and retransmits the segment. Let us discuss this in detail with an example, as shown in Fig. 4.16.

Figure 4.16 shows how retransmission happens with the help of the acknowledgement mechanism. The sending computer sends an IP datagram and its TCP software waits for acknowledgement from the receiving computer in a stipulated time set, using the timer. As can be seen in case of the second datagram, the sending computer does not get any response from the receiving computer before the timer

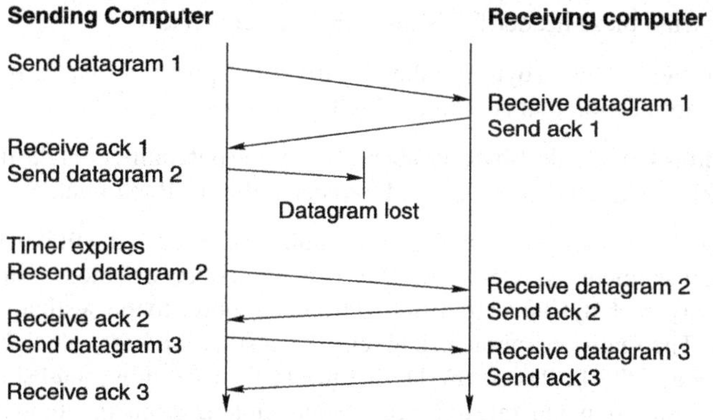

Fig. 4.16 *Retransmission example*

elapses. As a result, it retransmits the second datagram. In case of datagrams 1 and 3, retransmission is not required because the acknowledgement from the receiving computer arrives at the sender's end before the timer expires.

TCP SEGMENT FORMAT 4.8

Figure 4.17 shows the format of a TCP segment. A TCP segment consists of a header of size 20 to 60 bytes, followed by the actual data. The header consists of 20 bytes if the TCP segment does not contain any options. Otherwise, the header consists of 60 bytes. That is, a maximum of 40 bytes are reserved for options. Options can be used to convey additional information to the destination. However, we shall ignore them, as they are not very frequently used.

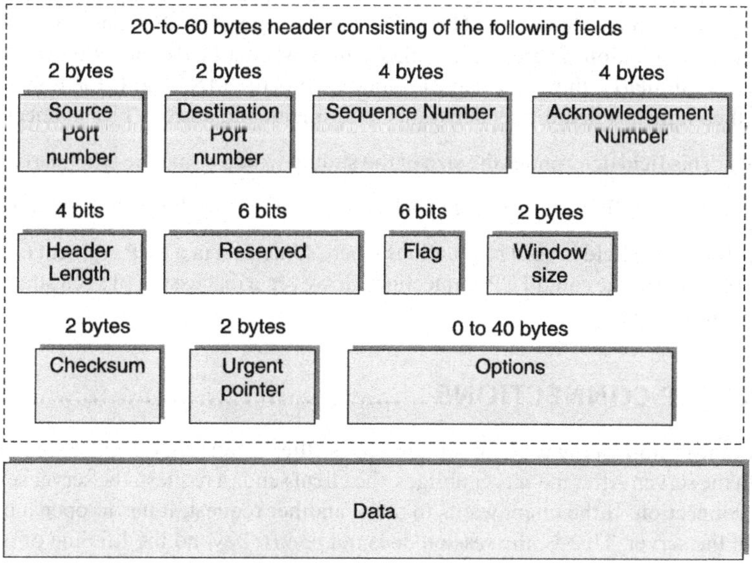

Fig. 4.17 *TCP segment format*

Let us briefly discuss these header fields inside a TCP segment.

1. Source port number This 2-byte number signifies the port number of the source computer, corresponding to the application that is sending this TCP segment.

2. Destination port number This 2-byte number signifies the port number of the destination computer, corresponding to the application that is expected to receive this TCP segment.

3. Sequence number This 4-byte field defines the number assigned to the first byte of the data portion contained in this TCP segment. As we know, TCP is a connection-oriented protocol. For ensuring a continuous connectivity, each byte to be transmitted from the source to the destination is numbered in an increasing sequence. The sequence number field tells the destination host, which byte in this sequence comprises the first byte of the TCP segment. During the TCP connection establishment phase, both the source as well as the destination generate different unique random numbers. For instance, if this random number is 3130 and the first TCP segment is carrying 2000 bytes of data, then the sequence number field for that segment would contain 3132 (bytes 3130 and 3131 are used in connection establishment). The second segment would then have a sequence number of 5132 (3132 + 2000), and so on.

4. Acknowledgement number If the destination host receives a segment with sequence number X correctly, it sends $X + 1$ as the acknowledgement number back to the source. Thus, this 4-byte number defines the sequence number that the source of TCP segment is expecting from the destination as a receipt of the correct delivery.

5. Header length This 4-bit field specifies the number of four-byte words in the TCP header. As we know, the header length can be between 20 and 60 bytes. Therefore, the value of this field can be between 5 (because $5 \times 4 = 20$) and 15 (because $15 \times 4 = 60$).

6. Reserved This 6-byte field is reserved for future and is currently unused.

7. Flag This 6-bit field defines six different control flags, each one of them occupying one bit. Out of the six flags, two are most important. The SYN flag indicates that the source wants to establish a connection with the destination. Therefore, this flag is used when a TCP connection is being established between two hosts. Similarly, the other flag of importance is the FIN flag. If the bit corresponding to this flag is set, then it means that the sender wants to terminate the current TCP connection.

8. Window size This field determines the size of the sliding window that the other party must maintain.

9. Checksum This 16-bit field contains the checksum for facilitating the error detection and correction.

10. Urgent pointer This field is used in situations where some data in a TCP segment is more important or urgent than other data in the same TCP connection. However, a discussion of such situations is beyond the scope of the current text.

PERSISTENT TCP CONNECTIONS 4.9

A TCP connection is **non-persistent**. In simple terms, this means that a client requests for a TCP connection with the server. After the server obliges, the client sends a request, the server sends a response, and closes the connection. If the client wants to make another request, it has to open a brand new TCP connection with the server. That is, the session does not *persist* beyond the lifetime of one request and one response.

There are situations when non-persistent connections are not desirable. As we shall study, on the Internet, a single Web page can contain text, images, audio and video. Suppose a client requests a server for a Web page containing some text and two images. The images reside on the server as separate files, and therefore, normally, the client would have to open three *separate* TCP connections with the server for obtaining the complete Web page. This is shown in Fig. 4.18.

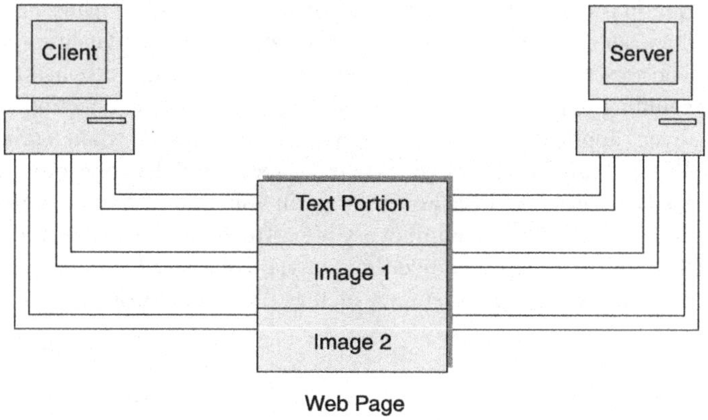

In the traditional Internet, even for fetching different parts of a single Web page, the browser must open separate connections with the server

Fig. 4.18 *Persistent connection*

Instead, the new version 1.1 of the HTTP protocol (which runs on top of TCP/IP, and uses TCP/IP for communication) allows for **persistent connections**. Here, the server serves the request, and does not terminate the TCP connection. Instead, it keeps it open. Thus, the client can reuse the same connection for all forthcoming requests (such as images in a Web page). So, in our example, just one connection would suffice.

Persistent connections can be of two types. In persistent connections **without pipelining**, the client sends the next request within the same TCP connection to the server only after receiving a response to its previous request. In persistent connections **with pipelining**, the client can send multiple requests to the server within the same TCP connection without waiting for any responses from the server. Thus, multiple requests are possible in this case.

Persistent connections are expected to improve the throughput in case of Web pages that contain many non-textual data, such as images, audio and video, because a single TCP connection can suffice all portions of the Web page.

USER DATAGRAM PROTOCOL (UDP) 4.10

We know that the TCP/IP suite of protocols offers two protocols at the transport layer. The first of them is Transmission Control Protocol (TCP), which we have studied in detail. The other protocol in the transport layer is **User Datagram Protocol (UDP)**. We shall study UDP now. UDP is far simpler but less reliable than TCP.

UDP is a connectionless protocol, unlike TCP. UDP allows computers to send data without needing to establish a virtual connection. Since there is no error checking involved here, UDP is simpler than TCP. UDP does not provide for any acknowledgement, sequencing or reordering mechanisms. Thus, UDP datagrams may be lost, duplicated or arrive out of order at the destination. UDP contains very primitive means of error checking (such as checksums). The UDP datagrams are not numbered, unlike TCP segments. Thus, even when multiple UDP datagrams are sent by the same source to the same destination, each datagram is completely independent of all previous UDP datagrams. Since there is no connection between the sender and the destination, the path taken by a UDP datagram cannot be predicted.

Thus, it is left to the application program that uses UDP to accept full responsibility to handle issues such as reliability, including data loss, duplication, delay, and loss of connection. Clearly, this is not such a good idea for every application program to perform these checks, when a reliable data transport mechanism such as TCP is available. However, when the speed of delivery is more important than the reliability of data, UDP is preferred to TCP. For instance, in voice and video transmissions, it is all right to lose a few bits of information, than sending every bit correctly at the cost of transmission speed. In such a situation, UDP would be a better choice. In contrast, computer data transmission must be very reliable. Therefore, for transferring computer data such as files and messages, TCP is used.

UDP DATAGRAM 4.11

Figure 4.19 shows the format of a UDP datagram. Each UDP datagram has a fixed 8-byte header that is subdivided into four fields, each of two bytes. This is followed by the actual data to be transmitted using this UDP datagram, as the figure depicts.

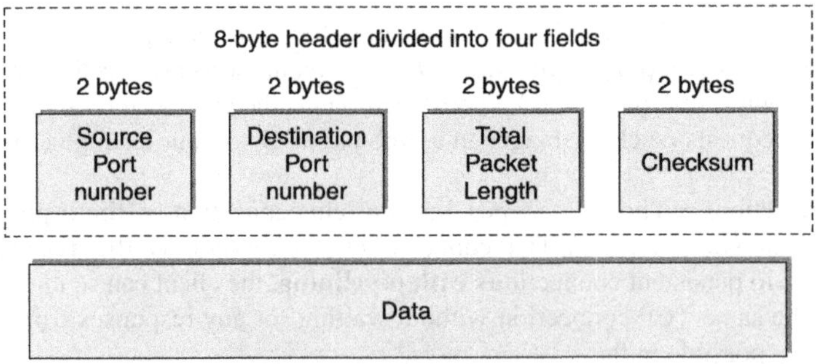

Fig. 4.19 *UDP datagram format*

Let us briefly examine the fields in the UDP datagram header.

1. Source port number This is the port number corresponding to the application running on the source computer. Since it can take up to two bytes, it means that a source port number can be between 0 and 65,535.

2. Destination port number This is the port number corresponding to the application running on the destination computer. Since it can also take up to two bytes, it means that a destination port number can also be between 0 and 65,535.

3. Total packet length This 2-byte field defines the total length of the UDP datagram, i.e., header plus data. Actually, this field is not required at all, because there is a similar *packet* length field in the IP datagram, which encapsulates a UDP datagram inside it before sending it to the destination. Therefore, the following equation is always true.

UDP datagram length = IP datagram length – IP header length

However, this field is retained in the UDP datagram header as an additional check.

4. Checksum This field is used for error detection and correction, as usual.

We can summarize as follows:

(a) *Higher-layer data transfer* An application sends a message to UDP software.

(b) *UDP message encapsulation* The higher-layer message is encapsulated into the *Data* field of a UDP message. The UDP headers are filled (e.g., source and destination ports, and optionally checksum).

(c) *Transfer message to IP* The UDP datagram is passed to IP for transmission.

As a result, when we use UDP, the following happens.

(a) Connectionless service
  (i) Each UDP datagram is independent
  (ii) No connection establishment
  (iii) No numbering of datagrams
  (iv) No chopping of user data into smaller datagrams: User data must be small enough to fit inside an UDP datagram

(b) Flow and error control
  (i) No flow control
  (ii) Error control: Checksum
  (iii) Packets can be lost or duplicated

DIFFERENCES BETWEEN UDP AND TCP 4.12

We shall now understand the broad level difference between UDP and TCP with a simple example. Suppose three clients want to send some data to a server. Let us first understand how this can be done with the help of UDP. We shall then examine what happens in the case of TCP.

4.12.1 Using UDP for Data Transfer

In the case of UDP, a server is called an **iterative**. It means that when a server is dealing with UDP requests, it processes only one request at a time. A client prepares a UDP request datagram, encapsulates it inside an IP datagram, and sends it to the server. The server processes the request, forms a UDP response datagram and sends it back to the client. In the meanwhile, if more UDP requests arrive at the server, the server does not pay any attention to them. It completes servicing a UDP request before taking up any other UDP request. In order to ensure that the UDP requests received in the meantime are not lost, the server stores them in a queue of waiting UDP requests, and processes them one after the other. Note that the UDP requests could arrive from the same client, or from different clients. In any case, they are strictly processed one after another in a sequence. Since UDP is connection-less, this is fine. This is shown in Fig. 4.20.

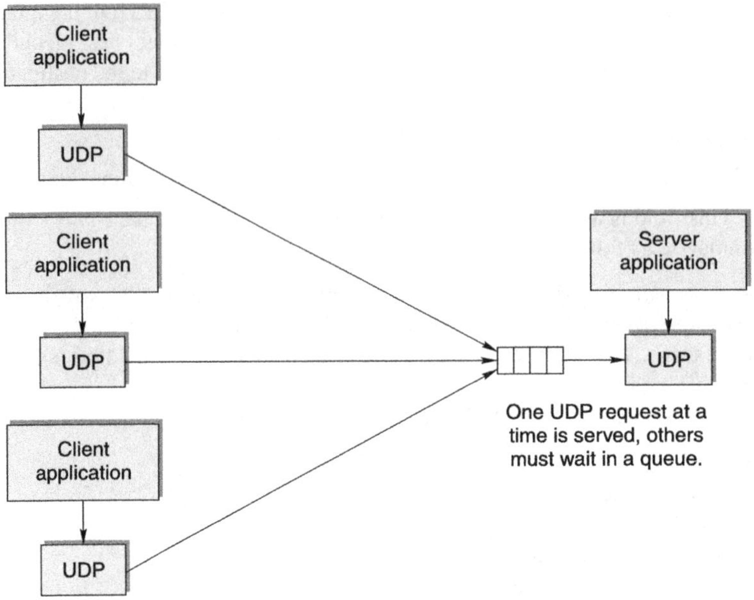

Fig. 4.20 *UDP datagrams are queued*

4.12.2 Using TCP for Data Transfer

In contrast to the UDP model, TCP works strictly on the basis of connections. That is a connection (virtual connection) must be first established between a client and a server before they can send data to each other. As a result, if multiple clients attempt to use the same server at the same time, a separate connection is established for each client. Therefore, the server can process many client requests at the same time unlike what happens in UDP. For this reason, when using TCP, a server is said to be in **concurrent** mode. It means that a server can concurrently serve the requests of multiple clients at the same time, similar to the way a multiprogramming operating system executes many programs at the same time. A connection is established between the server and each client, and each such connection remains open until the entire data stream is processed.

At the implementation level, the concept of parent and child processes is used. That is, when a request for a connection is received from a new client, the server creates a child process, and allocates it to the new client. The new client and the child server processes then communicate with each other. Thus, there is a separate connection between each client and a server child process. Once a parent server process creates a child process to serve the requests of a particular client, the parent process is free to accept more client requests, and create more child processes, as and when necessary. This is shown in Fig. 4.21.

When the communication between a client and a server is over, the parent process kills that particular server child process.

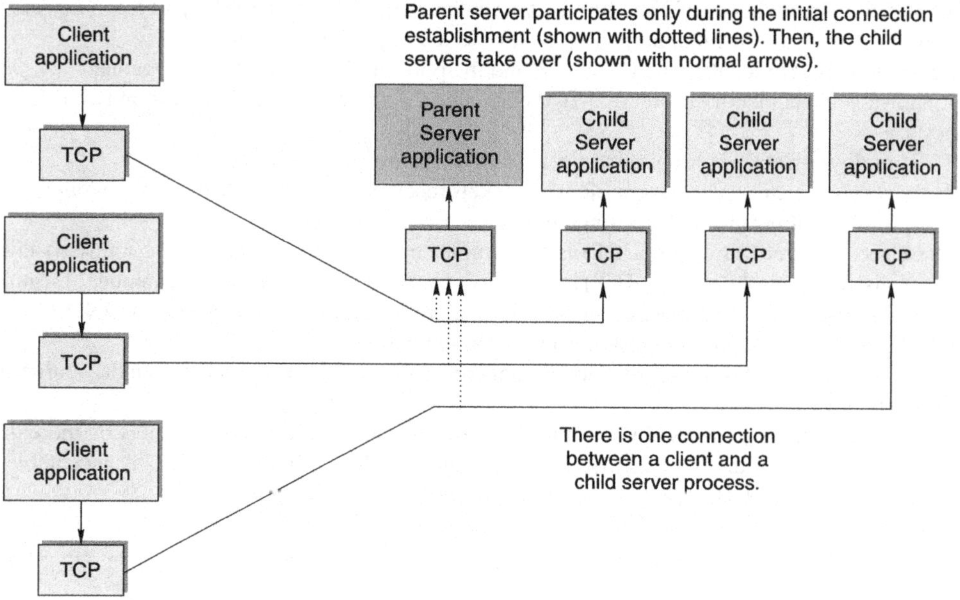

Fig. 4.21 *TCP transmission*

Key Terms and Concepts

Acknowledgement • Active open • Duplication control • Checksum • Concurrent • Connection-oriented • Duplication control • End to end delivery • Error control • Iterative • Loss control • Non-persistent connection • Packet retransmission • Pair of sockets • Passive open • Persistent connection • Point-to-point communication • Port • Port-to-port communication • Segment • Sequence control • Socket • Three way handshake • Transport Layer Protocol (TCP) • User datagram • User Datagram Protocol (UDP) • Well-known ports • Window size changes • With pipelining • Without pipelining

SUMMARY

- The Transmission Control Protocol (TCP) is one of the two transport layer protocols—the other is User Datagram Protocol (UDP).
- The main function of TCP is to ensure a correct delivery of packets between the end points.
- Since the lower layer protocol (IP) is a connection-less, best-effort delivery mechanism that does not worry about issues such as transmission impairments, loss of data and duplicate data, these features have been built into a higher layer protocol, i.e., TCP.
- The main features offered by TCP are reliability, end-to-end communication and connection management.

- Applications running on different hosts communicate with TCP with the help of a concept called as ports. A port is a 16-bit unique number allocated to a particular application.
- A socket is used to identify the IP address and the port number concatenated together.
- A pair of sockets identifies a unique TCP connection between two applications on two different hosts.
- TCP employs an acknowledgement mechanism to ensure correct delivery.
- At the receiver's end, TCP reassembles the packets received, sequences them, removes duplicates, if any, and constructs back the original message as was sent by the sender.
- The User Datagram Protocol (UDP) is the simpler of the two protocols in the transport layer. Transmission Control Protocol (TCP) is a sophisticated protocol that provides a number of features for error control, flow control, accurate delivery, end-to-end communication, etc. UDP is a far simpler protocol that does not provide any of these features.
- UDP is a connectionless protocol that does not create a virtual connection between the source and the destination.
- In multimedia transmissions or voice transport, transmission speed is a major concern, more than accurate delivery of the message itself. The change of values of a few data bits is acceptable in such transmissions. UDP is a suitable candidate for such transmissions.
- UDP is never used for transmitting critical data.

MULTIPLE-CHOICE QUESTIONS

1. Transport layer protocols are useful for ensuring ________ delivery.
(a) host-to-host (b) host-to-router
(c) network-to-network (d) end-to-end

2. ________ is reliable delivery mechanism.
(a) IP (b) TCP (c) UDP (d) ARP

3. When a packet is lost in transit, it should be handled by ________.
(a) sequence control (b) error control
(c) loss control (d) duplication control

4. When a single packet reaches the destination twice, it should be handled by ________.
(a) sequence control (b) error control
(c) loss control (d) duplication control

5. When packet 2 reaches packet 1 at the destination, it should be handled by ________.
(a) sequence control (b) error control
(c) loss control (d) duplication control

6. Combination of ________ and ________ makes a socket.
(a) TCP address, IP address (b) IP address, UDP address
(c) IP address, port number (d) IP address, physical address

7. Well-known ports are generally required ________.
(a) only on the client (b) on the client and the server
(c) on the client but not on the server (d) on the server

8. The client does ________.
(a) active open (b) passive open
(c) both (a) and (b) (d) None of these

9. UDP is iterative because __________.
   (a) it processes multiple requests at the same time
   (b) it performs round-robin checks
   (c) it processes only one request at a time
   (d) it performs parallel processing
10. TCP is concurrent because __________.
   (a) it processes multiple requests at the same time
   (b) it performs round-robin checks
   (c) it processes only one request at a time
   (d) it performs parallel processing

DETAILED QUESTIONS

1. Briefly discuss when to use TCP and when to use UDP.
2. Describe the broad-level features of TCP.
3. Discuss the idea of a port.
4. What is the difference between a port and a socket?
5. Discuss the idea of *passive open* and *active open.*
6. How does the three-way handshake for creating a TCP connection work?
7. What factors make TCP reliable?
8. What is the purpose of the field sequence number inside a TCP segment header?
9. Describe the main fields of UDP datagram header.
10. What is a persistent TCP connection? When is it useful?

EXERCISES

1. Transport layer programming using TCP or UDP involves the use of sockets. Learn the basics of socket programming, using either C or Java.
2. Investigate why it is a lot easier to do socket programming in Java as compared to C or other languages.
3. Try opening a socket on a server, and then communicate with that from a client socket.
4. What different things does one have to do in socket programming while using TCP vis-à-vis UDP?
5. What is your idea of persistent connections? Compare that with the persistent connections in a client-server environment.

5 TCP-IP PART III (DNS, EMAIL, FTP, TFTP)

INTRODUCTION

In the last few chapters, we have discussed various protocols in the network/Internet layer and the transport layer of the TCP/IP protocol suite. These protocols such as IP, ARP, TCP and UDP are responsible for providing lower layer services such as delivery of packets from one host to another, and optionally error-checking and retransmission, etc.

The network and transport layer protocols in TCP/IP would have no meaning without the application layer protocol services such as **Domain Name System (DNS)**, **Simple Mail Transfer Protocol (SMTP)** for **electronic mails (emails)**, **File Transfer Protocol (FTP)** and **Trivial File Transfer Protocol (TFTP)**. We shall study all these protocols that are akin to passengers in a transport system. Of course, these are not the only protocols in the application layer of TCP/IP suite of protocols. We shall discuss the remaining application layer protocols in TCP/IP later.

DOMAIN NAME SYSTEM (DNS) ... 5.1

5.1.1 Introduction

Although computers work at their best when dealing with numbers, humans feel quite at home, dealing with names, instead. For instance, we would certainly prefer if someone asks us to send a message to Sachin's computer than telling us to send it to a computer whose IP address is 150.21.90.101. (Though this is much better than having to talk about an address as a string of 32 bits). Sachin's computer might correspond to this IP address. But for you, it is far better to call it as Sachin's computer, or even better, simply Sachin! This simple idea of identifying computer networks and computers on those networks by some names is the basis for **domain names**.

A domain name is a name given to a network for ease of reference by humans. The term *domain* actually refers to a group of computers that are called by a single common name. Of course, somebody ultimately has to translate these domain names into IP addresses, because, it is only these 32-bit IP addresses of computers that the TCP/IP or the Internet understands while sending or receiving any messages such as emails or files. This is conceptually shown in Fig. 5.1 where a computer's domain name is *Atul*, and its IP address is 150.21.90.101. The diagram shows the perspectives from both the point of views of a user and a network.

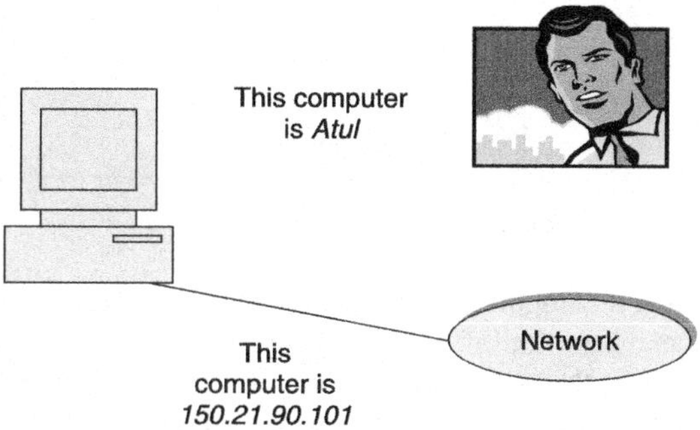

Fig. 5.1 *Domain name and IP address are different representations of the same computer*

People often name their computers with pride. In some organizations, naming computers is standardized. But in many other cases, computers are identified by the names of the people that use them, or by planet names. Jokingly, you could hear a comment such as *Anita is down today*, which actually means Anita's computer is not working for some reason! To summarize, we humans like to call computers by, well, names. There is only one problem here. Two computers in a network cannot have the same name. Otherwise, a computer cannot be identified uniquely. For this reason, it is necessary to ensure that the computer names are always unique and that too globally, if we want to use them on the Internet.

In order to make computer names unique, the Internet naming convention uses a simple and frequently used idea. Additional strings or suffixes are added to the names. The full name of a computer consists of its local name followed by a period and the organization's suffix. For example, if Radhika works in IBM, her computer's name would be Radhika.IBM. Of course, if there are two or more persons with the same name in an organization, another convention (e.g., Radhika1 and Radhika2 in this case) could be used.

We would realize that this is not good enough. The names of the organization themselves could be same or similar. For example, Atul.techsystems may not suffice, since there can be many organizations with the name *techsystems*. (Moreover, there could be many *Atuls* in each of them). This means, having the organization's suffix to the local name is not adequate. As a result, another suffix is added to the computer names after the organization's name. This indicates the type of the organization. For example, it could be a commercial organization, a non-profit making concern or a university. Depending on the type, this last suffix is added. Normally, this last suffix is three characters long. For example: *com* indicates a commercial organization, *edu* indicates an university and *net* indicates a network. As a result, Radhika's computer would now become Radhika.IBM.com. In general terms, all computers at IBM would have the last portion of their names as IBM.com. If an IBM university crops up tomorrow, it would not clash with IBM.com. Instead, it would become IBM.edu. This is shown in Fig. 5.2.

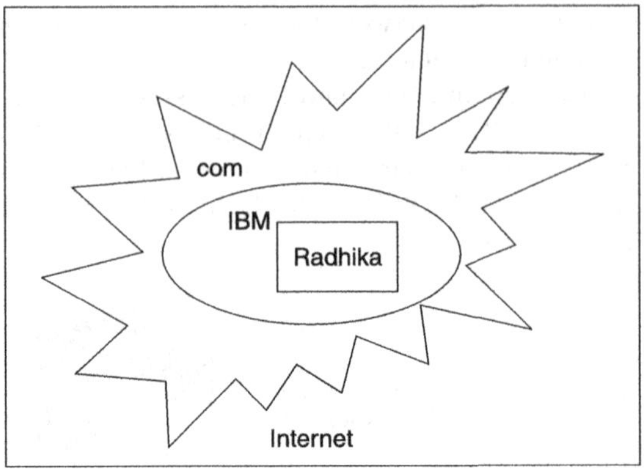

Fig. 5.2 *Domain name example*

It must be mentioned that a computer's name on the Internet need not necessarily be made up of only three parts. Once the main portion of the name is allocated to an organization (e.g., IBM.com), the organization is free to add further subnames to computers. For instance, IBM's US division might choose to have a prefix of IBM-US.com or IBM.US.com to all their computers instead of IBM.com.

Initially, all domain names had to end with a three-character suffix such as *com* or *org*. However, as the Internet became more popular and widespread, people thought of adding country-specific prefixes to the domain names. These prefixes were two-characters long. Examples of these suffixes are *in* for India, *uk* for England, *jp* for Japan and *de* for Germany. So, if the computer containing the information about the site (called **Web server**, which we shall study in detail later) were hosted in England, the prefix would not be *com*, instead it would be *co.uk*. For instance, BBC's site is www.bbc.co.uk and not www.bbc.com. Basically, it is decided on the physical location of the Web server as well as where the domain name is registered. However, any site in the US does not have a two-character suffix (such as *us*). All commercial domain names in the US end with *com* and not *co.us*. The reason for this is simple. The Internet was born in the US, and therefore, the US is taken as default. Remember that the country name is not written on the postal stamps in England – after all the postal system started there, and no one then thought that it would one day become so popular that all other countries would adopt it. In a similar way, people did not thought that one day, **Web sites** (a term used to refer to the existence of an organization on the Internet, or the *Web*) would come up in so many different parts of the world. Therefore, *com* meant US – at least, initially!

The general domain names are shown in Fig. 5.3.

Domain name	*Description*
com	Commercial organization
edu	Educational institution
gov	Government institution
int	International organization
mil	Military group
net	Network support group
org	Non-profit organization

Fig. 5.3 *General domain names*

The proposed additional general name labels are shown in Fig. 5.4.

Domain name	*Description*
arts	Cultural organization
firm	Business unit or firm
info	Information service provider
nom	Personal nomenclature
rec	Recreation or entertainment group
store	Business offering goods/services
web	Web-related organization

Fig. 5.4 *Proposed general domain names*

Thus, humans use domain names when referring to computers on the Internet, whereas computers work only with IP addresses, which are purely numeric. For instance, suppose while using the Internet, I want to send a message to my friend Umesh who works in a company called Sunny software solutions. Therefore, there should be some screen on my computer that allows me to type umesh.sunny.com. However, when I do so, for the Internet to understand this, clearly, there must be a mechanism to translate this computer name (*umesh.sunny.com*) into its corresponding IP address (say *120.10.71.93*). Only then, the correct computer can be contacted. This problem is shown in Fig. 5.5.

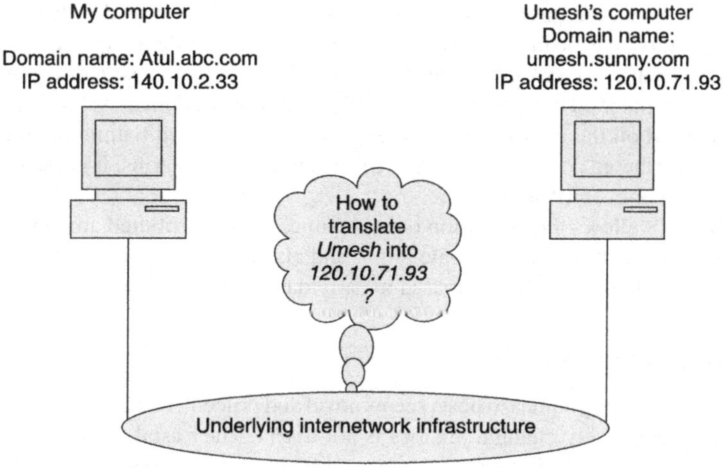

Fig. 5.5 *How to translate domain names into IP addresses?*

How is this achieved? We shall study this now.

5.1.2 Domain Name System (DNS)

In the early days of the Internet, all domain names (also called **host names**) and their associated IP addresses were recorded in a single file called *hosts.txt*. The Network Information Center (NIC) in the US maintained this file. A portion of the hypothetical *hosts.txt* file is shown in Fig. 5.6 for conceptual understanding.

Host name	IP address
Atul.abc.com	120.10.210.90
Pete.xyz.co.uk	131.90.120.71
Achyut.pqr.com	171.92.10.89
…	…

Fig. 5.6 *Hosts.txt file – a logical view*

Every night, all the hosts attached to the Internet would obtain a copy of this file to refresh their domain name entries. As the Internet grew at a breathtaking pace, so did the size of this file. By mid-1980s, this file had become extremely huge. Therefore, it was now too large to copy it to all systems and almost impossible to keep it up-to-date. These problems of maintaining *hosts.txt* on a single server can be summarized as shown in Fig. 5.7.

Problem	*Description*
Traffic volumes	A single name server handling all domain name queries would make it very slow and lead to a lot of traffic from and to the single server.
Failure effects	If the single domain server fails, it would almost lead to the crash of the full Internet.
Delays	Since the centralized server might be *distant* for many clients (e.g., if it is located in the US, for someone making a request from New Zealand, it is too far). This would make the domain name requests-responses very slow.
Maintenance	Maintaining single file would be very difficult as new domain name entries keep coming, and some of the existing ones become obsolete. Also, controlling changes to this single file can become a nightmare.

Fig. 5.7 *Problems with a centralized domain name mechanism*

To solve this problem, the Internet **Domain Name System (DNS)** was developed as a **distributed database**. By distributed, we mean that the database containing the mapping between the domain names and IP addresses was scattered across different computers. This DNS is consulted whenever any message is to be sent to any computer on the Internet. It is simply a mapping of domain names versus IP addresses.

The DNS is based on the creation of a hierarchical domain-based naming architecture, which is implemented as a distributed database, as remarked earlier. In simple terms, it is used for mapping host names and email addresses to IP addresses.

Additionally, DNS allows the allocation of host names to be distributed amongst multiple naming authorities, rather than centralized at a single point, and also facilitates quicker retrievals. This makes the Internet a lot more democratic as compared to early days. We shall study this in the next section.

5.1.3 The DNS Name Space

Although the idea of assigning names to hosts seems novel and prudent, it is not an easy one to implement. Managing a pool of constantly changing names is not trivial. The postal system has to face a similar problem. It deals with it by requiring the sender to specify the country, state, city, street name and house number of the addressee. Using this hierarchy of information, distinguishing Atul Kahate of 13th East Street, Pune, India from the Atul Kahate of 13th East Street, Chelmsford, England becomes easy. DNS uses the same principle.

The Internet is theoretically divided into hundreds of top-level domains. Each of these domains, in turn, has several hosts underneath. Also, each domain can be further subdivided into subdomains, which can be further classified into subsubdomains, and so on. For instance, if we want to register a domain called *Honda* under the category *auto*, which is within *in* (for India), the full path for this domain would be *Honda.auto.in*. Similarly, from Fig. 5.8, it can be seen that Atul.maths.oxford.edu identifies the complete path for a computer under the domain *Atul*, which is under the domain *maths*, which is under the domain *oxford*, and which is finally under the domain *edu*.

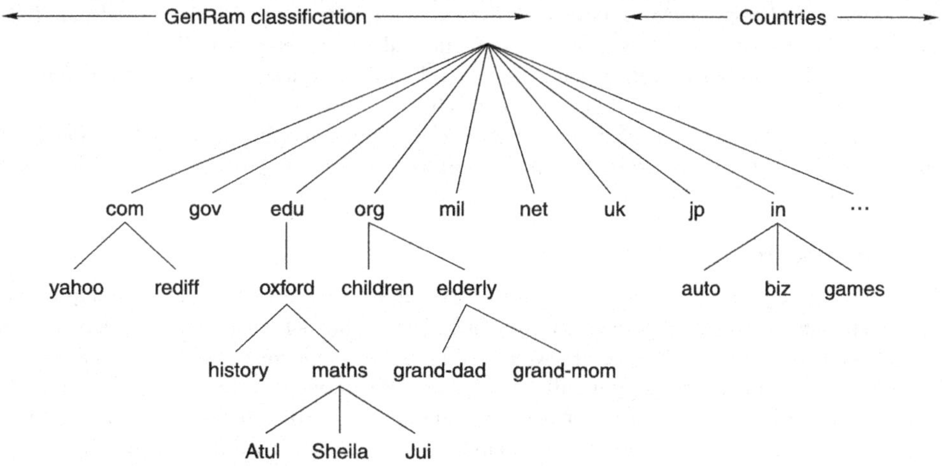

Fig. 5.8 *A portion of the Internet's domain name space*

This creates a tree-like structure as shown in Fig. 5.8. Note that a leaf represents a lowest-level domain that cannot be classified further (but contains hosts). The figure shows a hypothetical portion of the Internet.

The topmost domains are classified into two main categories: **General** (which means, the domains registered in the US) and **countries**. The General domains are subclassified into categories such as com (commercial), gov (the US federal government), edu (educational), org (non-profit organizations) mil (the US military) and net (network providers). The country domains specify one entry for each country. For instance, uk (United Kingdom), jp (Japan), in (India) and so on.

Each domain is fully qualified by the path upward from it to the topmost (unnamed) root. The names within a full path are separated by a dot. Thus, Microsoft's Technology section could be named as tech.microsoft.com; whereas Sun Microsystem's downloads section could be named downloads.sun.com. Domain names are case insensitive. Thus, com and COM are the same thing in a domain name. A full path name can be up to 255 characters long including the dots, and each component within it can be up to a maximum of 63 characters. Also, there could be as many dots in a domain name you could have – within each component, separated by dots.

5.1.4 DNS Server

Introduction

There is no doubt that we should have a central authority keeping track of the database of names in the topmost level domains such as com, edu and net. However, it is not prudent to centralize the database of all of the entries within the com domain. For example, IBM has hundreds of thousands of IP addresses and domain names. IBM would like to maintain its own **Domain Name System Server (DNS Server)**, also called just **Domain Name Server**, for the IBM.com domain. A domain name server is simply a computer that contains the database and the software for mapping between domain names and IP addresses. Similarly, India wants to govern the *in* top-level domain; and Australia wants to take care of the *au* domain, and so on. That is why DNS is a distributed database. IBM is totally responsible for maintaining the name server for IBM.com. It maintains the computers and the software (databases, etc.) that implement its portion of the DNS, and IBM can change the database for its own domain (*IBM.com*) whenever it wants to, simply because it owns its domain name servers. Similarly, for IBM.au, IBM can provide a cross-reference entry in its IBM.com domain, and take its responsibility.

Thus, every domain has a domain name server. It handles requests coming to computers owned by it and also maintains the various domain entries. This might surprise you. In fact, this is one of the most amazing facts about the Internet. The DNS is completely distributed throughout the world on millions of computers. It is administered by millions of people. Still, it appears to be a single, integrated worldwide database!

How the DNS Server Works

The DNS works pretty similar to a telephone directory inquiry service. You dial up the inquiry service and ask for a person's telephone number, based on the name. If the person is local, the directory service immediately comes up with the answer. However, if the person happens to be staying in another state, the directory service either directs your call to that state's telephone directory inquiry service, or asks you to call them. Furthermore, if the person is in another country, the directory service takes help of their international counterparts. This is very similar to the way a DNS server works. In case of the telephone directory service, you tell a person's name and ask for the telephone number. In case of DNS, you specify the domain name and ask for its corresponding IP address.

Basically, the DNS servers do two things tirelessly:

1. Accepting requests from programs for converting domain names into IP addresses.
2. Accepting requests from other DNS servers to convert domain names into IP addresses.

When such a request comes in, a DNS server has the following options:

1. It can supply the IP address because it already knows the IP address for the domain.
2. It can contact another DNS server and try to locate the IP address for the name requested. It may have to do this more than once. Every DNS server has an entry called as *alternate DNS server*, which is the DNS server it should get in touch with for unresolved domains. The DNS hierarchy specifies how the chains between the various DNS servers should be established for this purpose. That discussion is beyond the scope of the current text.
3. It can simply say, "I do not know the IP address for the domain name you have requested, but here is the IP address for a name server that knows more than I do." In other words, it suggests the name of another DNS server.
4. It can return an error message because the requested domain name is invalid or does not exist.

This is shown in Fig. 5.9.

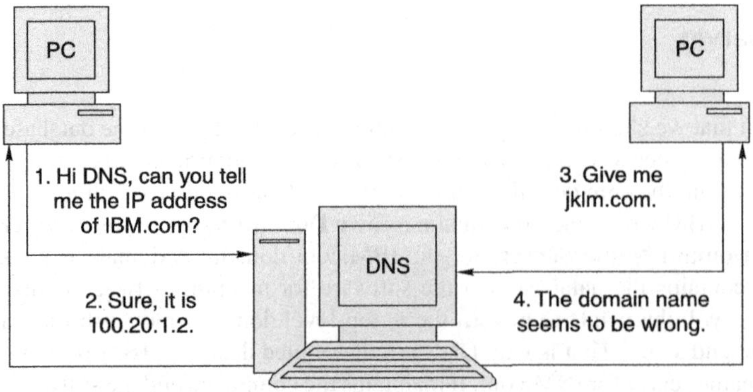

Fig. 5.9 *Interactions between hosts and a DNS server*

As the figure shows, one host is interested in knowing the IP address of the server at *IBM.com*. For this purpose, it contacts its nearest DNS server. The DNS server looks at the list of domain names and their IP addresses. It finds an entry for the domain and sends it back to the client computer. However, when the DNS server receives another request from another computer for *jklm.com*, it replies back saying that such a domain name does not exist. As we know, for this, it might need to consult other DNS servers to see if they have any idea about this domain name, or it might need to suggest the name of the DNS server that the host should contact itself.

For using DNS, an application program performs the following operations:

1. The application program interested in obtaining the IP address of another host on the Internet calls a library procedure called **resolver**, sending it the domain name for which the corresponding IP address is to be located. The resolver is an application program running on the host.
2. The resolver sends a UDP packet to the nearest DNS server (called the **local DNS server**).
3. The local DNS server looks up the domain name and returns the IP address to the resolver.
4. The resolver returns the IP address back to the calling application.

Using the IP address thus obtained, the calling application establishes a transport layer (TCP) connection with the destination, or sends UDP packets, as appropriate. All this happens without the end user being aware of it. When you key in the domain name such as *honda.auto.com*, to see its Website, internally, the DNS is used to get the IP address and then the connection is established.

ELECTRONIC MAIL (EMAIL).. 5.2

5.2.1 Introduction

Electronic mail (email) was created to allow two individuals to communicate using computers. In early days, the email technology allowed one person to type a message and then send it to another person over the Internet. It was like posting a card, except that the communication was electronic, instead of on paper. These days, email facility allows many features such as:

1. Composing and sending / receiving a message.
2. Storing/forwarding/deleting/replying to a message with normally expected facilities, such as carbon copy (CC), blind carbon copy (BCC), etc.
3. Sending a single message to more than one person.
4. Sending text, voice, graphics and video.
5. Sending a message that interacts with other computer programs.

The best features of email are:

1. The speed of email is almost equal to that of telephonic conversations.
2. The recording of the email messages in some form is like the postal system (which is even better than the telephone system).

Thus, email combines the best of the features of the telephone system and the postal system, and is yet very cheap.

From the view point of users, email performs the following five functions:

1. **Composition** The email system can provide features in addition to the basic text editor features, such as automatic insertion of the receiver's email address when replying to a message.
2. **Transfer** The email system takes upon itself the responsibility of moving the message from the sender to the receiver, by establishing connections between the two computers and transferring the message using TCP/IP.

3. **Reporting** The sender needs to know whether the email message was successfully delivered to the receiver, or it did not reach the receiver for whatever reason. The email system performs this reporting task as well.
4. **Displaying** The email system displays the incoming messages in a special pop-up window, or informs the user in some way that an email message has arrived. The user can then open that message on the screen.
5. **Disposition** This includes features such as forwarding, archiving, and deleting messages that have been dealt with. The user can decide what to do with such an email message, and instruct the email system accordingly.

There is a tremendous similarity between the postal system using which we send letters, and the email system. When we write a letter to someone, we put it in an envelope, write the intended recipient's name and the postal address on the envelope and drop it in a post box. The letter then goes via one or more interfaces, such as inter-state or inter-country postal services. It also passes through various *nodes*, where sorting and forwarding of letters take place. Remember, the pin code comes handy for this! Finally, it arrives in the personal mailbox of the recipient. (Here, we imagine that each resident has a post mailbox near his house. We may also assume that the person checks the mailbox for any letters twice a day). This is shown in Fig. 5.10. Here, a person from New York wants to send a letter to her friend in Brighton (England).

Fig. 5.10 *Postal communication system used by humans*

Email does not work a lot differently than this. The major difference between postal mail and email is the interface. Whereas postal system has humans coordinating most of the communication (say New York to London, London to Brighton) in terms of moving the letter ahead, in case of emails, it is all handled by one or more intermediate routers, as studied earlier. Email uses TCP/IP as the underlying protocol. This means that when a person X writes a message to Y, it is broken down into packets according to the TCP/IP format, routed through various routers of the Internet and reassembled back into the complete email message at the destination before it is presented to Y for reading.

Interestingly, email first started with people sending files to each other. The convention followed was that when it was required to send an electronic message, the person would send a file instead, with the desired recipient's name written in the first line of the file. However, people soon discovered problems with this approach, some of which are as follows:

1. There was no provision for creating a message containing text, audio and video.
2. The sender did not receive any acknowledgement from the receiver, and therefore, did not know if the message indeed reached the receiver.
3. Sending the same message to a group of people was difficult with this approach. Examples of such situations are memos or meeting invitations sent to many people.
4. The user interface was poor. The user had to first invoke an editor, type the message into a file, close the editor, invoke the file transfer program, send the file, and close the file transfer program.
5. The messages did not have a predefined structure, making viewing or editing cumbersome.

Considering these problems, it was felt that a separate application was needed to handle electronic messaging.

5.2.2 Mailbox

Just as we usually have our own personal mailbox outside the building for receiving postal mails, for receiving emails, we have an electronic **mailbox**. An email mailbox is just a storage area on the disk of the computer. This area is used for storing received emails; similar to the way a postal mailbox stores postal mails.

The postman arrives some time during the day to deliver postal mails. At that time, the recipient may not be at home. Therefore, the postman deposits the letters in the mailbox. We check our mailbox after returning home from work. Therefore, usually there is some gap between the times the mail is actually delivered in the box and the time it is actually opened. That is why this type of communication is called *asynchronous*, as opposed to the *synchronous* telephonic conversation, where the both parties are communicating at the same time. Similarly, when you write an email to somebody, that person may not have started his computer. Should this email reach that computer only to find that it cannot accept it? To solve this problem, another computer is given the responsibility of storing email messages before they are forwarded. This computer, along with the software is called **email server**. The email server is dedicated to his task of storing and distributing emails, but can, in theory, also perform other tasks. There is a mailbox (i.e., some disk space) on the email server computer for each client computer connected to it and wanting to use the email facility. That server has to be kept *on* constantly. When the user types in his email, it is sent from his computer to the email server of the sender, where it is stored first.

Similarly, all emails received for all the users connected to the email server are received and stored on this server first. The reason is that this email server is always *on*, even if the user (client) computers are *shut off*. When the client computer starts and connects to the server computer, the client can pick up the email from his mailbox on the server and either bring it on to his hard disk of the client PC, or just read it without bringing it to its own computer (i.e., download) and retain it or delete it. Thus, the user of the client computer can read all mails one by one and reply to them or delete them or forward them, etc. Therefore, in this regard, emails are similar to the postal mails. They can be stored until the recipient wants to have a look at them. However, unlike postal mails, which take days, or even weeks to travel from the sender to the recipient, emails travel very fast—in a few minutes. In this aspect, emails are similar to telephone calls.

Thus, we will realize that there are two email servers that participate in any email communication as shown in Fig. 5.11.

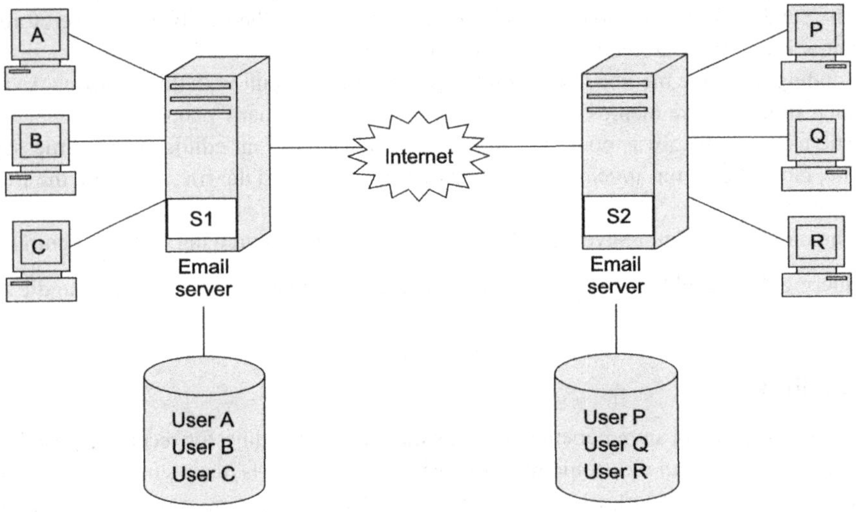

Fig. 5.11 *Overview of the email system*

When a user A wants to write an email to P, A creates a message on his PC and sends it. It is first stored on its email server (S1). From there, it travels through the Internet to the email server of P (i.e., S2). It is stored in the mailbox of P on the hard disk of S2. When P logs on, his PC is connected to his server (S2) and he is notified that there are new messages in his mailbox. P can then read them one by one, redirect them, delete them or transfer them to his local PC (i.e., download).

The email service provided by the Internet differs from other communication mechanisms in one more respect. This feature, called **spooling**, allows a user to compose and send an email message even if his network is currently disconnected or the recipient is not currently connected to his end of the network. When an email message is sent, a copy of the email is placed in a storage area on the server's disk, called spool.

A spool is a queue of messages. The messages in a spool are sent on a *first come first searched* basis. That is, a background process on the email server periodically searches every message in a spool automatically after a specified time interval, and an attempt is made to send it to the intended recipient.

For instance, the background process can attempt to send every message in a spool after every 30 seconds. If the message cannot be sent due to any reasons such as too many messages in the queue, the date and time when an attempt was made to send it is recorded. After a specified number of attempts or time interval, the message is removed from the spool and is returned back to the original sender with an appropriate error message. Until that time, the message remains in the spool. In other words, a message can be considered as delivered successfully only when both the client and the server conclude that the recipient has received the email message correctly. Till that time, copies of the email message are retained in both the sending spool and the receiving mailbox.

The postal system worldwide identifies the recipient using his unique postal address – usually some combination of city/zip code and street name and numbers, etc. In a similar fashion, an email is sent to a person using the person's **email address**. An email address is very similar to postal address – it helps the email system to uniquely identify a particular recipient. We shall look at email addresses in more depth.

5.2.3 Sending and Receiving an Email

The person sending a postal mail usually writes or types it and puts it in the envelope having the recipient's postal address. The software that enables the email system to run smoothly, i.e., the email software, has two parts. One that runs on the client (user's) PC called as **email client software** and the other that runs on the email server, called **email server software**. For writing an email, the sender runs **email client software** on his computer. The email client software is a program that allows the user to compose an email and specify the intended recipient's email address. The composing part is very similar to simple word processing. It allows features such as simple text to be typed in, adjusting the spacing, paragraphs, margins, fonts and different ways of displaying characters (e.g., bold, italics, underlining, etc.). The email is composed using this software, which asks for the address of the recipient. The user then types it in. The email client software knows the sender's address anyway. Thus, a complete message with the sender's and the recipient's addresses is created and then sent across.

Using the recipient's email address, the email travels from the source to the email server of the source, and then to the recipient's email server – of course, through many routers. As we know, the underlying protocol used is again TCP/IP. That means that the bits in the contents of the email (text, image, etc.) are broken down into packets as per TCP/IP format and re-assembled at the recipient's end. In-between the nodes, the error/flow control and routing functions are performed as per the different protocols of different networks. The TCP/IP software running on the email server ensures the receipt of the complete email message. This server also has to have a part of the email server software, which manages the email boxes for different clients. After receiving the message, this software deposits it in the appropriate mailbox. When the recipient logs on to the server, the message is transferred to his computer. The recipient also has to have email client software application running on his computer. It is used to read the received email, and reply if necessary. The receiver can also forward the email thus, received to other users of email anywhere on the Internet, or he can delete it. All this is done by using the email client software on the recipient's computer. Obviously, as this software also allows replying to the message, it also has to have the word processing capabilities.

Thus, the email software itself is divided into two parts: client portion and server portion. The client portion allows you to compose a message, forward it, reply to a message, and also display a received message. The server portion essentially manages the mailbox to store the messages temporarily and deliver them when directed.

Each company normally installs an email server, using which, all the employees can communicate with each other, and also with the outside world. Alternatively, most of the ISPs provide the email service, who then have to take care of email server hardware and software. Apart from this, there are organizations like Yahoo, Hotmail, etc., who create a large pool of servers, with the server part of email software. Now, you can communicate with anyone freely on the Internet. Why does Yahoo do this? Because Yahoo feels that many people will subscribe to Yahoo, due to its free email service, and then while sending/receiving emails, will also see the advertisements displayed. Yahoo, in turn, gets the money from the advertisers, who want to advertise on the Yahoo Web site, due to its large number of subscribers. It is exactly like a TV channel and their advertisements.

Having understood the basic concepts, let us look at the email message anatomy in more detail.

5.2.4 Email Anatomy

Here is a sample email message, as shown in Fig. 5.12.

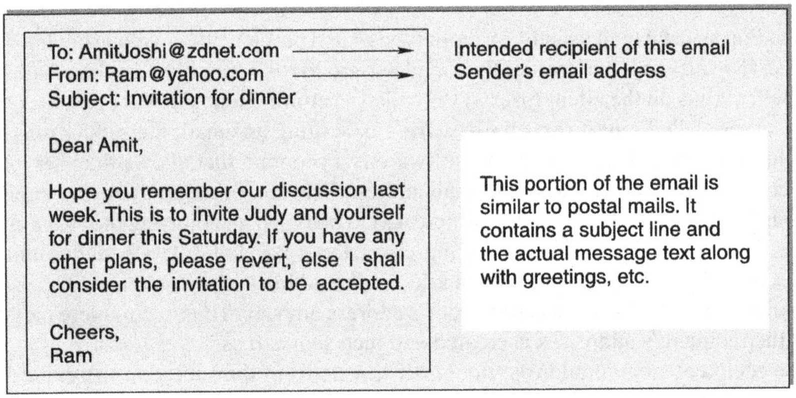

Fig. 5.12 *A sample email message*

Each electronic mailbox on the server has a unique email address. This consists of two parts – the name of the user and the name of the domain. The @ symbol joins them to form the email address as shown in Fig. 5.13.

User name	@	Domain name

Fig. 5.13 *Email address format*

As we have seen before, the domain name usually identifies the organization or university of the user, like the street and city names. The user name is like the house number. For example, Amit Joshi works for an organization called zdnet in the above example (AmitJoshi@zdnet.com). Therefore, zdnet is the name of the organization and Amit Joshi is one of the users belonging to that organization. This is similar to writing the name of the person along with the house number and then the street name, city, etc., on the envelope. Note that the user name syntax is not very strict in many cases. If the email service is provided by an organization where the person is working (i.e., the email server hardware/software is hosted by the organization) itself, some standard is usually established (e.g., all email ids would be in the form name.surname@domainname). However, if the person subscribes to a free email service provider (such as Yahoo, Hotmail, USA.net, Rediffmail, etc.), he is free to choose the user name portion. Thus, an email id can be as silly as shutup@hotmail.com, where shutup is a user name! This is possible because there are no naming standards in case of the email service providers.

Google, Hotmail, Yahoo are some of the most popular networks within the Internet - with thousands of subscribers. All the people connected to Yahoo would have the domain name as yahoo.com. Thus, if the sender of our letter is Ram on the Yahoo domain, his full email address is Ram@yahoo.com. Fig. 5.14 shows this.

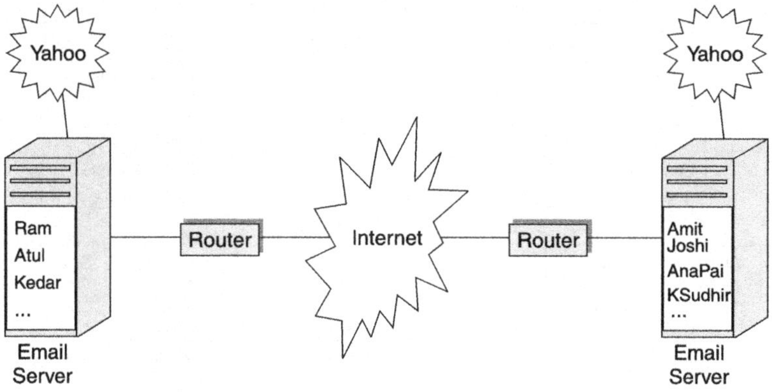

Fig. 5.14 *Concept of domains and email servers*

The corresponding block diagram for this is as shown in Fig. 5.15.

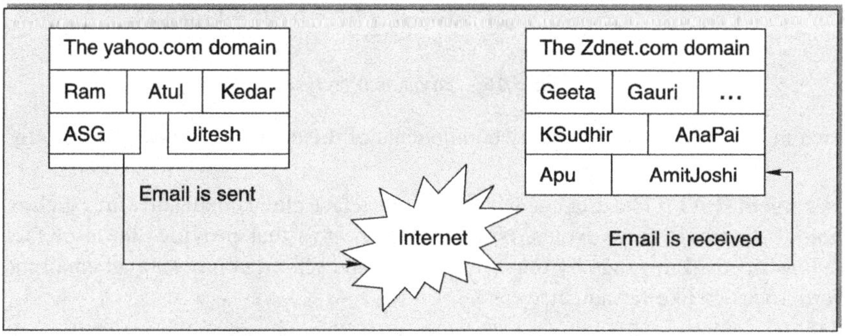

Fig. 5.15 *Domains and mailboxes on domains*

Several terms are used in the email technology. Let us understand them with the help of Fig. 5.16.

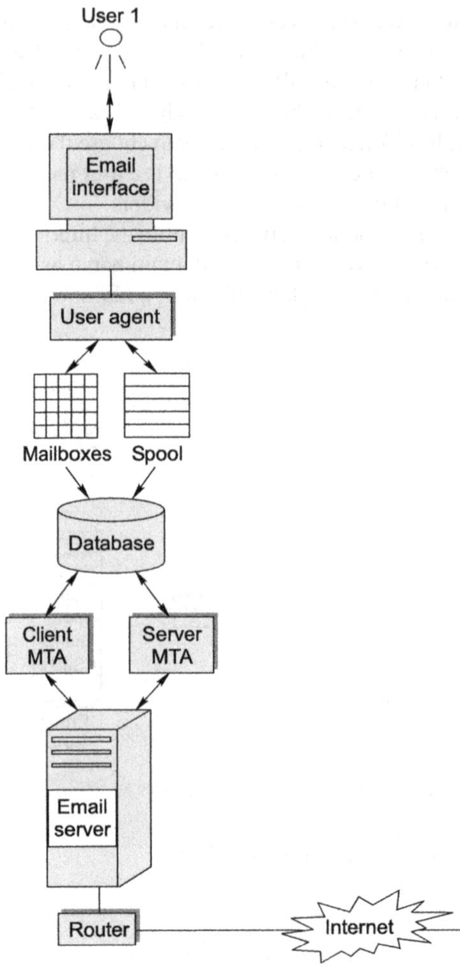

Fig. 5.16 *Email architecture*

As shown in Fig. 5.16, there are many components of the email architecture, as briefly described below.

1. **User Agent (UA)** The user agent is the user interface client email software (such as Microsoft Outlook Express, Lotus Notes, Netscape Mail, etc.) that provides the user facilitates for reading an email message by retrieving it from the server, composing an email message in a Wordprocessor like format, etc.
2. **Mailbox** We have discussed mailboxes as well. There is one mailbox per user, which acts as the email storage system for that user.
3. **Spool** We have already discussed spool. It allows storing of email messages sent by the user until they can be sent to the intended recipient.
4. **Mail Transfer Agent (MTA)** The mail transfer agent is the interface between the email system and the local email server.

5.2.5 Simple Mail Transfer Protocol (SMTP)

Simple Mail Transfer Protocol (SMTP) is at the heart of the email system. In SMTP, the server keeps waiting on well-known port 25. SMTP consists of two aspects, UA and MTA, which are explaiend earlier.

SMTP actually performs two transfers: (a) from the sender's computer to the sender's SMTP server, and (b) from the sender's SMTP server to the receiver's SMTP server. The last leg of transferring emails between the receiver's SMTP server and the end receiver's computer is done by one of the two other email protocols, called as POP or IMAP (which we shall discuss shortly). The concept is illustrated in Fig. 5.17.

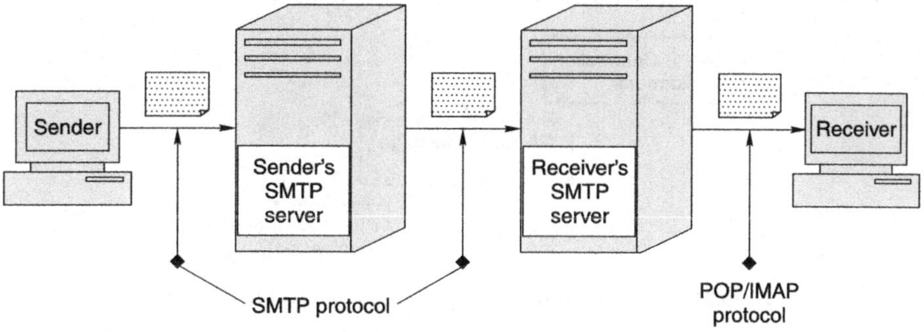

Fig. 5.17 *SMTP and POP*

We should remember that SMTP is different from other protocols, because it is asynchronous – in other words, it allows a delayed delivery. The delays can happen at both the sender's side, as well as at the receiver's side. At the sender's side, email messages are spooled so that the sender can send an email and without waiting to see its progress, continue her other work. On the receiver's side, received emails are deposited in the user's mailbox so that the user need not interrupt her ongoing work, and open her mailbox only when she wants it.

In SMTP, client sends one or more commands to the server. Server returns responses.

Figure 5.18 shows examples of commands sent by a client to a server.

Command	*Explanation*
HELO	Client identifies the server using client's domain name.
MAIL FROM	Client identifies its email address to the server.
RCPT TO	Client identifies the intended recipient's email address.

Fig. 5.18 *Types of responses returned by the server to the client*

Response	*Explanation*
2yz	Positive completion reply
3yz	Positive intermediate reply
4yz	Transient negative reply
5yz	Permanent negative completion reply

Fig. 5.19 *Types of responses returned by the server to the client*

Based on these, Fig. 5.20 shows examples of responses returned by the server to the client.

Response	*Explanation*	*Response type*
220	Service ready	2yz
354	Start of mail input	3yz
450	Mailbox not available	4yz
500	Syntax error	5yz

Fig. 5.20 *Types of responses returned by the server to the client*

The SMTP mail transfer happens in three phases, as shown in Fig. 5.21.

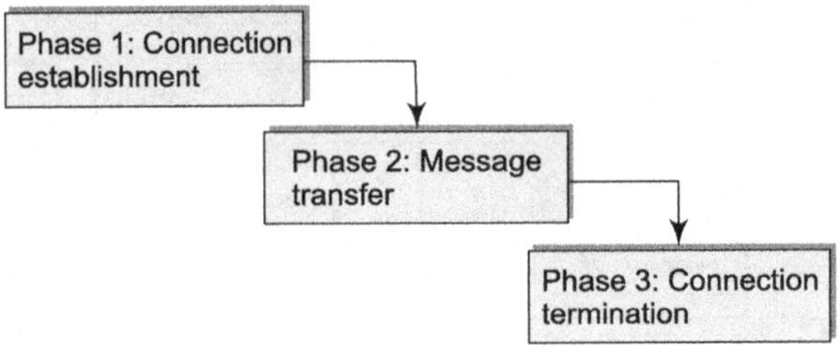

Fig. 5.21 *Types of responses returned by the server to the client*

Let us understand all these phases with an example.

Phase 1: Connection establishment

Here, the following steps happen:

1. Client makes active TCP connection with the server on server's well-known port number 25.
2. Server sends code 220 (service ready), else 421 (service not available).
3. Client sends HELO message to identify itself using its domain name.
4. Server responds with code 250 (request command completed) or an error.

A sample interaction to depict this is shown in Fig. 5.22.

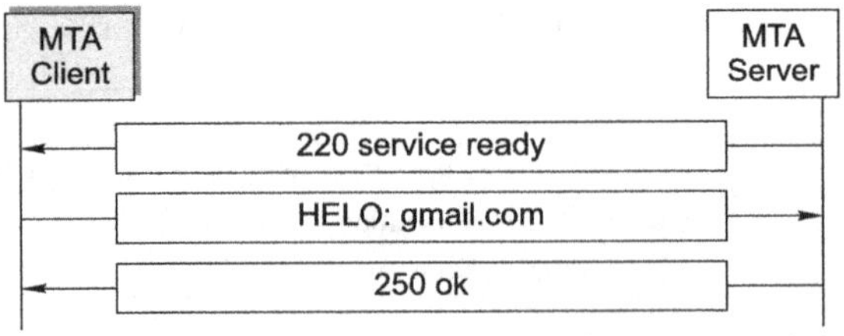

Fig. 5.22 *Connection establishment phase*

Phase 2: Mail transfer

This step is the most important one, as it actually involves the transfer of email contents from the sender to the receiver. This step consists of the following steps as an example:

1. Client sends MAIL message, identifying the sender.
2. Server responds with 250 (ok).
3. Client sends RCPT message, to identify the receiver.
4. Server responds with 250 (ok).
5. Client sends DATA to indicate start of message transfer.

6. Server responds with 354 (start mail input).
7. Client sends email header and body in consecutive lines.
8. The message is terminated with a line containing just a period.
9. The server responds with 250 (ok).

This is shown in Fig. 5.23.

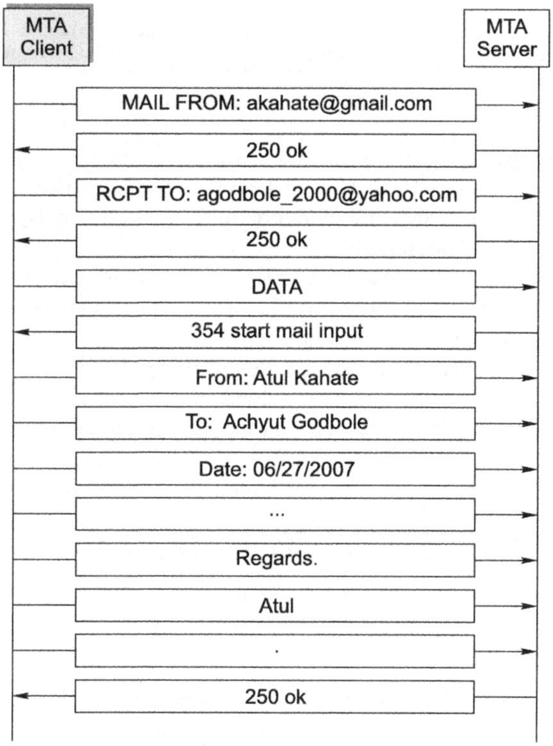

Fig. 5.23 *Mail transfer phase*

Note that after the server asks the client to send email data (i.e., after the server sends the client a command with code 354), the client keeps on sending email contents to the server. Server keeps absorbing that content. When the client has to indicate to the server that the email contents have been completely transferred, the client sends a dot character without anything else on that line to the server. SMTP uses this convention to indicate to the server that the email contents have been completely transferred by the client to the server. The server acknowledges this with a 250 OK response.

Phase 3: Connection termination

This step is very simple. Here, the client sends a QUIT command, which the server acknowledges, as mentioned below:

1. Client sends the QUIT message.
2. Server responds with 221 (service closed) message.
3. TCP connection is closed.

This is depicted in Fig. 5.24.

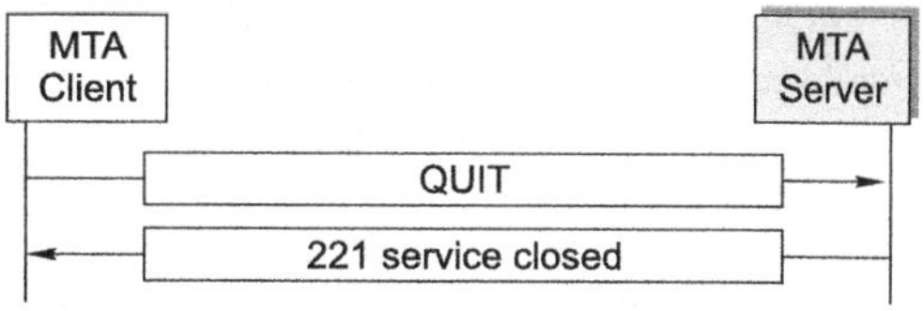

Fig. 5.24 *Connection termination phase*

5.2.6 Email Access and Retrieval (POP and IMAP)

There are three primary email access models, as mentioned in Fig. 5.25.

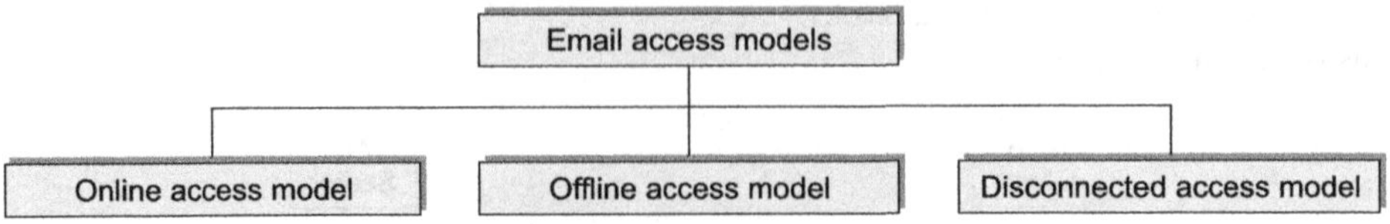

Fig. 5.25 *Email access models*

Let us discuss these now.

1. **Online access model** It is the most ideal, but often not a practical approach. Every user needs to be connected to the Internet, and therefore, to the mailbox managed by the SMTP server at all times. Clearly, this is not possible.
2. **Offline access model** Here, the user connects to the mailbox from a remote client computer, downloads emails to the client computer, and disconnects from the mailbox. Once this happens, emails are deleted from the server mailbox.
3. **Disconnected access model** This is a mixed approach. Here, the user can download emails to the client computer, but they are also retained on the server. Synchronization between client and server email states is possible (e.g., mark emails are read/unread, tag emails that need to be responded to, etc.).

In this context, two email access and retrieval protocols are important, as shown in Fig. 5.26.

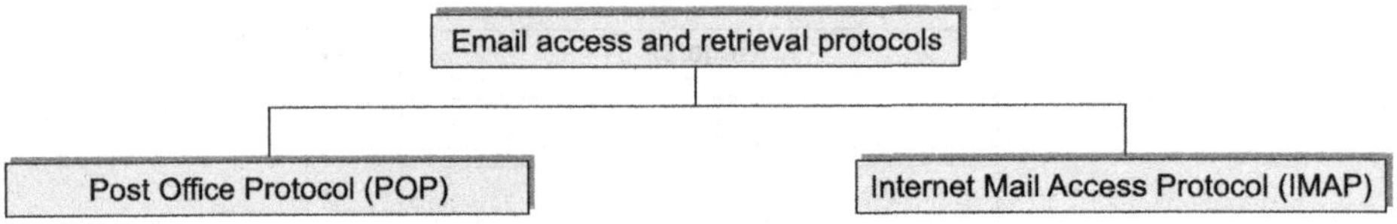

Fig. 5.26 *Email access and retrieval protocols*

Let us now discuss these protocols one after the other.

Post Office Protocol (POP)

The **Post Office Protocol (POP)** allows a user to retrieve the incoming mails from her email server. In effect, SMTP transfers emails from the sender's computer to the sender's email server and from there to the receiver's email server. POP then allows the receiver to remotely or locally log on to the receiver's email server and retrieve those *waiting* emails. In other words, POP (like IMAP) works only at the receiver's end, and has no role to play at the sender's side. Therefore, all the description below applies only to the receiver.

POP has two parts: a client POP (i.e., the receiver's POP) and a server POP (which uses the receiver's email server). The client (i.e., the receiver) opens a TCP connection with the receiver's POP server on well-known port 110. The client user name and password to access the mailbox are sent along with it. Provided these are correct, the receiver user can list and receive emails from the mailbox. POP supports *delete mode* (i.e., delete emails from the mailbox on the email server once they are downloaded to the receiver's computer) and *keep mode* (i.e., keep emails in the mailbox on the email server once they are downloaded to the receiver's computer). The default option is *delete*.

POP uses TCP. The server listens to well-known port 110. Client sends commands to server; server responds with replies and/or email contents and deletes emails from server. POP commands are 3-4 letters long and are case-insensitive. They are actually plain ASCII text, terminated with a CR-LF pair. Server replies are simple: either +OK or –ERR.

A POP session between a client and a server has three states, one after the other:

1. **Authorization state** Here, the server does a passive open and the client authenticates itself.
2. **Transaction state** Here, the client is allowed to perform mailbox operations (view/retrieve/delete/... mails).
3. **Update state** Here, the server deletes messages marked for deletion, session is closed, and TCP connection is terminated.

Here is an example of what happens in the *authorization state*. At this stage, we assume that the client and the server have already negotiated a three-way TCP connection successfully. For understanding purposes, we have shown client commands in **bold** and server replies in *italics*.

```
+OK POP3 server ready
USER atul.kahate@iflexsolutions.com
+OK
PASS ********
+OK atul.kahate@iflexsolutions.com has 3 messages
```

Fig. 5.27 *POP authentication*

This is now followed by the *transaction state*. The client can send commands to the server now. Examples of client commands are STAT (Mailbox status), LIST (List of messages in the mailbox), RETR (Retrieve a particular message), etc.

Figure 5.28 depicts an example of this state. The same convention as earlier applies, to distinguish between client commands and server replies.

```
STAT
+OK 2 574
LIST
+OK
1 414
2 160
.
RETR 1
+OK
(Message 1 is sent)
.
DELE 1
+OK message 1 deleted
RETR 2
+OK
(Message 2 is sent)
.
DELE 2
+OK message 2 deleted
QUIT
```

Fig. 5.28 *POP transaction state*

We can see that initially, the client asks for the mailbox status. The server informs that there are two mails waiting for the user, with a total size of 574 bytes on the disk. The client asks for a list of both. The server responds with their serial numbers and sizes. The client retrieves the first email and deletes it from the mailbox. It repeats it for the second one and then quits this state.

In the *update state*, some housekeeping functions are performed and then the TCP connection is broken. At this stage, the client can request the server to *undo* earlier deletions by using a RSET command. Else, the connection is closed after deletions are made permanent.

Internet Mail Access Protocol (IMAP)

POP is very popular but is offline (mail is retrieved from the server and deleted from there). POP was made disconnected to achieve this functionality (i.e., retrieve mail on to the client computer, but do not delete from the server; synchronize changes, if any). This is not always desired. Hence, a different email access and retrieval protocol is necessary. That protocol is **Internet Mail Access Protocol (IMAP).**

IMAP is more powerful and also more complex than POP. It allows folder creation on the server, reading the mail before retrieval, search for email contents on the server, etc. Here, work is focused on email server, rather than downloading emails on the client before doing anything else (unlike what happens in the case of POP).

In this protocol, the server does a passive open on well-known port number 143. TCP three-way handshake happens and client and server can use IMAP over a new session that gets created. There are four possible IMAP session states:

1. Not authenticated state
2. Authenticated state
3. Selected state
4. Logout state

Of these, the first three are interactive. Let us understand the meaning and purpose of these.

1. **Not authenticated state** Session normally begins in this state after a TCP connection is established.
2. **Authenticated state** Client completes authentication. Client is now allowed to perform mailbox operations. Client selects a mailbox to work with.
3. **Selected state** Client can access/manipulate individual messages in the mailbox. Thereafter, client can close the mailbox and return to the *authenticated state* to work with another mailbox, or log out of the IMAP session.
4. **Logout state** Client can explicitly log out by sending a *Logout* command, or session can also expire because of timeout. Server sends a response and connection is terminated.

IMAP commands are grouped into various categories, as mentioned in Fig. 5.29. The categorization is based on which commands can be used in which state.

Command group	*Description*
Any state commands	These commands can be used at any stage (e.g., LOGOUT command).
Not authenticated state commands	These are commands for authentication (e.g., LOGIN command).
Authenticated state commands	These are commands for mailbox operations (e.g., LIST command).
Selected state commands	These are commands for individual messages (e.g., SEARCH command).

Fig. 5.29 *IMAP commands*

After processing a client command, the server can send back two things:

1. **Result** This indicates status of a command, usually tagged to the command sent earlier by the client. Examples of this are OK, NO, BAD, and BYE.
2. **Response** This provides additional information about the processing results. Examples of this are ALERT, READ-ONLY, and READ-WRITE.

5.2.7 Web-based Emails

This is an interesting phenomenon. Examples of this category of emails are Hotmail, Yahoo, Gmail, etc. Assuming that both the sender and the receiver are using Web-based email system:

1. The mail transfer from the sender to her mail server is done using HTTP.
2. The mail is transferred from sender's mail server to the receiver's mail server using SMTP.
3. Receiver retrieves mail from the receiver's mail server using HTTP.
4. There is no need for POP or IMAP in such a case.

Of course, if the receiver is using the traditional (non-Web based) email system, then we need POP or IMAP for email retrieval at the receiver's end.

The concept is shown in Fig. 5.30.

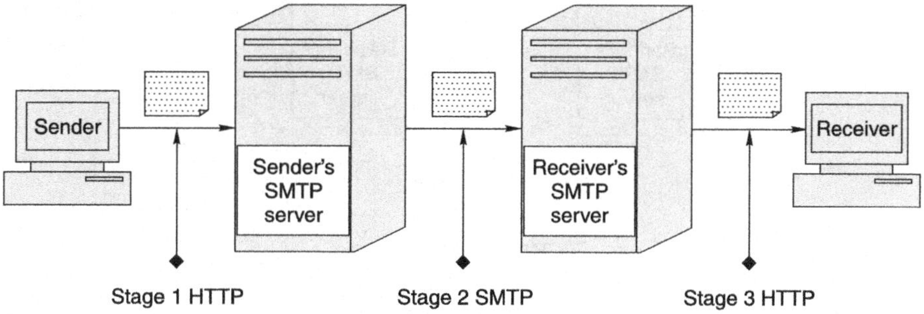

Fig. 5.30 *Web-based emails*

How is this possible?

Stage 1: At the sender's end, HTML forms technology is used. When the sender wants to compose a new email message, the email service provider site (e.g., gmail) shows the user an HTML form, containing fields such as TO, CC, BCC, SUBJECT, etc. The user enters all this information and clicks on the *Send* button. This causes the HTML form to be submitted to the user's email service provider.

Stage 2: This form is parsed by the email service provider's application and transformed into an SMTP connection between itself and the receiver's SMTP server. The email message is sent to the receiver's SMTP server like any other email message transferred using the SMTP protocol.

Stage 3: For retrieval of incoming emails, the receiver logs on to her email service provider's site by using HTTP. The incoming email is shown to the user in the form of an HTML page (and hence POP or IMAP is not necessary).

5.2.8 Multipurpose Internet Mail Extensions (MIME)

The SMTP protocol can be used to send only NVT 7-bit ASCII text. It cannot work with some languages (French, German, etc., ...). Furthermore, it cannot be used to send multimedia data (binary files, video, audio, etc.). Here is where the **Multipurpose Internet Mail Extensions (MIME)** protocol extends SMTP to allow for non-ASCII data to be sent. We should note that it is not an email transfer/access/retrieval protocol, unlike SMTP, POP, and IMAP.

The way MIME works is quite simple from a conceptual view point. MIME transforms non-ASCII data at the sender's end into NVT ASCII and delivers it to the client SMTP for transmission. At the receiver's end, it receives NVT ASCII data from the SMTP server and transforms it back into the original (possibly non-ASCII) data. This is shown in Fig. 5.31.

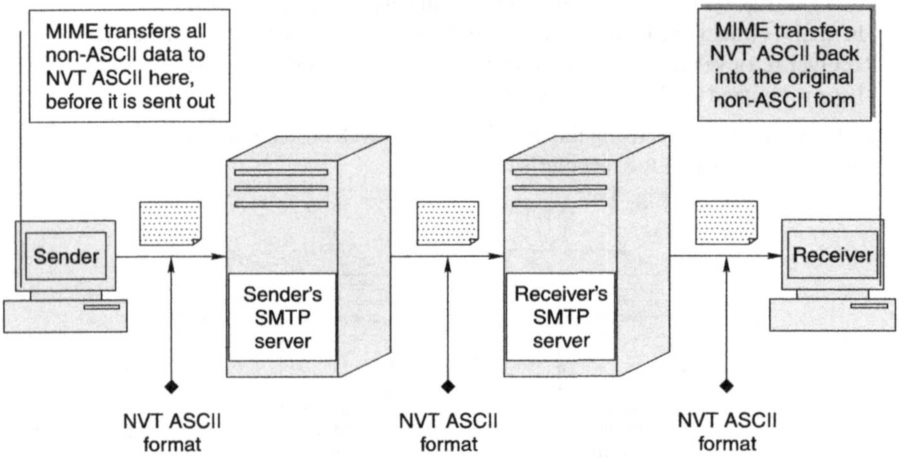

Fig. 5.31 *MIME concept*

While it is ok to say this conceptually, how is this done in actual practice? To convert non-ASCII data to ASCII format, MIME uses the concept of **Base-64 encoding**. It is a very interesting and effective process. In Base-64 encoding, three bytes are considered at a time, each of which consists of eight bits. Thus, we have $3 \times 8 = 24$ bits. Base-64 then represents these 24 bits as four printable characters, each consisting of 6 bits, in the ASCII standard. Why is this done? Let us understand.

The whole aim of MIME is to transform non-ASCII data to ASCII. We know that ASCII is 7-bit in the basic form. That is, in ASCII, each character occupies 7 bits. Hence, if something has to be transformed into or represented in ASCII, it must occupy not more than 7 bits per character. Therefore, Base-64 encoding chooses something closest to this pattern of 7 bits per character, which happens to be 6 bits per character. We know that Base-64 only uses 6 bits (corresponding to $2^6 = 64$ characters) to ensure that encoded data is printable and humanly readable. Therefore, special ASCII characters are not used. The 64 characters (hence the name Base-64) consist of 10 digits, 26 lowercase characters, 26 uppercase characters as well as the + and / characters.

These steps in Base-64 encoding are outlined in Fig. 5.32 with an example.

Step 1 *Here, we convert three 8-bit bytes to four 6-bit characters.*

Suppose that our non-ASCII data that needs to be converted into ASCII using Base-64 encoding is 100110111010001011101001. Using 8-bit ASCII, it looks as follows:

10011011 in binary = 155 in decimal
10100010 in binary = 162 in decimal
11101001 in binary = 233 in decimal

We split the bit pattern into four 6-bit bytes, as follows:

100110 in binary = 38 in decimal
111010 in binary = 58 in decimal
001011 in binary = 11 in decimal
101001 in binary = 41 in decimal

Step 2 *Here, we assign the symbols equivalent to the above bit patterns by using the Base-64 table. The table is as shown below:*

Value	Char	Value	Char	Value	Char	Value	Char
0	A	16	Q	32	g	48	w
1	B	17	R	33	h	49	x
2	C	18	S	34	i	50	y
3	D	19	T	35	j	51	z
4	E	20	U	36	k	52	0
5	F	21	V	37	l	53	1
6	G	22	W	38	m	54	2
7	H	23	X	39	n	55	3
8	I	24	Y	40	o	56	4
9	J	25	Z	41	p	57	5
10	K	26	a	42	q	58	6
11	L	27	b	43	r	59	7
12	M	28	c	44	s	60	8
13	N	29	d	45	t	61	9
14	O	30	e	46	u	62	
15	P	31	f	47	v	63	/

Hence, our four 6-bit slots can now be mapped to the corresponding Base-64 letters, as follows:

100110 in binary = 38 in decimal = m as per the Base-64 mapping table
111010 in binary = 58 in decimal = 6 as per the Base-64 mapping table
001011 in binary = 11 in decimal = L as per the Base-64 mapping table
101001 in binary = 41 in decimal = p as per the Base-64 mapping table

Hence, our original non-ASCII text of 155, 162, and 233 in decimal (or 100110111010001011101001 in binary) would be sent as m6Lp (i.e., as the binary equivalent of this text).

Fig. 5.32 *MIME example*

For performing all these operations, the concept of **MIME headers** is used. MIME defines five headers that can be added to the original SMTP header section to define the transformation parameters. These five headers are:

1. MIME-Version
2. Content-Type
3. Content-Transfer-Encoding
4. Content-Id
5. Content-Description

Such an email message looks as shown in Fig. 5.33.

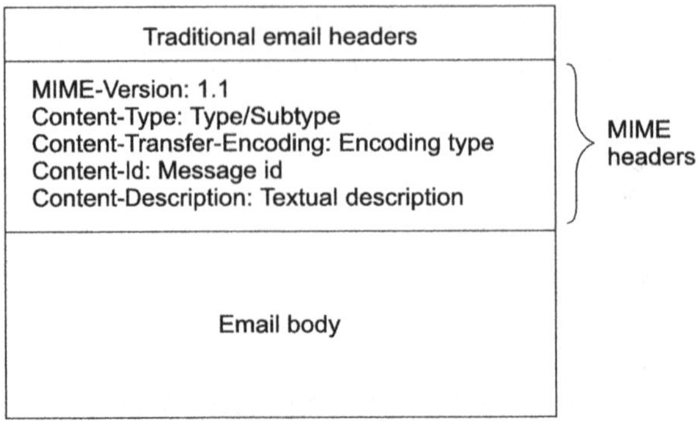

Fig. 5.33 *MIME headers*

Figure 5.34 explains the five MIME headers.

MIME header	*Description*
MIME-Version	This contains the MIME version number. Currently, it has a value of 1.1. This field is reserved for the future use, when newer versions of MIME are expected to emerge. This field indicates that the message conforms to RFCs 2045 and 2046.
Content-Type	Describes the data contained in the body of the message. The details provided are sufficient so that the receiver email system can deal with the received email message in an appropriate manner. The contents are specified as: Type/Subtype. MIME specifies 7 content types, and 15 content subtypes. These types types and subtypes are shown later.
Content-Transfer-Encoding	Specifies the type of transformation that has been used to represent the body of the message. In other words, the method used to encode the messages into zeroes and ones is defined here. There are five content encoding methods, as shown later.
Content-Id	Identifies the whole message in a multiple-message environment.
Content-Description	Defines whether the body is image, audio, or video.

Fig. 5.34 *MIME header details*

The Content-Type header can contain the following types and subtypes, as shown in Fig. 5.35.

Type	*Subtype*	*Description*
Text	Plain	Free form text.
	Enriched	Text with formatting details.
Multipart	Mixed	Email contains multiple parts. All parts must be delivered together, and in sequence.
	Parallel	Email contains multiple parts. All parts must be delivered diffferently, in different sequence.
	Alternative	Email contains multiple parts. These parts represent the alternative vesions of the same information. They are sent so that the receiver's email system can select the *best fit* from them.

(Contd.)

Fig. 5.35 *Contd...*

Type	*Subtype*	*Description*
	Digest	Similar to mixed. Detailed discussion is out of scope of the current text.
Message	RFC822	The body itself is an encapsulated message that conforms to RFC 822.
	Partial	Used in fragmentation of larger email messages.
	External-body	Contains a pointer to an object that exists somewhere else.
Image	Jpeg	An image in JPEG format.
	Gif	An image in GIF format.
Video	Mpeg	A video in MPEG format.
Audio	Basic	Sound format.
Application	PostScript	Adobe PostScript.
	octet-stream	General binary data (8-bit bytes).

Fig. 5.35 *MIME content types and subtypes*

The Content-Transfer-Encoding header can specify one of the following, as shown in Fig. 5.36.

Type	*Description*
7-bit	NVT ASCII characters and short lines
8-bit	Non-ASCII characters and short lines
Binary	Non-ASCII characters with unlimited-length lines
Base-64	6-bit blocks of data encoded into 8-bit ASCII characters
Quoted-Printable	Non-ASCII characters encoded as an *equal to* sign, followed by an ASCII code

Fig. 5.36 *Content-Transfer-Encoding*

Figure 5.37 shows an example of a real-life email message containing some MIME headers.

```
Microsoft Mail Internet Headers Version 2.0
x-mimeole: Produced By Microsoft Exchange V6.5
Content-class: urn:content-classes:message
MIME-Version: 1.0
Content-Type: application/ms-tnef;
        name="winmail.dat"
Content-Transfer-Encoding: binary
Subject: Great news! We have done it!
Date: Wed, 27 Jun 2007 16:05:38 +0530
Message-ID: <3683ACA470CF1049840B1FFC9BAD1236C86D39@MUM-MSG-02.i-flex.com>
In-Reply-To: <2F7965ADFBA5814F86BA9E530F78425EA0B537@MUM-MSG-02.i-flex.com>
X-MS-Has-Attach: yes
X-MS-TNEF-Correlator: <3683ACA470CF1049840B1FFC9BAD1236C86D39@MUM-MSG-02.i-flex.com>
From: "Umesh Aherwadikar-AMB" <Umesh.Aherwadikar@iflexsolutions.com>
To: "Atul Kahate-AMB" <Atul.Kahate@iflexsolutions.com>
```

Fig. 5.37 *MIME example*

5.2.9 Email Privacy

As we have discussed, when one person sends an email to another, the email message can potentially travel through a number of intermediate routers and networks before it reaches the recipient. Consequently, there is a concern among email users about its privacy. What if the email message gets trapped on its way and is read by an unintended recipient? To resolve this issue, the **Pretty Good Privacy (PGP)** is widely used. A slightly older protocol called **Privacy Enhanced Mail (PEM)** also exists, which we would quickly review as well. We shall discuss them in brief, as a detailed discussion of these techniques is beyond the scope of the current text.

Pretty Good Privacy (PGP)

Phil Zimmerman is the father of the **Pretty Good Privacy (PGP)** protocol. He is credited with the creation of PGP. The most significant aspects of PGP are that it supports the basic requirements of cryptography, is quite simple to use, and is completely free, including its source code and documentation. Moreover, for those organizations that require support, a low-cost commercial version of PGP is available from an organization called Viacrypt (now Network Associates). PGP has become extremely popular and is far more widely used, as compared to PEM. The email cryptographic support offered by PGP is shown in Fig. 5.38.

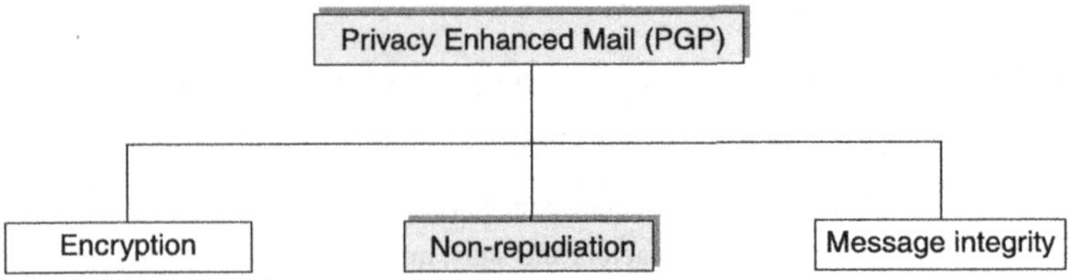

Fig. 5.38 *Security features offered by PGP*

How PGP Works?

In PGP, the sender of the message needs to include the identifiers of the algorithm used in the message, along with the value of the keys. The broad level steps in PEM are illustrated in Fig. 5.39. As shown, PGP starts with a digital signature, which is followed by compression, then by encryption then by digital enveloping and finally, by Base-64 encoding.

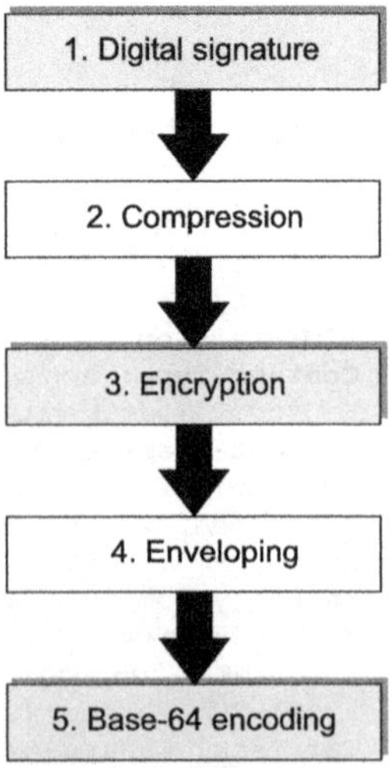

Fig. 5.39 *PGP operations*

PGP allows for four security options when sending an email message. These options are:

1. Signature only (Steps 1 and 2)
2. Signature and Base-64 encoding (Steps 1, 2 and 5)
3. Signature, encryption, enveloping and Base-64 encoding (Steps 1 to 5)

An important concept in PGP is that of key rings. When a sender wants to send an email message to a single recipient, there is not too much of a problem. Complexities are introduced when a message has to be sent to multiple recipients. If Alice needs to correspond with 10 people, Alice needs the public keys of all these 10 people. Hence, Alice is said to need a **key ring** of 10 public keys. Additionally, PGP specifies a ring of public-private keys. This is because Alice may want to change her public-private key pair, or may want to use a different key pair for different groups of users (e.g., one key pair when corresponding with someone in her family, another when corresponding with friends, a third in business correspondence, etc.). In other words, every PGP user needs to have two sets of key rings: (i) A ring of her own public-private key pairs, and (ii) A ring of the public keys of other users.

The concept of key rings is shown in Fig. 5.40. Note that in one of the key rings, Alice maintains a set of key pairs; while in the other, she just maintains the public keys (and not key pairs) of other users. Obviously, she cannot have the private keys of the other users. Similarly, other users in a PGP system will have their own two key rings.

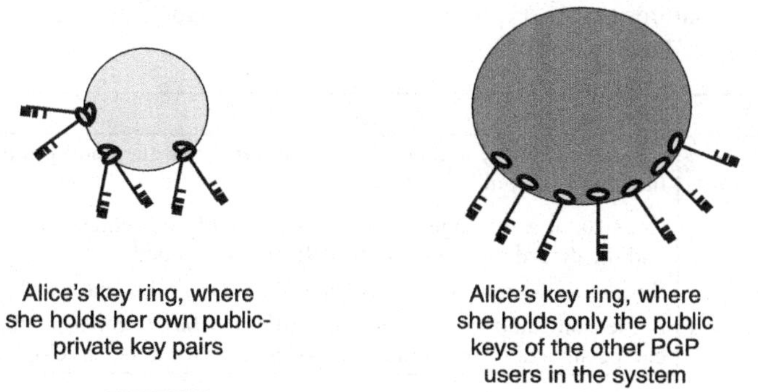

Fig. 5.40 *Key rings maintained by a user in PGP*

The usage of these key rings should be fairly easy to understand. Nevertheless, we provide a brief explanation below.

There would be two possible situations:

1. Alice needs to send a message to another user in the system.
   (a) Alice creates a message digest of the original message (using SHA-1), and encrypts it using her own private key (via the RSA or DSS algorithm) from one of the key pairs shown in the left side of the diagram. This produces a digital signature.
   (b) Alice creates a one-time symmetric key.
   (c) Alice uses the public key of the intended recipient (by looking up the key ring shown on the right side for the appropriate recipient) to encrypt the one-time symmetric key created above. RSA algorithm is used for this.
   (d) Alice encrypts the original message with the one-time symmetric key (using IDEA or DES-3 algorithm).
   (e) Alice encrypts the digital signature with the one-time symmetric key (using IDEA or DES-3 algorithm).
   (f) Alice sends the output of steps (d) and (e) above to the receiver. What would the receiver need to do? This is explained below.
2. Now suppose that Alice has received a message from one of the other users in the system.
   (a) Alice uses her private key to obtain the one-time symmetric key created by the sender. Refer to steps (b) and (c) in the earlier explanation if you do not understand this.
   (b) Alice uses the one-time symmetric key to decrypt the message. Refer to steps (b) and (d) in the earlier explanation if you do not understand this.
   (c) Alice computes a message digest of the original message (say *MD1*).
   (d) Alice now uses this one-time symmetric key to obtain the original digital signature. Refer to steps (b) and (e) in the earlier explanation if you do not understand this.

(e) Alice uses the sender's public key from the key ring shown in the right side of the diagram to decrypt the digital signature and gets back the original message digest (say *MD2*).

(f) Alice compares message digests *MD1* and *MD2*. If they match, Alice is sure about the message integrity and authentication of the message sender.

S/MIME

To secure emails containing MIME content, the technology of **Secure MIME (S/MIME)** is used.

In terms of the general functionality, S/MIME is quite similar to PGP. Like PGP, S/MIME provides for digital signatures and encryption of email messages. More specifically, S/MIME offers the functionalities as depicted in Fig. 5.41.

Functionality	*Description*
Enveloped data	Consists of encrypted content of any type, and the encryption key encrypted with the receiver's public key.
Signed data	Consists of a message digest encrypted with the sender's private key. The content and the digital signature are both Base-64 encoded.
Clear-signed data	Similar to Signed data. However, only the digital signature is Base-64 encoded.
Signed and enveloped data	Signed-only and enveloped-only entities can be combined, so that the enveloped data can be signed, or the signed/clear-signed data can be enveloped.

Fig. 5.41 *S/MIME functionalities*

In respect of the algorithms, S/MIME prefers the usage of the following cryptographic algorithms:

1. Digital Signature Standard (DSS) for digital signatures
2. Diffie-Hellman for encrypting the symmetric session keys
3. RSA for either digital signatures or for encrypting the symmetric session keys
4. DES-3 for symmetric key encryption

Interestingly, S/MIME defines two terms: *must* and *should* for describing the usage of the cryptographic algorithms. What is the meaning of these? Let us understand:

1. **Must** This word specifies that these cryptographic algorithms are an absolute requirement. The user systems of S/MIME have to necessarily support these algorithms.
2. **Should** There could be reasons because of which algorithms in this category cannot be supported. However, as far as possible, these algorithms should be supported.

Based on these terminologies, S/MIME supports the various cryptographic algorithms as shown in Fig. 5.42.

Functionality	*Algorithm support recommended by S/MIME*
Message digest	*Must* support *MD5* and SHA-1. *Should* use SHA-1.
Digital signature	Sender and receiver both *must* support DSS. Sender and receiver *should* support RSA.
Enveloping	Sender and receiver *must* support Diffie-Hellman. Sender and receiver *should* support RSA.
Symmetric key encryption	Sender *should* support DES-3 and RC4. Receiver *must* support DES-3 and *should* support RC2.

Fig. 5.42 *Guidelines provided by S/MIME for cryptographic algorithms*

As we have mentioned, for an email message, S/MIME supports digital signature, encryption or both. S/MIME processes the email messages along with the other security-related data, such as the algorithms used and the digital certifiates to produce what is called a **Public Key Cryptography Standard (PKCS) object**. A PKCS object is then treated like a message content. This means that appropriate MIME headers are added to it. For this purpose, S/MIME two new content types and six new subtypes, as shown in Fig. 5.43.

Type	*Subtype*	*Description*
Multipart	Signed	A clear signed message consisting of the message and the digital signature.
Application	PKCS#7 MIME Signed data	A signed MIME entity.
	PKCS#7 MIME Enveloped data	An enveloped MIME entity.
	PKCS#7 MIME Degenerate signed data	An entity that contains only digital certificates.
	PKCS#7 Signature	The content type of the signature subpart of a multipart/signed message.
	PKCS#10 MIME	A certificate registration request.

Fig. 5.43 *S/MIME content types*

The actual processing to perform message digest creation, digital signature creation, symmetric key encryption and enveloping is quite similar to the way it happens in PGP, and therefore, we will not discuss it here again.

FILE TRANSFER PROTOCOL (FTP).. 5.3

5.3.1 Introduction

We have seen how email works. However, there are situations when we want to receive or send a file from or to a remote computer. Emails are usually just short messages. Transferring files from one computer to another is quite different. A special software and set of rules called **File Transfer Protocol (FTP)** exists for this purpose. FTP is a high level (application layer) protocol that is aimed at providing a very simple interface for any user of the Internet to transfer files. At a high level, a user (the client) requests the FTP software to either retrieve from or upload a file to a remote server. We shall study how this works in detail.

Figure 5.44 shows at a broad level, how a FTP client can obtain a file *ABC* from a FTP server.

For this, a user at the FTP client host might enter a command such as *GET ABC*, which means that the client is interested in obtaining a file called as *ABC* from the specified server. FTP supports other commands such as *PUT*, *OPEN*, *CLOSE*, etc. The commands are self-explanatory.

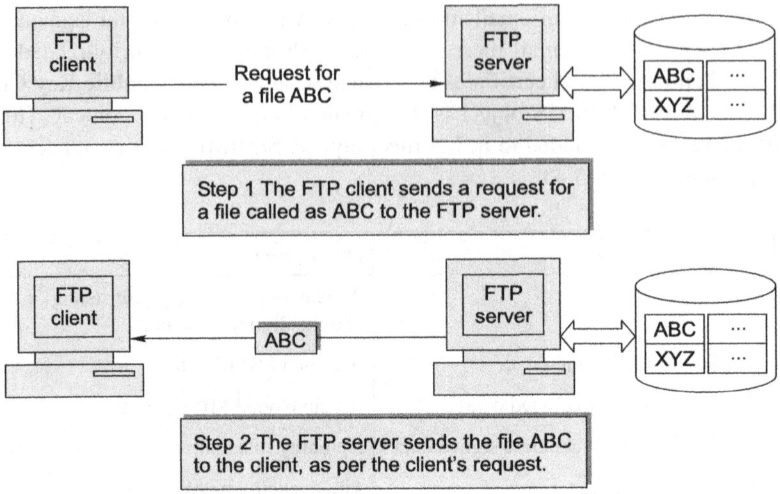

Fig. 5.44 *A high level view of File Transfer Protocol (FTP)*

5.3.2 Issues With File Transfers

Emails are meant for short message transfers. FTP is meant for file transfers. But that is not the sole reason why FTP was born in the first place. When a user wants to download a file from a remote server, several issues must be dealt with. First of all, the client must have the necessary authorizations to download that file. Secondly, the client and server computers could be different in terms of their hardware and/or operating systems. This means that they might represent and interpret data in different formats (e.g., floating point representation). Thirdly, an end user must not be concerned with these issues as long as he has the necessary access rights.

FTP provides a simple file transfer mechanism for the end user, and internally handles these complications without bothering him.

5.3.3 FTP Basics

Let us first discuss the user perspective of FTP. FTP presents the user with a prompt and allows entering various commands for accessing and downloading files that physically exist on a remote computer. After invoking an FTP application, the user identifies a remote computer and instructs FTP to establish a connection with it. FTP contacts the remote computer using the TCP/IP software. Once the connection is established, the user can choose to download a file from the remote computer, or he can send a file from his computer to be stored on the remote computer.

However, FTP differs from other application layer protocols in one respect. All other application layer protocols use a single connection between a client and a server for their inter-communication. However, FTP uses two connections between a client and a server. One connection is used for the actual file's data transfer, and the other is used for control information (commands and responses). This separation of data transfer and commands makes FTP more efficient. Internally, this means that FTP uses two TCP/IP connections between the client and the server. This basic model of FTP is shown in Fig. 5.45.

As shown in Fig. 5.22, the client has three components: the user interface, the client control process and the client data transfer process. On the other hand, the server has just two components: the server control process and the server data transfer process. Since there is no interaction required at the server

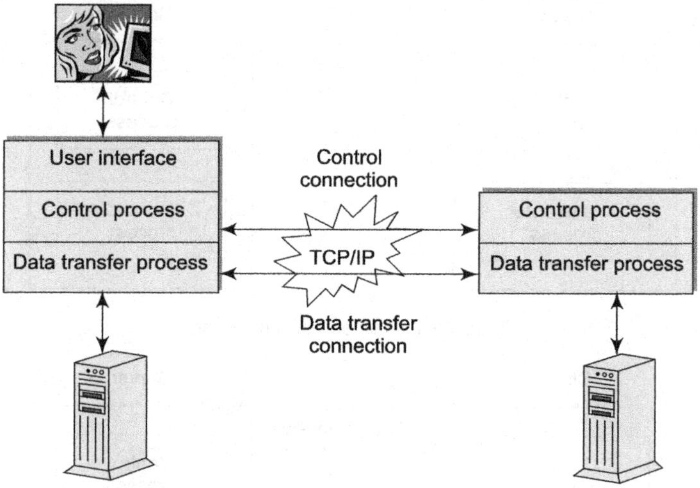

Fig. 5.45 *Two connections are used in the FTP process*

side exactly at the time of file transfer, the user interface component is not required at the server. The TCP **control connection** is made between the control processes of the client and the server. The TCP **data transfer connection** is made between the data transfer processes of the client and the server. While the data of the file is sent (in the form of IP packets and TCP/IP protocol) from the server to the client, the server keeps a track of how much data is sent (number of bytes sent, percentage of the total file size in bytes, etc.) and how much is remaining. It keeps on sending this information simultaneously on the second connection, viz, the control connection. This is how, the control connection reassures the user downloading/uploading the file that the file transfer is going on successfully, by displaying messages about the number of bytes transferred so far, the number of bytes remaining to be transferred, the completion percentage, etc.

Note that if multiple files are to be transferred in a single FTP session, then the control connection between the client and the server must remain active throughout the entire FTP session. The data transfer connection is opened and closed for each file that is to be transferred. The data transfer connection opens every time the commands for transferring files are used, and it gets closed when the file transfer is complete.

5.3.4 FTP Connections

Let us understand how the control and data transfer connections are opened and closed by the client and the server during a FTP session.

Control Connection

The process of the creation of a control connection between a client and a server is pretty similar to the creation of other TCP connections between a client and a server. Specifically, two steps are involved here:

1. The server passively waits for a client (passive open). In other words, the server waits endlessly for accepting a TCP connection from one or more clients.
2. The client actively sends an open request to the server (active open). That is, the client always initiates the dialog with the server by sending a TCP connection request.

This is shown in Fig. 5.46.

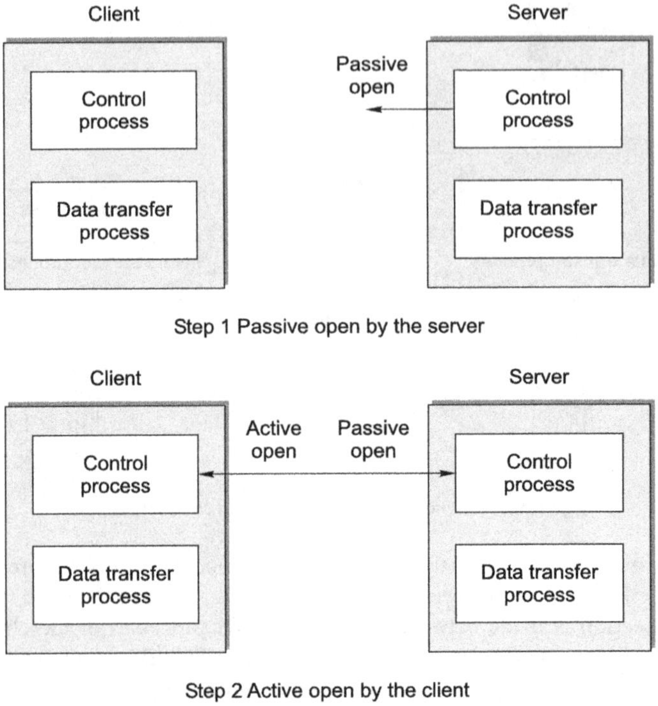

Fig. 5.46 *Opening of the control connection between the client and the server*

The opening of a control connection internally consists of the following steps:

1. The user on the client computer opens the FTP client software. The FTP client software is a program that prompts the user for the domain name / IP address of the server.
2. When the user enters these details, the FTP software on the client issues a *TCP connection* request to the underlying TCP software on the client. Of course, it provides the IP address of the server with which the connection is to be established.
3. The TCP software on the client computer then establishes a TCP connection between the client and the server using a three-way handshake as we have discussed previously in the topic on TCP. Of course, internally it uses protocols such as IP and ARP for this as discussed many times before.
4. When a successful TCP connection is established between the client and the server, it means that a FTP server program is ready to serve the client's requests for file transfer. Note that the client can either download a file from the server, or upload a file on to the server. This is when we say that the control connection between the client and the server is successfully established.

As we have noted earlier, the control connection is open throughout the FTP session.

Data Transfer Connection

The connection for data transfer, in turn, uses the control connection established previously. Note that unlike the control connection, which always starts with a passive open from the server, the data transfer connection is always first requested for by the client. Let us understand how the data transfer connection is opened.

The client issues a passive open command for the data transfer connection. This means that the client has opened a data transfer connection on a particular port number, say X, from its side.

The client uses the control connection established earlier, to send this port number (i.e., *X*) to the server.

The server receives the port number (*X*) from the client over the control connection, and invokes an open request for the data transfer connection on its side. This means that the server has also now opened a data transfer connection. This connection is always on port 20 – the standard port for FTP on any Web server (not specifically shown in the figure).

This is shown in Fig. 5.47.

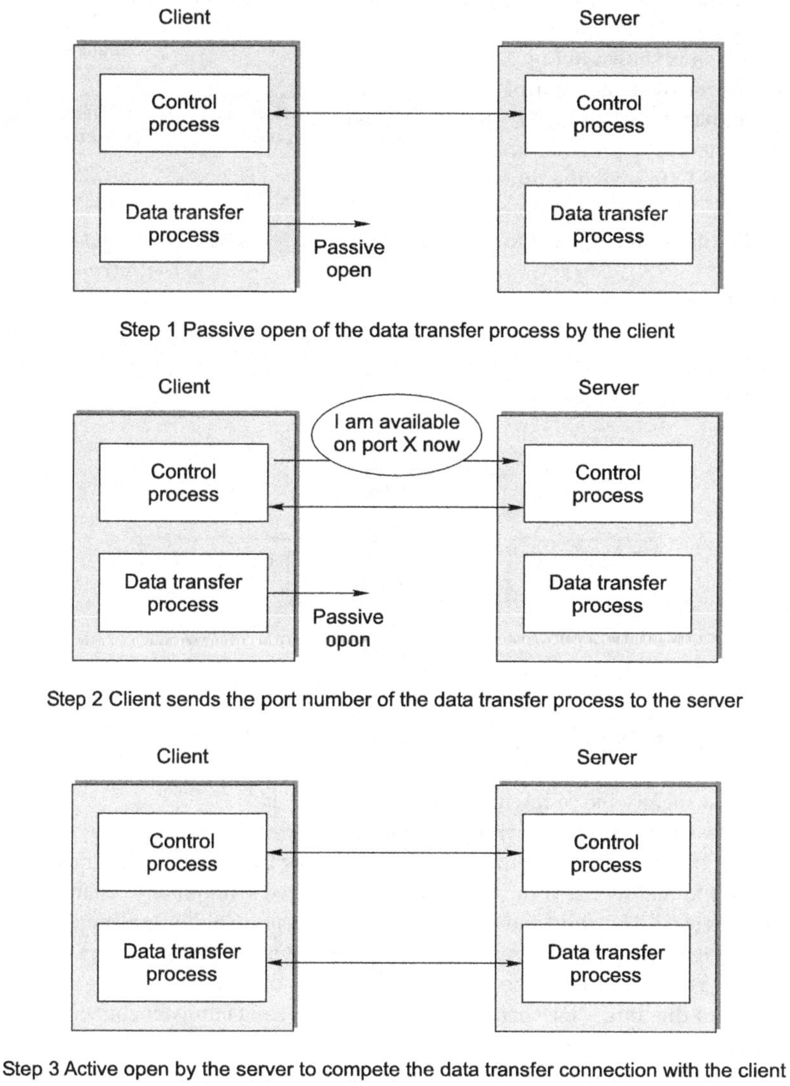

Fig. 5.47 *Opening of the control connection between the client and the server*

5.3.5 Client-Server Communication Using FTP

Having opened the control and data transfer connections, the client and the server are now ready for transferring files. Note that the client and the server can use different operating systems, file formats, character sets and file structures. FTP must resolve all these incompatibility issues. Let us now study how FTP achieves this using the control connection and the data transfer connection.

Control Connection

The control connection is pretty simple. Over the control connection the FTP communication consists of one request and one response. This request-response model is sufficient for FTP, since the user sends one command to the FTP server at a time. This model of the control connection is shown in Fig. 5.48.

The requests sent over the control connection are four-character commands such as QUIT (to log out of the system) ABOR (to abort the previous command), DELE (to delete a file), LIST (to view the directory structure), RETR (to retrieve a file from the server to the client), STOR (to upload a file from the client to the server), etc.

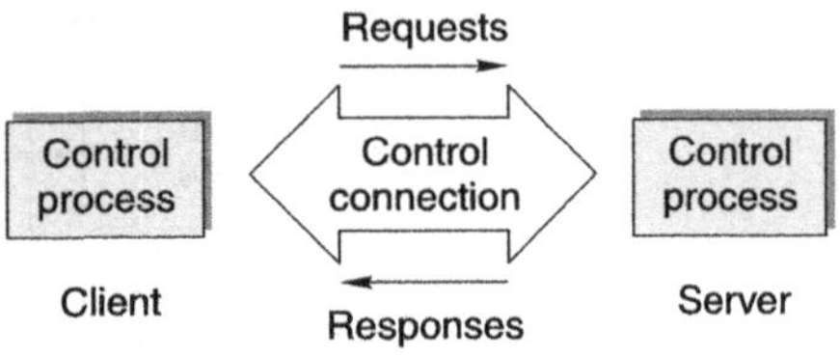

Fig. 5.48 *Command processing using the control connection*

Data Transfer Connection

The data transfer connection is used to transfer files from the server to the client or from the client to the server, as shown in Fig. 5.49. As we have noted before, this is decided based on the commands that travel over the control connection.

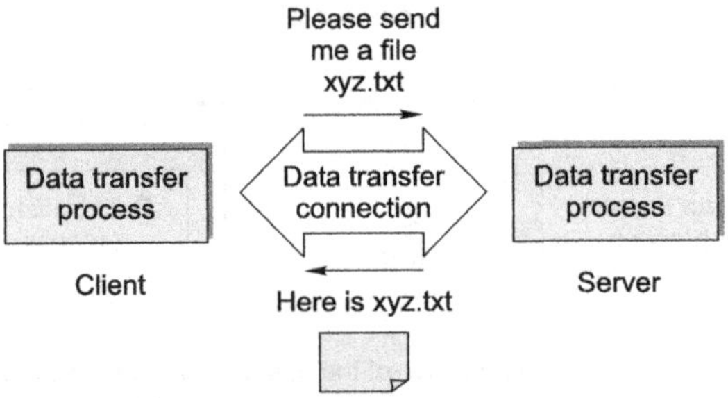

Fig. 5.49 *File transfer using the data transfer connection*

The sender must specify the following attributes of the file:

1. **Type of the file to be transferred** The file to be transferred can be an ASCII, EBCDIC or Image file. If the file has to be transferred as ASCII or EBCDIC, the destination must be ready to accept it in that mode. If the file is to be transferred without any regard to its content, the third type is used. This third and last type – image file – is actually a misnomer. It has nothing to do with images. Actually, it signifies a binary file that is not interpreted by FTP in any manner, and is sent as it is. Compiled programs are examples of image files.
2. **Structure of the data** FTP can transfer a file across a data transfer connection by interpreting it its structure in the following ways:
   (a) *Byte-oriented structure* The file can be transmitted as a continuous stream of data (byte-oriented structure), wherein no structure for the file is assumed.

(b) *Record-oriented structure* The other option for the structure of the file being transferred is the record-oriented structure, where the file is divided into records and these records are then sent one by one.

3. **Transmission mode** FTP can transfer a file by using one of the three transmission modes as described here:
   (a) *Stream mode* If the file is transmitted in stream mode, which is the default mode, data is delivered from FTP to TCP as a continuous stream of data. TCP is then responsible for splitting up the data into appropriate packets. If the data uses the byte-oriented structure (see earlier point), then no end-of-file character is needed. When the sender closes the TCP connection, the file transfer is considered to be complete. However, if the file follows the record-oriented structure, then each record will have an end-of-record character, and the file would have a end-of-file character at the end.
   (b) *Block mode* Data can be delivered from FTP to TCP in terms of blocks. In this case, each data block follows a three-byte header. The first byte of the header is called block descriptor, whereas the remaining two bytes define the size of the block.
   (c) *Compressed mode* If the file to be transferred is being, it can be compressed before it is sent. Normally, the Run Length Encoding (RLE) compression method is used for compressing a file. This method replaces repetitive occurrences of a data block by the first occurrence only, and a count of how many times it repeats is stored along with it. For example, the most compressed data blocks in case of a text file are blank spaces, and those in a binary file are null characters.

This information is used by FTP to resolve the heterogeneity problem. In any case, we must note that the data travels from the sender to the recipient as IP packets. That is, the file is broken down into TCP packets, and then into IP packets. The IP packets are then sent one by one by the sender to the recipient. We have discussed this earlier, and shall not elaborate on it here.

5.3.6 FTP Commands

Using the control connection, the client sends commands to the server. The server sends back responses on the same connection. FTP commands can be classified into the following types:

1. **Access commands** These commands let the user access the remote system. Examples of this type of commands are:
   (a) USER (User ID): Identifies the user
   (b) PASS (Password): Password
   (c) QUIT (): Logoff
2. **File management commands** These commands let the user access the file system on the remote computer. Examples of this type of commands are:
   (a) CWD (Directory): Change to another directory
   (b) DELE (File): Delete a file
   (c) LIST (Directory): Provide a directory listing
3. **Data formatting commands** These commands let the user define the data structure, file type, and transmission type. Examples of this type of commands are:
   (a) TYPE (A, E, I): ASCII, EBCDIC, Image, etc., – Ensures the correct interpretation of characters
   (b) STRU (F, R, P): File, Record, Page – *File* is mostly preferred, which indicates that every byte in the file is equal, and that the file is not divided into logical records, etc.
   (c) MODE (S, B, C): Stream, Block, Compressed – *Stream* is most preferred, since it allows the transmission of data as continuous stream of bytes to the receiver without any header

4. **Port defining commands** These commands define the port number for the data connection on the client side. There are two options:
   (a) Client uses the PORT command to choose an ephemeral port number and sends it to the server using a passive open. Server does an active open to connect to the client on that port
   (b) Client uses the PASV command to ask the server to choose a port number. Server does a passive open on that port and sends it as a response to the client. Client does an active open
5. **File transferring commands** These commands actually let the user transfer files. Examples of this type of commands are:
   (a) RETR (File): Retrieves files from server to client
   (b) STOR (File): Stores files from client to server
   (c) APPE (File): Appends to the end of an already existing file
6. **Miscellaneous commands** These commands deliver information to the FTP user at the client side. Examples of this type of commands are:
   (a) HELP: Ask for help
   (b) NOOP: Check if server is alive

5.3.7 FTP responses

Every FTP command generates at least one response from the server. A response consists of two parts:

1. Three digit number (Code), say *xyz*
   (a) *x* (1st digit): Defines status of the command
   (b) *y* (2nd digit): Provides more details on the status of the command
   (c) *z* (3rd digit): Provides additional information
2. Text (Contains parameters or extra information)

Figure 5.50 explains the relevance of the first digit of the response code.

Command	*Meaning*
1*yz*	Action has started, server will send another reply before accepting another command.
2*yz*	Action has been completed. Server is ready to accept another command.
3*yz*	Command has been accepted, but more information is needed.
4*yz*	Action did no take place.
5*yz*	Command was rejected.

Fig. 5.50 *FTP responses – Part 1*

Figure 5.51 explains the usage of the second digit in the response code.

Command	*Meaning*
x0z	Syntax
x1z	Information
x2z	Connections
x3z	Authentication and accounting
X4z	Unspecified
X5z	File system

Fig. 5.51 *FTP responses – Part 2*

Figure 5.52 shows the relevance of the third digit in the response code.

Command	*Meaning*
125	Data connection open; data transfer will start shortly
150	File status is ok; data connection will be open shortly
200	Command ok
230	User login ok
331	User name ok, enter password
425	Cannot open data connection
426	Connection closed; transfer aborted
500	Syntax error; unrecognized command
530	User not logged in

Fig. 5.52 *FTP responses – Part 3*

Figure 5.53 shows a sample FTP interaction.

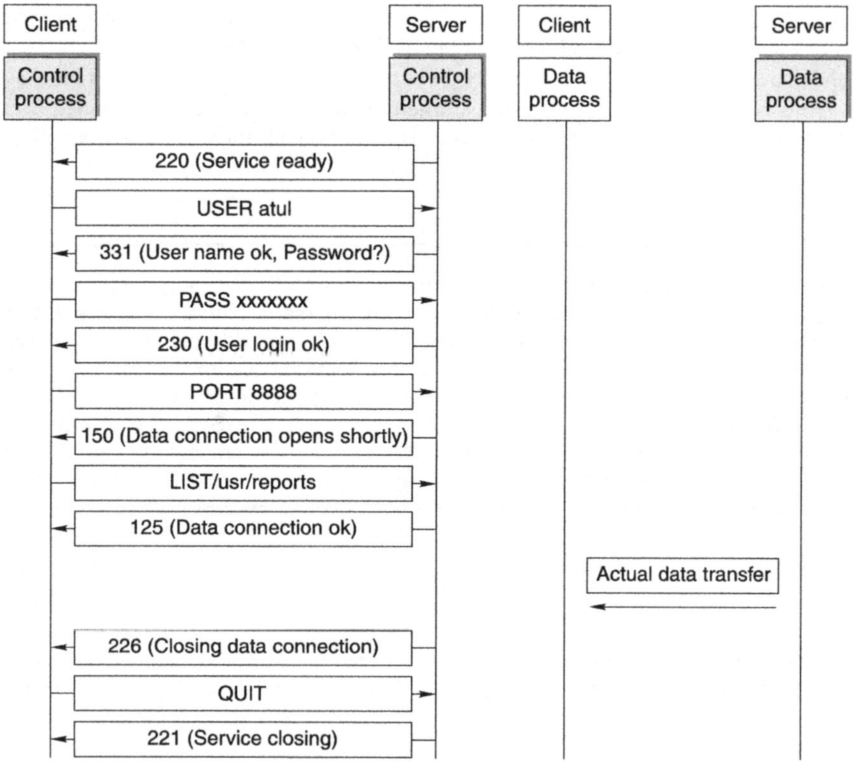

Fig. 5.53 *Sample FTP interaction*

TRIVIAL FILE TRANSFER PROTOCOL (TFTP).. 5.4

The **Trivial File Transfer Protocol (TFTP)** is a protocol used for transferring files between two computers, similar to what FTP is used for. However, TFTP is different from FTP is one major respect. Whereas FTP uses the reliable TCP as the underlying transport layer protocol, TFTP uses the unreliable UDP protocol for data transport. Other minor differences between FTP and TFTP are that while FTP allows changing directory of the remote computer or to obtain a list of files in the directory of the remote computer, TFTP does not allow this. Also, there is no interactivity in TFTP. It is a protocol designed for purely transferring files.

There are situations where we need to simply copy a file without needing to use the sophisticated features provided by FTP. In such situations, TFTP is used. For example, when a diskless workstation or a router is booted, it is required to download the bootstrap and configuration files to that workstation or router. The device (workstation or router) in such a case simply needs to have the TFTP, UDP and IP software hard coded into its Read Only Memory (ROM). After receiving power, the device executes the code in ROM, which broadcasts a TFTP request across the network. A TFTP server on that network then sends the necessary files to the device, so that it can boot. Not much of error checking and authentication is required here. TFTP is a suitable candidate for such situations.

TFTP does not allow for user authentication unlike FTP. Therefore, TFTP must not be used on computers where sensitive/confidential information is stored.

TFTP transfers data in fixed-size blocks of 512 bytes each. The recipient must acknowledge each such data block before the sender sends the next block. Thus, the sender sends data packets in the form of blocks and expects acknowledgement packets, whereas the recipient receives data blocks and sends acknowledgement packets. Either of them must time out and retransmit if the expected data block or acknowledgement, as appropriate, does not arrive. Also, unlike FTP, there is no provision for resuming an aborted file transfer from its last point.

Key Terms and Concepts

Block mode • Browser-based emails • Byte oriented structure • Compressed mode • Control connection • Data transfer connection • Distributed database • Domain name • Domain Name System (DNS) • DNS server • Electronic mail (Email) • Email address • Email client • Email server • File Transfer Protocol (FTP) • Host name • Internet Mail Access Protocol (IMAP) • Local DNS server • Mailbox • Mail Transfer Agent (MTA) • Multipurpose Internet Mail Extensions (MIME) • Post Office Protocol (POP) • Pretty Good Privacy (PGP) • Resolver • Simple Mail Transfer Protocol (SMTP) • Spooling • Stream mode • Stream oriented structure • Transmission mode • Trivial File Transfer Protocol (TFTP) • UDP packet • User agent • Web server • Web site •

SUMMARY

- Computers work best with numbers: humans don't. Humans prefer names.
- Every computer on the Internet has a unique IP address. Since the IP addresses used on the Internet to identify computers are in the numerical form, it would be very difficult for humans to remember the IP addresses of even a few computers.
- This difference between the perceptions of humans and computers is resolved by assigning names to computers. Thus, the name of a computer is mapped to its IP address.

- The name given to a group of computers – that is, to a computer network, is called its domain name.
- The Domain Name System (DNS) is a distributed database that contains the mappings between domain names and IP addresses.
- A client computer contacts its nearest DNS server to find out the IP address of the computer with which it wants to communicate. The DNS server consults its database to find a match. If it does not find a match, it relays the query on to another DNS server, which might relay it to a third DNS server, and so on, until either a match is found or it is detected that the domain name specified by the user is invalid.
- Electronic mail (email) was created to allow two individuals to communicate using computers.
- Email combines the best features of a telephone call (immediate delivery) and a letter delivered via post/courier (an immediate response is not compulsory, but is always possible).
- The underlying transport mechanism for email messages, like all Internet communications, is TCP/IP.
- An email mailbox is just a storage area on the disk of the email server computer. This area is used for storing received emails on behalf of the users similar to the way a postal mailbox stores postal mails.
- Simple Mail Transfer Protocol (SMTP) is actually responsible for transmitting an email message between the sender and the recipient.
- The Post Office Protocol (POP) is concerned with the retrieval of an email message stored on a server computer,
- Multipurpose Internet Mail Extensions (MIME) allow an email to not only contain text data, but also any binary file such as an image, audio, video, documents in different formats, etc.
- Two email privacy standards are available: Pretty Good Privacy (PGM) and Privacy Enhanced Mail (PEM).
- The File Transfer Protocol (FTP) is used to transfer files between the two computers.
- FTP presents the user with a prompt and allows entering various commands for accessing and downloading files that physically exist on a remote computer.
- Unlike other applications at the application layer, FTP opens two connections between the client and the server computers. One connection (called data transfer connection) is used for the actual file transfer, while the other connection (called control connection) is used for exchanging control information.
- A simpler version of FTP, called as Trivial File Transfer Protocol (TFTP) also exists. Unlike in FTP, TFTP does not perform any validations or error control.

MULTIPLE-CHOICE QUESTIONS

1. The hosts.txt file used to contain ________ and ________.
   (a) IP address, physical address (b) IP address, domain name
   (c) Domain name, IP address (d) Domain name, physical address
2. The com domain name refers to ________.
   (a) common (b) commercial (c) computer (d) None of these
3. ________ is a storage area to store emails.
   (a) Database (b) File (c) Mailbox (d) Server

4. The ________ symbol is used to connect the user name and the domain name portions of an email id.
   (a) & (b) @ (c) * (d) $
5. ________ protocol is used to retrieve emails from a remote server.
   (a) POP (b) IP (c) POP (d) SMTP
6. ________ protocol is used for transferring mails over the Internet.
   (a) POP (b) IP (c) POP (d) SMTP
7. ________ allows non-text data to be sent along with an email message.
   (a) PGP (b) MIME (c) PEM (d) MTA
8. For transferring big files over the Internet, the ________ protocol is used.
   (a) SMTP (b) POP (c) HTTP (d) FTP
9. ________ uses TCP as the transport protocol.
   (a) FTP (b) TFTP
   (c) Both (a) and (b) (d) None of these
10. FTP uses the control connection for transferring ________.
   (a) data (b) control information
   (c) data and control information (d) All of these

DETAILED QUESTIONS

1. What is the need for additional suffixes such as *com*, *edu* and *gov*?
2. What is DNS? Why is it required?
3. Explain the significance of a DNS server.
4. What is the purpose of an email server?
5. Why is email client required?
6. Discuss email architecture in brief along with its main components.
7. Discuss SMTP.
8. What is the purpose of FTP?
9. Discuss the FTP connection mechanism between the client and the server.
10. What are the specific purposes of the control connection?

EXERCISES

1. Find out how the DNS server is configured in your organization. Also find out how much money is required to register a new domain name, and what the procedure is for the same.
2. Try sending an attachment along with an email message through an email client like Outlook Express, and try the same using a Web-based email service (such as Yahoo or Hotmail). Note the differences.
3. Normally, when you download a file, HTTP and not FTP is used. Try downloading a file by using HTTP and then try the same using FTP. What are the differences according to you?
4. Investigate how you can send emails through programming languages/tools such as ASP.NET, JSP and Servlets.
5. Try to find out more information about the SMTP, POP, IMAP servers used in your organization, college or university.

6 TCP-IP PART IV (WWW, HTTP, TELNET)

INTRODUCTION

Apart from email, the most popular application running on the Internet is the **World Wide Web (WWW)**. It is so important that people often confuse it with the Internet itself. However, WWW is just an application such as email and File Transfer that uses the Internet for communications, i.e., TCP/IP as an underlying transport mechanism. Many companies have Internet **Websites**. What is meant by a Website? It is a collection of **Web pages** like a brochure (a collection of paper pages), except that the pages are stored digitally on the **Web server**. You could have a dedicated server computer in your company for storing these Web pages (or for *hosting the Website, as it is popularly called*), or you could lease some disk space from a large server installed at your ISP's location.

In either case, the server has a piece of software running on it, which is actually the Web server software. However, commonly, the server computer itself is called the *Web server* (actually inaccurately in a strict sense). The function of the Web server hardware and software is to store the Web pages and transmit them to a client computer as and when it requests for the Web pages to be sent to them from the server, after locating them. The Website address (also called **Uniform Resource Locator** or **URL**) will be that of the first page (also called **home page**) of your Website installed on the server of your ISP. Internally, each Web page is a computer file stored on the disk of the server. The file contains *tags* written in a codified form – as we shall see – that decide how the file would look like when displayed on a computer's screen.

In your company's Website, you can display the information about your products, employees, policies or even the practices. It can, therefore, be used as a company news bulletin and it can be made more attractive using different colors, sound and animation (multimedia). A company can use it like a window in a shop where you display what you want to sell. On a Website, not only what is to be sold is displayed, but there can be Websites which are dedicated to specialized tasks such as displaying news, share prices, sports, directory services, or indeed a combination of one or more of these services. For example, CNN's Website is www.CNN.com. Sometimes, you might also type the **HTTP** prefix, which makes the name of the same Website http://www.CNN.com. This only indicates that we use the HTTP protocol to communicate with the Website. Mentioning this is optional. If nothing is mentioned, the system assumes HTTP. We shall see what this HTTP means, later, but will stop mentioning this explicitly as this is assumed.

BRIEF HISTORY OF WWW 6.1

The term WWW refers to a set of Internet protocols and software, which together present information to a user in a format called **hypertext**, as we shall study. The WWW became quite popular in mid 1990s. Tim Berners-Lee did the primary work in the development of the WWW at the European Laboratory for Particle Physics (CERN). The original motivation for the development of the WWW, now more commonly known as the Web, was to try and improve the CERN's research-document handling and sharing mechanisms. CERN was connected to the Internet for over two years, but the scientists were looking for better ways of circulating their scientific papers and information among the high-energy Physics research world.

In a couple of years' time, Berners-Lee developed the necessary software application for a hypertext server program, and made it available as a free download on the Internet. As we shall see, a hypertext server stores documents in a hypertext format, and makes them available over the Internet, to anyone interested. This paved the way for the popularity of the Web. Berners-Lee called his system of hypertext documents as the World Wide Web (WWW). The Web became very popular among the scientific community in a short span of time. However, the trouble with the Web was the lack of availability of software to read the documents created in the hypertext format, for the general public.

In 1993, Marc Andreessen and his team, at the University of Illinois, wrote a program called Mosaic, which could read a document created using the hypertext format, and interpret its contents, so that they could be displayed on the user's screen. This program, later known as the world's first **Web browser**, essentially opened the gates of the Web for the general public. Anybody who had a copy of the Mosaic Web browser, could download any hypertext document from any other corner of the world, as long as it was a part of the Web, and read it on his PC. Mosaic was a free piece of software, too.

Soon, people realized that the Web's popularity was something to cash on. Here was a potentially worldwide network of computers, which was accessible to anybody who had a PC, an Internet connection, and a Web browser. So, business interests in the Web started developing fast. In 1994, Andreessen and his colleagues at the University of Illinois joined hands with James Clarke of Silicon Graphics to form a new venture, named as Netscape Communications. Their first product was Netscape Navigator, a Web browser, based on Mosaic. Netscape Navigator was an instant hit. It became extensively popular in a very short time period, before Microsoft realized the potential of the Web, and came up with their own browser – the Internet Explorer. Although many browsers exist in the market today, Internet Explorer and Netscape Navigator dominate the Web browser market.

Since the last few years, the World Wide Web Consortium (W3C) oversees the standards related to the WWW.

BASICS OF WWW AND BROWSING 6.2

6.2.1 Introduction

Most of the companies and organizations have their Websites consisting of a number of pages, each. In addition, there are many **portals**, which you can use to do multiple activities. Yahoo, for instance, can be used to send/receive emails, sell/buy goods, or carry out auctions, etc. In order to attract more customers to their site, they create large Web pages ("content"), which give you different news, information and entertainment items. The idea is that you would visit this site again and again and notice some *sale* going on somewhere, buy that product on line, so that Yahoo will get a small portion of that transaction amount as commission. Or companies pay Yahoo to put up the advertisements for their products, because Yahoo's site is popular and many people visit it (called *number of eyeballs* or *number of hits*), and they will notice the advertisement. Like the TV or newspaper, more the viewers/readers, more is the cost of the advertisements; and therefore, sites such as Yahoo give a lot of content (i.e., infotainment) to make it popular, which is why, in turn other companies will pay higher rates for their advertisements displayed on yahoo Website. For instance, a site for buying/selling trains/plane tickets can also give information about hotels, tourist places, etc. This is called the *content.* There are literally thousands of such sites or portals in the WWW in addition to the various company Websites. That is why WWW contains a tremendous amount of information.

Thus, WWW consists of thousands of such Websites for thousands of individuals and companies giving tremendous amount of information about people, companies, events, history, news, etc. WWW is a huge, on-line repository of information that users can view using a program called a Web browser. Modern browsers allow a graphical user interface. So, a user can use the mouse to make selections, navigate through the pages, etc. Earlier Web browsers were purely text based, which meant that users had to type commands and more importantly, could not view any graphics.

You would realize that the same concepts of client-server communication and the use of TCP/IP software apply here. In the case of email, it is the email client and the email server software that communicate. In the case of FTP, it is the FTP client and FTP server programs that communicate. In case of the WWW, the roles are performed by the Web browser (the client) and Web server (the server). In all the cases, whatever is sent from the client to the server (request for a Web page) and from the server to the client (actual Web page) is sent using TCP/IP as an underlying protocol – i.e., the message is broken into IP packets and routed through various routers and networks within the internet until they reach the final destination where they are reassembled after verifying the accuracy, etc.

6.2.2 How Does a Web Server Work?

A Web server is a program running on a server computer. Additionally, it consists of the Website containing a number of Web pages. A Web page constitutes simply a special type of computer file written in a specially designed language called **Hyper Text Markup Language (HTML)**. Each Web page can contain text, graphics, sound, video and animation that people want to see or hear.

The Web server constantly and passively waits for a request for a Web page from a browser program running on the client and when any such request is received, it locates that corresponding page and sends it to the requesting client computer. To do this, every Website has a server **process** (a running instance of a program) that listens to TCP connection requests coming from different clients all the time. After a TCP connection is established, the client sends one request and the server sends one response. Then the server releases the connection. This request-response model is governed by a protocol called **Hyper Text Transfer Protocol (HTTP)**. For instance, HTTP software on the client prepares the request for a Web page, whereas the HTTP software on the server interprets such a request and prepares a response to be sent back to the client. Thus, both client and server computers need to have HTTP software running on them. Do not confuse HTTP with HTML. HTML is a special language in which the Web pages are written and stored on the server. HTTP is a protocol, which governs the dialog between the client and server.

You would realize that this is a typical client-server interaction, as we have discussed so far – the Web server obviously acting as a server, in this case. Rather than requesting for a file as in case of FTP, a client requests for a specific Web page here. As we know, each Web page is stored in HTML format on the server. The server receives a request for a specific Web page, locates it with the help of the operating system, and sends it back to the client using TCP/IP as the basic message transport mechanism. After receiving the Web page in the HTML format in the memory of the client computer, the browser *interprets* it – i.e., displays it on the screen of the client computer.

Two of the most popular Web servers are Apache and IIS. They have Web containers, namely Tomcat and IIS. Apache Tomcat is used for Java-based server-side technologies, such as Java Servlets and JSP. On the other hand, Microsoft's IIS is used for Microsoft-based technologies, such as ASP.NET.

6.2.3 How does a Web browser Work?

A Web browser acts as the client in the WWW interaction. Using this program, a user requests for a Web page (which is a disk file, as we have noted) stored on a Web server. The Web server locates this Web page and sends it back to the client computer. The Web browser then interprets the Web page written in the HTML language/format and then displays it on the client computer's screen.

The typical interaction between a Web browser (the client) and a Web server (the server) is as shown in Fig. 6.1 and happens as explained below:

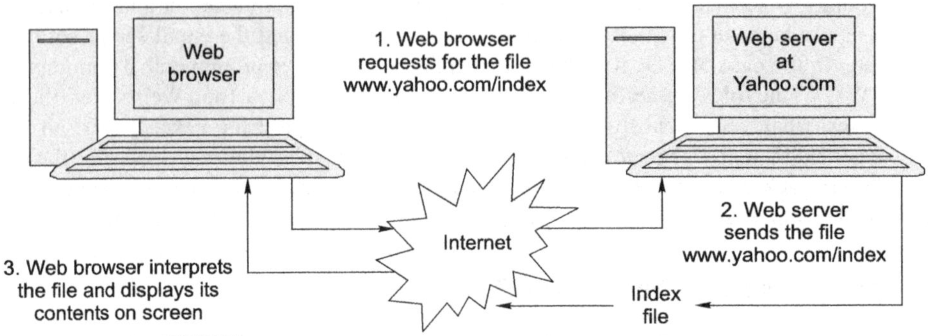

Fig. 6.1 *Interaction between a Web browser and a Web server*

1. The user on the client computer types the full file name including the domain name of the Web server that hosts the Web page that he is interested in. This name is typed on a screen provided by the Web browser program running on his computer. As we know, this full file name is called Uniform Resource Locator (URL). A URL signifies the full, unique path of any file on the Internet.

   For instance, a URL could be http://www.yahoo.com/index or only www.yahoo.com/index, because specifying http is optional, as we have mentioned. First let us understand its anatomy using Fig. 6.2.

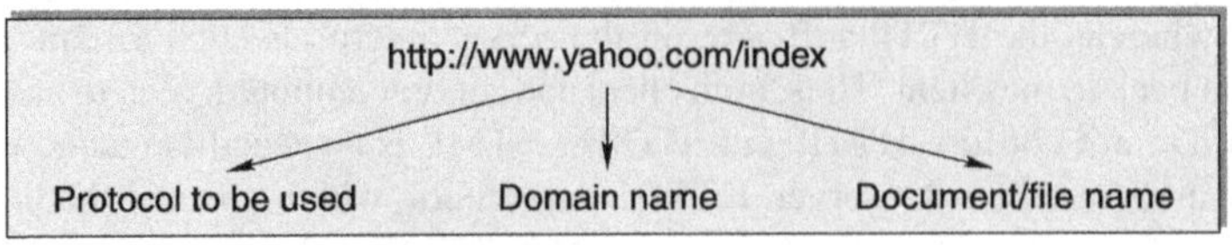

Fig. 6.2 *Anatomy of a URL*

Here, *http* indicates the protocol (discussed later). *Index* is the name of the file. It is stored on the Web server whose domain name is *yahoo.com*. Because it is a WWW application, it also has a www prefix. The forward slash (/) character indicates that the file is one of the many files stored in the domain yahoo.com. Suppose, the user wants another file called newsoftheday, from this site, he would type http://www.yahoo.com/newsoftheday. Alternatively, the user can just type the name of the domain (e.g., www.yahoo.com). Every Web server has one default file, which can be used in these cases. When the user types just the domain name without mentioning the file name, this default file is used. This default file is returned to the Web browser in such cases. If index file is such a default file, this will be another way of reaching the index file at yahoo.com. The page displayed from the default file (in this case the index file) may then provide links to other files (or Web pages) stored at that domain. If a user clicks on one of them (e.g., finance), the finance file stored at the yahoo domain is then displayed.

2. The browser requests DNS for the IP address corresponding to www.yahoo.com.
3. DNS replies with the IP address for www.yahoo.com (let us say, it is 120.10.23.21).
4. The browser makes a TCP connection with the computer 120.10.23.21.
5. The client makes an explicit request for the Web page (in this case, the file corresponding to the page *index* at *yahoo.com*) to the Web server using **HTTP request**. The HTTP request is a series of lines, which, among other things, contains two important statements *GET* and *HOST*, as shown with our current example (all HTTP and HTML keywords are case-insensitive):
   GET /index.htm and
   Host: yahoo.com
   The *GET* statement indicates that the *index.htm* file needs to be retrieved (the *.htm* extension indicates that the file is written in HTML). The *Host* parameter indicates that the *index* file needs to be retrieved from the domain *yahoo.com*.
6. The request is handed over to the HTTP software running on the client machine to be transmitted to the server.
7. The HTTP software on the client now hands over the HTTP request to the TCP/IP software running on the client.
8. The TCP/IP software running on the client breaks the HTTP request into packets and sends them over TCP to the Web server (in this case, *yahoo.com*).
9. The TCP/IP software running on the Web server reassembles the HTTP request using the packets thus, received and gives it to the HTTP software running on the Web server, which is *yahoo.com* in this case.
10. The HTTP software running on the Web server interprets the HTTP request. It realizes that the browser has asked for the file *index.htm* on the server. Therefore, it requests the operating system running on the server for that file.
11. The operating system on the Web server locates *index.htm* file and gives it to the HTTP software running on the Web server.
12. The HTTP software running on the Web server adds some headers to the file to form a **HTTP response**. The HTTP response is a series of lines that contains this header information (such as date and time when the response is being sent, etc.) and the HTML text corresponding to the requested file (in this case, *index.htm*).
13. The HTTP software on the Web server now hands over this HTTP response to the TCP/IP software running on the Web server.
14. The TCP/IP software running on the Web server breaks the HTTP response into packets and sends it over the TCP connection to the client. Once all packets have been transmitted correctly

to the client, the TCP/IP software on the Web server informs the HTTP software on the Web server.

15. The TCP/IP software on the client computer checks the packets for correctness and reassembles them to form the original Web page in the HTML format. It informs the HTTP software on the server that the Web page was received correctly.
16. Realizing this, the HTTP software on the Web server terminates the TCP connection between itself and the client. Therefore, HTTP is called **stateless protocol**. The TCP connection between the client and the server is established for every page, even if all the pages requested by the client reside on the same server. Moreover, if the Web page contains images (photographs, icons, images, etc.), for each such image, or sound, etc., a separate file is required, which stores it in specific formats (GIF, JPEG, PNG, etc.). Therefore, if a Web page contains text, sound and image, it will take three HTTP requests to locate and bring three files residing on the same or different servers to the client, after which the browser on the client can compose these together to display that Web page. Needless to say that this involves a DNS search as many times as well. This is the reason why retrieving a Web page that contains many graphical elements is very slow.
    Thus, HTTP does not remember anything about the previous request. It does not maintain any information about the state – and hence the term *stateless*. Keeping HTTP stateless was aimed at keeping the Web simple: usually more clients would be requesting Web pages from a lesser number of servers. If each such request from a client is to be *remembered*, the Web server would shortly run out of processing power and memory.
17. The TCP/IP software on the client now hands over the Web page to the Web browser for interpretation. It is only the browser, which understands the "HTML code language" to decipher which elements (text, photo, video) should be displayed where and how. This is the meaning of "interpretation". How does the browser do this?

To understand this, we shall study the Web pages more in depth.

6.2.4 HTTP Commands

Let us discuss a few commands in the HTTP protocol when a client requests a server for a Web page, as summarized in Fig. 6.3.

HTTP command	*Description*
GET	Request for obtaining a Web page.
HEAD	Request to read the header of a Web page.
PUT	Requests the server to store a Web page.
POST	Similar to PUT, but is used for updating a Web page.
DELETE	Remove a Web page.
LINK	Connects two resources.
UNLINK	Disconnects two resources.

Fig. 6.3 *HTTP request commands*

A browser uses the commands shown in Fig. 6.3 when it sends a HTTP request to a Web server. Let us discuss each of them. Note that these commands are case-sensitive.

1. **GET** A browser uses this command for requesting a Web server for sending a particular Web page.

2. **HEAD** This command does not request for a Web page, but only requests for its header. For instance, if a browser wants to know the last modified date of a Web page, it would use the HEAD command, rather than the GET command.
3. **PUT** This command is exactly opposite of the GET command. Rather than requesting for a file, it sends a file to the server for storing it there.
4. **POST** This command is very similar to the PUT command. However, whereas the PUT command is used to send a new file, the POST command is used to update an existing file with additional data.
5. **DELETE** This command allows a browser to send a HTTP request for deleting a particular Web page.
6. **LINK** This command is used to establish hyperlinks between two pages.
7. **UNLINK** This command is used to remove existing hyperlinks between two pages.

Note that GET is the most common command sent by a client browser as a part of the HTTP request to a Web server. This is because, not many Web servers would allow a client to delete/add/link/unlink files. This can be fatal. However, for the sake of completeness, we have discussed them briefly.

When a browser sends such an HTTP request command to a Web server, the server sends back a status line (indicating the success or failure, as a result of executing that command) and additional information (which can be the Web page itself). The status line contains error codes. For example, a status code of 200 means success (OK), 403 means authorization failure, etc.

For instance, the following line is an example command sent by a browser to a server for obtaining a Web page named *information.html* from the site www.mysite.com, as shown in Fig. 6.4.

GET *http://WWW.mysite.com/information.html* HTTP/1.0

Fig. 6.4 *Example of GET command sent by a browser*

This GET command requests the Web server at www.mysite.com for a file called *information.html*. The HTTP/1.0 portion of the command indicates that the browser uses the 1.0 version of the HTTP protocol.

In response, the server might send the following HTTP response back to the browser, as shown in Fig. 6.5.

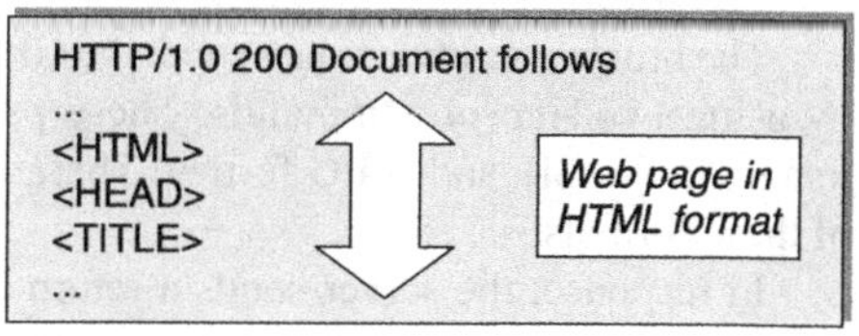

Fig. 6.5 *HTTP response from the server*

The first line indicates to the browser that the server is also using HTTP 1.0 as its protocol version. Also, the return code of 200 means that the server processed the browser's HTTP request successfully. After that, there would be a few other parameters, which are not shown. After these parameters, the following line start:

```
<HTML>
<HEAD>
<TITLE>
```

This is a Web page codified in HTML format.

We shall see what these statements mean when discussing HTML. However, for now, just keep in mind that the actual contents of the Web page are sent by the Web server to the browser with the help of these **tags**. A tag is a HTML keyword usually enclosed between less than and greater than symbols. For instance, the <HTML> statement (i.e., tag) indicates that the HTML contents of the Web page start now.

6.2.5 Example of a HTTP Interaction

Let us study an example of an HTTP request and response model. In this example, the browser (i.e., the client) retrieves a HTML document from the Web server. We shall assume that the TCP connection between the client and the server is already established, and we shall not discuss it further.

As shown in Fig. 6.6, the client sends a GET command to retrieve an image with the path /files/new/image1. That is, the name of the file is image1, and it is stored in the files/new directory of the Web server. Instead, the Web browser could have, of course, requested for a HTML page (i.e., a file with *html* extension).

In response, the Web server sends an appropriate return code of 200, which means that the request was successfully processed, and also the image data, as requested. We shall discuss the details shown in Fig. 6.6 after taking a look at it.

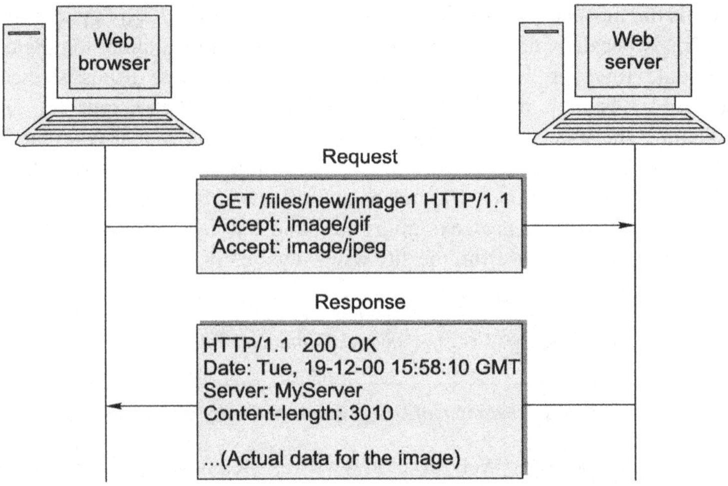

Fig. 6.6 *Sample HTTP request and response interaction between a Web browser and a Web server*

The browser sends a request with the GET command, as discussed. It also sends two more parameters by using two *Accept* commands. These parameters specify that the browser is capable of handling images in the GIF and JPEG format. Therefore, the server should send the image file only if it is in one of these formats.

In response, the server sends a return code of 200 (OK). It also sends the information about the date and time when this response was sent back to the browser. The server's name is the same as the domain name. Finally, the server indicates that it is sending 3010 bytes of data (i.e., the image file is made up of bits equivalent to 3010 bytes). This is followed by the actual data of the image file (not shown in the figure).

HYPER TEXT MARKUP LANGUAGE (HTML) 6.3

6.3.1 What is HTML?

Physicists at CERN (*Centre Europeen pour la Recherche Nucleaire*) needed a way to easily share information. In 1980, Tim Berners-Lee developed the initial program for linking documents with each other. A decade of development led to WWW and the **Hyper Text Markup Language (HTML)**, including Web browsers.

HTML stands for Hyper Text Markup Language. An HTML file is a text file containing small **markup tags**. The markup tags tell the Web browser how to display the page. An HTML file must have an htm or html file extension. An HTML file can be created using a simple text editor.

Figure 6.7 shows an example of a Web page.

```
<html>
  <head>
    <title>Title of page</title>
  </head>
  <body>
    This is my first homepage.
    <b>This text is bold</b>
  </body>
</html>
```

Fig. 6.7 *Example of an HTML page*

We can create the above file by using any simple text editor, such as Notepad. We can save it in a directory of our choice and then open it in a browser. The browser shows the output as shown in Fig. 6.8.

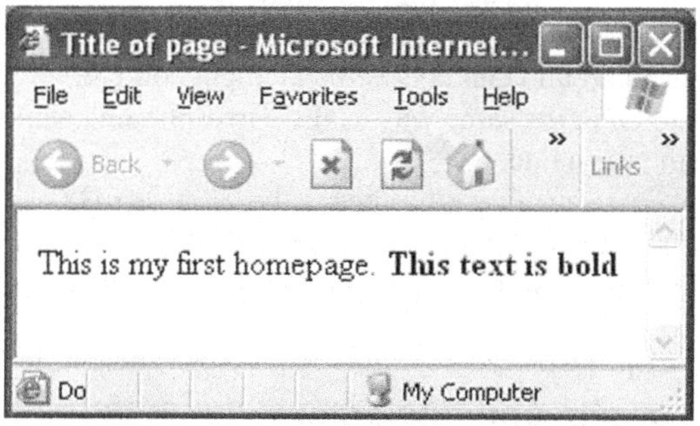

Fig. 6.8 *Output of a simple HTML page*

As we can see, we can format the output the way we want. Let us examine what we have done in terms of coding now.

```
<html>
```

Every HTML page must begin with this line. This line indicates that the current page should be interpreted by the Web browser (when we ask the browser to open it) as an HTML page. Because we enclose the word *html* inside the characters < and >, it is called a *tag*. A tag in HTML conveys some information to the browser. For example, here, the tag <html> tells the browser that the HTML page starts here. We shall see more such examples in due course of time.

```
<head>
  <title>Title of page</title>
</head>
```

These lines define the head part of an HTML page. An HTML page consists of two sections: the head of the page, and the body of the page. The title of the page is defined in the head section. We can see that we have defined the title of the page as *Title of page*. If we look at the browser output, we will notice that this value is displayed at the top of the page. This is where the output of the title is shown. Incidentally, like *title*, there can be many other tags inside the head section, as we shall see subsequently.

```
<body>
  This is my first homepage.
  <b>This text is bold</b>
</body>
```

As mentioned earlier, the HTML page has a head section and a body section. The body section contains the tags that display the output on the browser screen other than the title. Here, the body section contains some text, which is displayed as it is. Thereafter, we have some text inside tags <b> and </b>. This indicates that whatever is enclosed inside these tags should be displayed in bold (b stands for bold). Hence, we see that the text enclosed inside the <b>and </b> tags is displayed in bold font in the browser output.

```
</html>
```

This tag indicates the end of the HTML document.

We need to note some points regarding what we have discussed so far.

1. HTML tags are used to mark-up HTML elements.
2. HTML tags are surrounded by the two characters < and >.
3. HTML tags normally come in pairs like <b> and </b>.
4. The first tag in a pair is the start tag, the second tag is the end tag.
5. The text between the start and end tags is the element content.
6. An ending tag is named in the same way as the corresponding starting tag, except that it has a / character before the tag name.
7. HTML tags are not case sensitive, <b> means the same as <B>.
8. We are specifying all tags in lower case. Although this was not a requirement until HTML version 4.0, in the future versions, it is likely to become mandatory. Hence, we should stick to lower case tags only.

6.3.2 Headings, Paragraphs, and Line breaks

Headings in HTML are defined with the <h1> to <h6> tags. For example, <h1> defines the largest heading, whereas <h6> defines the smallest heading. HTML automatically adds an extra blank line before and after a heading. Figure 6.9 shows an example.

```
<html>
  <head>
    <title>Headings Example</title>
  <head>
  <body>
    <h1>This is heading H1</h1>
    <h2>This is heading H2</h2>
    <h3>This is heading H3</h3>
    <h4>This is heading H4</h4>
    <h5>This is heading H5</h5>
    <h6>This is heading H6</h6>
  </body>
</html>
```

Fig. 6.9 *Headings*

Figure 6.10 shows the corresponding output.

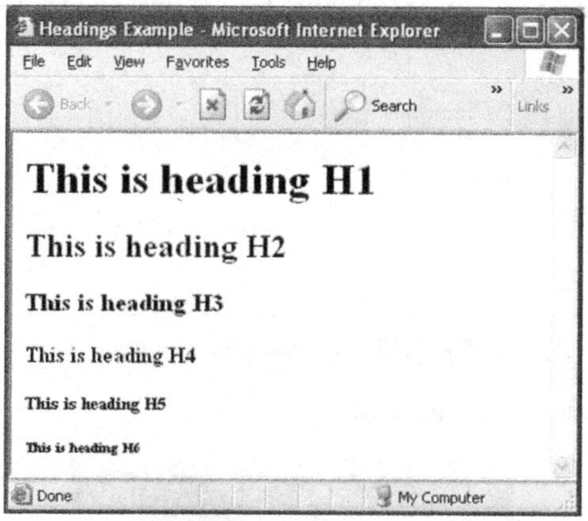

Fig. 6.10 *Heading output*

Paragraphs are defined with the <p> tag. HTML automatically adds an extra blank line before and after a paragraph. Figure 6.11 shows an example.

```
<html>
  <head>
    <title>Paragraphs Example</title>
  <head>
  <body>
    <h1>This is heading H1</h1>
    <p>This is a paragraph</p>
    <p>This is another paragraph</p>
</body>
</html>
```

Fig. 6.11 *Paragraphs example*

Figure 6.12 shows the corresponding output.

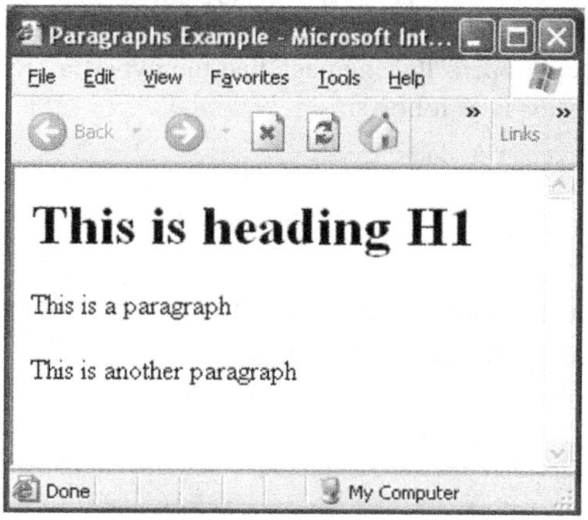

Fig. 6.12 *Paragraphs output*

The <br> tag is used when we want to end a line. This tag does not start a new paragraph. The <br> tag forces a line break wherever you place it. Figure 6.13 shows an example.

```
<html>
  <head>
    <title>Line Breaks Example</title>
  <head>
  <body>
    <p>This <br> is a para<br>graph with line breaks</p>
  </body>
</html>
```

Fig. 6.13 *Line breaks example*

The resulting output is shown in Fig. 6.14.

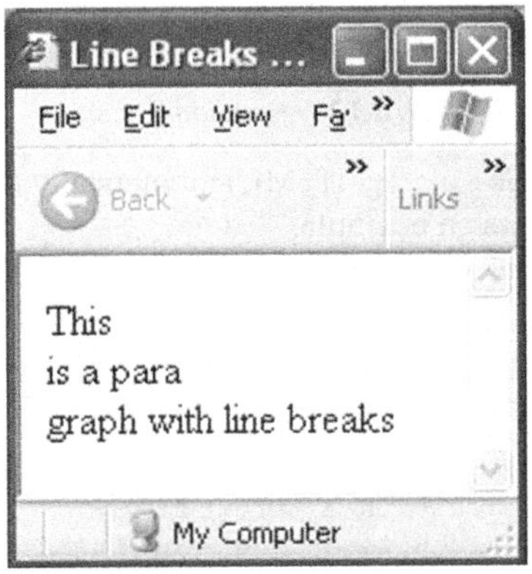

Fig. 6.14 *Line breaks output*

6.3.3 Creating Links to Other Pages

The anchor tag can be used to create a link to another document. This is called hyperlink or Uniform resource Locator (URL). The tag causes some text to be displayed as underlined. If we click on that text in the Web browser, our browser opens the site/page that the hyperlink refers to. The tag used is <a>. The general syntax for doing this is as follows:

```
<a href="url">Text to be displayed</a>
```

Here:

`a` = Create an anchor
`href` = Target URL
`Text` = Text to be displayed as substitute for the URL

For example, if we code the following in our HTML page:

```
<a href="http://www.yahoo.com/">Visit Yahoo!</a>
```

The result is

visit Yahoo!

A full example is shown in Fig. 6.15.

```
<html>
  <head>
    <title>Hype link Example</title>
  <head>
  <body>
       <h3> This tag will create a hyper link </h3>
       <br> <br>
       <h5> <a href="http://www.yahoo.com/">Visit Yahoo!</a></h5>
  </body>
</html>
```

Fig. 6.15 *Hyper link example*

The resulting output is shown in Fig. 6.16.

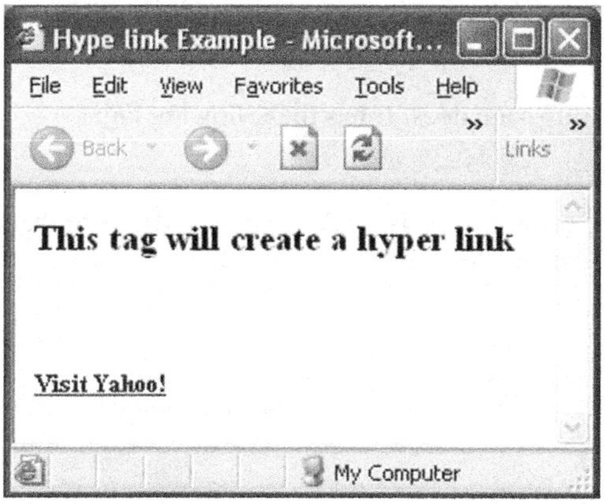

Fig. 6.16 *Hyper link output*

6.3.4 Frames

The technology of **frames** allows us to split the HTML page window (i.e., the screen that the user sees) into two or more sections. Each section of the page contains its own HTML document. The original HTML page, which splits itself into one or more frames, is also an HTML page. If this sounds complex, refer to Fig. 6.17.

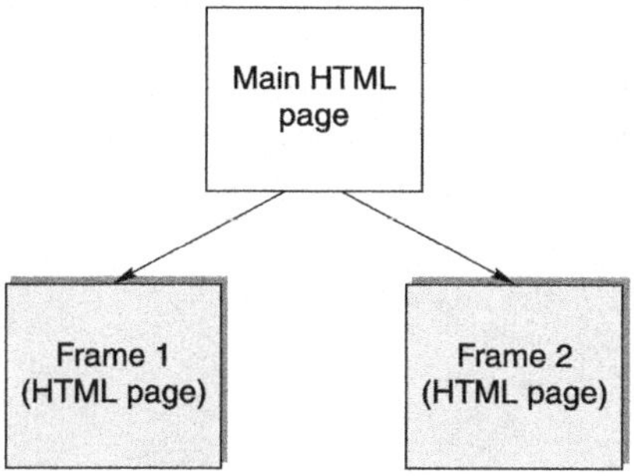

Fig. 6.17 *Frames concept*

How do we achieve this? The main HTML page contains reference to the two frames. An example would help clarify this point. A sample main HTML page is shown in Fig. 6.18.

```
<html>
  <head>
    <title>Frames Example!</title>
  </head>

  <frameset cols = "50%, 50%">
    <frame src = "page1.html">
    <frame src = "page2.html">
  </frameset>

</html>
```

Fig. 6.18 *Frames example*

Let us understand what this page does. It has the following tag:

```
<frameset cols="50%,50%">
```

This tag indicates to the browser that is loading this HTML page that the HTML page is not like a traditional HTML page. Instead, it is a set of frames. There are two frames, each of which occupies 50% of the screen space.

```
<frame src="page1.html">
```

This tag tells the browser that in the first 50% reserved area, the contents of the HTML page titled *page1.html* should be loaded.

```
<frame src="page2.html">
```

Needless to say, this tag tells the browser that in the second 50% reserved area, the contents of the HTML page titled *page2.html* should be loaded.

The output would be similar to what is shown in Fig. 6.19, provided the two HTML pages (*page1.html* and *page2.html*) contain the specified text line.

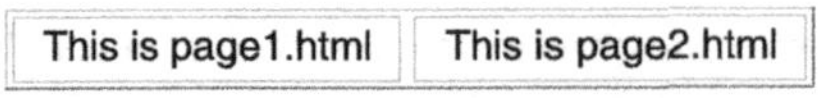

Fig. 6.19 *Frames output*

We should note that the browser reads our *frame src* tags for the columns from left to right. Therefore, we should keep everything in the order we want it to appear. Now, suppose we wanted three frames across the page, and not two. To achieve this, we need to modify our *frameset* tag and add another *frame src* tag for the third frame, as follows:

```
<frameset cols = "33%, 33%, 33%">
  <frame src = "page1.htm">
  <frame src = "page2.htm">
  <frame src = "page3.htm">
</frameset>
```

Interestingly, this covers only 99% of the space on the page. What about the remaining 1%? The browser would fill it up on its own. This may lead to slightly unpredictable results, so it is better to increase one of the 33% by 1 to make it 34%.

We can also create frames in other formats. An example is shown in Fig. 6.20.

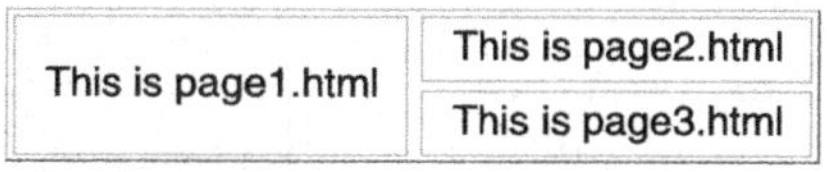

Fig. 6.20 *Another frames output*

How do we code the main HTML page for doing this? It is shown in Fig. 6.21.

```
<html>
  <head>
    <title>Another Frames Example!</title>
  </head>

    <frameset cols="65%, 35%">

    <frame src="page1.htm">

    <frameset rows="50%, 50%">
      <frame src = "page2.htm">
      <frame src = "page3.htm">
    </frameset>

  </frameset>

</html>
```

Fig. 6.21 *Frames code*

Let us understand this now.

1. The first *frameset* tag tells the browser to divide the page into two columns of 65% and 35% sizes, respectively.
2. The *frame src* tag after it tells the browser the first column should be filled with the contents of page1.html.
3. The next *frameset* tag is nested inside the first *frameset* tag. This tag tells the browser to divide the second column into two rows, instead of using a single HTML page to fill the column.
4. The ext two *frame src* tags tell the browser to fill the two rows with *page2.html* in the top row and page3.html in the bottom row, in the order of top to bottom.
5. We must close all of our *frameset* tags after they have been used.

Based on all the concepts discussed so far, let us now take a look at a real-life example. Figure 6.22 shows code for three HTML pages: one test page (*test.html*), which contains a frameset that specifies two frames (*left.html* and *right.html*).

test.html

```
<html>
  <head>
    <title>Simple Frames Example</title>
  </head>

  <frameset cols="20%, 80%">
    <frame src="left.html" name="left">
    <frame src="right.html" name="right">
  </frameset>

</html>
```

left.html

```
<html>
  <head>
    <title>Left Frame</title>
  </head>
  <body>
    Left Frame
  </body>
</html>
```

```
<html>
  <head>
    <title>Right Frame</title>
  </head>
  <body>
    Right Frame
  </body>
</html>
```

right.html

Fig. 6.22 *Frames inside a frameset*

The resulting output is shown in Fig. 6.23.

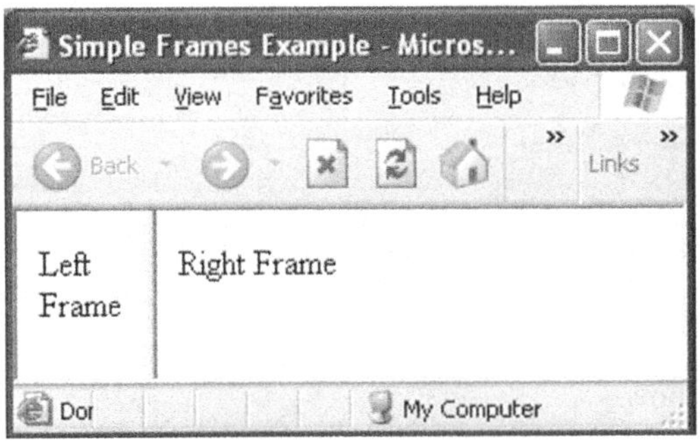

Fig. 6.23 *Frameset concept*

We will not discuss more features of frames, since they are not relevant to the current context.

6.3.5 Working With Tables

Figure 6.24 summarizes the tags that can be used to create an HTML table.

Tag	*Use*
<table>	Marks a table within an HTML document.
<tr>	Marks a row within a table. Closing tag is optional.
<td>	Marks a cell (table data) within a row. Closing tag is optional.
<th>	Marks a heading cell within a row. Closing tag is optional.

Fig. 6.24 *Table tags*

For example, suppose we want to create the following table in HTML, as shown in Fig. 6.25.

Book Name	*Author*
Operating Systems	Godbole
Data Communications and Networks	Godbole

Fig. 6.25 *Sample table output*

Let us understand this step by step.

Step 1: Start with the basic <table> and </table> tags.

```
<table>
</table>
```

Step 2: Add <tr> and </tr> tags for the number of rows needed. We have one header row and three data rows. Hence, we would have four instances of <tr> and </tr>.

```
<table>
  <tr>
  </tr>
  <tr>
  </tr>
  <tr>
  </tr>
  <tr>
  </tr>
</table>
```

Step 3: Add <th> and </th> tags for table headings.

```
<table>
  <tr>
    <th></th>
    <th></th>
  </tr>
  <tr>
  </tr>
  <tr>
  </tr>
  <tr>
  </tr>
</table>
```

Step 4: Add <td> and </td> tags for adding actual data.

```
<table>
  <tr>
    <th></th>
    <th></th>
  </tr>
    <td></td>
    <td></td>
  <tr>
```

```
      <td></td>
      <td></td>
    </tr>
    <tr>
      <td></td>
      <td></td>
    </tr>
  </table>
```

Step 5: Add actual heading and data values.

```
<table>
  <tr>
    <th>Book Name</th>
    <th>Author</th>
  </tr>
    <td>Operating Systems</td>
    <td>Godbole</td>
  <tr>
    <td>Data Communications and Networks</td>
    <td>Godbole</td>
  </tr>
  <tr>
    <td>Cryptography and Network Security</td>
    <td>Kahate</td>
  </tr>
</table>
```

The full HTML page is shown in Fig. 6.26.

```
<html>
  <head>
    <title>Table Example</title>
  </head>
  <body>
       <h1> Here is a Table in HTML</h1>
    <table>
       <tr>
         <th>Book Name</th>
         <th>Author</th>
       </tr>
         <td>Operating Systems</td>
         <td>Godbole</td>
       <tr>
         <td>Data Communications and Networks</td>
         <td>Godbole</td>
       </tr>
       <tr>
         <td>Cryptography and Network Security</td>
         <td>Kahate</td>
       </tr>
    </table>
  </body>
</html>
```

Fig. 6.26 *HTML code for a table*

The resulting output is shown in Fig. 6.27.

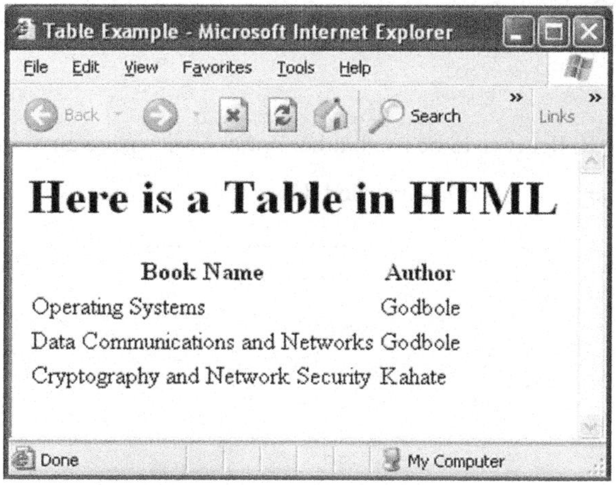

Fig. 6.27 *Output of HTML table*

We can see that the table does not have any borders. We can easily add them using the *border* attribute. The modified *table* tag is as follows (other things being exactly the same as before):

```
<table border="1">
```

The resulting output is as shown in Fig. 6.28.

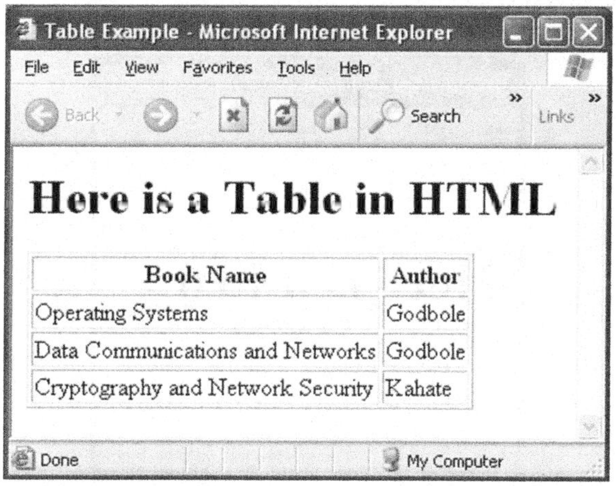

Fig. 6.28 *Adding border to a table*

6.3.6 Lists

In HTML, there are two types of lists: unordered and ordered. An unordered list is a list of items marked with bullets. It starts with <ul>. Inside, each item starts with <li>. On the other hand, an ordered list is a list of items marked with numbers. It starts with <ol>. Inside, each item starts with <li>.

The allowed types of lists are:

1. **Numbered lists**

   `Type="A"` Number or letter with which the list should start; other options are a, I, i, or 1 (Default)

2. **Bulleted lists**

   `Type="disc"` Bullet type to be used; other options are square and circle

Figure 6.29 shows an example of an unordered list.

```
<html>
  <head>
    <title>Unordered List Example</title>
  </head>
  <body>
    <h1> Here is a List</h1>
    <ul>
      <li>Coffee</li>
      <li>Milk</li>
      <li>Tea</li>
    </ul>
  </body>
</html>
```

Fig. 6.29 *Unordered list example*

The resulting output is shown in Fig. 6.30.

Fig. 6.30 *Unordered list output*

Suppose we want the bulleted list to have filled squares as the bullets, instead of filled circles. We can then modify the <ul> tag to the following (remaining things being the same as before):

```
<ul type="square">
```

The resulting output is shown in Fig. 6.31.

Fig. 6.31 *Unordered list with square bullets*

Instead of bullets, we can have the items numbered, by using an ordered list. The code is shown in Fig. 6.32.

```
<html>
  <head>
    <title>Ordered List Example</title>
  </head>
  <body>
    <h1> Here is a List</h1>
    <ol>
      <li>Coffee</li>
      <li>Milk</li>
      <li>Tea</li>
    </ol>
  </body>
</html>
```

Fig. 6.32 *Ordered list example*

Note that we have used the <ol> and </ol> tags, instead of <ul> and </ul>. The resulting output is shown in Fig. 6.33.

Fig. 6.33 *Ordered list output*

Lists can be nested as well. Figure 6.34 shows an example of a nested unordered list.

```
<html>
  <head>
    <title>Unordered List Example</title>
  </head>
  <body>
    <h1> Here is a List</h1>
    <ul>
      <li>Coffee</li>
      <li>Tea
        <ul>
          <li>Black tea</li>
          <li>Green tea</li>
        </ul>
      </li>
      <li>Milk</li>
    </ul>
  </body>
</html>
```

Fig. 6.34

The resulting output is shown in Fig. 6.35.

Fig. 6.35 *Nested unordered list*

6.3.7 Forms Processing

Form is an area containing form elements. A form element allows user to enter information. The various form elements can be text fields, drop-down lists, radio buttons, check boxes, and so on. These form elements need to be enclosed inside the <form> and </form> tags.

The <input> tag is the most commonly used form element. The type of input being accepted is specified with the type attribute. For example, to accept values in a text box, we can specify the following:

```
<form>
<input type="text" ...>
...
</form>
```

Figure 6.36 shows how to create a simple form.

```
<html>
  <head>
    <title>Forms Example</title>
  <head>
  <body>
    <h3>Please fill in the Form below</h3>
    <form>
      First name:
      <input type="text" name="firstname">
      <br>
      Last name:
      <input type="text" name="lastname">
     </form>
  </body>
</html>
```

Fig. 6.36 *HTML form*

The resulting HTML form on the browser screen is shown in Fig. 6.37.

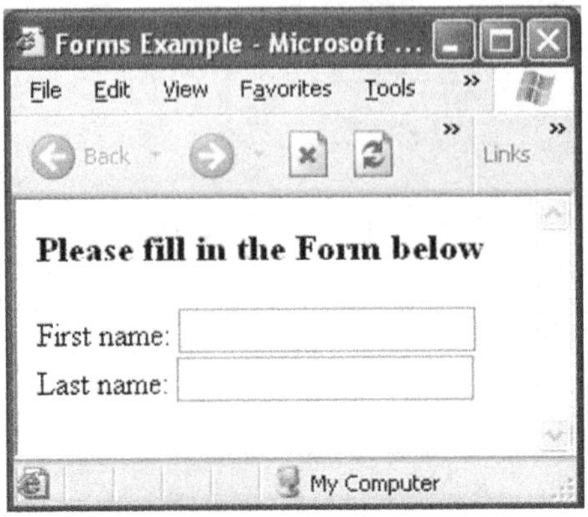

Fig. 6.37 *Form output*

Figure 6.38 shows the various attributes of the input tag that is used to create forms.

Tag/Attribute	*Use*
<input>	Sets an area in a form for user input
Type="..."	Text, Password, Checkbox, Radio, File, Hidden, Image, Submit, Reset
Name="..."	Processes form results
Value="..."	Provide default values
Size="*n*"	Sets visible size for text inputs
Maxlength="*n*"	Maximum input size for text fields
Selected	Default selection when form is initially displayed or reloaded

Fig. 6.38 *Form attributes*

In our earlier example, we saw that *<input type="text">* created a text box. Similarly, we can create radio buttons by changing the type to radio, as shown in Fig. 6.39.

```
<html>
  <head>
    <title>Forms Example</title>
  <head>
  <body>
    <h3>Please fill in the Form below</h3>
    <form>
      <input type="radio" name="fruit" value="apple"> Apple
      <br>
      <input type="radio" name="fruit" value="orange"> Orange
      <br>
      <input type="radio" name="fruit" value="grapes"> Grapes
     </form>
  </body>
</html>
```

Fig. 6.39 *Creating radio buttons*

Let us understand what we are doing here in the *input* tag.

```
<input type="radio" name="fruit" value="apple"> Apple
```

This means that we want a radio button, which would be known programmatically as *fruit*. We shall later study how to make use of these variable names. The internal value of this variable is *apple*. In other words, whenever we want to check whether the user has selected this radio button, we will compare it with this value. Finally, the on-screen display for this button would be *Apple* (which is what we see on the screen).

The resulting output is shown in Fig. 6.40.

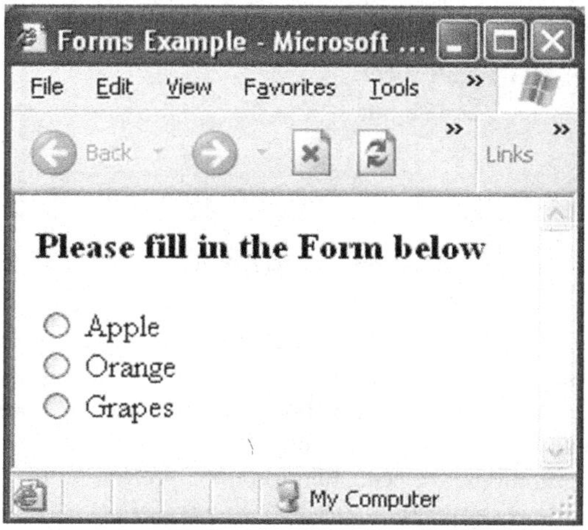

Fig. 6.40 *Radio buttons output*

We can create checkboxes. An example is shown in Fig. 6.41.

```
<html>
  <head>
    <title>Forms Example</title>
  <head>
  <body>
    <h3>Please fill in the Form below</h3>
    <form>
      <input type="checkbox" name="bike">
      I have a bike
      <br>
      <input type="checkbox" name="car">
      I have a car
      <br>
      <input type="checkbox" name="bus">
      I have a bus
     </form>
  </body>
</html>
```

Fig. 6.41 *Using checkboxes*

The resulting output is shown in Fig. 6.42.

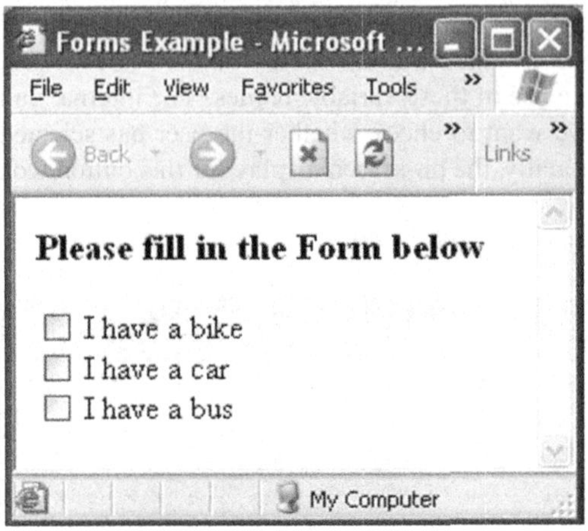

Fig. 6.42 *Checkbox output*

Whenever we key in any input (either using text boxes or by way of radio buttons, check boxes, etc.), we ideally want to also click a button to initiate an action. For example, we may want to submit all this information to a program, which would validate all information, store it somewhere, and do the necessary processing. For example, we may use a form to select books of interest, make a payment using credit card, etc. In all such situations, we need a button to be present on the screen. For this purpose, a button is needed. Sample code is shown in Fig. 6.43.

```
<html>
  <head>
    <title>Forms Example</title>
  <head>
  <body>
    <h3>Please fill in the Form below</h3>
    <form name="input" action="html_form_action" method="get">
     User name: <input type="text" name="user"> <br><br>
                <input type="submit" value="Submit">
    </form>
  </body>
</html>
```

Fig. 6.43 *Adding a button*

Here, we are saying that we want to accept the user's name on this screen. Once the user enters her name, we want to send this name to a program called *html_form_action*. What and how this program will process is a separate topic, which we shall deal with separately. For now, we need not bother about it. We can see that *<input type="submit">* enables the creation of a button.

The resulting output is shown in Fig. 6.44.

Fig. 6.44 *Output with a button*

Figure 6.45 shows an example of creating a drop down list.

```
<html>
  <head>
    <title>Forms Example</title>
  <head>
  <body>
  <form>
    <select name=”cars”>
      <option value=”volvo”>Volvo
      <option value=”saab”>Saab
      <option value=”fiat”>Fiat
      <option value=”audi”>Audi
    </select>
   </form>
  </body>
</html>
```

Fig. 6.45 *Drop down list*

The resulting output is shown in Fig. 6.46.

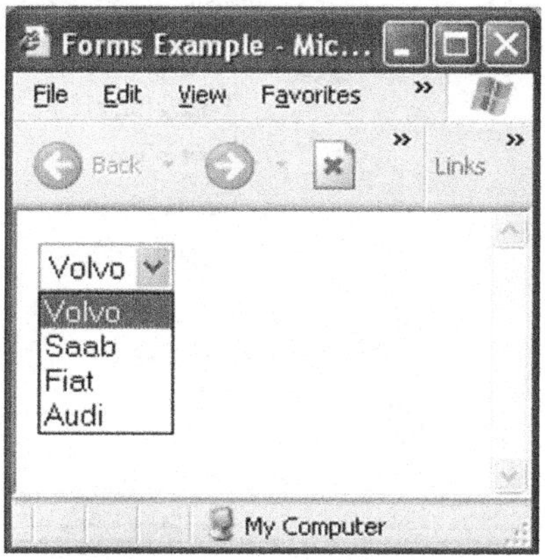

Fig. 6.46 *Drop down list output*

Combining several of the above features, we create a more meaningful form, the code for which is in Fig. 6.47.

```
<html>
  <head>
     <title>Forms Example</title>
  <head>
  <body>
   <form>
      <input type="text" name="firstname" size="40" maxlength="50">First Name<br>
      <input type="text" name="lastname" size="40" maxlength="50">Last Name<br>
      <input type="text" name="email" size="40" maxlength="50">Email Address<br>
      <input type="text" name="address" size="40" maxlength="50">Postal Address<br>
      <input type="text" name="city" size="20" maxlength="40">City
      <select name="state">
         <option value="ap">AP
         <option value="bi">Bi
         <option value="ma">MH
         <option value="mp">MP
         <option value="mp">TN
      </select>
      State
      <input type="text" name="pin" size="10" maxlength="15">Pin code<br>
      <input type="text" name="country" size="40" maxlength="50">Country<br>
    </form>
  </body>
</html>
```

Fig. 6.47 *Full form*

The resulting output is shown in Fig. 6.48.

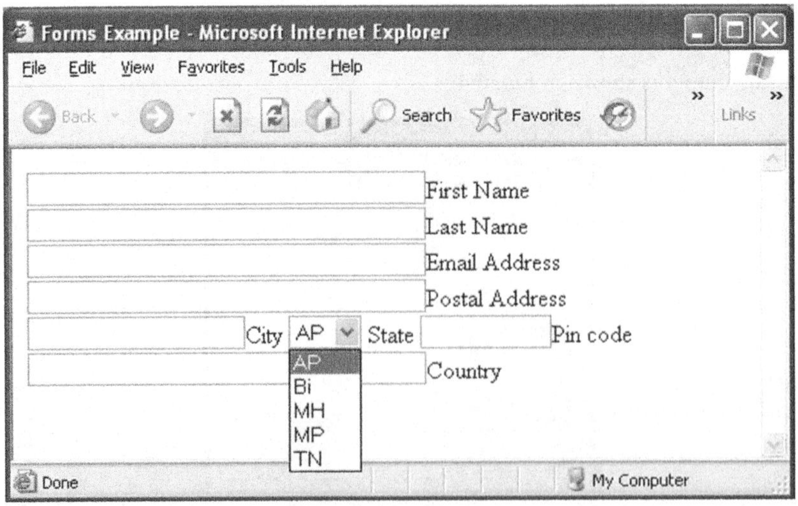

Fig. 6.48 *Full form output*

6.3.8 Images

We can also insert images inside an HTML page by using the *img* tag, as shown in Fig. 6.49.

```
<html>
  <head><title>Image Example</title></head>
  <body background="mickey.bmp">
    <h3>Look: A background image!</h3>
    <p>Both gif and jpg files can be used as HTML backgrounds.</p>
    <p>If the image is smaller than the page, the image will repeat itself.</p>
  </body>
</html>
```

Fig. 6.49 *Image example*

The image is supposed to be stored in a file called *background.jpg*. The result is shown in Fig. 6.50.

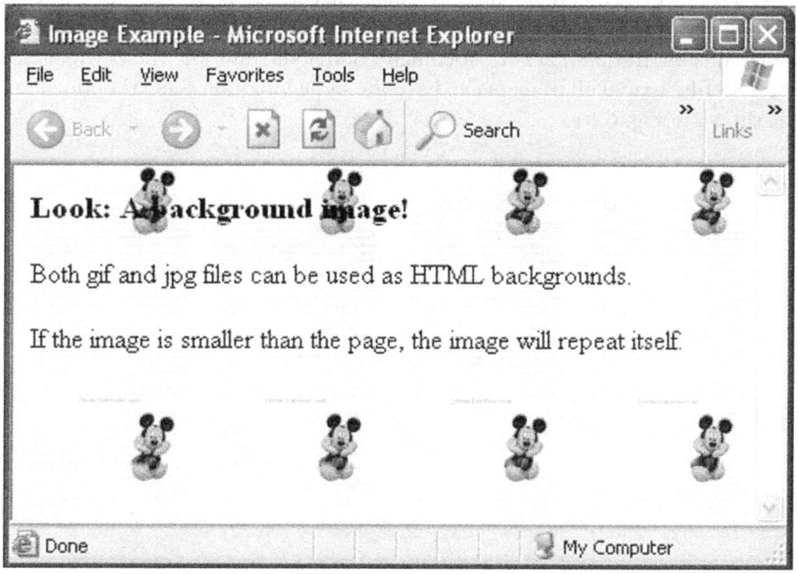

Fig. 6.50 *Image output*

6.3.9 Style Sheets

The whole purpose for defining HTML tags originally was to specify the content of a document. For example, they were supposed to inform the browser that *This is a header*, *This text should be displayed in bold*, or *This is a table*, by using tags such as <h2>, <b>, or <table>, and so on. However, implementing them, i.e., utilizing the appropriate layout was supposed to be taken care of by the browser. That is, when we say "h2", what should be the font size, and font family? This was left to the individual Web browsers to decide.

The two major Web browsers of those times, namely Netscape Navigator and Internet Explorer, did not always follow the HTML specifications as defined by the standards body. Instead, they went on adding new HTML tags and attributes (e.g., the <font> tag and the color attribute) to the original HTML specifications. As a result, two problems arose:

1. Applications were no longer browser-independent. Something that worked on Netscape Navigator was not guaranteed to work on Internet Explorer, and vice versa. This was because these browsers were also adding proprietary tags to their implementation of the HTML specifications.
2. It became increasingly more difficult to create Websites where the content of HTML document and its presentation layout were very cleanly separated.

In order to resolve this problem and come up with a general solution, the World Wide Web Consortium (W3C) - the non-profit, standard setting consortium responsible for standardizing HTML - created **styles** in addition to HTML 4.0. Styles, as the name suggests, define how HTML elements should be displayed, very similar to the way the font tag and the color attribute in HTML 3.2 work. Styles control the output (i.e., display) of the HTML tags, and remove ambiguity. They also help reduce the clutter from HTML pages (we shall see an example of this to understand its meaning clearly).

Technically, style sheets are implemented by using what are called **Cascading Style Sheets (CSS)**. The idea is simple. We keep all styling details separate (e.g., in an external file with a CSS extension), and we can refer to this file from our HTML document. Better yet, multiple HTML documents can make use of the same CSS file, so that all of them can have the same look-and-feel, as defined in the CSS file. This concept is shown in Fig. 6.51.

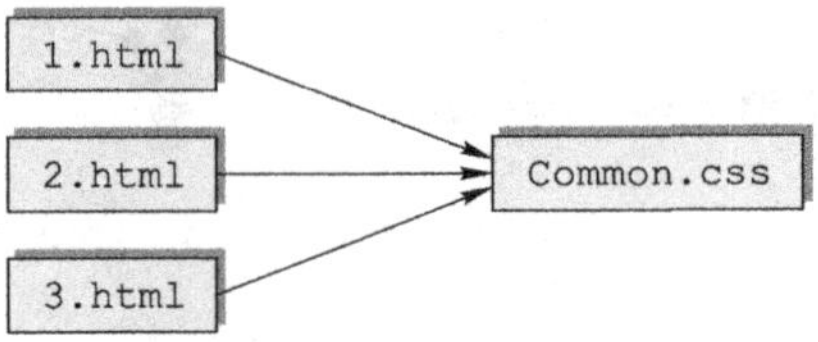

Fig. 6.51 *Style sheet concept*

How does this work? Let us understand with an example, as shown in Fig. 6.52.

one.html

```
<html>
  <head>
    <link rel="stylesheet" type="text/css" href="one.css">
  </head>
  <body>
    <h1>This HTML page uses CSS</h1>
    <h2>This is a new header</h2>
    <p>See the effects of CSS here </p>
  </body>
</html>
```

one.css

```
body {color: black}
h2 {text-align:center; color:blue; font-family: "verdana"}
p {font-family: "sans serif"; color:red}
```

Fig. 6.52 *Style sheet example*

Let us understand how this works. The HTML page has the following line inside its *<head>* tag:

```
<link rel="stylesheet" type="text/css" href="one.css">
```

It means that the HTML page wants to link with a separate file, named *one.css*. In other words, the HTML page would be handed over to the CSS file for applying styles. Let us see now how this actually happens. For this purpose, let us go through our CSS file:

```
body {color: black}
h2 {text-align:center; color:blue; font-family: "verdana"}
p {font-family: "sans serif";color:red}
```

Figure 6.53 explains each line of the CSS code.

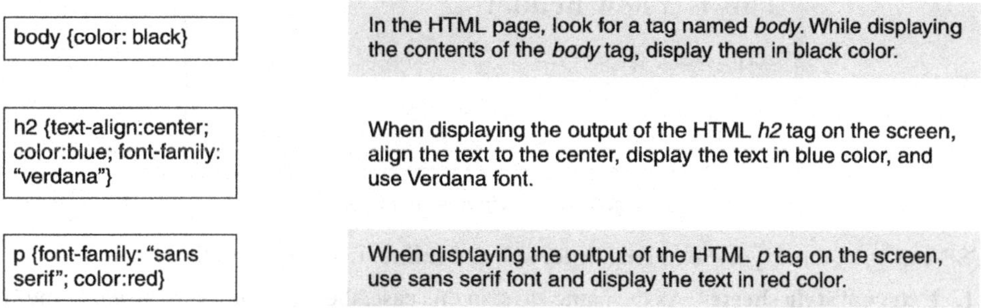

Fig. 6.53 *Understanding CSS code*

As we can see, the CSS file instructs the browser as to how to display the output of an HTML page with very precise formatting details. The resulting page is shown in Fig. 6.54.

Fig. 6.54 *CSS output*

The same HTML page, without using the CSS, would look as shown in Fig. 6.55. We would not notice the differences in color in the black-and-white print of this book, but at least the differences in alignment and font of the *h2* header should be clear.

Fig. 6.55 *Output without CSS*

CSS can be of three types: **external**, **internal**, and **inline**. Let us discuss these now.

1. **External style sheets** As the name says, in this case, the style sheet is *external* to the HTML document. In other words, the HTML document and the CSS file are separate. This type of CSS is ideal when the same style is applied to many HTML pages. With the help of an external style sheet, we can change the look of an entire Website by changing just one file! This is because all HTML files can potentially link to the same CSS file! Of course, in real practice, this is not how it is done. Instead, many CSS files are created, and HTML pages link with them on needs basis. In general, an HTML page must link to the style sheet using the <link> tag. The <link> tag goes inside the head section. We have seen an example of this earlier, and hence we will not repeat the discussion here.
2. **Internal style sheets** These style sheets should be used when a single document has a unique style. We define internal styles in the *head* section of the HTML document with the <style> tag. Figure 6.56 shows an example.

```
<html>
  <head>
     <title>CSS Example</title>
        <style type="text/css">
          body {background-color: lightblue}
          h1 {font-family:tahoma}
          p {margin-left: 50px; font-family:comic sans ms}
        </style>
  </head>
  <body>
     <h1>This is an Internal Style Sheet</h1>
     <p>Hello World</p>
  </body>
</html>
```

Fig. 6.56 *Internal style sheet*

Let us understand what we are doing here. Inside the *head* section, we do not specify a link to an external CSS file now. Instead, we have a *style* tag, which defines all the styles that we want to define for the current HTML page. As a result of which, both the HTML document and the CSS tags are in the same physical document (hence the name *internal*). For example, the background color of the HTML body has been defined to consist of light blue color. Similarly, other styles define how the header h1 should be displayed, how paragraphs are to be displayed, etc.

The resulting output is shown in Fig. 6.57.

Fig. 6.57 *Internal style sheet output*

3. **Inline style sheets** The inline style sheets should be used when a unique style is to be applied to a single occurrence of an element. To use inline styles, we can use the style attribute in the relevant tag. The style attribute can contain any CSS property. Here, we do not define styles in the *<head>* section, but define them at the place where they are actually used in the HTML body. An example of inline style sheets is shown in Fig. 6.58.

```
<html>
  <head>
    <title>CSS Example</title>
  </head>
  <body>
    <h1 style="margin-left: 50px; text-decoration: underline; font-family:
        times">This is an Internal Style sheet</h1>
    <p>This is a paragraph</p>
   <p style="color: red; margin-left: 30px; font-weight: bold; font-family: courier">
       This is another paragraph
    </p>
  </body>
</html>
```

Fig. 6.58 *Inline style sheet*

As we can see, we have defined styles inline, i.e., at the same place where the HTML tags are defined. Also, we have defined styles for one *h1* and one *p* tags. On the other hand, we have not defined any styles for the remaining *p* tag. This is perfectly ok. We can define styles only wherever we want to use them.

We can also combine some of the style sheet types. In other words, the same HTML document can have both inline and internal style sheets, or just one of them, and an external style sheet as well. The same tag can have references in multiple types of style sheets as well. That is, let us say that the external style sheet says that the heading <h1> should be displayed in font with size 12 and type Times New Roman. On the other hand, suppose that there is an internal style declaration for the same <h1> tag, with different display characteristics (say with font size 10 and font type as Tahoma). In any such cases, the order of preference is always Inline -> Internal -> External. In other words, if the same HTML tag has references from multiple types of style sheets, inline takes the highest preference, followed by internal, and followed by external. This is depicted in Fig. 6.59.

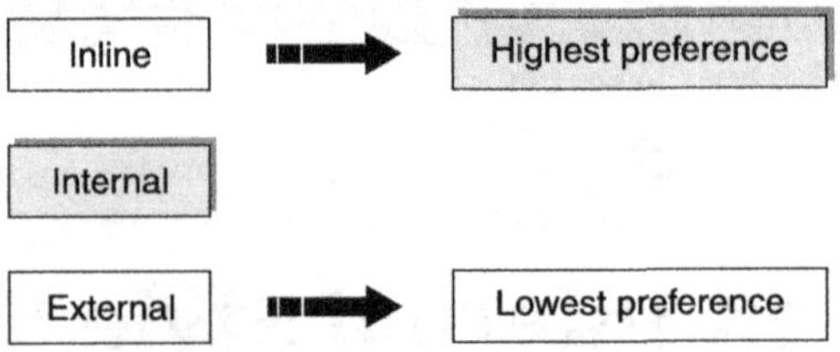

Fig. 6.59 *Style sheet priorities*

Here is an example. We have used all the three types of style sheets (inline, internal, and external). See how the inline style sheet overrides the internal style sheet, which in turn, overrides the external one, a shown in Fig. 6.60.

```
<html>
  <head>
    <title>CSS Example</title>
    <!-- Internal style sheet -->
    <style type = "text/css">
        p {font-family: "Tahoma";color: blue; font-size = 50}
    </style>
    <!—External style sheet reference -->
    <link rel="stylesheet" type="text/css" href="one.css">
  <body>
   <!-- Inline style sheet -->
     <h1 style="margin-left: 50px; text-decoration: underline; font-family:
         times">This is an Internal Style Sheet</h1>
   <p>This is a paragraph</p>
   <!-- Inline style sheet -->
   <p style="color: blue; margin-left: 20px; font-weight: bold; font-family: courier">
       This is another paragraph
     </p>
  </body>
</html>
```

Fig. 6.60 *Multiple types of style sheet used in a single HTML page*

As we can see, there is an internal style sheet defined in the <head> section of the HTML page using the *style* tag. We also have a reference to an external style sheet with the help of the *link* tag. On top of this, we also have an inline style defined inside the *p* tag in the body of the HTML page.

Let us now take a look at the external style sheet, as shown in Fig. 6.61.

```
body {color: green}
h2 {text-align:center;color:blue;font-family: "verdana"}
p {font-family: "sans serif";color: brown; font-size: 100}
```

Fig. 6.61 *External style sheet*

The resulting output is shown in Fig. 6.62. See how the principle of inline -> internal -> external style sheet holds good.

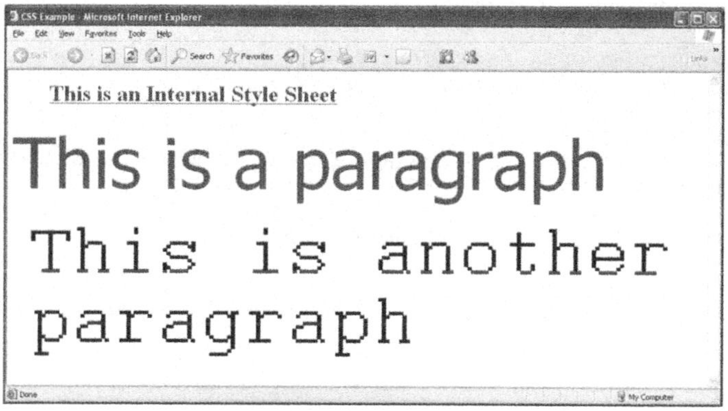

Fig. 6.62 *Style sheet output*

COMMON GATEWAY INTERFACE (CGI)... 6.4

6.4.1 CGI Introduction

Common Gateway Interface (CGI) is the oldest dynamic Web technology. It is still in use, but is getting replaced by other technologies such as Microsoft's ASP.NET and Sun's Servlets and JSP. Many people think that **CGI** is a language. But it is not actually the case. Instead, we should remember that CGI is a specification for communication between a Web browser and a Web server using the HTTP protocol. A CGI program (also called a *CGI script*) can be written in any language that can read values from a standard input device (usually the keyboard), write to a standard output device (usually the screen), and read environment variables. Most well-known programming languages such as C, PERL, and even simple UNIX shell scripting provide these features, and therefore, they can be used to write CGI scripts.

CGI scripts execute on a Web server, similar to ASP.NET and JSP/Servlets. Hence, CGI is also a server-side dynamic Web page technology.

The typical manner in which a CGI script executes is shown in Fig. 6.63.

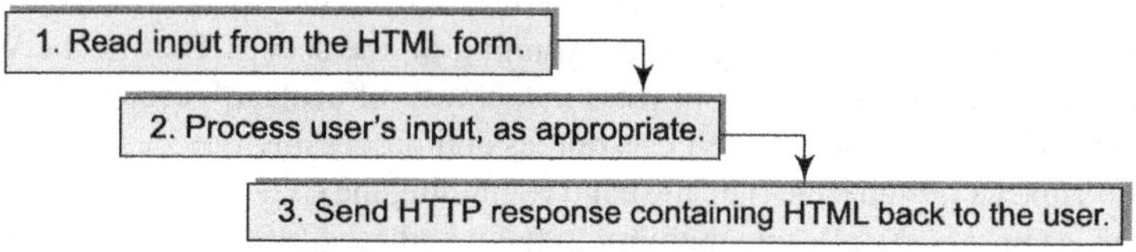

Fig. 6.63 *Typical steps in CGI script execution*

Let us take a look at these steps now.

6.4.2 Read Input From the HTML Form

We know that the HTML form is an area where the user can enter the requested information. The form has various controls, such as text boxes, text areas, checkboxes, radio buttons, dropdown lists, and so on; which capture the user inputs. When the user submits the form, these user inputs are sent to the Web server, as a part of the browser's HTTP request.

As we have seen earlier, we can read the user inputs in ASP.NET or JSP/Servlets with the help of the *request* object. In CGI, the syntax for doing the same thing is a bit more complex. Figure 6.64 shows a sample PERL script for reading user input.

```
if (($ENV{'REQUEST_METHOD'} eq 'GET') ||
    ($ENV{'REQUEST_METHOD'} eq 'HEAD') ) {
        $in= $ENV{'QUERY_STRING'} ;
    } elsif ($ENV{'REQUEST_METHOD'} eq 'POST') {
        if ($ENV{'CONTENT_TYPE'}=~ m#^application/x-www-form-urlencoded$#i) {
            length($ENV{'CONTENT_LENGTH'})
                || &HTMLdie("No Content-Length sent with the POST request.");
            read(STDIN, $in, $ENV{'CONTENT_LENGTH'});
        }
                else {
&HTMLdie("Unsupported Content-Type: $ENV{'CONTENT_TYPE'}");
                      }
} else {
        &HTMLdie("Script was called with unsupported REQUEST_METHOD.");
}
```

Fig. 6.64 *CGI script to read form variables in PERL*

The script first attempts to see whether the user's request was received in the form of a GET or HEAD method. Accordingly, it read the contents of the *query string* (i.e., the area of memory where the user's form data is kept for the server to access and process it). If the user's request was POST, it performs some necessary conversions and then reads the content. Otherwise, it displays an error message.

6.4.3 Send HTTP Response Containing HTML Back to the User

This process is even simpler. Here, we first need to write the following statement:

Content-type: text/html

Then we need to send one blank line to the standard output. After this, we can write our HTML contents page to the standard output. Once the end of the contents is reached, the HTML content would automatically be sent to the browser, as a part of the server's HTTP response.

The example in Fig. 6.65 is reproduced from http://www.jmarshall.com/easy/cgi/.

6.4.4 CGI Problems

However, there is one problem with CGI, which is that for each client requesting a CGI Web page, a new process has to be created by the operating system running on the server. That is, the Web server must request the operating system to start a new process in memory, allocate all resources such as stack for it and schedule it, etc. This takes a lot of server resources and processing time, especially when multiple clients request the same CGI Web page (i.e., the page containing the CGI program). The operating system has to queue all these processes, allocate memory to them and schedule them. This is a large overhead.

This is shown in Fig. 6.66. Here, three different clients are shown to request for the same CGI Web page (named *CGI-1*). However, the Web server sends a request to create a different process for each of them to the operating system.

```
#!/usr/local/bin/perl
#
#   hello.pl-- standard "hello, world" program to demonstrate basic
#       CGI programming, and the use of the &getcgivars() routine.
#
# First, get the CGI variables into a list of strings
%cgivars= &getcgivars ;
# Print the CGI response header, required for all HTML output
# Note the extra \n, to send the blank line
print "Content-type: text/html\n\n" ;
# Finally, print out the complete HTML response page
print <<EOF ;
<html>
<head><title>CGI Results</title></head>
<body>
<h1>Hello, world.</h1>
Your CGI input variables were:
<ul>
EOF
# Print the CGI variables sent by the user.
# Note that the order of variables is unpredictable.
# Also note this simple example assumes all input fields had unique names,
#   though the &getcgivars() routine correctly handles similarly named
#   fields-- it delimits the multiple values with the \0 character, within
#   $cgivars{$_}.
foreach (keys %cgivars) {
    print "<li>[$_] = [$cgivars{$_}]\n" ;
}
# Print close of HTML file
print <<EOF ;
</ul>
</body>
</html>
EOF
exit ;
```

Fig. 6.65 *CGI sample program to send output back to the user*

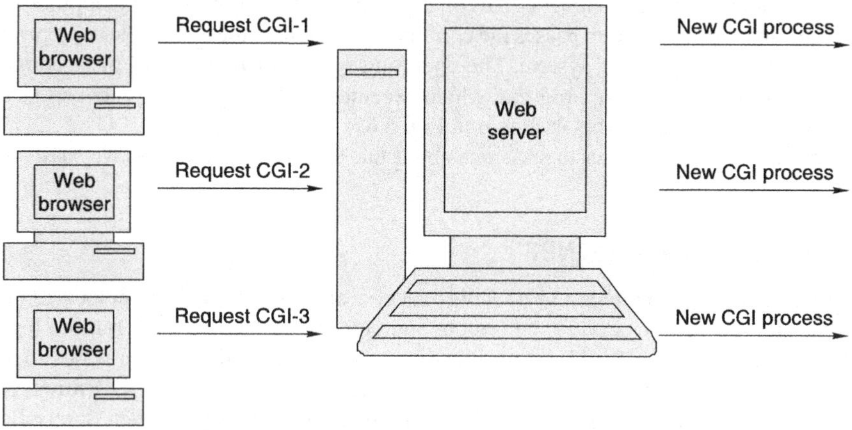

Fig. 6.66 *Each CGI request results into a new process creation*

REMOTE LOGIN (TELNET) 6.5

6.5.1 Introduction

The **TELNET** protocol allows remote login services, so that a user on a client computer can connect to a server on a remote system. TELNET has two parts: a client and a server. The client portion of TELNET software resides on an end user's machine, and the server portion resides on a remote server machine. That is, the remote server is the TELNET server, which provides an interactive terminal session to execute commands on the remote host. Once a user using the services of a TELNET client connects to the remote TELNET server computer, the keystrokes typed by the user on the client are sent to the remote server to be interpreted/acted upon to give an impression as if the user is using the server computer directly.

The TELNET protocol emerged in the days of timesharing operating systems such as Unix. In a timesharing environment, a common server computer serves the requests of multiple users in turns. Although many users use the server at the same time, the speed is normally so fast that every user gets an illusion that he is the only user, using that server computer. The interaction between a user and the server computer happens through a *dumb* terminal. Such a dumb terminal also has to have a microprocessor inside. Thus, it can be considered to be a very primitive computer that simply has a keyboard, mouse and a screen and almost no processing power. In such an environment, all the processing is essentially done by the central server computer. When a user enters a command using the keyboard, for example, the command travels all the way to the server computer, which executes it and sends the results back to the user's terminal. At the same time, another user might have entered another command. This command also travels to the server, which processes it and sends the results back to that user's terminal. Neither user is concerned with the fact that the server is processing the requests from another user as well. Both users feel that they have exclusive access to the server resources.

Thus, timesharing creates an environment in which every user has an illusion of using a dedicated computer. The user can execute a program, access the system's resources, switch between two or more programs, and so on. How is this possible?

6.5.2 Local Login

In timesharing systems, all users log into the central server computer and use its resources. This is called **local login**. A user's terminal sends the commands entered by the user to a program called **terminal driver**, which is running on the central server computer. It is a part of the server computer's operating system. The terminal driver program passes the commands entered by the user to the appropriate module of the server computer's operating system. The operating system then processes these commands and invokes the appropriate application program, which executes on the server computer and its results are sent back to the user's terminal. This is shown in Fig. 6.67.

This forms the basis for further discussions about the TELNET protocol, as we shall study in the next section.

6.5.3 Remote Login and TELNET

In contrast to local login, sometimes a user wants to access an application program located on a remote computer. For this, the user logs on to the remote computer in a process called **remote login**. A user specifies the domain name or IP address to select a remote server with which it wants to establish a TELNET session. This is where TELNET comes into picture. TELNET stands for **TERminal NETwork**. This is shown in Fig. 6.68. The step numbers shown in the figure followed by their descriptions depict how TELNET works, in detail.

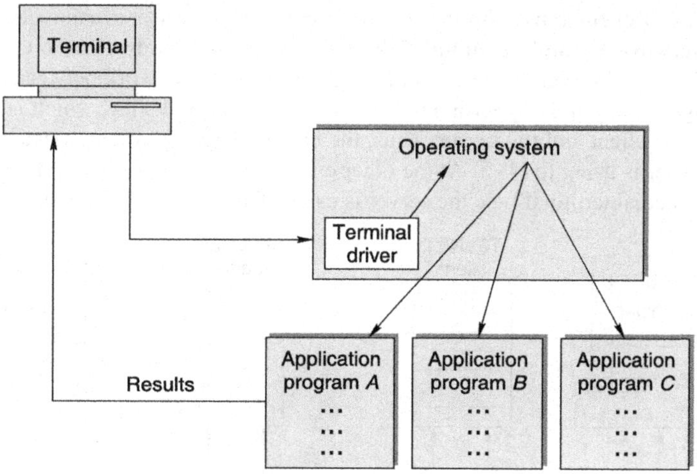

Fig. 6.67 Local login

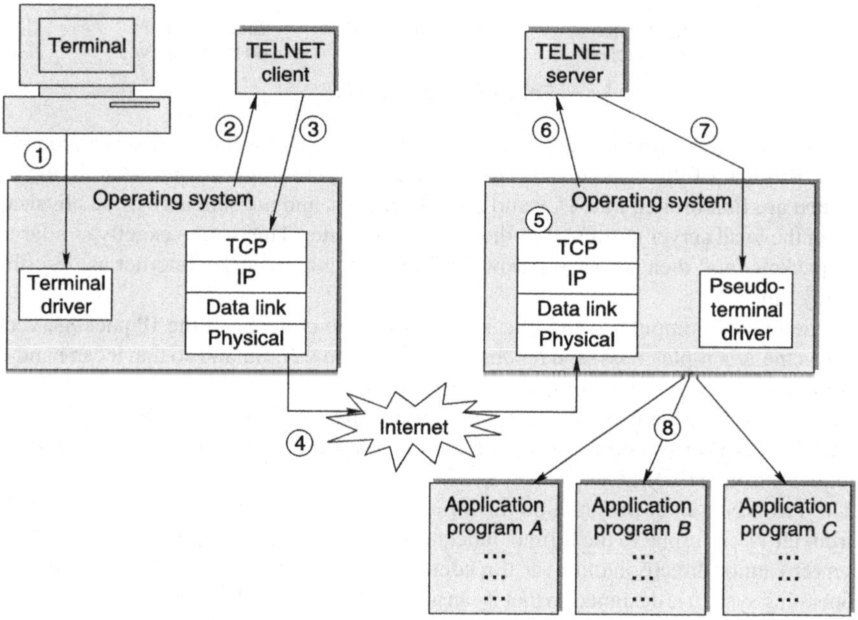

Fig. 6.68 Remote login using TELNET

1. As usual, the commands and characters typed by the user are sent to the operating system on the common server computer. However, unlike a local login set up, the operating system now does not interpret the commands and characters entered by the user.
2. Instead, the local operating system sends these commands and characters to a **TELNET client** program, which is located on the same server computer.

3. The TELNET client transforms the characters entered by the user to a universally agreed format called **Network Virtual Terminal (NVT)** characters and sends them to the TCP/IP protocol stack of the local server computer. TELNET was designed to work between any host (i.e., any operating system) and any terminal. NVT is an imaginary device, which is the commonality between the client and the server. Thus, the client operating system maps whatever terminal type the user is using to NVT. At the other end, the server operating system maps NVT on to whatever actual terminal type the server is using. This concept is illustrated in Fig. 6.69.

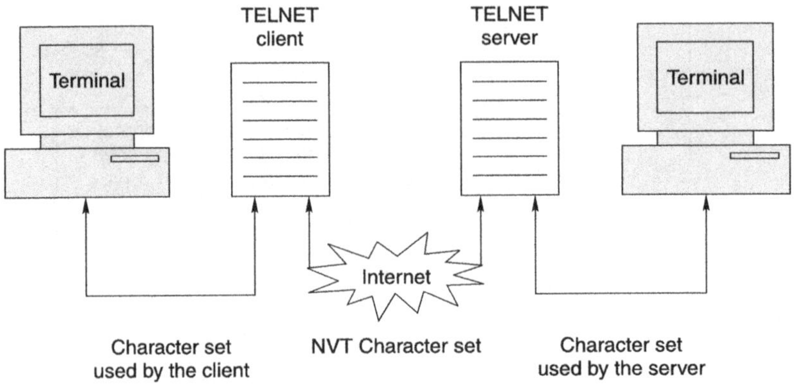

Fig. 6.69 *Concept of NVT*

4. The commands or text in the NVT format then travel from the local server computer to the TCP/IP stack of the remote computer via the Internet infrastructure. That is, the commands or text are first broken into TCP and then IP packets, and are sent across the physical medium from the local server computer to the remote computer. This works exactly similar to the way IP packets (and then physical hardware frames) travel over the Internet as described earlier many times.
5. At the remote computer's end, the TCP/IP software collects all the IP packets, verifies their correctness/completeness, and reconstructs the original command so that it can hand over these commands or text to that computer's operating system.
6. The operating system of the remote computer hands over these commands or text to the **TELNET server** program, which is executing on that remote computer, passively waiting for requests from TELNET clients.
7. The TELNET server program on the remote computer then transforms the commands or text from the NVT format to the format understood by the remote computer. However, the TELNET server cannot directly hand over the commands or text to the operating system, because the operating system is designed so that it can accept characters only from a terminal driver: not from a TELNET server. To solve this problem, a software program called **pseudo-terminal driver** is added, which pretends that the characters are coming from a terminal and not from a TELNET server. The TELNET server hands over the commands or text to this pseudo-terminal driver.
8. The pseudo-terminal driver program than hands over the commands or text to the operating system of the remote computer, which then invokes the appropriate application program on the remote server.

The client using the terminal on the other side, can, thus, access this remote computer as if it is a local server computer!

6.5.4 TELNET: A Technical Perspective

Technically, the TELNET server is actually quite complicated. It has to handle requests from many clients at the same time. These concurrent requests must be responded to in real time, as the users perceive TELNET as a real-time application. To handle this issue effectively, the TELNET server uses the principle of delegation. Whenever there is a new client request for a TELNET connection, the TELNET server creates a new child process and lets that child process handle that client's TELNET connection. When the client wants to close down the TELNET connection, the child process terminates itself. Thus, if there are 10 clients utilizing TELNET services at the same time, there would be 10 child processes running, each servicing one client. There would, of course, be the main TELNET server process executing to coordinate the creation and handling of child processes.

TELNET uses only one TCP connection (unlike FTP, which uses two). The server waits for TELNET client connection requests (made using TCP) at a well-known port 23. The client opens a TELNET connection (made using TCP) from its side whenever the user requests for one. The same TCP connection is used to transfer data and control characters. The control characters are embedded inside data characters. How does TELNET then distinguish a control character from a data character? For this, it mandates that each sequence of control characters must be preceded by a special control character called **Interpret As Control** (IAC).

6.5.5 TELNET as an Alternative to a Web browser

Interestingly, TELNET software can be used as a poor alternative to a Web browser. As we have seen, a Web browser is essentially a software program that runs on the computer of an Internet user. It can be used to request an HTML page from a Web server and then interpret the HTML page and display its contents on the user's screen. Supposing that a user, for some reason, does not have a Web browser, but knows how to enter TELNET commands, and has some software that can interpret HTML pages.

In such a case, the user can actually type TELNET commands that mimic the function of a Web browser, by requesting Web pages from a Web server. This happens as if the request is sent from a Web browser. Of course, in such a case, the user must be knowledgeable and should know how the Web works. However, the point is not that – it actually is that TELNET can actually be used to send HTTP commands to a Web server.

Key Terms and Concepts

Anchor tag • Crawler • DELETE • GET • HEAD • Home page • Hyper link • Hyper Text Markup Language (HTML) • Hyper Text Transfer Protocol (HTTP) • HTTP request • HTTP response • IMG • Knowbot • Link • LINK • Local login • Mailto • Network Virtual Terminal (NVT) • Plug-in • Portal • POST • Process • Proxy server • Pseudo-terminal driver • PUT • Remote login • Search engine • Stateless protocol • Tag • TELNET • TELNET client • TELNET server • Terminal client • Terminal driver • Uniform Resource Locator (URL) • UNLINK • Web browser • Web page • Web server • Website • World Wide Web (WWW) • Worm

SUMMARY

- The World Wide Web (WWW) is the second most popular application on the Internet, after email. It also works on the basis of client-server architecture, and uses a request-response paradigm.
- An organization hosts a Website, consisting of Web pages. Anybody armed with a Web browser and wanting to access these Web pages can do so.
- Each Website has a unique identifier, called Uniform Resource Locator (URL), which is essentially an address of home page of the Website.
- The WWW application uses the Hyper Text Transfer Protocol (HTTP) to request for and serve Web pages.
- A Web server is a program running on a server computer. Additionally, it consists of the Website containing a number of Web pages.
- The contents of a Web page are written using a special tag language, called Hyper Text Markup Language (HTML).
- There are various HTTP commands to request, upload, and delete Web pages that a browser can use.
- HTTP is a stateless protocol. This means that the TCP connection between a client and a server is established and broken for every Web page request.
- The Hyper Text Markup Language (HTML) is used for creating Web pages. HTML is a presentation language that uses tags to demark different text formats such as boldface, italics, underline, paragraphs, headings, colors, etc.
- The TELNET protocol allows remote login services, so that a user on a client computer can connect to a server on a remote system.
- In TELNET, the user's commands are not processed by the local operating system. Instead, they are directed to a remote server to which the user is connected.

MULTIPLE-CHOICE QUESTIONS

1. The main page of a Website is generally called the ________.
   (a) chief page (b) main page (c) home page (d) house page
2. The world's first real Web browser was ________.
   (a) Mosaic (b) Internet Explorer
   (c) Netscape Navigator (d) None of these
3. Web pages are created in the ________ language.
   (a) HTTP (b) WWW (c) Java (d) HTML
4. The portion after the words WWW identify a ________.
   (a) client (b) Web server (c) database server (d) application server
5. GET and PUT commands are used to ________ a HTML document.
   (a) download (b) upload (c) delete (d) modify
6. HTTP is called a ________ protocol.
   (a) stateful (b) stateless
   (c) state-aware (d) connection-oriented
7. The ________ command allows a client to remove a file from a Web server using HTTP.
   (a) GET (b) POST (c) UNLINK (d) DELETE

8. Proxy server is used to transform ________ protocol to ________ format.
(a) TCP/IP, OSI (b) OSI, TCP/IP
(c) non-HTTP, HTTP (d) TCP/IP, HTTP

9. Generally, the closing HTML tag is indicated by the ________ character.
(a) * (b) / (c) \ (d) @

10. The ________ tag can be used to create hyper links.
(a) anchor (b) arrow (c) link (d) pointer

DETAILED QUESTIONS

1. Define the terms Website, Web page, Web server, URL and home page.
2. What is the purpose of HTTP?
3. How does a Web browser work?
4. Describe the steps involved when a Web browser requests for and obtains a Web page from a Web server.
5. Why is HTTP called a stateless protocol? Why is it so?
6. Discuss any three HTTP commands.
7. What is the purpose of a proxy server?
8. Why is the job of search engines not easy?
9. Discuss the idea of HTML tags with an example.
10. Describe any three HTML tags.

EXERCISES

1. Discuss the differences between GET and POST commands. (*Hint: Use technical books on Web technologies such as ASP.NET, servlets and JSP - which we shall study later*).
2. Investigate how you can set up your own Website. What are the requirements for the same?
3. Create a Web page that displays your own details in about 100 words, and also includes your photograph. Use different fonts, colors and character-spacing tricks to see the change in the output.
4. Try to find out the major differences between the two major Web browsers – Internet Explorer and Netscape Navigator.
5. Try connecting to a remote server using TELNET. What are your observations in terms of look and feel, communication speed and features available?

7 JAVASCRIPT AND AJAX

INTRODUCTION

HTML Web pages are static. They do not react to events. Also, they do not produce different outputs when different users ask for them; or even when the same user asks for them, but under different conditions. Therefore, there is a lot of predictability about HTML pages. Moreover, the output is always the same. This means that there is no programming involved at all. Therefore, attempts were made to add interactivity to HTML pages. This was done both at the client (Web browser) side, as well as the server (Web server) side. Thus, we have both client-side as well as server-side programming on the Internet. The server-side programming techniques will be discussed at length later. This chapter looks at the client-side programming techniques. Several have come and gone, but the one that has stayed on is the **JavaScript** language. JavaScript is a *quick and dirty* programming language, which can be used on the client (Web browser) for performing a number of tasks, such as validating input, doing local calculations, etc.

In addition to JavaScript, the technology of **AJAX** has gained prominence in the last few years. We shall also discuss AJAX in detail.

JAVASCRIPT 7.1

7.1.1 Basic Concepts

We know that HTML pages are static. In other words, there is no interactivity in the case of plain HTML pages. To add interactivity to HTML inside the browser itself, the technology of JavaScript was developed. JavaScript involves programming. We can write small programs that execute inside the HTML page, based on certain events or just like that. These programs are written in JavaScript. Earlier, there were a few other scripting languages such as VBScript and JScript. However, these technologies are obsolete now, and JavaScript is the only one that has survived.

JavaScript is an interpreted language. It can be directly embedded inside HTML pages, or it can be kept in a separate file (with extension *.js*) and included in the HTML page. It is supported by all the major browsers, such as Internet Explorer, Firefox, and Netscape Navigator. We need to remember that Java and JavaScript do not have anything in common, except for the naming. It was *cool* to call everything *Java something* when these technologies were coming up for the first time. Hence, we have the name JavaScript.

JavaScript has several features:

1. **Programming tool** JavaScript is a scripting language with a very simple syntax.
2. **Can produce dynamic text into an HTML page** For example, the JavaScript statement *document.write ("<h1>" + name + "</h1>");* results into the HTML output *<h1>Atul</h1>*, if the variable *name* contains the text *Atul*.
3. **Reacting to events** JavaScript code executes when something happens, like when a page has finished loading or when a user clicks on an HTML element.
4. **Read and write HTML elements** JavaScript can read and change the content of an HTML element.
5. **Validate data** JavaScript can be used to validate form data before it is submitted to a server. This saves the server from extra processing.

The first JavaScript is shown in Fig. 7.1.

```
<html>
  <body>
     <script type="text/javascript">
       document.write ("Hello World!");
     </script>
  </body>
</html>
```

Fig. 7.1 *JavaScript example*

7.1.2 Controlling JavaScript Execution

As we can see JavaScript is a part of the basic HTML page. It is contained inside the *<script>… </script>* tags. Here, *document* is the name of an object, and *write* is a method of that object.

We can control when JavaScript code executes. By default, scripts in a page will be executed immediately while the page loads into the browser. This is not always what we want. Sometimes we want to execute a script when a page loads, and at other times when a user triggers an event.

Scripts that we want to execute only when they are called, or when an event is triggered, go in the head section. When we place a script in the head section, we ensure that the script is loaded before anyone uses it. That is, it does not execute on its own. However, if we put scripts in the body section, then they automatically get executed when the page loads in the browser.

This difference is shown in Fig. 7.2.

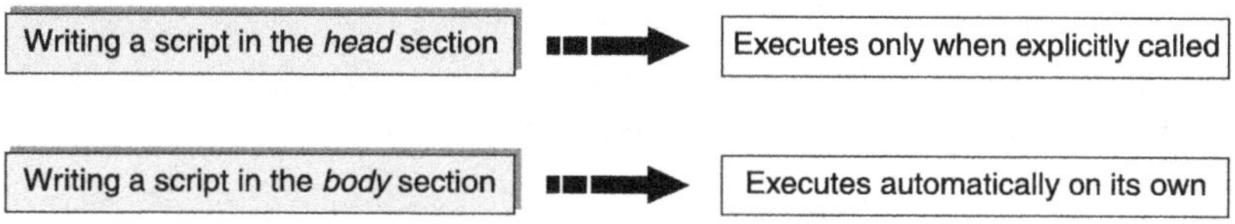

Fig. 7.2 *Where to place JavaScript*

Of course, we can put as many scripts as we like, in an HTML page. Also, there is no limitation on how many of them should be in the *<head>* section, and how many of them should be in the *<body>* section. In the example we had shown earlier, the script was written inside the *<body>* section, and therefore, it executed without needing to make any explicit call. Instead, if we had written it inside the *<body>* section, then we would have needed to call it explicitly from some part of the *<body>* section.

Let us understand the differences between the two clearly. Figure 7.3 shows the code for writing a script inside the *<head>* section, versus in the *<body>* section.

```
<html>
  <head>
    <script type="text/javascript">
      function message () {
       alert ("Called from the <body> section")
      }
    </script>
  </head>

  <body onload = "message ()">
  </body>
</html>
```

(a) Script in the *<head> section*

```
<html>

  <head>
  </head>

  <body>
    <script type="text/javascript">
      window.document.write ("Directly executed")
    </script>
  </body>
</html>
```

(b) Script in the *<body> section*

Fig. 7.3 *Writing scripts in <head> and <body> sections*

As we can see, the difference is where we have put the script. In case (a), the script is inside the *<head>* section, and therefore, must explicitly get called to get executed. We call the script from the *onload* event of the *<body>* section. In other words, we tell the browser that as soon as it starts loading the HTML page (i.e., the contents of the *<body>* section), it should call the *message ()* function written in the *<head>* section. In case (b), the script is a part of the *<body>* section itself, and therefore, would get executed as soon as the HTML page gets loaded in the browser. There is no need to call this script from anywhere.

Figure 7.4 shows how to put the JavaScript in an external file and include it in our HTML page. We have not shown the script code itself, as the example is only to illustrate the concept.

```
<html>
  <head>
  </head>
  <body>
    <script src="MyScript.js"></script>
  </body>
  </html>
```

Fig. 7.4 *How to declare external JavaScript?*

As we can see, the JavaScript code is supposed to be contained in a separate file called *MyScript.js*.

7.1.3 Miscellaneous Features

Variables

JavaScript allows us to define and use variables just like other programming languages. Variables are declared using the keyword *var*. However, this keyword is optional. In other words, following two declarations are equivalent:

```
var name = "test";
name = test;
```

Variables can be local or global.

1. **Local variables** When we declare a variable within a function, the variable can only be accessed within that function. When we exit the function, the variable is destroyed. This type of variable is a local variable.
2. **Global variables** If we declare a variable outside a function, all the functions on our HTML page can access it. The lifetime of these variables starts when they are declared, and ends when the page is closed.

Figure 7.5 shows an example of using variables.

```
<html>
   <head>
     <title>Seconds in a day</title>

     <script type = "text/javascript">

        var seconds_per_minute = 60;
        var minutes_per_hour  = 60;
        var hours_per_day = 60;

        var seconds_per_day = seconds_per_minute * minutes_per_hour * hours_per_day;

      </script>
    </head>

    <body>

     <h1> We can see that ...</h1>

     <script type="text/javascript">

        window.document.write ("there are ");
        window.document.write (seconds_per_day);
        window.document.write (" seconds in a day.");
      </script>
   </body>
</html>
```

Fig. 7.5 *Variables example*

The resulting output is shown in Fig. 7.6.

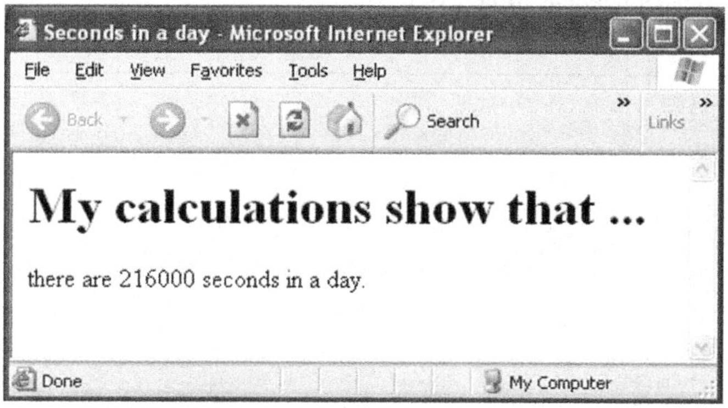

Fig. 7.6 *Output of variables example*

Operators

JavaScript supports a variety of operators. Figure 7.7 summarizes them.

Operator classification	*List of operators*
Arithmetic	+ - * / % ++ --
Assignment	= += -= *= /= %=
Comparison	= < > <= >= !=
Logical	&& || !

Fig. 7.7 *JavaScript operators*

Functions

A function contains block of code that needs to be executed repeatedly, or based on certain event. Another part of the HTML page calls a JavaScript function on needs basis. Usually, all functions should be defined in the *<head>* section, right at the beginning of the HTML page, and should be called as and when necessary. A function can receive arguments, or it can also be a function that does not expect any arguments. A function is declared by using the keyword *function*, followed by the name of the function, followed by parentheses. If there are any arguments that the function expects, they are listed inside the parentheses, separated by commas. A function can return a single value by using the *return* statement. However, unlike standard programming languages, a function does not have to mention its *return data type* in the function declaration.

Enough of theory! Let us now look at a function example, as shown in Fig. 7.8.

As we can see, the name of the function is *total*. It expects two arguments. What should be their data types? This is not needed to be mentioned. The function adds the values of these two arguments and stores the result into a third variable called *result*. It then returns this value back to the caller. How would the caller call this function? It would say something like *sum = total (5, 7).*

```
function total (a, b) {
  result = a+b;
  return result;
}
```

Fig. 7.8 *Function example*

Conditional Statements

JavaScript supports three types of conditional statements: *if*, *if-else*, and *switch*. They work in a manner that it quite similar to what happens in Java or C#.

Figure 7.9 shows an example of the *if* statement.

```
<html>
  <body>
     <script type="text/javascript">
        var d = new Date ();
        var time = d.getHours ();

        if (time > 12) {
           document.write ("<b>Good afternoon</b>");
        }
     </script>
  </body>
</html>
```

Fig. 7.9 *Example of if statement*

The resulting output is shown in Fig. 7.10, assuming that currently it is the afternoon.

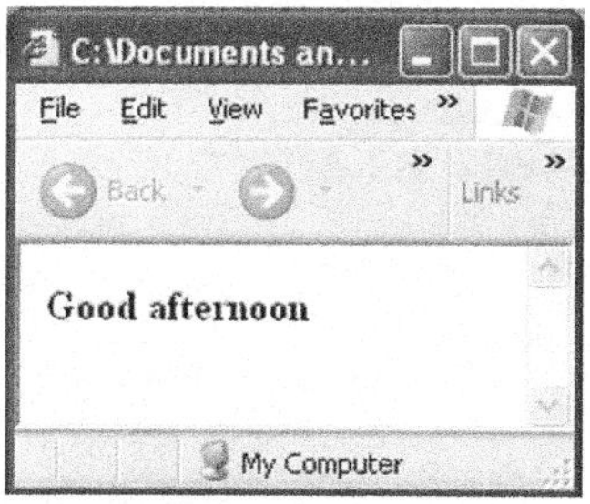

Fig. 7.10 *Output of if example*

On the other hand, an *if-else* statement allows us to write alternative code whenever the *if* statement is not true. Figure 7.11 shows an example of the *if-else* statement.

```
<html>
   <body>
      <script type=”text/javascript”>
         var d = new Date ();
         var time = d.getHours ();

         if (time < 12) {
            document.write (“Good morning!”);
         }
         else {
            document.write (“Good day!”);
         }
      </script>
   </body>
</html>
```

Fig. 7.11 *Example of if-else statement*

The resulting output is shown in Fig. 7.12.

Fig. 7.12 *Output of if-else example*

Figure 7.13 shows the example of the *switch* statement.

```
<html>
   <body>
      <script type = “text/javascript”>
         var d = new Date ();
         theDay = d.getDay ();

         switch (theDay) {
            case 5:
               document.write (“Finally Friday”);
               break;
            case 6:
            case 0:
               document.write (“Super Weekend”);
               break;
            default:
               document.write (“I’m looking forward to this weekend!”);
         }
      </script>
   </body>
</html>
```

Fig. 7.13 *Example of switch statement*

Figure 7.14 shows the resulting output.

Fig. 7.14 *Output of the switch example*

We can also use the ?: conditional operator in JavaScript. For example, we can have the following code block:

```
greeting = (visitor == “Senior”) ? “Dear sir”: “Dear”;
```

Loops

JavaScript provides three kinds of loops: *while, do-while*, and *for*. The *while* loop first checks for the condition being tested, and if it is satisfied, only then executes the code. The *do-while* loop first executes the code and then checks for the condition being tested. In other words, it executes at least once, regardless of whether the condition being tested is successful or no. The *for* loop executes in iteration, usually incrementing or decrementing the loop index.

Figure 7.15 shows the example of the *while* loop.

```
<html>
   <body>

      <script type = "text/javascript">
         var i = 0;

         while (i <= 5) {
            document.write ("The number is" + i);
            document.write ("<br>");
            i++;
         }
      </script>


      <p><p>
      <b>We have seen an example of the <i>while</i> loop</b>

   </body>
</html>
```

Fig. 7.15 *Example of while loop*

Figure 7.16 shows the output of the *while* example.

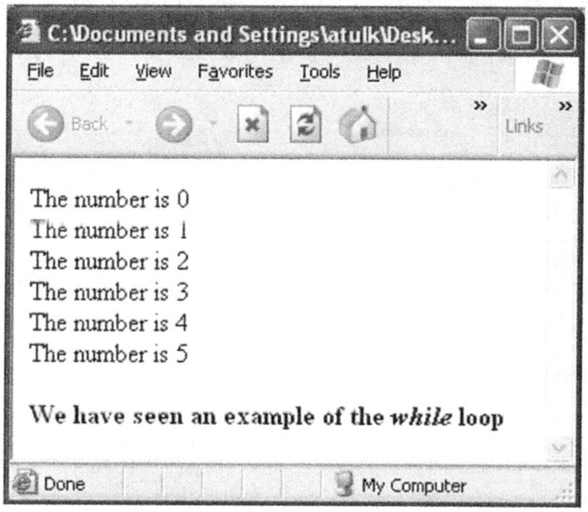

Fig. 7.16 *Output of while example*

Figure 7.17 shows the example of the *do-while* loop.

```
<html>
  <body>

    <script type="text/javascript">
      i = 0;
      do {
          document.write ("The number is" + i);
          document.write ("<br>");
          i++;
      }
      while (i <= 5);
    </script>

    <p><p>
    <b>We have seen an example of the <i>do-while</i> loop</b>

  </body>
</html>
```

Fig. 7.17 *Example of do-while loop*

Figure 7.18 shows the output of the *do-while* example.

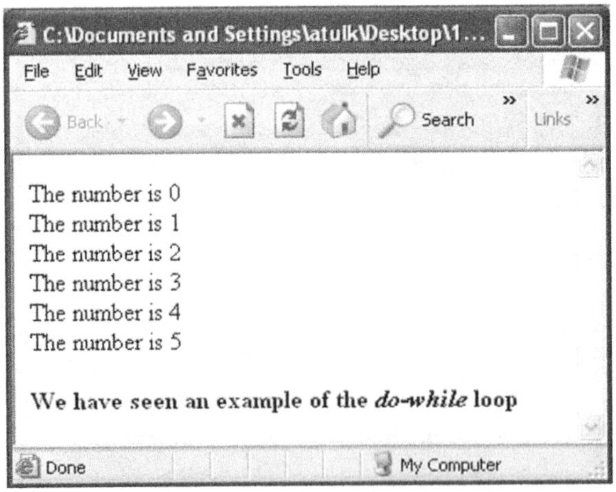

Fig. 7.18 *Output of the do-while example*

Figure 7.19 shows the example of the *for* loop.

```
<html>
   <body>

     <script type="text/javascript">
        for (i = 0; i <= 5; i++) {
           document.write ("The number is" + i);
           document.write ("<br>");
        }
     </script>

      <p><p>
      <b>We have seen an example of the <i>for</i> loop</b>

   </body>
</html>
```

Fig. 7.19 *Example of the for loop*

Figure 7.20 shows the output of the *for* example

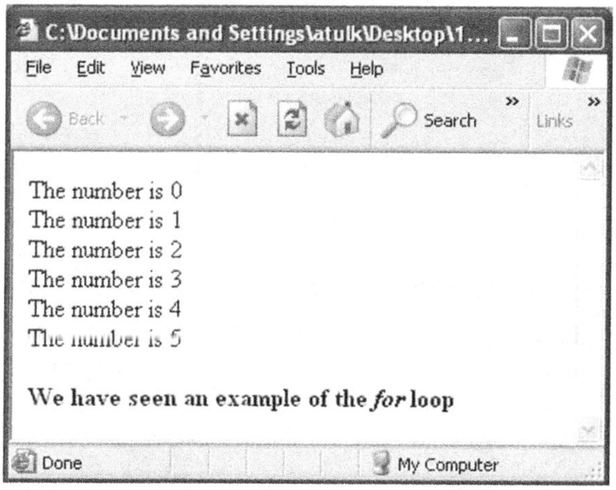

Fig. 7.20 *Output of the for example*

Standard Objects

JavaScript provides several standard objects, such as Array, Boolean, Date, Math, String, etc. We shall quickly review some of them.

Figure 7.21 shows the example of the *Date* object.

```
<html>
   <body>

      <script type="text/javascript">
         var d = new Date ();
         document.write (d.getDate ());
         document.write (".");
         document.write (d.getMonth () + 1);
         document.write (".");
         document.write (d.getFullYear ());
      </script>

   </body>
</html>
```

Fig. 7.21 *Date object example*

In the code, we create a new instance of the *Date ()* object. From this object, we get the day number, the month number (and increment by one, since it starts with 0), and the four-digit year; all concatenated with each other by using a dot symbol. The output is shown in Fig. 7.22.

Fig. 7.22 *Output of the Date object*

We can manipulate values of the date object as well. For example, we can display the current date and time in the full form, change the year value to a value of our choice, and then display the full date and time again. This is shown in Fig. 7.23.

```
<html>
   <body>

      <script type="text/javascript">
         var d = new Date ();
         document.write (d);
         document.write ("<br />");
         d.setFullYear ("2100");
         document.write (d);
      </script>

   </body>
</html>
```

Fig. 7.23 *Manipulating dates*

The resulting output is shown in Fig. 7.24.

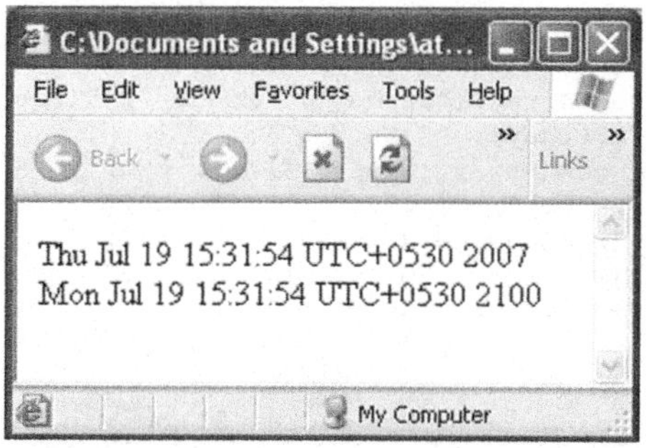

Fig. 7.24 *Output of the date manipulation example*

Here is another example related to dates, as shown in Fig. 7.25. Here, we use the Array default object as well.

```
<html>
   <body>
      <script type = "text/javascript">
         var d = new Date ();
         var weekday = new Array ("Sunday", "Monday", "Tuesday", "Wednesday",
            "Thursday",  "Friday", "Saturday");
         document.write ("Today is" + weekday [d.getDay ()]);
      </script>
   </body>
</html>
```

Fig. 7.25 *Use of Date and Array objects*

The resulting output is shown in Fig. 7.26.

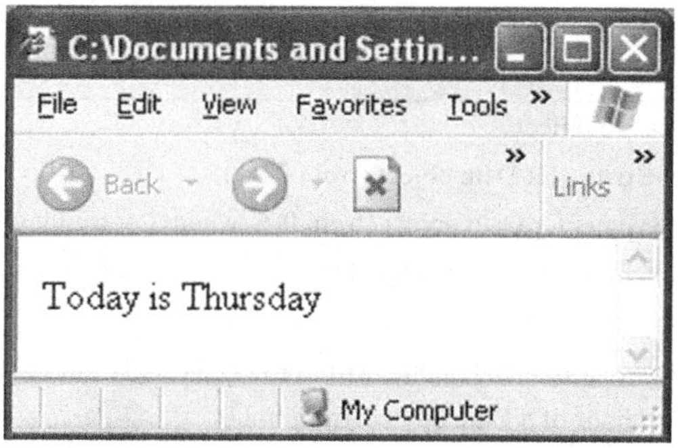

Fig. 7.26 *Output of the Date and Array objects*

The same example is modified further, as shown in Fig. 7.27.

```
<html>
   <body>
      <script type=”text/javascript”>
         var d = new Date ();
         var weekday = new Array (“Sunday”, “Monday”, “Tuesday”, “Wednesday”,
            “Thursday”, “Friday”, “Saturday”);
         var monthname = new Array (“Jan”, “Feb”, “Mar”, “Apr”, “May”, “Jun”,
            “Jul”, “Aug”, “Sep”, “Oct”, “Nov”, “Dec”);
         document.write (weekday [d.getDay ()] + “ ”);
         document.write (monthname [d.getMonth ()] + “ ”);
         document.write (d.getFullYear ());
      </script>
   </body>
</html>
```

Fig. 7.27 *Another Date example*

The resulting output is shown in Fig. 7.28.

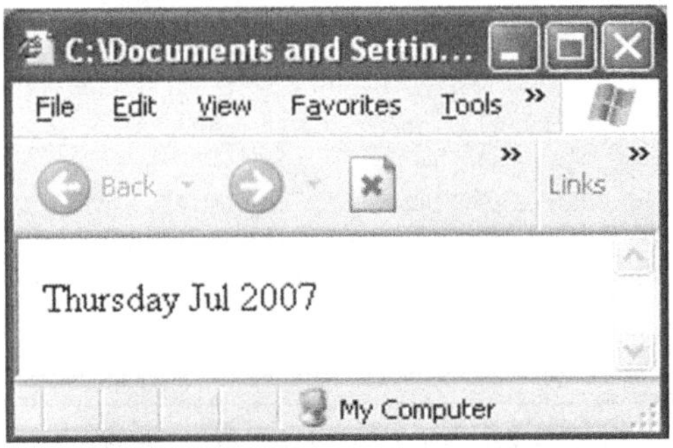

Fig. 7.28 *Output of the modified example*

Figure 7.29 shows the most useful date functions.

Method	*Description*
Date()	Returns a Date object
getDate()	Returns the date of a Date object (from 1-31)
getDay()	Returns the day of a Date object (from 0-6, where 0 = Sunday, 1 = Monday, etc.)
getMonth()	Returns the month of a Date object (from 0-11, where 0 = January, 1 = February, etc.)
getFullYear()	Returns the year of a Date object (four digits)
getYear()	Returns the year of a Date object (from 0-99). Use getFullYear instead.
getHours()	Returns the hour of a Date object (from 0-23)
getMinutes()	Returns the minute of a Date object (from 0-59)
getSeconds()	Returns the second of a Date object (from 0-59)

Fig. 7.29 *Date functions*

Figure 7.30 shows an example of using the *Math* object.

```
<html>
   <body>

      <script type = "text/javascript">
         document.write (Math.round (7.80))
      </script>

   </body>
</html>
```

Fig. 7.30 *Math object example*

The resulting output is shown in Fig. 7.31.

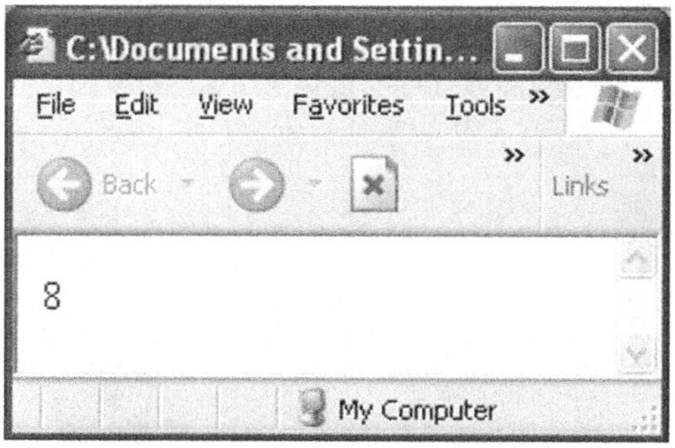

Fig. 7.31 *Output of using the Math object*

Figure 7.32 lists the important methods of the *Math* object.

Method	*Description*
abs (x)	Returns the absolute value of x
cos (x)	Returns the cosine of x
exp (x)	Returns the value of E raised to the power of x
log (x)	Returns the natural log of x
max (x, y)	Returns the number with the highest value of x and y
min (x, y)	Returns the number with the lowest value of x and y
pow (x, y)	Returns the value of the number x raised to the power of y
random ()	Returns a random number between 0 and 1
round (x)	Rounds x to the nearest integer
sin (x)	Returns the sine of x
sqrt (x)	Returns the square root of x
tan (x)	Returns the tangent of x

Fig. 7.32 *Math functions*

JavaScript provides a few functions for handling strings. These are summarized below:

1. **indexOf ()** Finds location of a specified set of characters (i.e., of a *substring*) Starts counting at 0, returns starting position if found, else returns –1.
2. **lastIndexOf ()** Similar to the above, but looks for the *last* occurrence of the sub-string.
3. **charAt ()** Returns a single character inside a string at a specific position.
4. **subString ()** Returns a substring inside a string at a specific position.
5. **split ()** Divides a string into substrings, based on a delimiter.

We shall discuss a few string processing examples when we study form validations.

Figure 7.33 shows a sample of the *indexOf ()* function.

```
<html>
  <head>
    <title>Validate Email Address</title>

    <script type = "text/javascript">

      function validateEmailAddress (the_email_address) {

        var the_at_symbol = the_email_address.indexOf ("@");
        var the_dot_symbol = the_email_address.lastIndexOf (".");
        var the_space_symbol = the_email_address.indexOf (" ");

        /////////////////////////////////////////////////////
        // Now see if the email address is valid
        /////////////////////////////////////////////////////
        if(
          (the_at_symbol != -1)  && // There must be an @ symbol
          (the_at_symbol != 0)   && // The @ symbol must not be at the first position
          (the_dot_symbol != -1) && // There must be a . symbol
          (the_dot_symbol != 0) && // The . symbol must not be at the first position
          (the_dot_symbol > the_at_symbol + 1) && // Must have something after @ and before .
          (the_email_address.length > the_dot_symbol + 1) && // Must have something after .
          (the_space_symbol == -1) // Must not have a space anywhere
          ) {
          alert ("Email address seems to be correct.");
          return true;
        }
        else {
          alert ("Error!!! Email address seems to be incorrect.");
          return false;
        }
      }

    </script>
  <head>

  <body>

    <h1>Please enter your email address below</h1>

    <form name = "the_form" action = "" method = "post"
     onSubmit = "var the_result = validateEmailAddress (this.email_address.value);
                return the_result;">

      Email address:<input type = "text" name = "email_address">
      <input type = "submit" value = "Submit Form">
    </form>
  </body>
</html>
```

Fig. 7.33 *Example of indexOf ()*

7.1.4 JavaScript and Form Processing

JavaScript has a big role to play in the area of form processing. We know that HTML forms are used for accepting user inputs. JavaScript helps in validating these inputs and also to perform some processing on the basis of certain events.

Figure 7.34 shows a simple example of capturing the event of a button getting clicked.

```
<html>
   <head>
      <script type="text/javascript">
         function show_alert() {
            alert("Hello World!")
         }
      </script>
   </head>

   <body>
      <form>
         <input type = "button" value = "Click me!" name="myButton"
           onClick = "show_alert ()" />
      </form>
   </body>
</html>
```

Fig. 7.34 *Button click example*

As we can see, we have a simple button on the screen. On clicking of this button, we are calling a JavaScript function to display an alert box. The resulting output is shown in Fig. 7.35.

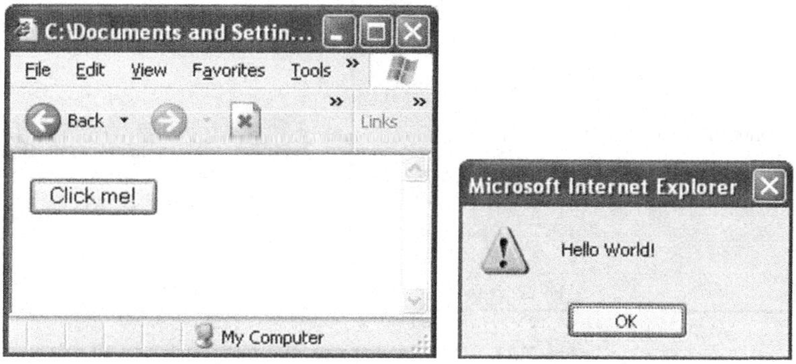

(a) (b)

Fig. 7.35 *(a) Original screen (b) Result when the button is clicked*

Now let us take a look at a more useful example. Here, we accept two numbers from the user and display a hyper link where the user can click to compute their multiplication. When the user does so, we display the resulting multiplication value inside an alert box. The code for this functionality is shown in Fig. 7.36.

```
<html>
   <head>
      <title>Simple Multiplication</title>
         <script type=”text/javascript”>
            function multiply () {
               var number_one = document.the_form.field_one.value;
               var number_two = document.the_form.field_two.value;
                  var result = number_one * number_two;
                  alert (number_one + “ times ” + number_two + “ is: ” + result);
            }
         </script>
   </head>

   <body>
      <form name = “the_form”>
         Number 1: <input type = “text” name = “field_one”> <br>
         Number 2: <input type = “text” name = “field_two”> <br>
         <a href = “#” onClick = “multiply (); return false;”>Multiply them! </a>
      </form>
   </body>
</html>
```

Fig. 7.36 *Using JavaScript to multiply two numbers*

The resulting output is shown in Fig. 7.37.

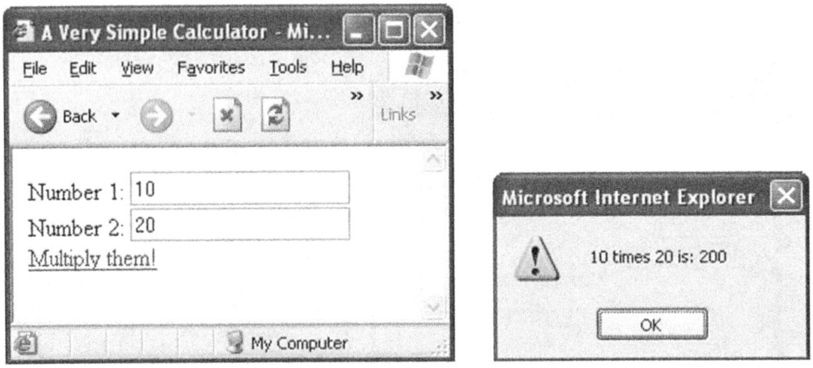

Fig. 7.37 *Multiplying two numbers*

We will now modify the same example to display the resulting multiplication value inside a third text box, instead of displaying it inside an alert box. The code for this purpose is shown in Fig. 7.38.

```
<html>
   <head>
      <title>A Simple Calculator</title>
      <script type="text/javascript">
         function multiply () {
            var number_one = document.the_form.field_one.value;
            var number_two = document.the_form.field_two.value;
            var result = number_one * number_two;
            document.the_form.the_answer.value = result;
         }
      </script>
   </head>

   <body>
      <form name = "the_form">
         Number 1: <input type = "text" name = "field_one"> <br>
         Number 2: <input type = "text" name = "field_two"> <br>
         The Product: <input type = "text" name = "the_answer"> <br>
         <a href = "#" onClick = "multiply (); return false;">Multiply them! </a>
      </form>
   </body>

</html>
```

Fig. 7.38 *Displaying result of multiplication in a separate text box*

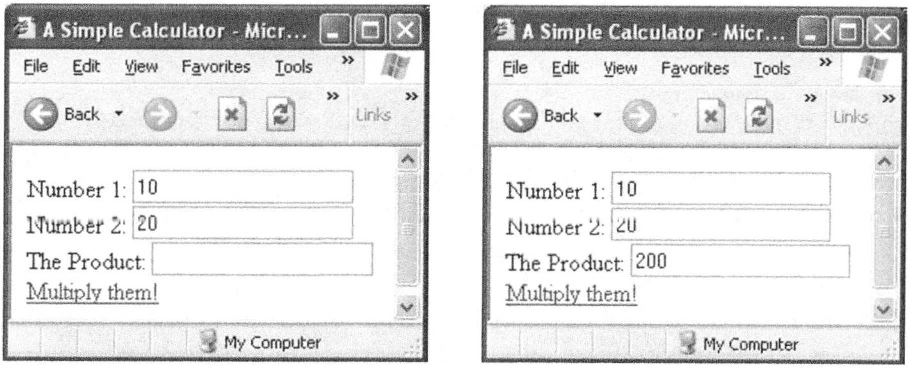

Fig. 7.39 *Displaying result of multiplication in a separate text box*

Let us now take an example of using checkboxes. Figure 7.40(a) shows the code, where we display three checkboxes. Depending on the number of selections, the JavaScript just displays the score, assigning one mark per selection. The result is shown in Fig. 7.40(b).

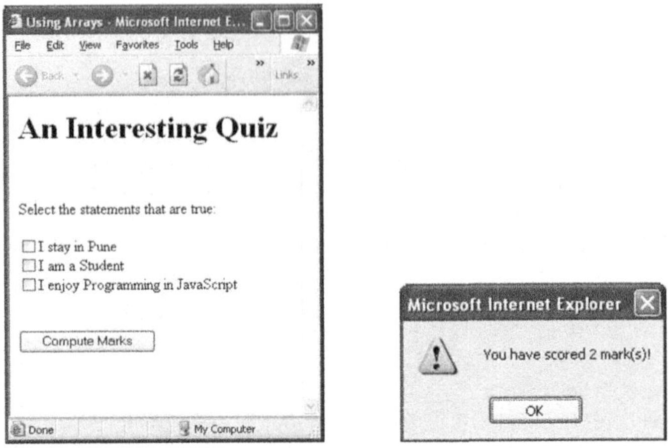

(a) (b)

Fig. 7.40 *(a) Checkbox example (b) Output*

Note that JavaScript offers short hands for certain syntaxes. For example, every time writing the complete window.document.the_form syntax is quite tedious. However, a solution is available whereby the following two syntaxes are equivalent:

```
<form name = "my_form"
  onSubmit = "window.location = window.document.my_form.the_url.value;
  return false;">

<form name = "my_form"
  onSubmit = "window.location = this.the_url.value; return false;">
```

As we can see, the second syntax is quite handy.

Here is another example:

```
<form name = "my_form">
  <input type = "text" name = "age" onChange = "checkAge (window.document.
  my_form.age.value);" />
</form>

<form name = "my_form">
  <input type = "text" name = "age" onChange = "checkAge (this.value);" />
</form>
```

Inside onChange event, implicitly it is the current element, and hence, we can directly say *this. value*, even without saying age!

In the following example (Fig. 7.41), we illustrate the usage of arrays and loops. The functionality achieved is actually the same as what we had achieved in the checkbox example shown earlier. But the code is quite compact here, as we can see.

```
<html>
  <head>
    <title>Using Arrays</title>

    <script type = "text/javascript">

      function computeScore () {

         var index = 0, correct_answers = 0;

         while (index < 3) {

           if (window.document.the_form.elements[index].checked == true) {
            correct_answers++;
          }

          index++;

        }

        alert ("You have scored" + correct_answers + " mark(s)!");
      }
    </script>
  </head>

  <body>
    <h1>An Interesting Quiz</h1>
    <br><br>
    Select the statements that are true:

    <form name = "the_form">
      <input type = "checkbox" name = "question1">I stay in Pune<br>
      <input type = "checkbox" name = "question2">I a a Student<br>
      <input type = "checkbox" name = "question3">I enjoy Programming in JavaScript<br>
      <br><br>

      <input type = "button" value = "Compute Marks" onClick = "computeScore();">
    </form>
  </body>
</html>
```

Fig. 7.41 *Usage of arrays and loops*

The resulting output is not shown, as we have already had one look at it earlier.

Of course, we can also use either the *do-while* or the *for* loop, instead. Figure 7.42 shows an example of the *for* loop.

```
<html>
  <head>
    <title>Rainbow!</title>

    <script = "text/javascript">

      function rainbow () {

        var rainbow_colours = new Array ("red", "orange", "yellow", "green", "blue", "violet");
        var index = 0;

        for (index = 0; index < rainbow_colours.length; index++) {
          window.document.bgColor = rainbow_colours [index];
          //window.document.writeln (index);
        }
      }
    </script>
  </head>

  <body>
    <form>
      <input type = "button" value = "Rainbow" onClick = "rainbow();">
    </form>
  </body>

</html>
```

Fig. 7.42 *Example of the for loop*

Figure 7.43 shows an example where we want to validate the contents of an HTML form.

```
<html>
  <head>
    <title>Form Validation</title>

    <script type = "text/javascript">
      function checkMandatoryFields () {
        var error_Message = "";

        // Check text box
        if (window.document.the_form.the_text.value == "") {
           error_Message += "Please enter your name.\n";
        }

        // Check scrolling list
        if (window.document.the_form.state.selectedIndex < 0) {
            error_Message += "Please select a state.\n";
        }

        // Check radio buttons
        var radio_Selected = "false";
        for (var index = 0; index < window.document.the_form.gender.length; index++) {
          if (window.document.the_form.gender[index].checked == true) {
             radio_Selected = "true";
          }
        }

        if (radio_Selected == "false") {
          error_Message += "Please select a gender.\n";
        }

        if (error_Message == "") {
          return true;
        }
```

(Contd.)

Fig. 7.43 *Contd...*

```
        else {
          error_Message = “Please correct the following errors:\n\n” + error_Message;
          alert (error_Message);
          return false;
        }
      }
      </script>
    <head>
<body bgColor = “lightblue”>

      <h1>Please provide your details below</h1>

      <form name = “the_form” action = “” method = “post” onSubmit = “var the_result =
      checkMandatoryFields (); return the_result;”>

        <table border = “2” bgColor = “yellow”>
          <tr>
             <td><b>Name:</b></td>
             <td><input type = “text” name = “the_text”></td>
          </tr>

             <tr /><tr />

             <tr>
             <td><b>State:</b></td>
             <td>
                <select name = “state” size = “5”>
                  <option value = “andhra”>Andhra Pradesh</option>
                  <option value = “bihar”>Bihar</option>
                  <option value = “Karnataka”>Karnataka</option>
                  <option value = “goa”>Goa</option>
                  <option value = “maharashtra”>Maharashtra</option>
                  <option value = “mp”>Madhya Pradesh</option>
                  <option value = “rajasthan”>Rajasthan</option>
                  <option value = “up”>Uttar Pradesh</option>
                </select>
              </td>
            </tr>

            <tr /><tr />

             <tr>
              <td><b>Gender:</b></td>
              <td>
                <input type = “radio” name = “gender”>Female
                <input type = “radio” name = “gender”>Male
              </td>
            </tr>

            <tr /> <tr />

            <tr>
                <td><input type = “submit” value = “Submit Form”></td>
                </tr>

                <tr /> <tr />

        </table>
      </form>
    </body>
  </html>
```

Fig. 7.43 *Form validations*

Figure 7.44 shows a sample of the *indexOf ()* string function. This example attempts to accept an email address from the user in an HTML form and then validates it. The particulars of the validation logic are mentioned inside the code comments. So, we will not repeat them here.

```
<html>
  <head>
    <title>Validate Email Address</title>

    <script type = "text/javascript">

      function validateEmailAddress (the_email_address) {

        var the_at_symbol = the_email_address.indexOf ("@");
        var the_dot_symbol = the_email_address.lastIndexOf (".");
        var the_space_symbol = the_email_address.indexOf (" ");

        ////////////////////////////////////////////////////////
        // Now see if the email address is valid
        ////////////////////////////////////////////////////////
        if (
          (the_at_symbol != -1)  && // There must be an @ symbol
          (the_at_symbol != 0)   && // The @ symbol must not be at the first position
          (the_dot_symbol != -1) && // There must be a . symbol
          (the_dot_symbol != 0) && // The . symbol must not be at the first position
          (the_dot_symbol > the_at_symbol + 1) && // Must have something after @ and before .
          (the_email_address.length > the_dot_symbol + 1) && // Must have something after .
          (the_space_symbol == -1) // Must not have a space anywhere
          ) {
          alert ("Email address seems to be correct.");
          return true;
        }
        else {
          alert ("Error!!! Email address seems to be incorrect.");
          return false;
        }
      }

    </script>
  <head>

  <body>

    <h1>Please enter your email address below</h1>

    <form name = "the_form" action = "" method = "post"
     onSubmit = "var the_result = validateEmailAddress (this.email_address.value);
     return the_result;">

     Email address:<input type = "text" name = "email_address">
     <input type = "submit" value = "Submit Form">
    </form>
  </body>
</html>
```

Fig. 7.44 *Using the indexOf () string function*

We can write the same logic using another string function, namely *charAt ()*. The resulting code is shown in Fig. 7.45.

```
<html>
  <head>
    <title>Validate Email Address - charAt Version</title>

    <script type = "text/javascript">

      function validateEmailAddress (the_email_address) {

        var the_at_symbol = the_email_address.indexOf ("@");
        var the_dot_symbol = the_email_address.lastIndexOf (".");
        var the_space_symbol = the_email_address.indexOf (" ");
        var is_invalid = false;

        /////////////////////////////////////////////////////
        // Now see if the email address is valid
        /////////////////////////////////////////////////////
        if (
          (the_at_symbol != -1)  && // There must be an @ symbol
          (the_at_symbol != 0)   && // The @ symbol must not be at the first position
          (the_dot_symbol != -1) && // There must be a . symbol
          (the_dot_symbol != 0) && // The . symbol must not be at the first position
          (the_dot_symbol > the_at_symbol + 1) && // Must have something after @ and before .
          (the_email_address.length > the_dot_symbol + 1) && // Must have something after .
          (the_space_symbol == -1) // Must not have a space anywhere
          ) {
          is_invalid = false; // do nothing
        }
        else {
          is_invalid = true;
        }

        if (is invalid == true) {
              alert ("Error!!! Email address is invalid.");
              return false;
          }

        /////////////////////////////////////////////////////
        // Now check for the presence of illegal characters
        /////////////////////////////////////////////////////

        var the_invalid_characters = "!#$%^&*()+=:;?/<>";
        var the_char = "";
for (var index = 0; index < the_invalid_characters.length; index++) {
        the_char = the_invalid_characters.charAt (index);

        if (the_email_address.indexOf (the_char) != -1) {
          is_invalid = true;
         }
       }
```

(Contd.)

Fig. 7.45 *Contd...*

```
      if (is_invalid == true) {
         alert ("Error!!! Email address is invalid.");
         return false;
      }
      else {
         alert ("Email address seems to be valid.");
         return true;
      }
    }
    </script>

  <head>

  <body>

    <h1>Please enter your email address below</h1>

    <form name = "the_form" action = "" method = "post"
     onSubmit = "var the_result = validateEmailAddress (this.email_address.value);
     return the_result;">

     Email address:<input type = "text" name = "email_address">
     <input type = "submit" value = "Submit Form">
   </form>
  </body>
</html>
```

Fig. 7.45 *Using the charAt () function*

Another string function, *substring ()* is a bit tricky. The general syntax for this function is *substring (from, until)*. This means return a string starting with *from* and ending with one character less than *until*. That is, *until* is at a position that is greater than the last position of the *substring* by one. As a result, some of the tricky examples shown in Fig. 7.46 need to be observed carefully.

Example	*Result*	*Explanation*
the_word.substring (0, 4)	"Java"	from = 0, until = 4 – 1 = 3. So, returns characters at positions 0, 1, 2, and 3.
the_word.substring (1, 4)	"ava"	from = 1, until = 4 – 1 = 3. So, returns characters at positions 1, 2, and 3.
the_word.substring (1, 2)	"a"	from = 1, until = 2 – 1 = 1. So, returns character at position 1 only.
the_word.substring (2, 2)	""	from = 2, until = 2 – 1 = 1. So, returns an empty string.

Fig. 7.46 *Examples of the substring () function*

7.1.5 Pop-up Boxes

JavaScript supports three types of **pop-up boxes**, namely **alert box**, **confirm box**, and **prompt box**. An alert box displays a message for the user and expects the user to acknowledge the message. In other words, here the user does not have an option to reject/cancel the message. Confirm box does something similar, but in addition also displays a cancel button. The idea being that the user can either acknowledge the message or cancel it. In the prompt box case, the user has an area to type back some message and then press the OK or Cancel button.

Figures 7.47, 7.48, and 7.49 illustrate the three pop-up boxes and the corresponding results.

```
<html>
<head>
</head>
<script type="text/javascript">
alert("Please acknowledge this first!");
</script>
<body>
<h1> Test page </h1>
Hello Web Technologies!
</body>
</html>
```

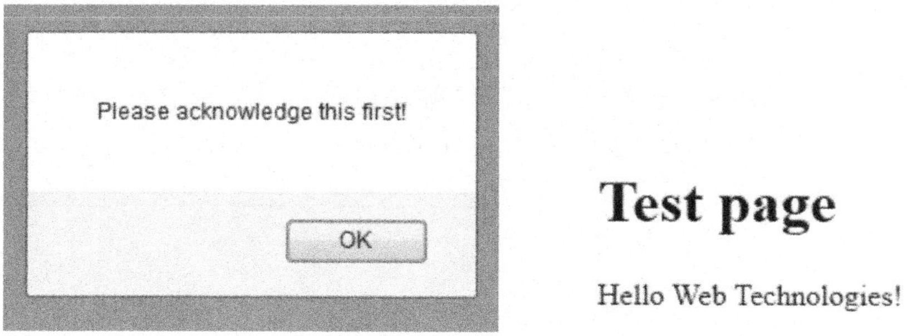

Fig. 7.47 *Alert box example*

```
<html>
<head>
</head>
<script type="text/javascript">
if (confirm("Do you Agree?"))
        {alert("You Agree!")}
else
        {alert ("You do not Agree!")};
</script>
<body>
<h1> My Website </h1>
Good bye!
</body>
</html>
```

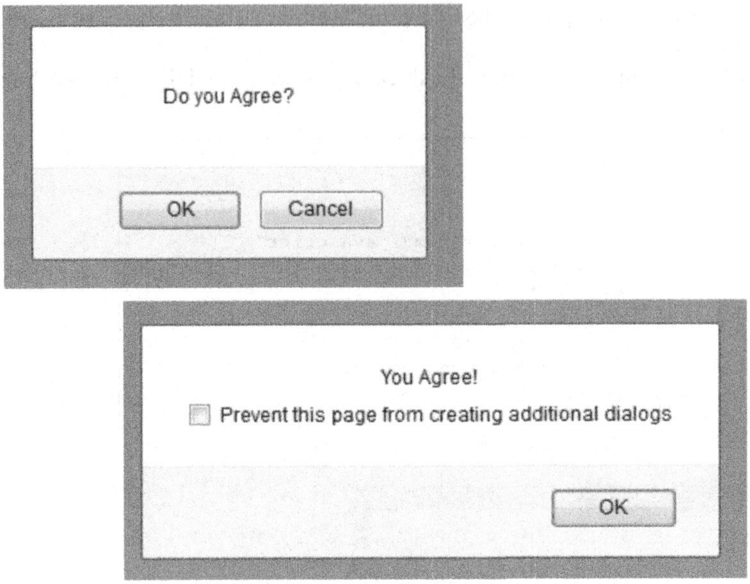

Fig. 7.48 *Confirm box example*

```
<html>
  <head>
    <title>Prompt box Example</title>
    <script type = “text/javascript”>
      var the_name = prompt (“What is your name?”, “Please enter your name here.”);
    </script>
  </head>
  <body>
    <h1>Hello
      <script type = “text/javascript”>
        document.write (the_name);
      </script>
    ,</h1>
  </body>
</html>
```

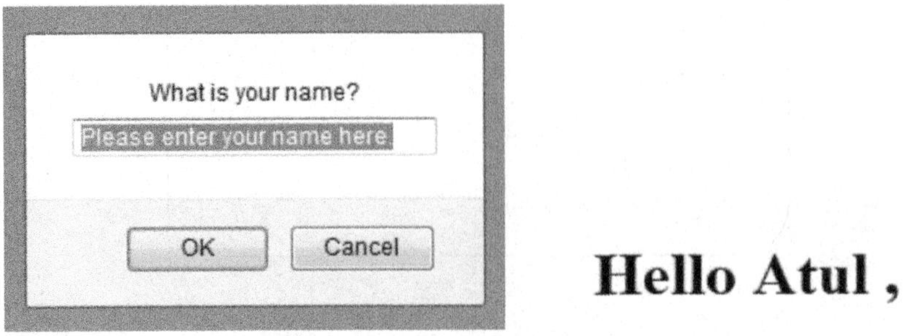

Fig. 7.49 *Prompt box example*

AJAX 7.2

7.2.1 Introduction

The term **AJAX** is used quite extensively in the Information Technology area these days. Everyone seems to want to make use of AJAX, but a few may not know where exactly it fits in, and what it can do. In a nutshell:

AJAX can be used for making user experience better by using clever techniques for communication between a Web browser (the client) and the Web server.

How can AJAX do this? Let us understand this at a conceptual level.

In traditional Web programming, we have programs that execute either on the client (e.g., written using JavaScript) or on the server (e.g., written using Java's Servlets/JSP, Microsoft's ASP.NET, or other technologies such as PHP, Struts, etc.). This is shown in the Fig. 7.50.

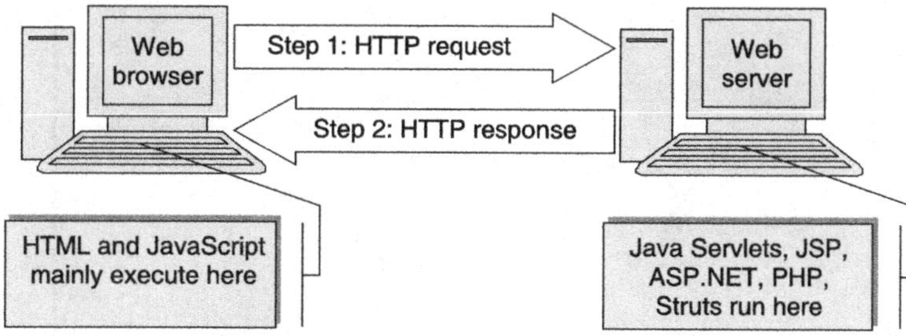

Fig. 7.50 *Technologies and their location*

What do these programs do? They perform a variety of tasks. For example,

1. Validate that the amount that the user has entered on the screen is not over 10,000.
2. Ensure that user's age is numeric and is over 18.
3. If city is entered as Pune, then country must be India.

Mind you, these are simple examples of validating user inputs. They are best done on the client-side itself, using JavaScript. However, all tasks are not validations of these kinds alone. For example,

1. From the source account number specified by the user, transfer the amount mentioned by the user into the target account number specified by the user.
2. Produce a report of all transactions that have failed in the last four hours with an appropriate reason code.
3. Due to 1% increase in the interest rates, increase the EMI amount for all the customers who have availed floating loans.

These are examples of business processes. These are best run on the server-side, using the technologies listed earlier.

We can summarize:

Client-side technologies, such as JavaScript, are used for validating user inputs. Server-side technologies, such as Java Servlets, JSP, ASP.NET, PHP, etc., are used for ensuring that business processes happen as expected.

Sometimes, we run into situations where we need a mixture of the two. For instance, suppose that there is a text box on the screen, where the user needs to type the city name. As the user starts typing the city name, we want to automatically populate a list of all city names that match what the user has started typing. (For example, when the user types *M*, then we want to show Madrid, Manila, Mumbai, and so on). The user may select one of these, or may type the next character, say a. If the user has typed the second character as a, the user's input would now have become *Ma*. Now, we want to show only Madrid and Manila, but not Mumbai (which has the first two characters as *Mu*). We may perhaps even show a warning to the user, in case the user is typing the name of a city, which does not exist at all!

The best example of this is Google Suggest (*http://www.google.com/webhp?complete=1&hl=en*). You can visit this URL and try what we have shown below. Suppose that we are trying to search for the word *i-flex*.

In the search window, type i. We would get a list of all the matching entries, starting with *i* from Google's database, as shown in Fig. 7.51.

Fig. 7.51 *Google Suggest – 1*

Now add a hyphen to get the following screen. As we can see, the list is now filtered for entries starting with *i-*. The result is shown in Fig. 7.52.

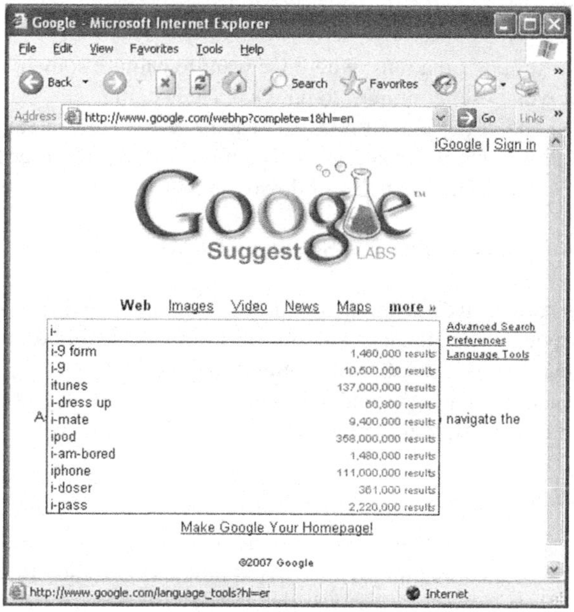

Fig. 7.52 *Google Suggest – 2*

Now I add an f to make it *i-f*. This is shown in Fig. 7.53.

Fig. 7.53 *Google Suggest – 3*

We get what we want!

This uses AJAX.

We can use AJAX in similar situations, where we want to capture something the user is typing or has typed, and process it while user continues to do what she is doing.

Of course, this is just one of the uses of AJAX. It can be used in any situation, where we want the client to send a request to the server for taking some action, without the user having to abandon her current task. This tells us that AJAX helps us to do something behind the scenes, without impacting the user's work.

The name says it all: **Asynchronous JavaScript And XML**.

AJAX is

1. **Asynchronous** because it does not disturb the user's work, and does not refresh the full screen (unlike what happens when the user submits a form to the server, for example.)
2. **JavaScript** because it uses JavaScript for the actual work
3. **And XML** because XML is supposed to be there everywhere today (Jokes apart, using AJAX, the server can return XML to the browser)

7.2.2 How AJAX Works?

AJAX uses the following technique, described in a generic fashion.

Whenever AJAX needs to come into picture, based on the user action (e.g., typing something) it sends a request from the Web browser to the Web server.

On the Web server, a program written in a server-side technology (any one from those listed earlier) receives this request from the Web browser, sent by AJAX.

The program on the Web server processes this request, and sends a response back to the Web browser. Note that while this happens, the user does not have to wait – actually, the user does not even notice that the Web browser has sent a request to the Web server!

The Web browser processes the response received from the Web server, and takes an appropriate action (e.g., in Google Suggest, the browser would show us a list of all the matching entries for the text typed so far, which was sent by the Google server to the browser in Step 3 above).

This concept is shown in Fig. 7.54.

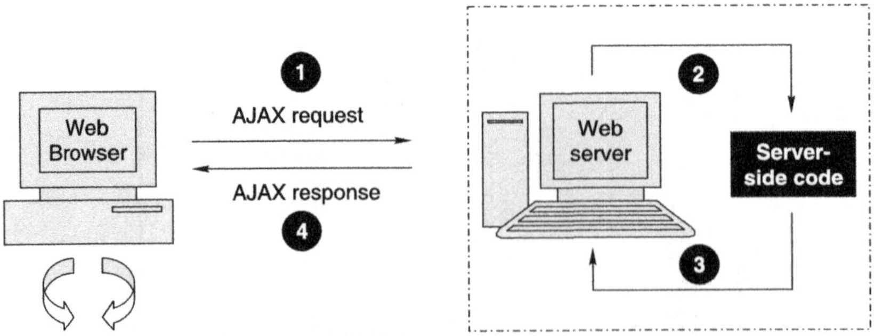

Fig. 7.54 AJAX process

Let us understand how this works.

1. While the user (client) is filling up an HTML form, based on certain event, JavaScript in the client's browser prepares and sends an AJAX request (usually called as an XMLHttpRequest) to the Web server.

2. While the user continues working as if nothing has happened (shown with two *processing* arrows at the bottom part of the diagram), the Web server invokes the appropriate server-side code (e.g., a JSP/Servlet, an ASP.NET page, a PHP script, as we shall learn later).
3. The server-side code prepares an AJAX response and hands it over to the Web server.
4. While the user continues working with the remainder of the HTML form, the server sends the AJAX response back to the browser. The browser automatically reflects the result of the AJAX response (e.g., populate a field on the HTML form). Note that the user would not even notice that Steps 1 to 3 have happened behind the scene!

Therefore, we can differentiate between non-AJAX based processing and AJAX-based processing a shown in Figs. 7.55 and 7.56.

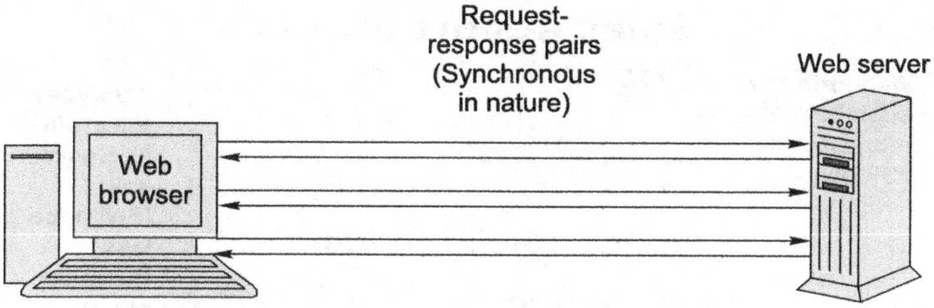

Fig. 7.55 *Traditional HTTP processing (without AJAX)*

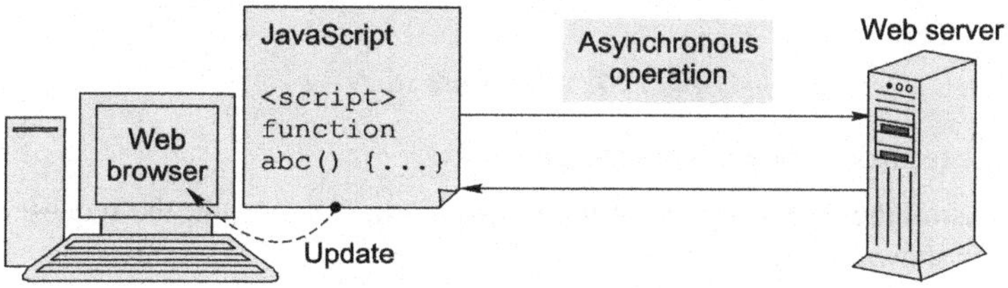

Fig. 7.56 *AJAX-based processing*

7.2.3 AJAX FAQ

In the beginning, people have a lot of questions regarding AJAX. We summarize them along with their answers below:

1. Do we not use request/response model in AJAX?

Ans. We do, but the approach is different now. We do not submit a form now, but instead send requests using JavaScript

2. Why not submit thc form? Why AJAX?

Ans. AJAX processing is asynchronous. Client does not wait for server to respond. When server responds, JavaScript does not refresh the whole page.

3. How does a page get back a response, then?

Ans. When the server sends a response, JavaScript can update a page with new values, change an image, or transfer control to a new page. The user does not have to wait while this happens.

4. Should we AJAX for all our requests?

Ans. No. Traditional form filling is still required in many situations. But for immediate and intermediate responses/feedbacks, we should use AJAX.

5. Where is the XML in AJAX?

Ans. Sometimes the JavaScript can use XML to speak with the server back and forth.

7.2.4 Life Without AJAX

Suppose that we have a book shop, where we want to constantly view the amount of profit we have made. For this purpose, an application sends us the latest number of copies sold, as on date. We multiply that with the profit per copy, and compute the total profit made. We shall get into coding details subsequently.

The conceptual view of this is shown in Fig. 7.57.

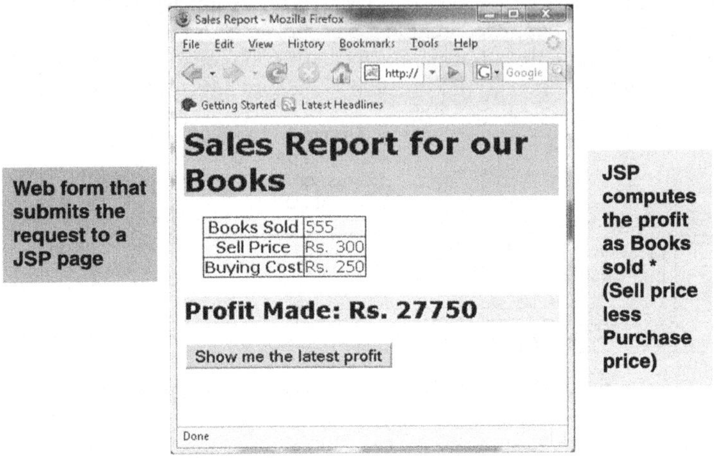

Fig. 7.57 *AJAX case study – 1*

The way this executes is shown step-by-step below.

Step 1: User clicks on the button shown in the HTML form. As a result, the request would go to the Web server. This is shown in Fig. 7.58.

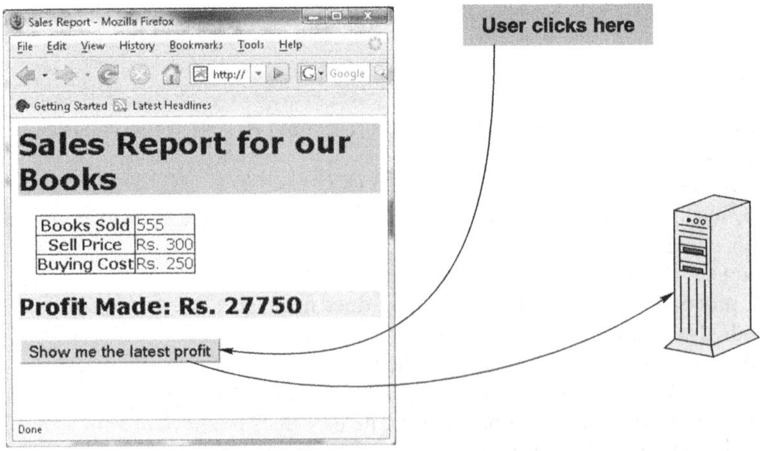

Fig. 7.58 *AJAX case study -2*

Step 2: The server-side program (maybe a JSP) processes the user's request, and sends back an HTTP response to the user. This response refreshes or reloads the screen completely. This is shown in Fig. 7.59.

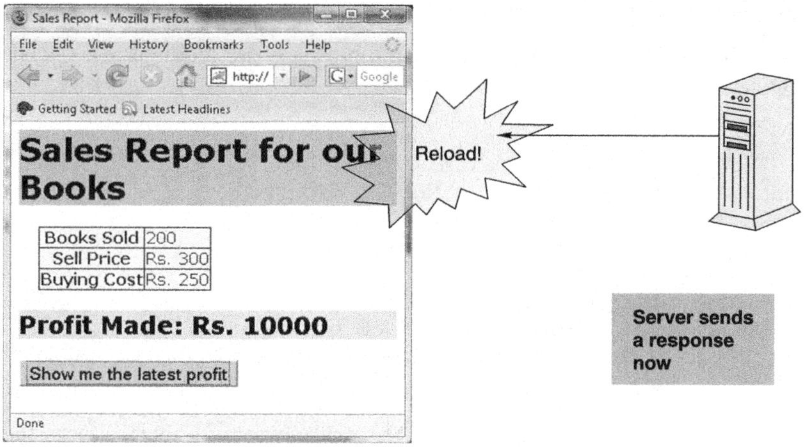

Fig. 7.59 *AJAX case study -2*

At this stage, let us reinforce our AJAX ideas.

AJAX has ability to fetch data from the server without having to refresh a page.

1. **Applications without AJAX**
   (a) Normal Web applications communicate with the server by referring to a new URL
   (b) Example: When a form is submitted, it is processed by a server-side program, which gets invoked
2. **AJAX applications**
   (a) Use an object called XMLHttpRequest object built into the browser, using JavaScript to communicate with the server
   (b) HTML form is not needed to communicate with the server

What is this XMLHttpRequest object all about? It is an alternative for HTML forms. It is used to communicate with the server side code, from inside a browser. The server side code now returns text or XML data, not the complete HTML Web page. The programmer has to extract data received from the server via the XMLHttpRequest object, as per the needs.

7.2.5 AJAX Coding

Figure 7.60 outlines the way we can write code for AJAX-based applications.

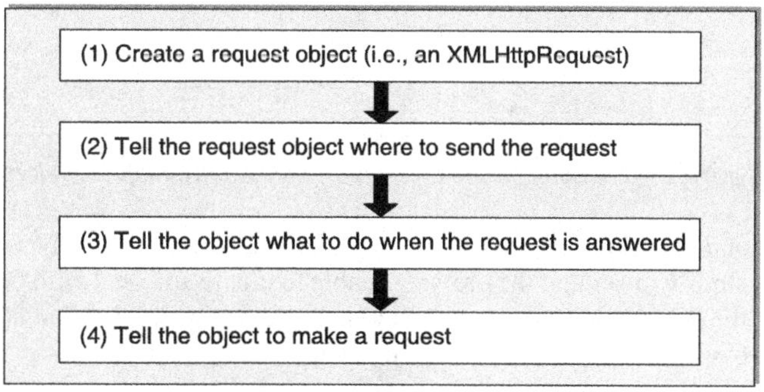

Fig. 7.60 *AJAX processing steps*

Let us now discuss these steps in detail.

1. Create the XMLHttpRequest object Two main browsers are required to be handled: Internet Explorer and Others.

```
Code for non-Internet Explorer browsers
var XMLHttpRequestObject = false;
if (window.XMLHttpRequest) { // Non-IE browser
   XMLHttpRequestObject = new XMLHttpRequest ();
}

Code for Internet Explorer
else if (window.ActiveXObject) { // IE browser
   XMLHttpRequestObject = new ActiveXObject ("Microsoft.XMLHTTP");
}
```

We can write a complete HTML page to ensure that our browser was able to successfully create the XMLHttpRequest object, as shown in Fig. 7.61.

```
<html>
   <head>
      <title>AJAX Example</title>

      <script language = "javascript">

         var XMLHttpRequestObject = false;

         if (window.XMLHttpRequest) {
            XMLHttpRequestObject = new XMLHttpRequest ();
         }
         else if (window.ActiveXObject) {
            XMLHttpRequestObject = new ActiveXObject ("Microsoft.XMLHTTP");
         }

         if (XMLHttpRequestObject) {
            document.write ("<h1>Welcome to AJAX</h1>");
         }

      </script>
   </head>

   <body>
   </body>

</html>
```

Fig. 7.61 *Checking for the presence of the XMLHttpRequest object*

This code does not do anything meaningful, except for checking that the browser is *AJAX enabled.* Of course, by this we simply mean that the browser is able to create and deal with the XMLHttpRequest object, as needed by the AJAX technology. If it is able to do so (which is what should happen for all modern browsers), we will see the output as shown in Fig. 7.62.

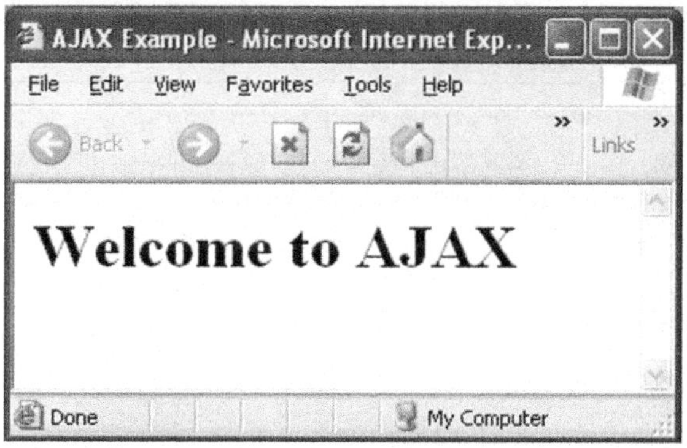

Fig. 7.62 *Output of the earlier HTML page*

2. Tell the XMLHttpRequest object as to where to send the request We need to open the XMLHttpRequest object now by calling its open method. It expects two parameters: the type of the method (GET/POST), and the URL where the asynchronous AJAX request is to be sent. An example is shown below.

```
XMLHttpRequestObject.open ("GET", "test.dat");
```

Here, we are saying that we want to send a GET request to fetch a file named *test.dat*.

3. Tell the XMLHttpRequest object what to do when the request is answered We can download data from the server using the XMLHttpRequest object. This process happens *behind the scenes*, i.e., in an asynchronous manner. When data comes from the server, the following two things happen:

(a) The readyState property of the HTTPRequestObject changes to one of the following possible values:
0 – Uninitialized, 1 – Loading, 2 – Loaded, 3 – Interactive, 4 – Complete

(b) The status property holds the results of the HTTP download
200 – OK, 404 – Not found, etc.

Thus, we can check this status as follows:

```
if ((XMLHttpRequestObject.readyState == 4) &&
            (XMLHttpRequestObject.status == 200)) {
                ...
            }
```

4. Tell the XMLHttpRequest object make a request In this step, we download the data received from the server and use it in our application, as desired.

7.2.6 Life with AJAX

Let us now continue our earlier example to understand how *AJAX enabling* makes it so much more effective.

Our code would have the following JavaScript functions:

1. **getBooksSold ()** This function would create a new object to talk to the server.
2. **updatePage ()** This function would ask the server for the latest book sales figures.
3. **createRequest ()** This function would set the number of books sold and profit made.

Let us write the HTML part first. The code is shown in Fig. 7.63.

```
<html>
   <head>
      <title>Sales Report</title>
      <link rel="stylesheet" type="text/css" href="books.css" />
   </head>

   <body>
      <h1>Sales Report for our Books</h1>

      <div id="Books">
         <table>
            <tr><th>Books Sold</th>
            <td><span id="books-sold">555</span></td></tr>
            <tr><th>Sell Price</th>
          <td>Rs. <span id="price">300</span></td></tr>
          <tr><th>Buying Cost</th>
          <td>Rs. <span id="cost">250</span></td></tr>
       </table>

         <h2>Profit Made: Rs. <span id="cash">27750</span></h2>

         <form method="GET" action="getUpdatedBookSales.jsp">
            <input value="Show me the latest profit" type="button" />
         </form>
      </div>
   </body>
</html>
```

Fig. 7.63 *HTML code for AJAX-enabled page – Initial version*

The resulting screen is shown in Fig. 7.64.

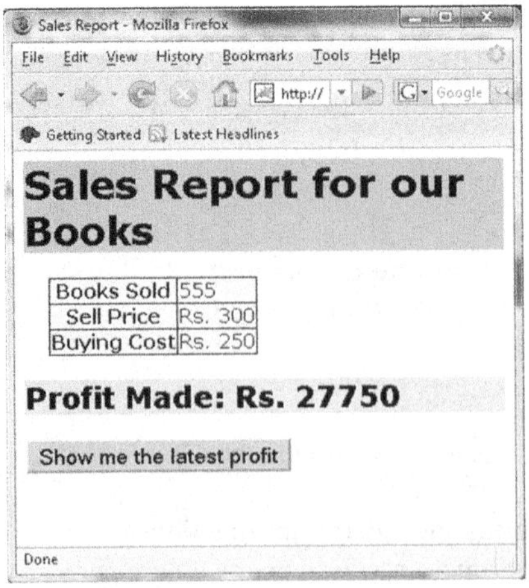

Fig. 7.64 *Result of our HTML code*

We now want to add JavaScript so that at the click of the button, the function *getBooksSold ()* will get called. This is shown in Fig. 7.65.

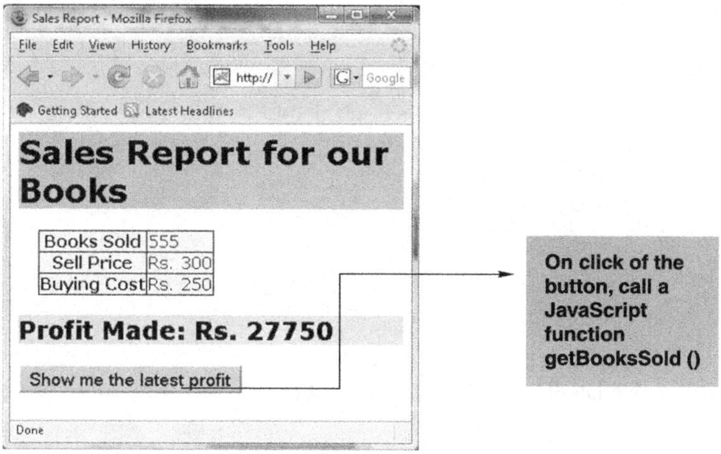

Fig. 7.65 *Adding JavaScript*

The *getBooksSold ()* function

What should the *getBooksSold ()* function do? We can summarize:

1. Create a new request by calling the createRequest () function.
2. Specify the URL to receive the updates from.
3. Set up the request object to make a connection.
4. Request an updated number of books sold.

Here is the outline of the JavaScript code so far.

```
<script language="javascript" type="text/javascript">

   function createRequest ()
   // JavaScript code

   function getBooksSold () {
      createRequest ();
   }

</script>
```

Now, let us think about the contents of the *createRequest ()* function.

The *createRequest ()* function

This function would simply create an instance of the XMLHttpRequest object, as per the browser type:

```
 function createRequest () {
   if (window.XMLHttpRequest) {
      XMLHttpRequestObject = new XMLHttpRequest ();
```

```
    }
    else
       if (window.ActiveXObject) {
         XMLHttpRequestObject = new ActiveXObject ("Microsoft.XMLHTTP");
     }
}
```

Now let us modify the *getBooksSold ()* function suitably, as follows:

```
function getBooksSold () {
        createRequest ();
        var url = "getUpdatedBookSales.jsp";

        XMLHttpRequestObject.open ("GET", url);
}
        ...
```

This would call getUpdatedBookSales.jsp. We want to process the response sent by this JSP now.

```
function getBooksSold () {
        createRequest ();
        var url = "getUpdatedBookSales.jsp";
        XMLHttpRequestObject.open ("GET", url);

        XMLHttpRequestObject.onreadystatechange = updatePage;
        XMLHttpRequestObject.send (null);

        ...
}
```

Here, *updatePage ()* is a function that will get called when the JSP on the server side has responded to our XMLHttpRequest. What should this function have? Let us see. First, it should receive the value sent by the JSP:

```
function updatePage () {
        var newTotal = XMLHttpRequestObject.responseText;
```

Note that normally, the server-side JSP would have returned a full HTML page. But now the JSP is dealing with an AJAX request (i.e., XMLHttpRequest object). Hence, the JSP does not send a full HTML page. Instead, it simply returns a number in which the *updatePage ()* function is interested. This number is stored inside a JavaScript variable called as *newTotal*.

Now, we want to also read the current values of the HTML form variables *books-sold* and *cash*. Hence, we amend the above function further:

```
function updatePage () {
        var newTotal = XMLHttpRequestObject.responseText;

        var booksSoldElement = document.getElementById ("books-sold");
        var cashElement = document.getElementById ("cash");
```

Now, we want to replace the current value of the books sold element with the on received from the server now. Hence, we add one more line to the code:

```
function updatePage () {
            var newTotal = XMLHttpRequestObject.responseText;

           var booksSoldElement = document.getElementById ("books-sold");
            var cashElement = document.getElementById ("cash");
            replaceText (booksSoldElement, newTotal);
}
```

This would *refresh* only the tag of interest, which is the *booksSoldElement*, which, in turn, means the *books-sold* HTML form variable.

What should the JSP do? It is expected to simply return the latest number of books sold at this juncture. Hence, it has a single line:

```
out.print (300);
```

Key Terms and Concepts

JavaScript • AJAX • Validate data • Local variables • Global variables • Standard objects • Asynchronous JavaScript And XML • Asynchronous • XMLHttpRequest • indexOf() • lastIndexOf() • charAt () • subString () • split () • Loops

SUMMARY

- JavaScript adds dynamic content to Web pages on the client side.
- A JavaScript program is a small program that is sent by the Web server to the browser along with the standard HTML content.
- The JavaScript program executes in the boundaries of the Web browser, and performs things such as client-side validations, responding to user inputs, performing basic checks, and so on.
- JavaScript does not perform any operations on the server, but is clearly a client-side technology.
- JavaScript is a full-fledged programming language in its own right. It allows us to use operators, functions, loops, conditions, and so on.
- Ajax allows us to invoke server-side code from the client, but without submitting an HTML form, contrary to what happens in the normal processing. Instead, when we use Ajax, the requests are sent from the browser to the server in an asynchronous fashion. This means that the client-side user can continue doing what she was doing while the request is sent to the server and the response is returned by the server.
- This allows for writing very creative code for a number of situations. For example, while the user is entering data, we can perform *on the fly* server-side validations, provide online help, and so on, which was not possible with the earlier client-only or server-only programming models.

MULTIPLE-CHOICE QUESTIONS

1. JavaScript is __________ language.
   (a) interpreted (b) compiled
   (c) interpreted and compiled (d) None of these
2. JavaScript is contained inside the __________ tags.
   (a) <font>...</font> (b) <script>...</script>
   (c) <head>...</head> (d) <body>...</body>
3. All functions should be defined in the __________ section.
   (a) <head> (b) <script> (c) <body> (d) <font>
4. The function __________ returns the month of a Date object.
   (a) getHours() (b) getMonth() (c) getDay() (d) getMinutes()
5. The function __________ Returns a random number between 0 and 1.
   (a) pow (x, y) (b) random () (c) round (x) (d) sin (x)
6. The __________ function Returns the second of a Date object.
   (a) getSeconds() (b) getMonth() (c) getDay() (d) getMinutes()
7. Client-side technology, such as __________ is used for validating user inputs.
   (a) JavaScript (b) ASP.NET (c) PHP (d) JSP
8. The __________ function used to create an instance of the XMLHttpRequest object, as per the browser type.
   (a) createRequest () (b) getRequest () (c) putRequest () (d) Request()
9. AJAX application uses __________ object built into the browser, using JavaScript to communicate with the server
   (a) XMLFtpRequest (b) XMLHttpRequest (c) HttpRequest (d) HttpResponse
10. The __________ function that will get called when the JSP on the server side has responds to XMLHttpRequest.
    (a) updateRequest() (b) updatePage() (c) HttpRequest (d) HttpResponse

DETAILED QUESTIONS

1. Explain how to call JavaScript from an HTML page.
2. What are the various kinds of functions in JavaScript?
3. Can JavaScript be in a separate file? Give details.
4. What are the key usages of JavaScript?
5. How are HTML form and JavaScript related?
6. What is the purpose of Ajax?
7. Differentiate between synchronous and asynchronous processing.
8. Why is Ajax different from traditional request-response model?
9. How do we refer to some server-side script/program from an Ajax-enabled page?
10. Explain the XMLHttpRequest object.

EXERCISES

1. Write an HTML page and also provide a JavaScript for accepting a user ID and password from the user to ensure that the input is not empty.
2. In the above page, stop the user if the user attempts to tab out of the user ID or password fields without entering anything.
3. Make the same HTML page now Ajax-enabled, so that the server-side code can check if the user id and password are correct (by comparing it with corresponding database fields). [Hint: We would need to make use of ASP.NET or JSP/Servlets for this].
4. Find out how XML and Ajax are related.
5. Explore any possible sites that make use of Ajax.

8 PHP/MySQL – AN OVERVIEW

INTRODUCTION

PHP is a widely-used open source general-purpose scripting language that is especially suited for web development and can be embedded into HTML. It has gained enormous popularity in the community as the free and efficient alternative to commercial competitors such as Microsoft's ASP. PHP is distributed under a license that makes the source code available to anyone. But before dwelling much into PHP and subsequently MySQL, lets understand the concept of scripting language, its types and uses.

WHAT IS SCRIPTING LANGUAGE? 8.1

In simple words, a scripting language is a special type of programming language meant to deal with Web page interactions. Scripting language adds dynamic behavior to a Web page. Scripting languages came about largely because of the development of the Internet as a communications tool. To show content and add effects such as color and other formatting in Web pages we have HTML and CSS. But these are used only for presentation of information. In scenarios where we have to take some action on base of any activity done by user on web page we need to use some programming logic on the web page. That is where scripting language comes into picture. For example, activities like validating user input on forms, displaying dynamic advertisements on page, image slideshow on web pages and so on can be done using scripting language. So if we describe a dynamic Web page then we can conceive its presentation part to be made of HTML and CSS and programming logic part to be consisting of scripting language. So based on understanding and definition, scripting language differs from a normal programming language on below points:

1. It can be embedded inside HTML and adds programming logic to a Web page.
2. Scripting language does not contain any entry point like main function/method in a program.

3. Scripting language is never compiled. So as many times we execute/load the Web page, statements will be interpreted from scratch again and again.

On the base of functionality scripting can be done on either server or client side.

CLIENT SIDE SCRIPTING VS SERVER SIDE SCRIPTING 8.2

A client side scripting language is different from server side scripting on below points:

Client side scripting	*Server side scripting*
Adds interactivity on client browser.	Performs interaction from server side.
Runs on the client browser, no extra software is needed.	Requires a Web server with language parser/interpreter support.
Used mainly for form validations, controlling behavior of browser.	Used for request/response manipulation and handling.
Cannot connect to database or read/write files.	Interacts with db and can do file operations.
Can view the source code by clicking on view source on browser.	Since its executed on server side, you cannot view source code by clicking on view source on client browser.
Example Javascript, VBscript.	Example PHP, ASP, JSP, etc.

FEATURES OF PHP 8.3

1. **Fast and efficient** As a standard CGI program, PHP can be installed on any UNIX machine running any UNIX web server. With support for the new FastCGI standard, PHP can take advantage of the speed improvements gained through this mechanism. As an Apache module, PHP becomes an extremely powerful and lightning fast alternative to CGI programmimg.
2. **Access logging** With the access logging capabilities of PHP, users can maintain their own hit counting and logging. It does not use the system's central access log files in any way, and it provides real-time access monitoring. The Log Viewer Script provides a quick summary of the accesses to a set of pages owned by an individual user. In addition to that, the package can be configured to generate a footer on every page which shows access information. See the bottom of this page for an example of this.
3. **Access control** A built-in web-based configuration screen handles access control configuration. It is possible to create rules for all or some Web pages owned by a certain person which place various restrictions on who can view these pages and how they will be viewed. Pages can be password protected, completely restricted, logging disabled and more based on the client's domain, browser, e-mail address or even the referring document.
4. **MySQL and PostgresSQL support** MySQL and Postgres are advanced free RDBMS. PHP supports lots of inbuilt functions and liabraries to support MySQL and PostgreSQL. It had good support for other popular databases as well.
5. **Mail and file upload support** PHP has huge list of functions to support mailing and file upload. Its very easy to send mails to someone using PHP. Also it lets users upload files to a Web server. PHP provides the actual Mime decoding to make this work and also provides the additional framework to do something useful with the uploaded file once it has been received.

6. **Variables, arrays, associative arrays** PHP supports typed variables, arrays and even Perl-like associative arrays. These can all be passed from one Web page to another using either GET or POST method forms.
7. **Extended regular expressions** Regular expressions are heavily used for pattern matching, pattern substitutions and general string manipulation. PHP supports all common regular expression operations.
8. **Raw HTTP header control** The ability to have Web pages send customized raw HTTP headers based on some condition is essential for high-level Web site design. A frequent use is to send a location: URL header to redirect the calling client to some other URL. It can also be used to turn off cacheing or manipulate the last update header of pages.
9. **On-the-fly GIF image creation** PHP has support for Thomas Boutell's GD image library which makes it possible to generate GIF images on the fly.
10. **ISP "Safe Mode" support** PHP supports an unique "Safe Mode" which makes it safe to have multiple users run PHP scripts on the same server.
11. Many more new features are being added in newer releases of PHP. Visit the main web site at http://www.php.net
12. **It's free!** One final essential feature. The package is completely free. It is licensed under the GNU/GPL which allows you to use the software for any purpose, commercial or otherwise.

GETTING STARTED WITH PHP 8.4

Here in this section, we will know about how to install PHP, what all other components are needed in running a PHP program and will go through steps to run a basic PHP "Hello World" program.

8.4.1 Installation

For smoothly running a PHP page you need below components installed on your machine:

1. **PHP Parser** This is required for interpreting your PHP program while execution. Latest version can be downloaded from official PHP Web site, i.e., www.php.net
2. **Web server** Since PHP is a server side scripting language so we need a Web server (like Apache or IIS) to run it. Below is the download link of apache server. Its widely used as its free: http://httpd.apache.org/download.cgi
3. **Database (optional)** Usually in order to create a Web application we need to have a database. For that purpose, we can download and install MySQL or PgSQL s these two have very good connectivity and in built functions for various operations.

Since downloading different things from different places and configuring them can be a tedious task, therefore, we can say that there are various packages available for different operating systems. Some of the most popular packages are WAMP (stands for Windows Apache, MySQL, PHP and available for windows operating System) and LAMP (stands for Linux Apache MySQL PHP and available for linux operating system). Now we will see the steps for installation using WAMP server package.

8.4.2 Installation Using WAMP

WAMP server is a free software and can be downloaded from below link:

http://www.wampserver.com/en/

After downloading from the above source, below are the screenshots for installation steps of WAMP:

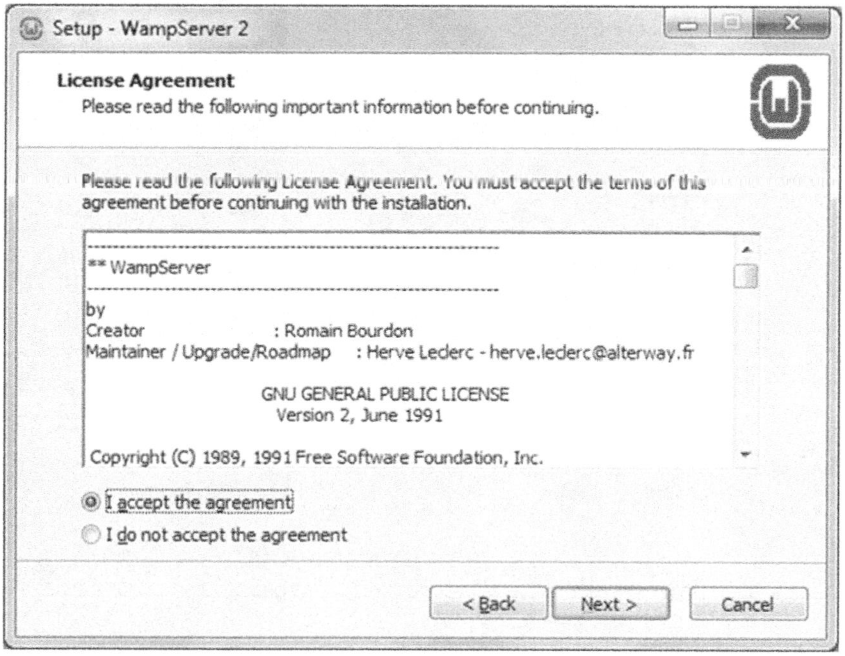

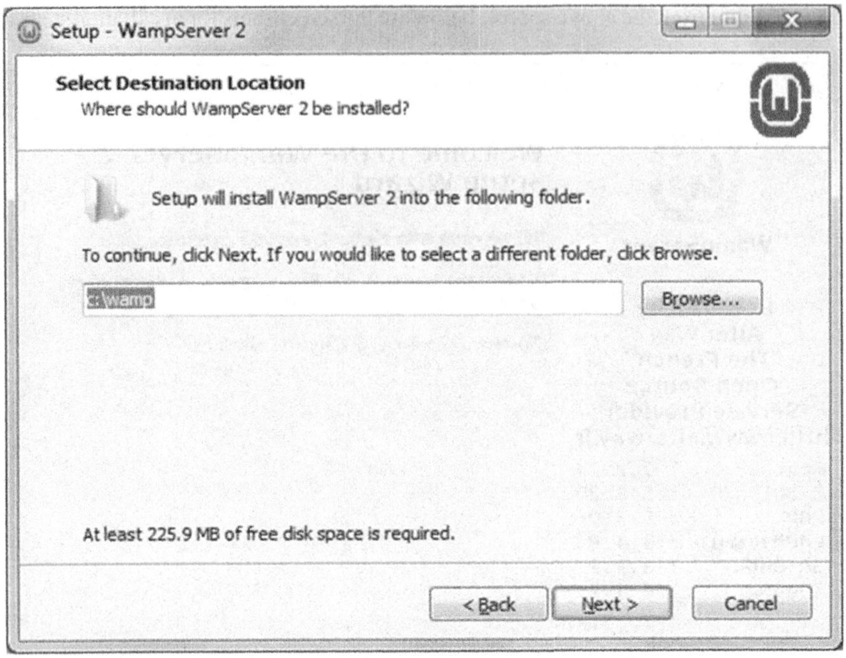
Setup - WampServer 2
Select Destination Location
Where should WampServer 2 be installed?
Setup will install WampServer 2 into the following folder.
To continue, click Next. If you would like to select a different folder, click Browse.
c:\wamp
Browse...
At least 225.9 MB of free disk space is required.
< Back
Next >
Cancel

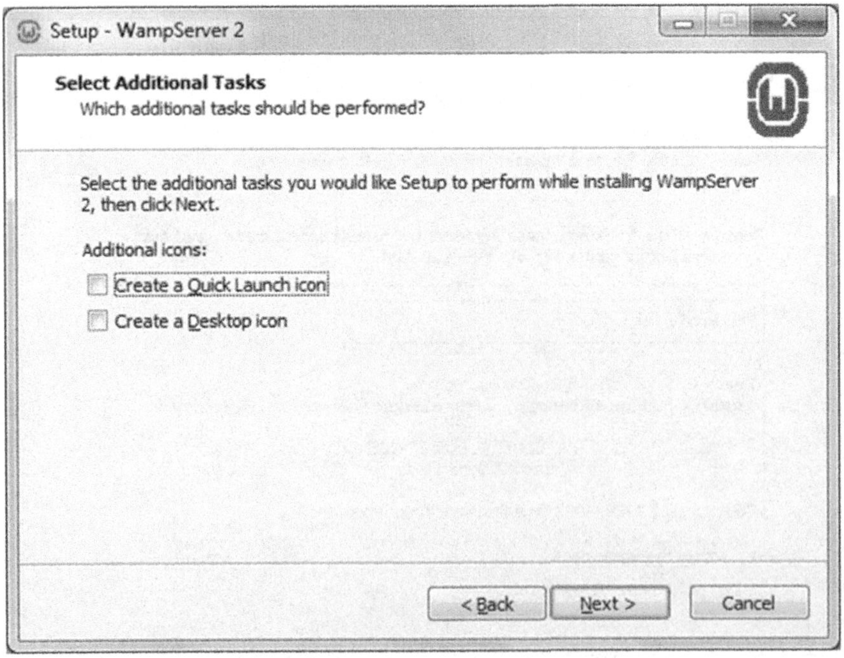
Setup - WampServer 2
Select Additional Tasks
Which additional tasks should be performed?
Select the additional tasks you would like Setup to perform while installing WampServer 2, then click Next.
Additional icons:
Create a Quick Launch icon
Create a Desktop icon
< Back
Next >
Cancel

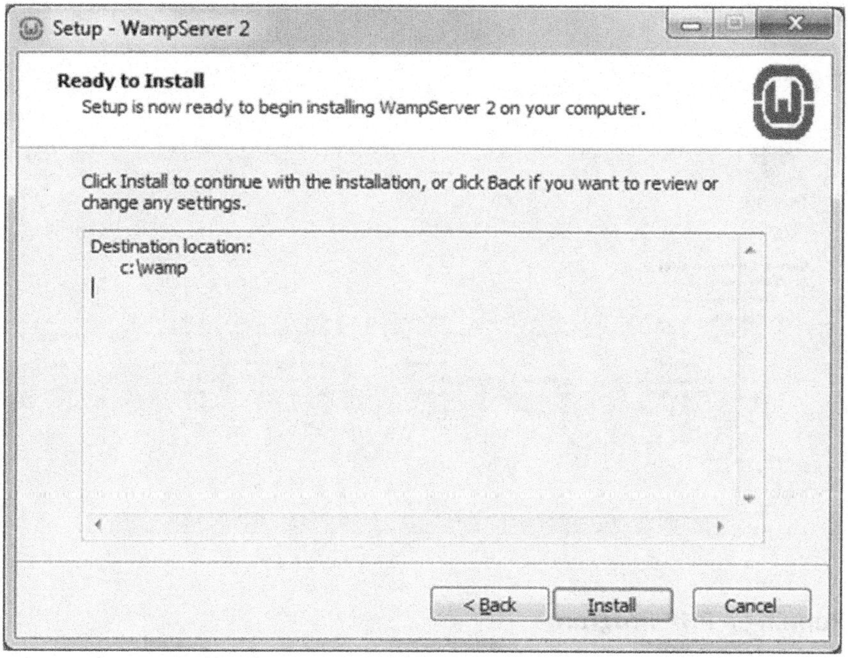
Setup - WampServer 2
Ready to Install
Setup is now ready to begin installing WampServer 2 on your computer.
Click Install to continue with the installation, or click Back if you want to review or change any settings.
Destination location:
c:\wamp
< Back
Install
Cancel

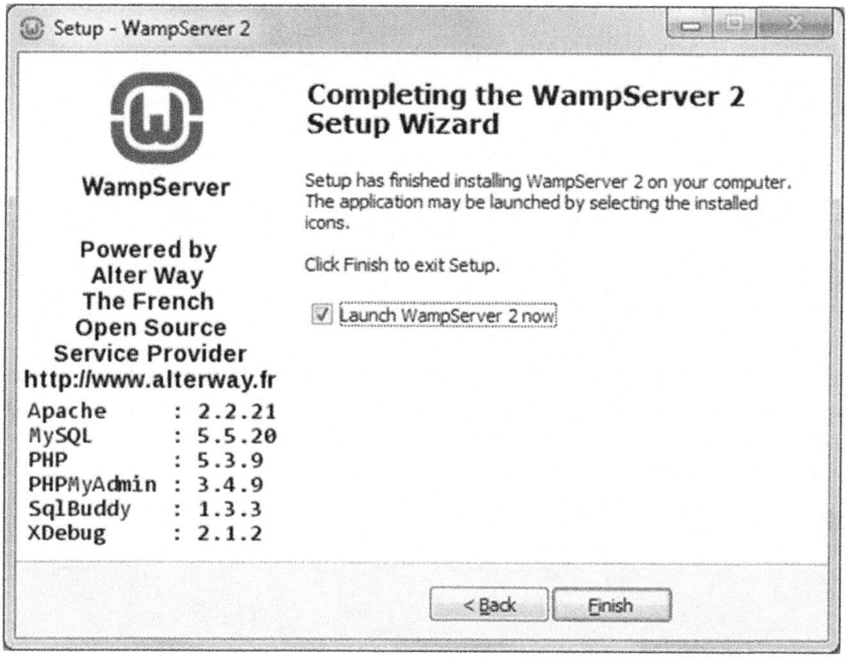
Setup - WampServer 2
WampServer
Powered by
Alter Way
The French
Open Source
Service Provider
http://www.alterway.fr
Apache : 2.2.21
MySQL : 5.5.20
PHP : 5.3.9
PHPMyAdmin : 3.4.9
SqlBuddy : 1.3.3
XDebug : 2.1.2
Completing the WampServer 2 Setup Wizard
Setup has finished installing WampServer 2 on your computer. The application may be launched by selecting the installed icons.
Click Finish to exit Setup.
Launch WampServer 2 now
< Back
Finish

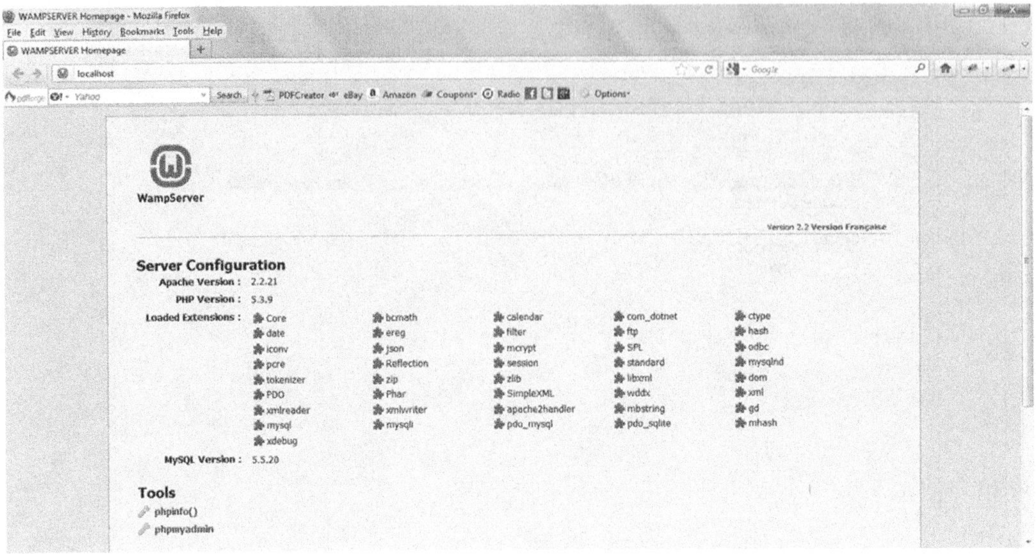

8.4.3 Running a PHP Program

Now after doing the WAMP server setup we will go through the steps to write and run a basic “Hello World” program in PHP:

1. Write below code in any text editor like notepad:

```
<html>
<body>
<?php
echo "Hello World";
 ?>
</body>
</html>
```

2. Save this file as hello_world.php inside the c:\wamp\www directory (assuming that WAMP is installed inside c:\ of your system). www is the directory name where all the PHP applications and files are stored for WAMP server. Its also called document root.
3. Start the WAMP server if not started.
4. Type the path http://localhost/hello_world.php in browser. You will see the below screen:

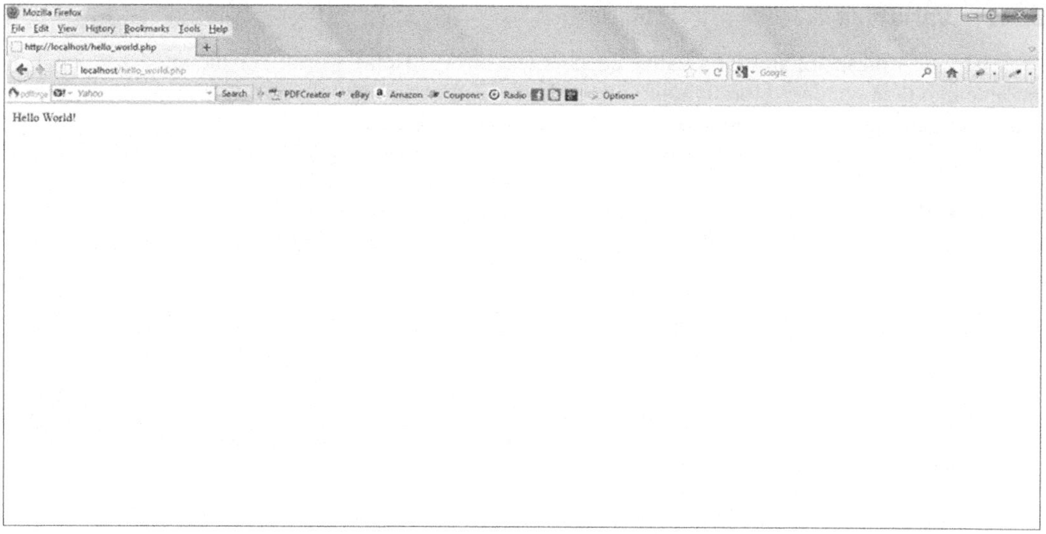

8.4.4 Some Key Points

Here are some key points related to a PHP program:

1. PHP files have a file extension of ".php", ".php3", or ".phtml".
2. You cannot view the PHP source code by selecting "View source" in the browser. This is because the scripts are executed on the server before the result is sent back to the browser. So you will only see the output from the PHP file, which is plain HTML.
3. The output is displayed usually on web browser.
4. Echo and print statements are used for outputting any text .print returns a value on successful display whereas echo doesn't.

LANGUAGE REFERENCE - BASICS 8.5

Now in order to get familiar with the language we will now go through the basics of PHP. When someone visits your PHP Web page, your Web server processes the PHP code. It then sees which parts it needs to show to visitors (content and pictures) and hides the other stuff (file operations, math calculations, etc.) then translates your PHP into HTML. After the translation into HTML, it sends the Web page to your visitor's Web browser.

8.5.1 Syntax

Much of its syntax is borrowed from C, Java and Perl with a couple of unique PHP-specific features thrown in. The goal of the language is to allow web developers to write dynamically generated pages quickly. As evident in the above "Hello World" example, a PHP scripting block always starts with <?php and ends with ?>. On servers with shorthand support enabled you can start a scripting block with <? and end with ?>. Also, each code line in PHP must end with a semicolon. A PHP file normally contains HTML tags, just like an HTML file, and some PHP scripting code.

8.5.2 Variables

A variable is a means of storing a value, such as text string "Hello World!" or the integer value 4. A variable can then be reused throughout your code, instead of having to type out the actual value over and over again. In PHP you define a variable with the following form:

```
$variable_name = Value;
```

Note: If you forget that dollar sign at the beginning, it will not work.

Below is sample PHP code

```
<?php
$hello = "Hello World!";
$a_number = 4;
$anotherNumber = 8;
?>
```

Following are the variable naming rules for PHP:

1. PHP variables must start with a letter or underscore "_".
2. A variable name should not contain spaces.
3. PHP variables may only be comprised of alpha-numeric characters and underscores. a-z, A-Z, 0-9, or _.
4. Variables are case sensitive this means $myvariable is different from $myVariable.
5. Variables with more than one word should be separated with underscores like $my_variable or with capitalization, e.g., $myVariable.

8.5.3 Constants

As per the definition, a constant contains a value which does not change during the execution of program. In PHP, define() function is used to declare a constant.PHP constants unlike variables do not begin with the "$" sign. Constant names are usually uppercase as per coding conventions. Constant names can contain letters, numbers, and the (_) underscore character. Constants cannot, however, begin with numbers.

Below are some examples of constant declaration:

```
<html>
<body>
<?php
define("STRING_CONST","My PHP program");
define("INTEGER_CONST",500);
define("FLOAT_CONST",2.25);
echo STRING_CONST;
echo INTEGER_CONST;
echo FLOAT_CONST;
?>
</body>
 </html>
```

8.5.4 Data Types

Most PHP scripts deal with data in one form or another, usually stored in variables. In PHP you don't have to explicitly define type of the data. When you assign a value to a variable, it automatically converts it into the type based on value. PHP can work with different types of data. For example, a whole number is said to have an integer data type, while a string of text has a string data type. On broader way, we can classify PHP data types into below forms:

1. Scalar types
2. Compound data types
3. Special types

Scalar Types

Scalar data is data that only contains a single value. As of version 6, PHP features 5 scalar data types:

Type	*Description*	*Example*
Integer	A whole number	5, 120, –1250
Float	A floating point number	7.89, –3.56.
String	A sequence of characters	"Hello", "abc123!@#".
Binary	A sequence of binary (non-unicode) characters	"Hello", "abc123!@#".
Boolean	True or false	True, false

Note: Since we do not have to specify the type explicitly, following will result in boolean false if we convert them:

1. integer 0
2. float 0.0
3. empty string or string "0"
4. an array with zero elements
5. the type NULL

Compound Types

Compound types can contain multiple values in one variable. Below are compound variables supported in PHP:

Type	*Description*
Array	Can hold multiple values indexed by numbers or strings. Will describe it more later on in this chapter.
Object	Can hold multiple values (properties), and can also contain methods (functions) for working on properties.

Special Types

As well as scalar and compound types, PHP has 2 special data types that don't fall into the other categories:

Type	*Description*
Resource	Used to access an external resource (for example, a file handle or database connection)
Null	Can only contain the value null, which means "no value"

Loose Typing in PHP

Some languages, such as Java, are strongly typed: once you have created a variable, you can't change the type of data stored in it. PHP, in contrast, is loosely typed: you can change a variable's data type at any time. Please see the below example:

```
<?php
$x = 10;
$x .="Hello";
$x = 5.67;
?>
```

The above code will run without any error and old values will get flushed and will be replaced by new ones. In the above example, $x starts off by holding integer data (10). The next line appends the string "hello" to the data using the concatenation operator (.), which changes $x's value to "10hello" (a string data type). Finally, 5.67 is assigned to $x, changing its data type to a float.

8.5.5 Comments

If you want something to be ignored (a comment for example) you can put // before it as. There are a few other ways of creating comments within PHP, which are demonstrated below:

```
<?php
 //A comment on a single line

 #Another single line comment

 /*
 Using this method
 you can create a larger block of text
 and it will all be commented out
 */

 ?>
```

One reason you may want to put a comment in your code is to make a note to yourself about what the code is doing for reference when you edit it later. You may also want to put comments in your code if you plan on sharing it with others and want them to understand what it does, or to include your name and terms of use within the script.

8.5.6 Operators

Below is the list of operators supported in PHP:

1. Arithmetic operators :- +,-,*,/,%;
2. Increment/decrement :- ++,--;
3. Assignment operators :- =,+=,-=,*=,/= etc;
4. Comparison operators:- ==,===, !=, !==,>=,<=,>,< etc.;
5. Logical operators :- &&,||,! .

8.5.7 Conditions

Conditions are backbone of any programming language. Conditional statements are used to perform different actions based on different scenarios. Very often when you write code, you want to perform different actions for different decisions. In PHP, you have if... else, elseif, and switch statements for condition checking.

Here are the conditions supported by PHP:

If Condition

Use the if statement to execute some code only if a specified condition is true.

Syntax:
if (condition) code to be executed if condition is true;

Example:

```
<html>
<body>

<?php
$num= -5;
if ($num<0) echo "This is a negative number";
?>

</body>
</html>
```

Output:
Above example will print "This is a negative number" as the given condition is true.

If...Else Condition

Use the if....else statement to execute some code if a condition is true and another code if a condition is false.

Syntax:

```
if (condition)
   code to be executed if condition is true;
else
   code to be executed if condition is false;
```

Example:

```
<html>
<body>

<?php
$n= 4;
if ($n<0)
```

```
    echo "This is negative number";
else
    echo "This is positive number";
?>

</body>
</html>
```

Output:

This will print “this is positive number” on Web page.

If...Elseif.. Else Condition

Use the if....elseif...else statement to select one of several blocks of code to be executed.

Syntax:

```
if (condition)
    code to be executed if condition is true;
elseif (condition)
    code to be executed if condition is true;
else
    code to be executed if condition is false;
```

Example:

```
<html>
<body>

<?php
$d=date("D");
if ($d=="Fri")
    echo "Have a nice weekend!";
elseif ($d=="Sun")
    echo "Have a nice Sunday!";
else
    echo "Have a nice day!";
?>

</body>
</html>
```

Output:

The above example will output “Have a nice weekend!” if the current day is Friday, and “Have a nice Sunday!” if the current day is Sunday. Otherwise it will output “Have a nice day!”

Switch...Case Statement

Use the switch statement to select one of many blocks of code to be executed.

Syntax:

```
switch (n)
{
case label1:
    code to be executed if n=label1;
    break;
case label2:
    code to be executed if n=label2;
    break;
default:
    code to be executed if n is different from both label1 and label2;
}
```

This is how it works: First we have a single expression n (most often a variable), that is evaluated once. The value of the expression is then compared with the values for each case in the structure. If there is a match, the block of code associated with that case is executed. Use break to prevent the code from running into the next case automatically. The default statement is used if no match is found.

Example:

```
<html>
<body>

<?php
$x=1;
switch ($x)
{
case 1:
    echo "Number 1";
    break;
case 2:
    echo "Number 2";
    break;
case 3:
    echo "Number 3";
    break;
default:
    echo "No number between 1 and 3";
}
?>

</body>
</html>
```

Output:

Output of above code will be “Number 1”.

8.5.8 Looping

Looping, also known as iteration is the process of executing the line of codes for a specified number of times or till a particular condition is satisfied. In simple words, if you need to execute a statement 10 times then you don't need to write it 10 times and put it inside a loop will do the trick for you.

Following are loops supported in PHP:

1. while
2. do….while
3. for
4. foreach

Now we will see details about each loop. Details about foreach loop will be available on next section later on in order to understand it in better way.

While Loop

The while loop executes a block of code while a condition is true.

Syntax:

```
while (condition)
    {
    code to be executed;
    }
```

Example:

```
<html>
<body>

<?php
$i=1;
while($i<=5)
    {
    echo "The number is " . $i . "<br/>";
    $i++;
    }
?>

</body>
</html>
```

Output:

The number is 1
The number is 2
The number is 3
The number is 4
The number is 5

do...while Loop

The do...while statement will always execute the block of code once, it will then check the condition, and repeat the loop while the condition is true.

Syntax:

```
do
    {
    code to be executed;
    }
while (condition);
```

Example:

```
<html>
<body>

<?php
$i=1;
do
  {
  $i++;
  echo "The number is" . $i . "<br/>";
  }
while ($i<=5);
?>

</body>
</html>
```

Output:

The number is 2
The number is 3
The number is 4
The number is 5
The number is 6

for Loop

The for loop is used when you know in advance how many times the script should run.

Syntax:

```
for (init; condition; increment)
    {
    code to be executed;
    }
```

Below is a brief about for loop parameters:

1. **init** Mostly used to set a counter (but can be any code to be executed once at the beginning of the loop)
2. **condition** Evaluated for each loop iteration. If it evaluates to TRUE, the loop continues. If it evaluates to FALSE, the loop ends.
3. **increment** Mostly used to increment a counter (but can be any code to be executed at the end of the loop)

Example:

```
<html>
<body>

<?php
for ($i=1; $i<=5; $i++)
    {
    echo "The number is" . $i . "<br/>";
    }
?>

</body>
</html>
```

Output:

The number is 1
The number is 2
The number is 3
The number is 4
The number is 5

LANGUAGE REFERENCE – ADVANCE 8.6

After getting familiar with basic languages constructs now we will move on to some advanced topics. The things which we have already seen till now are the backbone of any programming language. Now in order to build more complex applications we will study some advanced topics.

8.6.1 Arrays

In PHP, array is a variable which can hold a collection of data. Since in PHP we don't have explicit declaration of data type, so here we can have multiple type of data in a single array.

Example:

$weekdays = array("Sunday","Monday",Tuesday","Wednesday"."Thursday",Friday","Saturday");

There are three types of arrays in PHP:

1. Numeric
2. Associative
3. Multi-dimensional

Numeric Arrays

A numeric array is a traditional array which stores each element with a numeric index.

Example:

1. In the following example the index are automatically assigned (the index starts at 0):

```
$cars=array("Maruti","Hyundei","BMW","Toyota");
```

2. In the following example we assign the index manually:

```
$cars[0]="Maruti";
$cars[1]="Hyundei";
$cars[2]="BMW";
$cars[3]="Toyota";
```

Associative Arrays

This is a bit of deviation from normal array in PHP. When storing data about specific named values, a numerical array is not always the best way to do it. With associative arrays we can use the values as keys and assign values to them.

Example:
In this example we use an array to assign ages to the different persons:

```
$ages = array("Peter"=>32, "Quagmire"=>30, "Joe"=>34);
```

Multi-dimensional Arrays

In a multi-dimensional array, each element in the main array can also be an array. And each element in the sub-array can be an array, and so on. In this we can either have numeric arrays or associative or a combination of both.

Example:

```
$families = array
    (
    "Griffin"=>array
    (
    "Peter",
    "Lois",
    "Megan"
    ),
    "Quagmire"=>array
    (
    "Glenn"
    ),
    "Brown"=>array
    (
    "Cleveland",
    "Loretta",
    "Junior"
    )
    );
```

8.6.2 Foreach Loop

In order to traverse arrays and access elements of those, PHP supports an advanced version of for loop. This is known as *foreach loop*.

Syntax:

```
foreach ($array as $value)
  {
  code to be executed;
  }
```

For every loop iteration, the value of the current array element is assigned to $value (and the array pointer is moved by one) - so on the next loop iteration, you'll be looking at the next array value.

Example:

```
<html>
<body>

<?php
$x=array("one","two","three");
foreach ($x as $value)
    {
    echo $value . "<br/>";
a}
?>

</body>
</html>
```

Output:

one
two
three

8.6.3 Functions

In simple words, function is a set of instructions which carries out a specific task. A function is not executed unless it gets called from within the program. These functions are either provided in the languages itself of can be defined by the programmer. The real power of PHP comes due to its vast list of its built in functions. Due to open source nature of PHP many new functions keep getting added giving it more usability. While creating a user defined function, the function name should be given in such a way that it shows what activity is dine inside the function body. Also, a function name can start with either an alphabet or underscore (and not any digit or any other special symbol).

Syntax:

```
function functionName()
{
code to be executed;
}
```

Example:

Below is a simple function that writes a name given in the parameter:

```
<html>
<body>

<?php
function writeName($fname)
{
echo $fname . "Kumar.<br/>";
}

echo "My name is";
writeName("Ram");
echo "My sister's name is";
writeName("Meera");
echo "My brother's name is";
writeName("Shyam");
?>

</body>
</html>
```

Output:

My name is Ram Kumar.
My sister's name is Meera Kumar.
My brother's name is Shyam Kumar.

8.6.4 Server Side Includes

Code reusability is one of the very important aspects for any language. It will make code look modular and will minimize changes to common pages. Due to this it becomes easier to maintain the code. You also don't need to write code again and again and can use one code wherever you need. Functions are one of the bases to provide this reusability but it has limited scope (i.e., inside one file). Server Side Includes (or File Includes) achieve this goal with broader scope, i.e., across multiple files. You can insert the content of one PHP file into another PHP file before the server executes it, with the include() or require() function.

The two functions are identical in every way, except how they handle errors:

1. **include**() generates a warning, but the script will continue execution
2. **require**() generates a fatal error, and the script will stop

These two functions are used to create functions, headers, footers, or elements that will be reused on multiple pages.

Server side includes saves a lot of work. This means that you can create a standard header, footer, or menu file for all your Web pages. When the header needs to be updated, you can only update the include file, or when you add a new page to your site, you can simply change the menu file (instead of updating the links on all your Web pages).

Syntax:

You can include files by writing include(filename) or require(filename) statement. Here filename is a string containing path of the file to be included.

Examples:

Suppose we have a file named **menu.php** which has below code:

```
<a href="/index.php">Home</a>
<a href="/about.php">About Me</a>
<a href="/blog.php">Blog</a>
<a href="/contact.php">Contact</a>
```

Now in other page, e.g., **index.php** we can include it in below way:

```
<html>
<body>

<div class="leftmenu">
<?php include("menu.php"); ?>
</div>

<h1>Welcome to my home page.</h1>
<p>Some text.</p>

</body>
</html>
```

Now lets say if we include any wrong file (which does not exist) in our code then in case of include and require functions below will be errors displayed in the browser:

```
<html>
<body>

<?php
include("wrongFile.php");
echo "Hello World!";
?>

</body>
</html>
```

Below will be the error message for the same:

Warning: include(wrongFile.php) [function.include]:
failed to open stream:
No such file or directory in C:\wamp\www\test.php on line 5

Warning: include() [function.include]:
Failed opening 'wrongFile.php' for inclusion
(include_path='.;C:\php5\pear')
in C:\wamp\www\test.php on line 5

Hello World!

Now if we use require function and change code to below:

```
<html>
<body>

<?php
require("wrongFile.php");
echo "Hello World!";
?>

</body>
</html>
```

Below is the error message for above code:

Warning: require(wrongFile.php) [function.require]:
failed to open stream:
No such file or directory in C:\wamp\www\test.php on line 5

Fatal error: require() [function.require]:
Failed opening required 'wrongFile.php'
(include_path='.;C:\php5\pear')
in C:\wamp\www\test.php on line 5

Note: The echo statement is not executed, because the script execution stopped after the fatal error.

8.6.5 Form Handling

A Web application receives input from the user via form input. Handling form input is the cornerstone of a successful Web application – everythingelse builds on it. User enters values in html form fields (like <input>, ,<Textarea>, select an option inside <select>, etc.) and after sumiting that form it goes to the url mentioned in the action attricute of form. in that page we can retrieve the data using server side scripting languages (like PHP) and then can manipulate it as per our requirement. to retrieve the values PHP uses pre defined arrays like $_GET (for all request whose method is get), $_POST (for all requests whose method is post) and $_REQUEST (its a superset of $_GET and $_POST). Now let us understand this concept with an example.

Example:
Lets say we have a file named **"user.php"** where we are asking name and email id of the user. Code for the same is given below:

```
<html>
<body>

<form action="user_result.php" method="post">
Name: <input type="text" name="name"/>
Email Id: <input type="text" name="email"/>
<input type="submit"/>
</form>

</body>
</html>
```

Now in the next file which is **user_result.php** (given in the form action), we will have below code to retrieve and display the values:

```
<html>
<body>
<?php
$name = $_POST["name"];
$email = $_POST["email"];
?>
Welcome <?php echo $name; ?>!<br/>
Your email id is <?php echo $email; ?> .

</body>
</html>
```

In the above code inside $_POST array the key names (name and email) should be same as the value of form field attribute name. The most important thing to notice when dealing with HTML forms and PHP is that any form element in an HTML page will automatically be available to your PHP scripts.

INTRODUCTION TO MySQL 8.7

MySQL is one of the most popular relational database management system on the Web. The MySQL Database has become the world's most popular open source database, because it is free and available on almost all the platforms. The MySQL can run on Unix, window, and Mac OS. MySQL is used for the internet applications as it provides good speed and is very secure. MySQL was developed to manage large volumes of data at very high speed to overcome the problems of existing solutions. MySQL can be used for verity of applications but it is mostly used for the Web applications on the internet. Programming libraries for C, Python, PHP, Java, Delphi, etc., are available to connect to MySQL database. It is available for Windows operating system Window NT, from earlier versions like Windows 95 to latest Windows 7. It is a very fast thread-based memory allocation system and is available for the most Unix operating platform.

Modern day Web sites seem to be relying more and more on complex database systems. These systems store all of their critical data, and allow for easy maintenance in some cases. Also for Web applications space and performance is major area of concern. That is where MySQL has an edge over some other RDBMS. It is light weight this means consumes less space and delivers good performance with high accuracy.

8.7.1 Features of MySQL

Below are the main features/benefits of MySQL:

1. **Reliability and performance** MySQL is very reliable and high performance relational database management system. It can used to store many GB's of data into database.
2. **Availability of source** MySQL source code is available; that's why now you can recompile the source code.
3. **Cross-platform support** MySQL supports more than twenty different platform including the major Linux distribution .Mac OS X ,Unix and Microsoft windows.
4. **Powerful uncomplicated software** The MySQL has most capabilities to handle most corporate database application and used to very easy and fast

5. **Client/Server architecture** MySQL is a client/server system. There is a database server (MySQL) and arbitrarily many clients (application programs), which communicate with the server; that is, they query data, save changes, etc. The clients can run on the same computer as the server or on another computer (communication via a local network or the Internet).
6. **SQL compatibility** MySQL supports as its database language, as its name suggests: SQL (Structured Query Language). SQL is a standardized language for querying and updating data and for the administration of a database. There are several SQL dialects (about as many as there are database systems). MySQL adheres to the current SQL standard (at the moment SQL:2003), although with significant restrictions and a large number of extensions.
7. **Unicode support** MySQL has supported all conceivable character sets since version 4.1, including Latin-1, Latin-2, and Unicode (either in the variant UTF8 or UCS2). This means it can store non-English characters as well along with the special symbols.
8. **Lightweight** As stated earlier PHP is less resource consuming. So it does not take much space and also it does not make the system slow after installation so in this way its preferred over its competitors.

BASICS OF MySQL 8.8

In this section, we will see some basic commands supported by MySQL which are used to interact with database. Since MySQL supports most of the SQL commands so first we will have a look on those. SQL in itself is very vast topic in itself so we will go through some basic overview of few commands only here.

SQL statements can be categorized in three types:

1. **DDL (Data Definition Language) statements** These statements work on the structures of database or tables. Example: CREATE, ALTER, DROP, etc.
2. **DML (Data Manipulation Language) statements** These statements work on the values stored in the database tables. Example: UPDATE,DELETE,SELECT, etc.
3. **TCL (Transaction Control Language) statements** These statements work on the SQL transactions (i.e., set of DML operations) in order to control those. Example: COMMIT, ROLLBACK, etc.

Now we will have a look on some useful SQL commands.

8.8.1 CREATE Command

In SQL CREATE Command is used to create databases, users for the databases, tables or other SQL objects.

Syntax: To create a database below is the syntax for command:

```
CREATE database <database name>;

To create table below is syntax:
CREATE TABLE <table name>
(
column_name1 data_type,
column_name2 data_type,
column_name3 data_type,
....
)
```

Example:

```
For creating a database: CREATE database my_db;
For creating a table: CREATE TABLE persons
(
p_id int,
last_name varchar(255),
first_name varchar(255),
address varchar(255),
city varchar(255)
);
```

8.8.2 ALTER Command

The ALTER statement is used to add, delete, or modify columns in an existing table.

Syntax:

```
To add a column:
ALTER TABLE <table name>
ADD <column name>  datatype

To modify/delete a column:

ALTER TABLE <table name>
DROP/MODIFY COLUMN <column name>  datatype
```

Example:

Below is example to add a column:

```
ALTER TABLE persons
ADD date_of_birth date;

Below is example to modify a column:

ALTER TABLE persons
MODIFY COLUMN date_of_birth varchar(50);

Below is example to delete a column

ALTER TABLE persons
DROP COLUMN date_of_birth;
```

8.8.3 DROP Command

Drop command is used to delete either database or table from the database.

Syntax:

```
To delete database: DROP database <db name>;

To delete table: DROP table <table name>;
```

Example:

```
To delete database:  DROP database my_db;

To delete table: DROP table persons;
```

8.8.4 INSERT Command

INSERT statement is used to input a new row/record in the table.

Syntax:

It is possible to write the INSERT INTO statement in two forms.

The first form doesn't specify the column names where the data will be inserted, only their values:

```
INSERT INTO <table name>
VALUES (value1, value2, value3,...)
```

The second form specifies both the column names and the values to be inserted:

```
INSERT INTO <table name> (column1, column2, column3,...)
VALUES (value1, value2, value3,...)
```

Example:

Below is example for first form of insert statement:

```
INSERT INTO persons
VALUES (4,'Nilsen', 'Johan', 'Street 1', 'Bangalore')
```

Below is the example for second form:

```
INSERT INTO persons (p_id,  last_name,  first_name)
VALUES (5, 'Singh', 'Manish')
```

8.8.5 UPDATE Command

UPDATE command is used to modify any value inside the table.

Syntax:

```
UPDATE <table name>
SET column1=value, column2=value2,...
WHERE some_column=some_value
```

Example:

```
UPDATE persons
SET Address='Teachers Colony', City='Bangalore'
WHERE last_name='Singh' AND first_name='Manish'
```

8.8.6 DELETE Command

DELETE command is used to delete any value from table. We cannot delete just one column value using DELETE statement. It will always delete the complete row.

Syntax:

```
DELETE FROM <table name>
WHERE some_column=some_value
```

Example:

```
DELETE from persons where last_name = 'Singh' and first_name =  'Manish'
```

8.8.7 SELECT Command

SELECT is perhaps most widely used SQL command. It retrieves data from a table and present to the user.

Syntax:
To get all the columns below is the syntax:

```
SELECT * FROM <table name> WHERE some_column = some_value;
```

In order to retrieve values off some specific columns we use below syntax:

```
SELECT column1, column2,column3… FROM <table name> where come_column =
some_value;
```

Example:

```
SELECT * from persons WHERE p_id = 4;

For some specific columns below is the example:

SELECT last_name,first_name,city from persons where p_id = 5;
```

USING MySQL WITH PHP 8.9

As stated earlier, PHP has lot of inbuilt functions for connecting to MySQL and some packages like WAMP, LAMP, etc., contain both MySQL and PHP in product suit. Also unlike .NET platform, PHP-MySQL applications are cross-platform means you can make an application on windows and then can run it in Linux and vice versa and you don't need to do any extra configuration for this. Due to this platform, independent nature PHP/MySQL applications are quite popular choices for developer who can use linux (which does not license fees and open source) to develop applications and host them either on windows or linux servers.

8.9.1 Connecting to MySQL with PHP

Below are the steps for connecting MySQL from PHP and performing any database related task and closing connection:

Step 1: Connect to MySQL First step is to establish a connection to the MySQL database. This is an extremely important step because if your script cannot connect to its database, your queries to the database will fail. A good practice when using databases is to set the username, the password and the database name values at the beginning of the script code. If you need to change them later, it will be an easy task.

```
$username="your_username";
$password="your_password";
$database="your_database";
```

You should replace "your_username", "your_password" and "your_database" with the MySQL username, password and database that will be used by your script.

Next you should connect your PHP script to the database. This can be done with the MySQL_connect PHP function:

```
$conn = MySQL_connect("localhost",$username,$password);
```

This line tells PHP to connect to the MySQL database server at 'localhost' (localhost is the MySQL server which usually runs on the same physical server as your script).

Step 2: Select the database After the connection is established you should select the database you wish to use. This should be a database to which your username has access to. This can be completed through the following command:

```
$db = MySQL_select_db($dbname,$conn) or die("error in selecting database,
please check database name");
```

It tells PHP to select the database stored in the variable $database (in our case it will select the database "your_database"). If the script cannot connect it will stop executing and will show the error message given in die function.

Step 3: Query the database Next step is to write a SQL query and execute that. Suppose we have a query as:

```
$query = "select from persons where p_id=5";
```

Then we would use below function to query the table:

```
$resultSet = MySQL_query($query);
```

MySQL_query function returns a result set for every query.

Step 4: Process the result After executing the query we get a result set which contains all the data that we get from database. This may be either all the rows or number of rows affected due to insert/update query. Depending upon the result set there are different functions which process the data. Some of the commonly used functions are:

1. **MySQL_fetch_array($recordSet)** Returns an array that corresponds to the fetched row and moves the internal data pointer ahead.
2. **MySQL_num_rows($recordSet)** Determines the number of rows contained in a recordset returned by the previous SQL SELECT operation. The function returns a value of FALSE if the operation fails.
3. **MySQL_affected_rows($recordSet)** Determines the number of rows affected by the previous SQL INSERT, DELETE, or UPDATE operation. The function returns a value of -1 if the operation fails.

Step 5: Close the connection After doing the manipulation on data we need to close the connection for performance reasons. Below is the function for that:

```
MySQL_close($conn).
```

8.9.2 Sample Registration Flow with PHP-MySQL

In order to understand PHP MySQL connectivity in better way, we will go through a sample registration flow and go through the code as well.

First of all, we need to have a MySAL database. Here we assume that we have a database named php_demo which contains table named user. User table has fields username,password,first_name,last_name,email and city.

Now below is the code for html form in the registration page named **"register.php"**.

```
<html>
    <head>
        <title>Registration Page
        </title>


            <style type="text/css">
                                legend
                                  {
                                      font-weight: bold;
                                     border: 1px solid #888;
                                     border-right: 1px solid #666;
                                     border-bottom: 1px solid #666;
                                     padding: .5em;
                                     background-color: #CCC;
                                  }

        </style>

    </head>

    <body>
        <form method = "GET" action  = "register_submit.php">

<fieldset>
        <legend align="center"> REGISTRATION  FORM </legend>
  <table align = center>
      <tr>
        <td align="right"> USERNAME: <input type="text" name="username"
size="30"/></td>
      </tr>
      <br>

      <tr>
         <td> </td>
      </tr>

      <tr>
       <td align="right">PASSWORD:<input type="password" name="password"
size="30" id="password" /></td>
      </tr>
      <br>
```

```
        <tr>
         <td> </td>
        </tr>

         <tr>
         <td align="right">FIRST NAME: <input type="text" name="firstName"
size="30" id="firstName"/></td>
         </tr>
         <br>

         <tr>
            <td> </td>
         </tr>

         <tr>
           <td align="right">LAST NAME: <input type="text" name="lastName"
size="30" id="lastName"/></td>
         </tr>
         <br>

         <tr>
            <td> </td>
          </tr>

         <tr>
          <td align="right">EMAIL ADDRESS: <input type="text" name="email"
size="30" id="email"/></td>
        </tr>
        <br>

        <tr>
          <td> </td>
        </tr>

        <tr>
         <td align="right"> CITY: <input type="text" name="city" size="30"
id="city"/></td>
        </tr>

</table>
<center> <input type="submit" value="SUBMIT"/>   <input
type="reset" value=" RESET "/>
</center>
          </fieldset>
              </form>
         </body>
</html>
```

Now we will have one file named **"db.php"** which contains database connection code. Having it in separate files means we can utilize it at any place by including this file:

```
$host = 'localhost';
$dbname = 'php_demo';
```

```
$user = 'root';
$pass = '';


//Get the Connection
$con = mysql_connect($host,$user,$pass) or die("Could Not Connect to
database with the provided credentials!!");
//Select the DB
$db = mysql_select_db($dbname,$con) or die("error in selecting database,
please check database name");
```

And now we have a file named **"register_submit.php"** where we will receive the data from register page and insert it into database. Below is its code:

```
<?php
include('db.php');

$user = $_REQUEST['username'];
$pass = $_REQUEST['password'];
$firstname= $_REQUEST['firstName'];
$lastname= $_REQUEST['lastName'];
$email = $_REQUEST['email'];
$city = $_REQUEST['city'];
$rs = mysql_query("select * from user where username = '$user'");
$affected_rows = mysql_num_rows($rs);
if ($affected_rows == 0){

$query = "insert into user (username,password,first_name,last_
name,email,city) values ('$user','$pass','$firstname','$lastname',
'$email','$city')";
mysql_query($query);
$affected_rows = mysql_affected_rows();
if ($affected_rows > 0){

    $msg = "<strong>Registration Success<br/><br/><br/>Now please login to
access your acccount!!</strong><br/><br/><br/>";
echo $msg;
    }
else {
    $msg = "<strong>Registration Failed<br/><br /><br/>Please Try Again!!
</strong><br/><br/><br/>" ;
    echo $msg;
    include("register.php");
}
}
else {
  $msg = "<strong>Registration Failed<br/><br/><br/>This user already
exist!!</strong><br/><br/><br/>" ;
                echo $msg;
    include("register.php");
}
?>
```

Below are screenshots for the above mentioned pages. First of them is registration form page:

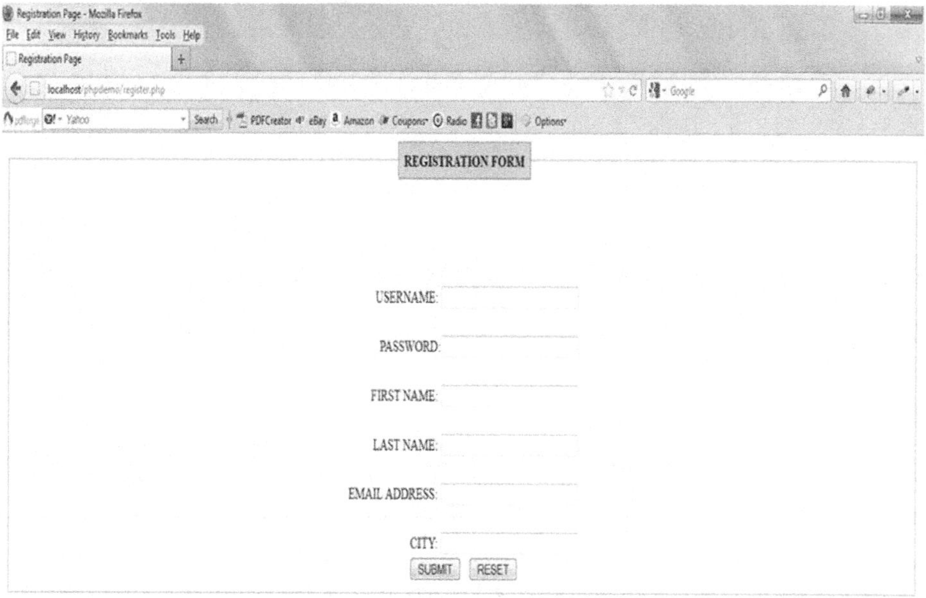

Below is the screenshot while filling up the form:

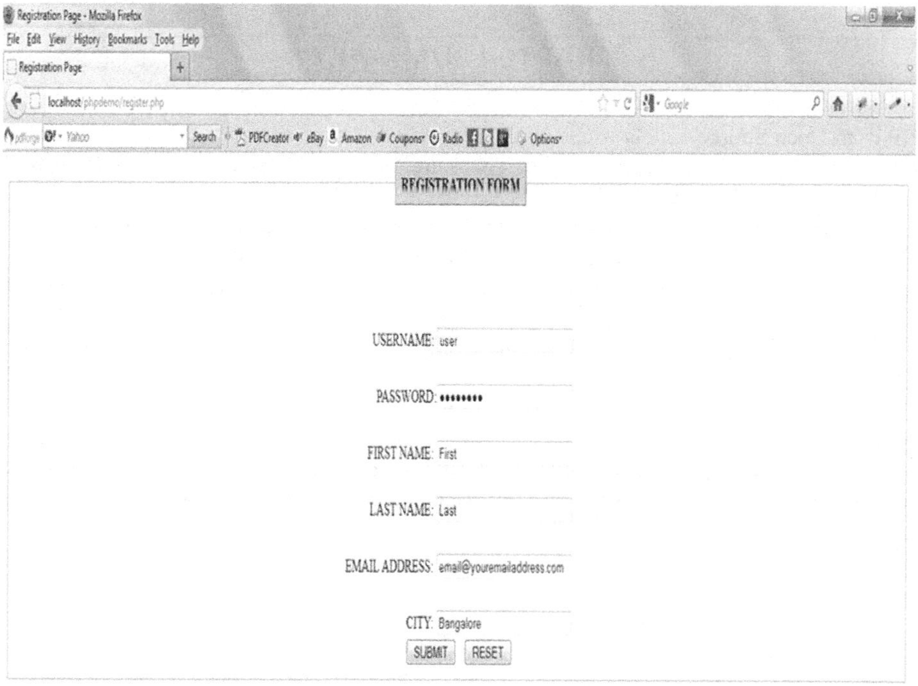

Below is screenshot of register submit page:

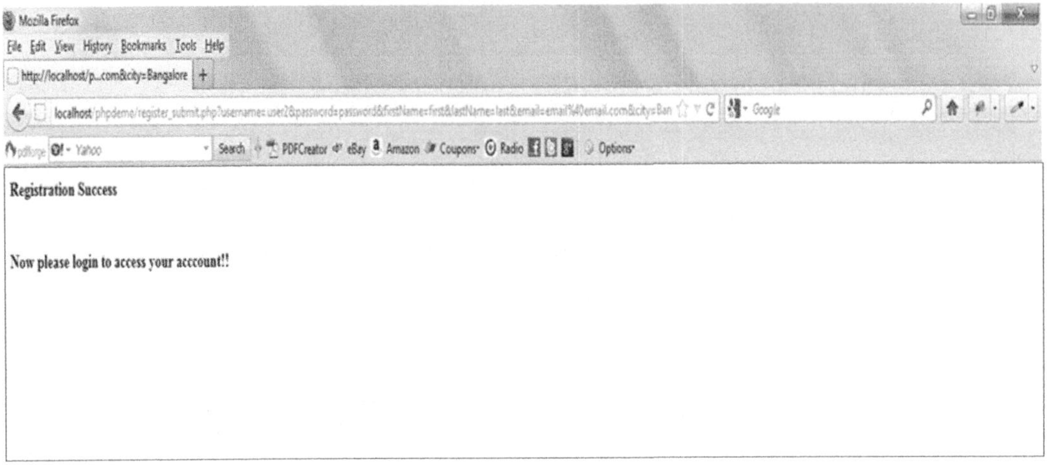

Key Terms and Concepts

PHP • Scripting Language • Client Side Scripting • Server Side Scripting • Web Server • WAMP • LAMP • Perl • Interpreter • Loosely typed • Foreach loop • Arrays • Associative arrays • Functions • Server Side includes • MySQL • DDL • DML • DCL • Cross-Platform • Die

CHAPTER SUMMARY

- PHP is an Open Source widely used server side scripting language.
- PHP is easy to install, fast and efficient. There are Operating System specific install packages available for PHP along with MySQL.
- In PHP variable names begin with $sign. Its syntaxes are borrowed from perl and C.
- You cannot see the PHP code when you click on view source in browser.
- PHP supports lots of in built functions to perform various tasks. Users can easily create their own user defined functions as well.
- PHP supports server side Includes to allow one file to be included inside other to promote reusability.
- PHP uses super global arrays $_GET and $_POST to handle form parameters.
- MySQL is one of the polular open source relational database which allows users to create database
- PHP along with MySQL is very popular tool to create database driven Web applications.
- PHP provides in built functions for MySQL connectivity. No other API or liabrary is needed for that.
- There are several Web development tools such as Drupal, Wordpress, Joomla, etc., that are available, and which are build on top of PHP and MySQL.

MULTIPLE-CHOICE QUESTIONS

1. PHP stands for _____.
   (a) PHP Hypertext Preprocessor (b) Personal Hypertext Preprocessor
   (c) Personal HTML Processor (d) None of these
2. Which of the following activities cannot be done by client side scripting language?
   (a) Form validation (b) Disabling mouse click
   (c) Connecting to databases (d) Opening a popup window
3. In WAMP, A stands for ______.
   (a) Active (b) Apache
   (c) Adverb (d) Administration
4. In PHP, a constant is defined using ______ function.
   (a) declare (b) do
   (c) start (d) define
5. The arrays which contain a user defined key as index are called __________.
   (a) special Array (b) associative Array
   (c) key Array (d) string Array
6. Which of the following statements act on the values stored in the tables?
   (a) DDL (b) DML
   (c) TCL (d) None of these
7. _____ function creates a connection with database.
   (a) MySQL_query (b) MySQL _fetch_array
   (c) MySQL _connect (d) MySQL _select_db
8. ______ function is used to include one file inside other.
   (a) include (b) require
   (c) include_once (d) all of the above
9. _____ is the global array of all the parameters which come as POST form method.
   (a) $_GET (b) $_POST
   (c) $_POSTPARAM (d) $_PARAM

DETAILED QUESTIONS

1. What is a client side scripting language?
2. What are the activities which can be done using server side scripting language?
3. Explain benefits of PHP.
4. What is a Web server? Why do we need a web server while installing PHP?
5. Explain variables and constants in PHP.
6. Explain the decision control structure in PHP.
7. What are the different types of statements in MySQL.
8. Explain all the steps required to connect to MySQL from PHP page and fetch the data from table and show in the page.
9. What are the benefits of using PHP-MySQL for developing Web applications?
10. Compare and contrast PHP and ASP.

EXERCISES

1. Why is PHP-MySQL a popular platform for Web development?
2. Examine the difference between PHP, ASP and JSP.
3. What are the enhancements in latest stable version of PHP? Investigate.
4. What are different libraries required from PHP to connect to different databases?
5. How do we install LAMP and run PHP program in that? Investigate.

9 ASP.NET—AN OVERVIEW

INTRODUCTION

Web technologies have evolved at a breathtaking pace since the development of the Internet. So many technologies have come and gone, and yet, so many of them have successfully stayed on as well! In this chapter, we attempt to understand how all of them work, and how they fit in the overall scheme of things.

At the outset, Web technologies classify Web pages into three categories, as shown in Fig. 9.1.

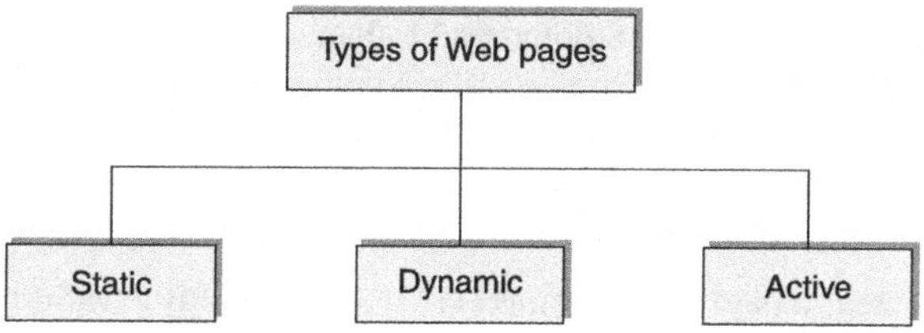

Fig. 9.1 *Types of Web pages*

Let us understand all the three types of Web pages in brief.

1. Static Web pages A Web page is **static**, if it does not change its behavior in response to external actions. The name actually says it all. A static Web page remains the same, i.e., static, for all its life, unless and until someone manually changes its contents. Any time any user in the world sends an HTTP request to a Web server, the Web server returns the same contents to the user via an HTTP response. Such a Web page is static. Examples of static Web pages are some home pages, pages specifying the contact details, etc., which do not change that often.

The process of retrieving a static Web page is illustrated in Fig. 9.2. As we can see, when the client (Web browser) sends an HTTP request for retrieving a Web page, the client sends this request to the Web server. The Web server locates the Web page (i.e., a file on the disk with a `.html` or `.htm` extension) and sends it back to the user inside the HTTP response. In other words, the server's job in this case is simply to locate a file on the disk and send its contents back to the browser. The server does not perform any extra processing. This makes the Web page processing *static*.

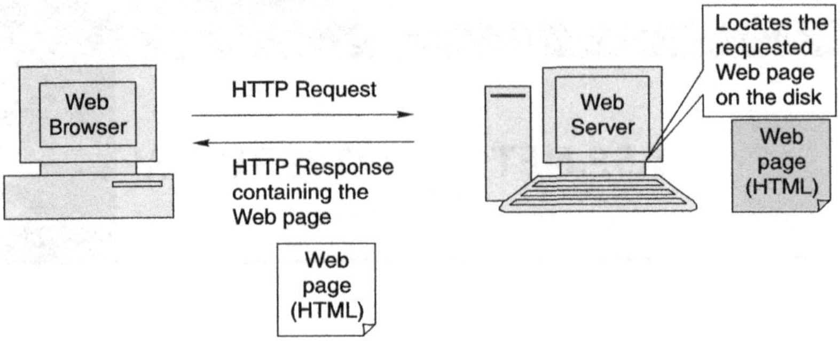

Fig. 9.2 *Static Web page*

Static Web pages can mainly contain HTML, JavaScript, and CSS. We have discussed all these technologies earlier. Therefore, we would not repeat this discussion here. All we would say is that using these technologies, or even with plain HTML, we can create static Web pages.

2. Dynamic Web pages A Web page is **dynamic**, if it changes its behavior (i.e., the output) in response to external actions. In other words, in response to a user's HTTP request, if the Web page possibly produces different output every time, it is a dynamic Web page.

Of course, the output need not always be different, but usually it is. For example, if we ask for current foreign exchange rate between US dollar and Indian rupee, a dynamic Web page would show the latest rate (and hence, it is dynamic). However, if we immediately refresh the page, the rate may not have changed in a second's time, and hence, the output may not change. In that sense, a dynamic Web page may not always produce different output.

In general, we should remember the following.

(a) A static Web page is a page that contains HTML and possibly JavaScript and CSS, and is pre-created and stored on the Web server. When a user sends an HTTP request to fetch this page, the server simply sends it back.

(b) A dynamic Web page, on the other hand, is not pre-created. Instead, it is prepared *on the fly*. Whenever a user sends an HTTP request for a dynamic Web page, the server looks at the name of the dynamic Web page, which is actually a program. The server executes the program locally. The program produces output at run time—on the fly—which is again in the HTML format. It may also contain JavaScript and CSS like a static Web page. This HTML (and possibly JavaScript and CSS) output is sent back to the browser as a part of the HTTP response.

The concept of dynamic Web pages is illustrated in Fig. 9.3.

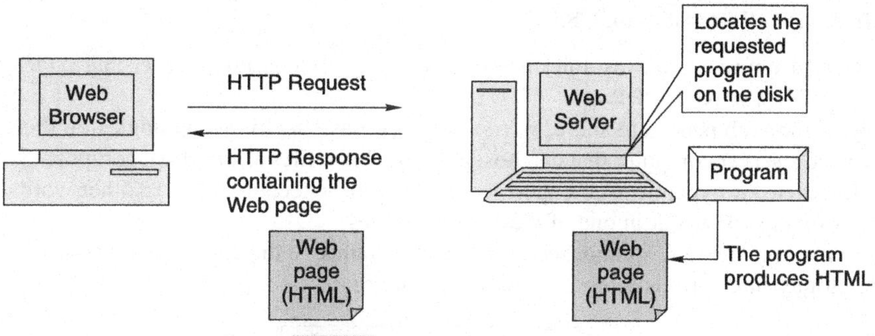

Fig. 9.3 *Dynamic Web page*

Thus, we can summarize:

A static Web page is pre-created in the HTML and associated languages/technologies and stored on the Web server. Whenever a user sends a request for this page, the server simply returns it. On the other hand, a dynamic Web page is actually a program, which produces HTML and associated output and sends it back to the user.

3. Active Web pages There is yet another category of Web pages as well, called as **active** Web pages. A Web page is active, if it executes a program (and here we are not talking about client-side JavaScript) on the client, i.e., Web browser. In other words, if a static or dynamic Web page not only sends HTML, JavaScript, and CSS to the browser, but in addition a program; the Web page is active. Remember that we are talking about a program getting executed on the client, and not on the server, here.

Now, what can that program be? It can be a **Java applet**, or an **ActiveX control**. We shall discuss some of these details later. The concept is shown in Fig. 9.4.

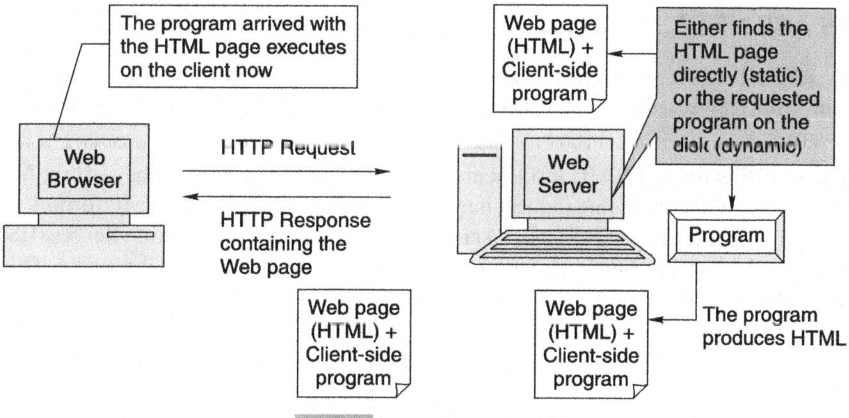

Fig. 9.4 *Active Web page*

POPULAR WEB TECHNOLOGIES 9.1

Web technologies involve the concept of a **tier**. A tier is nothing but a layer in an application. In the simplest form, the Internet is a **two-tier application**. Here, the two tiers are the Web browser and the Web server. The technologies that exist in these tiers are as follows:

1. Client tier HTML, JavaScript, CSS

2. Server tier Common Gateway Interface (CGI), Java Servlets, Java Server Pages (JSP), Apache Struts, Microsoft's ASP.NET, PHP, etc.

Clearly, if the Web pages are static, we do not need any specific technologies on the server tier. We simply need a server computer that can host and send back files to the client computer as and when required. However, for dynamic Web pages, we do need these technologies. In other words, we write our programs on the server tier in one of these technologies.

We would now review a few major server-side technologies. At the outset, let us classify the available set of technologies into various categories, as shown in Fig. 9.5.

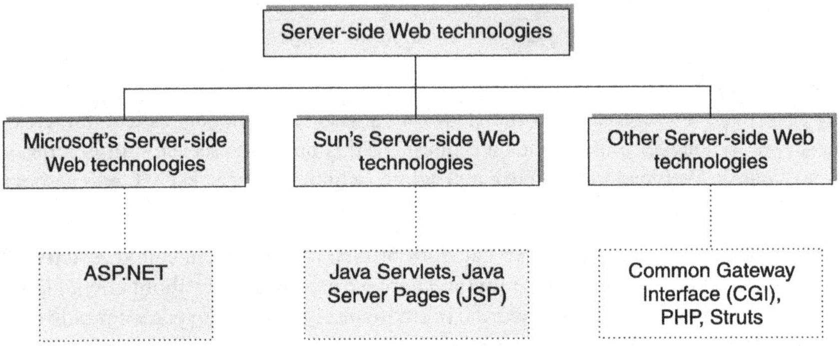

Fig. 9.5 *Classification of server-side Web technologies*

Let us now discuss these technologies in reasonable detail in the following sections.

WHAT IS ASP.NET? 9.2

Microsoft's ASP.NET is a wonderful technology to rapidly develop dynamic Web pages. It eases development with features that were earlier unheard of. The basic idea of this technology is quite straightforward.

1. The user fills up an HTML form, which causes an HTTP request to be sent to the ASP.NET Web server. Of course, this request need not necessarily go via an HTML form. It can also be sent without a form. The ASP.NET server is called Internet Information Server (IIS).
2. The IIS Web server runs a program in response to the user's HTTP request. This program is written to adhere to a specification, which we call ASP.NET. The actual programming language is usually C# (pronounced *C sharp*) or VB.NET. We shall discuss this shortly. This program performs the necessary operations, based on the user's inputs and selection of options, etc.
3. This program prepares and sends the desired output back to the user inside an HTTP response.

At this stage, let us understand the fact that ASP.NET is a specification. When we say that ASP.NET is a specification, we simply mean that Microsoft has said that if an HTTP request is sent by the user to the Web server, a certain number of things should happen (for example, the Web server should be able to read values entered by the user in the HTML form in a certain manner; or that the database access should be possible in a certain way, and so on). A language such as C# or VB.NET would implement these specifications in the specific language syntax. Figure 9.6 shows an example.

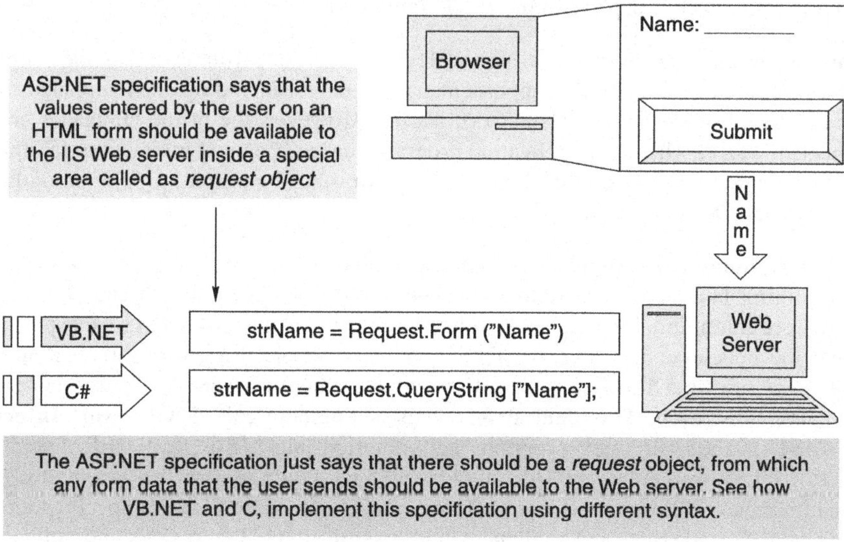

Fig. 9.6 *ASP.NET concept*

ASP.NET provides a number of features for dealing with user requests, working with server-side features, and sending responses back to the user. It also reduces a lot of coding effort by providing drag-and-drop features. To work with ASP.NET, ideally we need a software called Microsoft Visual Web Developer 2008. However, as a wonderful gesture, Microsoft has provided a completely free downloadable version of this development environment (called the *Express Edition*). This free edition can be downloaded from the Microsoft site and used for developing ASP.NET pages.

AN OVERVIEW OF THE .NET FRAMEWORK 9.3

.NET is a development platform. Some people allege that Microsoft is trying to sell old wine (read technology) in a new bottle (read development platform). However, it is difficult to agree with this theory. `.NET` is very powerful and rich in features. Figure 9.7 shows the make-up of the `.NET` framework.

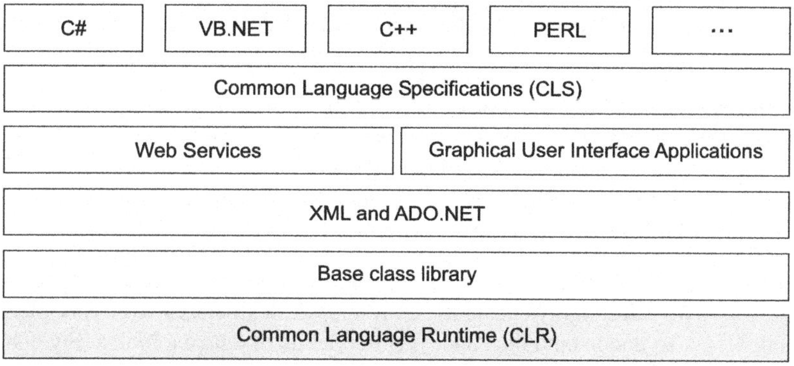

Fig. 9.7 *Overview of the .NET framework*

Let us understand the key aspects of the .NET framework.

1. Programming languages layer The highest level in the `.NET` framework is the programming languages layer. The `.NET` framework supports many languages, including such languages as PERL, which were not heard of in the Microsoft world earlier. However, the prime languages are C# and `VB.NET`. This is the layer where the application programmer has the most interaction. In other words, a programmer can write programs in the C# or `VB.NET` (or other supported) programming languages, which execute on the `.NET` platform.

2. Common Language Specifications (CLS) At this layer, the differences between all the `.NET` programming languages are addressed. The CLS is the common thread between all the varying `.NET` programming languages. In other words, regardless of what is the programming language that the developer is using, the CLS makes the whole thing uniform. We can think of CLS as a *neutral* run-time format/specification, which transforms all the source code into this neutral format/specification. This neutral format is a language called **Microsoft Intermediate Language (MSIL)**. Thus, all `.NET` programs get compiled into MSIL, and MSIL operates under the umbrella of CLS. Remember the idea about ASP.NET being a specification, and C# being a language that implements those specifications? Here is a similar idea. CLS is a specification, and the programming languages adhere to and implement those specifications. This raises some really innovative possibilities:

(a) Run-time differences between programming languages go away. A class written in C# can extend another class that is written in VB.NET! Remember, as long as both *speak in* CLS at run time, the source languages do not matter.
(b) All languages have similar run-time performance. The notion of C++ being faster than Visual Basic in the earlier days does not any longer hold true.

3. Web Services and GUI applications The concept of Web Services would be discussed later in this book. However, for now we shall simply say that a Web Service is a *program-to-program communication using XML-based standards*. GUI applications are any traditional client-server or desktop applications that we want to build using the .NET framework.

4. XML and ADO.NET At this layer, the data representation and storage technologies come into picture.`XML`, as we shall discuss separately, is the preferred choice for data representation and exchange in today's world. ADO.NET, on the other hand, is the database management part of the .NET framework. ADO.Net provides various features using which we can persist our application's data into database tables.

5. Base class library The base class library is the set of pre-created classes, interfaces, and other infrastructure that are reusable. For example, there are classes and methods to receive inputs from the screen, send output to the screen, perform disk I/O, perform database operations, create various types of data structures, perform arithmetic and logical operations, etc. All our application programs can make use of functionalities of the base class library.

6. Common Language Runtime (CLR) The **Common Language Runtime (CLR)** is the heart of the `.NET` framework. We can roughly equate the CLR in `.NET` with the **Java Virtual Machine (JVM)** in the Java technology. To understand the concept better, let us first take a look at Fig. 9.8.

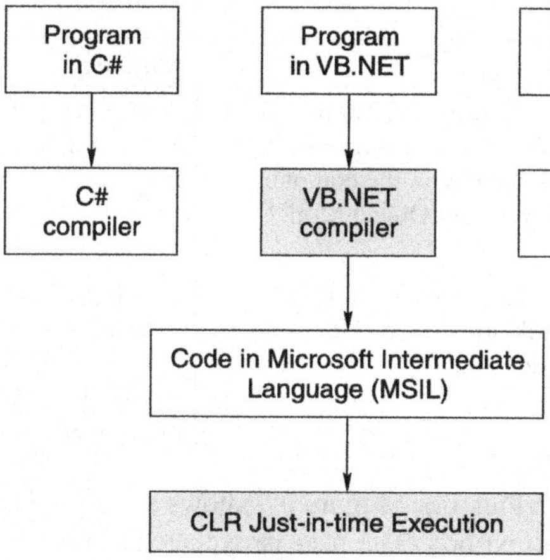

Fig. 9.8 *CLR concept*

As we can see, programs written in the source language are translated by the appropriate language compilers into a universal Microsoft Intermediate Language (MSIL). The MSIL is like the Java byte code, or an *intermediate language* like the Assembly language. That is, it is neither a High Level Language, nor a Low Level Language. Instead, the MSIL is the language that the CLR *understands*. Thus, the CLR receives a program in MSIL as the input, and executes it step-by-step. In that sense, the CLR is basically a language interpreter, the language that is interpreted in this case being MSIL.

This also tells us that the .NET framework embeds the various language compilers (e.g., a C# compiler, a VB.NET compiler, and so on). Also, the CLS specifies what should happen, and the CLR enforces it at run time.

The CLR performs many tasks, such as creating variables at run time, performing **garbage collection** (i.e., automatically removing variables no longer in use from the computer's memory), and ensuring that no unwanted behavior (e.g., security breaches) is exhibited by the executing program.

ASP.NET DETAILS 9.4

Before we discuss more on ASP.NET, we would like to do a quick comparison between ASP.NET and its predecessor: ASP. ASP.NET provides several advantages over ASP, major ones of which can be summarized as shown in Table 9.1.

Table 9.1 *ASP versus ASP.NET*

Point of discussion	*ASP*	*ASP.NET*
Coding style	ASP relied on scripting languages such as JavaScript and VBScript. These languages are quick to learn and use. However, they are also languages that are easier to debug, do not provide extensive programming support for good error handling, and in general, are not elegant unlike traditional programming languages, such as Java and C#.	ASP.NET uses full-fledged programming languages such as C# and VB.NET.

(Contd.)

Table 9.1 *Contd...*

Point of discussion	*ASP*	*ASP.NET*
Deployment and Configuration	Deploying and configuring ASP applications was a big headache, since it needed multiple settings in IIS, working with the complex technology of Component Object Model (COM), etc.	Deploying ASP.NET applications is very easy, with no complicated installations needed.
Application structuring	ASP applications have intermixed HTML and JavaScript code. It is often difficult to read, maintain, and debug.	In ASP.NET, we can keep the HTML code and the programming code (written in C# or VB.NET) separate. This makes the whole application easy to maintain, understand, and debug.

How does an ASP.NET program look like? Figure 9.9 shows an example. The first page (`a.aspx`) shows an HTML form, which has a text box. The user is expected to type her name in that text box. Once the user enters her name and clicks on the button in the HTML form, the HTTP request goes to the server. This request is expected to be sent to another ASP.NET program, called as a1.aspx. This ASP.NET program (`a1.aspx`) reads the contents of the textbox sent by the HTTP request, and displays the value of the text box back to the user.

If we run this application, a.aspx displays a screen as shown in Fig. 9.10(a).

If I type my name and click on the button, the browser sends an HTTP request to `a1.aspx`, passing my name. As a result, the screen shown in Fig. 9.10(b) appears.

a.aspx

```
<%@ Page Language="C#" %>

<html>
<body>

 <form id="form1" action = "a1.aspx">
 <input type = "text" value = "Hi" name = "aa" /> <br />
 <input type = "submit" value = "Click here" />
 </form>

</body>
</html>
```

a1.aspx

```
<%@ Page Language="C#" %>

<html>
<body>
 Hi in a1.aspx

 <%
 String a;
 a = Request.QueryString ["aa"];
 Response.Write(a);
 %>

</body>
</html>
```

Fig. 9.9 *Simple ASP.NET example*

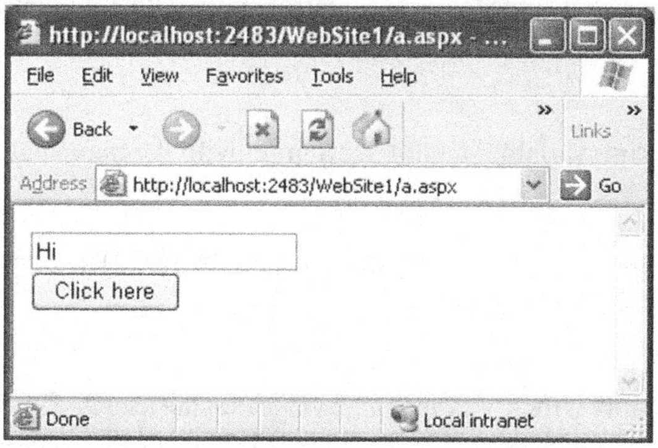

(a) Output of the ASP.NET page—Part 1

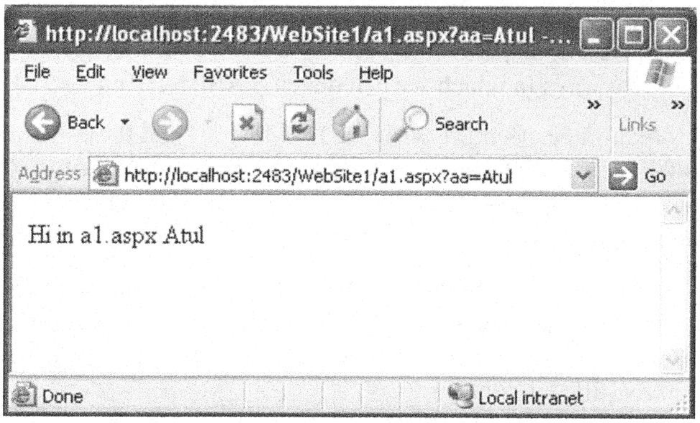

(b) Output of the ASP.NET page—Part 2

Fig. 9.10

How does the magic happen? We can see in the URL bar the following string.

```
http://localhost:2483/WebSite1/a1.aspx?aa=Atul
```

It means that the browser is asking the server to execute a1.aspx whenever the browser's request is to be processed. In addition, the browser is telling the server that a variable named *aa*, whose value is *Atul*, is also being passed from the browser to the a1.aspx program. If we look at the code of a1.aspx again, we shall notice the following lines.

```
<%
    String a;
    a = Request.QueryString["aa"];
    Response.Write(a);
%>
```

Let us understand this line-by-line.

```
<%
```

The <% symbol indicates that some C# code is starting now. This is how we can distinguish between HTML code and C# code inside an ASP.NET page.

```
String a;
```

This line declares a string variable in our C# program with the name *a*.

```
a = Request.QueryString ["aa"];
```

This line reads the value of the text box named *aa* from the HTML screen, and populates that value into the C# variable *a*, which was declared earlier.

```
Response.Write(a);
```

This statement now simply writes back the same value that the user had initially entered in the HTML form. *Response* is an object, which is used to send the HTTP response back to the user, corresponding to the user's original HTTP request.

```
%>
```

This line concludes our C# code part.

In general, there are two ways in which we can develop ASP.NET pages:

1. Single-page model In this approach, we write the HTML code and the corresponding programming language code (in say C# or VB.NET) in a single file with an extension of `.aspx`. This approach is similar to the traditional manner of the older ASP days. This is useful in the case of smaller projects, or for study/experimentation purposes.

2. Code-behind page model In this approach, all the HTML part is inside one .aspx file, and the actual functionality resides in various individual files. For example, if the application code is written in the C# programming language, then we will have as many .cs files as needed, one per class written in C#. This is more practical in real-life situations.

SERVER CONTROLS AND WEB CONTROLS 9.5

ASP.NET provides rich features for creating HTML forms and for performing data validations. For this purpose, it provides modified versions of the basic HTML form controls, such as text boxes, radio buttons, drop down lists, submit buttons, and so on. In a nutshell, when using ASP.NET, we have three basic choices for creating an HTML form, as illustrated in Fig. 9.11.

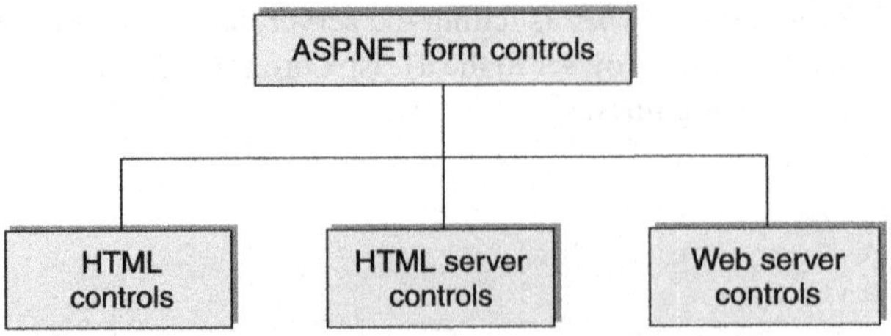

Fig. 9.11 *Types of HTML controls*

Table 9.2 distinguishes between the three types of controls.

Table 9.2 *Classification of ASP.NET HTML controls*

Type of control	*Description*	*Example*
HTML controls	These are the traditional HTML controls. We can use them in ASP.NET in exactly the same way as we can use them in HTML, or any other server-side technology. There is nothing new here.	<input type = "text" name = "user_name">
HTML server controls	We can add an attributed titled *runat = "server"* to the above HTML controls to make them HTML *server* controls. This allows us to create HTML controls/tags that are understood by the Web server. This has certain implications, as we shall study shortly. This feature is not in the plain HTML syntax, but has been added by ASP.NET.	<input type = "text" name = "user_name" runat = "server">
Web server controls	This is a completely new way of adding HTML controls/tags to an HTML form. By using these types of controls, we can make our HTML page very interactive, and can provide a very rich interface to the user of the application. We shall discuss this shortly.	<asp:TextBox id="user_name" Text="Hello World!" runat="server" />

Let us now understand these types of controls in more detail.

1. HTML controls HTML controls are traditional, standard HTML-based controls, as shown in Fig. 9.12. As mentioned earlier, there is nothing unique here. We can use these types of controls in plain HTML or in other Web technologies as well. As much as possible, these controls are discouraged in ASP.NET, since the usage of these controls deprives the programmer from the real power of ASP.NET form processing and validations.

```
<html>
<head>
  <title>Server Control and HTML Control Example</title>
</head>
<body>
  <form id="Form1" >
    <a id="link1" href="http://www.google.com">Visit Google!</a>
  </form>
</body>
</html>
```

Fig. 9.12 *Simple HTML page*

As we can see, this is a straightforward HTML form, which specifies an anchor tag that leads us to the URL of Google. There is nothing new or unique about this code.

We will not discuss these controls any further.

2. HTML server controls These controls are very similar in syntax to the standard, traditional HTML controls, with one difference. As mentioned earlier, we add the `runat = "server"` attribute to traditional HTML controls to make them **HTML server controls**. Figure 9.13 shows the difference.

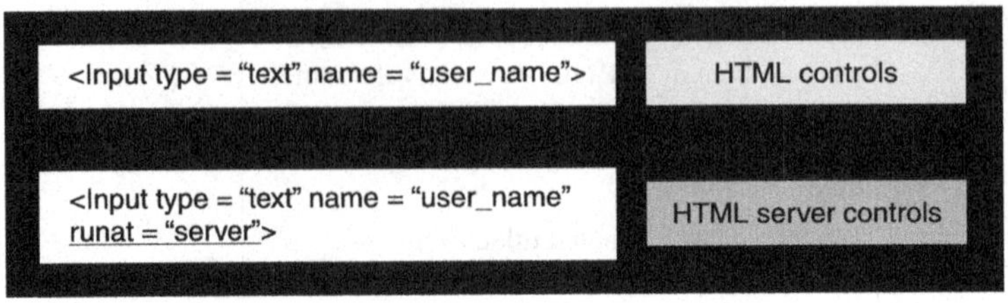

Fig. 9.13 *HTML controls and HTML server controls*

As we can see, HTML server controls are special HTML tags. These are processed by the Web server in a manner somewhat to the way HTML tags are interpreted by the Web browser. We can know that an HTML tag is an HTML server tag because it contains a `runat="server"` attribute. This attributes helps the server in differentiating between standard HTML controls and HTML server controls.

Once the Web server sees an HTML server control, it creates an in-memory object, corresponding to the HTML server control. This server-side object can have properties, methods, and can expose or raise server–side events while processing the ASP.NET page. Once the processing is completed, the control produces its resulting output in the of HTML form. It is then sent to the browser as part of the resulting HTML page for actual display.

The server controls help us simplify the process of dealing with the properties and attributes of the various HTML tags. They also allow us to hide the logic affecting the tags from the tags themselves, thus helping us to write a cleaner code.

Figure 9.14 shows an example of HTML server control. We have modified our earlier example of the simple HTML control to convert it into an HTML server control.

```
<html>
<head>
 <title>Server Control and HTML Control Example</title>

 <script language="c#" runat="server">

  void page_load()
  {
   link1.HRef = "http://www.google.com";
  }

 </script>

</head>
<body>
 <form id="Form1" runat="server">
  <a id="link1" runat="server">Visit Google!</a>
 </form>
</body>
</html>
```

Fig. 9.14 *HTML server control*

As we can see, an HTML control is specified for the anchor tag, to create a hyper link. However, the actual hyper link is not specified in the anchor tag. Instead, it is added by the `page_load ()` method. The `page_load ()` method is actually an event, that gets called whenever the Web page loads in the Web browser. However, and this is the point, this is not client-side JavaScript code. Instead, it is C# code that executes on the Web server, not on the client. This can really confuse us at the beginning. However, we should remember that when we use HTML server controls, we ask ASP.NET to automatically execute the server-side code as if it is running on the client-side. That is, we write code using a syntax that makes it look like server-side code, but it actually executes on the client. Therefore, in this case, the `page_load ()` event causes the Web page to be loaded on the HTML client (i.e., the browser), and yet executes code that is written in a server-side manner.

To take this point further, Fig. 9.15 shows what the user gets to see, if she/he does a *View-Source*.

```
<html>
<head>
 <title>Server Control and HTML Control Example</title>
</head>
<body>
 <form name="Form1" method="post" action="a.aspx" id="Form1">
<div>
<input type="hidden" name="__VIEWSTATE" id="__VIEWSTATE" value="/ wEPDwUJLTY0Mzkz
Mjg0D2QWAgICD2QWAgIBDxYCHgRocmVmBRVodHRwOi8vd3d3Lmdvb2dsZS5jb21kZG/Ua00rKHN8+a9/
j8EAE+pUMGYt" />
</div>

   <a href="http://www.google.com" id="link1">Visit Google!</a>
 </form>
</body>
</html>
```

Fig. 9.15 *Result of doing view source*

As we can see, there is no trace of any server-side code here. The user does not even know that a method called `page_load ()` has got executed. Thus, HTML server controls hide the complexity from the user, and yet perform the necessary functions as if the code is on the client.

However, we shall notice that the effect of adding the hyperlink via the `page_load ()` method can be seen in the end result. The *href* tag is indeed added to the resulting Web page.

We will also notice that the source code has a *hidden* variable with strange contents for name, id, and value. This hidden variable is what ASP.NET internally uses to make our traditional HTML control an HTML server control. How it works and what are its contents is none of our business. It is managed internally by ASP.NET, and we must not make any attempts to directly access/manipulate it.

If, on the other hand, what if we had not coded the anchor tag as an ordinary HTML control (and not as an HTML server control)? Let us see the modified code, as shown in Fig. 9.16.

Notice that we do not have a `runat ="server"` attribute in the anchor tag anymore. Now, *link1* is an ordinary anchor. What if we try to compile this application? We get an error, as shown in Fig. 9.17.

As we can see, the compiler does not recognize *link1* in the `page_load ()` method now. Why is it so? It is because it is no longer an HTML server control. Instead, it is an ordinary HTML control. The moment we make it an ordinary HTML control, we lose the benefit of the ability of manipulating the contents of this control programmatically in server-side code. This is exactly what has happened here. Now, *link1* has become a client-only HTML control. This means that it can be manipulated by client-side JavaScript in the browser, but not by the server!

```
<html>
<head>
 <title>Server Control and HTML Control Example</title>

 <script language="c#" runat="server">

  void page_load()
  {
   link1.HRef = "http://www.google.com";
  }

 </script>

</head>
<body>
 <form id="Form1" runat="server">
  <a id="link1">Visit Google!</a>
 </form>
</body>
</html>
```

Fig. 9.16 *HTML control example*

```
Compiler Error Message: CS0103: The name 'link1' does not exist in the current context
Source Error:

Line 7:     void page_load()
Line 8:     {
Line 9:             link1.HRef = "http://www.google.com";
Line 10:    }
Line 11:

Source File: c:\Documents and Settings\atulk\My Documents\Visual Studio 2005\WebSites\WebSite1\a.aspx
Line: 9
```

Fig. 9.17 *Error in the example*

This should clearly outline the practical differences between an ordinary HTML control and an HTML server control.

We now summarize the advantages and disadvantages of the HTML server controls below:

Advantages

1. The HTML server controls are based on the traditional HTML-like object model.
2. The controls can interact with client-side scripting. Processing can be done at the client-side as well as at the server-side, depending on our logic.

Disadvantages

1. We would need to code for browser compatibility.
2. They have no way of identifying the capabilities of the client browser accessing the current page.
3. They have abstraction similar to the corresponding HTML tags, and they do not offer any added abstraction levels.

3. Web server controls Web server controls are an ASP.NET speciality. They are rich, powerful, and very easy to use. They go even beyond the HTML server controls. They exhibit behavior that makes the ASP.NET applications extremely easy and user/programmer friendly. All Web server controls have a special identifier, which is `<asp:...>`. These controls do not have the traditional HTML-like tags. Figure 9.18 distinguishes between the creation of a text box by using an HTML control, an HTML server control, and a Web server control.

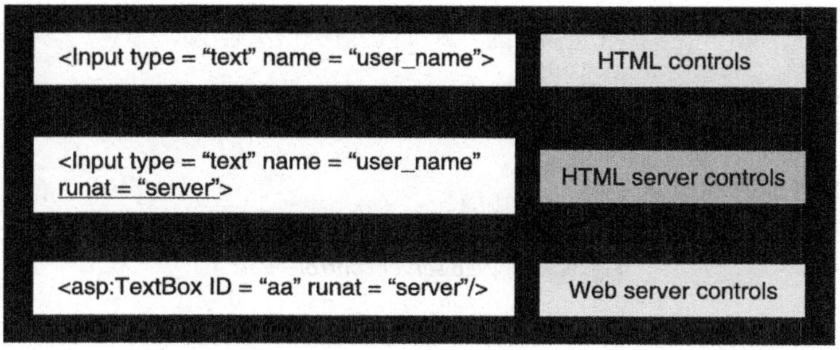

Fig. 9.18 *Difference between various control types*

As we can see, the way to define a text box by using the Web server control is given below:

```
<asp:TextBox ID = "aa" runat = "server" />
```

How does this work?

We code the above tag. ASP.NET, in turn, transforms this code into an HTML text box control, so that the text box can be displayed on the user's browser screen. However, in addition

(a) It also ensures that the same features that were provided to the HTML server control were retained.

(b) It adds a few new features of its own.

Suppose that our code is as shown in Fig. 9.19.

```
<%@ Page Language="C#"%>
<html>
<body>
 <form id="form1" method = "post" action = "Default.aspx" runat = "server">
 <asp:TextBox ID = "aa" runat = "server" /> <br />
 </form>
</body>
</html>
```

Fig. 9.19 *Web server control—Part 1*

This will cause a text box to be displayed on the screen. If we again do a *View-source*, the result is shown in Fig. 9.19.

```
<html>
<body>
 <form name="form1" method="post" action="a1.aspx" id="form1">
<div>
<input type="hidden" name="__VIEWSTATE" id="__VIEWSTATE" value="/
wEPDwULLTIwNDAwODk2OTNkZHJOn8VhbM/58LKu3kGkEe3CYxLE" />
</div>
 <input name="aa" type="text" id="aa" /> <br />
<div>
  <input type="hidden" name="__EVENTVALIDATION"
id="__EVENTVALIDATION"
value="/wEWAgK99OLgBAK/76bvDNVrcLGRSQtvYML9DNdJWW3EAzI6" />
</div>
</form>
</body>
</html>
```

Fig. 9.19 *Web server control—Part 2*

As we can see, our code for the text box has again been converted into a traditional text box. Plus, two hidden variables have been added.

Before we proceed, let us see what would have happened if we had used an HTML server control, instead of a Web server control. In other words, suppose that our source code is as shown in Fig. 9.22.

```
<%@ Page Language="C#"%>

<html>
<body>
 <form id="form1" method = "post" action = "Default.aspx" runat = "server">
 <input type = "text" ID = "aa" runat = "server" /> <br />
 </form>
</body>
</html>
```

Fig. 9.20 *HTML control—Part 1*

Note that we have replaced our Web server control for the text box with a corresponding HTML server control. Now if we do a *View-source*, what do we get to see? Take a look at Fig. 9.20.

We can see that this code is almost exactly the same as what was generated in the Web server control case. How does a Web server control then differ from an HTML server control? There are some key differences between the two, as follows:

(a) Web controls provide richer Graphical User Interface (GUI) features as compared to HTML server controls. For example, we have calendars, data grids, etc., in the Web controls.
(b) The object model (i.e., the programming aspects) in the case of Web controls is more consistent than that of HTML server controls.
(c) Web controls detect and adjust for browsers automatically, unlike HTML server controls. In other words, they are browser-independent.

A detailed discussion of these features is beyond the scope of the current text. However, we would summarize the advantages and disadvantages of Web server controls.

```
<html>
<body>
 <form name="form1" method="post" action="a1.aspx" id="form1">
<div>
<input type="hidden" name="__VIEWSTATE" id="__VIEWSTATE" value="/wEPDwULLTE5NzAxMTkz
  NTBkZKMTMfePQ5d1zwH0WY5bRAdtp+7w" />
</div>

 <input name="aa" type="text" id="aa" /> <br />

<div>
  <input type="hidden" name="__EVENTVALIDATION" id="__EVENTVALIDATION" value="/
   EWAgK6uokMAr/vpu8MZj0syjknPCVIRWpGyhxHCnsb8/g=" />
</div>

</form>
</body>
</html>
```

Fig. 9.20 *HTML control—Part 2*

Advantages

1. They can detect the target browser's capabilities and render themselves accordingly.
2. Additional controls, which can be used in the same manner as any HTML control, such as Calender controls are possible without any dependency on any external code.
3. Processing is done at the server side.
4. They have an object model, which is different from the traditional HTML model and they even provide a set of properties and methods that can change the outlook and behavior of the controls.
5. They have the highest level of abstraction.

Disadvantages

1. The programmer does not have a very deep control on the generated code.
2. Migration of ASP to any ASP.NET application is difficult if we want to use these controls. It is actually the same as rewriting our application.

VALIDATION CONTROLS 9.6

ASP.NET is a dynamic Web page, server-side technology. Therefore, it does not directly interact with the Web browser. For example, there are no ASP.NET properties/methods to get keyboard input from the user, respond to mouse events, or perform other tasks that involve user interaction with the browser. ASP.NET can get the results of such actions after the page has been posted, but cannot directly respond to browser actions. Therefore, in order to validate information (say whether the user has entered a numeric value between 0 and 99 for age), we must write JavaScript as per the traditional approach. This client-side JavaScript would travel to the user's browser along with the HTML page, and validate its contents before they are posted to the server. The other approach of validating all this information on the server is also available, but is quite wasteful.

ASP.NET has introduced something quite amazing to deal with user validations. Titled **validation controls**, these additional tags validate user information with very little coding. They are very powerful, browser-independent, and can easily handle all kinds of validation errors.

The way validation controls work is illustrated in Fig. 9.21.

1. ASP.NET checks the browser when generating a page.
2. If the browser can support JavaScript, ASP.NET sends client-side JavaScript to the browser for validations, along with the HTML contents.
3. Otherwise, validations happen on the server.
4. Even if client-side validation happens, server-side validation still happens, thus ensuring double checking.

Fig. 9.21 *Validation controls operation*

Table 9.3 summarizes the various validation controls provided by ASP.NET.

Table 9.3 *Validation controls*

Validation control	*Explanation*
RequiredFieldValidator	Ensures that a mandatory field must have some value
CompareValidator	Compares values of two different controls, based on the specified conditions
RangeValidator	Ensures that the value of a control is in the specified range
RegularExpressionValidator	Compares the value of a control to ensure that it adheres to a **regular expression**
CustomValidator	Allows the user to provide her own validation logic

Let us understand how validation controls work, with an example. Figure 9.22 shows an ASP.NET page that displays a text box to the user. It also makes this text box mandatory by using the RequiredFieldValidator validation control.

Let us understand how this works. We have an HTML form, which has a text box named *aaa*. Associated with this text box is a special control called as `<asp:RequiredFieldValidator>`. If we look at the syntax of this validation control, we shall notice that it specifies *ControlToValidate* as our text box (i.e., *aaa*). In other words, the validation control is intended to act upon the text box. Also, because this is a validation control that controls whether or not the user has entered something in the text box, it is called *RequiredFieldValidator*. Let us now see how this works in real life. As we can see, if the user does not type anything in the text box and clicks on the button, we see an error message as shown in Fig. 9.23.

How does this work? When we declare an HTML control to be of type *RequiredFieldValidator*, and associate it with some other HTML control (e.g., with a text box, in this case), ASP.NET generates the client-side JavaScript code behind to build the right association between them. In other words, it writes the code to ensure that whenever the user tabs out of the text box, the validation control should kick in. This is so convenient as compared to writing tedious JavaScript code ourselves! Better still, we can ensure multiple validations on the same control (e.g., the fact that it is mandatory, and that it should contain a numeric value between this and this range, and that it should be less than some value in some other control). The best part, though, is the fact that we need not write almost a single line of code to do all this! We can just use the drag-and-drop features of ASP.NET to do almost everything that we need here.

```
<%@ Page Language="C#" %>

<html>
<head>
 <title>Validation Control Example</title>
</head>
<body>
 <form id="Form1" action="a1.aspx" runat="server">
  <asp:TextBox ID="aaa" runat="server" />
  <asp:RequiredFieldValidator ID="RequiredFieldValidator1" ControlToValidate="aaa"
   ErrorMessage="Please enter something" runat="Server" /><br />
  <br />
  <asp:Button ID="Button1" Text="Click" runat="server" />
 </form>
</body>
</html>
```

Fig. 9.22 *RequiredFieldValidator example*

Fig. 9.23 *RequiredFieldValidator usage example*

Truly, this is something remarkable. Programmers, who have used JavaScript to do similar things in the past can vouch for the complexities they had to undergo to achieve similar objectives. JavaScript works, but it is quite tedious. And to an extent, it is browser-dependent, as well! We need not go through all that pain any more, if we are using ASP.NET. We can use the underlying features of this technology to implicitly implement all these features declaratively, rather than programmatically.

Just to illustrate the point further, we shall illustrate one more example. This time, we make use of the *RangeValidator*. As the name suggests, this validation control allows us to specify the range in which the value of a particular control must be. Have a look at Fig. 9.24.

```
<%@ Page Language="C#" %>

<script runat="server">

 void Button_Click(Object sender, EventArgs e)
 {
  if (Page.IsValid)
  {
   MessageLabel.Text = "Page submitted successfully.";
  }
  else
  {
   MessageLabel.Text = "There is an error on the page.";
  }
 }

</script>

<html>
<head id="Head1" runat="server">
 <title>Validator Example</title>
</head>
<body>
 <form id="form1" runat="server">
  <h3>
   Validator Example</h3>
  Enter a number from 1 to 10.
  <asp:TextBox ID="NumberTextBox" runat="server" />
  <asp:RangeValidator ID="NumberCompareValidator"
   ControlToValidate="NumberTextBox" Type="Integer" Display="Dynamic"
   ErrorMessage="Please enter a value from 1 to 10."
   MaximumValue="10" MinimumValue="1" Text="*" runat="server" />
  <asp:RequiredFieldValidator ID="TextBoxRequiredValidator"
   ControlToValidate="NumberTextBox" Display="Dynamic" ErrorMessage="Please enter a
   value." Text="*" runat="server" />
  <br />
  <br />
  <asp:Button ID="SubmitButton" Text="Submit" OnClick="Button_Click"
   runat="server" />
  <br />
  <br />
  <asp:Label ID="MessageLabel" runat="server" />
  <br />
  <br />
  <asp:ValidationSummary ID="ErrorSummary" runat="server" />
 </form>
</body>
</html>
```

Fig. 9.24 *RangeValidator and ValidationSummary validation controls*

Let us understand how this code works. We have defined a text box, which is actually a Web server control.

```
<asp:TextBox ID="NumberTextBox" runat="server" />
```

We then have a *RangeValidator*:

```
<asp:RangeValidator ID="NumberCompareValidator" ControlToValidate="Numbe
rTextBox"
    Type="Integer" Display="Dynamic" ErrorMessage="Please enter a value
from 1 to 10."
        MaximumValue="10" MinimumValue="1" Text="*" runat="server" />
```

This code tells us that we want to validate the text box control created earlier. We then say that the minimum value that the text box can accept is 1, and the maximum value is 10. We also specify the error message, in case the user has not entered a number in the text box adhering to this range.

We then also have a *RequiredFieldValidator*:

```
<asp:RequiredFieldValidator ID="TextBoxRequiredValidator"
ControlToValidate="NumberTextBox"
    Display="Dynamic" ErrorMessage="Please enter a value." Text="*" runat=
            "server" />
```

This validation control ensures that the user does not leave our text box empty.

Finally, we have an interesting piece of code:

```
<asp:ValidationSummary ID="ErrorSummary" runat="server" />
```

This is the *ValidationSummary* validation control. This validation control ensures that instead of displaying different validation errors differently, and at different places, all if them can be summarized and displayed at one place. In other words, we want to summarize all the validation errors at one place for better look and feel. Following are its key features:

1. Consolidates error reporting for all controls on a page
2. Usually used for forms containing large amounts of data
3. Shows list of errors in a bulleted list

Above this, we had the following code:

```
<asp:Button ID="SubmitButton" Text="Submit" OnClick="Button_
Click"runat="server" />
```

This code says that when the user submits the form, we want to call a method called as `Button_Click`. If we look at the code of this method, we realize that it is a server-side method, written in C#:

```
<script runat="server">

    void Button_Click(Object sender, EventArgs e)
    {
        if (Page.IsValid)
        {
            MessageLabel.Text = "Page submitted successfully.";
        }
        else
        {
            MessageLabel.Text = "There is an error on the page.";
        }
    }
```

This method checks if all the validation controls on the page have been successfully validated. If yes, the *Page.IsValid* property is considered to be *true*, else it is *false*. Accordingly, the appropriate message would get displayed on the screen. Let us see the output in various situations now. Figure 9.25 shows the first case.

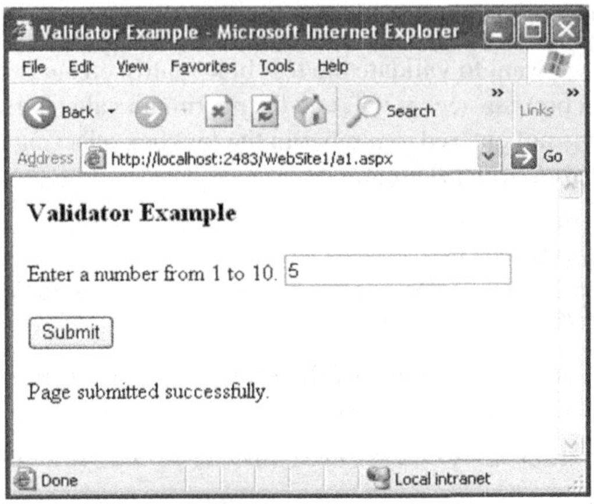

Fig. 9.25 *Correct input*

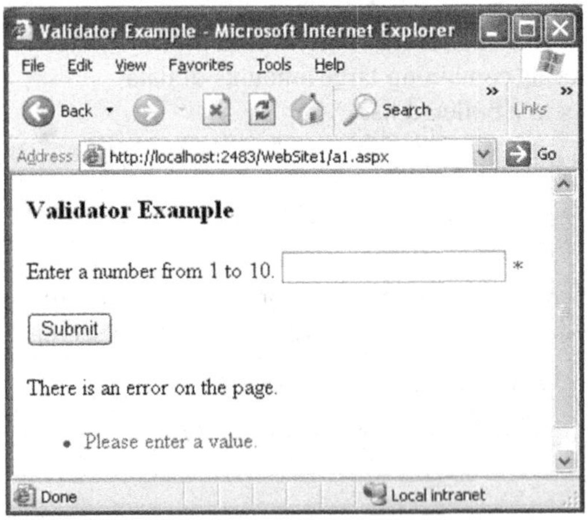

Fig. 9.26 *No input—RequiredFieldValidator in action*

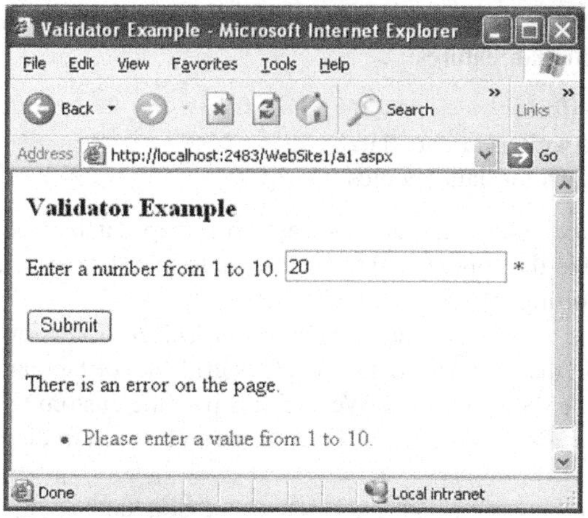

Fig. 9.27 *RangeValidator in action*

This completes our overview of validation controls.

DATABASE PROCESSING 9.7

Database processing in ASP.NET framework is handled by the ADO.NET technology. ADO.NET is the interface between ASP.NET application programs and the DBMS. ADO.NET database support is classified into two categories, as shown in Fig. 9.28.

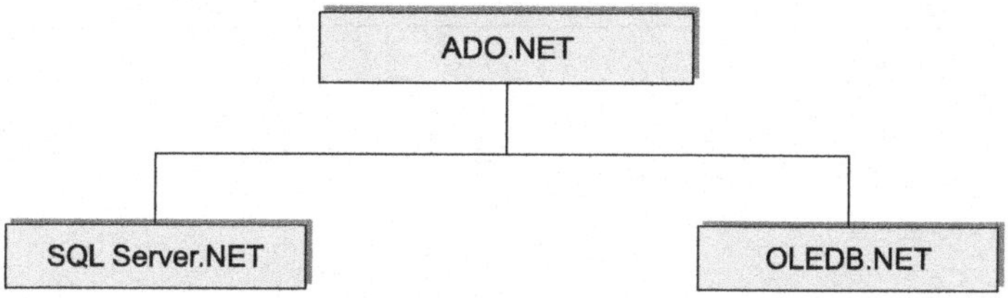

Fig. 9.28 *ADO.NET classification*

Like all other similar database technologies, ADO.NET supports the concept of **data binding**. The idea is interesting. We can display data in the form of HTML controls on the screen by designing the screen in the manner that we want. That is, we can have text boxes, drop down lists, radio buttons, etc., as usual. However, the source of data for some or all of these can be from database tables. ADO.NET facilitates this by using the concept of data binding. That is, controls on the HTML page are automatically linked or bound to some data in the database. Not only that, the controls help transform data from plain database row-and-column structure to the format of the appropriate control. For example, if the control is a drop-down list, data from the table would be populated inside the drop-down list with the appropriate format, conventions, etc.

In ASP.NET version 2.0, the concept of **Data source controls** was introduced. These controls provide the following additional features:

1. Minimal coding effort
2. Facility to read as well as update data
3. New HTML controls for data updates

Using these data source controls, it is very easy to set up database processing. By doing some drag-and-drop, we can make the source of data as any table in a database, and perform operations on the selected data such as sorting, pagination, and so on.

Similarly, **FormView** is also a new database control in ASP.NET version 2.0. This feature allows us to select and display data in the form of a data grid. This grid-like or tabular approach to data selection makes viewing and updating data very easy. We can also provide custom template for data display.

Similarly, another database control called **TreeView** can be used to display hierarchical data (such as XML).

We now take a look at the various approaches for accessing data using ADO.NET.

9.7.1 Using SqlDataSource

This data source control provides us database access to any source that has ADO.NET data provider. For example, it can be ODBC, OLE DB, SQL server, Oracle, etc. In the ASP.NET designer window, we simply need to use the SqlDataSource control to be dragged on to the screen. Then we can perform a series of very simple steps that allow us to link this control to an MS-Access database table (as an example). They are quite self-explanatory, and hence, we need not discuss them here. Then we can drag-drop a server control such as a drop-down list, and bind it to the SqlDataSource control. The resulting code-behind is shown in Fig. 9.29.

```
<%@ Page Language="C#" %>

<!DOCTYPE html PUBLIC "-//W3C//DTD XHTML 1.0 Transitional//EN" "http://www.w3.org/TR/
xhtml1/DTD/xhtml1-transitional.dtd">

<script runat="server">

</script>

<html xmlns="http://www.w3.org/1999/xhtml" >
<head runat="server">
  <title>Untitled Page</title>
</head>
<body>
  <form id="form1" runat="server">
  <div>
    <asp:SqlDataSource ID="SqlDataSource1" runat="server" ConnectionString="<%$
      ConnectionStrings:db1ConnectionString %>"
    ProviderName="<%$ ConnectionStrings:db1ConnectionString.ProviderName %>"
      SelectCommand="SELECT [Product_Name], [Price], [Quantity] FROM [Products]">
    </asp:SqlDataSource>
```

(Contd.)

Fig. 9.29 *Contd...*

```
    <br />
    <asp:DropDownList ID="DropDownList1"        runat="server"
     DataSourceID="SqlDataSource1"              DataTextField="Product_Name"
     DataValueField="Product_Name">
    </asp:DropDownList>
    </div>
  </form>
</body>
</html>
```

Fig. 9.29 *SqlDataSource example*

We can also add an *UpdateCommand* attribute to the SqlDataSource to allow the user to edit data.

9.7.2 GridView

This control allows us to access data without writing a single line of code! We can drag this control on to the screen, and link it to a data source. Simply by setting a couple of properties, we can have the data sorted, pagination enabled, and so on. The data that gets displayed is in a grid form.

9.7.3 FormView

This control allows us to display a single data item from a bound data source control and allows insertions, updates, and deletions to data. We can also provide a custom template for the data display. Figure 9.30 illustrates the usage of this control with an example.

```
<%@ Page Language="C#" %>
<html >
<head runat="server">
 <title>Untitled Page</title>
</head>
<body>
 <form id="form1" runat="server">
 <div>
   <asp:FormView ID="FormView1" runat="server" AllowPaging="True"
                         DataSourceID="AccessDataSource1">
  <ItemTemplate>
   lname:
   <asp:Label ID="lnameLabel" runat="server" Text='<%# Bind("lname") %>'></asp:Label>
    <br />
   fname:
   <asp:Label ID="fnameLabel" runat="server" Text='<%# Bind("fname") %>'></asp:Label>
    <br />
   hiredate:
   <asp:Label ID="hiredateLabel" runat="server" Text='<%# Bind("hiredate") %>'>
    </asp:Label><br />
```

(Contd.)

Fig. 9.30 *Contd...*

```
phone:
<asp:Label ID="phoneLabel" runat="server" Text='<%# Bind("phone") %>'></asp:Label>
  <br />
</ItemTemplate>
<EditItemTemplate>
 lname:
 <asp:TextBox ID="lnameTextBox" runat="server" Text='<%# Bind("lname") %>'>
 </asp:TextBox><br />
 fname:
 <asp:TextBox ID="fnameTextBox" runat="server" Text='<%# Bind("fname") %>'>
 </asp:TextBox><br />
 hiredate:
 <asp:TextBox ID="hiredateTextBox" runat="server" Text='<%# Bind("hiredate") %>'>
 </asp:TextBox><br />
 phone:
 <asp:TextBox ID="phoneTextBox" runat="server" Text='<%# Bind("phone") %>'>
 </asp:TextBox><br />
 <asp:LinkButton ID="UpdateButton" runat="server" CausesValidation="True"
            CommandName="Update"
  Text="Update">
 </asp:LinkButton>
 <asp:LinkButton ID="UpdateCancelButton" runat="server" CausesValidation="False"
            CommandName="Cancel"
  Text="Cancel">
 </asp:LinkButton>
</EditItemTemplate>
```

Fig. 9.30 *FormView example—Part 1*

```
<InsertItemTemplate>
 lname:
 <asp:TextBox ID="lnameTextBox" runat="server" Text='<%# Bind("lname") %>'>
 </asp:TextBox><br />
 fname:
 <asp:TextBox ID="fnameTextBox" runat="server" Text='<%# Bind("fname") %>'>
 </asp:TextBox><br />
 hiredate:
 <asp:TextBox ID="hiredateTextBox" runat="server" Text='<%# Bind("hiredate") %>'>
 </asp:TextBox><br />
 phone:
 <asp:TextBox ID="phoneTextBox" runat="server" Text='<%# Bind("phone") %>'>
 </asp:TextBox><br />
 <asp:LinkButton ID="InsertButton" runat="server" CausesValidation="True"
            CommandName="Insert"
  Text="Insert">
 </asp:LinkButton>
 <asp:LinkButton ID="InsertCancelButton" runat="server" CausesValidation="False"
   CommandName="Cancel"
  Text="Cancel">
 </asp:LinkButton>
</InsertItemTemplate>
```

(Contd.)

Fig. 9.30 *Contd...*

```
    </asp:FormView>
    <asp:AccessDataSource ID="AccessDataSource1" runat="server"
       DataFile="C:\Lectures\SICSR\Web
    Technologies\WT-2\Examples\employees.mdb"
   SelectCommand="SELECT [lname], [fname], [hiredate], [phone] FROM
    [employees]"></asp:AccessDataSource>
      <br />
   </div>
  </form>
</body>
</html>
```

Fig. 9.30 *FormView example—Part 2*

9.7.4 Database Programming

So far, we have discussed the options of performing database processing by using minimum code. However, ASP.NET also facilitates features whereby the programmer has full control over the database processing. The general steps for this approach are shown in Fig. 9.31.

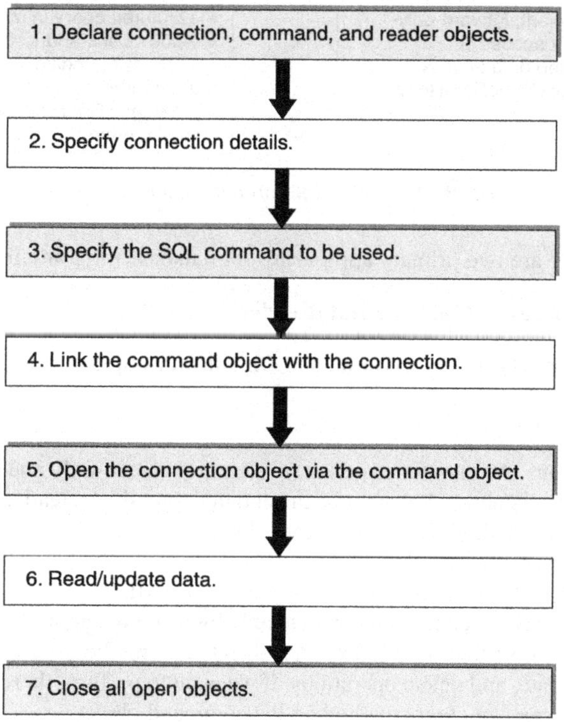

Fig. 9.31 *ASP.NET database programming steps*

The command object provides a number of useful methods, as summarized below:

1. ExecuteNonQuery This method executes the specified SQL command and returns the number of affected rows.

2. ExecuteReader This command provides a forward-only and read-only cursor; and executes the specified SQL command to return an object of type SqlDataReader (discussed subsequently).

3. ExecuteRow This method executes a command and returns a single row of type SqlRecord.

4. ExecuteXMLReader Allows processing of XML documents.

For the purpose of programming, there are two options, as specified in Fig. 9.32.

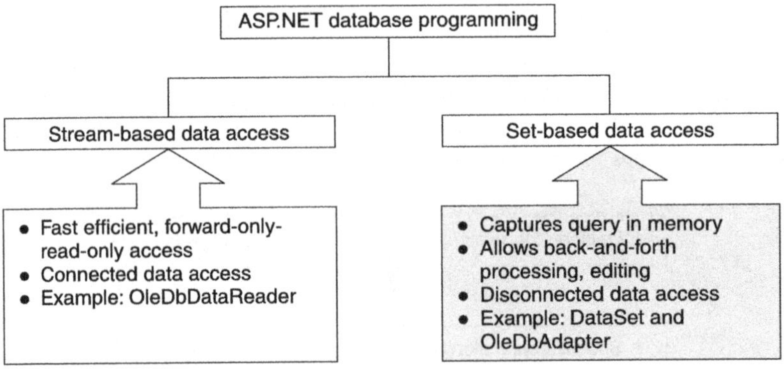

Fig. 9.32 *ASP.NET programming approaches*

As we can see, there are two primary approaches for database programming using ASP.NET.

1. Stream-based data access Using the **DataReader** object.

2. Set-based data access Using the **DataSet** and **DbAdapter** objects.

We shall discuss both now.

1. Using the DataReader As mentioned earlier, this control is read-only and forward-only. It expects a live connection with the database. It cannot be instantiated directly. Instead, it must be instantiated by calling the *ExecuteReader* method of the *Command* object.

Figure 9.33 shows an example.

As we can see, a *GridView* control is specified in the HTML page. It is bound to a *DataReader* object. The *DataReader* object fetches data from a table by using the appropriate SQL statement.

However, we should note that the *DataReader* object can only be used for reading data. It cannot be used in the insert, update, and delete operations. If we want to perform these kinds of operations, we can directly call the *ExecuteNonQuery* method on the command object.

```
<%@ Page Language="C#" Debug = "true"%>
<%@ Import Namespace = "System.Data" %>
<%@ Import Namespace = "System.Data.SqlClient" %>
<%@ Import Namespace = "System.Configuration" %>
<%@ Import Namespace = "System.Data.OleDb" %>

<!DOCTYPE html PUBLIC "-//W3C//DTD XHTML 1.0 Transitional//EN" "http://www.w3.org/TR/
 xhtml1/DTD/xhtml1-transitional.dtd">

<script runat="server">

 protected void Page_Load()
  {
    if (!Page.IsPostBack)
  {
     OleDbConnection MyConnection;
     OleDbCommand MyCommand;
     OleDbDataReader MyReader;

     MyConnection = new OleDbConnection
       ("Provider=Microsoft.Jet.OLEDB.4.0;Data Source=\"C:\\Lectures\\SICSR\\Web
       Technologies\\WT-2\\Examples\\employees.mdb\"");
     MyCommand = new OleDbCommand();
     MyCommand.CommandText = "SELECT lname FROM employees";
     MyCommand.CommandType = CommandType.Text;
     MyCommand.Connection = MyConnection;

     MyCommand.Connection.Open();

     MyReader = MyCommand.ExecuteReader(CommandBehavior.CloseConnection);

     gvEmployees.DataSource = MyReader;
     gvEmployees.DataBind();

     MyCommand.Dispose();
     MyConnection.Dispose();
    }
  }
</script>

<html xmlns="http://www.w3.org/1999/xhtml" >
<head runat="server">
 <title>SQL Example</title>
</head>
<body>
 <form id="form1" runat="server">
 <div>
  <asp:GridView ID="gvEmployees" runat="server">
  </asp:GridView>

 </div>
 </form>
</body>
</html>
```

Fig. 9.33 *Using the DataReader object*

Figure 9.34 shows an example for inserting data using the *ExecuteNonQuery* method of the *Command* object.

```
<%@ Page Language="C#" Debug = "true"%>
<%@ Import Namespace = "System.Data" %>
<%@ Import Namespace = "System.Data.SqlClient" %>
<%@ Import Namespace = "System.Configuration" %>
<%@ Import Namespace = "System.Data.OleDb" %>

<!DOCTYPE html PUBLIC "-//W3C//DTD XHTML 1.0 Transitional//EN" "http://www.w3.org/TR/
 xhtml1/DTD/xhtml1-transitional.dtd">

<script runat="server">

 protected void Page_Load()
 {
  if (!Page.IsPostBack)
  {
   OleDbConnection MyConnection;
   OleDbCommand MyCommand;

   MyConnection = new OleDbConnection
     ("Provider=Microsoft.Jet.OLEDB.4.0;Data Source=\"C:\\Lectures\\SICSR\\Web
     Technologies\\WT-2\\Examples\\employees.mdb\"");

   MyConnection.Open();

   MyCommand = new OleDbCommand
     ("INSERT INTO employees VALUES ('8000', 'Kahate', 'Atul', '13-08-2001', 0, 'D1',
      'Mr', 'atul@atul.com', '2101011')", MyConnection);

   MyCommand.ExecuteNonQuery ();

   MyConnection.Close();
   MyCommand.Dispose();
   MyConnection.Dispose();
  }
 }
</script>

<html xmlns="http://www.w3.org/1999/xhtml" >
<head id="Head1" runat="server">
 <title>SQL Example</title>
</head>
<body>
 <form id="form1" runat="server">
 <div>
  Hello
 </div>
 </form>
</body>
</html>
```

Fig. 9.34 *Inserting data using ExecuteNonQuery method of the Command object*

We can similarly update data, as shown in Fig. 9.35.

```
<%@ Page Language="C#" Debug = "true"%>
<%@ Import Namespace = "System.Data"  %>
<%@ Import Namespace = "System.Data.SqlClient"  %>
<%@ Import Namespace = "System.Configuration"  %>
<%@ Import Namespace = "System.Data.OleDb"  %>

<!DOCTYPE html PUBLIC "-//W3C//DTD XHTML 1.0 Transitional//EN" "http://www.w3.org/TR/
 xhtml1/DTD/xhtml1-transitional.dtd">

<script runat="server">

 protected void Page_Load()
 {
  if (!Page.IsPostBack)
  {
   OleDbConnection MyConnection;
   OleDbCommand MyCommand;

   MyConnection = new OleDbConnection
    ("Provider=Microsoft.Jet.OLEDB.4.0;Data Source=\"C:\\Lectures\\SICSR\\Web
     Technologies\\WT-2\\Examples\\employees.mdb\"");

   MyConnection.Open();

   MyCommand = new OleDbCommand
    ("UPDATE employees SET lname = 'test' WHERE empno = '8000'", MyConnection);

   MyCommand.ExecuteNonQuery ();

   MyConnection.Close();
   MyCommand.Dispose();
   MyConnection.Dispose();
  }
 }
</script>

<html xmlns="http://www.w3.org/1999/xhtml" >
<head id="Head1" runat="server">
 <title>SQL Example</title>
</head>
<body>
 <form id="form1" runat="server">
 <div>
  Hello
 </div>
 </form>
</body>
</html>
```

Fig. 9.35 *Updating data using ExecuteNonQuery method of the Command object*

We can also delete data, as shown in Fig. 9.36.

One of the nice features of SQL programming these days is to perform what are called as **parameterized operations**. In other words, we can decide at run time, what values should be provided to an SQL query for comparisons, insertions, updates, etc. For example, suppose that we want to accept some value from the user and allow the user to search for matching rows based on that value. Now, in this case, we cannot hard code that value in our SQL query, since that would stop the user from providing a different value each time. However, if we parameterize it, the user can provide the value at run time, and the query would take that value as the input for the look up. Figure 9.37 shows the example of a parameterized SELECT statement.

```
<%@ Page Language="C#" Debug = "true"%>
<%@ Import Namespace = "System.Data"  %>
<%@ Import Namespace = "System.Data.SqlClient"  %>
<%@ Import Namespace = "System.Configuration"  %>
<%@ Import Namespace = "System.Data.OleDb"  %>

<!DOCTYPE html PUBLIC "-//W3C//DTD XHTML 1.0 Transitional//EN" "http://www.w3.org/
TR/xhtml1/DTD/xhtml1-transitional.dtd">

<script runat="server">

 protected void Page_Load()
 {
  if (!Page.IsPostBack)
  {
   OleDbConnection MyConnection;
   OleDbCommand MyCommand;

   MyConnection = new OleDbConnection
     ("Provider=Microsoft.Jet.OLEDB.4.0;Data Source=\"C:\\Lectures\\SICSR\\Web
      Technologies\\WT-2\\Examples\\employees.mdb\"");

   MyConnection.Open();

   MyCommand = new OleDbCommand
     ("DELETE FROM employees WHERE empno = '3000'", MyConnection);

   MyCommand.ExecuteNonQuery ();

   MyConnection.Close();
   MyCommand.Dispose();
   MyConnection.Dispose();
  }
 }
</script>

<html xmlns="http://www.w3.org/1999/xhtml" >
<head id="Head1" runat="server">
<title>SQL Example</title>
</head>
<body>
  <form id="form1" runat="server">
  <div>
   Hello
  </div>
  </form>
</body>
</html>
```

Fig. 9.36 *Deleting data using ExecuteNonQuery method of the Command object*

```
<%@ Page Language="C#" %>
<%@ Import Namespace ="System.Data" %>
<%@ Import Namespace ="System.Data.SqlClient" %>
<%@ Import Namespace ="System.Configuration" %>
<%@ Import Namespace = "System.Data.OleDb"  %>

<script runat="server">
 protected void Page_Load(object sender, EventArgs e)
 {
  if (!Page.IsPostBack)
  {
   OleDbConnection MyConnection;
   OleDbCommand MyCommand;
   OleDbDataReader MyDataReader;

   MyConnection = new OleDbConnection
     ("Provider=Microsoft.Jet.OLEDB.4.0;Data Source=\"C:\\Lectures\\SICSR\\Web
      Technologies\\WT-2\\Examples\\employees.mdb\"");
   MyConnection.Open();

   MyCommand = new OleDbCommand();
   MyCommand.CommandText = " SELECT lname, fname FROM employees WHERE deptno = @deptno ";

   MyCommand.CommandType = CommandType.Text;
   MyCommand.Connection = MyConnection;
   MyDataReader = null;

   MyCommand.Parameters.Add("@deptno", OleDbType.Char);

   MyCommand.Parameters["@deptno"].Value = "D1";

   try
   {
    MyDataReader = MyCommand.ExecuteReader();

    if (MyDataReader.HasRows)
    Response.Write ("--- Found data ---<br>");
    else
    Response.Write("--- Did not find any data ---<br>");
   }
   catch (OleDbException ex)
   {
    Response.Write("*** ERROR *** ==> " + ex.Message.ToString());
   }

   while (MyDataReader.Read())
   {
    Response.Write("Last name = " + MyDataReader["lname"] + "  ");
    Response.Write("First name = " + MyDataReader["fname"]);
    Response.Write("<br>");
   }

   MyDataReader.Dispose();
   MyCommand.Dispose();
   MyConnection.Dispose();
  }
 }
</script>
```

Fig. 9.37 *Parameterized SELECT—Part 1*

```
<html xmlns="http://www.w3.org/1999/xhtml" >
<head id="Head1" runat="server">
 <title>Untitled Page</title>
</head>
<body>
 <form id="form1" runat="server">
 <div>
   </div>
 </form>
</body>
</html>
```

Fig. 9.37 *Parameterized SELECT—Part 2*

As we can see, the department number is not hardcoded into the SQL query. Instead, this is passed as a parameter value at run time. Of course, in this case, it is provided without any user intervention. But in real life, this value can come from the user or from another table/application, etc.

Figure 9.38 shows a parameterized UPDATE statement.

```
<%@ Page Language="C#" %>
<%@ Import Namespace ="System.Data" %>
<%@ Import Namespace ="System.Data.SqlClient" %>
<%@ Import Namespace ="System.Configuration" %>
<%@ Import Namespace = "System.Data.OleDb"  %>

<script runat="server">

 protected void Page_Load(object sender, EventArgs e)
 {
  if (!Page.IsPostBack)
  {
   OleDbConnection MyConnection;
   OleDbCommand MyCommand;

   OleDbParameter DeptnoParam;
   OleDbParameter DeptnameParam;

   MyConnection = new OleDbConnection
     ("Provider=Microsoft.Jet.OLEDB.4.0;Data Source=\"C:\\Lectures\\SICSR\\Web
      Technologies\\WT-2\\Examples\\employees.mdb\"");
   MyConnection.Open();

   MyCommand = new OleDbCommand();
   MyCommand.CommandText = " UPDATE departments SET deptname = @deptname WHERE deptno
      = @deptno ";

   MyCommand.CommandType = CommandType.Text;
   MyCommand.Connection = MyConnection;
```

Fig. 9.38 *Parameterized UPDATE—Part 1*

```
        MyCommand.Parameters.Add("@deptname", OleDbType.Char);
        MyCommand.Parameters.Add("@deptno", OleDbType.Char);

        MyCommand.Parameters["@deptname"].Value = "Test name";
        MyCommand.Parameters["@deptno"].Value = "D2";
    try
        {
         MyCommand.ExecuteNonQuery();
        }

        catch (OleDbException ex)
        {
         Response.Write("*** ERROR *** ==> " + ex.Message.ToString());
        }

        MyCommand.Dispose();
        MyConnection.Dispose();
      }
     }
    </script>

    <html xmlns="http://www.w3.org/1999/xhtml" >
    <head id="Head1" runat="server">
     <title>Untitled Page</title>
    </head>
    <body>
     <form id="form1" runat="server">
     <div>
       </div>
     </form>
    </body>
    </html>
```

Fig. 9.38 *Parameterized UPDATE—Part 2*

Just as we can select or update data based on the parameters provided by the user or another application, we can even create a new row in the table, depending on what data the user has provided. In other words, parameterized insert is also allowed. Figure 9.39 shows an example.

```
<%@ Page Language="C#" %>
<%@ Import Namespace ="System.Data" %>
<%@ Import Namespace ="System.Data.SqlClient" %>
<%@ Import Namespace ="System.Configuration" %>
<%@ Import Namespace = "System.Data.OleDb"  %>

<script runat="server">
 protected void Page_Load(object sender, EventArgs e)
 {
  if (Page.IsPostBack)
  {
   Label1.Text = "Result: ";

   OleDbConnection MyConnection;
```

(Contd.)

Fig. 9.39 *Contd...*

```
    OleDbCommand MyCommand;

    String Dept_No = TextBox1.Text.ToString();
    String Dept_Name = TextBox2.Text.ToString();
    String Dept_Mgr = TextBox3.Text.ToString();
    String Dept_Location = TextBox4.Text.ToString();

    MyConnection = new OleDbConnection
      ("Provider=Microsoft.Jet.OLEDB.4.0;Data Source=\"C:\\Lectures\\SICSR\\Web
       Technologies\\WT-2\\Examples\\employees.mdb\"");
    MyConnection.Open();
    MyCommand = new OleDbCommand();
    MyCommand.CommandText = "INSERT INTO departments VALUES (@deptno, @deptname, @deptmgr,
       @location) ";

    MyCommand.CommandType = CommandType.Text;
    MyCommand.Connection = MyConnection;

    MyCommand.Parameters.Add("@deptno", OleDbType.Char);
    MyCommand.Parameters.Add("@deptname", OleDbType.Char);
    MyCommand.Parameters.Add("@deptmgr", OleDbType.Char);
    MyCommand.Parameters.Add("@location", OleDbType.Char);

    MyCommand.Parameters["@deptno"].Value = Dept_No;
    MyCommand.Parameters["@deptname"].Value = Dept_Name;
    MyCommand.Parameters["@deptmgr"].Value = Dept_Mgr;
    MyCommand.Parameters["@location"].Value = Dept_Location;

    try
    {
      int i = MyCommand.ExecuteNonQuery();

      if (i == 1)
        Label1.Text += " One row added to the table";
    }
    catch (OleDbException ex)
    {
      Label1.Text += "*** ERROR *** ==> " + ex.Message.ToString();
    }

    MyCommand.Dispose();
    MyConnection.Dispose();
  }
}

</script>
```

Fig. 9.39 *Parameterized INSERT—Part 1*

```
<html xmlns="http://www.w3.org/1999/xhtml" >
<head id="Head1" runat="server">
 <title>Untitled Page</title>
</head>
<body>
 <form id="form1" runat="server">
 <div>
  <h2>Please provide following values<br /></h2>
  <br />
  <h5>
  <table style="width: 436px">
   <tr>
    <td style="width: 160px" bgcolor="#ffffcc">
     Department Number (Unique)</td>
    <td style="width: 346px" bgcolor="#ffffcc">
     <asp:TextBox ID="TextBox1" runat="server"></asp:TextBox></td>
   </tr>
   <tr>
    <td style="height: 21px; width: 160px;" bgcolor="#ffffcc">
     Department Name</td>
    <td style="width: 346px; height: 21px" bgcolor="#ffffcc">
     <asp:TextBox ID="TextBox2" runat="server"></asp:TextBox></td>
   </tr>
   <tr>
    <td style="width: 160px" bgcolor="#ffffcc">
     Department Manager</td>
    <td style="width: 346px" bgcolor="#ffffcc">
     <asp:TextBox ID="TextBox3" runat="server"></asp:TextBox></td>
   </tr>
   <tr>
    <td style="width: 160px" bgcolor="#ffffcc">
     Location</td>
    <td style="width: 346px" bgcolor="#ffffcc">
     <asp:TextBox ID="TextBox4" runat="server"></asp:TextBox></td>
   </tr>
  </table>
  </h5>
 </div>
  <br />
                         
            
  <asp:Button ID="Button1" runat="server" Text="Insert Data" /><br />
  <br />
  <asp:Label ID="Label1" runat="server" BorderStyle="Ridge" Font-Bold="True" Font-
   Italic="True"
   Font-Size="Medium" Text="Result: "></asp:Label>
 </form>
</body>
</html>
```

Fig. 9.39 *Parameterized INSERT—Part 2*

2. Using the DataSet, DataTable, and DataAdapter We have mentioned earlier that the DataSet offers disconnected data access. This is the most common form of database access. In other words, this technique allows the ASP.NET program to be disconnected from the database while performing the database operations. The final result of the operation, however, gets applied to the database by connecting once.

The DataSet object is a collection of many DataTable objects. A DataTable represents one database table in the memory of the application. We can choose to directly work with a DataTable object. Figure 9.40 shows an example.

```
<%@ Page Language="C#" %>
<%@ Import Namespace ="System.Data" %>
<%@ Import Namespace ="System.Data.SqlClient" %>
<%@ Import Namespace ="System.Configuration" %>
<%@ Import Namespace ="System.Data.OleDb"  %>

<script runat="server">

 protected void Page_Load(object sender, EventArgs e)
 {
   if (!Page.IsPostBack)
   {
    OleDbConnection MyConnection;
    OleDbCommand MyCommand;

    DataTable MyDataTable;
    OleDbDataReader MyReader;
    OleDbParameter EmpnoParam;

    MyConnection = new OleDbConnection
      ("Provider=Microsoft.Jet.OLEDB.4.0;Data Source=\"C:\\Lectures\\SICSR\\Web Technologies
       \\WT-2\\Examples\\employees.mdb\"");

    MyCommand = new OleDbCommand();
    MyCommand.CommandText = " SELECT * FROM employees WHERE empno = @empno ";

    MyCommand.CommandType = CommandType.Text;
    MyCommand.Connection = MyConnection;

    EmpnoParam = new OleDbParameter();
    EmpnoParam.ParameterName = "@empno";
    EmpnoParam.OleDbType = OleDbType.Char;
    EmpnoParam.Size = 50;
    EmpnoParam.Direction = ParameterDirection.Input;
    EmpnoParam.Value = "4000";

    MyCommand.Parameters.Add(EmpnoParam);

    MyCommand.Connection.Open();
    MyReader = MyCommand.ExecuteReader(CommandBehavior.CloseConnection);

    MyDataTable = new DataTable();
    MyDataTable.Load(MyReader);

    gvEmployees.DataSource = MyDataTable;
    gvEmployees.DataBind();

    MyDataTable.Dispose();
    MyCommand.Dispose();
    MyConnection.Dispose();
   }
 }
</script>
```

Fig. 9.40 *Using the DataTable for SELECT—Part 1*

```
<html xmlns="http://www.w3.org/1999/xhtml" >
<head runat="server">
 <title>Untitled Page</title>
</head>
<body>
 <form id="form1" runat="server">
 <div>
  <asp:GridView ID="gvEmployees" runat="server">
  </asp:GridView>

 </div>
 </form>
</body>
</html>
```

Fig. 9.40 *Using the DataTable for SELECT—Part 2*

In a similar fashion, we can insert data as shown in Fig. 9.41.

```
<%@ Page Language="C#" %>
<%@ Import Namespace  ="System.Data" %>
<%@ Import Namespace  ="System.Data.SqlClient" %>
<%@ Import Namespace  ="System.Configuration" %>
<%@ Import Namespace = "System.Data.OleDb"  %>

<!DOCTYPE html PUBLIC "-//W3C//DTD XHTML 1.0 Transitional//EN" "http://www.w3.org/
 TR/xhtml1/DTD/xhtml1-transitional.dtd">

<script runat="server">

 protected void Page_Load(object sender, EventArgs e)
 {
  if (!Page.IsPostBack)
  {
   OleDbConnection MyConnection;
   OleDbCommand MyCommand;

   DataTable MyDataTable;
   OleDbDataReader MyReader;
   OleDbParameter DeptNoParam;
   OleDbParameter DeptNameParam;
   OleDbParameter DeptMgrParam;
   OleDbParameter LocationParam;
```

Fig. 9.41 *Using the DataTable for INSERT—Part 1*

```
   MyConnection = new OleDbConnection
    ("Provider=Microsoft.Jet.OLEDB.4.0;Data Source=\"C:\\Lectures\\SICSR\\Web
     Technologies\\WT-2\\Examples\\employees.mdb\"");

   MyCommand = new OleDbCommand();
```

(Contd.)

Fig. 9.41 *Contd...*

```
    MyCommand.CommandText = " INSERT INTO departments VALUES (@deptno, @deptname, @deptmgr,
      @location)";

    MyCommand.CommandType = CommandType.Text;
    MyCommand.Connection = MyConnection;

    DeptNoParam = new OleDbParameter();
    DeptNoParam.ParameterName = "@deptno";
    DeptNoParam.OleDbType = OleDbType.Char;
    DeptNoParam.Size = 50;
    DeptNoParam.Direction = ParameterDirection.Input;
    DeptNoParam.Value = "D100";
    MyCommand.Parameters.Add(DeptNoParam);

    DeptNameParam = new OleDbParameter();
    DeptNameParam.ParameterName = "@deptname";
    DeptNameParam.OleDbType = OleDbType.Char;
    DeptNameParam.Size = 50;
    DeptNameParam.Direction = ParameterDirection.Input;
    DeptNameParam.Value = "New Department";
    MyCommand.Parameters.Add(DeptNameParam);

    DeptMgrParam = new OleDbParameter();
    DeptMgrParam.ParameterName = "@deptmgr";
    DeptMgrParam.OleDbType = OleDbType.Char;
    DeptMgrParam.Size = 50;
    DeptMgrParam.Direction = ParameterDirection.Input;
    DeptMgrParam.Value = "2000";
    MyCommand.Parameters.Add(DeptMgrParam);

    LocationParam = new OleDbParameter();
    LocationParam.ParameterName = "@location";
    LocationParam.OleDbType = OleDbType.Char;
    LocationParam.Size = 50;
    LocationParam.Direction = ParameterDirection.Input;
    LocationParam.Value = "Pune";
    MyCommand.Parameters.Add(LocationParam);

    MyCommand.Connection.Open();
    MyReader = MyCommand.ExecuteReader(CommandBehavior.CloseConnection);

    MyDataTable = new DataTable();
    MyDataTable.Load(MyReader);

    gvEmployees.DataSource = MyDataTable;
    gvEmployees.DataBind();

    MyDataTable.Dispose();
    MyCommand.Dispose();
    MyConnection.Dispose();
  }
 }
</script>
```

Fig. 9.41 *Using the DataTable for INSERT—Part 2*

```
<html xmlns="http://www.w3.org/1999/xhtml" >
<head id="Head1" runat="server">
 <title>Untitled Page</title>
</head>
<body>
 <form id="form1" runat="server">
 <div>
  <asp:GridView ID="gvEmployees" runat="server">
  </asp:GridView>

 </div>
 </form>
</body>
</html>
```

Fig. 9.41 *Using the DataTable for INSERT—Part 3*

Let us now worry about the DataSet and DataAdapter.

A DataSet does not interact with the database directly. It takes the help of the DataAdapter object. The job of the DataAdapter is to perform database operations and create DataTable objects. The DataTable objects contain the query results. It also writes the changes done to DataTable objects are reflected back on to the database. Conceptually, this can be depicted as shown in Fig. 9.42.

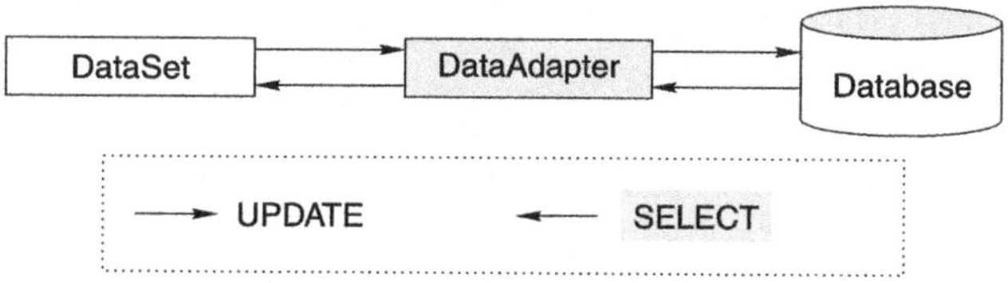

Fig. 9.42 *DataSet and DataAdapter*

The DataAdapter object has a method called as `Fill ()`, which queries a database and initializes a DataSet (actually a DataTable) with the results. Similarly, there is a method called `Update ()`, which is used to propagate changes back to the database.

Figure 9.43 shows an example of selecting data from a table using this idea.

```
<%@ Page Language="C#" %>
<%@ Import Namespace  ="System.Data" %>
<%@ Import Namespace  ="System.Data.SqlClient" %>
<%@ Import Namespace  ="System.Configuration" %>
<%@ Import Namespace = "System.Data.OleDb"  %>

<script runat="server">

 protected void Page_Load(object sender, EventArgs e)
 {
  if (!Page.IsPostBack)
```

(Contd.)

Fig. 9.43 *Contd...*

```
    {
     OleDbConnection MyConnection;
     OleDbCommand MyCommand;
     OleDbDataAdapter MyAdapter;
     DataTable MyTable = new DataTable();

     MyConnection = new OleDbConnection
       ("Provider=Microsoft.Jet.OLEDB.4.0;Data Source=\"C:\\Lectures\\SICSR\\Web
        Technologies\\WT-2\\Examples\\employees.mdb\"");
     MyConnection.Open();

     MyCommand = new OleDbCommand();
     MyCommand.CommandText = " SELECT lname, fname FROM employees WHERE deptno = 'D1' ";
     MyCommand.CommandType = CommandType.Text;
     MyCommand.Connection = MyConnection;

     MyAdapter = new OleDbDataAdapter();
     MyAdapter.SelectCommand = MyCommand;
     MyAdapter.Fill(MyTable);

     GridView1.DataSource = MyTable.DefaultView;
     GridView1.DataBind();

     MyAdapter.Dispose();
     MyCommand.Dispose();
     MyConnection.Dispose();
    }
  }
</script>

<html xmlns="http://www.w3.org/1999/xhtml" >
<head id="Head1" runat="server">
 <title>Untitled Page</title>
</head>
<body>
 <form id="form1" runat="server">
 <div>
   <asp:GridView ID="GridView1" runat="server">
   </asp:GridView>
    </div>
 </form>
</body>
</html>
```

Fig. 9.43 *Selecting data using the DataSet and DataAdapter classes*

Figure 9.44 shows a parameterized SELECT using the DataSet and DataAdapter objects.

```
<%@ Page Language="C#" %>
<%@ Import Namespace  ="System.Data" %>
<%@ Import Namespace  ="System.Data.SqlClient" %>
<%@ Import Namespace  ="System.Configuration" %>
<%@ Import Namespace = "System.Data.OleDb"  %>

<script runat="server">

 protected void Page_Load(object sender, EventArgs e)
 {
  if (!Page.IsPostBack)
  {
   OleDbConnection MyConnection;
   OleDbCommand MyCommand;
   OleDbDataAdapter MyAdapter;
   DataTable MyTable = new DataTable();

   MyConnection = new OleDbConnection
     ("Provider=Microsoft.Jet.OLEDB.4.0;Data Source=\"C:\\Lectures\\SICSR\\Web
      Technologies\\WT-2\\Examples\\employees.mdb\"");
   MyConnection.Open();

   MyCommand = new OleDbCommand();
   MyCommand.CommandText = " SELECT lname, fname FROM employees WHERE deptno = @deptno ";
   MyCommand.CommandType = CommandType.Text;
   MyCommand.Connection = MyConnection;

   MyCommand.Parameters.Add("@deptno", OleDbType.Char);
   MyCommand.Parameters["@deptno"].Value = "D1";

   MyAdapter = new OleDbDataAdapter();
   MyAdapter.SelectCommand = MyCommand;
   MyAdapter.Fill(MyTable);

   GridView1.DataSource = MyTable.DefaultView;
   GridView1.DataBind();

   MyAdapter.Dispose();
   MyCommand.Dispose();
   MyConnection.Dispose();
  }
 }
</script>

<html xmlns="http://www.w3.org/1999/xhtml" >
<head id="Head1" runat="server">
 <title>Untitled Page</title>
</head>
<body>
 <form id="form1" runat="server">
 <div>
  <asp:GridView ID="GridView1" runat="server">
  </asp:GridView>
   </div>
 </form>
</body>
</html>
```

Fig. 9.44 *Parameterized select using the DataSet and DataAdapter classes*

ACTIVEX CONTROLS.. 9.8

ActiveX controls (also called **ActiveX objects**) are similar to the Java applets in the sense that they are also tiny programs that can be downloaded from the Web server to the Web browser, and executed locally at the browser. However, there are two major differences between an applet and an ActiveX control, as discussed below:

1. An applet has to go through many security checks (for example, an applet cannot write to the hard disk of the browser computer), an ActiveX object can actually write to the local hard disk. This makes its behaviour suspect, although it can offer richer functionality as a compensation for this.
2. An applet gets downloaded every time it is accessed. This means that if a user accesses a Web page containing an applet, it gets downloaded to the user's browser and executes there. When the user closes the browser session, the applet is removed from the user's computer because the applet is stored in the main memory of the client computer during its execution. In contrast, when downloaded, ActiveX controls are stored on the hard disk of the client machine. They remain there even when the browser is closed. Therefore, when the user accesses the same Web page containing the same ActiveX control, the ActiveX control from the client's computer is used, and is not downloaded once again from the server.

ActiveX, as mentioned, is Microsoft technology. Therefore, ActiveX objects can run only on Internet Explorer browser. The reason for it being Microsoft-specific is again the Windows registry. All ActiveX objects must be recorded in the registry of the operating system that the Web server is running. This means the Web server must run on an operating system that supports the concept of registry, that is Windows. We shall not discuss ActiveX further, since the conceptual framework is similar to applets.

One more point needs to be noted. These days, the concept of **code signing** has gained prominence. In simple terms, the organization, which develops the program code, declares (digitally) that it has developed a particular piece of code, and the person who has downloaded it (in the form of applets or ActiveX controls) can trust it not to perform any malicious actions. For example, an applet coming from Sun Microsystems could declare that the applet is developed by Sun Microsystems, and that the user can trust it not to do any wrongdoings. Moreover, such **signed applets** or **signed ActiveX controls** can actually have more privileges than unsigned applets or ActiveX controls (e.g., that can perform disk operations). Of course, a signed applet can still contain malicious code, the only advantage here is that you know where this malicious code came from, and take an appropriate action.

The war between client side technologies is going to become hotter, as Microsoft has decided to remove Java support from Version 6 of its popular browser, Internet Explorer. This means that applets cannot execute inside Internet Explorer from Version 6, unless the user instals the Java Virtual Machine (JVM) by downloading it from the Internet—it would not be done automatically, anymore. Furthermore, as Internet Explorer is gaining in popularity, and as people realize that applets can make downloading and processing time slower, it appears that ActiveX controls, or some other client-side technology, if and when it appears on the scene, will become the key to active Web pages.

Key Terms and Concepts

ActiveX control • ASP • ASP.NET • Base class library • Code signing • Code-behind page model • Common Language Runtime (CLR) • Common Language Specifications (CLS) • Data binding • Garbage collection • HTML controls • HTML server controls • Java applet • Java Virtual Machine (JVM) • Microsoft Intermediate Language (MSIL) • Signed applets • Single-page model • Two-Tier application • Validation control • Web server controls • Web services

SUMMARY

- Microsoft's `.NET` platform is one of the best ways of creating Web applications.
- The ASP.NET specifications allow us to specify how Web applications can be constructed so as to have effective design, validations, and clarity.
- ASP.NET applications can be developed in a number of languages, but of most practical relevance are C# and VB.NET.
- Several features are available to make validations very easy in ASP.NET. An example is server controls.
- ASP.NET validations allow the developer to perform very complex validations without writing too much code.
- ASP.NET comes with an Integrated Development Environment (IDE), which allows development of applications very easily.
- ASP.NET provides database processing support in the form of ADO.NET.
- ADO.NET technology allows us to perform database processing in a number of ways, depending on the requirements.

MULTIPLE CHOICE QUESTIONS

1. A Web page is ________ if it does not change its behavior in response to external actions.
   (a) static (b) dynamic (c) active (d) frozen
2. A Web page is ________, if it changes its behavior (i.e., the output) in response to external actions.
   (a) static (b) dynamic (c) active (d) frozen
3. The highest level in the .NET framework is the ________.
   (a) programming languages layer (b) Common Language Specifications
   (c) Microsoft Intermediate Language (d) Web Services and GUI applications
4. ________ is the common thread between all the varying .NET programming languages.
   (a) Common Language Specifications (CLS) (b) XML and ADO.NET
   (c) Base class library (d) Common Language Runtime (CLR)
5. ASP.NET uses full-fledged programming languages such as ________.
   (a) C# and VB.NET (b) VB and C++
   (c) Base class library (d) BCPL and ASP
6. In the ________ approach, all the HTML part is inside one .aspx file, and the actual functionality resides in various individual files.
   (a) Single-page model (b) Code-behind page model
   (c) Double-page model (d) Multiple-page model
7. All ________ have a special identifier, which is `<asp:...>`.
   (a) Web server controls (b) single server controls
   (c) document server controls (d) server controls
8. ________ can run only on Internet Explorer browser and can actually write to the local hard disk.
   (a) Applet (b) ActiveX object (c) Dameon (d) Bean

9. __________ method executes a command and returns a single row of type SQLRecord.
   (a) ExecuteNonQuery (b) ExecuteReader
   (c) ExecuteRow (d) Execute Column

DETAILED QUESTIONS

1. Discuss in detail different types of Web pages.
2. Explain different kind of Web technologies.
3. Give an Overview of the .NET framework.
4. Discuss in detail ASP.NET form controls.
5. Discuss the advantages and disadvantages of Web server controls.
6. Explain how validation controls work. Write a program in ASP.NET, which will take the user name and password and perform effective validations.
7. Discuss in detail how database processing happens in ASP.NET, with an example.
8. What do you think will happen if we use JavaScript instead of ready-made controls for validations in ASP.NET?
9. Which is the best approach for database processing in ASP.NET?
10. How does the .NET framework support multiple languages?

EXERCISES

1. Examine the differences between ASP and ASP.NET.
2. Examine the equivalents of ASP.NET server controls in other technologies.
3. Why did Microsoft come up with the .NET framework? Investigate.
4. Why should we use ADO.NET, and not simple ODBC? Find out.
5. Is C# a better language than C++? Why?

JAVA WEB TECHNOLOGIES 10

INTRODUCTION

For some strange reasons, Sun had decided to name the second release of the Enterprise Java related technologies as **Java 2**. Hence, everything that was developed on top of it, became ***Java 2 xxxxx*** (please refer to the table shown later for more details). This left people wondering as to when would Java 3, Java 4, etc., would emerge. On the contrary, Java had already moved from the second release to the fifth release by then! Hence, **Java 2 Enterprise Edition 5.0** (or **J2EE 5.0** for short) actually meant Java Enterprise fifth edition (and not the second edition)! But the "2" after "Java" had somehow just stayed on! It served no real purpose or made any sense. This should have been **Java Enterprise Edition 5.0** (i.e., **JEE 5.0 in short**).

This was, clearly, confusing and unnecessary.

Thankfully, Sun has now simply dropped the "2" from the Java name, and the "dot zero" from the version number. Hence, the nomenclature has become quite simple now, compared to the dreadful days when everyone was confused about which version of which product one was referring to. To understand and appreciate this better, let us have a quick recap of what Sun had done earlier to create all this confusion, as shown in Table 10.1.

Table 10.1 *Confusion about Java terminology*

Old acronym	*Old long name*	*New long name, with the "2" gone*	*Description*
JDK	Java Development Kit	No change	This is needed if we wanted to just compile standard (core) Java programs, which do not make use of enterprise technologies such as JSP, Servlets, EJB, etc. In other words, these programs can make use of all the standard language features such as classes, strings, methods, operators,

(Contd.)

Table 10.1 *Contd...*

			loops, and even AWT or Swing for graphics. This would translate a java program (i.e., a file with .java extension) into its compiled byte code version (i.e., a file with a .class extension). Many .class files could be compiled into a Java archive file (i.e., a file with a .jar extension).
JRE	Java Runtime Environment	No change	This is the run time environment under which a Java program compiled above would execute.
~~*J2SE*~~	Java 2 Standard Edition	Java SE	It is basically JDK + JRE.
~~*J2EE*~~	Java 2 Enterprise Edition	Java EE	This is the 'enterprise version' of Java, which meant support for server-side technologies in the Web tier (e.g. Servlets and JSP) as well as in the application tier (e.g. EJB). People specialize in some or all of these tiers.

Note that not only is the "2" dropped, so also is the short-form of Java in the form of the letter "J". Now, we must not refer to the older J2SE as JSE. We must call it as Java SE, for example.

Enough about the naming fiasco! Let us have a quick overview about what Java EE 5.0 offers now. For this purpose, we have borrowed some really good diagrams from the official Java EE 5.0 tutorial developed by Sun microsystems.

Figure 10.1 depicts the communication between the various Java EE application layers. The *client tier* is usually made up of a Web browser, which means it can primarily deal with HTML pages and JavaScript (among others). These technologies communicate with the *Web tier* made up of JSP pages, Servlets, and JavaBeans (not EJB!). For example, a servlet may display a login page to the user, and after the user provides the login credentials, authenticate the user by checking the user id and password against a table maintained in the database, as discussed next. The JSP pages and Servlets then communicate with the *Business tier*, i.e., with one or more Enterprise JavaBeans (EJB). Note that the *Business tier* is optional, and is implemented only if the application needs to be able to handle very large volumes of data, provide high security, throughput, availability, robustness, etc. In any case, the *Web tier* usually talks to the *EIS tier* for database processing (either directly, or via the *Business tier*, as explained earlier).

Based on this, the Java EE APIs can be depicted as shown in Fig. 10.2.

Of course, it is not possible to explain any of these in detail here, but a small word on what is new, may perhaps help.

In the *Web tier (Web container* in the above diagram), we now have the following:

1. **Better support for Web services** This is provided by the APIs called as JAX-WS, JAXB, StAX, SAAJ, and JAXR. Some of these existed earlier, but were very clumsily stacked together.
2. **More modern way of developing dynamic Web pages** The JSP technology has become highly tag-oriented, rather than being code-intensive. In other words, the developer does not have to write a lot of code for doing things; but has to instead make certain declarations.
3. **Java Server Faces (JSF)**, which is user input validation technology, built in response to Microsoft's **Web controls** in **ASP.NET**.

In the *Business tier (EJB container* in the above diagram), we now have much easier way of writing Enterprise JavaBeans (EJB) EJB version 3.0 is again lot more declarative, than code-oriented, making the job of the developer far easier. There are several other changes in EJB, in line with these basic changes.

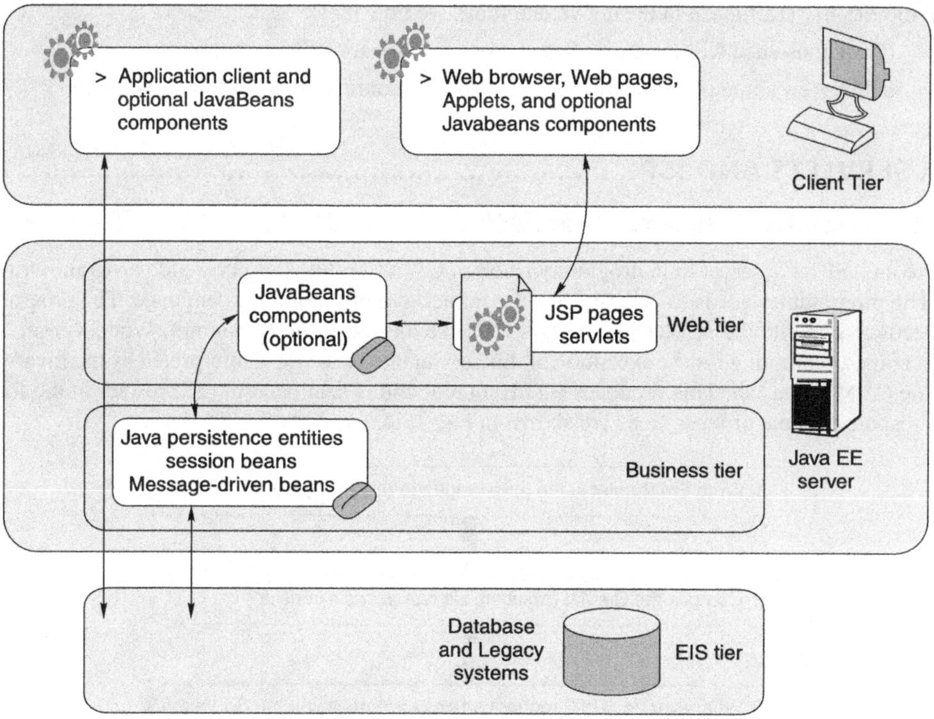

Fig. 10.1 *Sun's Java server architecture (Copyright Sun MicroSystems)*

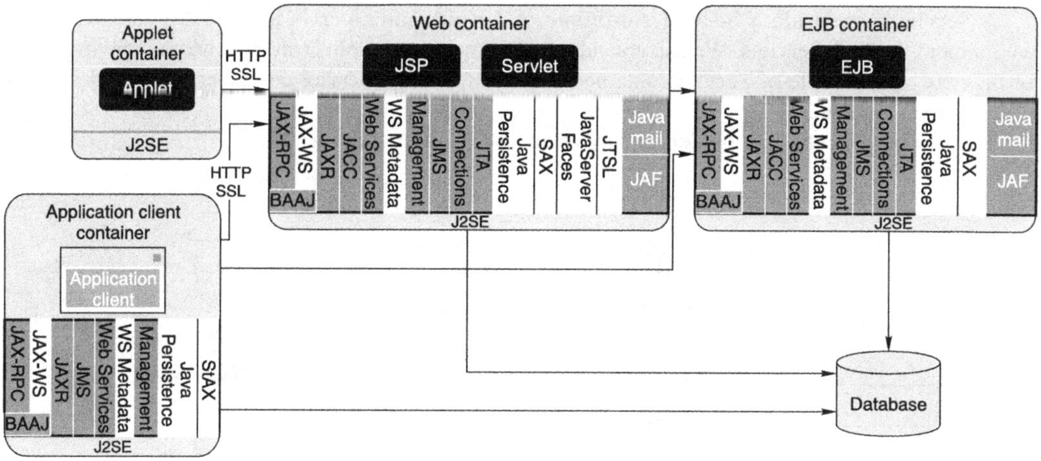

Fig. 10.2 *Sun's Java technologies (Copyright Sun MicroSystems)*

In the *EIS tier (Database* in the above diagram), we now have

Java Persistence API for easier integration of applications with database.

We shall review some of the key technologies in this context in the following sections.

JAVA SERVLETS AND JSP 10.1

10.1.1 Introduction to Servlets and JSP

Just like an ASP.NET server-side program written in C#, a Servlet is a server-side program written in Java. The programmer needs to code the Servlet in the Java programming language. The programmer then needs to compile the servlet into a class file, like any other Java program. Whenever an HTTP request comes, requesting for the execution of this servlet, the class file is interpreted by the Java Virtual Machine (JVM), as usual. This produces HTML output and is sent back to the browser in the form of HTTP response. Some of these steps are shown in Fig. 10.4.

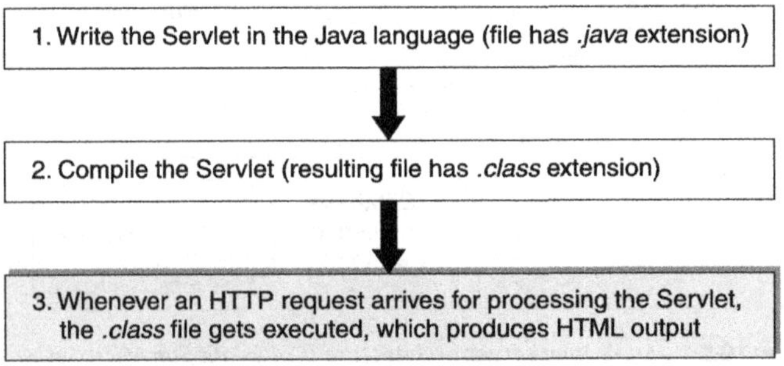

Fig. 10.4 *Servlet compilation process*

A Servlet runs inside a **Servlet container**. A Servlet container is the hosting and execution environment for Java Servlets. We can consider it to be a compiler plus run-time hosting environment for Servlets. An example of Servlet container is Tomcat. Such a Servlet container runs inside a Web server, such as Apache.

The flow of execution in the Servlet environment is as shown in Fig. 10.5.

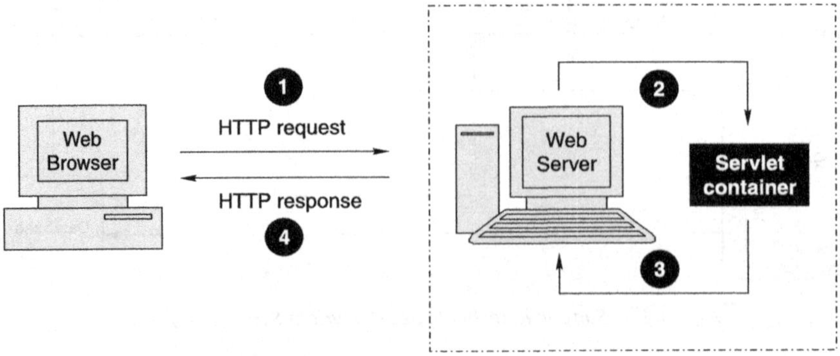

Fig. 10.5 *Servlet processing concept*

The step-by-step flow is explained below:

1. The browser sends an HTTP request to the Web server, as usual. This time, the request was for executing a Servlet.
2. The Web server notices that the browser has sent a request for the execution of a Servlet. Therefore, the Web server hands it over to the Servlet container, after it provides the appropriate execution environment to the Servlet container.
3. The Servlet container loads and executes the Servlet (i.e., the *.class* file of the Servlet) by interpreting its contents via the JVM. The result of the Servlet processing is usually some HTML output.
4. This HTML output is sent back to the Web browser via the Web server, as a part of the HTTP response.

Sometimes, the distinction between the Web server and the Servlet container is a bit blurred. People often mean the same thing when they either say Web server or Servlet container. As such, we shall also use these terms interchangeably now, since the distinction and context is clarified at this stage.

The next question then is what is a JSP? JSP stands for Java Server Pages (JSP). JSP offers a layer of abstraction on top of Servlets. A JSP is easier to code than a Servlet. Think about this in the same manner as that of the differences between a high-level programming language such as Java/C# and Assembly language. A programmer can write a program either in a high-level programming language, or in the Assembly language. Writing code in high-level language is easier and friendlier, but does not give us deep control the way Assembly language gives. In a similar manner, writing code in JSP is easier, but provides lesser finer control than what Servlets provide. In most situations, this does not matter.

Interestingly, when we write a JSP, the Servlet container (which now doubles up as a Servlet-JSP container) first translates the JSP into a temporary Servlet whenever a request arrives for the execution of this JSP. This happens automatically. The temporary Servlet is quickly compiled into a Java class file, and the class file is interpreted to perform the desired processing. This is depicted in Fig. 10.6.

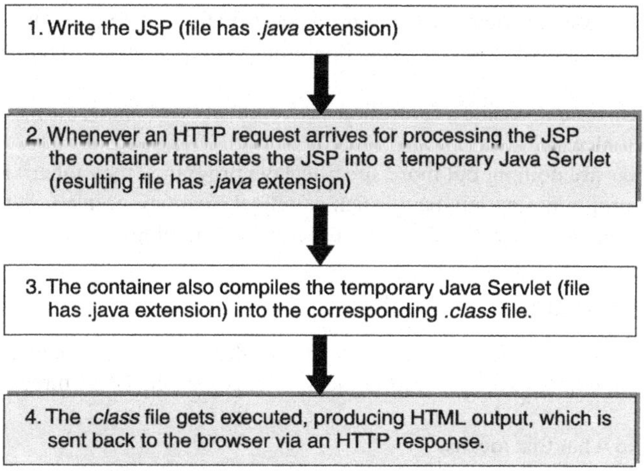

Fig. 10.6 *JSP compilation and execution process*

As we can see, there is some additional processing in the case of JSP, at the cost of ease of coding for the programmer.

10.1.2 Servlet Advantages

The advantages of Servlets can be summarized as follows:

1. Servlets are multi-threaded. In other words, whenever the Servlet container receives a request for the execution of a Servlet, the container loads the servlet in its memory, and assigns a thread of this Servlet for processing this client's requests. If more clients send requests for the same Servlet, the Servlet container does not create new Servlet instances (or processes). Instead, it creates new threads of the same Servlet instance, and allocates these thread instances to the different client requests. This makes the overall processing much faster, and also reduces the memory demands on the Servlet container/Web server. The idea is shown in Fig. 10.7.

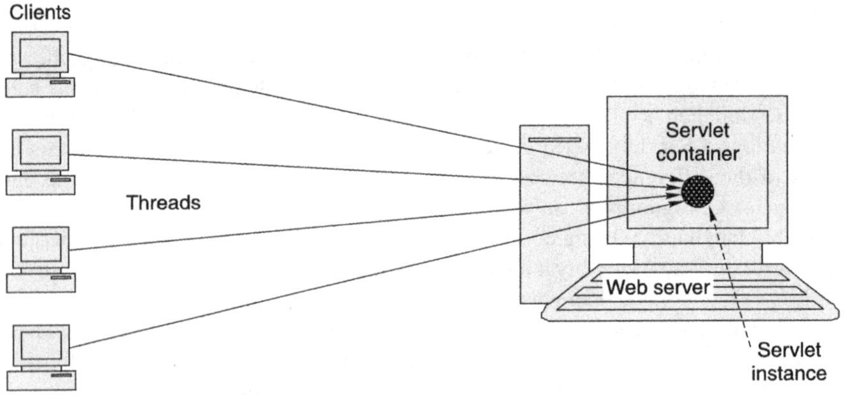

Fig. 10.7 *Servlet process and threads concept*

   As we can see, several clients are sending requests to the same Servlet in a concurrent fashion. The Servlet has created an instance (an operating system process) to handle them via multiple threads.

2. Since Servlets execute inside a controlled environment (container), they are usually quite stable and simple to deploy.
3. Since Servlets are nothing but more specific Java programs, they inherit all the good features of the Java programming language, such as object orientation, inherent security, networking capabilities, integration with other Java Enterprise technologies, etc.

10.1.3 Servlet Lifecycle

Java Servlets follow a certain path of execution during their life time. There are three phases that happen from the time the Servlet is deployed in the Servlet container. These three phases are illustrated in Fig. 10.8.

Let us understand what this means.

1. *Servlet initialization* happens only once. This is done by the Servlet container. Whenever a Servlet is deployed in a Servlet container, the container decides when to load a Servlet. The programmer cannot decide to or explicitly initialize a Servlet. As a result of initializing the Servlet, an instance of the Servlet is created in the memory. From this instance, as many Servlet threads as needed would get created to service the actual client requests.

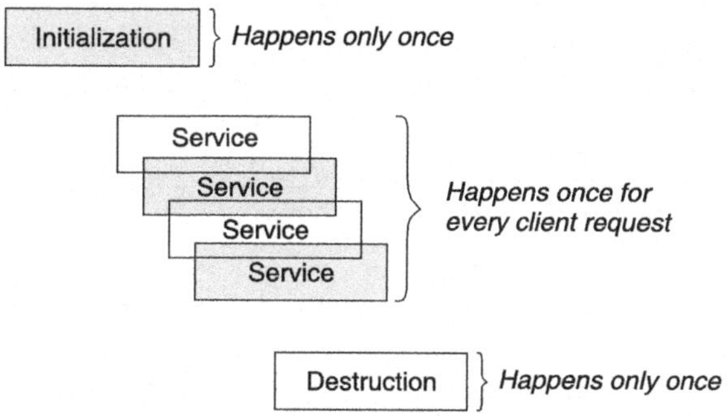

Fig. 10.8 *Phases in the Servlet lifecycle*

2. Once initialized, the Servlet can service client requests. This process is repeated for every client request. In other words, whenever an HTTP request arrives for a Servlet, the Servlet services it, as appropriate with the help of the particular thread of the Servlet instance.
3. Like initialization, the *Servlet destruction* also happens only once. Just as when to initialize a Servlet is decided and implemented by the Servlet container, so is the case of the Servlet destruction. The container chooses an appropriate moment to destroy the Servlet. Usually, when the container resources are getting exhausted because of memory shortage, etc., the container decides to destroy one of the Servlets. On what basis it decides it, and how it actually puts it into action is unpredictable. The programmer should not expect that the container would do the Servlet destruction at a particular point, or based on some condition.

How are these concepts implemented in reality? For this purpose, Sun has provided a Java class called HttpServlet. Whenever we want to write our own Servlet (e.g., an OrderServlet or a MakePaymentServlet), we need to write a Java class that extends this HttpServlet. Now, this base class titled HttpServlet has methods for initialization, servicing, and destruction of Servlets. This is shown in Fig. 10.9.

As we can see, our Servlet class extends the HttpServlet class provided by Sun. From this HttpServlet, our Servlet is able to inherit the *service ( )* Java method. Similarly, the HttpServlet itself, in turn, has been inherited from GenericServlet (see the diagram). The GenericServlet defines the other two methods, namely *init ( )* and *destroy ( )*. HttpServlet inherits these from GenericServlet, and passes them on to our OrderServlet.

Also, we can see that OrderServlet has some code written in all these three methods, namely *init ( )*, *service ( )*, and *destroy ( )*. Who calls these methods, and how would they execute? The simple answer is that we would not call these methods ourselves explicitly. Instead, the Servlet container would call them as and when it deems necessary. However, whenever it calls these methods, our code in the respective method would execute, producing three outputs in the server's log.

Just to make the picture complete, Fig. 10.10 shows the complete code for our OrderServlet.

The resulting output after deploying the Servlet is shown in Fig. 10.11.

Now, when we make any changes to the Servlet source code and recompile the Servlet, the Servlet container would destroy and reload the Servlet so as to be able to load the fresh instance of the Servlet in memory. The actual change to the Servlet could be quite artificial (e.g., just add one space somewhere). However, this causes the Servlet to be reloaded (destroyed + re-initialized). As such, the output would now look as shown in Fig. 10.12.

```
        Sun's standard definition of a Java Servlet
public abstract class HttpServlet extends GenericServlet {

   public void init ();
   public void service (HttpServletRequest request,
          HttpServletResponse response);
   void destroy ();
}
```

```
          Our own Servlet (e.g., orderServlet)
public class OrderServlet extends HttpServlet {

   public void init () {
      System.out.println ("In init …");
   }

   public void service (HttpServletRequest request,
              HttpServletResponse response) {
      System.out.println ("In service …");
   }

   void destroy () {
      System.out.println ("In destroy …");
   }
}
```

Fig. 10.9 *Servlet life cycle*

```
import java.io.*;
import javax.servlet.*;
import javax.servlet.http.*;

public class OrderServlet extends HttpServlet {


   public void init () {
          System.out.println ("In init () method");
   }


   public void service (HttpServletRequest request,
                        HttpServletResponse response) {
          System.out.println ("In doGet () method");
   }

   public void destroy () {
          System.out.println ("In destroy () method");
   }
}
```

Fig. 10.10 *Sample Servlet*

```
In init () method
In doGet () method
```

Fig. 10.11 *Output of Servlet*

```
In destroy () method
In init () method
In doGet () method
```

Fig. 10.12 *Output of Servlet*

This completes our overview of Servlet lifecycle.

At this stage, we would like to specify one technical detail. In general, although we can code of the *service ( )* method, the practice is discouraged. Instead, the recommended practice is to call one of "submethods" of the *service ( )* method, called as *doGet ( )* and *doPost ( )*. A detailed discussion of these is beyond the scope of the current text, but it should suffice to say that if we see *doGet ( )* or *doPost ( )* instead of *service ( )*, it should not surprise us.

10.1.4 Servlet Examples

We discuss some simple Servlet examples now, to get a better idea behind their working.

In the first example, we ask the user to enter her email ID on the screen. When the user provides this information and clicks on the *Submit* button on the screen, it causes an HTTP request to be sent to the server. There, we have a Servlet running, which captures this email ID and displays it back to the user. There is no other processing involved.

We start with the HTML page that requests the user to enter the email ID. This is shown in Fig. 10.13.

```
<html>
  <head>
    <title>Servlet Example Using a Form</title>
  </head>
  <body>
    <h1> Forms Example Using Servlets</h1>
    <form action = "EmailServlet">
    Enter your email ID: <input type = "text" name = "email">
    <input type ="submit">
    </form>
  </body>
</html>
```

Fig. 10.13 *HTML page to accept user's email ID*

As we can see, this HTML page would request the user to enter her email ID. When the user does so and clicks on the *submit* button, this will cause an HTTP request to be sent to the *EmailServlet* Servlet on the server. The result of viewing this HTML page in the browser is shown in Fig. 10.x.

Now let us look at the Servlet code that would execute in response to the HTTP request. It is shown in Fig. 10.14.

As we can see, our Servlet has the *doGet ( )* method, which is the rough equivalent of the *service ( )* method. This is the method that gets called when the HTTP request is submitted to the Servlet. We can also see that this method has two parameters: one is the *HttpServletRequest* object and the other is the *HttpServletResponse* object. As the names suggest, the former sends HTTP data from the browser

```
// import statements here ...

public class EmailServlet extends HttpServlet {

public void doGet (HttpServletRequest request, HttpServletResponse response)
                throws ServletException, IOException {

        String email;
        email = request.getParameter ("email");

        response.setContentType ("text/html");
        PrintWriter out = response.getWriter ();

        out.println ("<html>");
        out.println ("<head>");
        out.println ("<title>Servlet Example</title>");
        out.println ("</head>");

        out.println ("<body>");
        out.println ("<P> The email ID you have entered is: " + email +
"</P>");
        out.println ("</body>");
        out.println ("</html>");
        out.close ();
  }
}
```

Fig. 10.14 *EmailServlet*

to the server when a request is made; whereas the latter sends HTTP data from the server back to the browser when the server sends a response. This is illustrated in Fig. 10.15.

As we can see, the Servlet then uses the *HttpServletRequest* object (received as *request* here) to execute the following code:

```
String email;
email = request.getParameter ("email");
```

This code declares a Java string named *email*, and then reads the value of the on-screen field named *email* (received along with the HTTP request), which is assigned to the Java string. This is how communication between browser and server happens in servlets.

When the server is ready to send a response to the browser, the server uses the *HttpServletResponse* object as shown:

```
response.setContentType ("text/html");
PrintWriter out = response.getWriter ();

out.println ("<html>");
out.println ("<head>");
...
```

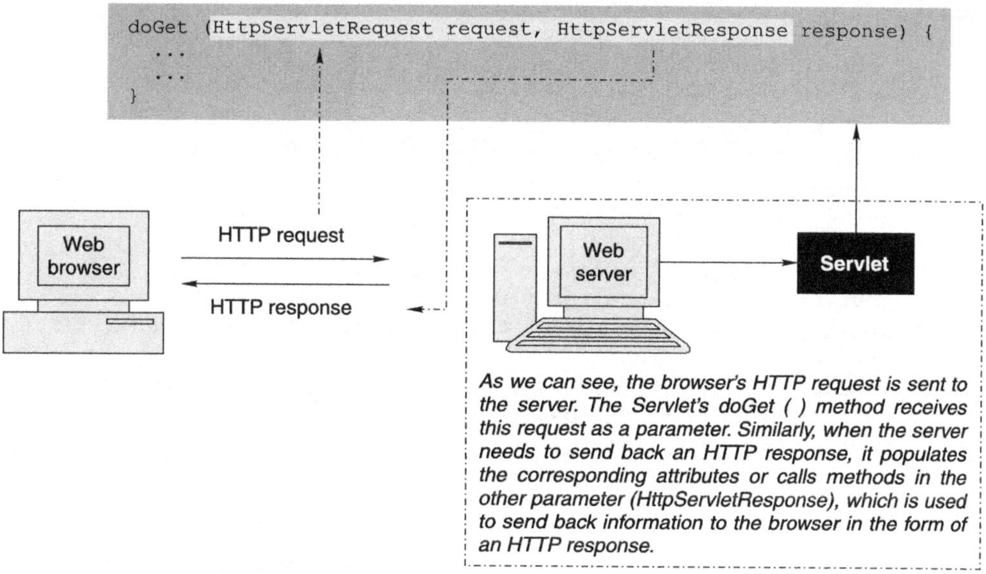

Fig. 10.15 *HTTP requests and responses with respect to Servlets*

In this code, we obtain an instance of the *PrintWriter* object, which is a special object used to help send HTTP responses to the browser. For this purpose, it calls the *println ( )* method with the HTML content that we want to send to the browser.

As we can see, this is actually quite clumsy way of writing code. We are writing HTML statements inside a Java method. This is not only a bit strange, but is also quite difficult to write at first. As such, people sometimes find it a bit unnerving to write Servlets to start with. However, one gets used to this style of coding easily.

Now let us take another example. Here, we write code for converting US Dollars into Indian Rupees, considering a rate of USD 1 = INR 40. The Servlet code is shown in Fig. 10.16.

```
import java.io.*;
import java.net.*;
import javax.servlet.*;
import javax.servlet.http.*;

public class CurrencyConvertor extends HttpServlet {

   protected void doGet (HttpServletRequest request,
         HttpServletResponse response) throws ServletException,
IOException {

      response.setContentType («text/html»);
```

(Contd.)

Fig. 10.16 *Contd...*

```
        PrintWriter out = response.getWriter ();

        out.println («<html>»);
        out.println («<head>»);
        out.println («<title>Dollars to Rupees Conversion Chart</title>»);
        out.println («</head>»);
        out.println («<body>»);
        out.println («<center>»);
        out.println («<h1>Currency Conversion Chart</h1>»);
        out.println («<table border='1' cellpadding='3' cellspacing='0'>»);
        out.println («<tr>»);
        out.println («<th>Dollars</th>»);
        out.println («<th>Rupees</th>»);
        out.println («</tr»);

        for (int dollars = 1; dollars <= 50; dollars++) {
            int rupees = dollars * 40;
            out.println («<tr>» + «<td align='right'>» + dollars + «</td>»
                    + «<td align='right'>» + rupees + «</td>» + «</tr>»);
        }

        out.println («</table>»);
        out.println («</center>»);
        out.println («</body>»);
        out.println («</html>»);

        out.close ();
    }
}
```

Fig. 10.16 *Servlet for doing currency conversions*

Let us understand what the code is doing. As before, the Servlet has a *doGet ( )* method, which will get invoked when the Servlet executes. Inside this method, we have a series of *println ( )* method calls to send various HTML tags to the browser for display. Then it has a simple *for* loop, which displays the values of dollars from 1 to 50, and the equivalent values in rupees.

Note that the Servlet displays the dollar-rupee conversion in an HTML table. For this purpose the appropriate HTML table related tags are included in the Servlet.

The Servlet produces output as shown in Fig. 10.17.

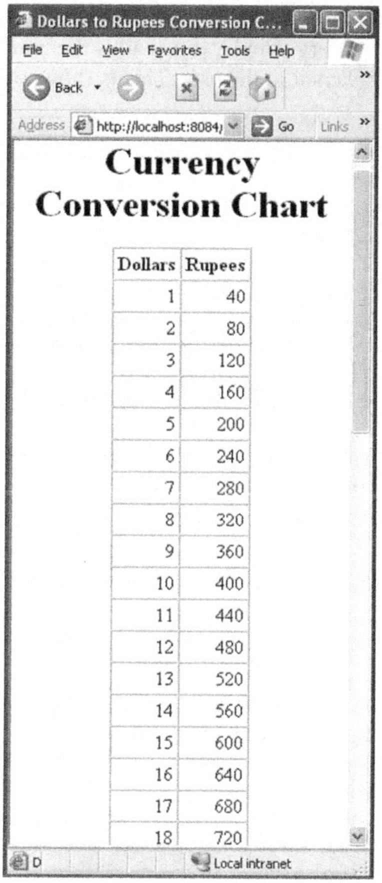

Fig. 10.17 *Output of the Servlet*

CREATING AND TESTING SERVLETS.. 10.2

There are several ways to create and test Servlets. We shall take two of the possible examples.

1. A lot of Interactive Development Environment (IDE) software programs such as NetBeans, Oracle JDeveloper, Eclipse, etc., are now available, which allow for the creation and testing of Servlets with ease. This is the simpler of the two approaches.
2. We can also download and use a Web server and use a simple editor such as Notepad++.

SERVLET EXAMPLES.. 10.3

We discuss some simple Servlet examples now, to get a better idea behind their working.

Example 1: Display sum of two numbers

The first Servlet is deliberately kept very simple. It just adds the numbers stored inside two variables, stores the sum in the third, and displays it to the user. This is shown in Fig. 10.18.

```
package example;

import java.io.IOException;
import java.io.PrintWriter;
import javax.servlet.ServletException;
import javax.servlet.http.HttpServlet;
import javax.servlet.http.HttpServletRequest;
import javax.servlet.http.HttpServletResponse;

public class SumServlet extends HttpServlet {

    public void doGet(HttpServletRequest request, HttpServletResponse
response) throws ServletException, IOException {

        int n1, n2, n3;

        n1 = 10;
        n2 = 20;
        n3 = n1 + n2;

        response.setContentType("text/html");
        PrintWriter out = response.getWriter();

        out.println("<html>");
        out.println("<head>");
        out.println("<title>Sum of Two Numbers</title>");
        out.println("</head>");

        out.println("<body>");
        out.println("Sum of " + n1 + " and " + n2 + " is " + n3);
        out.println("</body>");
        out.println("</html>");
        out.close();
    }
}
```

Fig. 10.18 *Servlet to add two numbers*

As we can see, our Servlet has the *doGet ( )* method, which is the rough equivalent of the *service ( )* method. This is the method that gets called when the HTTP request is submitted to the Servlet. We can also see that this method has two parameters: one is the *HttpServletRequest* object and the other is the *HttpServletResponse* object. As the names suggest, the former sends HTTP data from the browser to the server when a request is made; whereas the latter sends HTTP data from the server back to the browser when the server sends a response. This is illustrated in Fig. 10.19.

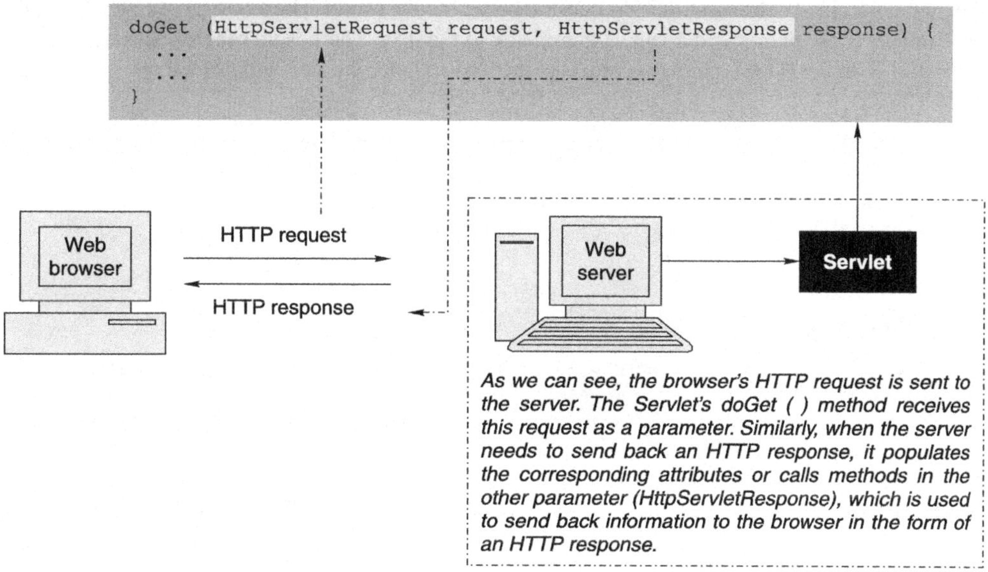

Fig. 10.19 *HTTP requests and responses with respect to Servlets*

When the Servlet is called, the *doGet ()* method would get called. It would initialize two integer variables n1 and n2 to values 10 and 20 respectively. It would then add them together to store the results in n3. It would then display the result in the HTML format.

When the server is ready to send a response to the browser, the server uses the *HttpServletResponse* object as shown:

```
response.setContentType ("text/html");
PrintWriter out = response.getWriter ();

out.println ("<html>");
out.println ("<head>");
...
```

In this code, we obtain an instance of the *PrintWriter* object, which is a special object used to help send HTTP responses to the browser. For this purpose, it calls the *println ( )* method with the HTML content that we want to send to the browser.

As we can see, this is actually quite clumsy way of writing code. We are writing HTML statements inside a Java method. This is not only a bit strange, but is also quite difficult to write at first. As such, people sometimes find it a bit unnerving to write servlets to start with. However, one gets used to this style of coding easily.

The resulting output is shown in Fig. 10.20.

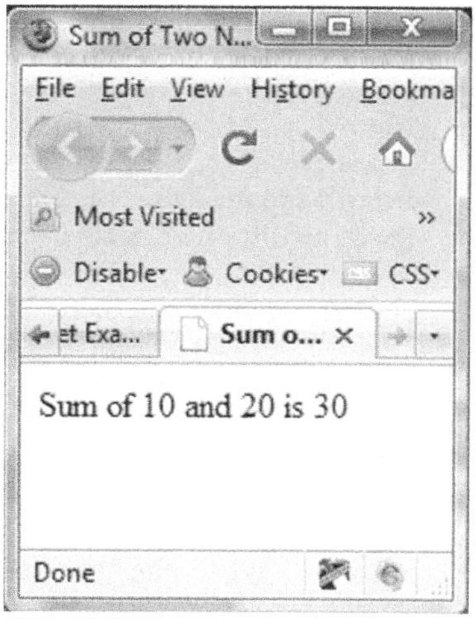

Fig. 10.20 *Result of Servlet to add two numbers*

Example 2: Accept and display back user's name

Now we ask the user to enter her first and last name on the screen. When the user provides this information and clicks on the *Submit* button on the screen, it causes an HTTP request to be sent to the server. There, we have a Servlet running, which captures these names and displays them back to the user. There is no other processing involved.

We start with the HTML page that requests the user to enter the first and last names. This is shown in Fig. 10.21.

```
<html>
  <head>
    <title>Servlet Example Using a Form</title>
  </head>
  <body>
    <h1>User Name Capturing</h1>
    <form action = "UserNameServlet">
    Enter your first name: <input type = "text" name = "firstName">
        <br />
    Enter your last name: <input type = "text" name = "lastName">
        <br />
    <input type ="submit">
    </form>
  </body>
</html>
```

Fig. 10.21 *HTML page to accept user's email ID*

The HTML page has a form. It accepts the user's first and last name. When the user provides this information, the form is submitted to a Servlet named *UserNameServlet*.

Now let us look at the Servlet code that would execute in response to the HTTP request. It is shown in Fig. 10.22.

```
package example;

import java.io.IOException;
import java.io.PrintWriter;
import javax.servlet.ServletException;
import javax.servlet.http.HttpServlet;
import javax.servlet.http.HttpServletRequest;
import javax.servlet.http.HttpServletResponse;

public class UserNameServlet extends HttpServlet {

     public void doGet(HttpServletRequest request, HttpServletResponse
response) throws ServletException, IOException {

        String myFirstName, myLastName;
        myFirstName = request.getParameter("firstName");
        myLastName = request.getParameter("lastName");
```

(Contd.)

Fig. 10.22 *Contd...*

```
            response.setContentType("text/html");
            PrintWriter out = response.getWriter();

            out.println("<html>");
            out.println("<head>");
            out.println("<title>servlet Example</title>");
            out.println("</head>");

            out.println("<body>");
            out.println("<p> Your first name is: " + myFirstName + "</p>");
            out.println("<p> Your last name is: " + myLastName + "</p>");
            out.println("</body>");
            out.println("</html>");
            out.close();
        }
    }
```

Fig. 10.22 *UserNameServlet*

As we can see, the servlet then uses the *HttpServletRequest* object (received as *request* here) to execute the following code:

```
String myFirstName, myLastName;
myFirstName = request.getParameter("firstName");
myLastName = request.getParameter("lastName");
```

This code declares Java strings named *myFirstName* and *myLastName*, and then reads the value of the on-screen fields named *firstName* and *lastName* (received along with the HTTP request), which are assigned to the Java strings. This is how communication between browser and server happens in Servlets.

Example 3: Miles to kilometers conversion

In this example, we would demonstrate the usage of a simple *for* Java loop. The loop runs through a counter 15 times, and in each case, displays the equivalent of the mile value in kilometers. The results are formatted and tabulated appropriately. The Servlet code is shown in Fig. 10.23.

```
package example;

import java.io.*;
import java.text.DecimalFormat;
import java.text.NumberFormat;
import javax.servlet.*;
import javax.servlet.http.*;

public class MileToKMConversion extends HttpServlet {
```

(Contd.)

Fig. 10.23 *Contd...*

```
    protected void doGet(HttpServletRequest request,
              HttpServletResponse response) throws ServletException,
  IOException {

        response.setContentType(«text/html»);
        PrintWriter out = response.getWriter();

        out.println(«<html>»);
        out.println(«<head>»);
      out.println(«<title>Kilometers to Miles Conversion Chart</title>»);
        out.println(«</head>»);
        out.println(«<body>»);
        out.println(«<center>»);
        out.println(«<h1>Distance Conversion Chart</h1>»);
      out.println(«<table border='1' cellpadding='3' cellspacing='0'>»);
        out.println(«<tr>»);
        out.println(«<th>Miles</th>»);
        out.println(«<th>KM</th>»);
        out.println(«</tr»);

        for (int miles = 1; miles <= 15; miles++) {
            double km = miles * 1.609344;
            NumberFormat fmt = new DecimalFormat(«###.000»);

            String formattedKm = fmt.format(km);
            out.println("<tr>" + "<td align='right'>" + miles + "</td>"
  + "<td align='right'>" + formattedKm + "</td>" + "</tr>");
        }

        out.println("</table>");
        out.println("</center>");
        out.println("</body>");
        out.println("</html>");

        out.close();
    }
  }
```

Fig. 10.23 *Servlet for doing distance conversion*

Let us understand what the code is doing. As before, the servlet has a *doGet ( )* method, which will get invoked when the Servlet executes. Inside this method, we have a series of *println ( )* method calls to send various HTML tags to the browser for display. Then it has a simple *for* loop, which displays the values of miles from 1 to 15 and the corresponding values in kilometers.

Note that the Servlet displays the mile-kilometer conversion in an HTML table. For this purpose, the appropriate HTML table related tags are included in the servlet.

The Servlet produces output as shown in Fig. 10.24.

Distance Conversion Chart

Miles	KM
1	1.609
2	3.219
3	4.828
4	6.437
5	8.047
6	9.656
7	11.265
8	12.875
9	14.484
10	16.093
11	17.703
12	19.312
13	20.921
14	22.531
15	24.140

Fig. 10.24 *Output of the Servlet*

Example 4: Factorial of a number

In this example, we ask the user to enter a number and compute its factorial and show it to the user. There is an HTML form that accepts the number from the user and calls a Servlet. The servlet does the job of computing and displaying the factorial. Figure 10.25 shows the HTML page and Fig. 10.26 shows the corresponding Servlet.

```
<html>
    <head>
        <title>Factorial</title>
    </head>
    <body>
        <h1>Factorial Computation</h1>
        <form action = "FactorialServlet">
            Enter number for factorial computation:
            <input type = "text" name = "userInput">
            <input type ="submit" value ="Compute Factorial">
        </form>
    </body>
</html>
```

Fig. 10.25 *HTML page to accept a number from the user for factorial computation*

```
package example;

import java.io.IOException;
import java.io.PrintWriter;
import javax.servlet.ServletException;
import javax.servlet.http.HttpServlet;
import javax.servlet.http.HttpServletRequest;
import javax.servlet.http.HttpServletResponse;

public class FactorialServlet extends HttpServlet {

    public void doGet(HttpServletRequest request, HttpServletResponse
response) throws ServletException, IOException {

        String stringUserInput;
        int userInput, factorial = 1, storeUserInput;

        stringUserInput = request.getParameter ("userInput");
        userInput = Integer.parseInt (stringUserInput);
        storeUserInput = userInput;

        while (userInput > 1) {
            factorial *= userInput;
            userInput--;
        }
        response.setContentType("text/html");
        PrintWriter out = response.getWriter();

        out.println("<html>");
        out.println("<head>");
        out.println("<title>Factorial Calculation</title>");
        out.println("</head>");

        out.println("<body>");
        out.println("Factorial of" + storeUserInput + "is" + factorial);
        out.println("</body>");
        out.println("</html>");
        out.close();
    }
}
```

Fig. 10.26 *Factorial Servlet*

The result of running the example is shown in Fig. 10.27.

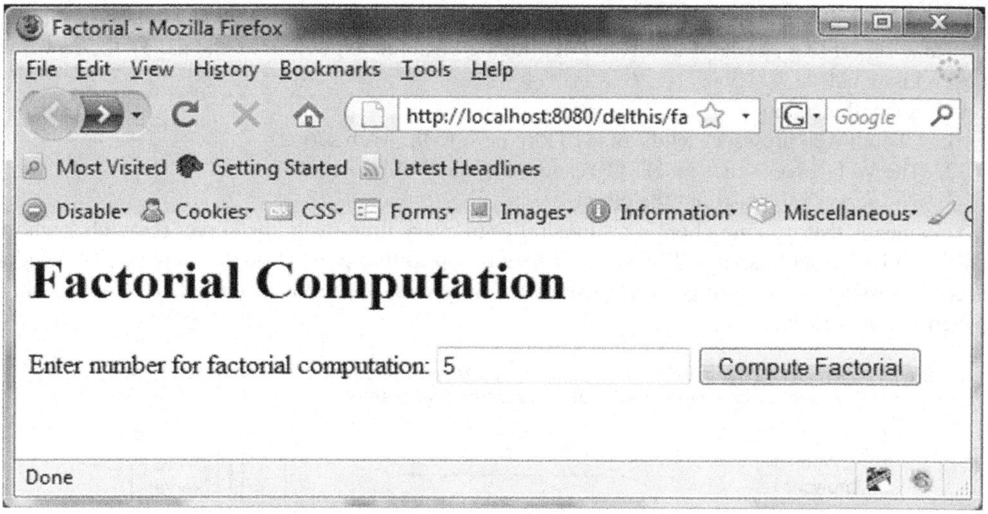

Fig. 10.27 *HTML page for accepting number from the user*

Fig. 10.28 *Result of factorial Servlet*

SESSION MANAGEMENT 10.4

HTTP is a stateless protocol. It means that it is a *forgetful* protocol. It forgets what it had done in the previous step. The straightforward way to describe this situation is:

1. Client (Web browser) sends an HTTP request to the Web server.
2. The Web server sends an HTTP response to the Web browser.
3. The server forgets about the client.

As we can see, this can be quite unnerving. For example, suppose our browser displays a login page, where we need to enter the user id and password and submit it to the server. Once we enter these details and send the HTTP request to the server, the server will check whether the user id and password are correct. Accordingly, it would generate the next HTML page and send to our browser. At this stage, it has already forgotten about us! This means that whenever our browser sends the next HTTP request to the same server (e.g., perhaps as a result of clicking on some hyper link on the page), the server will not even know us!

Let us say that again:

1. Client (Web browser) sends an HTTP request to the Web server.
2. The Web server sends an HTTP response to the Web browser.
3. The server forgets about the client.

This means that it is the client's responsibility to every time make the server remember who the client is, and what had happened in the conversation up to that point. For this purpose, we need the concept of **session state management** (also called only **session management**). The idea for doing is depicted in Fig. 10.29.

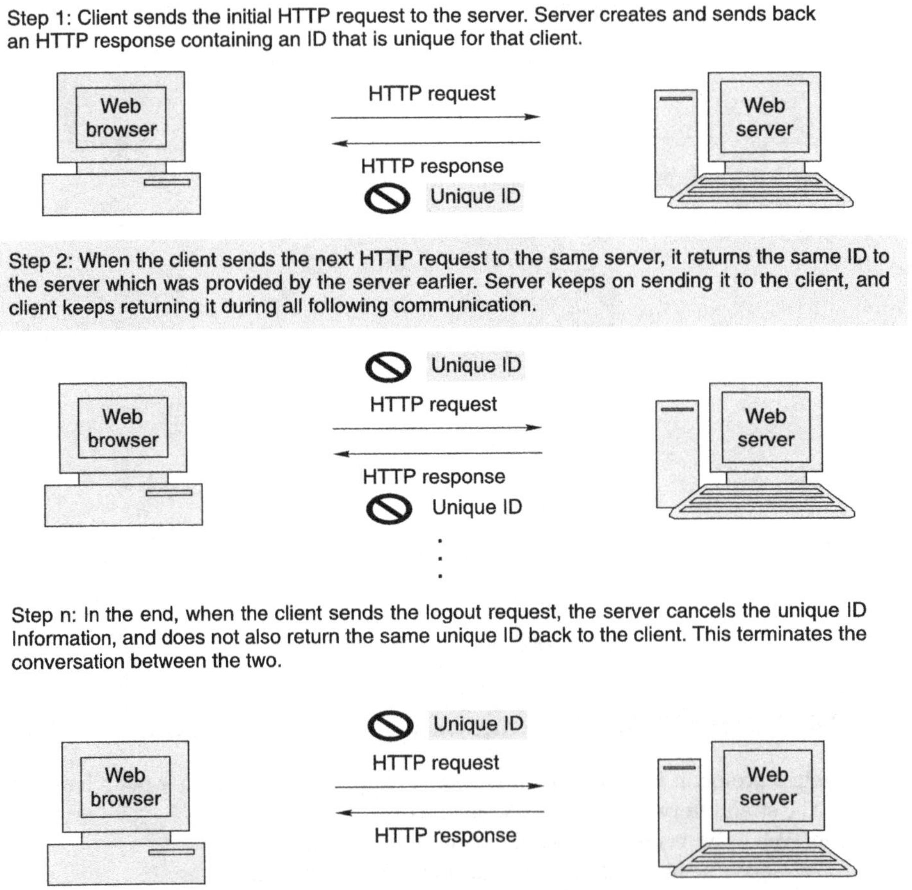

Fig. 10.29 *Session management concept*

The unique ID that keeps floating between the client and the server is called as **session ID**. It travels between the client and the server via a small piece of text called as **cookie**. Server creates a session

ID, puts it inside the cookie, and sends it to the client. Whenever the client sends the next request, it is supposed to return the same cookie back to the server. Based on the session ID contained in the cookie, the server identifies the client uniquely. This means that if there are 100 concurrent users (i.e., clients) accessing an application, the Web server would create 100 unique session IDs. It would map one user (i.e., one client) to one session ID. Hence, it would work as follows:

1. User U-1 accesses a Servlet. The Servlet creates session ID S-1 and maps user U-1 with S-1. It returns the session ID S-1 to U-1 inside a cookie. When user U-1 sends another request to the Servlet, it returns the same cookie back to the servlet. The Servlet opens this cookie, and gets session ID S-1. Therefore, it knows that this user is U-1, along with any other information that the Servlet would have created and mapped against this session ID S-1.
2. Now, a different user U-2 accesses the same Servlet. The servlet creates session ID S-2 and maps user U-2 with S-2. It returns the session ID S-2 to U-2 inside a different cookie. When user U-2 sends another request to the Servlet, it returns the same cookie back to the servlet. The Servlet opens this cookie, and gets session ID S-2. Therefore, it knows that this user is U-2, along with any other information that the Servlet would have created and mapped against this session ID S-2.
3. The same thing will happen for all the users accessing the Servlet. For every unique user, the Servlet would create a separate cookie.

The idea is shown in Fig. 10.30.

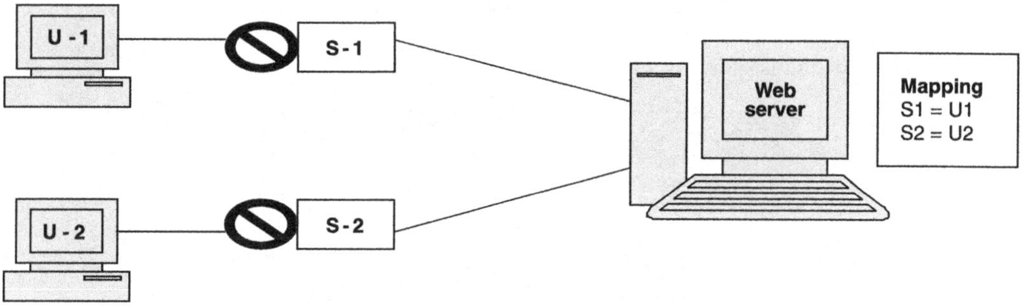

Fig. 10.30 *Users and sessions*

To create a session object in a Servlet, we need to write the following code:

```
HttpSession session = request.getSession();
```

Interestingly, the above code returns the session object arrived from the client if one exists. If not, it creates a new session for the user.

To retrieve the session ID from the session object, we can use this line:

```
String id = session.getId();
```

This extracts the session ID (a string containing hexadecimal characters when viewed, and a large number internally) and stores it in a variable called id.

Figure 10.31 shows a Servlet that creates a session if none exists, and then displays the value of the session ID.

```
package example;

import java.io.*;
import javax.servlet.*;
import javax.servlet.http.*;

public class SessionIDServlet extends HttpServlet {

   protected void doGet(HttpServletRequest request, HttpServletResponse
response)
            throws ServletException, IOException {
         response.setContentType("text/html");
         PrintWriter out = response.getWriter();
         HttpSession session = request.getSession();
         String id = session.getId();
         out.println("Session Id is : " + id);
    }
}
```

Fig. 10.31 *Session-related code in a Servlet*

The resulting output is shown in Fig. 10.32.

Fig. 10.32 *Output of the session example*

We should note that the session ID is dynamically generated, and has an unpredictable value. It would keep changing as we keep running the example after some time intervals.

It should be clear by now that session management is quite necessary in Web applications to ensure that the server does not *forget* the client after sending a response, but can communicate with the client on an ongoing basis the way humans converse with each other.

We can figure out how many times a user has accessed a page during a session with the help of the code shown in Fig. 10.33.

```
package example;

import java.io.*;
import javax.servlet.*;
import javax.servlet.http.*;

public class HitCounterServlet extends HttpServlet {

     public void doGet(HttpServletRequest request, HttpServletResponse
response)
            throws ServletException, IOException {
        HttpSession session = request.getSession(true);
        response.setContentType("text/html");
        PrintWriter out = response.getWriter();
        Integer count = new Integer(0);
        String head;
        if (session.isNew()) {
            head = "This session is a newly created session ...";
        } else {
            head = "You are working with an old session ...";
            Integer oldcount = (Integer) session.getAttribute("count");
            if (oldcount != null) {
                count = new Integer(oldcount.intValue() + 1);
            }
        }
        session.setAttribute("count", count);
            out.println("<html> <body bgcolor=\"#fdf5e6\">\n" + "<h2
align=\"center\">" + head + "</h2>\n" + "<table border=1 align=center>\n"
+ "<tr bgcolor=\"#ffad00\">\n" + "   <th>Information Type<th>Session
Count\n" + "<tr>\n" + " <td>Session access count: \n" +  "<td>" + count
+ "\n" +  "</table>\n" + "</body></html>");
    }
}
```

Fig. 10.33 *Session counter servlet code*

Figures 10.34 to 10.36 show us the outcome of this Servlet when we access it three times in quick succession. The counter would keep getting incrementing every time we refresh the output.

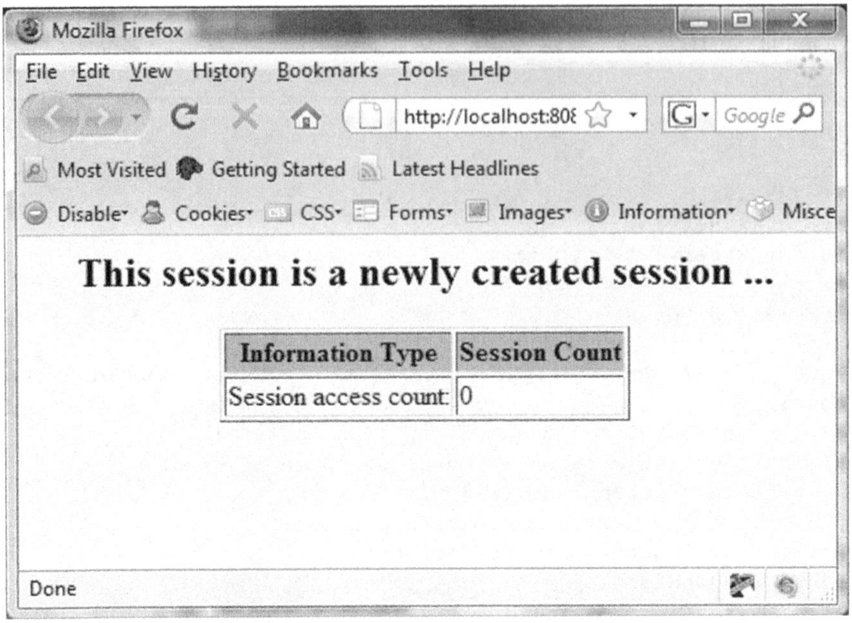

Fig. 10.34 *Initial output after the first access*

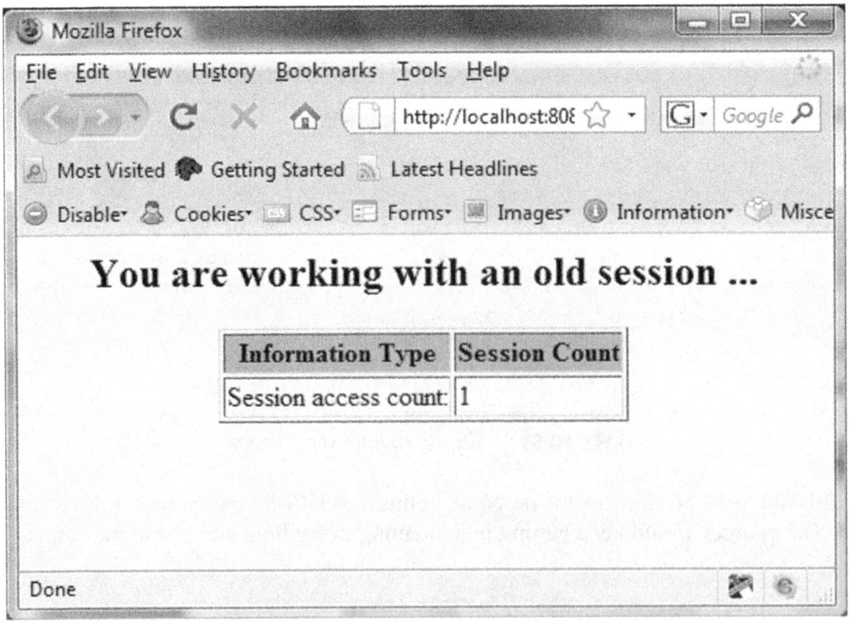

Fig. 10.35 *Output after the second access*

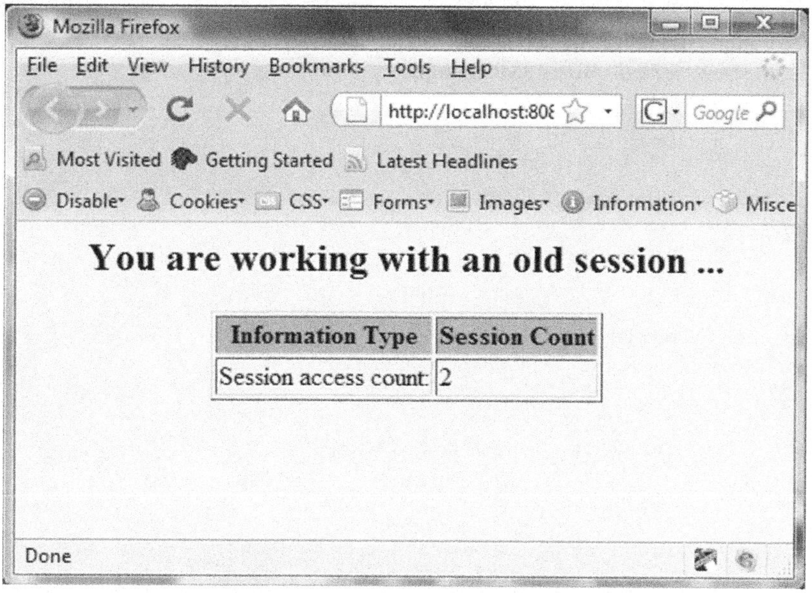

Fig. 10.36 *Output after the third access*

INTRODUCTION TO JSP 10.5

JSP is the *next version* of Servlets. Servlets are pretty complex to write in some situations, especially if the aim is to send HTML content to the user (instead of doing some business processing on the server). In such cases, we can look at Java Server Pages (JSP). JSPs are much easier to write than Servlets. However, we should quickly examine how the JSP technology has evolved.

When Java Servlets technology was developed by Sun, around the same time, Microsoft came up with Active Server Pages (ASP). ASP was a much simpler technology to use than Servlets. This was because ASP pages could be created in simple scripting languages, such as JavaScript and VBScript. However, to code Servlets, one needed to know Java, and moreover the syntax of Servlets was cumbersome (as we have already experienced here). To overcome the drawbacks of Servlets, instead of revamping the Servlets technology, Sun decided to come up with JSP, which was a layer on top of Servlets. We have already discussed how this works.

From a programmer's point of view, the advantages of using JSPs instead of Servlets in certain cases are immense. Simply to send the *<html>* tag to the browser, these two technologies take a completely different path, as illustrated in Fig. 10.37.

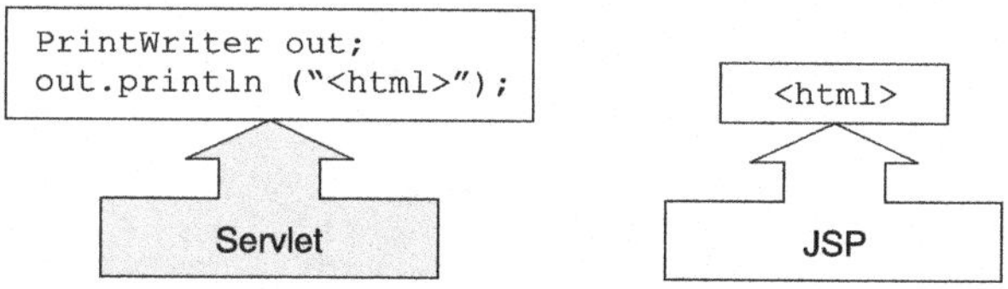

Fig. 10.37 *Servlet versus JSP*

The life cycle of a JSP does not greatly differ from that of a Servlet, since internally a JSP is anyway a Servlet, once compiled! Hence, we would not talk about it separately here.

Figure 10.38 shows a *Hello World* JSP example.

```
<html>
   <head>
      <title>Hello World</title>
   </head>

   <body>
      <h2>
         Hello World
      </h2>

      <%
         out.print ("<p><b>Hello World!</b>");
      %>

   </body>
</html>
```

Fig. 10.38 *Hello World JSP*

Before we proceed any further, we would like to have a look at the corresponding Servlet code to reemphasize the point about ease of coding JSPs versus Servlets. This is shown in Fig. 10.39.

```
import java.io.*;
import java.net.*;
import javax.servlet.*;
import javax.servlet.http.*;

public class HelloWorld extends HttpServlet {

   protected void doGet (HttpServletRequest request, HttpServletResponse
response)
      throws ServletException, IOException {

      response.setContentType ("text/html");
      PrintWriter out = response.getWriter ();

      out.println ("<html>");
      out.println ("<head>");
      out.println ("<title>Hello World</title>");
      out.println ("</head>");
      out.println ("<body>");
      out.println ("<h2>Hello World</h2>");
      out.println ("<p><b>Hello World</b>");
```

(Contd.)

Fig. 10.39 *Contd...*

```
        out.println ("</body>");
        out.println ("</html>");

        out.close ();
    }

}
```

Fig. 10.39 *Hello World Servlet*

As we can see, coding a JSP seems to be much simpler than coding the corresponding Servlet. In the JSP, we do not have to write complex Java code and worse yet, HTML inside that Java code. We can straightaway write HTML tags, and wherever needed, write Java code in between HTML tags. Hence, we can roughly say that Servlets are HTML inside Java, whereas JSPs are Java inside HTML. This is depicted in Fig. 10.40.

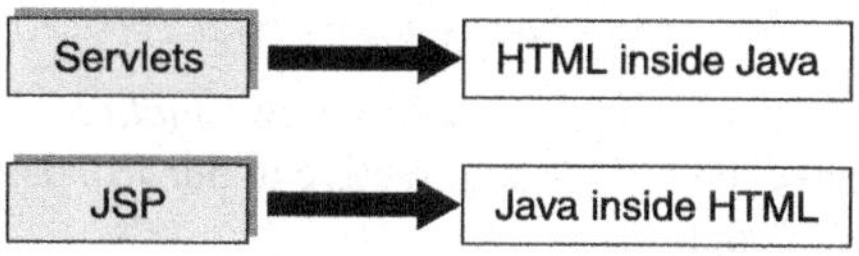

Fig. 10.40 *Servlets and JSP: Conceptual difference*

Having discussed this, let us now discuss the JSP way of coding now. We can see that our JSP page is nothing more than a simple HTML page, except for one part of the code:

```
<%
   out.print ("<p><b>Hello World!</b>");
%>
```

As we can see, there is an *out.print ( )* statement here, which is clearly not HTML syntax. It is a Java statement. This means that we can write Java in JSP. However, the Java part of a JSP page needs to be embedded inside the tag pair <% and %>. As we know, whenever the Servlet container receives a request for the execution of the JSP page, it first translates it into a Servlet. Hence, we can imagine that our JSP code would actually look like the Servlet code shown in the earlier diagram. Of course, there would not be an exact match between the Servlet code written by hand and a JSP translated into Servlet code by the Servlet container. However, from a conceptual point of view, the two code blocks would indeed look similar.

In summary, we can say that if producing HTML is the aim, JSP is a better choice. On the other hand, if performing business processing is more important, we should go for Servlets.

10.5.1 Elements of a JSP Page

A JSP page is composed of directives, comments, scripting elements, actions, and templates. This is shown in Fig. 10.41.

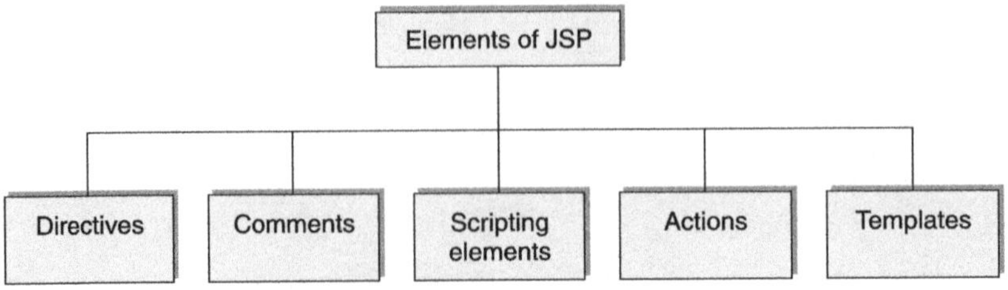

Fig. 9.22 *JSP elements*

Let us discuss these JSP elements now.

1. **Directives** Directives are instructions to the JSP container. These instructions tell the container that some action needs to be taken. For example, if we want to import some standard/non-standard Java classes or packages into our JSP, we can use a directive for that purpose. Directives are contained inside special delimiters, namely <%@ and %>. The general syntax for directives is:

```
<%@ Directive-name Attribute-Value pairs %>
```

   There are three main directives in JSP, namely *page*, *include*, and *taglib*.
   For example, we can have the following directive in our JSP page to explicitly say that our JSP is relying on some Java code:

```
<%@ page language = "Java" %>
```

   Here, *page* is the name of the directive, *language* is the name of the attribute, and *Java* is its value.
   Here is another directive example, this time to import a package:

```
<%@ page import = "java.text.*" %>
```

   As we can see, this time the *page* directive has an *import* attribute to import a Java package.

2. **Comments** Comments in JSP are of two types, as follows:
   (a) *HTML comments* These comments follow the standard HTML syntax, and the contents of these comments are visible to the end user in the Web browser, if the user attempts to view the source code of the HTML page. Thus, the syntax of HTML comments is as follows:

```
<%-- This is a an HTML style comment --%>
```

   (b) *JSP comments* These comments are removed by the JSP container before the HTML content is sent to the browser. The syntax of JSP comments is as follows:

```
<!-- This is a included inside the generated HTML -->
```

   As we can see, it is ok to have the end user view the contents of our comments; we should code them as HTML comments. Else, we should code them as JSP comments.

3. **Scripting elements** The scripting elements are the areas of the JSP page where the main Java code resides. We know that Java code is what makes JSPs dynamic. The Java code adds dynamism to an otherwise static HTML page. The JSP container interprets and executes this Java code, and mixes the results with the HTML parts of the JSP page. The final resulting output is sent to the browser. Scripting elements can be further sub-divided into three categories, as shown in Fig. 10.42.

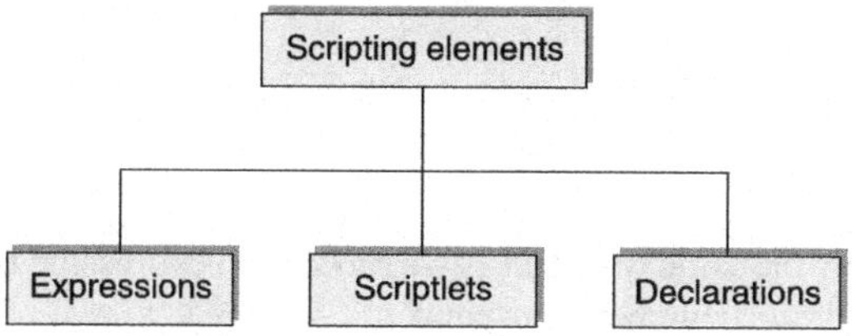

Fig. 10.42 *JSP scripting elements*

Let us understand these areas of JSP scripting elements now.

(*a*) *Expressions* Expressions are simple means of accessing the values of Java variables or other expressions that directly yield a value. The results of an expression can be merged with the HTML page that gets generated. The syntax of expressions is as follows:

```
<%= Expression %>
Some examples of using expression are:
The current time is: <%= new java.util.Date ( ) %>
Square root of 2 is <%= Math.sqrt (2) %>
The item you are looking for is <%= items [i] %>
Sum of a, b, and c is <%= a + b + c %>
```

(*b*) *Scriptlets* Scriptlets are one or more Java statements in a JSP page. The syntax of scriptlets is as follows:

```
<% Scriptlet code; %>
We have already seen some examples of scriptlet. Let us have
another one:
<table border = 2>
<%
    for (int i = 0; i < n; i++)   {
%>
        <tr>
        <td>Number</td>
        <td><%= i+1 %></td>
        </tr>
<%
    }
%>
</table>
```

As we can see, there is some HTML code for creating a table. Then we have a scriptlet (starting with <% and ending with %>). This is followed by some more HTML code, followed by one more scriptlet. Thus, we can see that in JSP, we can combine HTML code and JSP code the way we want.

Interestingly, our code snippet also has an expression:

```
<td><%= i+1 %></td>
```

This proves that we can inter-mix HTML, scriptlets, and expressions. Also, we need to observe that scriptlets can be alternatives to expressions, if we want. Thus, the above statement could be written as a scriptlet, instead of as an expression as shown:

```
<td>
   <%
         out.print (i + 1);
   %>
</td>
```

It would work in exactly the same way. But as we can see, an expression is a much better short-hand version, provided we are comfortable with its syntax.

Figure 10.43 shows an example that shows HTML code, directives, comments, scriptlets, and expressions.

```
<%@ page import="java.text.*" session = "false" %>

<html>
   <head>
      <title>Temperature conversion</title>
   </head>

   <body>
      <table border = "0" cellpadding = "3">
         <tr>
            <th>Fahrenheit</th>
            <th>Celsius</th>
         </tr>

            <%
            numberformat fmt = new decimalformat ("###.000");

            for (int f = 32; f <= 212; f += 20)
            {
                        double c = ((f - 32) * 5) / 9.0;
                        string cs = fmt.format (c);
            %>

            <tr>
                        <td align = "right"> <%= f %>    </td>
                        <td align = "right"> <%= cs %>   </td>
            </tr>

            <%
            }
            %>

      </table>
   </body>
</html>
```

Fig. 10.43 *Temperature conversion JSP*

(c) *Declarations* Declarations should be used, as the name suggests, when we need to make any declarations in the JSP page. The syntax of making declarations is as follows:

```
<%! Declarations; %>
```

Here are some declaration examples:

```
<%! int i = 0; %>
<%! int a, b; double c; %>
<%! Circle a = new Circle (2.0); %>
```

Figure 10.44 shows an example of using declarations in JSP.

```
<html>
   <body>
      <%! int counter = 0; %>
      The page count is now: <%= ++counter %>
   </body>
</html>
```

Fig. 10.44 *JSP declarations*

As we can see, we have declared a variable here by using the declaration syntax. Of course, we could have also declared this variable inside a scriptlet (as shown in Fig. 10.45), instead of specifying a declaration block. There are slight differences if we do that, and their discussion is out of scope of the current text. However, we are just explaining all the possibilities that exist.

```
<html>
   <body>
      <% int counter = 0; %>
      The page count is now: <%= ++counter %>
   </body>
</html>
```

Fig. 10.45 *Variable declaration inside a scriptlet*

4. **Actions** Actions are used in the context of some new areas in JSP, which we shall discuss later.
5. **Templates** Templates are also used in the context of some new areas in JSP, which we shall discuss later.

10.5.2 JavaBeans

Many times, it is useful to use a **JavaBean** in JSP. People often confuse between a JavaBean and an **Enterprise JavaBean (EJB)**. However, there is no resemblance between the two, and they must not be equated at all.

A JavaBean is a self-contained Java class, which provides *set* and *get* methods for accessing and updating its attributes from other classes. The *set* and *get* methods in a JavaBean are respectively called as *setters* and *getters*. Figure 10.46 shows an example of a JavaBean.

```
public class User {
   private String firstName;
   private String lastName;
   private String emailAddress;

   public User () { }

   public User (String first, String last, String email) {
       firstName = first;
       lastName = last;
       emailAddress = email;
   }

   public void setFirstName (String f) {
       firstName = f;
   }

   public String getFirstName () {
      return firstName;
   }

   public void setLastName(String l) {
       lastName = l;
   }

   public String getLastName () {
     return lastName;
   }

   public void setEmailAddress(String e) {
       emailAddress = e;
   }

   public String getEmailAddress () {
      return emailAddress;
   }
}
```

Fig. 10.46 *User JavaBean*

As we can see, we have a simple Java class, which has three private attributes; namely, firstName, lastName, and emailAddress. There are three methods to accept values from other methods to set the values of these three attributes of the User class (called the *setters*). Similarly, there are three methods to retrieve or get the values of these three attributes of the User class (called the *getters*). Thus, whenever any outside object needs to access/update values of attributes in the User class, that object can use these get/set methods. This allows the User class to keep these attributes private, and yet allow other objects to access/update their values. Whenever a class is written to support this functionality, it is called a JavaBean.

How are JavaBeans useful in a JSP? We can consider the fields/controls on an HTML form as attributes of a JavaBean. Whenever the HTML form is submitted to the server, the JSP on the server-side can use the JavaBean's get-set methods to retrieve/update the form values, as appropriate. This is much better than writing form processing code in the JSP itself.

10.5.3 Implicit JSP Objects

JSP technology provides a number of useful implicit (ready-made) objects. We can make use of these objects to make our programming easier, rather than having to code for every small thing ourselves. These implicit objects are shown in Fig. 10.47.

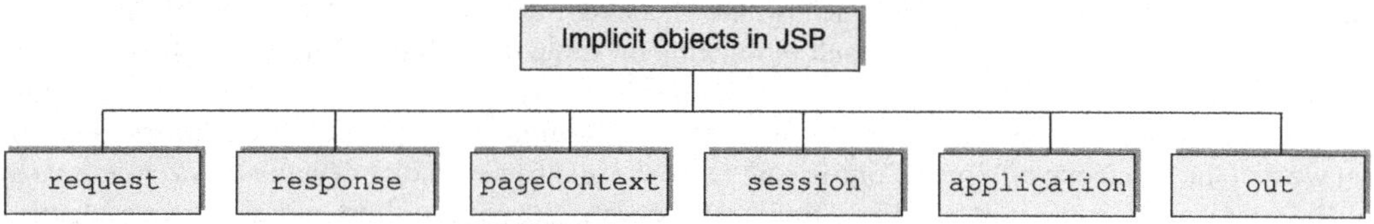

Fig. 10.47 *Implicit objects of JSP*

We have used some of these objects in our earlier examples. Let us have a formal explanation for them, among others. For that, we need to take a look at Fig. 10.48.

Object	*Description*	*Example*
request	**The request object is used to reed the values of the HTML form in a JSP, received as a part of the HTTP request sent by the client to the server.**	<% String uname; Uname = request.getParameter (name); %>
response	**The response object is used to send the necessary information from the server to the client. For example, we can send *cookies* (discussed separately) as shown in the example**	<% Cookie mycookie = new Cookie ("name", "atul"); response.addCookie (mycookie); %>
pageContext	**We can use a pageContext reference to get any attributes from any scope.**	· Setting a page-scoped attribute <% Float one = new Float (42.5); %> <% pageContext.setAttribute ("test", one); %> · Getting a page-scoped attribute <%= pageContext.getAttribute ("test"); %>
session	**We will discuss this separately.**	HttpSession session = request.getSession (); session.setAttribute ("name", "ram");
application	**It is the master object, and should not be used, since it puts a load on the JSP container.**	NA
out	**This object is used to send HTML content to the user's browser.**	<% String [] colors = {"red", "green", "blue"}; for (int i = 0; i < colors.length; i++) out.println ("<p>" + colors [i] + "</p>"); %>

Fig. 10.48 *JSP implicit objects*

10.5.4 Session Management in JSP/Servlets

HTTP is a stateless protocol. It means that it is a *forgetful* protocol. It forgets what it had done in the previous step. The straightforward way to describe this situation is:

1. Client (Web browser) sends an HTTP request to the Web server.
2. The Web server sends an HTTP response to the Web browser.
3. The server forgets about the client.

As we can see, this can be quite unnerving. For example, suppose our browser displays a login page, where we need to enter the user id and password and submit it to the server. Once we enter these details and send the HTTP request to the server, the server will check whether the user id and password are correct. Accordingly, it would generate the next HTML page and send to our browser. At this stage, it has already forgotten about us! This means that whenever our browser sends the next HTTP request to the same server (e.g., perhaps as a result of clicking on some hyper link on the page), the server will not even know us!

Perhaps the best way to understand this is to take the example of telephone conversations. Suppose that we dial the telephone number of our friend. Once we identify each other (with a *Hello I am so and so, How are you*, etc.), we start speaking. But what if our memory is too short and we forget each other after every turn in the conversation? It would lead to a very comical situation like this:

1. Person Atul (*picks up the ringing phone*): Hi, Atul here.
2. Person Achyut (*had dialed B's number*): Hi Atul, this is Achyut here. I wanted to know if you have completed the 7th chapter.
3. Person Atul: Yes, I have.
4. Person Achyut (*had dialed B's number*): Ok, what about the 8th?
5. Person Atul (*has forgotten about the previous conversation*): Who are you?

As we can see, after the initial handshake, Atul (equivalent of the *Web server*) has forgotten Achyut (equivalent of the *Web browser*)! This is very strange indeed. This means that Achyut (equivalent of the *Web browser*) needs to identify himself to Atul (equivalent of the *Web server*) every single time he needs to communicate something to him during the same conversation, and provide information as to what was discussed in the past.

Well, unfortunately, HTTP works in the same way. Let us say that again:

1. Client (Web browser) sends an HTTP request to the Web server.
2. The Web server sends an HTTP response to the Web browser.
3. The server forgets about the client.

This means that it is the client's responsibility to every time make the server remember who the client is, and what had happened in the conversation up to that point. For this purpose, we need the concept of **session state management** (also called as only **session management**). The idea for doing is depicted in Fig. 10.49.

The unique ID that keeps floating between the client and the server is called as **session ID**. How is this sent by the server to the browser? There are two techniques in JSP to work with session IDs. This is outlined in Fig. 10.50.

Let us understand them in brief.

1. Cookies In the first technique, the server creates a small text file, called as a **cookie** and associates this particular user with that cookie. The cookie is created by the server, and sent to the browser along with the first HTTP response. The browser accepts it and stores it inside the browser's memory. Whenever the browser sends the next HTTP request to the server, it reads this cookie from its memory and adds it

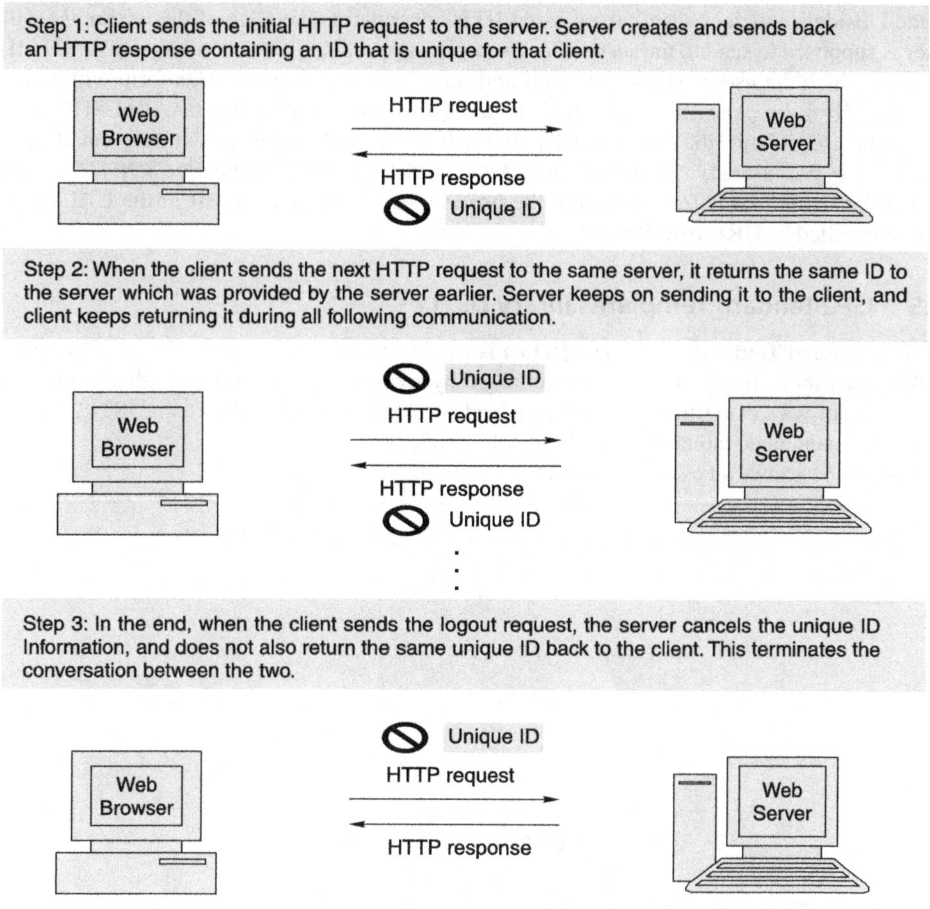

Fig. 10.49 *Session management concept*

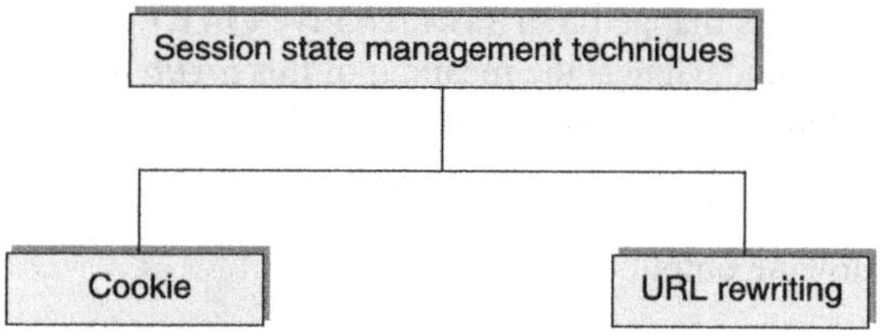

Fig. 10.50 *Session management techniques*

to the request. Thus, the cookie keeps traveling between the browser and the server for every request-response pair.

2. URL rewriting However, there is an option to disable cookies in the browser. If the user does so, session management will not work. Hence, another technique exists, whereby the session ID is not embedded inside a cookie. Instead, the session ID is appended to the URL of the *next request* that the browser is supposed to send to the server. For example, suppose that the server has sent an HTML form to the user, which the user is supposed to fill and send back to the server. This form will go to a JSP called *CheckForm.jsp*. Also, the server has created a session ID with value 0AAB6C8DE415. Then, whenever the user submits the form, the URL that will be seen in the browser window would not just be *CheckForm.jsp*, but instead, it would be *CheckForm.jsp&JSESSIONID=0AAB6C8DE415*. This would mean that the session ID is traveling from the browser to the server as a part of the URL itself. This technique is called as **URL rewriting**.

10.5.5 JSP Standard Template Library (JSTL)

The **JSP Standard Template Library (JSTL)** is used to reduce the amount of coding to achieve the same functionality as would normally be achieved by writing scriptlet code. In other words, JSTL is a more efficient way of writing JSP code, instead of using scriptlet code. Using JSTL, we do code development using tags, rather than writing a lot of code.

Figure 10.51 shows an example of JSTL.

```
<%@ taglib uri="http://java.sun.com/jstl/core" prefix="c" %>

<html>
    <body>
        <h1>JSP is as easy as ...</h1>

        <%-- Calculate the sum of 1, 2, and 3 dynamically -%>
        1 + 2 + 3 = <c:out value="${1 + 2 + 3}" />
    </body>
</html>
```

Fig. 10.51 *JSTL example*

Let us understand how this works.

At the beginning of the code, we have a directive that includes a *taglib* file. A *taglib* is the tag library, i.e., a collection of ready-made, precompiled tags used to accomplish a specific task. Although it would not be clear here, this directive is mapped to a **Java Archive (JAR)** file in the deployment descriptor file. That is how our JSP code understands the meaning of this *taglib* file.

The only other new statement in our code is this:

```
1 + 2 + 3 = <c:out value="${1 + 2 + 3}" />
```

This will print the following output:

```
1 + 2 + 3 = 6
```

How is this done? To compute the sum of 1, 2, and 3, the following code is used:

```
"${1 + 2 + 3}"
```

The above statement follows the syntax of what is called as **Expression Language (EL)**. EL is a short hand tag-oriented language. An EL expression always starts with ${ and ends with }. We have put this EL expression inside a *<c:out …>* statement. This is equivalent to an *out.println ( )* statement in the standard Java scriptlet code. Thus, the following two statements are equivalent:

```
JSTL version         1 + 2 + 3 = <c:out value="${1 + 2 + 3}" />
Scriptlet version    out.println ("1 + 2 + 3 = " + 1 + 2 + 3);
```

JSTL can be quite powerful. Figure 10.52 shows the scriptlet code to display numbers from 1 to 10, along with the version of the JSTL code.

```
<html>
   <head>
      <title>Count Example</title>
</head>

   <body>
      <%
         for (int i=1; i<=10; i++) {
      %>

      <%= i %>

      <br/>

      <%
         }
      %>

   </body>
</html>
```

(a) *Scriptlet version*

```
<%@ taglib uri="http://java.sun.com/jstl/core" prefix="c" %>

<html>
   <head>
      <title>Count Example</title>
</head>

   <body>
      <c:forEach var="i" begin="1" end="10" step="1">
         <c:out value="${i}" />
            <br/>
      </c:forEach>
   </body>
</html>
```

(b) *JSTL version*

Fig. 10.52 *Scriptlet and JSTL versions for program to display numbers from 1 to 10*

The JSTL version of the code has a tag *<c:forEach ...>*. As we can guess, this is a short hand notation for the standard Java *for* statement. Similarly, we again use the shorthand notation *<c:out ...>* instead of the standard JSP *out.println ( )* notation. We then use the EL syntax to display the current value of the variable *i* by using the EL syntax, as before.

Other than using these predefined tags such as *forEach* and *out*, we can also develop our own **custom tags**. These can be used in situations where we want to develop generic functionality, and use it in several JSP applications.

10.5.6 JSP Examples

Let us now discuss a few examples to understand the JSP syntax in more detail.

Example 1: Display sum of two numbers

Figure 10.53 shows JSP code for the addition of two numbers. We declare two variables in the declaration section, and one in scriptlet. This is just to show that it does not matter where we declare variables in JSP as long as we are not worried about multi-threading situations. In other words, we could have declared all the three variables inside the declaration section or all the three variables inside the scriptlet. The result would have been the same. We then assign values to two of the three variables thus declared, and store their sum in the third.

```
<html>
    <head>
        <title>Addition of two numbers | JSP Example</title>
    </head>
    <body>
        <h1>Addition Example!</h1>
        <%! int n1, n2; %>

        <%
        int n3;

        n1 = 10;
        n2 = 20;

        n3 = n1 + n2;

        out.println("Sum of " + n1 + " and " + n2 + " is " + n3);
        %>
    </body>
</html>
```

Fig. 10.53 *JSP implicit objects*

The result of running this code is shown in Fig. 10.54.

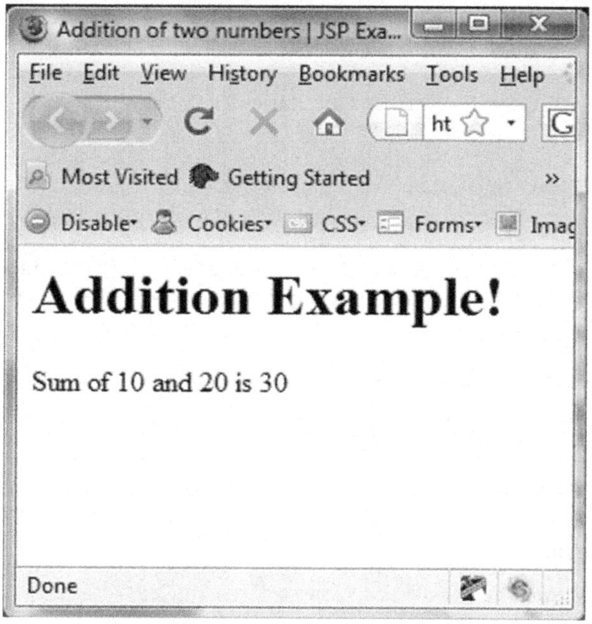

Fig. 10.54 *Output of addition JSP example*

Example 2: Accept and display back user's name

We ask the user to enter her first and last name on the screen. When the user provides this information and submits the HTML form, we show it back to the user via a JSP. Figure 10.55 shows the HTML page, and Fig. 10.56 shows the corresponding JSP.

```
<html>
  <head>
    <title>JSP Example Using a Form</title>
  </head>
  <body>
    <h1>User Name Capturing</h1>
    <form action = “username.jsp”>
    Enter your first name: <input type = “text” name = “firstName”>
        <br />
    Enter your last name: <input type = “text” name = “lastName”>
        <br />
    <input type =“submit”>
    </form>
  </body>
</html>
```

Fig. 10.55 *HTML page to accept user's name from the user*

```
<html>
    <head>
        <title>Accept and Display Name</title>
    </head>
    <body>
        <h1>Accept and Display Name!</h1>

        <%
        String firstName = request.getParameter("firstName");
        String lastName = request.getParameter("lastName");
        %>

        Hello <%= firstName%> <%= lastName%>
    </body>
</html>
```

Fig. 10.56 *JSP to display user's name accepted from the user*

Note the following line:

```
Hello <%= firstName%> <%= lastName%>
```

We have made use of an expression here. We could have written the same thing without using scriptlets in the normal syntax as:

```
out.println ("Hello " + firstName + lastName);
```

The resulting output is shown in Fig. 10.57 and 10.58.

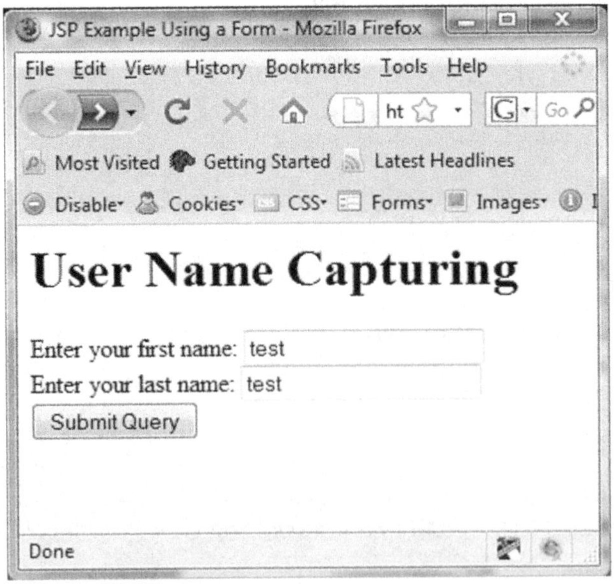

Fig. 10.57 *Output of the HTML page*

Fig. 10.58 *Output of the JSP*

Example 3: Miles to kilometers conversion

In this example, we would demonstrate the usage of a simple *for* Java loop in a JSP. The loop runs through a counter 15 times, converting miles to kilometers. Figure 10.59 shows the code.

```
<%@page import = “java.text.DecimalFormat” %>
<%@page import = “java.text.NumberFormat” %>

<html>
    <head>
        <title>Kilometers to Miles Conversion Chart</title>
    </head>
    <body>
        <h1>Kilometers to Miles Conversion Chart using JSP</h1>
        <%
        out.println(“<table border=‘1’ cellpadding=‘3’ cellspacing=‘0’>”);
        out.println(“<tr>”);
        out.println(“<th>Miles</th>”);
        out.println(“<th>KM</th>”);
        out.println(“</tr”);

        for (int miles = 1; miles <= 15; miles++) {
            double km = miles * 1.609344;
            NumberFormat fmt = new DecimalFormat(“###.000”);
```

(Contd.)

Fig. 10.59 *Contd...*

```
                String formattedKm = fmt.format(km);
                out.println("<tr>" + "<td align='right'>" + miles + "</td>"
    + "<td align='right'>" + formattedKm + "</td>" + "</tr>");
            }

            out.println("</table>");
            %>
        </body>
    </html>
```

Fig. 10.59 *Miles to kilometers conversion using Servlet*

Here, we have imported two files into the JSP page for formatting of the output. This is done by way of the *page import* directive, as shown below:

```
<%@page import = "java.text.DecimalFormat" %>
<%@page import = "java.text.NumberFormat" %>
```

The resulting output is shown in Fig. 10.60.

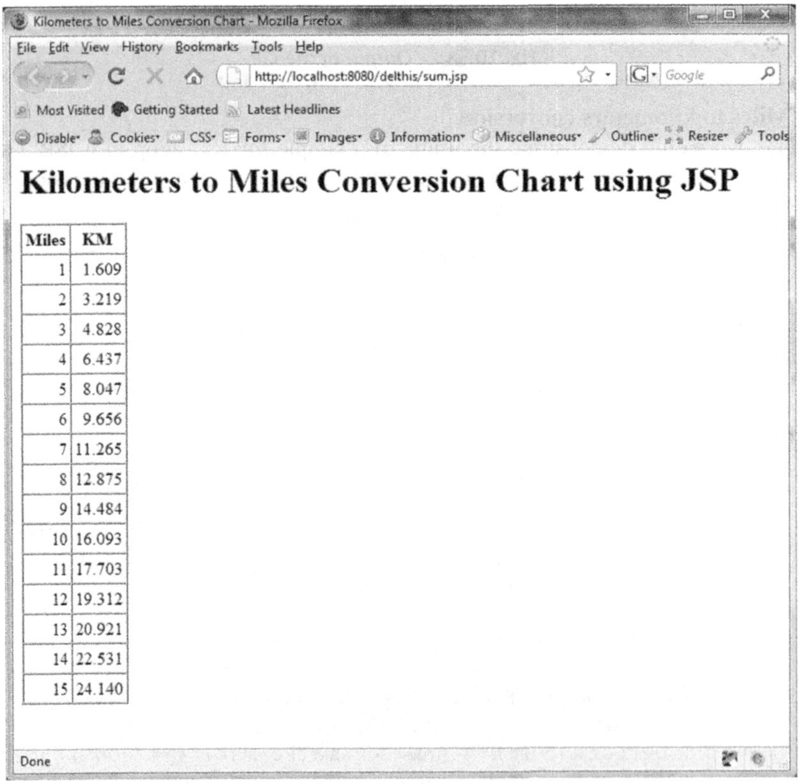

Fig. 10.60 *Miles to kilometers conversion using JSP*

Example 4: Factorial of a number

In this example, we ask the user to enter a number by displaying an HTML form and compute its factorial and show it to the user by using a JSP. Figure 10.61 shows the JSP.

```
<html>
    <head>
        <title>Factorial</title>
    </head>
    <body>
        <h1>Factorial Computation</h1>
        <form action = "factorial.jsp">
            Enter number for factorial computation:
            <input type = "text" name = "userInput">
            <input type ="submit" value ="Compute Factorial">
        </form>
    </body>
</html>
```

Fig. 10.61 *HTML page for accepting input from the user for factorial computation*

The JSP corresponding to this is shown in Fig. 10.62.

```
<%@page import = "java.text.DecimalFormat" %>
<%@page import = "java.text.NumberFormat" %>

<html>
    <head>
        <title>Factorial Example</title>
    </head>
    <body>
        <h1>Factorial Example</h1>
        <%

        String stringUserInput;
        int userInput, factorial = 1, storeUserInput;

        stringUserInput = request.getParameter("userInput");
        userInput = Integer.parseInt(stringUserInput);
        storeUserInput = userInput;

        while (userInput > 1) {
            factorial *= userInput;
            userInput--;
        }
        out.println("Factorial of " + storeUserInput + " is " + factorial);
        %>
    </body>
</html>
```

Fig. 10.62 *JSP for factorial computation*

The resulting output is shown in Figs. 10.62 and 10.63.

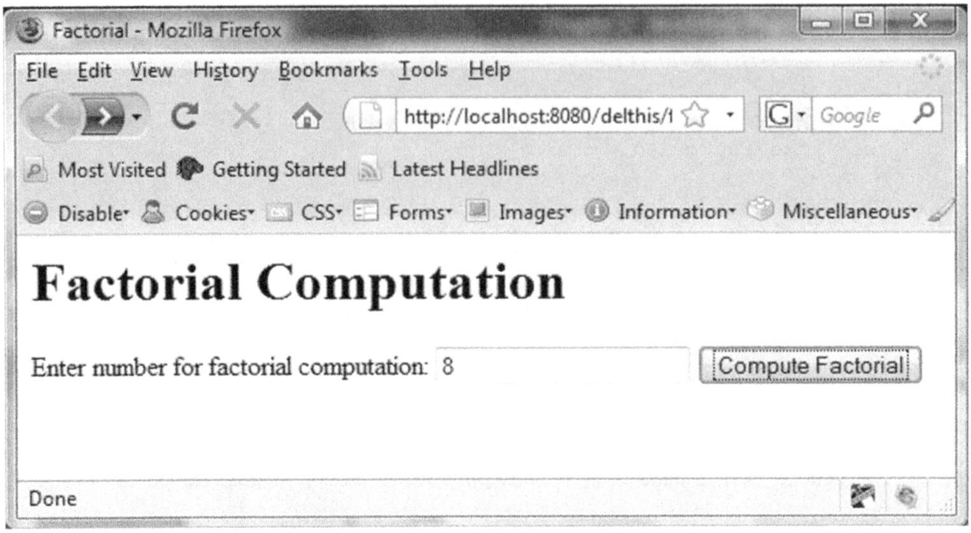

Fig. 10.62 *HTML output for factorial computation*

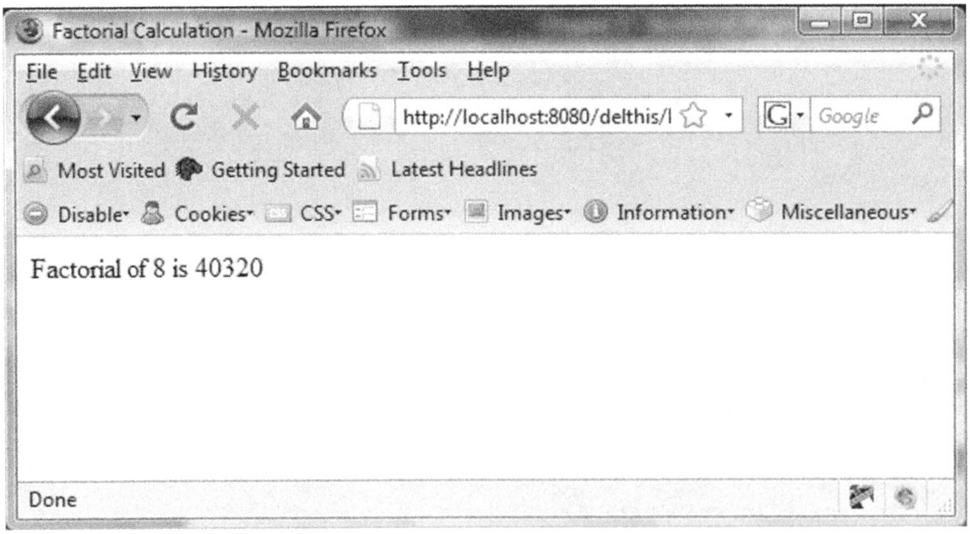

Fig. 10.63 *JSP output for factorial computation*

Example 5: Factorial of the largest of 3 numbers

We will now modify the previous example. Instead of accepting a number from the user and computing its factorial directly, we shall accept three numbers from the user and compute the factorial of the largest of those three numbers. Figure 10.64 shows the modified HTML page for this purpose.

```
<html>

<head>
<title>Compute Factorial of the Largest Number</title>
</head>

<body>
<h1>Compute Factorial of the Largest Number</h1>

<form action = "factorial.jsp">
Enter three numbers:
<input type = "text" name = "num_1">   
<input type = "text" name = "num_2">   
<input type = "text" name = "num_3">
<br />
<br />
<input type = "submit" value = "Compute the factorial of the largest">
</form>

</body>
</html>
```

Fig. 10.64 *Accepting three numbers from the user*

Figure 10.65 shows the JSP.

```
<html>

    <head>
        <title>Compute Factorial of the Largest Number</title>
    </head>

    <body>
        <h1>Compute Factorial of the Largest Number</h1>

        <%
        String num_1_str = request.getParameter("num_1");
        String num_2_str = request.getParameter("num_2");
        String num_3_str = request.getParameter("num_3");

        int num_1 = Integer.parseInt(num_1_str);
        int num_2 = Integer.parseInt(num_2_str);
        int num_3 = Integer.parseInt(num_3_str);

        int largest = 0, storeLargest = 0;

        if (num_1 > num_2 && num_1 > num_3) {
            largest = num_1;
        } else if (num_2 > largest && num_2 > num_3) {
            largest = num_2;
```

(Contd.)

Fig. 10.65 *Contd...*

```
        } else {
            largest = num_3;
        }

        storeLargest = largest;

        int fact = 1;

        while (largest > 1) {
            fact *= largest;
            largest--;
        }

        %>

        <h3> The numbers entered are: <%= num_1%>, <%= num_2%>, and <%=
num_3%>. </h3>

          <h2> The largest among them is: <%= storeLargest%>, and its
factorial is <%= fact%> </h2>

    </body>
</html>



</body>
</html>
```

Fig. 10.65 *JSP to compute factorial of the largest of three numbers*

The output of the HTML page is shown in Fig. 10.66.

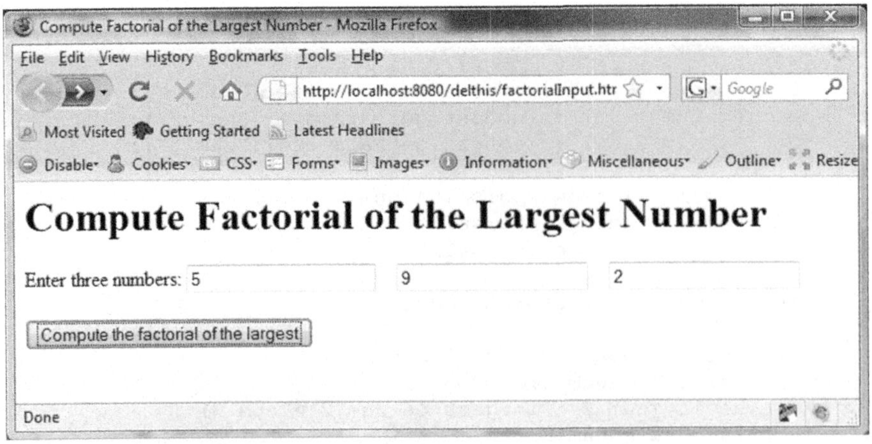

Fig. 10.66 *HTML page to accept three numbers from the user*

The result is shown in Fig. 10.67.

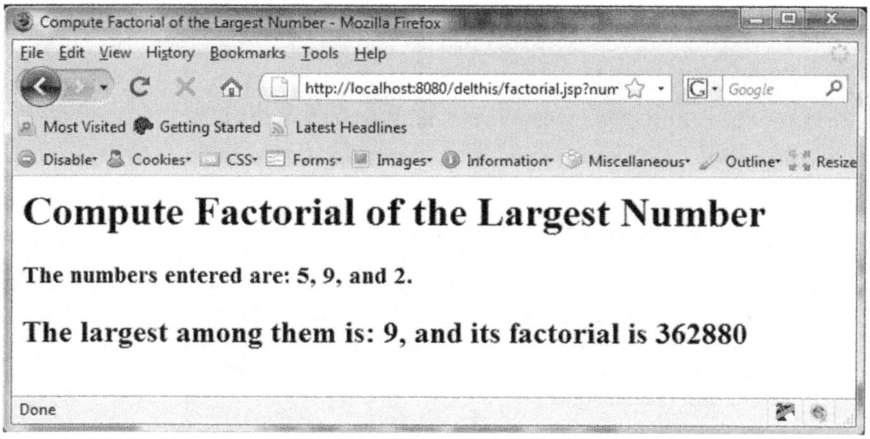

Fig. 10.67 *Output of the JSP that computes the factorial of the largest among three numbers*

Example 6: Cross-currency conversion

In this example, we allow the user to select either US dollars or Indian rupees as the source currency and also let the user enter the amount. We then convert it into the other currency equivalent and display to the user. The HTML page is shown in Fig. 10.68.

```
<html>

    <head>
        <title>Currency Cross-Conversion</title>
    </head>

    <body>
        <h1>Currency Cross-Conversion</h1>

        <form action = "currencyCrossConversion.jsp">
            Choose Source Currency <br />
           <input type = "radio" name ="currency" value="USD">USD<br />
           <input type = "radio" name ="currency" value="INR">INR<br />

            <br />

            Type amount: <input type = «text» name = «amount»>

            <br />
            <input type = "submit" value = "Convert">

        </form>
    </body>
</html>
```

Fig. 10.68 *Currency cross-conversion HTML page*

The JSP is shown in Fig. 10.69.

```
<html>

<head>
    <title>Currency Cross Conversion Results</title>
</head>

<body>
    <h1>Currency Cross Conversion Results</h1>

    <%
        String currency = request.getParameter(“currency”);
        String amount_str = request.getParameter(“amount”);
        int sourceAmount = Integer.parseInt(amount_str);
        float targetAmount = 0;

        if (currency.equals(“USD”)) {
            targetAmount = sourceAmount * 39;
        } else {
            targetAmount = sourceAmount / 39;
        }

        out.println(“Converted amount is: ” + targetAmount);
    %>

</body>
</html>
```

Fig. 10.69 *Currency cross-conversion JSP page*

The output of the HTML page and the JSP page are shown in Figs. 10.70 and 10.71.

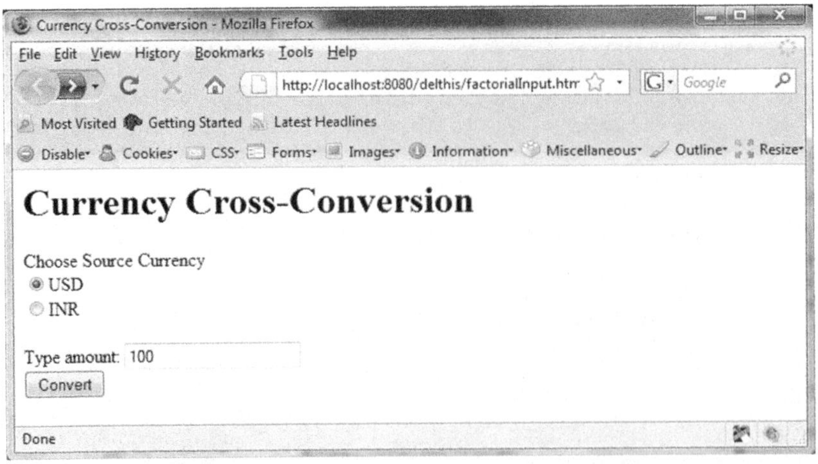

Fig. 10.70 *Currency cross-conversion – HTML output*

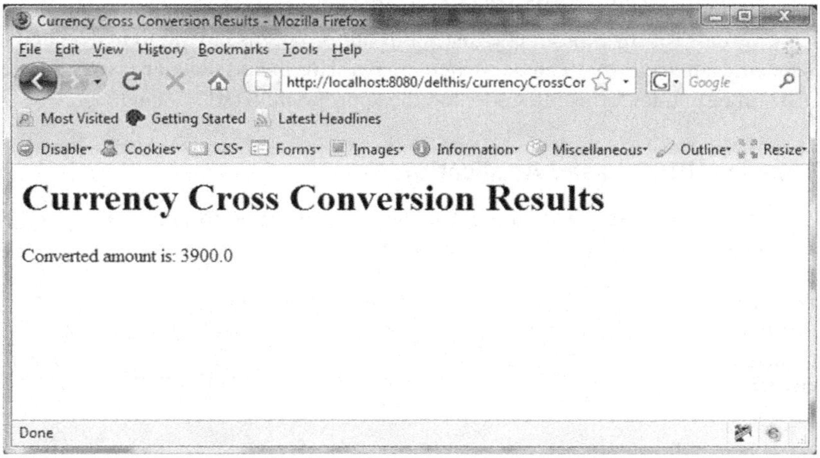

Fig. 10.71 *Currency cross-conversion – JSP output*

JSP AND JDBC.. 10.6

The Java programming language has in-built support for database processing. For this purpose, it uses the technology of **Java Database Connectivity (JDBC)**. JDBC is a set of classes and interfaces for allowing any Java application to work with an RDBMS in a uniform manner. In other words, the programmer need not worry about the differences in various RDBMS technologies, and can consider all RDBMS products as *some DBMS*, which all work in a similar fashion. Of course, it does not mean that the programmer can use any DBMS-specific (and not generic) functionalities and yet expect JDBC to support them across all other DBMS products. All we are saying is that the basic database accessing and processing mechanism is made uniform by JDBC; as long as the programmer sticks to the standard SQL/RDBMS features.

The conceptual view of JDBC is shown in Fig. 10.72.

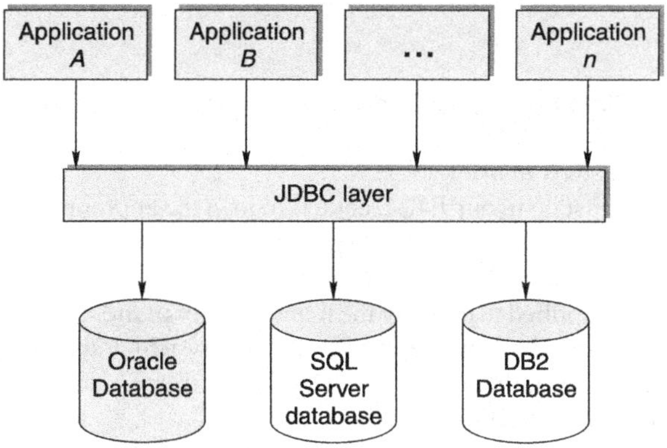

Fig. 10.72 *JDBC concept*

As we can see, the main idea of JDBC is to provide a layer of abstraction to our programs while dealing with the various RDBMS products. Instead of our programs having to understand and code in the RDBMS-specific language, they can be written in Java. This means that our Java code needs to *speak in JDBC*. JDBC, in turn, transforms our code into the appropriate RDBMS language.

10.6.1 Steps in a JDBC-based Application

Let us now outline the steps required in a JDBC-based application to perform the database-related programming operations. Figure 10.73 illustrates the idea.

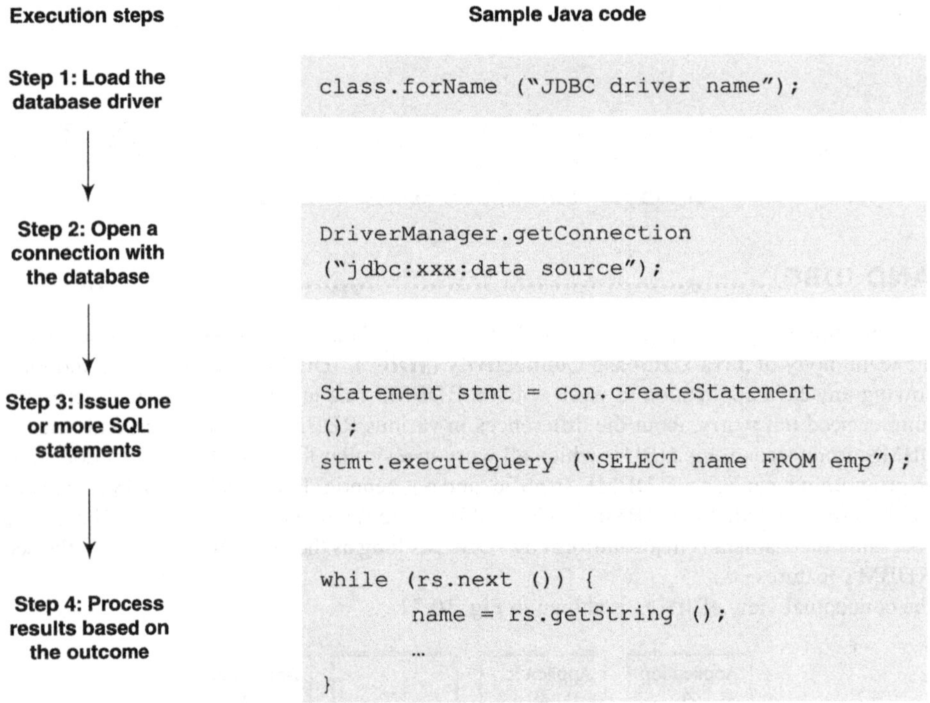

Fig. 10.73 *Steps in a JDBC-based program execution*

Let us understand these steps in brief.

1. The first thing we must do in our JDBC code is to load the appropriate database driver. Without loading the driver, we would not be able to perform any database operations. Sometimes, finding the right driver can be a challenge. But after some research, we should be able to locate the right driver. This is supplied usually by the manufacturer of the RDBMS product (e.g., Oracle).
2. Once the driver is loaded, using the driver, we specify which database we want to open, and whether it also requires authentication in the form of user id and password. For this purpose, we attempt to open a connection with the database.
3. In the next step, using the connection, we can execute any SQL statement of our choice. This statement is generally a Data Manipulation Language (DML) statement, i.e., SELECT/INSERT/UPDATE/DELETE.

Finally, we need to process the results of our query appropriately. Sometimes, this may also cause an exception, which we need to handle appropriately.

10.6.2 JDBC Driver Types

The various types of JDBC drivers are categorized into four *types*. These four types are shown in Table 10.1.

Table 10.1 *JDBC driver types*

JDBC driver type	*Name*	*Details*	*Advantages*	*Disadvantages*
Type 1	JDBC-ODBC bridge plus ODBC driver	This is a database driver implementation that employs Microsoft's ODBC driver to connect to the database. The driver converts JDBC method calls into the appropriate ODBC function calls. This driver is usually used when there is no pure-Java driver available for a particular database. This is used to easily enable users of Microsoft-based systems to make use of JDBC. The driver is implemented in the sun.jdbc.odbc. JdbcOdbcDriver class. It is the simplest of all but platform specific, i.e., only to Microsoft platform. The flow is: **Client -> JDBC Driver -> ODBC Driver -> Database**	Since ODBC availability is quite high, almost any database for which ODBC driver is installed can be accessed.	1. There is a performance overhead because of the JDBC-to-ODBC translation. 2. The ODBC driver needs to be installed on the client computer.
Type 2	Native API driver	This driver uses the client-side libraries of the database. The driver converts JDBC method calls into native calls of the database API. The driver is not written completely in Java because it interfaces with non-Java code that ultimately makes the final database calls. The driver is compiled for use with the particular operating system. For platform interoperability, the Type 4 driver, being a full-Java implementation, is preferred over this driver. The flow is: **Client -> JDBC Driver -> Vendor Client DB Library -> Database**	Provides better performance than Type 1 driver, since no JDBC to ODBC translation is needed here.	1. The vendor client library needs to be installed on every client computer. 2. This driver cannot be used on the Internet due the unavailability of the required client-side software. 3. Vendors may not provide the required client side library.

(Contd.)

Table 10.1 *Contd...*

Type 3	Network protocol driver	This is a database driver that makes use of a middle-tier between the calling program and the database. The middle-tier (application server) converts JDBC calls directly or indirectly into the vendor-specific database protocol. Here, the protocol conversion logic resides not at the client, but in the middle-tier. This driver is written entirely in Java. The same driver can be used for multiple databases. It depends on the number of databases the middleware has been configured to support. It is platform-independent as the platform-related differences are taken care by the middleware. Also, making use of the middleware provides additional advantages of security and firewall access. It does not need any specific client software installation. The flow is: **Client -> JDBC Driver -> Middleware server -> Database**	1. Since the communication between client and the middleware server is database independent, there is no need for the vendor library on the client computer. 2. The middleware server can provide useful middleware services such as caching (connections, query results), load balancing, logging, auditing, etc.	1. Requires database-specific coding to be done in the middle tier. 2. An extra layer results in a delay. But this is usually resolved by providing efficient middleware services as discussed earlier.
Type 4	Native protocol driver	This driver converts JDBC calls directly into the vendor-specific database protocol. It is written completely in Java and is hence is platform independent. It is installed inside the Java Virtual Machine of the client. It provides better performance over the type 1 and 2 drivers as it does not have the overhead of conversion of calls into ODBC or a vendor-specific database API calls. Unlike the type 1 and 2 drivers, it does not need any extra vendor libraries software to function. A native-protocol fully Java technology-enabled driver converts JDBC technology calls into the network protocol used by DBMSs directly. As the database protocol is vendor-specific, separate drivers, usually vendor-supplied, need to be used to connect to the database. The flow is: **Client Machine -> Native protocol JDBC Driver -> Database server**	There is no need to translate the requests into a vendor-specific database request or ODBC, etc. There is also no need for a middleware layer Hence, the performance is considerably improved.	At client side, the database-specific driver must be present.

The JDBC interface is contained in the packages:

1. java.sql – Core API, part of J2SE
2. Javax.sql – Optional extensions API, part of J2EE

JDBC uses more interfaces than classes, so that different vendors are free to provide an appropriate implementation for the specifications. Overall, about 30 interfaces and 9 classes are provided, such as Connection, Statement, PreparedStatement, ResultSet, and SQLException. We explain some of them briefly below:

1. **Connection object** It is the *pipe* between a Java program and the RDBMS. It is the object through which commands and data *flow* between our program and the RDBMS.
2. **Statement object** Using the *pipe* (i.e., the *Connection* object), the *Statement* object is used to send SQL commands that can be executed on the RDBMS. There are three types of commands that can be executed by using this object:
   (a) *Statement object* This object is used to define and execute static SQL statements.
   (b) *PreparedStatement* This object is used to define and execute dynamic SQL statements.
   (c) *CallableStatement* This object is used to define and execute stored procedures.
3. **ResultSet object** The result of executing a *Statement* is usually some data. This data is returned inside an object of type *ResultSet*.
4. **SQLException object** This object is used to deal with errors in JDBC.

10.6.3 JDBC Examples

Basic Concepts

Suppose we have two tables in our database, containing columns as shown in Fig. 10.74.

```
• CREATE TABLE departments (
  deptno  CHAR (2),
  deptname  CHAR (40),
  deptmgr CHAR (4)
  );

• CREATE TABLE employees (
  empno  CHAR (4),
  lname      CHAR (20),
  fname      CHAR (20),
  hiredate  DATE,
  ismgr      BOOLEAN,
  deptno CHAR (2),
  title      CHAR (50),
  email      CHAR (32),
  phone      CHAR (4)
  );
```

Fig. 10.74 *Sample tables*

Based on these, we want to display a list of departments, along with their manager name, title, telephone number, and email address. This can be done by using a JSP as shown in Fig. 10.74.

```
<%@page contentType="text/html"%>
<%@page pageEncoding="UTF-8"%>
<%@page session="false" %>
<%@page import="java.sql.*" %>
<%@page import="java.util.*" %>

<html>
    <head><title>Department Managers</title></head>
    <body>
<%
        // Open Database Connection
        Class.forName ("sun.jdbc.odbc.JdbcOdbcDriver");

        // Open a connection to the database
      Connection con = DriverManager.getConnection("jdbc:odbc:Employee");

          String sql = "SELECT D.deptname, E.fname, E.lname, E.title,
E.email, E.phone " +
                    "FROM departments D, employees E " +
                    "WHERE D.deptmgr = E.empno " +
                    "ORDER BY D.deptname";

// Create a statement object and use it to fetch rows in a resultset object
        Statement stmt = con.createStatement ();
        ResultSet rs = stmt.executeQuery (sql);

        while (rs.next ())
        {
            String dept = rs.getString (1);
            String fname = rs.getString (2);
            String lname = rs.getString (3);
            String title = rs.getString (4);
            String email = rs.getString (5);
            String phone = rs.getString (6);
%>

         <h5>Department: <%= dept %> </h5>
         <%= fname %> <%= lname %>, <%= title %>
         <br> (91 20) 2290 <%= phone %>, <%= email %>
<%
        }
        rs.close ();
        rs = null;
        stmt.close();
        stmt=null;
        con.close ();
%>
```

(Contd.)

Fig. 10.75 *Contd...*

```
<br> <br>
<b>-- END OF DATA --</b>
</body>
</html>
```

Fig. 10.75 *JSP containing JDBC code*

The Statement object provides a number of useful methods, as listed in Fig. 10.76.

Method	*Purpose*
executeQuery	Execute a SELECT and return result set
executeUpdate	INSERT/UPDATE/DELETE or DDL, returns count of rows affected
execute	Similar to (1) and (2) above, but does not return a result set (returns a Boolean value)
executeBatch	Batch update

Fig. 10.76 *Useful methods of the Statement object*

Let us discuss an example of the executeUpdate statement. Figure 10.77 shows code that allows us to update the value of the department column to some fixed text for all the rows in the table.

```
<%@page contentType="text/html"%>
<%@page pageEncoding="UTF-8"%>
<%@page session="false" %>
<%@page import="java.sql.*" %>
<%@page import="java.util.*" %>

<html>
    <head><title>Update Employees</title></head>
    <body>
    <H1> List of Locations BEFORE the Update</H1>
<%
        // Open Database Connection
        Class.forName ("sun.jdbc.odbc.JdbcOdbcDriver");

        // Open a connection to the database
      Connection con = DriverManager.getConnection("jdbc:odbc:Employee");

        String sql = "SELECT location FROM departments";

          // Create a statement object and use it to fetch rows in a
resultset object
        Statement stmt = con.createStatement ();
        ResultSet rs = stmt.executeQuery (sql);

        while (rs.next ())        {
```

(*Contd.*)

Fig. 10.77 *Contd...*

```
                    String location = rs.getString (1);
                        <h5><%= location %> </h5>
<%
          }
          rs.close ();
          rs = null;
%>
          <p><H1> Now updating ... </H1></P>
          <br> <br>
<%
try {
          String location = "Near SICSR";

          int nRows = stmt.executeUpdate ("UPDATE departments SET location
= '" + location + "'");
          out.println ("Number of rows updated:  " + nRows);

         stmt.close ();
         stmt=null;
         con.close ();
} catch (SQLException se) {
     out.println (se.getMessage ());
}
%>
 </body>
</html>
```

Fig. 10.77 *Using the executeUpdate () method*

Figure 10.78 shows an example of deleting data with the help of a result set.

```
<%@page import="java.util.*" %>

<html>
     <head><title>Delete Department Name using ResultSet</title></head>
     <body>
     <H1> Fetching data from the table ...</H1>
<%
       Class.forName ("sun.jdbc.odbc.JdbcOdbcDriver");
       Connection con = DriverManager.getConnection("jdbc:odbc:Employee");

       String sql = "SELECT deptname FROM departments WHERE deptno = 'Del'";

       Statement stmt = null;
       ResultSet rs = null;
       boolean foundInTable = false;
```

(Contd.)

Fig. 10.78 *Contd...*

```
        try {
                stmt   =   con.createStatement   (ResultSet.TYPE_SCROLL_
INSENSITIVE,            ResultSet.CONCUR_UPDATABLE);
          rs = stmt.executeQuery (sql);
          foundInTable = rs.next ();
        }
        catch (SQLException ex) {
          System.out.println («Exception occurred: « + ex);
        }

        if (foundInTable) {
            String str = rs.getString (1);
            out.println («Data found»);
            out.println («Old value = « + str);
        }
        else {
          out.println («Data not found»);
        }

        if (foundInTable) {
          try {
             rs.deleteRow ();           rs.close ();     rs = null;
          }
          catch (SQLException ex) {
          System.out.println («Exception occurred: « + ex);
      }
          out.println («Delete successful»);
        }

    try {
       stmt.close ();      stmt=null;    con.close ();
    }

    catch (SQLException ex) {
       System.out.println («Exception occurred: « + ex);
    }

%>

</body>
</html>
```

Fig. 10.78 *Deleting data through a result set*

There is something interesting in this JSP page:

```
stmt = con.createStatement (ResultSet.TYPE_SCROLL_INSENSITIVE, ResultSet.
CONCUR_UPDATABLE);
```

What does this line indicate? It tells us that the result set that is going to be produced should be *insensitive* as well as *updatable*. Let us understand these two parameters. They are first conceptually shown in Fig. 10.79.

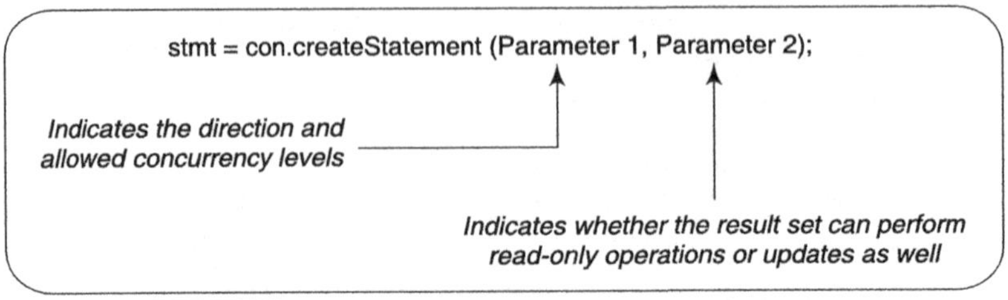

Fig. 10.79 *Understanding the createStatement parameters*

The first parameter can have values, as described with their meanings in Fig. 10.80.

Value	*Meaning*
TYPE_FORWARD_ONLY	Allow a cursor to move only in the forward direction on the result set
TYPE_SCROLL_SENSITIVE	Allow movement of the cursor on the result set in either direction, and if some other program is making any changes to the data under consideration, reflect those changes in our result set
TYPE_SCROLL_INSENSITIVE	Allow movement of the cursor on the result set in either direction, and if some other program is making any changes to the data under consideration, ignore those changes in our result set

Fig. 10.80 *Possible values for the first parameter*

Similarly, we describe the second parameter in Fig. 10.81.

Value	*Meaning*
CONCUR_READ_ONLY	Do not allow this result set to be updatable
CONCUR_UPDATABLE	Allow the result set to make changes to the database

Fig. 10.81 *Possible values for the second parameter*

Transactions in JDBC JDBC transaction management is quite simple. By default, all database changes in JDBC are automatically committed. However, if we want to control when commits or roll backs should happen, we need to do the following at the beginning of the JDBC code:

1. con.setAutoCommit (false);

Whenever we need to commit or update the changes, we need to execute either of the following:

1. con.commit (); or
2. con.rollback ();

Prepared Statements In order to allow the programmer to build the SQL statements dynamically at run time, JDBC supports the concept of prepared statements. A prepared statement specifies what operations will take place on the database, but does not indicate with what values. For example, consider the code block shown in Fig. 10.82.

```
// Prepare a string containing an SQL statement without a specific value
String preparedSQL = "SELECT location FROM departments WHERE deptno = ?";

// Now supply the SQL statement to the PreparedStatement instance
PreparedStatement ps = connection.prepareStatement (preparedSQL);

// Fill up the deptno value with whatever value we want to supply
ps.setString (1, user_deptno);

// Execute our prepared statement with the supplied value and store
results into a result set
ResultSet rs = ps.executeQuery ();
```

Fig. 10.82 *PreparedStatement concept*

As we can see, prepared statements allow us to *prepare* them at compile time, but with empty values. At run time, we supply the actual value of interest. Now, in this case, we could have either hard coded the value of the deptno, or as shown in the particular example, we can get it from another Java variable inside our JSP page. This allows us to execute the same prepared statement with different values for the deptno as many times as we wish. This means that we have the following advantages:

1. Reduced effort of checking and rechecking many statements
2. Write one statement and execute it as many times as desired, with different parameters
3. Better performance

We should note that the prepared statements need not always be only for selecting data. We can even insert data using the same concept, as illustrated in Fig. 10.83.

```
// Prepare a statement with no values for the paremeters
String preparedQuery = "INSERT INTO departments
    (deptno, deptname, deptmgr, location) VALUES (?, ?, ?, ?)";

// Make it available to the PreparedStatement object
PreparedStatement ps = con.prepareStatement (preparedQuery);

// Now supply the actual parameter values
ps.setString (1, user_deptno);
ps.setString (2, user_deptname);
ps.setString (3, user_deptmgr);
ps.setString (4, user_location);

// Execute the INSERT statement
ps.executeUpdate ();
```

Fig. 10.83 *PreparedStatement for INSERT*

We can similarly have prepared statements for deleting and updating data. We shall not discuss them here to avoid repetition.

Figure 10.84 shows a JSP page as an example of a preparedStatement.

```
<%@page pageEncoding="UTF-8"%>
<%@page session="false" %>
<%@page import="java.sql.*" %>
<%@page import="java.util.*" %>
<% boolean ucommit = true; %>

<html>
    <head><title>JDBC Transactions Application</title></head>
    <body>
    <h1> Account Balances BEFORE the transaction </h1>

    <table bgcolor = "yellow" border = "2">
    <tr>
       <th>Account Number</th>
       <th>Account Name</th>
       <th>Account Balance</th>
    </tr>

<%
      Class.forName ("sun.jdbc.odbc.JdbcOdbcDriver");
      Connection con = DriverManager.getConnection("jdbc:odbc:accounts");

// ********************************************************************
// THIS PART OF THE CODE DISPLAYS THE ACCOUNT DETAILS BEFORE THE TRANSACTION
// ********************************************************************

        String sql = "SELECT Account_Number, Account_Name, Balance " +
                     "FROM accounts " +
                     "ORDER BY Account_Name";

        Statement stmt = con.createStatement ();
        ResultSet rs = stmt.executeQuery (sql);

        while (rs.next ())
        {
            String account_Number = rs.getString (1);
            String account_Name = rs.getString (2);
            String balance = rs.getString (3);
%>

         <tr>
          <td><%= account_Number %> </td>
       <td><%= account_Name %> </td>
       <td><%= balance %> </td>
```

(Contd.)

Fig. 10.84 *Contd...*

```
    </tr>

<%
         }
         rs.close ();
         rs = null;
         stmt.close();
         stmt=null;
%>

    </table>
<br> <br>
<b>-- END OF DATA --</b>
<br><br>
```

Fig. 10.84 *PreparedStatement Example – Part 1*

```
<%
// ******************************************************************
// ATTEMPT TO EXECUTE THE TRANSACTION IF COMMIT WAS SELECTED
// ******************************************************************

if (request.getParameter ("Commit") == null)   { // Rollback was selected
   out.println ("<b> You have chosen to ROLL BACK the funds transfer. No
changes would be made to the database. </b>");
}

else {
   // Now try and execute the database operations
   int  fromAccount = Integer.parseInt (request.getParameter ("fromAcc"));
   int toAccount  = Integer.parseInt  (request.getParameter  ("toAcc"));
   int amount = Integer.parseInt (request.getParameter  ("amount"));
   int nRows = 0;

   // Debit FROM account
   PreparedStatement stmt_upd = con.prepareStatement  ("UPDATE accounts
" +
                   "SET Balance = Balance - ?" +
                   " WHERE Account_Number = ?");

   stmt_upd.setInt (1, amount);
   stmt_upd.setInt (2, fromAccount);

   out.print ("<br> Amount = " + amount);
   out.print ("<br> From Acc = " + fromAccount);
```

(Contd.)

Fig. 10.84 *Part 2 Contd...*

```
    try {
        nRows = stmt_upd.executeUpdate ();
        out.print ("<br>" + nRows);
        // out.print ("<br>" + stmt_upd);
        stmt_upd.clearParameters ();
    }

    catch (SQLException se) {
        ucommit = false;
        out.println (se.getMessage ());
    }

    // Credit TO account
    stmt_upd = con.prepareStatement ("UPDATE accounts " +
                    "SET Balance = Balance + ?" +
                    " WHERE Account_Number = ?");

    stmt_upd.setInt (1, amount);
    stmt_upd.setInt (2, toAccount);

    out.print ("<br> Amount = " + amount);
    out.print ("<br> To Acc = " + toAccount);
```

Fig. 10.84 *PreparedStatement Example – Part 2*

```
    try {
        nRows = stmt_upd.executeUpdate ();
        out.print ("<br>" + nRows);
        stmt_upd.clearParameters ();
    }
    catch (SQLException se) {
        ucommit = false;
        out.println (se.getMessage ());
    }

    if (ucommit) { // No problems, go ahead and commit transaction
        con.commit ();
        out.println ("<b> Transaction committed successfully! </b>");
    }
    else {
        con.rollback ();
        out.println ("<b> Transaction had to be rolled back! </b>");
    }
}
%>
```

(Contd.)

Fig. 10.84 *Part 3 Contd...*

```
<%
// ***********************************************************************
// DISPLAY THE ACCOUNT DETAILS AFTER THE TRANSACTION OPERATION
// ***********************************************************************
%>
    <table bgcolor = "lightblue" border = "2">
    <tr>
       <th>Account Number</th>
       <th>Account Name</th>
       <th>Account Balance</th>
    </tr>

<%
      sql = "SELECT Account_Number, Account_Name, Balance FROM accounts ";

        stmt = con.createStatement ();
        rs = stmt.executeQuery (sql);

        while (rs.next ())
        {
            String account_Number = rs.getString (1);
            String account_Name = rs.getString (2);
            String balance = rs.getString (3);
%>
         <tr>
          <td><%= account_Number %> </td>
      <td><%= account_Name %> </td>
      <td><%= balance %> </td>
    </tr>
<%
        }
        rs.close (),
        rs = null;
        stmt.close();
        stmt=null;
        con.close ();
%>

    </table>
<br> <br>
<b>-- END OF DATA --</b>
<br><br>


</body>
</html>
```

Fig. 10.84 *PreparedStatement Example – Part 3*

Fig. 10.84 *Part 3 Contd...*

```
        </table>
    <br> <br>
    <b>-- END OF DATA --</b>
    <br><br>


    </body>
    </html>
```

Fig. 10.84 *PreparedStatement Example – Part 4*

APACHE STRUTS 10.7

10.7.1 Model-View-Controller (MVC) Architecture

Over a period of time, it was realized that the best way to design and architect Web-based applications was to follow a technique known as **Model-View-Controller (MVC)** architecture. The idea of MVC is quite simple. We will understand it with the help of the JSP/Servlets technology, although it can be applied to other dynamic Web page technologies as well.

Instead of a single Servlet or JSP dealing with the user's HTTP request, performing the necessary processing, and also sending back the HTTP response to the user, the MVC approach recommends that we consider the whole Web application to be made up of three parts:

1. **Model** This is where the business logic resides. For example, it could be a simple Java class fetching data from a database using JDBC, or a JavaBean, or an Enterprise JavaBean (EJB), or even a non-Java application.
2. **View** The view is used to prepare and send the resulting output back to the user. Usually, this is done with the help of a JSP. In other words, the JSP constructs the HTML page that is sent to the browser as a part of the HTTP response.
3. **Controller** The controller is usually a Servlet. As the name suggests, the controller Servlet is responsible for controlling the overall flow of the application. In other words, it coordinates all the functions of the application and ensures that the user's request is processed appropriately.

The overall application architecture using the MVC approach looks as shown in Fig. 10.85.

Let us understand how this works, step-by-step. The step numbers refer to the corresponding sequence number depicted in the diagram.

1. The browser sends an HTTP request to the server, as usual.
2. The server passes the user's request on to the controller Servlet.
3. After performing the appropriate validations, etc., the controller calls the right model (depending on the business logic that needs to be executed). The model performs the business logic, and sends results back to the controller.
4. The controller invokes the view to prepare an HTML page that would eventually be sent out to the browser.
5. The HTML page is embedded inside an HTTP response message by the Web server.
6. The HTTP response is sent back to the browser.

As we can see, there is a very clear distinction between the responsibilities of the various components now. The controller, model, and view do not interfere with each other at all. Without MVC, the whole thing would have to be performed by a Servlet – worse yet, perhaps by the same single Servlet!

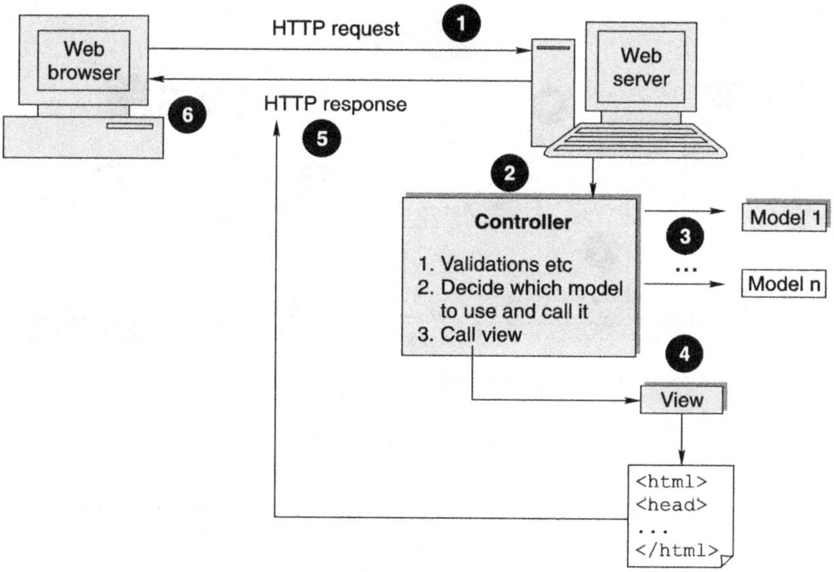

Fig. 10.85 *MVC concept*

10.7.2 Apache Struts and MVC

Struts from Apache is an open-source software that can be used to create applications in the MVC architecture by making use of declarative programming more than descriptive programming. In other words, Struts allows the programmer to specify a lot of functionality via configuration files and declarations, instead of having to write the code for those ourselves.

When an HTTP request is sent to a Struts application, it is handled by a special type of Servlet, called *ActionServlet*. When the *ActionServlet* receives a request, it checks the URL and consults the Struts configuration files. Accordingly, it delegates the handling of the request to an *Action* class. The *Action* class is part of the controller and is responsible for communicating with the model layer. The Struts framework provides an abstract *Action* class that we need to extend based on our application-specific requirements.

Let us understand all this terminology in a better manner now. Figure 10.86 shows the typical parts of a Struts application.

Let us understand this process step-by-step.

1. The client sends an HTTP request to the server, as usual. In Struts applications, an *action Servlet* receives HTTP requests.
2. The *action Servlet* consults a configuration file named *struts-config.xml* to figure out what to do next. It realizes that it has to forward this request to a *view component* (usually a JSP), as per the configuration done beforehand by the programmer.
3. The *action Servlet* forwards the request to the *form bean* (a Java representation of every field in the form data). The *form bean* is also called an *ActionForm* class. This is a JavaBean, which has getter and setter methods for the fields on the form.
4. It then consults the action *class* (for validating user input provided in the HTML form). The action class decides how to invoke the business logic now.

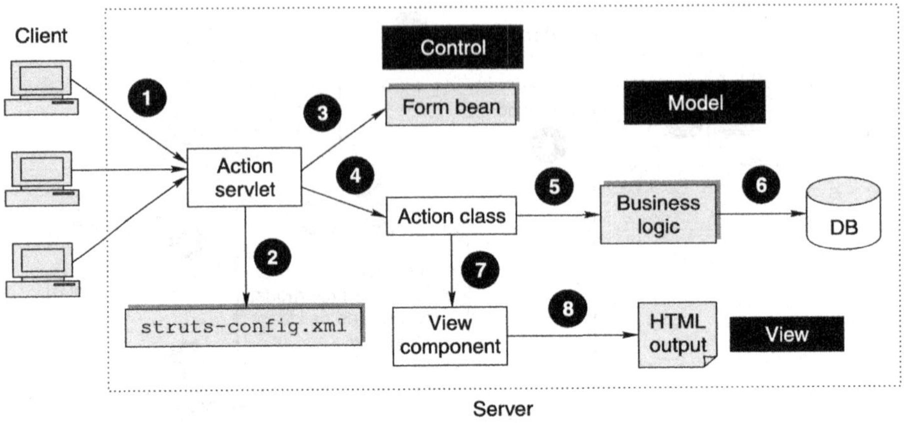

Fig. 10.86 *Struts application flow*

5. The business logic processing happens at this stage. The business logic can also be a part of the earlier class, i.e., the action class itself; or it can be a separate code (e.g., a Java class or an EJB).
6. Optionally, the database is also accessed.
7. The result of the above steps causes some output to be produced (which is not in the displayable HTML format yet). This is now passed to the *View component* (usually a JSP).
8. The JSP transforms this output into the final output format (usually HTML).

In essence, Struts takes the concept of MVC even further by providing built-in features for writing models, views and controllers and appropriately passing control back and fort between these components. If the programmer wants to do this herself, she would need to write the whole orchestrating logic herself.

JAVASERVER FACES (JSF).. 10.8

10.8.1 Background

Since the inception of the Internet programming, there has always been some debate as to where should one write the data input validation logic. Clearly, there are two ways to handle this. Either we write the validation code on the client-side (i.e., inside the Web browser in the form of JavaScript); or we can write it to execute on the server-side (i.e., inside the Web server). This is illustrated in Fig. 10.87.

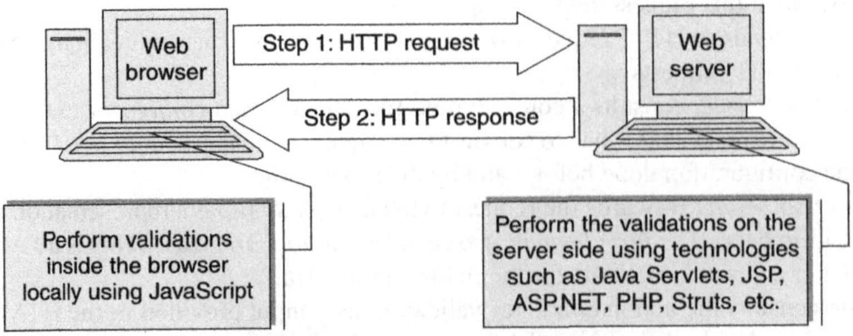

Fig. 10.87 *HTTP request/response*

Both approaches have their pros and cons. Over a period of time, it was almost standardized to keep the data entry related validations in JavaScript on the client-side. And then came ASP.NET. Until its arrival, validating anything on the server-side was possible, but quite cumbersome. ASP.NET changed all of that with the help of a novel concept titled **server controls**. These controls – basically drag-and-drop, can allow powerful validation logic to be built into ASP.NET pages with minimal effort, and the code also does not look ugly. In some sense, this actually transformed the whole Web programming model.

Quite clearly, Sun had to do something about it. The Java programming model for validations was still based on client-side JavaScript coding.

10.8.2 What is JSF?

With this in mind, Sun came up with what we now know as **JavaServer Faces (JSF)**. JSF is a technology that allows programmers to develop an HTML page using tags that are similar to the basic HTML tags, but have lot many features. For example, these tags *know* how to maintain their state (a huge problem in Web applications, otherwise), how and what sort of validations should take place, how to react to events, how to take care of internationalization, etc.

To understand this better, Fig. 10.88 shows a very simple example of defining the same tag first in plain HTML and then in JSF.

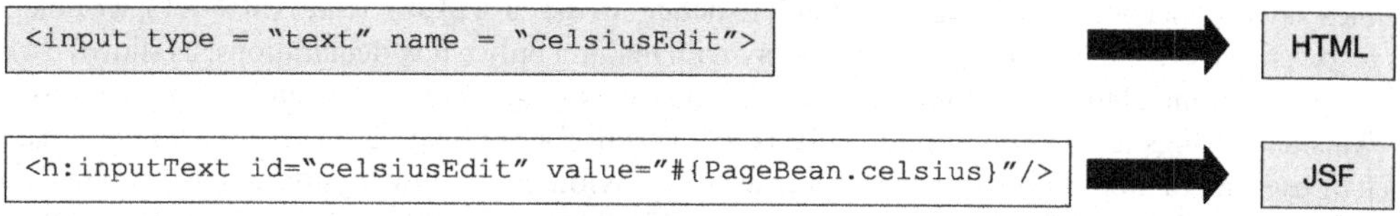

Fig. 10.88 *JSF concept*

Naturally, our first reaction would be that JSF seems to be quite complex. Well, we may feel that initially because the syntax looks a bit odd. However, when we play around a bit, and also see the benefits in lieu of using somewhat more syntax, it is easy to get convinced that JSF is a very powerful technology in many situations. In the same above case of JSF for example, what we are saying is that there is a textbox called *celciusEdit* that needs to be shown on the screen. Its value needs to be retrieved from the Web server. How? On the Web server, there would be a Java class (actually a simple JavaBean) named *PageBean*, which has an attribute called as *celcius*. The textbox is expected to show the value of this attribute on the Web page.

This should clearly tell us that unlike traditional Web programming model, where the client-side variables are quite de-linked from the corresponding server-side variables; here we are literally plumbing the server-side variable values straight into HTML pages! Moreover, we are doing this without writing any code on the client-side.

Now, it is also easy to imagine that we can manipulate the value of this variable in the server-side Java class the way we like. Essentially, we are allowing the server-side code to *prepare* the contents of this variable, and are sending them to the HTML screen in a very simple manner. Thus, the business logic need not be brought to the client, like the traditional JavaScript model. In other words, we are achieving the functionality of server-side business logic, as before.

However, what is more important to understand is that we not only achieve the above, but we would also be able to perform simple validations and formatting with almost no coding, but by using some simple declarations. For example, suppose that we want the user to be able to enter only a two-digit value in our input text box. Then, we can modify the declaration to look as shown in Fig. 10.89.

```
<h:inputText id="celsiusEdit" value="#{PageBean.celsius}"
    <f:validateLength minimum="2" maximum="2" />
</h:inputText>
```

Fig. 10.89 *JSF tags example*

Similarly, we can also restrict the minimum and maximum values to say 10 and 50, as shown in Fig. 10.90.

```
<h:inputText id="celsiusEdit" value="#{PageBean.celsius}"
    <f:validateLength minimum="2" maximum="2" />
    <f:validateLongRange minimum="10" maximum="50" />
</h:inputText>
```

Fig. 10.90 *More JSF syntax*

Of course, these are only a few of the possibilities that exist.

Also remember that do achieve the same thing in traditional Web pages, we need to write a lot of complex JavaScript code, which is also difficult to debug. In the case of JSF (like ASP.NET), we delegate this responsibility to the technology and get away with making only a few declarations, as shown earlier. This can be a tremendous boost to productivity in the case of user interface intensive applications.

This also brings us to another point. JSF is an overkill for applications where we do not have too much of user interaction. In other words, if the user is providing very few inputs, and instead the server is sending a lot of data back to the user in the form of HTML pages, then using JSF would not make sense at all!

Working with JSF is no longer a pain, either. All standard IDEs offer JSF support these days. For example, whenever we are creating a new Web application, NetBeans prompts us to say whether we want to use JSF in this application; and provides all the basic framework for enabling JSF.

Apache has provided an open source implementation of JSF titled MyFaces. It integrates nicely with Tomcat as the Web server.

10.8.3 JSF versus Struts

How does JSF compare with other frameworks, such as Apache Struts? In general, the consensus is that JSF fares better than Struts. The simple reasons for this view are that firstly JSF has been designed to mimic what ASP.NET does – something that the developers of Struts did not have in mind. Secondly, well, Struts came before JSF, and did not have the luxury of any hindsight!

Many developers feel that working with JSF is like working with Java Swing – in other words, having the ability to develop rich client applications, except that the client happens to be a thin client (Web browser), rather than the traditional Java client. However, everything in Struts is designed to work like a traditional Web application.

However, Struts has proved to be quite successful in production environments, and it may be some time before it can be replaced. But new applications can be straightaway developed in JSF, which promises to be an exciting technology for developing Web applications with rich client support.

Here are some guidelines for making that decision about using either Struts or JSF, or well, both! Figure 10.91 lists them.

Advantages	
Struts	*JSF*
Mature and proven framework.	User Interface is very powerful.
Easy to resolve problems since the developer community is quite large and documentation is quite good.	Event handling is very effective.
Good tool and IDE support.	Supported by a Java Community Support.
Open source framework.	Also open source now (Apache MyFaces).

Fig. 10.91 *Struts versus JSF – Part 1*

Use only this framework if ...	
Struts	*JSF*
We have an existing Struts application, that needs minor enhancements.	An application needs to be built from scratch and deadlines are not neck tight.
The project deadlines are very tight and unpredictability or lack of knowledgeable resources can become an issue.	Rich user interface is a very high priority item.
Good tool and IDE support.	There is a small existing Web application (even done using Struts) that needs major changes.

Fig. 10.92 *Struts versus JSF – Part 2*

Use *both* Struts and JSF if ...
There is a large Web application that needs significant changes. Here, we can write new code in JSF, retain existing Struts code with changes, as appropriate.

Fig. 10.93 *Struts versus JSF – Part 3*

10.8.4 JSF Case Study

Figure 10.94 shows a sample JSP page that contains some JSF tags.

```
<%@page contentType="text/html"%>
<%@page pageEncoding="UTF-8"%>

<%@ taglib uri="http://java.sun.com/jsf/core" prefix="f" %>
<%@ taglib uri="http://java.sun.com/jsf/html" prefix="h" %>

<html>
    <f:view>

    <head>
        <title>JSF Login Page Example</title>
    </head>

    <body bgcolor="pink">
```

(Contd.)

Fig. 10.94 *Contd...*

```
        <h:form>

            <h1 align="center">The Login Page</h1>

        <table border="1" bordecolor="maroon" cellspacing="1" cellpadding="1"
align="center">

                <tr>
                    <td>
                        <h:outputLabel for="txtName">
                            <h:outputText value="Name" />
                        </h:outputLabel>
                    </td>
                 <td><h:inputText id="txtName" value="#{UserBean.name}"
/></td>
                </tr>

                 <tr>
                    <td>
                        <h:outputLabel for="txtPassword">
                            <h:outputText value="Password" />
                        </h:outputLabel>
                    </td>
                 <td><h:inputSecret id="txtPassword" value="#{UserBean.
password}" /></td>
                </tr>

                <tr align="center">
                  <td colspan="2">
                <h:commandButton id="cmdLogin" value="Login"
action="login" />
                    </td>
                </tr>
            </table>

        </h:form>
    </body>
</html>
```

Fig. 10.94 *JSF sample*

This page would produce the following Web page in the browser, as shown in Fig. 10.95.
Let us understand how this works. Firstly, we see the following code in the JSP page:

```
<%@ taglib uri="http://java.sun.com/jsf/core" prefix="f" %>
<%@ taglib uri="http://java.sun.com/jsf/html" prefix="h" %>
```

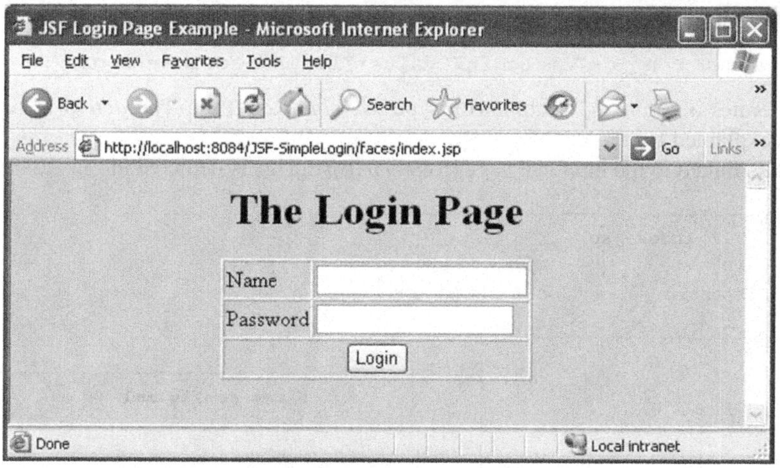

Fig. 10.95 *Sample output*

These taglib directives refer to the JSTL tags:

1. **jsf/core** Core library, contains custom action elements that represent JSF objects (which are independent of the page markup language)
2. **jsf/html** HTML library, contains custom action elements that represent JSF objects (which are to be rendered as HTML elements)

Next, we have the following statement:

```
<f:view>
```

This is an action element. A view in JSF is the grouping of components that make a specific UI screen. The view contains an instance of the *javax.faces.component.UIViewRoot* class. It does not display anything, but it is a container for other view components (e.g., input fields, buttons, etc.).

Then, we have the form elements:

```
<h:form>
```

This represents a form component. It acts as a container for all input components that hold values that needs to be processed together. Examples of these are *<h:inputText>*, *<h:inputSecret>*, *<h:commandButton>*.

```
For example:
<h:outputLabel for="txtName">
                <h:outputText value="Name" />
</h:outputLabel>
```

This identifies a component that generates an HTML label. Similarly, we can guess what happens with the following:

```
<h:inputText id="txtName" value="#{UserBean.name}" />
```

This generates a text box with id *txtName*. The value that user enters here would populate an attribute called as *name* of a server-side JavaBean titled *UserBean*.

On similar lines:

```
<h:commandButton id="cmdLogin" value="Login" action="login" />
```

This generates a command button with type as *submit* or *reset*. The *action* attribute here has relevance, as explained later.

How is this linked to the next JSP page (*welcome.jsp*)? This is depicted in Fig. 10.96.

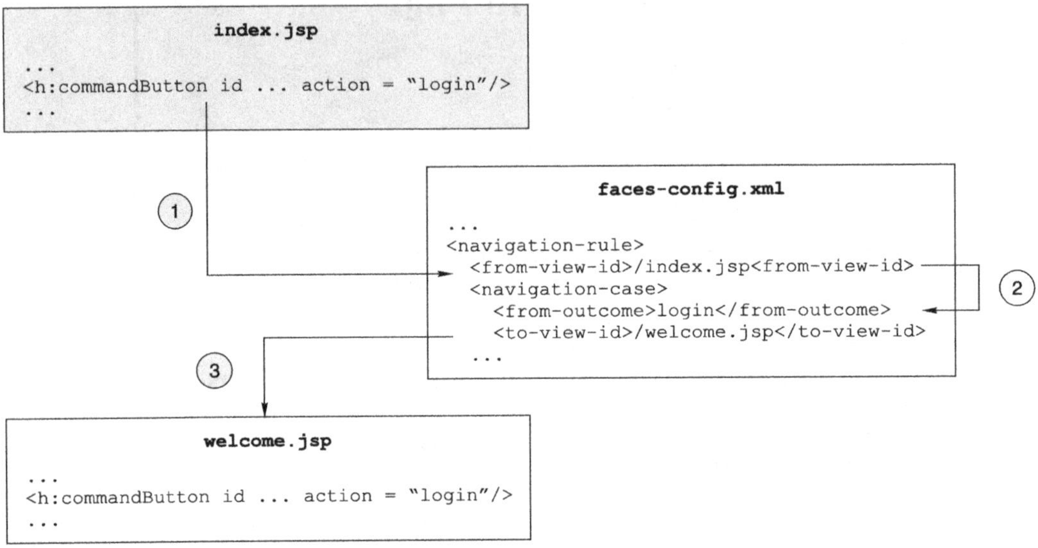

Fig. 10.96 *Understanding JSF flow*

There is a sequence of events when a request is sent to a JSF page is called as the *JSF request processing lifecycle*, or simply *JSF lifecycle*. For example:

```
<h:inputText value="#{modelBean.username}" />
```

This specifies that when the form is submitted, the value entered by the user in the input text box should be passed on to the corresponding property in the server-side JavaBean named *modelBean*.

Let us understand this.

1. As we can see, the *index.jsp* page is supposed to execute something called as *login*. Now, what is this login? It is a like a placeholder. It says that *if index.jsp is saying "login", then we want to do something*. Now, what is that *something*? It is *welcome.jsp*. In other words, we are saying that *if "login.jsp" says login, please transfer control to "welcome.jsp"*.
2. Therefore, control would now come to *welcome.jsp*. However, this would not happen directly. Remember, we had stated earlier that some of the user controls on the HTML page refer to some properties in the *UserBean* Java class? Hence, the control passes to the *UserBean* class first, and after that, it goes to the *welcome.jsp* page.
3. The *welcome.jsp* simply picks up the user name from the bean and displays a welcome message back to the user.

The *UserBean* class is shown in Fig. 10.97 and the *welcome.jsp* code is shown in Fig. 10.98.

```
package com.jsf.login;

public class UserBean {

    private String name;
    private String password;

    public String getName() {
        return name;
    }

    public void setName(String userName) {
        name = userName;
    }

    public String getPassword() {
        return password;
    }

    public void setPassword(String userPassword) {
        password = userPassword;
    }

}
```

Fig. 10.97 *UserBean.java*

```
<%@ taglib uri="http://java.sun.com/jsf/core" prefix="f" %>
<%@ taglib uri="http://java.sun.com/jsf/html" prefix="h" %>

<html>
   <f:view>
      <head>
         <title>Welcome to JSF!</title>
      </head>

      <body>
         <h:form>
              <h1 align="center">
                <h:outputText id="txtUserName" value="Welcome #{UserBean.
name}!" />
              </h1>
         </h:form>

      </body>
   </f:view>
</html>
```

Fig. 10.98 *welcome.jsp*

Figure 10.99 shows the output.

Fig. 10.99 *Output of welcome.jsp*

ENTERPRISE JAVABEANS (EJB) 10.9

10.9.1 Introduction

We develop applications to runs our business faster and with more efficiency. 'Business logic'- which is a program or a similar entity in an application - plays a key role in making the application perform the expected activity. In a Payroll application, the program that calculates the salary or generates the pay slip is some business logic. So, writing the business logic is the 'key' thing we application developers need to do. It is good practice to place business logic and presentations in separate layers. This helps in reducing the coupling between the presentation logic and business logic. Business logic can change with no or minimum impact to Presentation layer. Also the same business logic can be used by different presentation layers. Business logic to convert the currencies can be used by different module in the same application or altogether different applications.

For small applications, all the business logic or functionality could be written using few programs. However Enterprise applications have lots of functionalities to provide and the environment in which they run may be complex having database is at a different location or supporting lots of simultaneous users, etc. So writing the business logic or **Business Logic Layer (BLL)**, as it is commonly known as, for these applications would also involve handling the complexities, like interaction with remote database, managing parallel execution, etc. This would involve writing programs that would deal with low-level system details like managing transactions, threads, database access, load balancing, etc. These additional functionalities which need to be provided in Enterprise Application (Transaction Management, Security, etc.) would be needed for every such Enterprise Application and so it would be good if 'someone else' provides these and reduces the developer's task. This 'someone' is Application Server or precisely **EJB Container** inside the Application Server. When the Application Server can take care of these mundane, low-level activities, developers can concentrate on only implementing the business logic. How do developers now implement the business logic, so that container can execute it correctly along with performing its mundane activities when needed? *Enterprise JavaBeans* is one of the ways of implementing the business logic for Enterprise Applications.

10.9.2 What is 'Enterprise' Java Beans

Enterprise JavaBeans are server-side components which can be used to represent the business logic or data. Although it is possible to use standard Java objects to implement the business logic, using EJBs addresses Enterprise Application related requirements of scalability, life cycle management, and state management, which are not easy to implement using simple Java objects. We shall understand the EJB Technology, architecture and learn to use EJB in the next sections.

10.9.3 Need of Component Technology

An Enterprise Application can have functionality which may be used more than once (reuse) or may interact with other systems (external interfacing). If the reusable functionality, or external entity has clearly defined boundaries (input, output), managing the interactions is easier. This can be made possible by implementing the business functionality in form of components. Software **Component is a pluggable unit, consisting of one or more programs, that fulfils a clear function and is accessed through interfaces.** Components can be changed without impacting other components or entities which they interact with. The relationship between the components can be defined outside them, thus making it easy to manage. So using a clearly defined component for writing business logic in an Enterprises Application would help in reuse, separation of responsibilities[1], easier application maintenance. At design time the business logic or concepts are mapped to some artifact or component such as Salary calculation unit, Payslip Generation Component, etc. These components have clearly defined input, perform some activity and provide some output. Lets us understand how Enterprise JavaBeans are different from simple Java programs.

10.9.4 Enterprise Java Bean Compared to Java Beans

Table 10.2 *Java Bean compared with EJB*

Java Bean	*Enterprise Java Bean*
Java Beans are governed by Java Bean specifications.	EJB is governed by EJB specifications.
Java Bean is plain Java class which must have getter/setter methods and no value constructor.	EJB can be any Java component which is written as per EJB specifications.
Java Bean does not depend on container for its life cycle management. Client can directly create objects of Java Beans.	EJB depends of EJB Container and EJB clients cannot create objects on EJB.
Public methods of Java Bean are accessible to all the other classed. Precisely, the access is governed by only access specifies(public, private, protected).	Only those methods of EJB are accessible to clients that are exposed through the business interface.
Java Bean architecturally does not need any supporting class or interface.	EJB must have interface(s) which provide the view of the EJB.
Java Beans can be used in any type of Java Application.	EJB are typically used only in Enterprise Applications.
Same Java Bean instance may not be accessed by many clients.	Same EJB instance may be accessed by multiple clients.

[1] 'Separation of Concern' Design Pattern

10.9.5 EJB Technology

Enterprise JavaBeans (EJB) technology is an architecture which is based on EJB Specification provided by Sun Microsystems. EJB Technology is supposed to provide framework for business component that may be plugged in to compliant Application Server (Container) and will provide functionalities in addition to Application Servers. Enterprise JavaBeans are used to perform various types of task like interacting with the client, maintaining session for the clients retrieving and holding data from the database and communicating with the server.

EJB Technology has three main parts – EJB Specifications, EJB Containers and EJB Components.

1. EJB Specifications define the responsibilities of client, server (container) and the component. They are the contract which needs to be followed by all intending to use EJB Technology. When we refer to EJB version, EJB 2.1, EJB 3.0, etc., it is the EJB specification version that we are referring to, because everything else in EJB architecture is designed and implemented according to the specifications.

2. EJB Containers is a program that runs on server and implements EJB Specification. It takes care of EJB Components' life cycle management, security, transaction management, scalability, resource management, concurrency control, load balancing, persistence, etc. Single EJB Container can have multiple EJB Components.EJB Containers are provided by vendors (generally Application Server vendors, as EJB Container is part of Application server), ensuring that they provide all the functionality EJB Container is supposed to provide according to EJB Specifications. So popular EJB compliant Application Server are Oracle Weblogic, IBM WebSphere, GlassFish, JBoss. *Please refer to XXX for more details about Container.*

3. EJB Component is the actual program(s), written by developer, which contains the business logic. EJB Specifications ensure that same EJB Components can run in any EJB complaint container and developer code will be vendor-independent.

In this chapter, we will discuss the EJB Components in detail as developers create only EJB Components and only 'use' EJB Containers and 'refer' to EJB Specifications. For convenience, any further reference to EJB would mean EJB Component.

To summarize:
EJB Components are managed by and accessible through an EJB Container running inside EJB Server.

10.9.6 Accessing EJB Through Clients

EJB can be accessed by any Java or non-Java client (through CORBA). **EJB Client** is the code which will use the EJB functionality. Clients cannot create objects of EJB class/Component and Container manages the life cycle, i.e., creation, destroying of EJB Components. **Clients can access any EJB only through the EJB container.**

Some of the EJB clients can be

1. in an Enterprise Application, to access an EJB from the Web tier the client can be written using **JSP, Servlets** or any other server-side presentation tier technology.
2. an EJB can access another EJB on the same or a different Application Server.
3. a Web service can access an EJB (refer to chapter 9 for understanding Web services. In this chapter we are going to deal with making our EJB 'usable' by a Web Service.)
4. EJB can also be accessed from a simple Java class, Applet and other Java Technologies.

EJB Clients and EJB Component may be part of different application or different JVMs. This would involve using Java RMI (Remote Method Invocation) API to calling EJB from the client. We need not learn Java RMI separately to use EJBs; however we are including some relevant RMI basics to help us understand EJBs better. In Java RMI, the client does not call the methods directly on the remote object. Instead, the client calls methods on '*Stub*' (client side representative of remote object). Stub passes the information over network to '*Skeleton*' (server side entity to interact with remote object). Skeleton then speaks to remote object, EJB in this case. The figure below explains this RMI w.r.t to EJB.

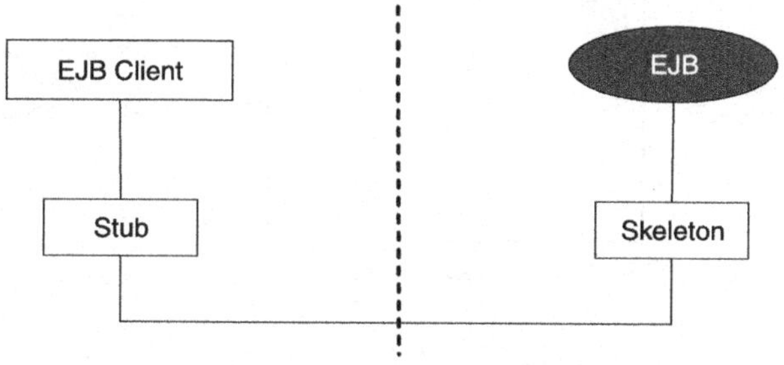

Fig. 10.100 *Client accessing Remote EJB*

Container provides the stub and skeleton at runtime to enable accessing EJBs as remote object.

EJB ARCHITECTURE — OVERVIEW.. 10.10

Development using EJB Technology is little different from distributed application development techniques. This is primarily because of EJB architecture.

EJB Architecture primarily comprises of - EJB Component, Application Server and its services (JNDI, JTA, JMS, JAAS, etc.), EJB Container, Container generated classes (which we shall not discuss as it does not have any impact on our application development) and EJB Client.

EJB Component contains the business logic, which is accessed by EJB Client through the EJB Container. Key role of EJB Container is to provide the low-level services, implemented by Application server, to the EJB Component. EJB class object cannot be directly created by client, nor can client create stub, skeleton or anything else in the architecture. Then, how will client be able to know what does the EJB do, or how will it tell the container to call the 'specific' EJB? Lets us understand this by exploring how EJB is visible at client side.

EJB exposes its methods in form of some interface(s) called business interface, which is accessed from client side. *Business interface* will have same method signatures as in EJB, so the client can access this interface and when client invokes a method on the business interface, container executes the corresponding method on the implementing EJB. for example, business interface and EJB both may have method getEmployeeData(String empid). Client will call method on business interface and the method implemented in the corresponding EJB will be invoked. Apart from shielding the access the EJB, accessing EJB through business interface secures the EJB code, as no implementation code is shared at the client side. We shall explore more about types of EJB interfaces little later. The Fig 10.101 explains the EJB architecture used by client to access the EJB.

Why is EJB accessible only through interfaces?

EJB Container needs to provide services like Distribution, Transaction Management, Security, Resource Management, etc., to the EJB. If EJB method has to be executed in a separate transaction the Container

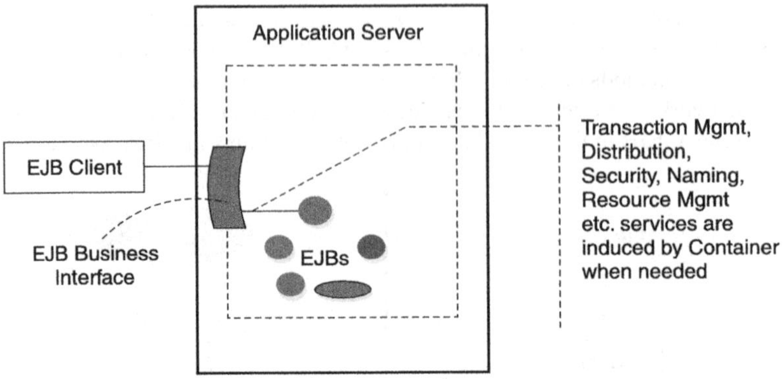

Fig. 10.101 *Client accessing the EJB through the Container*

has to ensure that a new transaction is started before the method starts and commit/rollback it after the method completes. All the other similar services, which are needed for large enterprise applications, can be provided only if Container is involved in between the client and EJB communication. In order to support these services Container now takes the responsibility of creating, invoking and destroying the EJB objects (life cycle management) depending on the client requests. Since the client cannot create EJB class objects, they get the business interface through which they can access the EJB methods. Also, accessing the EJB through interface helps in reducing the dependency between client and component; helps in maintaining the security of EJB classes and is required as per Component architecture. The separation of client reference and bean instance also allows container to provide efficient resource management, pooling, lazy initialization, transparent clustering support, concurrency control with guaranteed single-threaded bean instance and good error handling. We shall explore the container provided services in detail in relevant sections.

10.10.1 How to Design EJB?

When we design the application, the EJBs are part of Business tier. Which logic or components should be exposed as EJB is a question which needs should be thought over seriously to get maximum benefits of EJB technology. EJB are some coarse-grained components so generally, any large individual class or set of related classes which provide a complete functionality or deal with independent data unit can be implemented as EJB. For example, Class used for salary computation, bank account management, employee add/update/delete can be implemented using EJB.

10.10.2 Benefits of EJB

Some of the benefits of using EJB are:

1. EJBs simplify the development of large, distributed applications, as developer needs to concentrate only on business logic.
2. EJB Container provides system-level services to EJB and this ensures that tried-and-tested solutions are available to do this in form of different application servers.
3. EJBs help in separation and loose coupling between presentation and business logic. The helps in changing one without much impact on the other tier.

4. EJB Clients need not bother about implementing business rules or accessing databases. As a result, the clients are thinner, a benefit that is particularly important for clients that run on small devices.
5. EJBs are portable components, they can be developed once and then deployed on multiple platforms without recompilation or source code modification; the application assembler can build new applications from existing beans. These applications can run on any compliant application server.
6. The EJB specification that governs the use of enterprise beans is compatible with other Java™ APIs and CORBA. It also provides for interoperability between EJBs and non-Java applications.

10.10.3 When to Use EJB

According to EJB Specification- **EJB are scalable, transactional, distributed components**- this in itself defines when to use EJB. To use EJB or not is totally dependent on application requirements. We shall list some of the application requirements where using EJB can be beneficial:

1. **When the application must be scalable** If the application will need to scale beyond initial low usage levels then using EJB would help in accommodating a growing number of concurrent users. For example, for online banking where number of user would grow with increased awareness and access to technology.
2. **When the application is distributed** When the resources and data are distributed across multiple sites, then it is ideal to go for an application that is based on EJBs. Not only can the enterprise beans of an application run on different machines, but also their location will remain transparent to the clients. For example, for Tax calculation application, which may need to interact with multiple other applications.
3. **When application needs transactions** Transactions can be used to ensure data integrity and also manage the concurrent access of shared objects. EJBs support transactions so when transaction management is required, EJBs may be used. In EJB we can specify our transaction the EJB container will manage the transaction boundaries appropriately. In any other non-transactional technology, we will have to write code to manage the transaction, which is not easy especially when multiple resources need to be accessed. For example, when closing bank account, the corresponding checks and loan closures, etc., may have to be performed, ideally inside a transaction, to ensure it's all done or not done at all. This is best implemented using EJBs.
4. **When access to application modules changes with user roles** Using EJBs different security roles can be allowed or disallowed to access part of business functionality. Using this EJB security configuration feature, multiple user roles can be server in the application easily. For example, only admin user role can be given access to delete the employee records.
5. **When application may be accessed by variety of client** EJBs can be accessed by Java Client (simple Java Class, Applet, Servlet, any other presentation tier framework, from EJBs, Web services, etc.) or non-Java client. Client side code for accessing EJB from different clients does not vary much. So when the application may be accessed by variety of clients, it is better to use EJBs.
6. **When the application needs server cluster** Server cluster is when more than one servers (all sharing the application load) are used to cater to the application clients, mostly used for better performance. Applications Servers can use load balancing to ensure optimum use of each server in the cluster. Using EJBs help in writing code which can be handled well even in clustered environment.

7. **When application needs to be modular** When the presentation tier needs to be separated from business tier and needs to be managed separately, EJBs can be used for quick development. Also when business logic needs to be implemented in modules, it can be easily separated using different EJBs.

TYPES OF EJB.. 10.11

Enterprise JavaBeans, being a part of Enterprise application, are used to perform various types of task like interacting with the client, performing some business logic for the client, maintaining a conversational session for a particular client, retrieving and holding data from the database, communicating with the server and external resources. For facilitating all these and other various types of use EJBs can be put into, EJBs are categorized into 3 types. These 3 types of EJBs are structurally and architecturally different, each one being used in different situations.

Three types of EJBs are:

1. **Session beans** Session beans, also called SB, are most widely used type of EJBs. They can be used to perform any task for the client, so are typically used to implement the business logic. Session beans are non-persistent and should not be used for database interactions. To write a Session bean we need to define a business interface and the session bean class. Session beans can be used by variety of clients both local and remote. Session beans can also implement a Web service and can be used to cater to Web service. We will explore Session bean in detail in Sections 10.14.
2. **Message Driven bean** Message Driven Beans, also called MDB, are type of EJB which are invoked only by messages. They act as a listener for JMS message and can further process the message. Clients can invoke MDB by sending the message at the destination where the MDB is listening *asynchronously* at and not by calling any method on the MDB. To write a MDB we need to define the bean class which implements a particular message listener. No business interfaces are needed for MDBs as client cannot invoke any methods. MDBs can further use SBs to perform any other business activity and can provide separation between message processing and business logic. We shall explore Message Driven Bean in section 5.6.
3. **Entity bean** Entity Bean is type of EJB used for database persistence. They can be used to interact with database. Persistence in Entity Bean can be managed by the container or by the bean. Entity Beans are not very successful and have been replaced with Java Persistence API (JPA) since EJB3.0.

SESSION BEANS 10.12

Session beans are type of EJBs which primarily contain the business logic. According to EJB architecture, every session bean instance in the container would represent the client accessing it. **A session bean corresponds to a client server session**, a *single conversation* between the session bean client and the EJB container where the session bean is deployed. The client invokes the session bean's methods to access an application that is deployed on the server. One client-server session would last till the session bean method invoked by client is completed. Session Beans exists for the duration of this single the conversation (session) between the client and server. So **they are short-lived**. For example, if a client invokes processSalary(), the session bean would exist till the method completes, including calls to other methods or EJBs.

Session beans are generally the first type of EJB which would be accessed from clients outside the business tier. It is recommended to use session beans for implementing business logic rather than database interaction. Session beans are non-persistent EJBs, i.e., the values in the session bean instance cannot be persisted.

An application when used by multiple clients would have many session beans. It is not possible and feasible to **create** one session bean instance for each client request. However every client request would need a session bean to invoke the called method. How does the container manage to cater to large number of client requests with limited number of session beans? Container achieves this by '*pooling*' the bean instances. We know, the container manages the life-cycle of the EJB, so container can create and destroy EJBs whenever needed. **Instead of creating a new EJB instance for every client requests, container creates a predefined number of (can be configured) EJB instances. This is called 'pool' of EJB instances.** Whenever client request is received, one of the EJB instances - which is not doing some activity currently- can be picked from the pool and the client request can be executed by invoking the method on 'this' selected EJB instance. This pooling ensures optimum use of resources. The algorithm to pick the EJB instance is completely container vendor specific, and it does not impact our EJB implementation. For example, Pool of SalaryProcessingBean would mean all the instances of SalaryProcessingBean and when client request to invoke a method on this bean, one of these instances from the pool will be picked.

Pooling is managed differently for different types of EJBs. We shall explore the relevant details while discussing the specific EJB type. Figure below depicts client accessing EJB from the EJB pool.

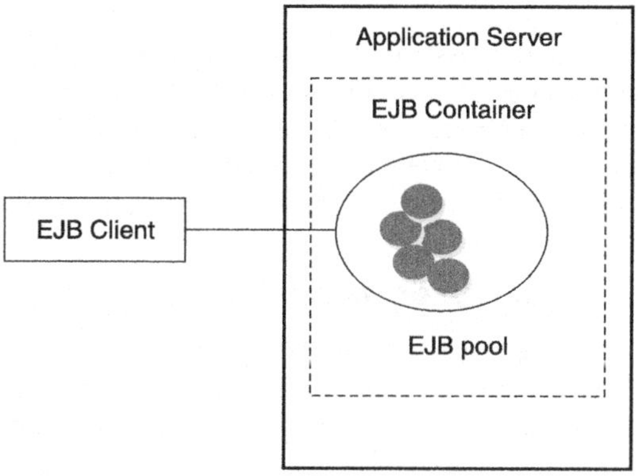

Fig. 10.102 *EJB Client accessing the pool of EJB instances*

Session bean cannot be shared across multiple clients, at any point of time one session bean caters to only one client request and represents the client. After the interaction with the client is over the session bean has no reference of client nor does the client know anything about the session bean instance. So no information that is part of session bean is available after the interaction between the client and session bean is over. This in other words this mean that session bean are non-persistent, i.e., they cannot be saved.

Session beans will remain as long as client invokes the methods. If the session bean remains idle long enough, more than defined idle timeout, the container can destroy the bean. Clients can call methods of session beans to use the functionality of the session bean. Session beans can also call to other session beans and entity beans.

The session between the client and session bean can be for a single invocation or multiple invocation in one session. There are two different types of session bean is used for both of these situations. They are:

1. Stateless Session bean session lasts for a single invocation
2. Stateful Session bean session lasts for multiple invocations

We shall explore the types of session beans in details in the following sections.

10.12.1 When to Use Session Beans

Session beans should be used to implement the business logic. If the need for EJB is finalized, session bean can be used in following situations:

1. To implement the business logic to be used again and again.
2. To perform the processing to be done before or after the database interaction and not actual database handling. For example, Appropriate data formatting to be done before or after data is saved/retrieved from database can be done using a session bean.
3. If the logic would be accessed by a single client at a time, i.e., no parallel executions on same bean object would be needed.
4. When Web service needs to be implemented for an enterprise application.
5. When the data in the bean need not be persisted.
6. When the container provided transaction, security management needs to use.
7. When the business logic needs to reside on different physical or logical tieOnce the decision to use session bean has been finalized, we can choose to use appropriate type of session bean – Stateless or Stateful.

Once we have decided to use the session Bean we will have to create:

1. Bean Class containing the implementations of business methods.
2. Business Interface containing the business method definition.

We shall discuss about writing the bean class in details in the subsequent sections. Let's now understand how to decide the type of business interface to be used to expose the bean to the clients.

10.12.2 Deciding to use Remote or Local Interface

Clients access the session bean using the business interface. Depending on the location of the client with respect to the bean class different types of business interface used are:

1. **Remote interface** Remote interface is used by the client that may be running on a different machine than the bean and needs to access the bean remotely using RMI.
2. **Local interface** Local interface is used by the client can coexist with the bean in the same JVM.

Session bean may provide both local and remote interface depending on the type of clients that will access the bean. When deciding between local and remote interface following aspects can be considered:

Table 10.3 *Remote or local interface*

Aspect	*Remote Interface*	*Local Interface*
Location transparency	Used when the client need not know the location of the EJB and accesses it transparently.	Used when the client knows that the EJB resides in the same JVM.
Protocol used	Client used RMI –IIOP to access the EJB.	Client accesses the EJB using local calls.

(Contd.)

Table 10.3 *Contd...*

Type of client	If the clients are application clients, Web components, EJBs, etc., executing on different machines.	If the client are Web component or other enterprise bean which will be executed in the same JVM as the EJB.
Coupling	If there is loose coupling between the client and the EJB. So when they may change without impacting each other using remote interface is a better choice.	If EJB is being accessed from another EJB/Web component which is tightly coupled and all of them put together form part of same business logic then local interface is a better choice.
Distributed components	If the components in the application may be distributed, i.e., may lie at different locations, remote interface would be used.	If the components or execution may not be distributed, local interface can be used.
Performance	Expensive remote call as RMI is involved. Distributed execution may help especially when the application may have heavy loads.	Better performance as locally accessed. For large applications distribution may help in better performance.
Parameter granularity	Since the remote calls are slower it is better to use fewer coarse grained parameters. Value object may be used as parameters.	Parameters can be fine grained.
Serialization	Objects must be serialized to be passed as parameters to remote EJB.	Serialization of objects is not involved.
Parameter passing	Objects are passed by value as client and the bean operate on different copies of the object.	Objects are passed by reference and client and bean can change the values of the same object.

If there is slightest possibility of remote clients or decision between the types of interface could not be made-choose remote interface. Using remote interface gives the flexibility to add variety of clients. Local clients can access EJB which have only remote interface but remote clients cannot access EJBs which have only local interface.

EJB can have any number of any type of (Remote or local) business interfaces. EJB may have more than one local interface or more than one remote interface if it needs to provide different views to different local and remote clients. However the same business interface cannot be both a local and remote business interface.

Local business interface will be accessible only if:

1. The client and EJB are in the same ejb-jar package as the EJB.
2. The client and EJB is in different ejb-jar but in the same ear file.
3. The client is packed in war (Servlet client), EJB is packed in ejb-jar and both are part of same ear.

In all the other cases remote interface needs to be used, including when the client is on same server but different ear.

For example, ManageEmployee bean may have following business interfaces:

1. Local interface L1 which provide methods to upload and retrieve employee details. This interface would be used by HR related EJB or Web component from to manage the employees of the same organization.
2. Local interface L2 which provide methods to only view the employee skills. This interface can be used by training department to check the training needs.
3. Remote interface R1 which provides methods to update employee salary. This interface would be used by third-party payroll service to update the payroll details.

4. Remote interface R2 which provides employee nomination and dependent details. This interface would be used by provident fund trust to get the nomination details.

JNDI LOOKUP 10.13

EJB clients can access using dependency injection engine or using JNDI lookup. Using JNDI lookup the bean interface has to be looked up using JNDI. JNDI lookup can be used even when dependency injection engine is available.

The JNDI service provider, which is part of the Application Server, might need specific information to connect to the directory service. This information can be location of machine in the network on which the directory server is running or the username and password to authenticate the client to the service. This information is provided to the service provider using the environment properties specified by the JNDI.

The steps to obtain bean reference through JNDI lookup are:

1. Acquire JNDI context referring to appropriate JNDI Service. JNDI Context is an object which contain object to name bindings.
2. Lookup the bean through the JNDI context.

10.13.1 Acquire JNDI Context

The information needed to define and use JNDI Service is are:

1. Server's DNS Host name
2. Socket Port number for JNDI service
3. JNDI Service class name, i.e., initial context factory class

Vendor specific additional information like credentials, etc., may be needed.

To acquire JNDI context the JNDI service information listed above needs to provided as environment properties to the application which needs to use JNDI Service to add or lookup the objects.

The application can access the properties defined in following ways:

1. Using environment variables or through command line arguments with java –D option.
2. Using `jndi.properties` file located at JRE home or `in classpath`.
3. Using a hashtable to define the properties in the code.

The first two options listed above are used to pre-configure JNDI for the entire environment. Using these options the properties can defined once and can be used in all the programs that run in the environment. These options are commonly used define JNDI properties in Application Server, Web server, etc.

Hashtable would be used in java classes that run outside a JNDI provider, say a simple java class, applet, etc.

We shall now write code to acquire JNDI Context in both the way- through predefined JNDI Service and using a new or different JNDI Service.

1. Using default JNDI properties For clients running on the server that has default JNDI service configured, the JNDI context can be obtained using InitialContext object. This can be used for JSP, Servlets, EJB running on the same server as EJB.

```
e.g.
    javax.naming.InitialContext  iCon =  new InitialContext();
```

2. Configuring separate JNDI properties For clients not having a default JNDI service configured, the JNDI properties can be specified using hahstable. The properties set in this hashtable can be used to create the JNDI Context.

This way of specifying JNDI properties can also be used to provide additional JNDI properties like security credentials, etc., or when a different JNDI service needs to be used. Also for accessing a Remote EJB from a non-Java EE Web container like Tomcat, JNDI properties have to be specified in the Java code using the Hashtable.

Hashtable is used to specify the following (minimum requirement) JNDI properties:

1. INITIAL_CONTEXT_FACTORY Specifies which initial context factory to use when creating initial context.
2. PROVIDER_URL The url that application client code uses to look up objects on the server. This includes the server name and JNDI Socket port number.

Application server references should be used to find additional JNDI parameters required.

For example,

```
Hashtable env = new Hashtable();
 env.put(Context.INITIAL_CONTEXT_FACTORY,"
jnp.interfaces.NamingContextFactory ");
env.put(Context.PROVIDER_URL, "127.0.0.1:1099");
javax.naming.InitialContext iCon = new InitialContext(env);
```

10.13.2 Lookup the EJB Through JNDI

To get the bean reference, we have to use lookup method and specify the JNDI name of the bean.

Syntax is

```
context.lookup(JNDIname);
```

For Sun Java Application Server EJB JNDI subcontext is **`java:comp/env/ejb`**

So the JNDI name for EJBs is java:comp/env/ejb/<bean name>

For example, JNDI name of EmployeeBean would be `java:comp/env/ejb/EmployeeBean`

Some containers allow specifying the lookup name relative to java:com/env or java:com/env/ejb [Check vendor specifications for details]

For looking up a bean in such container the only beanname or the `ejb/beanname` needs to specified, i.e., "`EmployeeBean`" or "`ejb/EmployeeBean`" can be used.

Bean can also be accessed by looking up the bean class name, i.e., `EmployeeBean.class`

Interface can be accessed by looking up the interface class name, i.e., `EmployeeBeanRemote.class`

If EJB is deployed in ear then the JNDI name can also be accessed relative to ear name as: `earname/ejbname`

As we lookup the bean business interface the **lookup name** depending on type of interface would be:

JNDI name of the bean/local or

JNDI name of the bean/remote

EmployeeBean having `EmployeeBeanRemote` and `EmployeeBeanLocal` interfaces, packed in ourEJB.ear, can be accessed by following lookup values:

```
context.lookup("java:comp/env/ejb/EmployeeBean")
contect.lookup("ejb/EmployeeBean")
context.lookup(EmployeeBeanRemote.class) or
```

```
context.lookup(EmployeeBeanLocal.class)
context.lookup("ourEJB/ EmployeeBean/remote") or context.
lookup("ourEJB/ EmployeeBean/local")
```

Key Terms and Concepts

Actions • Bean class • Bean-managed persistent entity beans • Business interface • Callable statement • Client code • Connection object • Container-managed persistent entity beans • Controller • Cookies • Custom tags • Declarations • Description • Directives • Enterprise JavaBean (EJB) • Entity beans • Expression Language (EL) • Expressions • J2EE 5.0 • Java Archive (JAR) • Java Database Connectivity (JDBC) • Java Enterprise Edition 5.0 • Java Naming and Directory API (JNDI) • Java Virtual Machine (JVM) • JavaBean • JavaServer Faces (JSF) • JDK • JEE 5.0 • JRE • JSF • JSP Standard Template Library (JSTL) • Location transparency • Message Driven Bean (MDB) • Model • Model-View-Controller (MVC) • Multi-user support • Object • Open source framework • Persistence • Remote awareness • Scripting elements • Scriptlets • Server controls • Servlet container • Session • Session beans • Session ID • Session management • Session state management • Stateful session beans • Stateless session beans • Struts • Templates • Transaction management • URL rewriting • View • Web controls

SUMMARY

- The Java Web technologies have evolved over a number of years, starting Java Servlets.
- Servlets are programs written in Java that execute on the Web server, in response to a request from the Web browser to produce HTML content dynamically.
- Servlets are a bit tedious to write. Hence, Sun microsystems came up with Java Server Pages (JSP).
- A JSP is a program written using HTML and Java languages, to produce and send back a Web page to the browser, in response to an HTTP request.
- JSPs are easier to write than Servlets.
- Over a period of time, Sun microsystems came up with a model, which could use both Servlets as well as JSPs in a single application.
- JSP and Servlets provide support for all kinds of Java technologies, e.g., JDBC for database access, JavaBeans for easier programming, etc.
- The Enterprise JavaBeans (EJB) technology allows us to write server-side business components, that can be used by programs such as Servlets and JSPs as and when needed.
- EJB should be used only if the application is quite demanding or intensive in nature, needing performance, security, load balancing, etc.
- The technology of Java Server Faces (JSF) has been developed to allow Web programmers to write extensive user validations and to provide richer user interface to the end users.
- JSF allows the developers to write user validations and perform other user interface related activities without writing too much of complex code, but instead, to do this in a declarative fashion.
- The technology of Struts is another technology for developing rapid Web applications. It allows the developers to quickly develop a Web-based application containing business rules and navigation.

MULTIPLE-CHOICE QUESTIONS

1. The ____ is usually made up of a Web browser, which means it can primarily deal with HTML pages and JavaScript.
   (a) client tier (b) server tier
   (c) Internet layer (d) proxy server
2. Support for Web services is provided by the_____ APIs.
   (a) TAPI (b) JAX-WS
   (c) SOAP (d) JAXB
3. A Servlet runs inside ____.
   (a) Servlet container (b) browser
   (c) applet (d) Web-enabled browser
4. A Servlet container is the _________ environment for a Java Servlet.
   (a) working (b) browsing
   (c) hosting and execution (d) broadcasting
5. A JSP page is composed of ________.
   (a) directives (b) scripting elements
   (c) actions (d) templates
6. The following snippet of code
   `<%= new java.util.Date ( ) %> is ____.`
   (a) comment (b) expression
   (c) variable (d) condition
7. The ______ object is used to reed read the values of the HTML form in a JSP, received as a part of the HTTP request sent by the client to the server.
   (a) Page (b) Request
   (c) Response (d) PageContext
8. ___ is the pipe between a Java program and the RDBMS.
   (a) Response (b) Object
   (c) Page (d) Connection object
9. _______ is used to define and execute dynamic SQL statements.
   (a) PreparedStatement (b) CallableStatement
   (c) ResultSet object (d) Page
10. The ____ is used to prepare and send the resulting output back to the user.
    (a) model (b) view
    (c) controller (d) JavaScript

DETAILED QUESTIONS

1. Discuss in detail Sun's Java server architecture.
2. What is a Servlet? Explain how a Servlet is processed.
3. What are the elements of a JSP page?
4. Write a Servlet which will accept user name and password in a form, which will compare both in the database display *success* or *failure*.

5. Why is session management is required in JSP/Servlet?
6. Write a JSP scriptlet for displaying even numbers between 1 to 50 and also its JSTL version.
7. How do transaction in JDBC happen?
8. Discuss MVC architecture in detail.
9. Explain JSF in detail and discuss how it affects the Web development.
10. Write a Java servlet which will display *Welcome to Servlet* message.

EXERCISES

1. Find out the different Servlet containers available. Study their features and also differences.
2. Examine how real-life Web sites perform user data entry validations.
3. Evaluate the various Java Integrated Development Environments (IDEs), such as NetBeans, Eclipse, and JDeveloper.
4. Mention all the plug-in available with the Apache MyJSF.
5. Explain where MVC can be used in real life Web sites (e.g., Amazon or ICICI Bank).

WEB SECURITY 11

INTRODUCTION

Most initial computer applications had *no*, or at best, *very little* security. This continued for a number of years until the importance of data was truly realized. Until then, computer data was considered to be useful, but not something to be protected. When computer applications were developed to handle financial and personal data, the real need for security was felt like never before. People realized that data on computers is an extremely important aspect of modern life. Therefore, various areas in security began to gain prominence. Two typical examples of such security mechanisms were as follows:

1. Provide a user id and password to every user, and use that information to authenticate a user.
2. Encode information stored in the databases in some fashion, so that it is not visible to users who do not have the right permissions.
3. Provide a user id and password to every user, and use that information to authenticate a user.
4. Encode information stored in the databases in some fashion, so that it is not visible to users who do not have the right permissions.

Organizations employed their own mechanisms in order to provide for these kinds of basic security mechanisms. As technology improved, the communication infrastructure became extremely mature, and newer and newer applications began to be developed for various user demands and needs. Soon, people realized the basic security measures were not quite enough.

Furthermore, the Internet took the world by storm, and there were many examples of what could happen if there was insufficient security built in applications developed for the Internet. Figure 11.1 shows such an example of what can happen when you use your credit card for making purchases over the Internet. From the user's computer, the user details such as user id, order details such as order id and item id, and payment details such as credit card information travel across the Internet to the server (i.e., to the merchant's computer). The merchant's server stores these details in its database.

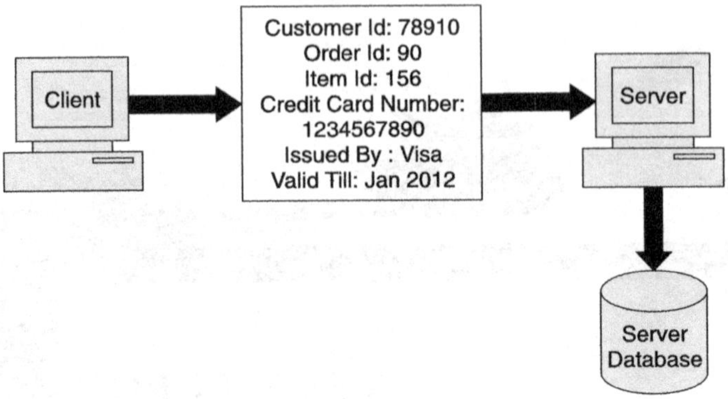

Fig. 11.1 *Example of information traveling from a client to a server over the Internet*

There are various security holes here. First of all, an intruder can capture the credit card details as they travel from the client to the server. If we somehow protect this transit from an intruder's attack, it still does not solve our problem. Once the merchant receives the credit card details and validates them so as to process the order and later obtain payments, the merchant stores the credit card details into its database. Now, an attacker can simply succeed in accessing this database, and therefore, gain access to all the credit card numbers stored therein! One Russian attacker (called Maxim) actually managed to intrude into a merchant Internet site and obtained 300,000 credit card numbers from its database. He then attempted extortion by demanding protection money ($100,000) from the merchant. The merchant refused to oblige. Following this, the attacker published about 25,000 of the credit card numbers on the Internet! Some banks reissued all the credit cards at a cost of $20 per card, and others forewarned their customers about unusual entries in their statements.

Such attacks could obviously lead to great losses – both in terms of finance and goodwill. Generally, it takes $20 to replace a credit card. Therefore, if a bank has to replace 3,00,000 such cards, the total cost of such an attack is about $6 million! How nice it would have been, if the merchant in the example just discussed had employed proper security measures!

Of course, this was just one example. Several such cases have been reported in the last few months, and the need for proper security is being felt increasingly with every such attack. In another example of this, in 1999, a Swedish hacker broke into Microsoft's Hotmail Web site, and created a mirror site. This site allowed anyone to enter any Hotmail user's email id, and read her emails!

In 1999, two independent surveys were conducted to invite people's opinions about the losses that occur due to successful attacks on security. One survey pegged the losses figure at an average of $256,296 per incident, and the other one's average was $759,380 per incident. Next year, this figure rose to $972,857!

PRINCIPLES OF SECURITY 11.1

Having discussed some of the attacks that have occurred in real life, let us now classify the principles related to security. This will help us understand the attacks better, and also help us in thinking about the possible solutions to tackle them. We shall take an example to understand these concepts.

Let us assume that a person A wants to send a check worth $100 to another person B. Normally, what are the factors that A and B will think of, in such a case? A will write the check for $100, put it inside an envelope, and send it to B.

1. A will like to ensure that no one except B gets the envelope, and even if someone else gets it, she does not come to know about the details of the check. This is the principle of **confidentiality**.
2. A and B will further like to make sure that no one can tamper with the contents of the check (such as its amount, date, signature, name of the payee, etc.). This is the principle of **integrity**.
3. B would like to be assured that the check has indeed come from A, and not from someone else posing as A (as it could be a fake check in that case). This is the principle of **authentication**.
4. What will happen tomorrow if B deposits the check in her account, the money is transferred from A's account to B's account, and then A refuses having written/sent the check? The court of law will use A's signature to disallow A to refute this claim, and settle the dispute. This is the principle of **non-repudiation**.

These are the four chief principles of security. There are two more, **access control** and **availability**, which are not related to a particular message, but are linked to the overall system as a whole.

We shall discuss all these security principles in the next few sections.

11.1.1 Confidentiality

The principle of *confidentiality* specifies that only the sender and the intended recipient(s) should be able to access the contents of a message. Confidentiality gets compromised if an unauthorized person is able to access a message. Example of compromising the confidentiality of a message is shown in Fig. 11.2. Here, the user of computer A sends a message to user of computer B. (Actually, from here onwards, we shall use the term A to mean the *user* A, B to mean *user* B, etc., although we shall just show the computers of user A, B, etc.). Another user C gets access to this message, which is not desired, and therefore, defeats the purpose of confidentiality. Example of this could be a confidential email message sent by A to B, which is accessed by C without the permission or knowledge of A and B. This type of attack is called **interception**.

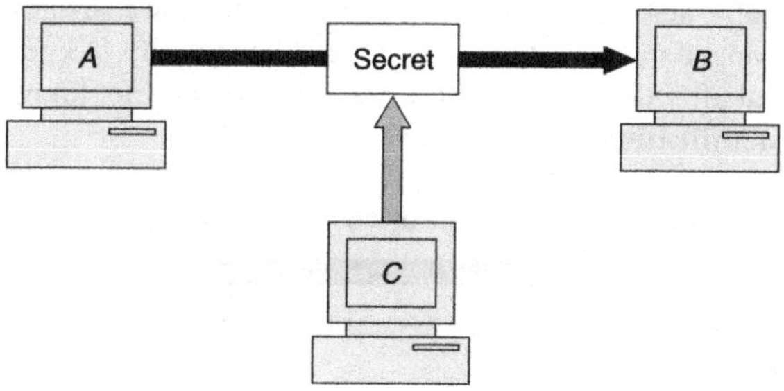

Fig. 11.2 *Loss of confidentiality*

Interception causes loss of message confidentiality.

11.1.2 Authentication

Authentication mechanisms help establish proof of identities. The authentication process ensures that the origin of a electronic message or document is correctly identified. For instance, suppose that user C sends an electronic document over the Internet to user B. However, the trouble is that user C had posed as user A when she sent this document to user B. How would user B know that the message has come from user C, who is posing as user A? A real life example of this could be the case of a user C, posing as user A, sending a funds transfer request (from A's account to C's account) to bank B. The bank might happily transfer the funds from A's account to C's account – after all, it would think that user A has requested for the funds transfer! This concept is shown in Fig. 11.3. This type of attack is called **fabrication**.

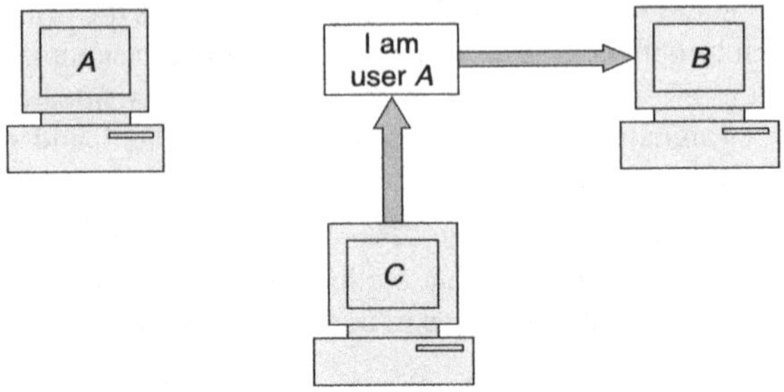

Fig. 11.3 *Absence of authentication*

Fabrication is possible in absence of proper authentication mechanisms.

11.1.3 Integrity

When the contents of a message are changed after the sender sends it, but before it reaches the intended recipient, we say that the *integrity* of the message is lost. For example, suppose you write a check for \$100 to pay for the goods bought from the US. However, when you see your next account statement, you are startled to see that the check resulted in a payment of \$1000! This is the case for loss of message integrity. Conceptually, this is shown in Fig. 11.4. Here, user C tampers with a message originally sent by user A, which is actually destined for user B. User C somehow manages to access it, change its contents, and send the changed message to user B. User B has no way of knowing that the contents of the message were changed after user A had sent it. User A also does not know about this change. This type of attack is called **modification**.

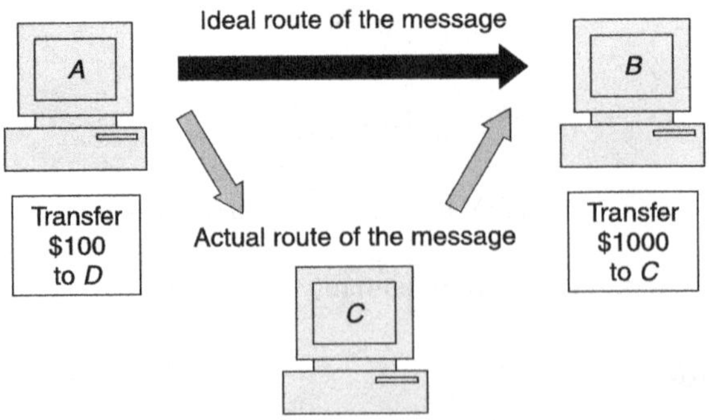

Fig. 11.4 *Loss of integrity*

Modification causes loss of message integrity.

11.1.4 Non-repudiation

There are situations where a user sends a message, and later on refuses that she had sent that message. For instance, user A could send a funds transfer request to bank B over the Internet. After the bank performs the funds transfer as per A's instructions, A could claim that she never sent the funds transfer instruction to the bank! Thus, A repudiates, or denies, her funds transfer instruction. The principle of *non-repudiation* defeats such possibilities of denying something, having done it. This is shown in Fig. 11.5.

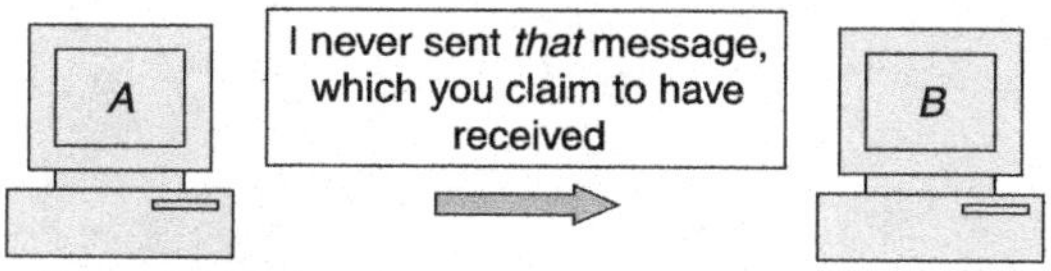

Fig. 11.5 *Establishing non-repudiation*

Non-repudiation does not allow the sender of a message to refute the claim of not sending that message.

11.1.5 Access Control

The principle of *access control* determines *who* should be able to access *what*. For instance, we should be able to specify that user A can view the records in a database, but cannot update them. However, user B might be allowed to make updates as well. An access control mechanism can be set up to ensure this. Access control is broadly related to two areas: *role management* and *rule management*. Role management concentrates on the user side (which user can do what), whereas rule management focuses on the resources side (which resource is accessible, and under what circumstances). Based on the decisions taken here, an access control matrix is prepared, which lists the users against a list of items they can access (e.g., it can say that user A can write to file X, but can only update files Y and Z). An **Access Control List (ACL)** is a subset of an access control matrix.

Access control specifies and controls who can access what.

11.1.6 Availability

The principle of *availability* states that resources (i.e., information) should be available to authorized parties at all times. For example, due to the intentional actions of another unauthorized user C, an authorized user A may not be able to contact a server computer B, as shown in Fig. 11.6. This would defeat the principle of availability. Such an attack is called **interruption**.

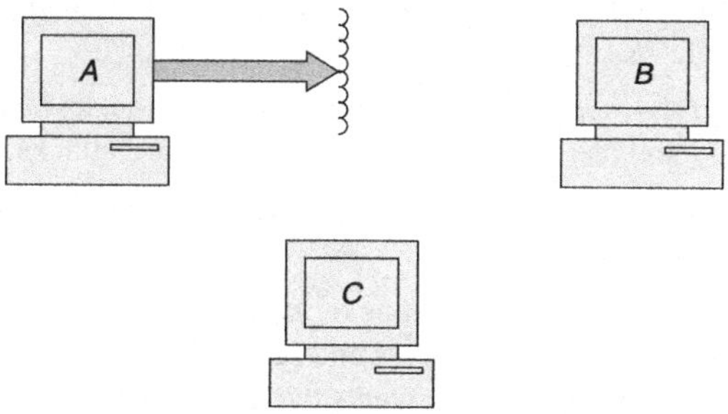

Fig. 11.6 *Attack on availability*

Interruption puts the availability of resources in danger.

We may be aware of the traditional OSI standard for Network Model (titled OSI Network Model 7498-1), which describes the seven layers of the networking technology (application, presentation, session, transport, network, data link, and physical). A very less known standard on similar lines is the **OSI standard for Security Model** (titled OSI Security Model 7498-2). This also defines seven layers of security in the form of

1. Authentication
2. Access control
3. Non-repudiation
4. Data integrity
5. Confidentiality
6. Assurance or availability
7. Notarization or signature

11.1.7 Specific Attacks

Sniffing and Spoofing On the Internet, computers exchange messages with each other in the form of small groups of data, called packets. A packet, like a postal envelope contains the actual data to be sent, and the addressing information. Attackers target these packets, as they travel from the source computer to the destination computer over the Internet. These attacks take two main forms: 1. **Packet sniffing** (also called **snooping**) and 2. **Packet spoofing**. Since the protocol used in this communication is called as Internet Protocol (IP), other names for these two attacks are: 1. **IP sniffing** and 2. **IP spoofing**. The meaning remains the same.

Let us discuss these two attacks.

1. Packet sniffing Packet sniffing is a passive attack on an ongoing conversation. An attacker need not *hijack* a conversation, but instead, can simply observe (i.e., *sniff*) packets as they pass by. Clearly, to prevent an attacker from sniffing packets, the information that is passing needs to be protected in some ways. This can be done at two levels: (a) The data that is traveling can be encoded in some ways, or (b) The transmission link itself can be encoded. To read a packet, the attacker somehow needs to access it in the first place. The simplest way to do this is to control a computer via which the traffic goes through. Usually, this is a router. However, routers are highly protected resources. Therefore, an attacker might not be able to attack it, and instead, attack a less-protected computer on the same path.

2. Packet spoofing In this technique, an attacker sends packets with an incorrect source address. When this happens, the receiver (i.e., the party who receives these packets containing false address) would inadvertently send replies back to this forged address (called **spoofed address**), and not to the attacker. This can lead to three possible cases:

(a) The attacker can intercept the reply If the attacker is between the destination and the forged source, the attacker can see the reply and use that information for *hijacking* attacks.

(b) The attacker need not see the reply If the attacker's intention was a Denial Of Service (DOS) attack, the attacker need not bother about the reply.

(c) The attacker does not want the reply The attacker could simply be *angry* with the host, so it may put that host's address as the forged source address and send the packet to the destination. The attacker does not want a reply from the destination, as it wants the host with the forged address to receive it and get confused.

Phishing

Phishing has become a big problem in recent times. In 2004, the estimated losses due to phishing were to the tune of USD 137 million, according to Tower Group. Attackers set up fake Web sites, which look like real Web sites. It is quite simple to do so, since creating Web pages involves relatively simple technologies such as HTML, JavaScript, CSS (Cascading Style Sheets), etc. Learning and using these technologies is quite simple. The attacker's modus operandi works as follows:

1. The attacker decides to create her own Web site, which looks very identical to a real Web site. For example, the attacker can clone Citibank's Web site. The cloning is so clever that human eye will not be able to distinguish between the real (Citibank's) and fake (attacker's) sites now.
2. The attacker can use many techniques to attack the bank's customers. The most common one is given below.

   The attacker sends an email to the legitimate customers of the bank. The email itself appears to have come from the bank. For ensuring this, the attacker exploits the email system to suggest that the sender of the email is some bank official (e.g., accountmanager@citibank.com). This fake email warns the user that there has been some sort of attack on the Citibank's computer systems and that the bank wants to issue new passwords to all its customers, or verify their existing PINs, etc. For this purpose, the customer is asked to visit a URL mentioned in the same email. This is conceptually shown in Fig. 11.7.

Subject: Verify your E-mail with Citibank

This email was sent by the Citibank server to verify your E-mail address. You must complete this process by clicking on the link below and entering in the small window your Citibank ATM/Debit Card number and PIN that you use on ATM.

This is done for your protection—because some of our members no longer have access to their email addresses and we must verify it.

To verify your E-mail address and access your bank account, click on the link below:

https://web.da-us.citibank.com/signin/citifi/scripts/email_verify.jsp

Fig. 11.7 *Attacker sends a forged email to the innocent victim (customer)*

3. When the customer (i.e., the victim) innocently clicks on the URL specified in the email, she is taken to the attacker's site, and not the bank's original site. There, the customer is prompted to enter confidential information, such as her password or PIN. Since the attacker's fake site looks exactly like the original bank site, the customer provides this information. The attacker gladly accepts this information and displays a *Thank you* to the unsuspecting victim. In the meanwhile, the attacker now uses the victim's password or PIN to access the bank's real site and can perform any transaction as if she is the victim!

A real-life example of this kind of attack is reproduced below from the site http://www.fraudwatchinternational.com.

Figure 11.8 shows a fake email sent by an attacker to an authorized PayPal user.

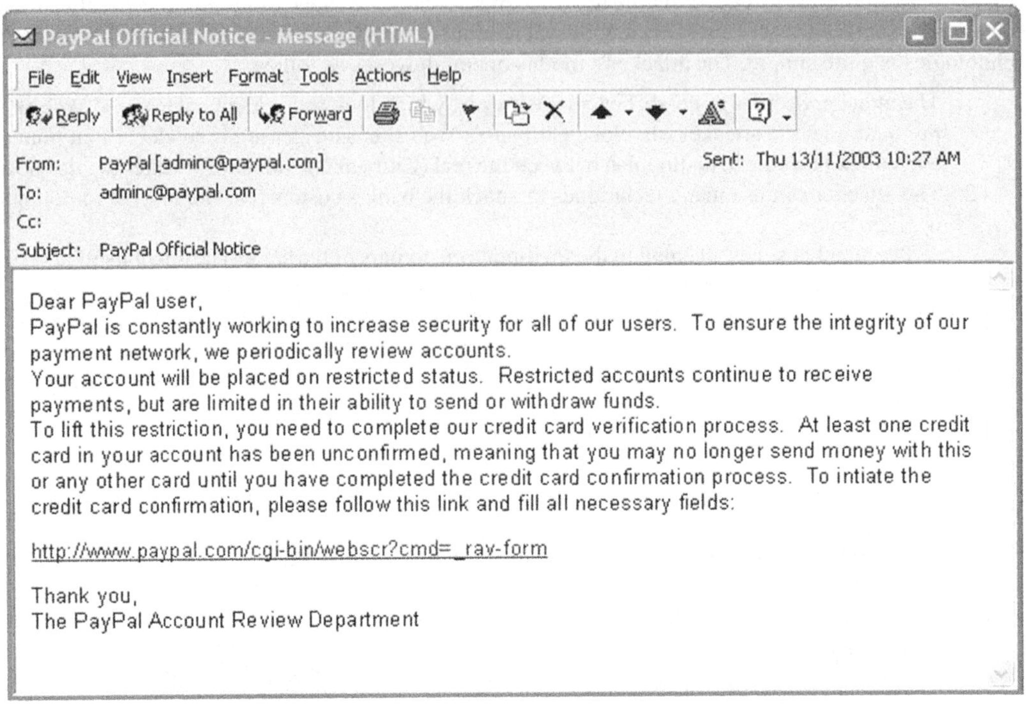

Fig. 11.8 *Fake email from the attacker to a PayPal user*

As we can see, the attacker is trying to fool the PayPal customer to verify her credit card details. Quite clearly, the aim of the attacker is to access the credit card information of the customer and then misuse it. Figure 11.9 shows the screen that appears when the user clicks on the URL specified in the fake email.

Once the user provides these details, the attacker's job is easy! She simply uses these credit card details to make purchases on behalf of the cheated card holder!

Pharming (DNS Spoofing) Another attack, known earlier as **DNS spoofing** or **DNS poisoning** is now called as **pharming** attack. As we know, using the **Domain Name System (DNS)**, people can identify Web sites with human-readable names (such as www.yahoo.com), and computers can continue to treat them as IP addresses (such as 120.10.81.67). For this, a special server computer called as a DNS server maintains the mappings between domain names and the corresponding IP addresses. The DNS server could be located anywhere. Usually, it is with the Internet Service Provider (ISP) of the users. With this background, the DNS spoofing attack works as follows:

1. Suppose that there is a merchant (Bob), whose site's domain name is www.bob.com, and the IP address is 100.10.10.20. Therefore, the DNS entry for Bob in all the DNS servers is maintained as follows:

   www.bob.com   100.10.10.20

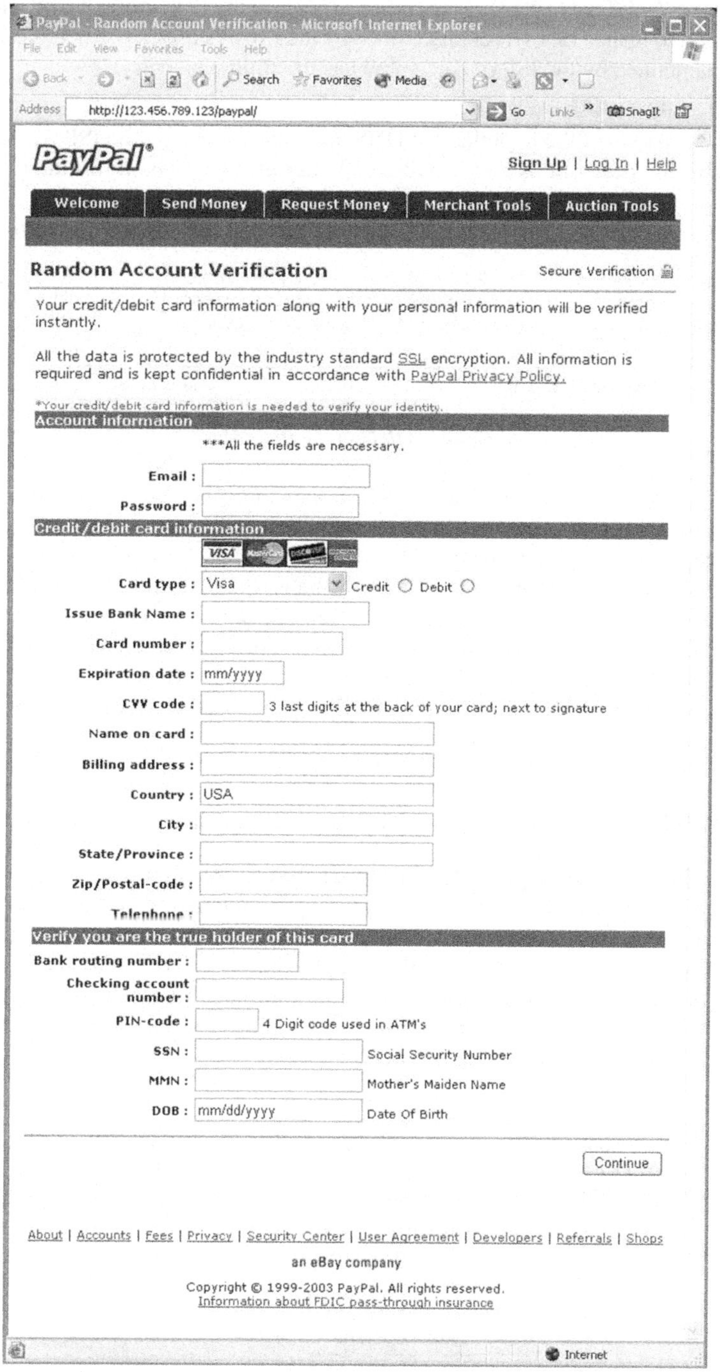

Fig. 11.9 *Fake PayPal site asking for user's credit card details*

2. The attacker (say Trudy) manages to hack and replace the IP address of Bob with her own (say 100.20.20.20) in the DSN server maintained by the ISP of a user, say Alice. Therefore, the DNS server maintained by the ISP of Alice now has the following entry:

   www.bob.com 100.20.20.20

   Thus, the contents of the hypothetical DNS table maintained by the ISP would be changed. A hypothetical portion of this table (before and after the attack) is shown in Fig. 11.10.

DNS Name	IP Address
www.amazon.com	161.20.10.16
www.yahoo.com	121.41.67.89
www.bob.com	100.10.10.20
...	...

Before the attack

DNS Name	IP Address
www.amazon.com	161.20.10.16
www.yahoo.com	121.41.67.89
www.bob.com	100.20.20.20
...	...

After the attack

Fig. 11.10 *Effect of the DNS attack*

3. When Alice wants to communicate with Bob's site, her Web browser queries the DNS server maintained by her ISP for Bob's IP address, providing it the domain name (i.e., www.bob.com). Alice gets the replaced (i.e., Trudy's) IP address, which is 100.20.20.20.
4. Now, Alice starts communicating with Trudy, believing that she is communicating with Bob!

   Such attacks of DNS spoofing are quite common, and cause a lot of havoc. Even worse, the attacker (Trudy) does not have to listen to the conversation on the wire! She has to simply be able to hack the DNS server of the ISP and replace a single IP address with her own!

   A protocol called **DNSSec (Secure DNS)** is being used to thwart such attacks. However, unfortunately it is not widely used.

CRYPTOGRAPHY 11.2

This chapter introduces the basic concepts in **cryptography**. Although this word sounds fearful, we shall realize that it is very simple to understand. In fact, most terms in computer security have very straightforward meaning. Many terms, for no reason, sound complicated. Our aim will be to demystify all such terms in relation to cryptography in this chapter. After we are through with this chapter, we shall be ready to understand computer-based security solutions and issues that follow in later chapters.

Cryptography is the art of achieving security by encoding messages to make them non-readable. Figure 11.11 shows the conceptual view of cryptography.

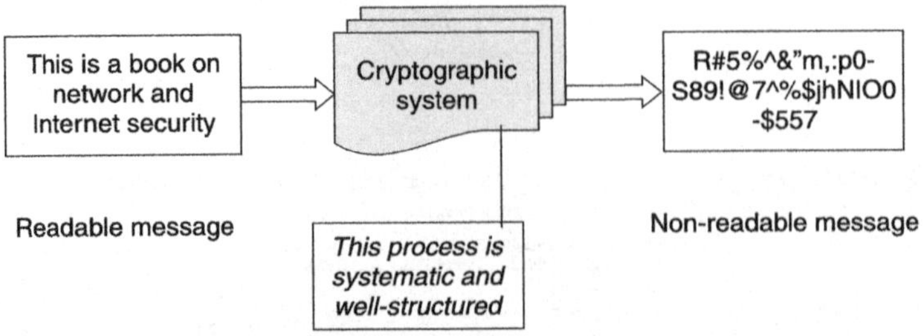

Fig. 11.11 *Cryptographic system*

PLAIN TEXT AND CIPHER TEXT 11.3

Any communication in the language that you and I speak – that is the human language, takes the form of **plain text** or **clear text**. That is, a message in plain text can be understood by anybody knowing the language as long as the message is not codified in any manner. For instance, when we speak with our family members, friends or colleagues, we use plain text because we do not want to hide anything from them. Suppose I say "Hi Anita", it is plain text because both Anita and I know its meaning and intention. More significantly, anybody in the same room would also get to hear these words, and would know that I am greeting Anita.

Notably, we also use plain text during electronic conversations. For instance, when we send an email to someone, we compose the email message using English (or these days, another) language. For instance, I can compose the email message as shown in Fig. 11.12.

> Hi Amit,
>
> Hope you are doing fine. How about meeting at the train station this Friday at 5 pm? Please let me know if it is ok with you.
>
> Regards.
>
> Atul

Fig. 11.12 *Example of a plain text message*

Now, not only Amit, but also any other person who reads this email would know what I have written. As before, this is simply because I am not using any codified language here. I have composed my email message using plain English. This is another example of plain text, albeit in written form.

Clear text or plain text signifies a message that can be understood by the sender, the recipient, and also by anyone else who gets an access to that message.

In normal life, we do not bother much about the fact that someone could be overhearing us. In most cases, that makes little difference to us because the person overhearing us can do little damage by using the overheard information. After all, we do not reveal many secrets in our day-to-day lives.

However, there are situations where we are concerned about the secrecy of our conversations. For instance, suppose that I am interested in knowing my bank account's balance and hence I call up my phone banker from my office. The phone banker would generally ask a secret question (e.g., What is your mother's maiden name?) whose answer only I know. This is to ascertain that someone else is not posing as me. Now, when I give the answer to the secret question (e.g., Leela), I generally speak in low voice, or better yet, initially call up from a phone that is isolated. This ensures that only the intended recipient (the phone banker) gets to know the correct answer.

On the same lines, suppose that my email to my friend Amit shown earlier is confidential for some reason. Therefore, I do not want anyone else to understand what I have written even if she is able to access the email by using some means, before it reaches Amit. How do I ensure this? This is exactly the problem that small children face. Many times, they want to communicate in such a manner that their little secrets are hidden from the elderly. What do they do in order to achieve this? Usually the simplest trick that they use is a code language. For instance, they replace each alphabet in their conversation with another character. As an example, they replace each alphabet with the alphabet that is actually three alphabets down the order. So, each A will be replaced by D, B will be replaced by E, C will be replaced by F, and so on. To complete the cycle, each W will be replaced by Z, each X will be replaced by A, each Y will be replaced by B and each Z will be replaced by C. We can summarize this scheme as shown in Fig. 11.13. The first row shows the original alphabets, and the second row shows what each original alphabet will be replaced with.

A	B	C	D	E	F	G	H	I	J	K	L	M	N	O	P	Q	R	S	T	U	V	W	X	Y	Z
D	E	F	G	H	I	J	K	L	M	N	O	P	Q	R	S	T	U	V	W	X	Y	Z	A	B	C

Fig. 11.13 *A scheme for codifying messages by replacing each alphabet with an alphabet three places down the line*

Thus, using the scheme of replacing each alphabet with the one that is three places down the line, a message *I love you* shall become *L ORYH BRX* as shown in Fig. 11.14.

I		L	O	V	E		Y	O	U
L		O	R	Y	H		B	R	X

Fig. 11.14 *Codification using the alphabet replacement scheme*

Of course, there can be many variants of such a scheme. It is not necessary to replace each alphabet with the one that is three places down the order. It can be the one that is four, five or more places down the order. The point is, however, that each alphabet in the original message can be replaced by another to hide the original contents of the message. The codified message is called **cipher text**. Cipher means a code or a secret message.

When a plain text message is codified using any suitable scheme, the resulting message is called cipher text.

Based on these concepts, let us put these terms into a diagrammatic representation, as shown in Fig. 11.15.

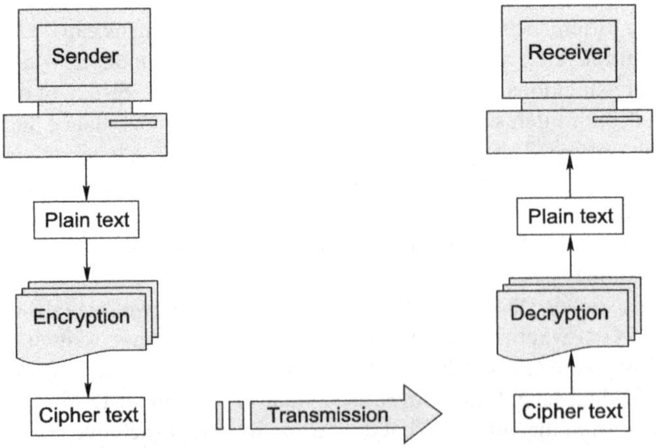

Fig. 11.15 *Elements of a cryptographic operation*

Let us now write our original email message and the resulting cipher text by using the alphabet-replacing scheme, as shown in Fig. 11.16. This will clarify the idea further.

Hi Amit,	Kl Dplw,
Hope you are doing fine. How about meeting at the train station this Friday at 5 pm? Please let me know if it is ok with you.	Krsh brx duh grlqj ilqh. Krz derxw phhwlqj dw wkh wudlq vwdwlrq wklv Iulgdb dw 5 sp? Sohdvh ohw ph nqrz li lw lv rn zlwk brx.
Regards.	Uhjdugv.
Atul	Dwxo
Plain text message	Corresponding cipher text message

Fig. 11.16 *Example of a plain text message being transformed into cipher text*

11.3.1 Types of Cryptography

Based on the number of keys used for encryption and decryption, cryptography can be classified into two categories:

1. Symmetric key encryption Also called **secret key encryption**, in this scheme, only one key is used and the same key is used for encryption and decryption of messages. Obviously, both the parties must agree upon the key before any transmission begins, and nobody else should know about it. The example in Fig. 11.17 shows how symmetric cryptography works. Basically at the sender's end, the key changes the original message to an encoded form. At the receiver's end, the same key is used to decrypt the encoded message, thus deriving the original message out of it. IBM's **Data Encryption Standard (DES)** uses this approach. It uses 56-bit keys for encryption.

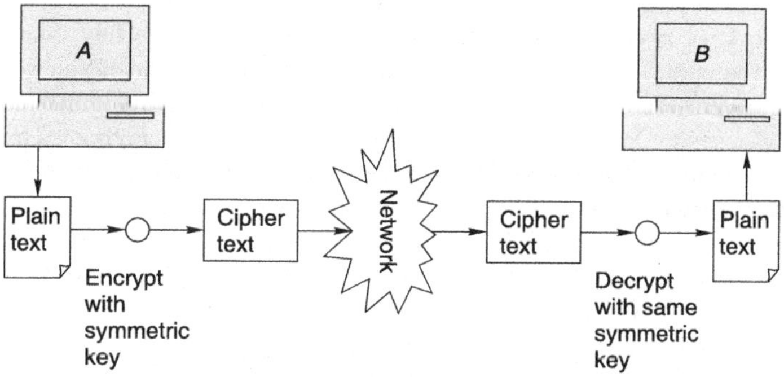

Fig 11.17 *Symmetric key encryption*

In practical situations, symmetric key encryption has a number of problems. One problem is that of key agreements and distribution. In the first place, how do two parties agree on a key? One way is for somebody from the sender (say A) to physically visit the receiver (say B) and hand over the key. Another way is to courier a paper on which the key is written. Both are not exactly not very convenient. A third way is to send the key over the network to B and ask for the confirmation. But then, if an intruder gets the message, he can interpret all the subsequent ones!

The second problem is more serious. Since the same key is used for encryption and decryption, one key per communicating parties is required. Suppose A wants to securely communicate with B and also with C. Clearly, there must be one key for all communications between A and B; and there must be another, *distinct* key for all communications between A and C. The same key as used by A and B cannot be used for communications between A and C. Otherwise, there is a chance that C can interpret messages going between A and B, or B can do the same for messages going between A and C! Since the Internet has thousands of merchants selling products to hundreds of thousands of buyers, using this scheme would be impractical because every buyer-seller combination would need a separate key!

DES has been found to be vulnerable. Therefore, better symmetric key algorithms have been proposed and are in active use. One way is simply to use DES twice with two different keys (called DES-2). A still stronger mechanism is DES-3, wherein key-1 is used to encrypt first, key-2 (a different key) is used to re-encrypt the encrypted block, and key-1 is used once again to re-encrypt doubly encrypted block. DES-3 is quite popular and is in wide use. Other popular algorithms are IDEA, RC5, RC2, etc.

2. Asymmetric key encryption This is a better scheme and is also called **public key encryption**. In this type of cryptography, two *different* keys (called **key pair**) are used. One key is used for encryption and only the other key must be used for decryption. No other key can decrypt the message – not even the original (i.e., the first) key used for encryption! The beauty of this scheme is that every communicating party needs just a key pair for communicating with any number of other communicating parties. Once someone obtains a key-pair, he can communicate with anyone else on the Internet in a secure manner, as we shall see later.

There is a simple mathematical basis for this scheme. If you have an extremely huge number that has only two factors that are prime numbers, you can generate a pair of keys. For example, consider a number 10. The number 10 has only two factors, 5 and 2. If you apply 5 as an encryption factor, only 2 can be used as the decryption factor. Nothing else – even 5 itself – can do the decryption. Of course, 10 is a very small number. Therefore, with a small effort, this scheme can be broken into. However, if the number is huge, even years of computation cannot break the scheme.

One of the two keys is called **public key** and the other is **private key**. Suppose you want to communicate over a computer network such as the Internet in a secure manner. You would need to obtain a public key and a private key. You can generate these keys using standard algorithms. The private key remains with you as a secret. You must not disclose your private key to anybody. However, the public key is for the general public. It is disclosed to all parties that you want to communicate with. In this scheme, in fact, each party or node publishes his public key. Using this, a directory can be constructed where the various parties or nodes (i.e., their ids) and their corresponding public keys are maintained. One can consult this and get the public key for any party that one wishes to communicate with by a simple table search. Suppose A wants to send a message to B without having to worry about its security. Then, A and B should each have a private key and a public key.

1. A's private key should be known only to A. However, A's public key should be known to B.
2. Only B should know B's private key. However, A should know B's public key.

How this works is simple:

1. When A wants to send a message to B, A encrypts the message using B's public key. This is possible because A knows B's public key.
2. A sends this message (encrypted using B's public key) to B.

3. B decrypts A' message using his private key. Note that only B knows about his private key. Thus, no one else can make any sense out of the message even if one can manage to intercept the message. This is because the intruder (hopefully) does not know about B's private key. It is only B's private key that can decrypt the message.
4. When B wants to send a message to A, exactly reverse steps take place. B encrypts the message using A's public key. Therefore, only A can decrypt the message back to its original form, using his private key.

This is shown in Fig. 11.18.

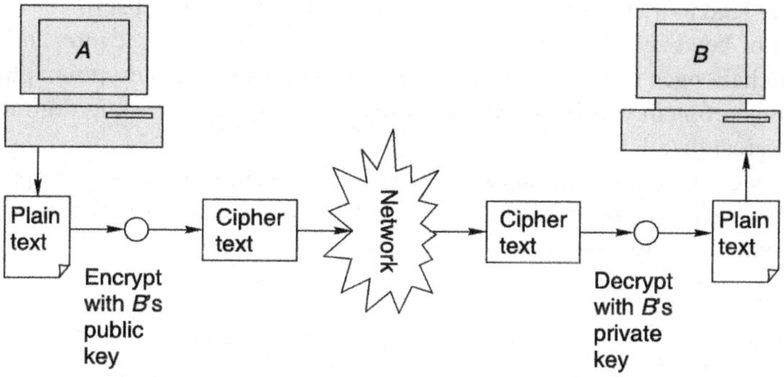

Fig. 11.18 *Public key encryption*

This can be shown in another way. For instance, suppose a bank needs to accept many requests for transactions from its customers. Then, the bank can have a private key – public key pair. The bank can then publish its public key to all its customers. The customers can use this public key of the bank for encrypting messages before they send them to the bank. The bank can decrypt all these encrypted messages with its private key, which remains with itself. This is shown in Fig. 11.19.

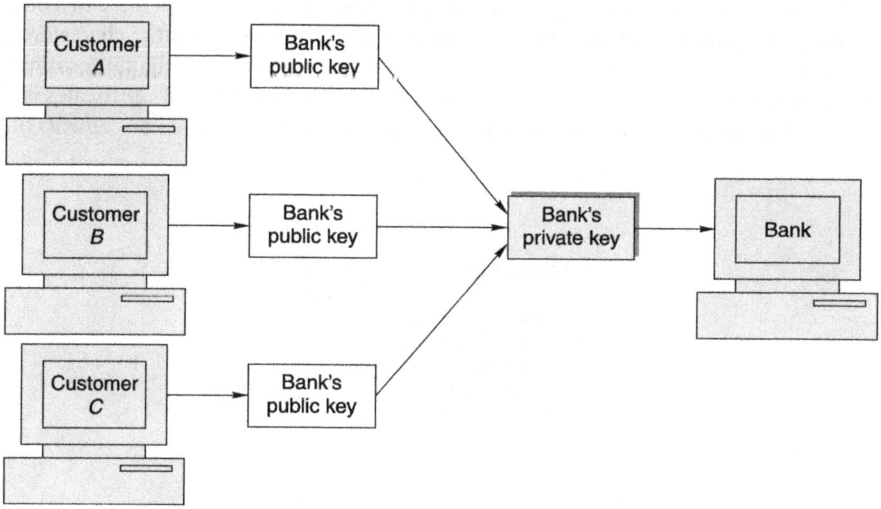

Fig. 11.19 *The use of a public key-private key pair by a bank*

DIGITAL CERTIFICATES 11.4

11.4.1 Introduction

We have discussed the problem of *key agreement* or *key exchange* in great detail. We have also seen how even the algorithm such as *Diffie-Hellman Key Exchange* designed specifically to tackle this problem also has its own pitfalls. The asymmetric key cryptography can be a very good solution. But it also has one unresolved issue, which is how do the parties/correspondents (i.e., the sender and the receiver of a message) exchange their public keys with each other. Obviously, they cannot exchange them openly – this can very easily lead to a *man-in-the-middle attack* on the public key itself!

This problem of key exchange or key agreement is, therefore, quite severe, and in fact, is one of the most difficult challenges to tackle in designing any computer-based cryptographic solution. After a lot of thought, this problem was resolved with a revolutionary idea of using **digital certificates**. We shall study this in great detail.

Conceptually, we can compare digital certificates to the documents such as our passports or driving licenses. A passport or a driving license helps in establishing our identity. For instance, a person's passport proves beyond doubt a variety of aspects, the most important ones being:

1. Full name
2. Nationality
3. Date and place of birth
4. Photograph and signature

Likewise, digital certificate would also prove something very critical, as we shall study.

11.4.2 Concept of Digital Certificates

A digital certificate is simply a small computer file. For example, my digital certificate would actually be a computer file with the file name such as atul.cer (where *.cer* signifies the first three characters of the word *certificate*. Of course, this is just an example: in actual practice, the file extensions can be different.) Just as my passport signifies the association between me and my other characteristics such as full name, nationality, date and place of birth, photograph and signature, my digital certificate simply signifies the association between my public key and me. This concept of digital certificates is shown in Fig. 11.20. Note that this is merely a conceptual view, and does not depict the actual contents of a digital certificate.

Fig. 11.20 *Conceptual view of a digital certificate*

We have not specified who is officially approving the association between a user and the user's digital certificate. Obviously, it has to be some authority in which all the concerned parties have a great amount of trust and belief. Imagine a situation where our passports are not issued by a government office, but by an ordinary shopkeeper. Would we trust the passports? Similarly, digital certificates must be issued by some trusted entity. Otherwise, we will not trust anybody's digital certificate.

As we have noted, a digital certificate establishes the relation between a user and her public key. Therefore, a digital certificate must contain the user name and the user's public key. This will prove that a particular public key belongs to a particular user. Apart from this, what does a digital certificate contain? A simplified view of a sample digital certificate is shown in Fig. 11.21.

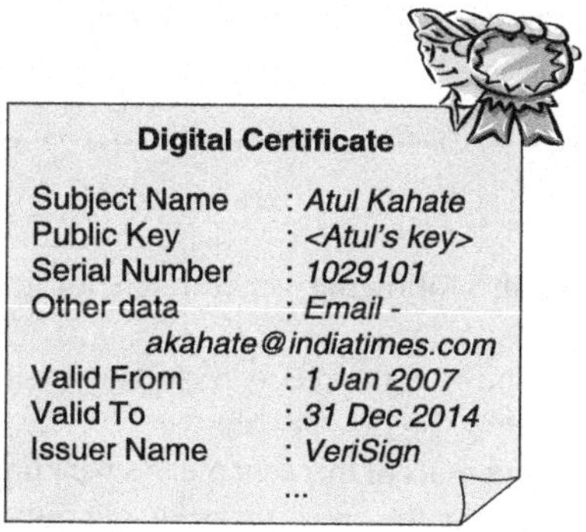

Fig. 11.21 *Example of a digital certificate*

We will notice a few interesting things here. First of all, my name is shown as **subject name**. In fact, any user's name in a digital certificate is always referred to as *subject name* (this is because a digital certificate can be issued to an individual, a group or an organization). Also, there is another interesting piece of information called **serial number**. We shall see what it means in due course of time. The certificate also contains other pieces of information, such as the validity date range for the certificate, and who has issued it (**issuer name**). Let us try to understand the meanings of these pieces of information by comparing them with the corresponding entries in my passport. This is shown in Fig. 11.22.

Passport entry	*Corresponding digital certificate entry*
Full name	Subject name
Passport number	Serial number
Valid from	Same
Valid to	Same
Issued by	Issuer name
Photograph and signature	Public key

Fig. 11.22 *Similarities between a passport and a digital certificate*

As the figure shows, the digital certificate is actually quite similar to a passport. Just as every passport has a unique passport number, every digital certificate has a unique serial number. As we know, no two passports issued by the same issuer (i.e., government) can have the same passport number. Similarly, no two digital certificates issued by the same issuer can have the same serial number. Who can issue these digital certificates? We shall soon answer this question.

11.4.3 Certification Authority (CA)

A **Certification Authority (CA)** is a trusted agency that can issue digital certificates. Who can be a CA? Obviously, not any Tom, Dick and Harry can be a CA. The authority of acting as a CA has to be with someone who everybody trusts. Consequently, the governments in the various countries decide who can and who cannot be a CA. (It is another matter that not everybody trusts the government in the first place!) Usually, a CA is a reputed organization, such as a post office, financial institution, software company, etc. Two of the world's most famous CAs are VeriSign and Entrust. Safescrypt Limited, a subsidiary of Satyam Infoway Limited, became the first Indian CA in February 2002.

Thus, a CA has the authority to issue digital certificates to individuals and organizations, which want to use those certificates in asymmetric key cryptographic applications.

DIGITAL SIGNATURES 11.5

11.5.1 Introduction

All along, we have been talking of the following general scheme in the context of asymmetric key cryptography:

If A is the sender of a message and B is the receiver, A encrypts the message with B's public key and sends the encrypted message to B.

We have deliberately hidden the internals of this scheme. As we know, actually this is based on digital envelopes as discussed earlier, wherein not the entire message but only the one-time session key used to encrypt the message is encrypted with the receiver's public key. But for simplicity, we shall ignore this technical detail, and instead, assume that the whole message is encrypted with the receiver's public key.

Let us now consider another scheme, as follows:

If A is the sender of a message and B is the receiver, A encrypts the message with A's private key and sends the encrypted message to B.

This is shown in Fig. 11.23.

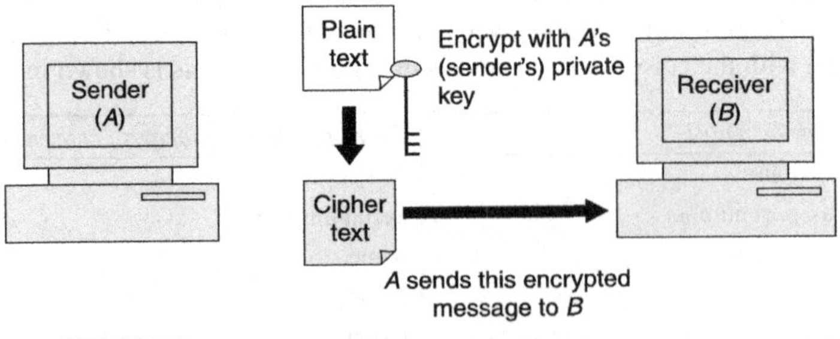

Fig. 11.23 *Encrypting a message with the sender's private key*

Our first reaction to this would be, what purpose would this serve? After all, A's public key would be, well, *public*, i.e., accessible to anybody. This means that anybody who is interested in knowing the contents of the message sent by A to B can simply use A's public key to decrypt the message, thus causing the failure of this encryption scheme!

Well, this is quite true. But here, when A encrypts the message with her private key, her intention is not to hide the contents of the message (i.e., not to achieve *confidentiality*), but it is something else. What can that intention be? If the receiver (B) receives such a message encrypted with A's private key,

B can use A's public key to decrypt it, and therefore, access the plain text. Does this ring a bell? If the decryption is successful, it assures B that this message was indeed sent by A. This is because if B can decrypt a message with A's public key, it means that the message must have been initially encrypted with A's private key (remember that a message encrypted with a public key can be decrypted only with the corresponding private key, and vice versa). This is also because only A knows her private key. Therefore, someone posing as A (say C) could not have sent a message encrypted with A's private key to B. A must have sent it. Therefore, although this scheme does not achieve confidentiality, it achieves *authentication* (identifying and proving A as the sender). Moreover, in the case of a dispute tomorrow, B can take the encrypted message, and decrypt it with A's public key to prove that the message indeed came from A. This achieves the purpose of *non-repudiation* (i.e., A cannot refuse that she had sent this message, as the message was encrypted with her private key, which is supposed to be known only to her).

Even if someone (say C) manages to intercept and access the encrypted message while it is in transit, then uses A's public key to decrypt the message, changes the message, that would not achieve any purpose. Because C does not have A's private key, C cannot encrypt the changed message with A's private key again. Therefore, even if C now forwards this changed message to B, B will not be fooled into believing that it came from A, as it was not encrypted with A's private key.

Such a scheme, wherein the sender encrypts the message with her private key, forms the basis of digital signatures, as shown in Fig. 11.24.

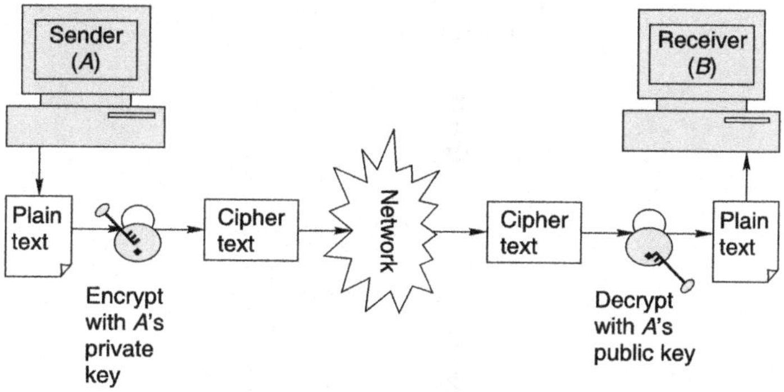

Fig. 11.24 *Basis for digital signatures*

Digital signatures have assumed great significance in the modern world of Web-commerce. Most countries have already made provisions for recognizing a digital signature as a valid authorization mechanism, just like paper-based signatures. Digital signatures have legal status now. For example, suppose you send a message to your bank over the Internet, to transfer some amount from your account to your friend's account, and digitally sign the message, this transaction has the same status as the one wherein you fill in and sign the bank's paper-based money transfer slip.

We have seen the theory behind digital signatures. However, there are some undesirable elements in this scheme, as we shall study next.

11.5.2 Message Digests

Introduction

If we examine the conceptual process of digital signatures, we will realize that it does not deal with the problems associated with asymmetric key encryption, namely slow operation and large cipher text size.

This is because we are encrypting the whole of the original plain text message with the sender's private key. As the size of the original plain text can be quite large, this encryption process can be really very slow.

We can tackle this problem using the digital envelope approach, as before. That is, A encrypts the original plain text message (PT) with a one-time symmetric key (K1) to form the cipher text (CT). It then encrypts the one-time symmetric key (K1) with her private key (K2). She creates a digital envelope containing CT and K1 encrypted with K2, and sends the digital envelope to B. B opens the digital envelope, uses A's public key (K3) to decrypt the encrypted one-time symmetric key, and obtains the symmetric key K1. It then uses K1 to decrypt the cipher text (CT) and obtains the original plain text (PT). Since B uses A's public key to decrypt the encrypted one-time symmetric key (K1), B can be assured that only A's private key could have encrypted K1. Thus, B can be assured that the digital envelope came from A.

Such a scheme could work perfectly. However, in real practice, a more efficient scheme is used. It involves the usage of a **message digest** (also called **hash**). A message digest is a *fingerprint* or the summary of a message.

We perform a hashing operation (or a message digest algorithm) over a block of data to produce its hash or message digest, which is smaller in size than the original message. This concept is shown in Fig. 11.25.

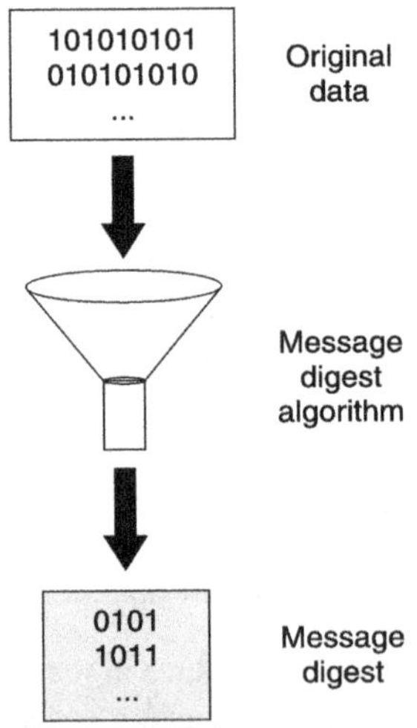

Fig. 11.25 *Message digest concept*

So far, we are considering very simple cases of message digests. Actually, the message digests are not so small and straightforward to compute. Message digests usually consist of 128 or more bits. This means that the chance of any two message digests being the same is anything between 0 to at least 2^{128}. The message digest length is chosen to be so long with a purpose. This ensures that the scope for two message digests being the same.

Digital Signature Process

We have mentioned that RSA can be used for performing digital signatures. Let us understand how this works in a step-by-step fashion. For this, let us assume that the sender (A) wants to send a message M to the receiver (B) along with the digital signature (S) calculated over the message (M).

Step 1: The sender (A) uses the SHA-1 message digest algorithm to calculate the message digest (MD1) over the original message (M). This is shown in Fig. 11.26.

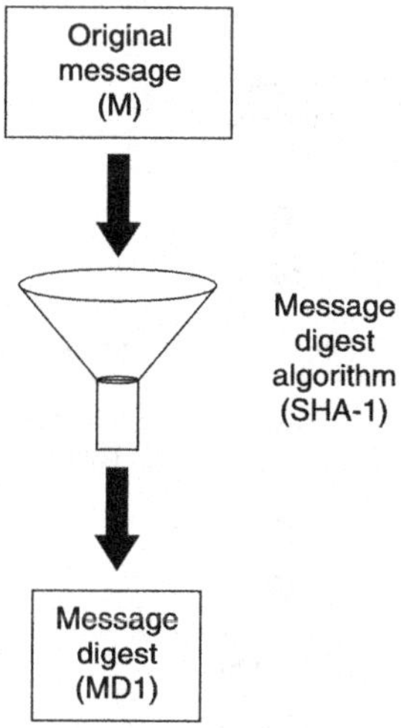

Fig. 11.26 *Message digest calculation*

Step 2: The sender (A) now encrypts the message digest with her private key. The output of this process is called as the digital signature (DS) of A. This is shown in Fig. 11.27.

Fig. 11.27 *Digital signature creation*

Step 3: Now the sender (A) sends the original message (M) along with the digital signature (DS) to the receiver (B). This is shown in Fig. 11.28.

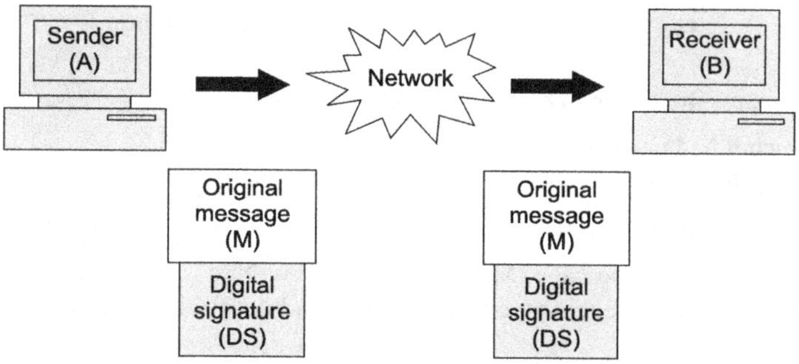

Fig. 11.28 *Transmission of original message and digital signature together*

Step 4: After the receiver (B) receives the original message (M) and the sender's (A's) digital signature, B uses the same message digest algorithm as was used by the A, and calculates its own message digest (MD2) as shown in Fig. 11.29.

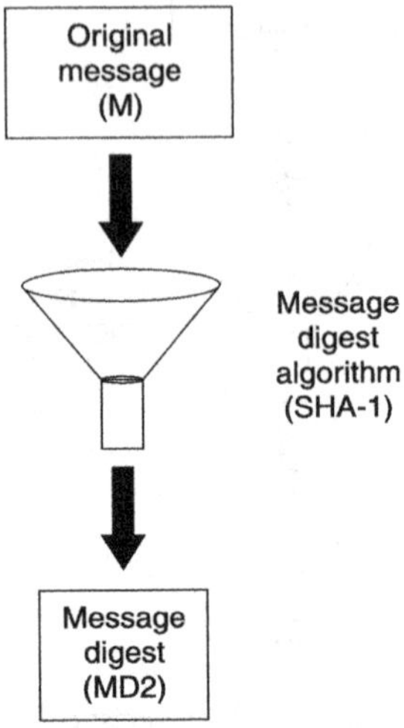

Fig. 11.29 *Receiver calculates its own message digest*

Step 5: The receiver (B) now uses the sender's (A's) public key to decrypt (sometimes also called as **de-sign**) the digital signature. Note that A had used her private key to encrypt her message digest (MD1) to form the digital signature. Therefore, only A's public key can be used to decrypt it. The output of this process is the original message digest as was calculated by A (MD1) in Step 1. This is shown in Fig. 11.30.

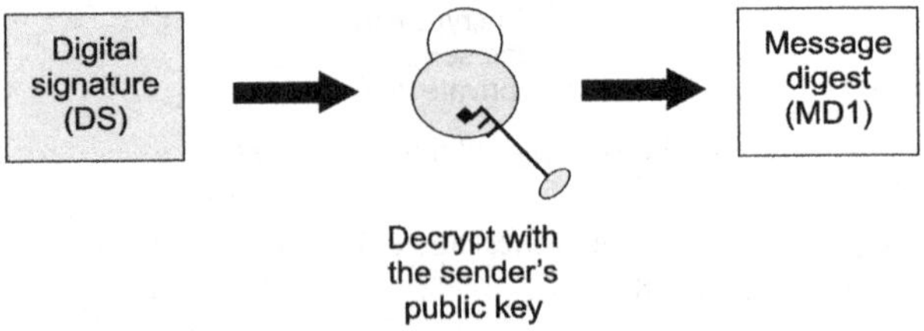

Fig. 11.30 *Receiver retrieves sender's message digest*

Step 6: B now compares the following two message digests:

1. MD2, which it had calculated in Step 4.
2. MD1, which it retrieved from A's digital signature in Step 5.

If MD1 = MD2, the following facts are established:

1. B accepts the original message (M) as the correct, unaltered, message from A.
2. B is also assured that the message came from A, and not from someone posing as A.

This is shown in Fig. 11.31.

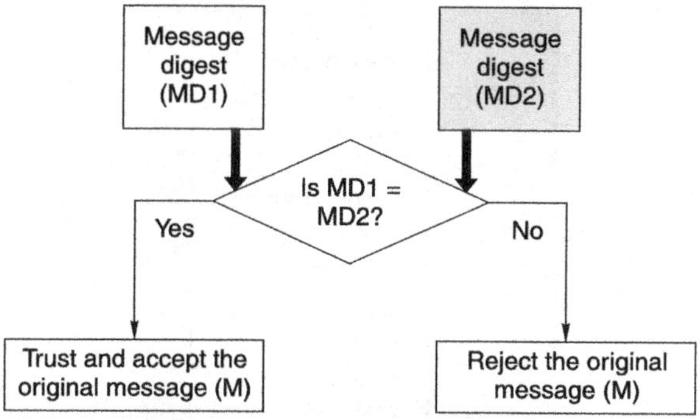

Fig. 11.31 *Digital signature verification*

The basis for the acceptance or the rejection of the original message on the basis of the outcome of the message digest comparison (i.e., step 6) is simple. We know that the sender (A) had used her private key to encrypt the message digest to produce the digital signature. If decrypting the digital signature produces the correct message digest, the receiver (B) can be quite sure that the original message and the digital signature came indeed from the sender (A). This also proves that the message was not altered by an attacker while in transit. Because, if the message was altered while in transit, the message digest calculated by B in Step 4 (i.e., MD2) over the received message would differ from the one sent (of course, in encrypted form) by A (i.e., MD1). Why can the attacker not alter the message, recalculate the message digest, and sign it again? Well, as we know, the attacker can very well perform the first two steps (i.e., alter the message, and recalculate the message digest over the altered message); but it cannot sign it again, because for that to be possible, the attacker needs A's private key. Since only A knows about A's private key, the attacker cannot use A's private key to encrypt the message digest (i.e., sign the message) again.

Thus, the principle of digital signatures is quite strong, secure and reliable.

SECURE SOCKET LAYER (SSL) 11.6

11.6.1 Introduction

The **Secure Socket Layer (SSL)** protocol is an Internet protocol for secure exchange of information between a Web browser and a Web server. It provides two basic security services: authentication and confidentiality. Logically, it provides a secure *pipe* between the Web browser and the Web server. Netscape Corporation developed SSL in 1994. Since then, SSL has become the world's most popular Web security mechanism. All the major Web browsers support SSL. Currently, SSL comes in three versions: 2, 3 and 3.1. The most popular of them is Version 3, which was released in 1995.

11.6.2 Position of SSL in TCP/IP Protocol Suite

SSL can be conceptually considered as an additional layer in the TCP/IP protocol suite. The SSL layer is located between the application layer and the transport layer, as shown in Fig. 11.32.

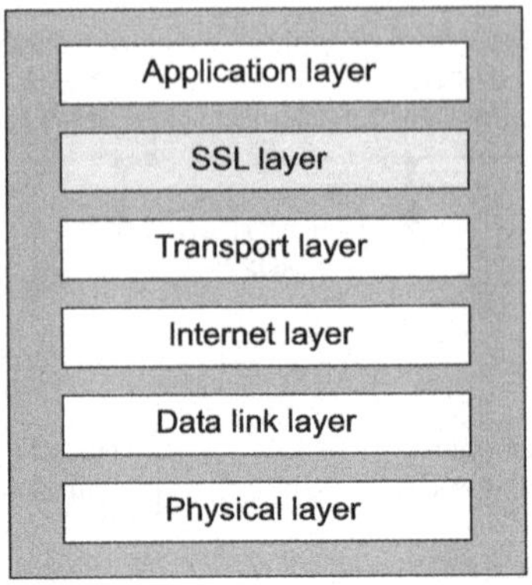

Fig. 11.32 *Position of SSL in TCP/IP*

As such, the communication between the various TCP/IP protocol layers is as shown in Fig. 11.33.

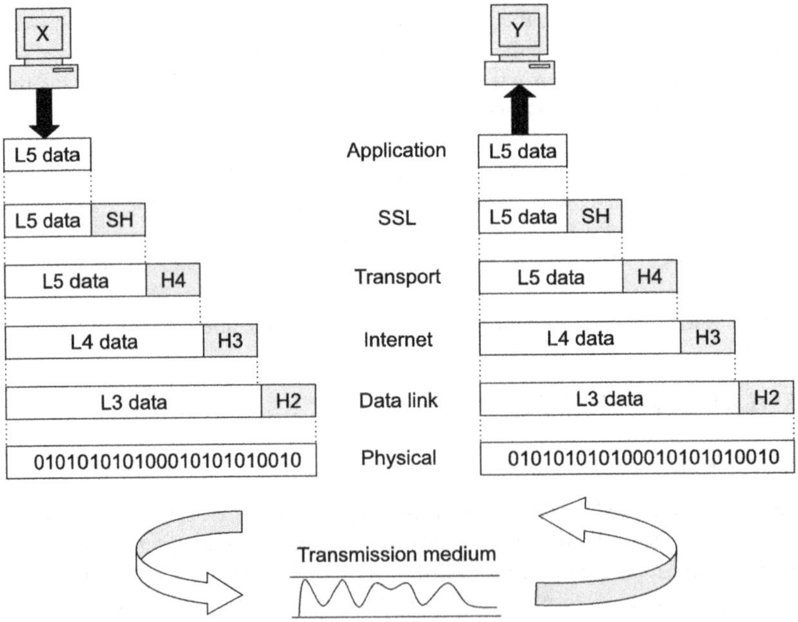

Fig. 11.33 *SSL is located between application and transport layers*

As we can see, the application layer of the sending computer (X) prepares the data to be sent to the receiving computer (Y), as usual. However, unlike what happens in the normal case, the application layer data is not passed directly to the transport layer now. Instead, the application layer data is passed to the SSL layer. Here, the SSL layer performs encryption on the data received from the application layer (which is indicated by a different color), and also adds its own encryption information header, called SSL Header (SH) to the encrypted data. We shall later study what exactly happens in this process.

After this, the SSL layer data (L5) becomes the input for the transport layer. It adds its own header (H4), and passes it on to the Internet layer, and so on. This process happens exactly the way it happens in the case of a normal TCP/IP data transfer. Finally, when the data reaches the physical layer, it is sent in the form of voltage pulses across the transmission medium.

At the receiver's end, the process happens pretty similar to how it happens in the case of a normal TCP/IP connection, until it reaches the new SSL layer. The SSL layer at the receiver's end removes the SSL Header (SH), decrypts the encrypted data, and gives the plain text data back to the application layer of the receiving computer.

Thus, only the application layer data is encrypted by SSL. The lower layer headers are not encrypted. This is quite obvious: if SSL has to encrypt all the headers, it must be positioned below the data link layer. That would serve no purpose at all. In fact, it would lead to problems. If SSL encrypted all the lower layer headers, even the IP and physical addresses of the computers (sender, receiver, and intermediate nodes) would be encrypted, and become unreadable. Thus, where to deliver the packets would be a big question. To understand the problem, imagine what would happen if we put the address of the sender and the receiver of a letter inside the envelope! Clearly, the postal service would not know where to send the letter! This is also why there is no point in encrypting the lower layer headers. Therefore, SSL is required between the application and the transport layers.

ONLINE PAYMENTS 11.7

Making online payments error-free and secure is one of the biggest challenges of the Internet world. Several challenges exist. For one, the payer and the payee do not meet or see each other, in contrast to what happens in many paper-based payments. There is no paper evidence for online transactions (e.g., there is no cheque or demand draft). Nobody signs anything by hand. And even if we can find some ways to thwart all these challenges so as to make the payment process possible, there are a number of risks to deal with. Since the payer and the payee do not see each other, or cannot even *feel* anything about the other, where is the question of trusting each other? Also, the payer can make a payment, and later on claim that someone else has used her credentials to make the payment, thereby forging the transaction. The payee can claim that she received a payment instruction, and therefore, went ahead with the payment transaction. The payee can be an attacker herself – thus accepting payments, and then running away with them; without actually supplying goods or services in return! In the case of a genuine payer making a successful payment to a genuine payee, an attacker can silently observe the payer's payment details (e.g., the credit card details) and later misuse them.

As we can see, this is quite an interesting headache to solve! In the late 1990s and the early part of the new century, several online payment protocols emerged. Every one of them was supposed to be the best available in the market, most secure, and quite authentic. Soon, the market was proliferated with so many online payment protocols that the situation was quite confusing and chaotic.

When the electronic commerce boom of the years 2000-2002 turned out to be a doom, most of the online payment protocols just withered away. Also, wiser decisions led to consolidation and standardization of a number of payment protocols into only a few. We review some of these key online payment protocols in this chapter.

This is a very dynamic area. So, chances are that the evolution in the space of online payment protocols will continue for quite some time to come.

PAYMENTS USING CREDIT CARDS 11.8

11.8.1 Brief History of Credit Cards

The first modern credit card was issued by the Franklin National bank in New York in 1951. They sent unsolicited credit cards to prospective customers without verifying their credit screening. Various merchants signed agreements with the bank, guaranteeing the acceptance of the cards. When a customer made purchases using the card, she would present the card to the merchant. The merchant would copy the information on the strip of the card on the sales slip. The merchant would then present a collection of these sales slips to the bank, which would credit the merchant with the sales amount. In the late 1950s, hundreds of other banks also started providing credit cards to their customers.

However, this approach had one major drawback. The customers could use their credit cards in their own geographic area, and could make payments using the card only at the merchants who had also signed up with their own bank (i.e., the customer's bank). To resolve this problem, Bank of America started the licensing of a few banks outside California to issue their card, the BankAmericard. That is, all the banks participating in this licensing scheme could issue a card to any of their customers. The customers could use the card at any of the merchants, who also had an account with one of the participating banks. For example, suppose that a customer had a credit card issued by bank A. The customer could use that card to make payment to a merchant who had tied up with bank B to accept card payments. This would work fine as long as both banks (A and B) had entered the licensing agreement with Bank of America.

This arrangement worked fine for the banks that obtained the BankAmericard license. (This network was later renamed to Visa in 1976.) However, this arrangement did not cover all the banks. Therefore, these *left out* banks got together in New York in 1966 to form their own card network, called Interbank Card Association, which later became MasterCard International.

As Visa and MasterCard gained popularity and acceptance, most banks started joining one of these groups, rather than entering the credit cards business on their own. All these participant banks agreed to display the bank name as well as the group name (Visa or MasterCard) on the card, to signify which group the bank belonged to. Now, both Visa and MasterCard have become immensely popular worldwide and every year, about 100 million customers get added to one of these groups.

What is the prime job of Visa and MasterCard? These associations perform the authorizations, clearing and settlement that allow a bank's credit card to be used at any merchant site that is a member of either of these associations. These associations also ensure security and fraud control. They are responsible for setting standards worldwide for card issuance, acceptance and compatibility among member banks.

11.8.2 Credit Card Transaction Participants

Having discussed the history of credit cards in brief, let us now pay our attention to the main parties in a credit card transaction. The four main parties are: (1) Cardholder, (2) Merchant, (3) Bank, (4) Association.

1. Cardholder Cardholder is the customer who uses a credit card to make payments for purchasing goods or services. A cardholder does not require carrying cash when making purchases. She does not also need to take loan every month to *buy first and pay later*. A credit card provides addresses both these issues. Using a credit card allows the customer to make purchases without needing to pay in cash. Secondly, the customer can make purchases first and then pay for them later (as per the credit card agreement with the bank). In the case of lost cash, there is a very high scope for misuse. However, in the case of a lost credit card, the customer's liability is limited.

2. Merchant From a merchant's perspective, credit cards provide several attractions. Generally, the convenience of credit cards induces customers to make high-value and impulsive purchases more often. Validating credit cards is also quite easy. To authorize a sale, the merchant can swipe the customer's credit card through a **Point Of Sale (POS)** terminal, via which the credit card information travels to the authorization network. This process results into the validation of the card.

3. Bank The usage of credit cards gives banks more customers: both the cardholders and the merchants. When a bank issues a credit card to a cardholder, it is called **issuing bank**. When a merchant ties up with a bank to accept credit card payments, that bank becomes the **acquiring bank**.

4. Association By association, we mean Visa or MasterCard. These bodies are owned by their member banks, and are governed by separate board of directors. Apart from licensing, setting up regulations, conducting research and analysis, etc., their main task is to process credit card payments. Processing millions of card transactions every day necessitates standardization and automation in clearing, interchange, and payment settlement.

11.8.3 Sample Credit Card Payment Flow

Let us now understand how a typical transaction using credit card takes place. There are two distinct phases in any credit card transaction: **clearing** and **settlement**.

1. Clearing is the process by which the transaction information is passed from the acquirer to the cardholder via the issuer to effect posting to the cardholder account. There is no transfer of funds in the clearing process.
2. Settlement is the process in which actual funds are transferred from the cardholder to the acquirer.

Let us understand this with an example, where the customer has made a purchase worth $100 using her card. Note that in the settlement process, the cardholder pays $100 to the issuer bank. The issuer bank pays only $98.50 to the association (Visa or MasterCard), retaining the $1.50 as its income. The association pays that amount to the acquirer bank. The acquirer bank pays only $97 to the merchant, retaining the $1 as its profit.

Figure 11.34 shows the clearing process, and Fig. 11.35 shows the settlement process. Note that the last step in the settlement process (the delivery of goods or services) is not usually the last in the sequence. It is many times done before the settlement phase is entered. However, it is shown here in the settlement phase simply to complete the logical flow.

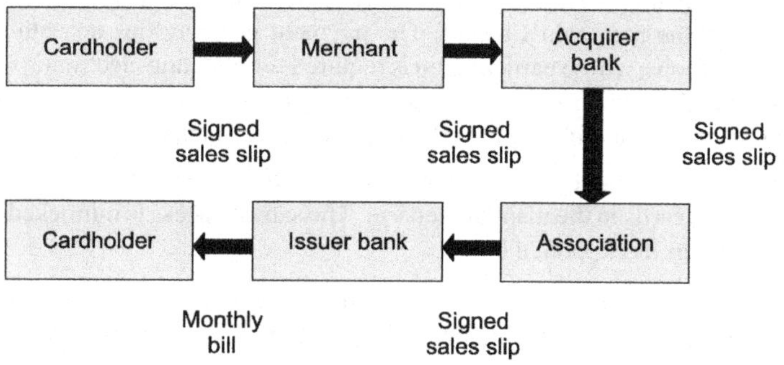

Fig. 11.34 *Clearing process*

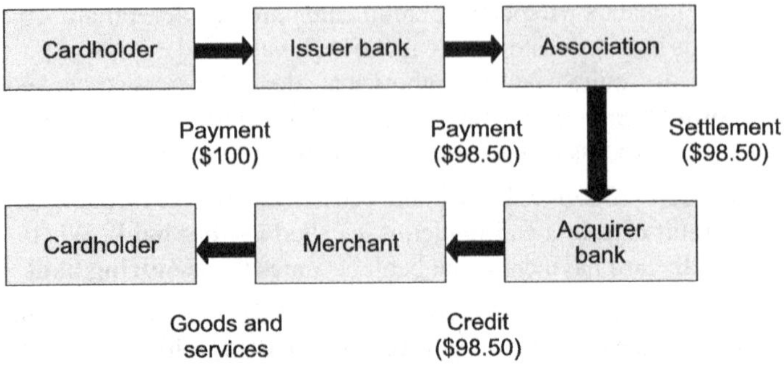

Fig. 11.35 *Settlement process*

At the broadest level, the credit card processing models in e-commerce transactions can be classified into two categories, based on who takes on the job of processing credit cards and making payments. These two models are:

1. Without involving a payment gateway This follows the traditional (manual) approach of credit card processing. Here, a third party (called a payment gateway) is not involved in the credit card processing. Therefore, it is left to the merchant to process credit cards online.

2. Involving a payment gateway In this type of credit card processing mechanism, a third party specializing in credit card processing, i.e., the payment gateway, is involved. A payment gateway is a third-party essentially taking care of the routing of messages between the merchant and the banks.

The payments related to e-commerce transactions pose the following difficulties:

1. Settlement of payment by physical means slows down the process and is inconvenient.
2. The buyer and seller are not physically present at the same place during the transaction and often may be completely unknown to each other. Therefore, although they may be genuine, their identities need to be authenticated.
3. The Internet being a public network raw transmission of payment data (for example credit card and amount details) to the merchant or any other party is highly unsafe.
4. A payment gateway facilitates e-commerce payments by authenticating the parties involved, routing payment related data between these parties and the concerned banks/financial institution in a highly secure environment and providing general support to them.
5. The merchant ties up with a payment gateway, which takes on the responsibility of processing credit cards on the merchant's behalf. The payment gateway ties up with all the banks and financial institutions, whose participation is required for effecting electronic payments, relieving the merchant of these requirements. The payment gateways are independent companies offering payment solutions to merchants for effecting online payments.

As we mentioned, this model of processing credit cards is very similar to the way shops and restaurants process credit cards in the manual scenario. The same process is mimicked using the Internet technologies. This happens as explained below.

Stage 1: Verification In this stage, the credit card details of the customer are verified with the help of a number of financial institutions. Let us first take a look at Fig. 11.36, which is explained later.

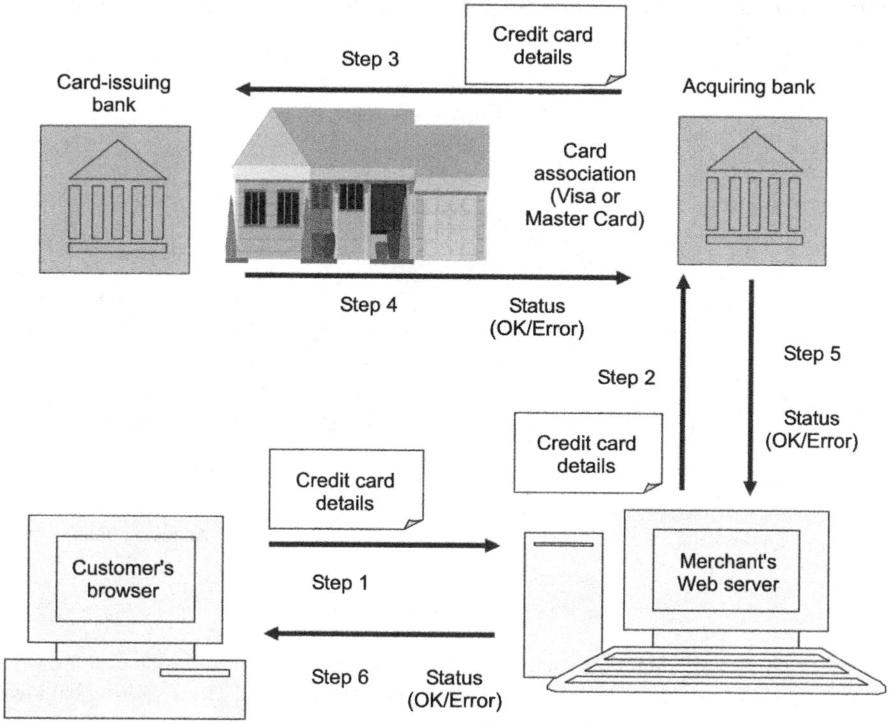

Fig. 11.36 *Payment verification process*

Let us understand the process.

1. The customer provides the credit card details such as the credit card number, expiry date and the customer's name as it appears on the credit card, to the merchant. In the early days of e-commerce transactions, the customer would send these details by email, or by filling up an online form. However, due to security issues realized later, the email approach is discouraged these days, and if the customer enters these details in an online form, this involves a SSL session between the merchant and the customer.
2. The merchant would forward this information (via another SSL-enabled session) to its own bank, called the acquiring bank.
3. The acquiring bank would then forward these credit cards details, in turn, all the way, to the customer's bank, called the issuing bank, via the card association.
4. The card-issuing bank would verify information such as the credit card details, the customer's credit limit, whether the credit card is in the list of stolen credit cards, etc., and send the appropriate status back to the merchant's acquiring bank.
5. The merchant's acquiring bank would then forward the status message back to the merchant.
6. Depending on whether the credit card was validated successfully or not, the merchant would either process the order, or reject it, and inform the customer accordingly.

Stage 2: Payment Having verified the credit card details of the customer, the actual payment processing has to now happen. This is shown in Fig. 11.37.

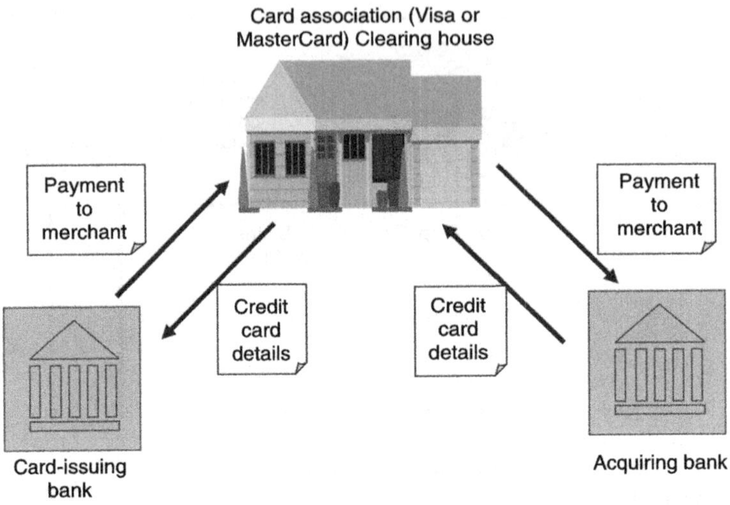

Fig. 11.37 *Payment process*

The merchant would collect all such credit card transactions that took place in a particular day, and send their list to its acquiring bank for obtaining payment for them. The acquiring bank would then interact with the various card-issuing banks through the card-association clearing house (a financial institution that settles credit card payments between banks, i.e., Visa or MasterCard, just as a clearing house settles check payments within banks), and debit the appropriate card-issuing bank accounts of the customers, and credit the merchant's acquiring bank account appropriately.

Notice that the merchant is directly dealing with its acquiring bank here. Over a period of time, people realized that the merchant had to take too many responsibilities in such a model, and that gave birth to the concept of a payment gateway. A payment gateway is a third party, that acts a middleman between merchants, acquiring banks and card issuing banks to authorize credit cards and ensure that the money is transferred from the customer's account to the merchant's account. This relieves the merchant from all these tasks, which it has to otherwise take upon itself.

3-D SECURE PROTOCOL 11.9

Secure Electronic Transaction (SET) was designed as a protocol for making online payments using credit cards. However, it was quite unsuccessful and was never really used in practice. Hence, search for newer mechanisms was on. In spite of its advantages, SET has one limitation: it does not prevent a user from providing someone else's credit card number. The credit card number is protected from the merchant. However, how can one prevent a customer from using another person's credit card number? That is not achieved in SET. Consequently, a new protocol developed by Visa has emerged, called as 3-D Secure.

The main difference between SET and 3-D Secure is that any cardholder who wishes to participate in a payment transaction involving the usage of the 3-D Secure protocol has to enroll on the issuer bank's *Enrollment Server*. That is, before a cardholder makes a card payment, she must enroll with the issuer bank's Enrollment server. This process is shown in Fig. 11.38.

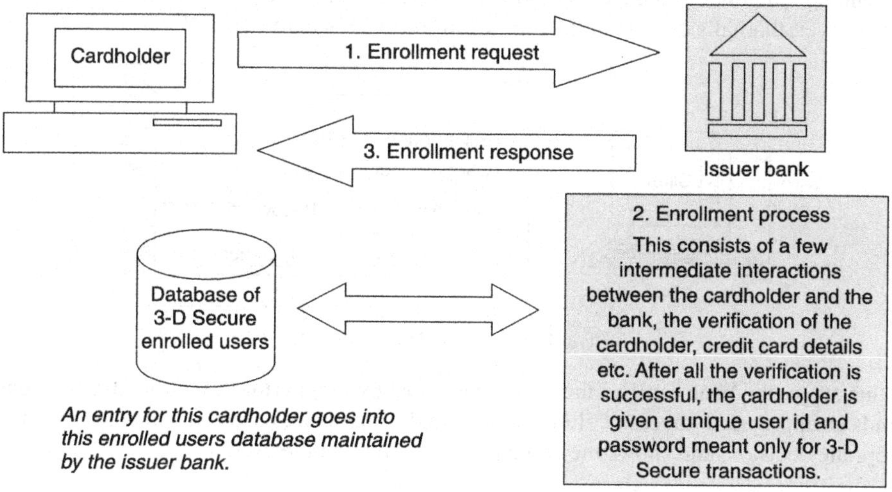

Fig. 11.38 *User enrollment*

At the time of an actual 3-D Secure transaction, when the merchant receives a payment instruction from the cardholder, the merchant forwards this request to the issuer bank through the Visa network. The issuer bank requires the cardholder to provide the user id and password that were created at the time of user enrollment process. The cardholder provides these details, which the issuer bank verifies against its 3-D Secure enrolled users database (against the stored card number). Only after the user is authenticated successfully that the issuer bank informs the merchant that it can accept the card payment instruction.

11.9.1 Protocol Overview

Let us understand how the 3-D Secure protocol works, step-by-step.

Step 1: The user shops using the shopping cart on the merchant site, and decides to pay the amount. The user enters the credit card details for this purpose, and clicks on the OK button, as shown in Fig. 11.39.

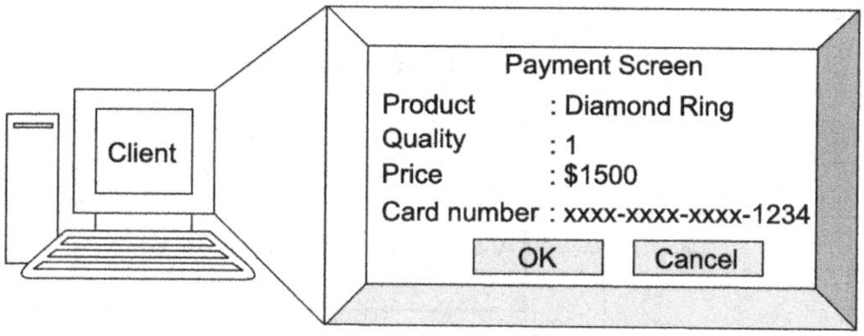

Fig. 11.39 *Step 1 in 3-D Secure*

Step 2: When the user clicks on the *OK* button, the user will be redirected to the issuer bank's site. The bank site will popup a screen, prompting the user to enter the password provided by the issuer bank. This is shown in Fig. 11.40. The bank (issuer) authenticates the user by the mechanism selected by the user earlier. In this case, we consider a simple static id and password based mechanism. Newer trends involve sending a number to the user's mobile phone and asking the user to enter that number on the screen. However, that falls outside of the purview of the 3-D Secure protocol.

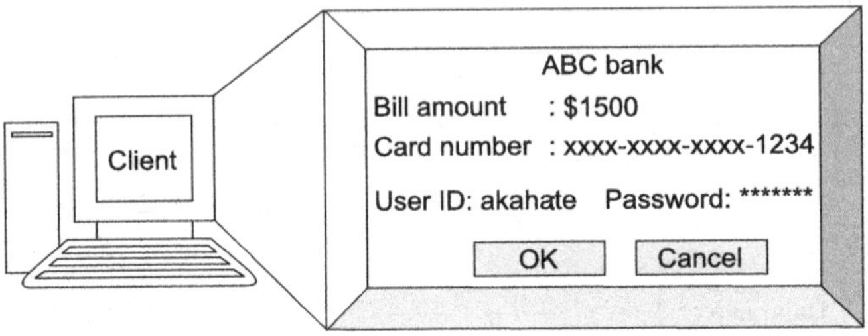

Fig. 11.40 *Step 2 in 3-D Secure*

At this stage, the bank verifies the user's password by comparing it with its database entry. The bank sends an appropriate success/failure message to the merchant, based on which the merchant takes an appropriate decision, and shows the corresponding screen to the user.

11.9.2 What Happens Behind the Scene?

Figure 11.41 depicts the internal operations of 3-D Secure. The process uses SSL for confidentiality and server authentication.

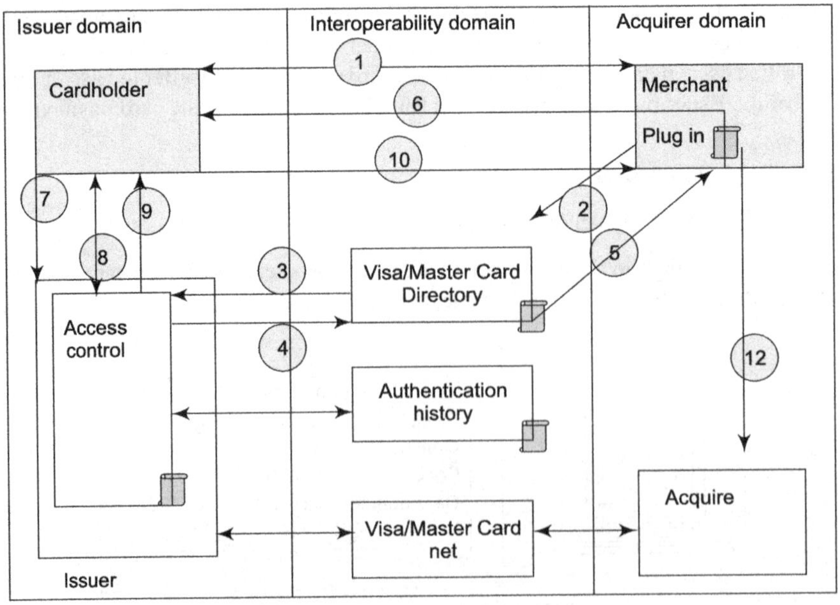

Fig. 11.41 *3-D Secure internal flow*

The flow can be described as follows:

1. The customer finalizes on the payment on merchant site (the merchant has all the data of this customer).
2. A program called *merchant plug in*, which resides at the merchant Web server, sends the user information to the Visa/MasterCard directory (which is LDAP-based).
3. The Visa/MasterCard directory queries access control server running at the issuer bank (i.e., the customer's bank), to check the authentication status of the customer.
4. The access control server forms the response for the Visa directory and sends it back to the Visa/MasterCard directory.
5. The Visa/MasterCard directory sends the payer's authentication status to the merchant plug in.
6. After getting the response, if the user is currently not authenticated, the plug in redirects the user to the bank site, requesting the bank or the issuer site to perform the authentication process.
7. The access control server (running on the bank's site) receives the request for authentication of the user.
8. The authentication server performs authentication of the user based on the mechanism of authentication chosen by the user (e.g., password, dynamic password, mobile, etc.)
9. The access control server returns the user authentication information to the merchant plug in running in the acquirer domain by redirecting the user to the merchant site. It also sends the information to the repository where the history of the user authentication is kept for legal purpose.
10. The plug in receives the response of the access control server through the user's browser. This contains the digital signature of the access control server.
11. The plug in validates the digital signature of the response and the response from the access control server.

If the authentication was successful and the digital signature of the access control server is validated, the merchant sends the authorization information to its bank (i.e., the acquire bank).

Key Terms and Concepts

Access control • Access Control List (ACL) • Authentication • Availability • Birthday attack • Certification Authority (CA) • Cipher text • Clear text • Confidentiality • Cryptanalysis • Cryptography • Cryptology • Data Encryption Standard (DES) • Digital certificate • DNS spoofing • DNSSec • Domain Name System (DNS) • DSN poisoning • Fabrication • Hash • Integrity • Interception • Interception • IP Sniffing • IP Spoofing • Message digest • Modification • Non repudiation • OSI standard for security model • Packet sniffing • Packet spoofing • Phishing • Plain text • Private key • Public key • Secure Socket Layer (SSL) • Snooping • Spoofed address • Symmetric key encryption

SUMMARY

- Cryptography is a technique of encoding and decoding messages, so that they are not understood by anybody except the sender and the intended recipient.
- The sender encodes the message (a process called as encryption) and the receiver decodes the encrypted message to get back the original message (a process called decryption).

- Encryption can be classified into symmetric key encryption and asymmetric key encryption.
- In symmetric key encryption, the same key is used for encryption and decryption.
- In asymmetric key encryption, each participant has a pair of keys (one private, the other public). If encryption is done using public key, decryption must be done using private key alone, and vice versa. The private key remains private with the participant; the public key is freely distributed to the general public.
- Digital signature has become a very critical technology for modern secure data communications. It involves a very intelligent combination of public key encryption techniques to achieve secure communication.
- To further strengthen the security mechanisms, the concept of digital certificates has gained popularity.
- Just as we have paper certificates to prove that we have passed a particular examination, or that we are eligible for driving a car (the certificate being a driver's license); a digital certificate is used for authenticating either a Web client or a Web server.
- The authority issuing a digital certificate is called certification authority (CA).
- CAs also have to maintain a Certificate Revocation List (CRL), which lets users know which digital certificates are no longer valid.
- The Secure Socket Layer (SSL) protocol is used to encrypt all communications between a Web browser and a Web server. It also provides message integrity.

MULTIPLE CHOICE QUESTIONS

1. When only the sender and the receiver want to be able to access the contents of a message, the principle of __________ comes into picture.
   (a) confidentiality (b) authentication (c) authorization (d) integrity
2. When the receiver wants to be sure of the sender's identity, ________ is important.
   (a) confidentiality (b) authentication (c) authorization (d) integrity
3. When the receiver wants to be sure that the contents of a message have not been tampered with, _______ is the key factor.
   (a) confidentiality (b) authentication (c) authorization (d) integrity
4. When the sender and the receiver use the same key for encryption and decryption, it is called ______________.
   (a) symmetric key encryption (b) asymmetric key encryption
   (c) public key encryption (d) Any of these
5. When the sender and the receiver use different keys for encryption and decryption, it is called ______________.
   (a) symmetric key encryption (b) asymmetric key encryption
   (c) public key encryption (d) Any of these
6. _________ is a public key encryption algorithm.
   (a) DES (b) RSA (c) RAS (d) DSE
7. _________ can be cracked if groups of characters repeat in the plain text.
   (a) Stream cipher (b) Character cipher (c) Block cipher (d) Group cipher
8. Digital signature uses ________.
   (a) array (b) table (c) chain (d) hash

9. In digital signature, at the sender's end, the sender's _________ is important.
   (a) public key
   (b) private key
   (c) None of the public or the private keys
   (d) Either public or private key
10. Digital certificate establishes the relation between a user and her _________.
    (a) private key
    (b) name
    (c) public key
    (d) credit card number

DETAILED QUESTIONS

1. Describe the risks involved in data communication over a network.
2. What is cryptography?
3. Explain how the symmetric encryption works.
4. Explain the technique used in the asymmetric cryptography.
5. Discuss the term digital signature.
6. Illustrate how digital signatures work by giving an example.
7. What are digital certificates? How are they useful?
8. Explain phising.
9. Discuss pharming attacks.
10. How does the SSL protocol work?

EXERCISES

1. Find out which algorithms are popular in message digests, digital signatures, symmetric as well as asymmetric key encryption and try to understand at least one of them in complete detail.
2. Read more about the IT laws in your home country. What is the significance of digital signatures?
3. Search for files with an extension .cer on your computer. Are there any such files? If there are, do they contain digital certificates?
4. Create a digital certificate using Java. Also try to investigate about the process involved and the payable fees in obtaining real-life digital certificates.
5. What does it take to implement the SSL protocol? Study the OpenSSL protocol.

12 NETWORK SECURITY

INTRODUCTION

In the previous chapter, we looked at the application layer security issues. While they are very critical and are worth examining in detail, equal importance needs to be given to network security-related issues also. Network security goes hand in hand with application security. While application security looks more at the transactional issues, network security deals with raw packets, and attempts to fix holes that appear at that layer. Various schemes can be used to provide network security, such as firewalls, VPNs, etc.

This chapter deals with all these issues at the network layer, and completes our overview of the Internet security issues and their solutions.

FIREWALLS 12.1

12.1.1 Introduction

The dramatic rise and progress of the Internet has opened possibilities that no one could have thought of earlier. We can connect any computer in the world to any other computer, no matter how far the two are located from each other. This is undoubtedly a great advantage for individuals and corporates as well. However, this can be a nightmare for network support staff, which is left with a very difficult job of trying to protect the corporate networks from a variety of attacks. At a broad level, there are two kinds of attacks.

1. Most corporations have large amounts of valuable and confidential data in their networks. Leaking of this critical information to competitors can be a great setback.
2. Apart from the danger of the insider information leaking out, there is a great danger of the outside elements (such as viruses and worms) entering a corporate network to create havoc.

We can depict this situation in Fig. 12.1.

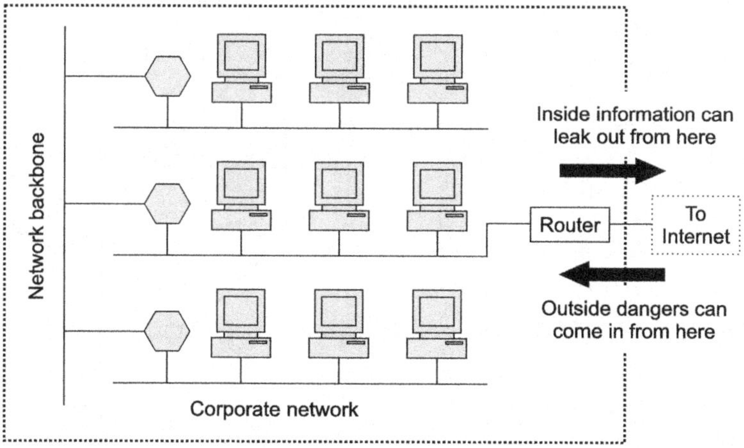

Fig. 12.1 *Threats from inside and outside a corporate network*

As a result of these dangers, we must have mechanisms which can ensure that the inside information remains inside, and also prevent the outside attackers from entering inside a corporate network. As we know, encryption of information (if implemented properly) renders its transmission to the outside world redundant. That is, even if confidential information flows out of a corporate network, if it is in an encrypted form, outsiders cannot make any sense of it. However, encryption does not work in the other direction. Outside attackers can still try to break inside a corporate network. Consequently, better schemes are desired to achieve protection from outside attacks. This is where a **firewall** comes into picture.

Conceptually, a firewall can be compared with a sentry standing outside an important person's house (such as the nation's president). This sentry usually keeps an eye on and physically checks every person that enters into or comes out of the house. If the sentry senses that a person wishing to enter the president's house is carrying a knife, the sentry would not allow the person to enter. Similarly, even if the person does not possess any banned objects, but somehow looks suspicious, the sentry can still prevent that person's entry.

A firewall acts like a sentry. If implemented, it guards a corporate network by standing between the network and the outside world. All traffic between the network and the Internet in either direction must pass through the firewall. The firewall decides if the traffic can be allowed to flow, or whether it must be stopped from proceeding further. This is shown in Fig. 12.2.

Of course, technically, a firewall is a specialized version of a router. Apart from the basic routing functions and rules, a router can be configured to perform the firewall functionality, with the help of additional software resources.

The characteristics of a good firewall implementation can be described as follows:

1. All traffic from inside to outside, and vice versa, must pass through the firewall. To achieve this, all the access to the local network must first be physically blocked, and access only via the firewall should be permitted.
2. Only the traffic authorized as per the local security policy should be allowed to pass through.
3. The firewall itself must be strong enough, so as to render attacks on it useless.

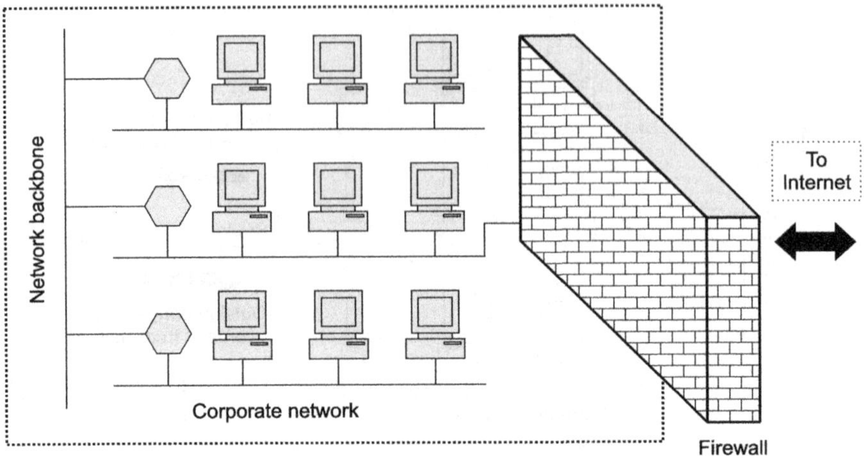

Fig. 12.2 *Firewall*

12.1.2 Types of Firewalls

Based on the criteria that they use for filtering traffic, firewalls are generally classified into two types, as shown in Fig. 12.3.

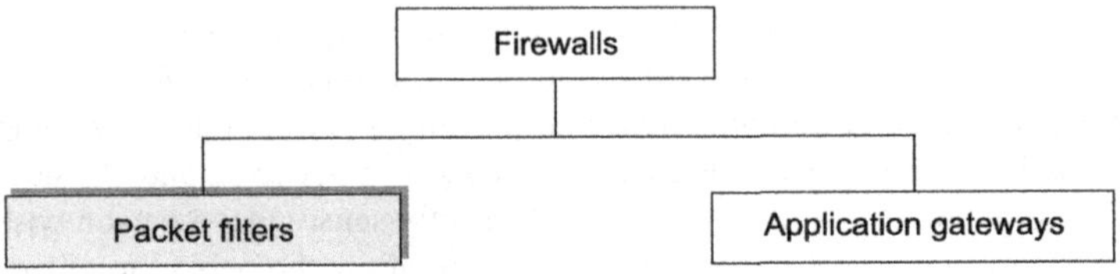

Fig. 12.3 *Types of firewalls*

Let us discuss these two types of firewalls one by one.

1. Packet filters As the name suggests, a packet filter applies a set of rules to each packet, and based on the outcome, decides to either forward or discard the packet. It is also called screening router or screening filter. Such a firewall implementation involves a router, which is configured to filter packets going in either direction (from the local network to the outside world, and vice versa). The filtering rules are based on a number of fields in the IP and TCP/UDP headers, such as source and destination IP addresses, IP protocol field (which identifies if the protocol in the upper transport layer is TCP or UDP), TCP/UDP port numbers (which identify the application which is using this packet, such as email, file transfer or World Wide Web).

The idea of a packet filter is shown in Fig. 12.4.

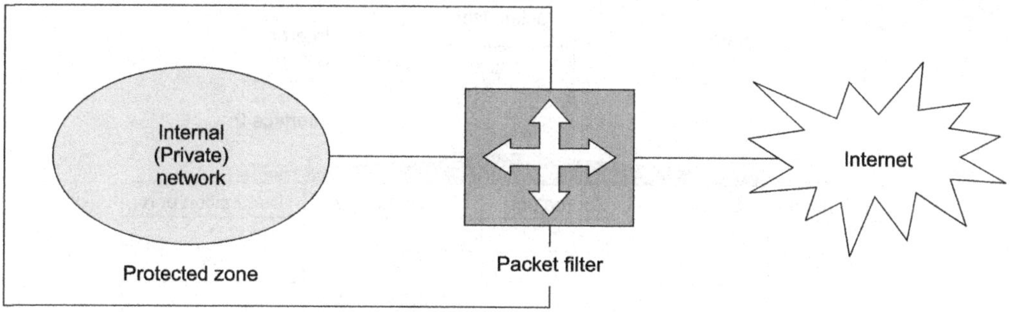

Fig. 12.4 *Packet filter*

Conceptually, a packet filter can be considered as a router that performs three main actions, as shown in Fig. 12.5.

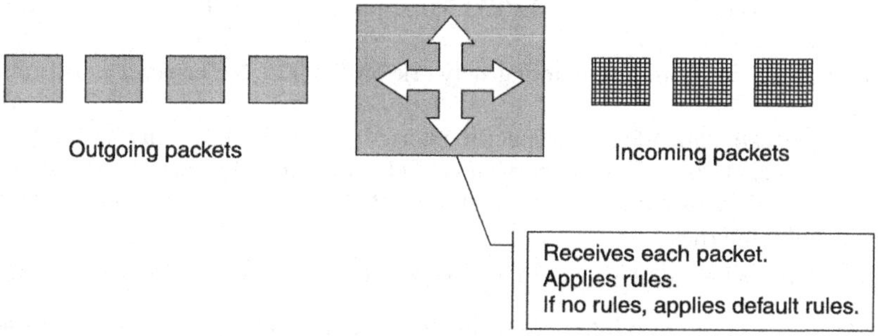

Fig. 12.5 *Packet filter operation*

A packet filter performs the following functions:

(a) It receives each packet as it arrives.
(b) It passes the packet through a set of rules, based on the contents of the IP and transports header fields of the packet. If there is a match with one of the set rules, it decides whether to accept or discard the packet based on that rule. For example, a rule could specify either to disallow all incoming traffic from an IP address 157.29.19.10 (this IP address is taken just as an example), or to disallow all traffic that uses UDP as the higher (transport) layer protocol.
(c) If there is no match with any rule, the packet filter takes the default action. The default can be *discard all packets*, or *accept all packets*. The former policy is more conservative, whereas the latter is more open. Usually, the implementation of a firewall begins with the default *discard all packets* option, and then rules are applied one by one to enforce packet filtering.

The chief advantage of the packet filter is its simplicity. The users need not be aware of a packet filter at all. Packet filters are very fast in their operating speed. However, the two disadvantages of a packet filter are the difficulties in setting up the packet filter rules correctly, and lack of support for authentication.

Figure 12.6 shows an example where a router can be converted into a packet filter by adding the filtering rules in the form of a table. This table decides which of the packets should be allowed (forwarded) or discarded.

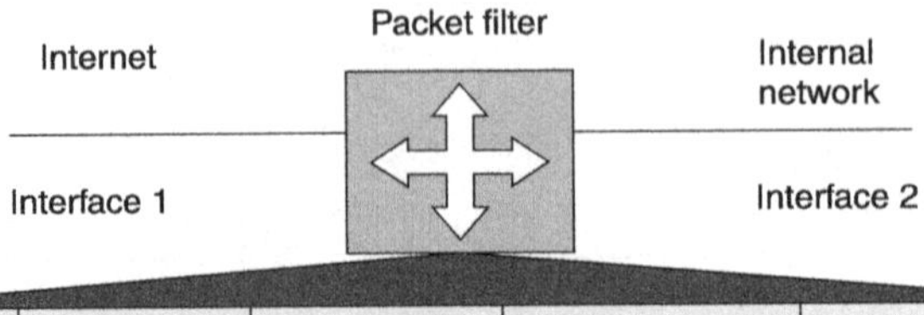

Interface	Source IP	Source port	Destination IP	Destination port
1	130.33.0.0	*	*	*
1	*	*	*	23
1	*	*	193.77.21.9	*
2	*	*	*	80

Fig. 12.6 *Example of packet filter table*

The rules specified in the packet filter work as follows:

(a) Incoming packets from network 130.33.0.0 are not allowed. They are blocked as a security precaution.

(b) Incoming packets from any external network on the TELNET server port (number 23) are blocked.

(c) Incoming packets intended for a specific internal host 193.77.21.9 are blocked.

(d) Outgoing packets intended for port 80 (HTTP) are banned. That is, this organization does not want to allow its employees to send requests to the external world (i.e., the Internet) for browsing the Internet.

Attackers can try and break the security of a packet filter by using the following techniques.

(a) *IP address spoofing* An intruder outside the corporate network can attempt to send a packet towards the internal corporate network, with the source IP address set equal to one of the IP addresses of the internal users. This is shown in Fig. 12.7. This attack can be defeated by discarding all the packets that arrive at the incoming side of the firewall, with the source address equal to one of the internal addresses.

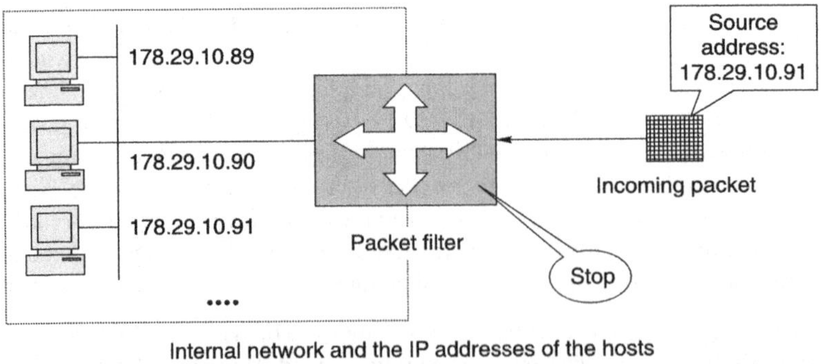

Fig. 12.7 *Packet filter defeating the IP address spoofing attack*

(b) *Source routing attacks* An attacker can specify the route that a packet should take as it moves along the Internet. The attacker hopes that by specifying this option, the packet filter can be fooled to bypass its normal checks. Discarding all packets that use this option can thwart such an attack.

(c) *Tiny fragment attacks* IP packets pass through a variety of physical networks, such as Ethernet, Token Ring, X.25, Frame Relay, ATM, etc. All these networks have a pre-defined maximum frame size (called the Maximum Transmission Unit or MTU). Many times, the size of the IP packet is greater than this maximum size allowed by the underlying network. In such cases, the IP packet needs to be fragmented, so that it can be accommodated inside the physical frame, and carried further. An attacker might attempt to use this characteristic of the TCP/IP protocol suite by intentionally creating fragments of the original IP packet and sending them. The attacker feels that the packet filter can be fooled, so that after fragmentation, it checks only the first fragment, and does not check the remaining fragments. This attack can be foiled by discarding all the packets where the (upper layer) protocol type is TCP and the packet is fragmented (refer to *identification* and *protocol* fields of an IP packet discussed earlier to understand how we can implement this).

An advanced type of packet filter is called **dynamic packet filter** or **stateful packet filter**. A dynamic packet filter allows the examination of packets based on the current state of the network. That is, it adapts itself to the current exchange of information, unlike the normal packet filters, which have routing rules hard coded. For instance, we can specify a rule with the help of a dynamic packet filter as follows:

Allow incoming TCP segments only if they are responses to the outgoing TCP segments that have gone through our network.

Note that the dynamic packet filter has to maintain a list of the currently open connections and outgoing packets in order to deal with this rule. Hence, it is called *dynamic* or *stateful*. When such a rule is in effect, the logical view of the packet filtering can be illustrated, as shown in Fig. 12.8.

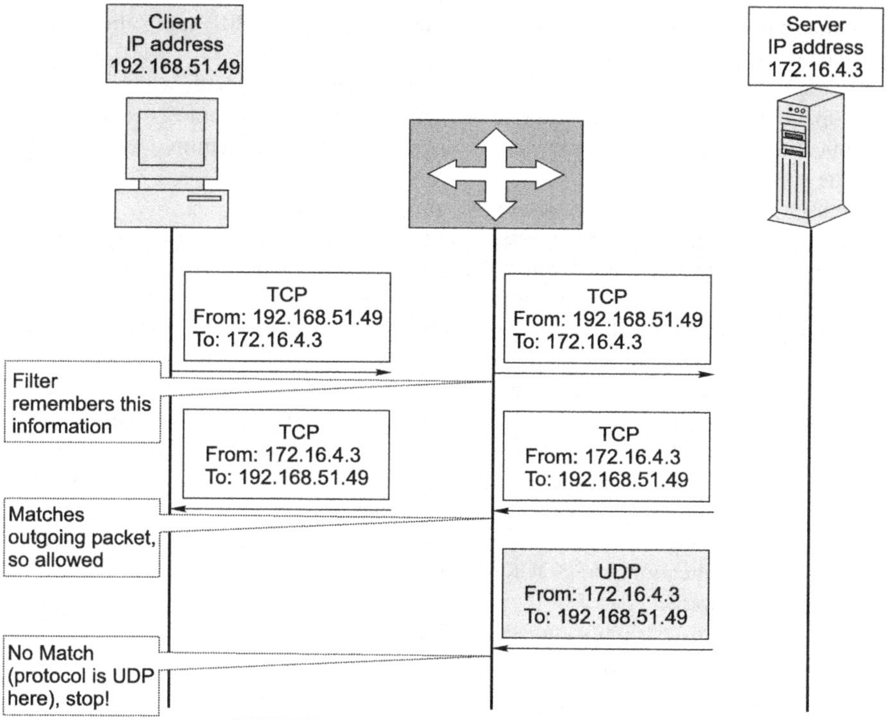

Fig. 12.8 *Dynamic packet filter technology*

As shown in the figure, firstly, an internal client sends a TCP segments to an external server, which the dynamic packet filter allows. In response, the server sends back a TCP segments, which the packet filter examines, and realizes that it is a response to the internal client's request. Therefore, it allows that packet in. However, next, the external server sends a new UDP datagram, which the filter does not allow, because previously, the exchange of the client and the server packets happened using the TCP protocol. However, this packet is based on the UDP protocol. Since this is against the rule that was set up earlier, the filter drops the packet.

Application Gateways An **application gateway** is also called a **proxy server**. This is because it acts like a proxy (i.e., deputy or substitute), and decides about the flow of application level traffic. The idea is shown in Fig. 12.9.

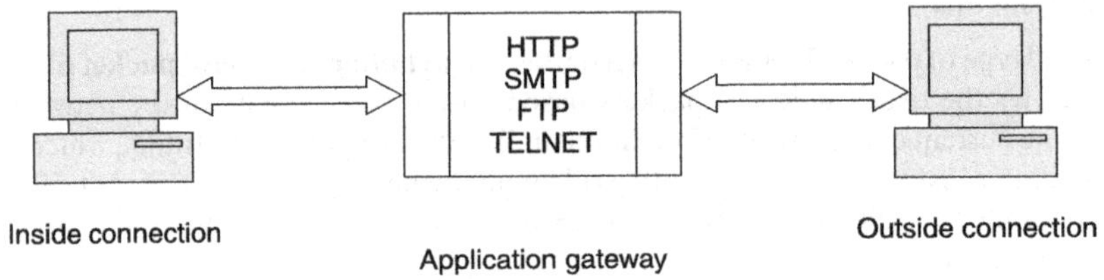

Fig. 12.9 *Application gateway*

Application gateways typically work as follows:

1. An internal user contacts the application gateway using a TCP/IP application, such as HTTP or TELNET.
2. The application gateway asks the user about the remote host with which the user wants to set up a connection for actual communication (i.e., its domain name or IP address, etc.). The application gateway also asks for the user id and the password required to access the services of the application gateway.
3. The user provides this information to the application gateway.
4. The application gateway now accesses the remote host on behalf of the user, and passes the packets of the user to the remote host. Note that there is a variation of the application gateway, called **circuit gateway**, which performs some additional functions as compared to those performed by an application gateway. A circuit gateway, in fact, creates a new connection between itself and the remote host. The user is not aware of this, and thinks that there is a direct connection between himself and the remote host. Also, the circuit gateway changes the source IP address in the packets from the end user's IP address to its own. This way, the IP addresses of the computers of the internal users are hidden from the outside world. This is shown in Fig. 12.10. Of course, both the connections are shown with a single arrow to stress on the concept, though in reality, both are two-way connections.

   The SOCKS server is an example of the real-life implementation of a circuit gateway. It is a client-server application. The SOCKS client runs on the internal hosts, and the SOCKS server runs on the firewall.
5. From here onwards, the application gateway acts like a proxy of the actual end user, and delivers packets from the user to the remote host and vice versa.

Application gateways are generally more secure than packet filters, because rather than examining every packet against a number of rules, here we simply detect whether a user is allowed to work with a TCP/IP application, or not. The disadvantage of application gateways is the overhead in terms of connections. As we noticed, there are actually two sets of connections now, one between the end user and the application gateway, and another between the application gateway and the remote host. The application gateway has to manage these two sets of connections, and the traffic going between them. This means that the actual communicating internal host is under an illusion, as illustrated in Fig. 12.11.

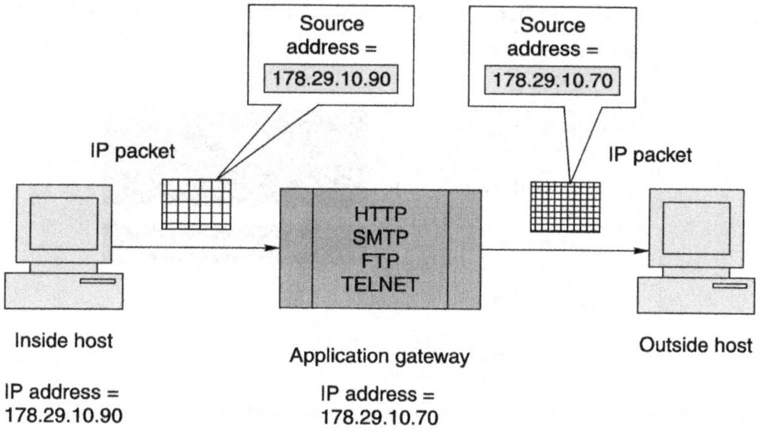

Fig. 12.10 *Circuit gateway operation*

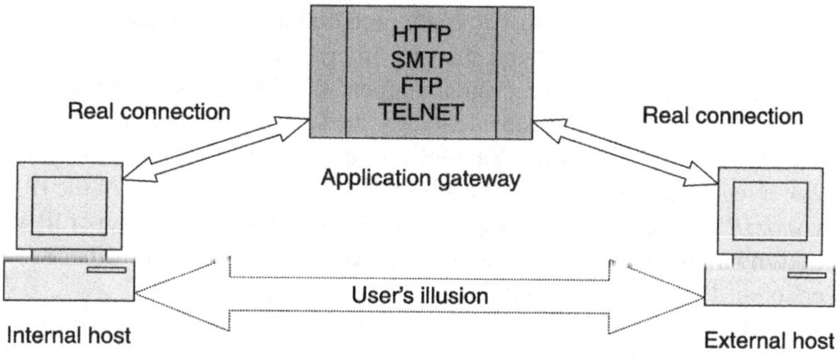

Fig. 12.11 *Application gateway creates an illusion*

An application gateway is also called **bastion host**. Usually, a bastion host is a very key point in the security of a network.

IP SECURITY 12.2

12.2.1 Introduction

The IP packets contain data in plain text form. That is, anyone watching the IP packets pass by can actually access them, read their contents, and even change them. We have studied higher-level security mechanisms (such as SSL, SHTTP, PGP, PEM, S/MIME and SET) to prevent such kinds of attacks.

Although these higher-level protocols enhance the protection mechanisms, there was a general feeling for a long time to make IP packets themselves secure. If we can achieve this, then we need not rely only on the higher-level security mechanisms. The higher-level security mechanisms can then serve as additional security measures. Thus, we will have two levels of security in this scheme.

1. First offer security at the IP packet level itself.
2. Continue implementing higher-level security mechanisms, depending on the requirements.

This is shown in Fig. 12.12.

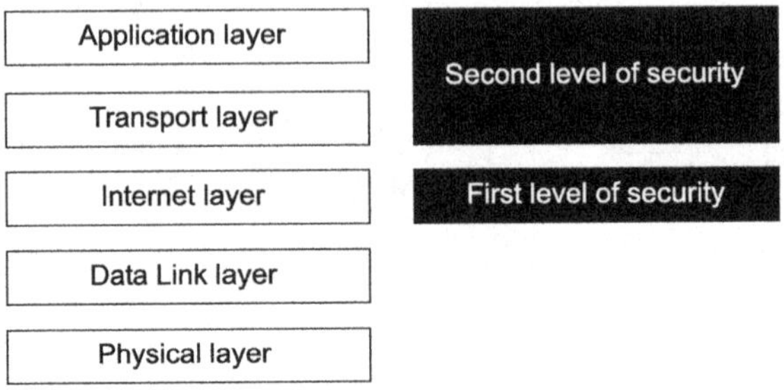

Fig. 12.12 *Security at the Internet layer as well as the above layers*

We have already discussed the higher-level security protocols. Our focus of discussion in this chapter is the first level of security (at the Internet layer).

In 1994, the Internet Architecture Board (IAB) prepared a report called *Security in the Internet Architecture* (RFC 1636). This report stated that the Internet was a very open network, which was unprotected from hostile attacks. Therefore, said the report, the Internet needs better security measures, in terms of authentication, integrity and confidentiality. In 1997 above, about 150,000 Web sites were attacked in various ways, proving that the Internet was quite unsafe. Consequently, the IAB decided that authentication, integrity and encryption must be a part of the next version of the IP protocol, called *IP version 6 (Ipv6)* or *IP new generation (IPng)*. However, since the new version of IP was to take some years to be released and implemented, the designers devised ways to incorporate these security measures in the current version of IP, called as *IP version 4 (IPv4)*, as well.

The outcome of the study and IAB's report is the protocol for providing security at the IP level, called **IP Security (IPSec)**. In 1995, the Internet Engineering Task Force (IETF) published five security-based standards related to IPSec, as shown in Table 12.1.

Table 12.1 *RFC documents related to IPSec*

RFC Number	*Description*
1825	An overview of the security architecture
1826	Description of a packet authentication extension to IP
1827	Description of a packet encryption extension to IP
1828	A specific authentication mechanism
1829	A specific encryption mechanism

IPv4 *may* support these features, but IPv6 *must* support them. The overall idea of IPSec is to encrypt and seal the transport and application layer data during transmission. It also offers integrity protection for the Internet layer. However, the Internet header itself is not encrypted, because of which the intermediate routers can deliver encrypted IPSec messages to the intended recipient. The logical format of a message after IPSec processing is shown in Fig. 12.13.

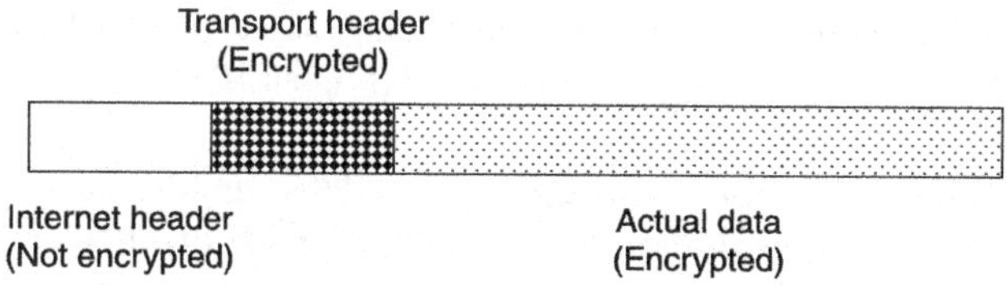

Fig. 12.13 *Result of IPSec processing*

Thus, the sender and the receiver look at IPSec, as shown in Fig. 12.14, as another layer in the TCP/IP protocol stack. This layer sits in between the transport and the Internet layers of the conventional TCP/IP protocol stack.

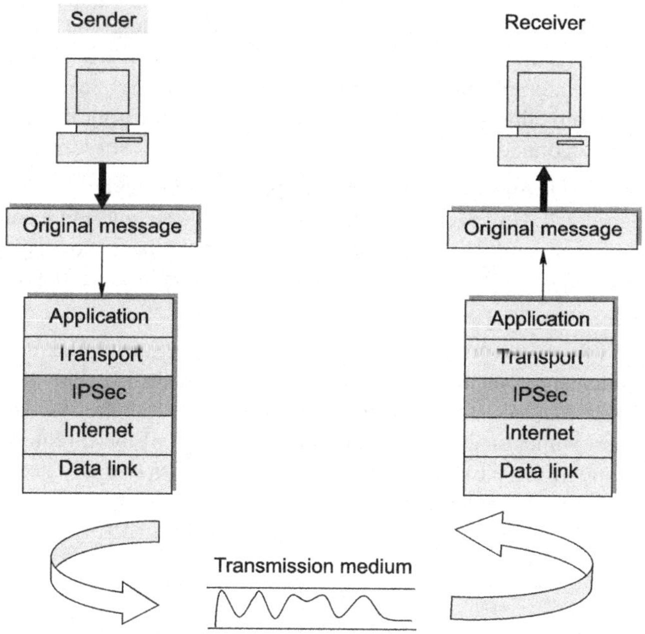

Fig. 12.14 *Conceptual IPSec positioning in the TCP/IP protocol stack*

12.2.2 IPSec Overview

1. Applications and advantages Let us first list the applications of IPSec.

(a) Secure remote Internet access Using IPSec, we can make a local call to our Internet Service Provider (ISP) so as to connect to our organization's network in a secure fashion from our home or hotel. From there, we can access the corporate network facilities or access remote desktops/servers.

(b) Secure branch office connectivity Rather than subscribing to an expensive leased line for connecting its branches across cities/countries, an organization can set up an IPSec-enabled network to securely connect all its branches over the Internet.

(c) Set up communication with other organizations Just as IPSec allows connectivity between various branches of an organization, it can also be used to connect the networks of different organizations together in a secure and inexpensive fashion.

Following are the main advantages of IPSec:

(i) IPSec is transparent to the end users. There is no need for user training, key issuance or revocation.
(ii) When IPSec is configured to work with a firewall, it becomes the only entry-exit point for all traffic, thus making it extra secure.
(iii) IPSec works at the network layer. Hence no changes are needed to the upper layers (application and transport).
(iv) When IPSec is implemented in a firewall or a router, all the outgoing and incoming traffic gets protected. However, the internal traffic does not have to use IPSec. Thus, it does not add any overheads for the internal traffic.
(v) IPSec can allow traveling staff to have secure access to the corporate network.
(vi) IPSec allows interconnectivity between branches/offices in a very inexpensive manner.

2. Basic concepts We must learn a few terms and concepts in order to understand the IPSec protocol. All these concepts are interrelated. However, rather than looking at these individual concepts straightaway, we shall start with the big picture. We will first take a look at the basic concepts in IPSec, and then elaborate each of the concepts. In this section, we shall restrict ourselves to the broad overview of the basic concepts in IPSec.

3. IPSec protocols As we know, an IP packet consists of two portions, IP header and the actual data. IPSec features are implemented in the form of additional IP headers (called as **extension headers**) to the standard, default IP headers. These extension IP headers follow the standard IP headers. IPSec offers two main services, authentication and confidentiality. Each of these requires its own extension header. Therefore, to support these two main services, IPSec defines two IP extension headers, one for authentication and another for confidentiality.

IPSec actually consists of two main protocols, as shown in Fig. 12.15.

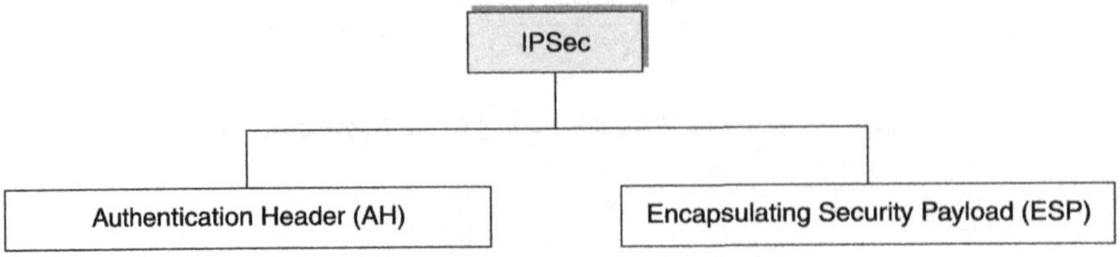

Fig. 12.15 *IPSec protocols*

These two protocols are required for the following purposes:

(a) *Authentication Header (AH)* protocol provides authentication, integrity and an optional anti-replay service. The IPSec AH is a header in an IP packet, which contains a cryptographic checksum (similar to a message digest or hash) for the contents of the packet. The AH is simply inserted between the IP header and any subsequent packet contents. No changes are required to the data contents of the packet. Thus, security resides completely in the contents of the AH.

(b) *Encapsulating Security Payload (ESP)* protocol provides data confidentiality. The ESP protocol also defines a new header to be inserted into the IP packet. ESP processing also includes the transformation of the protected data into an unreadable, encrypted forma. Under normal circumstances, the ESP will be *inside* the AH. That is, encryption happens first, and then authentication.

On receipt of an IP packet that was processed by IPSec, the receiver processes the AH first, if present. The outcome of this tells the receiver if the contents of the packet are all right, or whether they have been tampered with, while in transit. If the receiver finds the contents acceptable, it extracts the key and algorithms associated with the ESP, and decrypts the contents.

There are some more details that we should know. Both AH and ESP can be used in one of the two *modes*, as shown in Fig. 12.16.

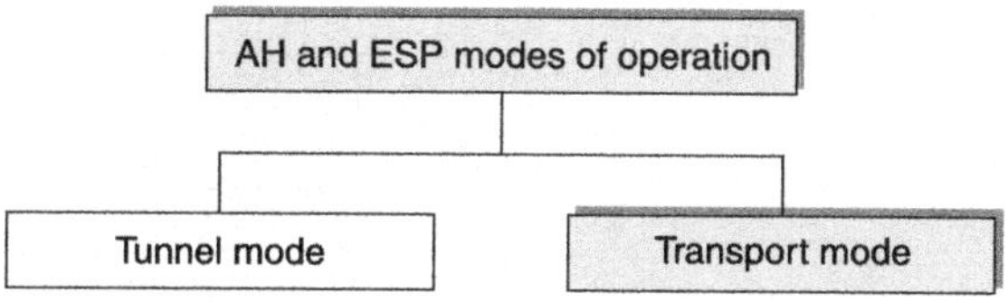

Fig. 12.16 *AH and ESP modes of operation*

We shall later study more about these modes. However, a quick overview would help.

In the **tunnel mode**, an encrypted *tunnel* is established between two hosts. Suppose *X* and *Y* are two hosts, wanting to communicate with each other using the IPSec tunnel mode. What happens here is that they identify their respective proxies, say P1 and P2, and a *logical encrypted tunnel* is established between P1 and P2. *X* sends its transmission to P1. The tunnel carries the transmission to P2. P2 forwards it to *Y*. This is shown in Fig. 12.17.

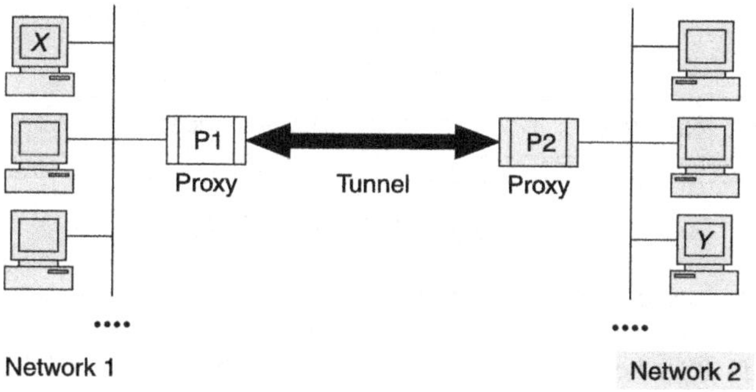

Fig. 12.17 *Concept of tunnel mode*

How do we implement this technically? As we shall see, we will have two sets of IP headers, internal and external. The internal IP header (which is encrypted) contains the source and destination addresses as *X* and *Y*, whereas the external IP header contains the source and destination addresses as P1 and P2. That way, *X* and *Y* are protected from potential attackers. This is shown in Fig. 12.18.

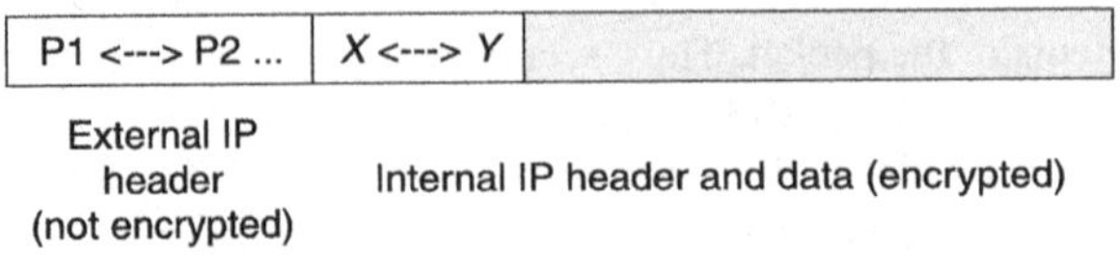

Fig. 12.18 *Implementation of tunnel mode*

(c) In the tunnel mode, IPSec protects the entire IP datagram. It takes an IP datagram (including the IP header), adds the IPSec header and trailer, and encrypts the whole thing. It then adds new IP header to this encrypted datagram.

This is shown in Fig. 12.19.

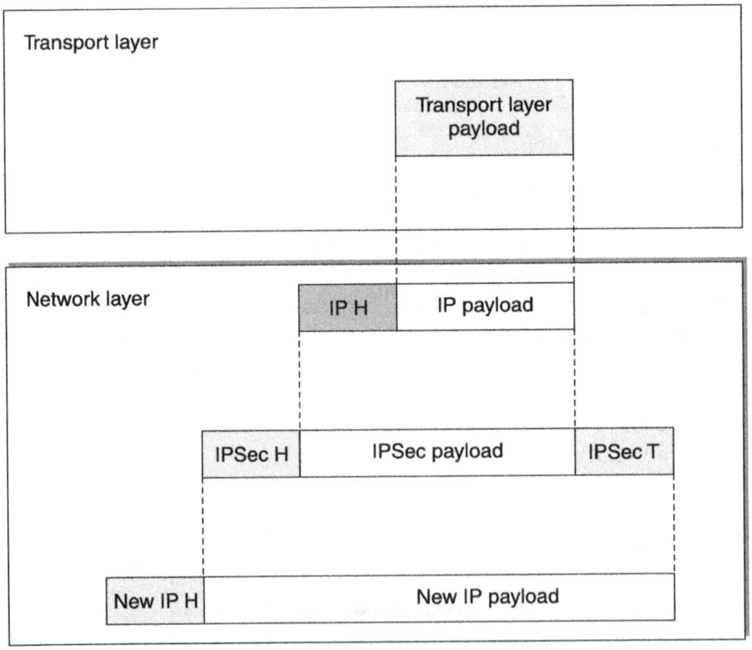

Fig. 12.19 *IPSec tunnel mode*

(d) In contrast, the transport mode does not hide the actual source and destination addresses. They are visible in plain text, while in transit. In the transport mode, IPSec takes the transport layer payload, adds IPSec header and trailer, encrypts the whole thing, and then adds the IP header. Thus, the IP header is not encrypted.

This is shown in Fig. 12.20.

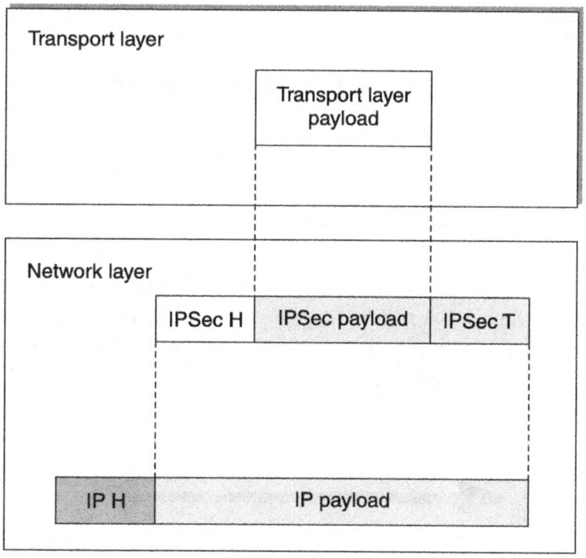

Fig. 12.20 *IPSec transport mode*

How does the user decide which mode should be used?

(i) We will notice that in the tunnel mode, the new IP header has information different from the information in the original IP header. The tunnel mode is normally used between two routers, a host and a router, or a router and a host. In other words, it is generally not used between two hosts, since the idea is to protect the original packet, including its IP header. It is as if the whole packet goes through an imaginary tunnel.

(ii) The transport mode is useful when we are interested in a host-to-host (i.e., end-to-end) encryption. The sending host uses IPSec to authenticate and/or encrypt the transport layer payload, and only the receiver verifies it.

4. Internet Key Exchange (IKE) Protocol Another supporting protocol used in IPSec for the key management procedures is called as **Internet Key Exchange (IKE)** protocol. IKE is used to negotiate the cryptographic algorithms to be later used by AH and ESP in the actual cryptographic operations. The IPSec protocols are designed to be independent of the actual lower-level cryptographic algorithms. Thus, IKE is the initial phase of IPSec, where the algorithms and keys are decided. After the IKE phase, the AH and ESP protocols take over. This process is shown in Fig. 12.21.

5. Security Association (SA) The output of the IKE phase is a **Security Association (SA)**. SA is an agreement between the communicating parties about factors such as the IPSec protocol version in use, mode of operation (transport mode or tunnel mode), cryptographic algorithms, cryptographic keys, lifetime of keys, etc. By now, we would have guessed that the principal objective of the IKE protocol is to establish an SA between the communicating parties. Once this is done, both major protocols of IPSec (i.e., AH and ESP) make use of SA for their actual operation.

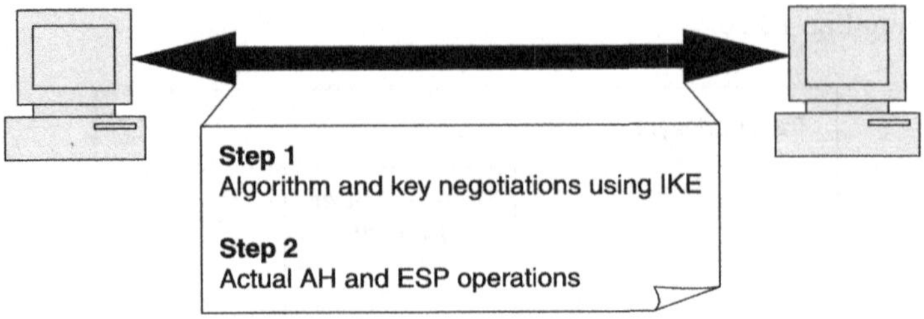

Fig. 12.21 *Steps in IPSec operation*

Note that if both AH and ESP are used, each communicating party requires two sets of SA, one for AH and one for ESP. Moreover, an SA is simplex, i.e., unidirectional. Therefore, at a second level, we need two sets of SA per communicating party, one for incoming transmission and another for outgoing transmission. Thus, if the two communicating parties use both AH and ESP, each of them would require four sets of SA, as shown in Fig. 12.22.

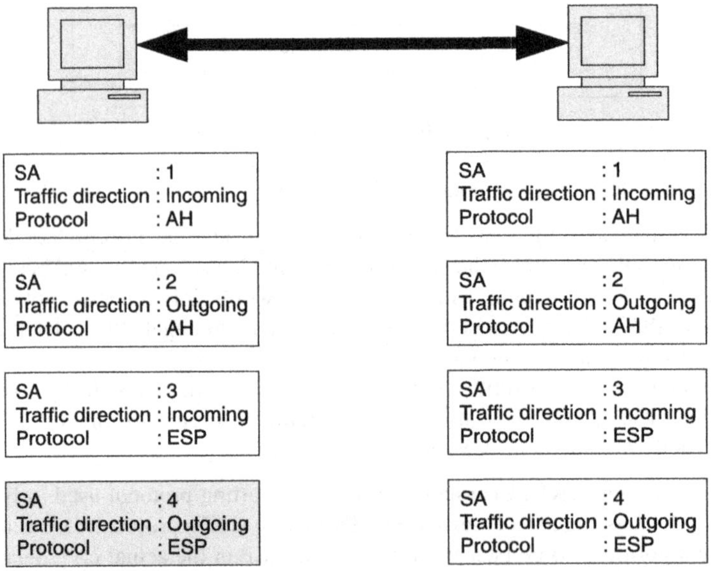

Fig. 12.22 *Security association types and classifications*

Obviously, both the communicating parties must allocate some storage area for storing the SA information at their end. For this purpose, a standard storage area called **Security Association Database (SAD)** is pre-defined and used by IPSec. Thus, each communicating party requires maintaining its own SAD. The SAD contains active SA entries. The contents of a SAD are shown in Table 12.2.

Table 12.2 *SAD fields*

Field	*Description*
Sequence number counter	This 32-bit field is used to generate the sequence number field, which is used in the AH or ESP headers.
Sequence counter overflow	This flag indicates whether the overflow of the sequence number counter should generate an audible event and prevent further transmission of packets on this SA.
Anti-replay window	A 32-bit counter field and a bit map, which are used to detect if an incoming AH or ESP packet is a replay.
AH authentication	AH authentication cryptographic algorithm and the required key.
ESP authentication	ESP authentication cryptographic algorithm and the required key.
ESP encryption	ESP encryption algorithm, key, Initial Vector (IV) and IV mode.
IPSec protocol mode	Indicates which IPSec protocol mode (e.g., transport or tunnel) should be applied to the AH and ESP traffic.
Path Maximum Transfer Unit (PMTU)	The maximum size of an IP datagram that will be allowed to pass through a given network path without fragmentation.
Lifetime	Specifies the life of the SA. After this time interval, the SA must be replaced with a new one.

Having discussed the background of IPSec, let us now discuss the two main protocols in IPSec, which are AH and ESP.

12.2.3 Authentication Header (AH)

1. AH format The Authentication Header (AH) provides support for data integrity and authentication of IP packets. The data integrity service ensures that data inside IP packets is not altered during the transit. The authentication service enables an end user or a computer system to authenticate the user or the application at the other end, and decide to accept or reject packets, accordingly. This also prevents the IP spoofing attacks. Internally, AH is based on the MAC protocol, which means that the two communicating parties must share a secret key in order to use AH. The AH structure is shown in Fig. 12.23.

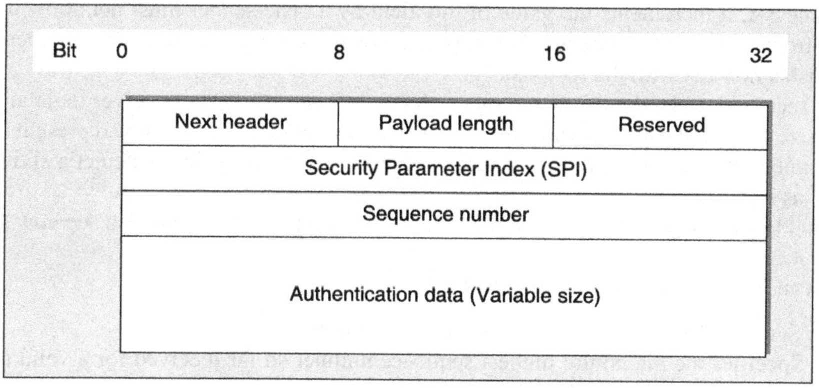

Fig. 12.23 *Authentication Header (AH) format*

Let us discuss the fields in the AH now, as shown in Table 12.3.

Table 12.3 *Authentication header field descriptions*

Field	*Description*
Next header	This 8-bit field identifies the type of header that immediately follows the AH. For example, if an ESP header follows the AH, this field contains a value 50, whereas if another AH follows this AH, this field contains a value 51.
Payload length	This 8-bit field contains the length of the AH in 32-bit words minus 2. Suppose that the length of the authentication data field is 96 bits (or three 32-bit words). With a three-word fixed header, we have a total of 6 words in the header. Therefore, this field will contain a value of 4.
Reserved	This 16-bit field is reserved for future use.
Security Parameter Index (SPI)	This 32-bit field is used in combination with the source and destination addresses as well as the IPSec protocol used (AH or ESP) to uniquely identify the Security Association (SA) for the traffic to which a datagram belongs.
Sequence number	This 32-bit field is used to prevent replay attacks, as discussed later.
Authentication data	This variable-length field contains the authentication data, called as the Integrity Check Value (ICV), for the datagram. This value is the MAC, used for authentication and integrity purposes. For IPv4 datagrams, the value of this field must be an integral multiple of 32. For IPv6 datagrams, the value of this field must be an integral multiple of 64. For this, additional padding bits may be required. The ICV is calculated generating a MAC using the HMAC digest algorithm.

2. Dealing with replay attacks Let us now study how AH deals with and prevents the replay attacks. To reiterate, in a replay attack, the attacker obtains a copy of an authenticated packet and later sends it to the intended destination. Since the same packet is received twice, the destination could face some problems because of this. To prevent this, as we know, the AH contains a field called as *sequence number*.

Initially, the value of this field is set to 0. Every time the sender sends a packet to the same sender over the same SA, it increments the value of this field by 1. The sender must not allow this value to circle back from $2^{32} - 1$ to 0. If the number of packets over the same increases this number, the sender must establish a new SA with the recipient.

On the receiver's side, there is some more processing involved. The receiver maintains a sliding window of size W, with the default value of $W = 64$. The right edge of the window represents the highest sequence number N received so far, for a valid packet. For simplicity, let us depict a sliding window with $W = 8$, as shown in Fig. 12.24.

Let us understand the significance of the receiver's sliding window, and also see how the receiver operates on it.

As we can see, the following values are used:

(a) W: Specifies the size of the window. In our example, it is 8.
(b) N: Specifies the maximum highest sequence number so far received for a valid packet. N is always at the right edge of the window.

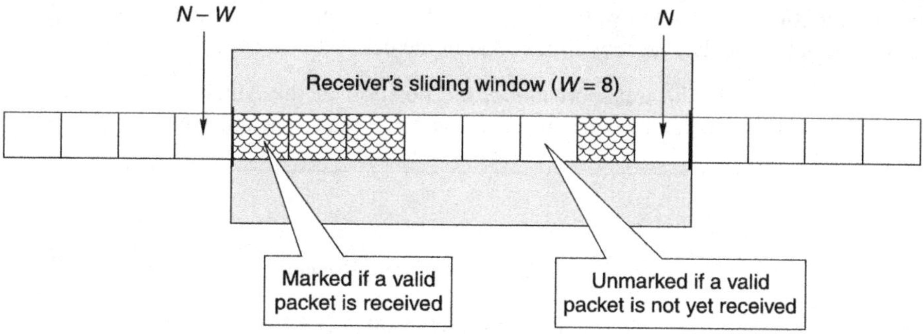

Fig. 12.24 *Receiver's sliding window*

For any packet with a sequence number in the range from $(N - W + 1)$ to N that has been correctly received (i.e., successfully authenticated), the corresponding slot in the window is marked (see figure). On the other hand, any packet in this range, which is not correctly received (i.e., not successfully authenticated), the slot is unmarked (see figure).

Now, when a receiver receives a packet, it performs the following action depending on the sequence number of the packet, as shown in Fig. 12.25.

1. If the sequence number of the received packet falls within the windows, and if the packet is new, its MAC is checked. If the MAC is successfully validated, the corresponding slot in the window is marked. The window itself does not move to the right-hand side.
2. If the received packet is to the right of the window [i.e., the sequence number of the packet is > N], and if the packet is new, the MAC is checked. If the packet is authenticated successfully, the window is advanced to the right in such a way that the right edge of the window now matches with the sequence number of this packet. That is, this sequence number now becomes the new N.
3. If the received packet is to the left of the window [i.e., the sequence number of the packet is < $(N - W)$], or if the MAC check fails, the packet is rejected, and an audible event is triggered.

Fig. 12.25 *Sliding window logic used by the receiver for each incoming packet*

Note that the third action thwarts replay attacks. This is because if the receiver receives a packet whose sequence number is less than $(N - W)$, it concludes that someone posing as the sender is attempting to resend a packet sent by the sender earlier.

We must also realize that in extreme conditions, this kind of technique can make the receiver believe that a transmission is in error, even though it is not the case. For example, suppose that the value of W is 64 and that of N is 100. Now suppose that the sender sends a burst of packets, numbered 101 to 500. Because of network congestions and other issues, suppose that the receiver somehow receives a packet with sequence number 300 first. It would immediately move the right edge of the window to 300 (i.e., $N = 300$ now). Now suppose that the receiver next receives packet number 102. From our calculations, $N - W = 300 - 64 = 236$. Therefore, the sequence number of the packet just received (102) is less than $(N - W = 236)$. Thus, our third condition in the earlier list would get triggered, and the receiver would reject this valid packet, and raise an alarm.

However, such situations are rare, and with an optimized value of W, such situations can be avoided.

3. Modes of operation As we know, both AH and ESP can work in two modes, that is, the transport mode and the tunnel mode. Let us now discuss AH in the context of these two modes.

(a) AH transport mode In the transport mode, the position of the Authentication Header (AH) is between the original IP header and the original TCP header of the IP packet. This is shown in Fig. 12.26.

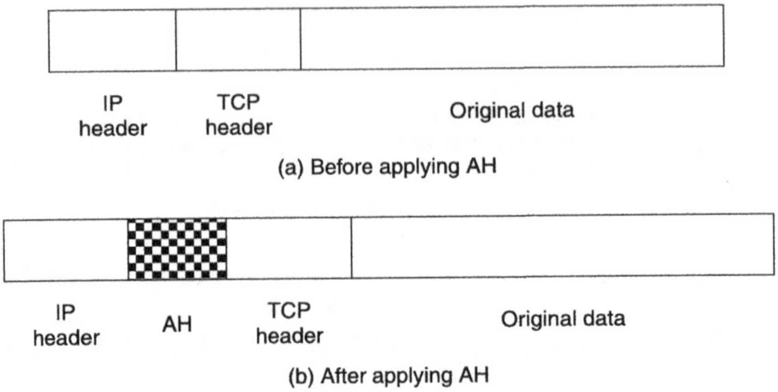

Fig. 12.26 *AH transport mode*

(b) AH tunnel mode In the tunnel mode, the entire original IP packet is authenticated and the AH is inserted between the original IP header and a new outer IP header. The inner IP header contains the ultimate source and destination IP addresses, whereas the outer IP header possibly contains different IP addresses (e.g., IP addresses of the firewalls or other security gateways). This is shown in Fig. 12.27.

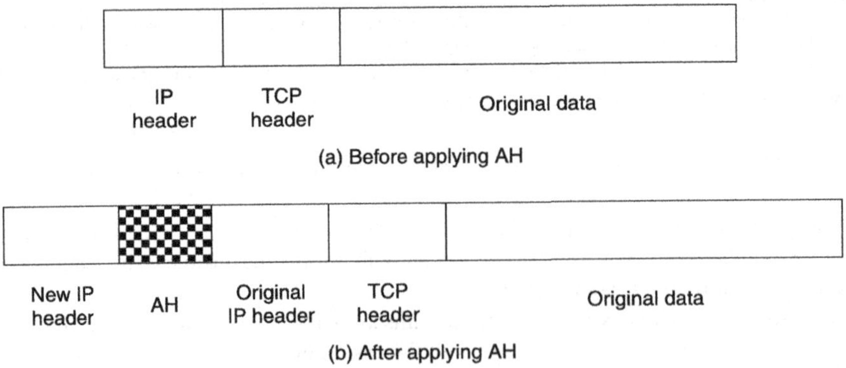

Fig. 12.27 *AH tunnel mode*

12.2.4 Encapsulating Security Payload (ESP)

1. ESP format The Encapsulating Security Payload (ESP) protocol provides confidentiality and integrity of messages. ESP is based on symmetric key cryptography techniques. ESP can be used in isolation, or it can be combined with AH.

The ESP packet contains four fixed-length fields, and three variable-length fields. Figure 12.28 shows the ESP format.

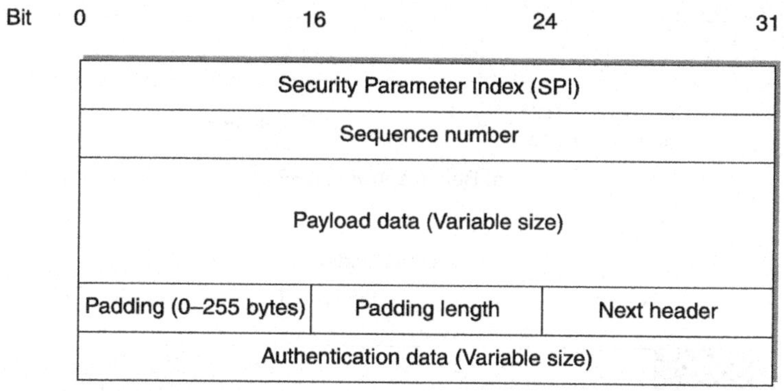

Fig. 12.28 *Encapsulating Security Payload (ESP) format*

Let us discuss the fields in the ESP now, as shown in Table 12.4.

Table 12.4 *ESP field descriptions*

Field	*Description*
Security Parameter Index (SPI)	This 32-bit field is used in combination with the source and destination addresses as well as the IPSec protocol used (AH or ESP) to uniquely identify the Security Association (SA) for the traffic to which a datagram belongs.
Sequence number	This 32-bit field is used to prevent replay attacks, as discussed earlier.
Payload data	This variable-length field contains the transport layer segment (transport mode) or IP packet (tunnel mode), which is protected by encryption.
Padding	This field contains the padding bits, if any. These are used by the encryption algorithm, or for aligning the padding length field, so that it begins at the third byte within the 4-byte word.
Padding length	This 8-bit field specifies the number of padding bytes in the immediately preceding field.
Next header	This 8 bit field identifies the type of encapsulated data in the payload. For example, a value 6 in this field indicates that the payload contains TCP data.
Authentication data	This variable-length field contains the authentication data, called as the Integrity Check Value (ICV), for the datagram. This is calculated over the length of the ESP packet minus the Authentication Data field.

2. Modes of operation ESP, like AH, can operate in the transport mode or the tunnel mode. Let us discuss these two possibilities now.

(a) ESP transport mode Transport mode ESP is used to encrypt, and optionally authenticate the data carried by IP (for example, a TCP segment). Here, the ESP is inserted into the IP packet immediately before the transport layer header (i.e., TCP or UDP), and an ESP trailer (containing the fields Padding, Padding length and Next header) is added after the IP packet. If authentication is also used, the ESP Authentication Data field is added after the ESP trailer. The entire transport layer segment and the ESP trailer are encrypted. The entire cipher text, along with the ESP header is authenticated. This is shown in Fig. 12.29.

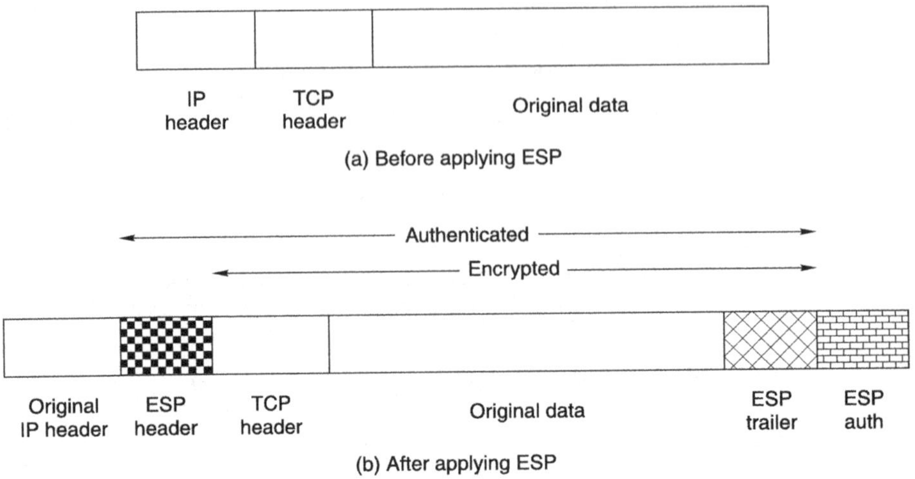

Fig. 12.29 *ESP transport mode*

We can summarize the operation of the ESP transport mode as follows:

(i) At the sender's end, the block of data containing the ESP trailer and the entire transport layer segment is encrypted and the plain text of this block is replaced with its corresponding cipher text to form the IP packet. Authentication is appended, if selected. This packet is now ready for transmission.

(ii) The packet is routed to the destination. The intermediate routers need to take a look at the IP header as well as any IP extension headers, but not at the cipher text.

(iii) At the receiver's end, the IP header plus any plain text IP extension headers are examined. The remaining portion of the packet is then decrypted to retrieve the original plain text transport layer segment.

(b) ESP tunnel mode The tunnel mode ESP encrypts an entire IP packet. Here, the ESP header is pre-fixed to the packet, and then the packet along with the ESP trailer is encrypted. As we know, the IP header contains the destination address as well as intermediate routing information. Therefore, this packet cannot be transmitted as it is. Otherwise, the delivery of the packet would be impossible. Therefore, a new IP header is added, which contains sufficient information for routing. This is shown in Fig. 12.30.

We can summarize the operation of the ESP tunnel mode as follows:

(i) At the sender's end, the sender prepares an inner IP packet with the destination address as the internal destination. This packed is pre-fixed with an ESP header, and then the packet and ESP trailer are encrypted and Authentication Data is (optionally) added. A new IP header is added to the start of this block. This forms the outer IP packet.

(ii) The outer packet is routed to the destination firewall. Each intermediate router needs to check and process the outer IP header, along with any other outer IP extension headers. It need not know about the cipher text.

(iii) At the receiver's end, the destination firewall processes the outer IP header plus any extension headers, and recovers the plain text from the cipher text. The packet is then sent to the actual destination host.

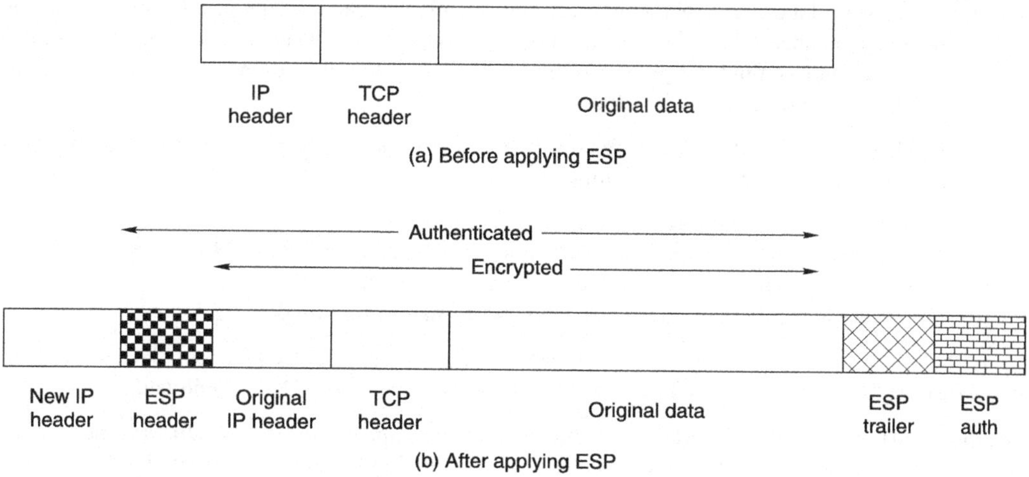

Fig. 12.30 *ESP tunnel mode*

12.2.5 IPSec Key Management

1. Introduction Apart from the two core protocols (AH and ESP), the third most significant aspect of IPSec is key management. Without a proper key management set up, IPSec cannot exist. This key management in IPSec consists of two aspects, which are, key agreement and distribution. As we know, we require four keys if we want to make use of both AH and ESP: two keys for AH (one for message transmissions, one for message receiving), and two keys for ESP (one for message transmissions, one for message receiving).

The protocol used in IPSec for key management is called **ISAKMP/Oakley**. The **Internet Security Association and Key Management Protocol (ISAKMP)** protocol a platform for key management. It defines the procedures and packet formats for negotiating, establishing, modifying and deleting SAs. ISAKMP messages can be transmitted via the TCP or UDP transport protocol. TCP and UDP port number 500 is reserved for ISAKMP.

The initial version of ISAKMP mandated the use of the Oakley protocol. Oakley is based on the Diffie-Hellman key exchange protocol, with a few variations. We will first take a look at Oakley, and then examine ISAKMP.

2. Oakley key determination protocol The Oakley protocol is a refined version of the Diffie-Hellman key exchange protocol. We will not discuss the concepts of Diffie-Hellman, as they are not relevant here. However, we will note here that Diffie-Hellman offers two desirable features.

(a) Creation of secret keys is possible as and when required.
(b) There is no requirement for any pre-existing infrastructure.

However, Diffie-Hellman also suffers from a few problems, as follows:

(a) It does not contain mechanism for authentication of the parties.
(b) It is vulnerable to man-in-the-middle-attack.

(c) It involves a lot of mathematical processing. An attacker can take undue advantage of this by sending a number of hoax Diffie-Hellman requests to a host. The host can unnecessarily spend a large amount of time in trying to compute the keys, rather than doing any actual work. This is called **congestion attack** or **clogging attack**.

The Oakley protocol is designed to retain the advantages of Diffie-Hellman, and to remove its drawbacks. The features of Oakley are as follows:

(a) It has features to defeat replay attacks.
(b) It implements a mechanism called as cookies to defeat congestion attacks.
(c) It enables the exchange of Diffie-Hellman public key values.
(d) It provides authentication mechanisms to thwart man-in-the-middle attacks.

We have already discussed the Diffie-Hellman key exchange protocol in great detail. Here, we shall simply discuss the approaches taken by Oakley to tackle the issues with Diffie-Hellman.

1. Authentication Oakley supports three authentication mechanisms: digital signatures (generation of a message digest, and its encryption with the sender's private key), public key encryption (encrypting some information such as the sender's user id with the recipient's public key), and secret key encryption (a key derived by using some out-of-band mechanisms).

2. Dealing with congestion attacks Oakley uses the concept of cookies to thwart congestion attacks. As we know, in this kind of attack, an attacker forges the source address of another legitimate user and sends a public Diffie-Hellman key to another legitimate user. The receiver performs modular exponentiation to calculate the secret key. A number of such calculations performed rapidly one after the other can cause congestion or clogging of the victim's computer. To tackle this, each side in Oakley must send a pseudo-random number, called cookie, in the initial message, which the other side must acknowledge. This acknowledgement must be repeated in the first message of Diffie-Hellman key exchange. If an attacker forges the source address, she does not get the acknowledgement cookie from the victim, and her attack fails. Note that at the most the attacker can force the victim to generate and send a cookie, but not to perform the actual Diffie–Hellman calculations.

The Oakley protocol provides for a number of message types. For simplicity, we shall consider only one of them, called as *aggressive key exchange*. It consists of three message exchanges between the two parties, say *X* and *Y*. Let us examine these three messages.

Message 1 To begin with, *X* sends a cookie and the public Diffie–Hellman key of *X* for this exchange, along with some other information. *X* signs this block with its private key.

Message 2 When *Y* receives *message 1*, it verifies the signature of *X* using the public key of *X*. When *Y* is satisfied that the message indeed came from *X*, it prepares an acknowledgement message for *X*, containing the cookie sent by *X*. *Y* also prepares its own cookie and Diffie–Hellman public key, and along with some other information, it signs the whole package with its private key.

Message 3 Upon receipt of *message 2*, *X* verifies it using the public key of *Y*. When *X* is satisfied about it, it sends a message back to *Y* to inform that it has received *Y*'s public key.

3. ISAKMP The ISAKMP protocol defines procedures and formats for establishing, maintaining and deleting SA information. An ISAKMP message contains an ISAKMP header followed by one ore more payloads. The entire block is encapsulated inside a transport segment (such as TCP or UDP segment). The header format for ISAKMP messages is shown in Fig. 12.31.

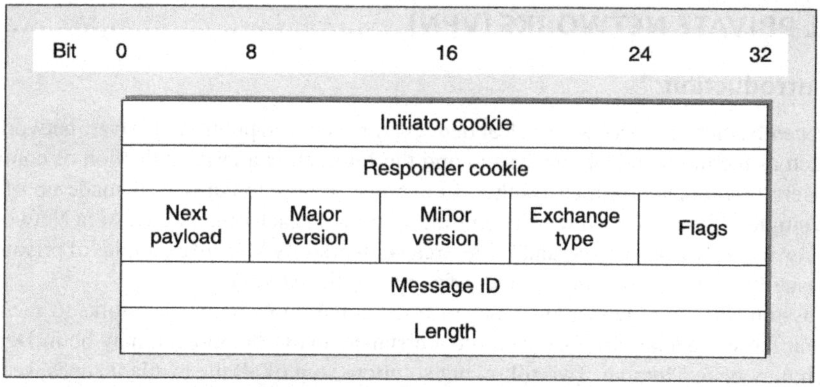

Fig. 12.31 *ISAKMP header format*

Let us discuss the fields in the ISAKMP header now, as shown in Table 12.5.

Table 12.5 *ISAKMP header field descriptions*

Field	*Description*
Initiator cookie	This 64-bit field contains the cookie of the entity that initiates the SA establishment or deletion.
Responder cookie	This 64-bit field contains the cookie of the responding entity. Initially, this field contains null when the initiator sends the very first ISAKMP message to the responder.
Next payload	This 8-bit field indicates the type of the first payload of the message (discussed later).
Major version	This 4-bit field identifies the major ISAKMP protocol version as used in the current exchange.
Minor version	This 4-bit field identifies the minor ISAKMP protocol version as used in the current exchange.
Exchange type	This 8-bit field indicates the type of exchange (discussed later).
Flags	This 8-bit field indicates the specific set of options for this ISAKMP exchange.
Message ID	This 32-bit field identifies the unique Id for this message.
Length	This 32-bit field specifies the total length of the message, including the header and all the payloads in octets.

Let us quickly discuss the fields not explained yet.

4. Payload types ISAKMP specifies different *payload types*. For example, an *SA payload* is used to start establishment of an SA. The *proposal payload* contains information used during the SA establishment. The *key exchange payload* indicates for exchanging keys using mechanisms such as Oakley, Diffie-Hellman, RSA, etc. There are many other *payload types*.

5. Exchange types There are five *exchange types* defined in ISAKMP. The *base exchange* allows the transmission of the key and authentication material. The *identity protection exchange* expands the *base exchange* to protect the identities of the user. The *authentication only exchange* is used to perform mutual authentication. The *aggressive exchange* attempts to minimize the number of exchanges at the cost of hiding the user's identities. The *information exchange* is used for one-way transmission of information for SA management.

VIRTUAL PRIVATE NETWORKS (VPN) 12.3

12.3.1 Introduction

Until very recently, there has been a very clear demarcation between public and private networks. A public network, such as the public telephone system and the Internet, is a large collection of communicators who are generally unrelated with each other. In contrast, a private network is made up of computers owned by a single organization, which share information with each other. Local Area Networks (LAN), Metropolitan Area Networks (MAN) and Wide Area Networks (WAN) are examples of private networks. A firewall usually separates a private network from a public network.

Let us assume that an organization wants to connect two of its branch networks to each other. The trouble is that these branches are located quite a distance apart. One branch may be in Delhi, and the other branch may be in Mumbai. Two following solutions, out of all the available ones, seem logical:

1. Connect the two branches using a personal network, i.e., lay cables between the two offices yourself, or obtain a leased line between the two branches.
2. Connect the two branches with the help of a public network, such as the Internet.

The first solution gives far more control and offers a sense of security, as compared to the second solution. However, it is also quite complicated. Laying cables between two cities is not easy, and is usually not permitted either. The second solution seems easier to implement, as there is no special infrastructure setup required. However, it also seems to be vulnerable to possible attacks. It would be a perfect situation if we could combine the two solutions!

Virtual Private Networks (VPN) offers such a solution. A VPN is a mechanism of employing encryption, authentication and integrity protection so that we can use a public network (such as the Internet) like a private network (i.e., a physical network created and controlled by you). VPN offers a high amount of security, and yet does not require any special cabling to be laid by the organization that wants to use it. Thus, a VPN combines the advantages of a public network (cheap and easily available) with those of a private network (secure and reliable).

A VPN can connect distant networks of an organization, or it can be used to allow traveling users to remotely access a private network (e.g., the organization's intranet) securely over the Internet.

A VPN is thus a mechanism to simulate a private network over a public network, such as the Internet. The term *virtual* signifies that it depends on the use of virtual connections. These connections are temporary, and do not have any physical presence. They are made up of packets.

12.3.2 VPN Architecture

The idea of a VPN is actually quite simple to understand. Suppose an organization has two networks, *Network 1* and *Network 2*, which are physically apart from each other, and we want to connect them using the VPN approach. In such a case, we set up two firewalls, *Firewall 1* and *Firewall 2*. The encryption and decryption are performed by the firewalls. The architectural overview is shown in Fig. 12.32.

We have shown two networks, *Network 1* and *Network 2*. Network 1 connects to the Internet via a firewall named Firewall 1. Similarly, *Network 2* connects to the Internet with its own firewall, *Firewall 2*. We shall not worry about the configuration of the firewall here, and shall assume that the best possible configuration is selected by the organization. However, the key point to note here is that the two firewalls are *virtually* connected to each other via the Internet. We have shown this with the help of a *VPN tunnel* between the two firewalls.

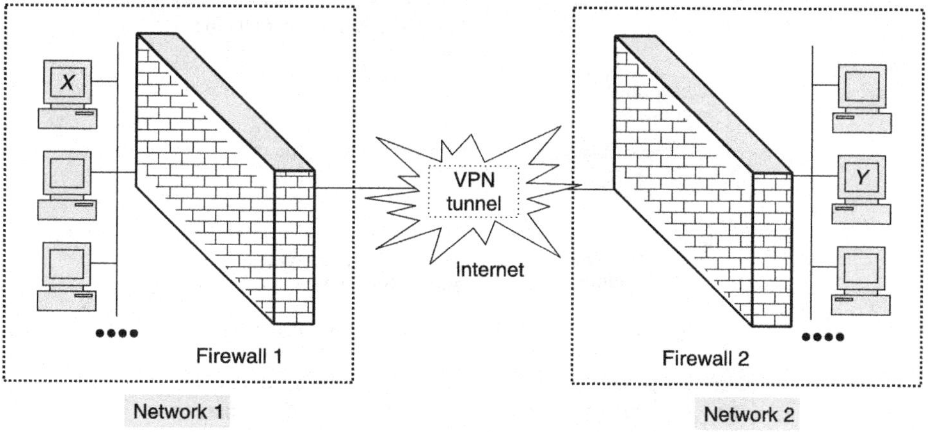

Fig. 12.32 VPN between two private networks

With this configuration in mind, let us understand how the VPN protects the traffic passing between any two hosts on the two different networks. For this, let us assume that host *X* on *Network 1* wants to send a data packet to host *Y* on *Network 2*. This transmission would work as follows:

1. Host *X* creates the packet, inserts its own IP address as the source address, and the IP address of host *Y* as the destination address. This is shown in Fig. 12.33. It sends the packet using the appropriate mechanism.
2. The packet reaches *Firewall 1*. As we know, *Firewall 1* now adds new headers to the packet. In these new headers, it changes the source IP address of the packet from that of host *X* to its own address (i.e., the IP address of *Firewall 1*, say F1). It also changes the destination IP address of the packet from that of host *Y* to the IP address of *Firewall 2*, say F2). This is shown in Fig. 12.34. It also performs the packet encryption and authentication, depending on the settings, and sends the modified packet over the Internet.
3. The packet reaches *Firewall 2* over the Internet, via one or more routers, as usual. *Firewall 2* discards the outer header and performs the appropriate decryption and other cryptographic functions as necessary. This yields the original packet, as was created by host *X* in Step 1. This is shown in Fig. 12.35. It then takes a look at the plain text contents of the packet, and realizes that the packet is meant for host *Y* (because the destination address inside the packet specifies host *Y*). Therefore, it delivers the packet to host *Y*.

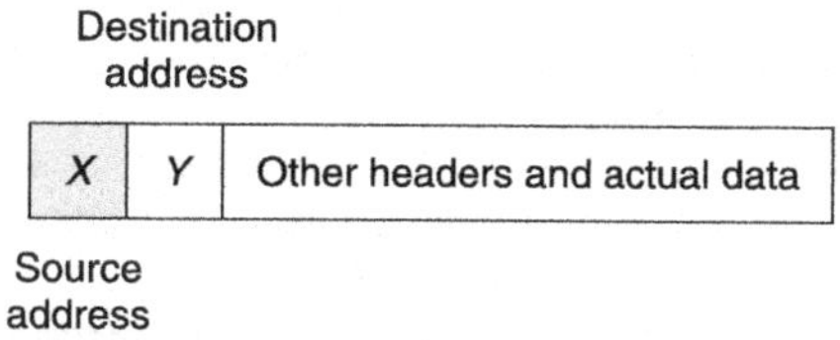

Fig. 12.33 Original packet

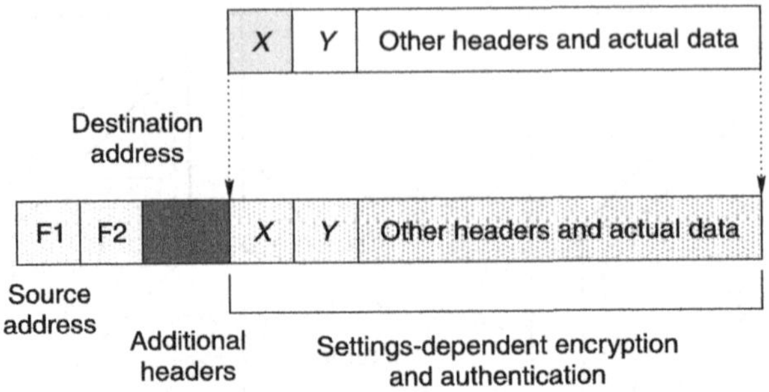

Fig. 12.34 *Firewall 1 changes the packet contents*

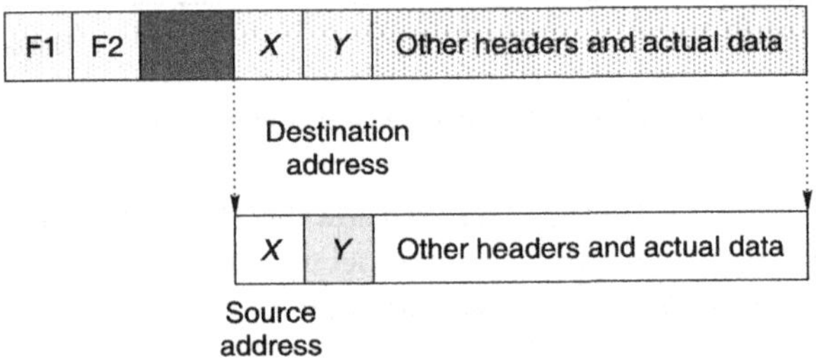

Fig. 12.35 *Firewall 2 retrieves the original packet contents*

There are three main VPN protocols. A detailed study of these protocols is beyond the scope of the current text. However, we shall briefly discuss them for the sake of completeness.

1. Point-to-Point Tunnelling Protocol (PPTP) is used on Windows NT systems. It mainly supports the VPN connectivity between a single user and a LAN, rather than between two LANs.
2. Developed by IETF, the **Layer 2 Tunnelling Protocol (L2TP)** is an improvement over PPTP. L2TP is considered as the secure open standard for VPN connections. It works for both combinations: user-to-LAN and LAN-to-LAN. It can include the IPSec functionality as well.
3. Finally, IPSec can be used in isolation. We have discussed IPSec in detail earlier.

Key Terms and Concepts

AH transport mode • AH tunnel mode • Application gateway • Authentication Header (AH) • Bastion host • Circuit gateway • Clogging attack • Congestion attack • Dynamic packet filter • Encapsulating Security Payload (ESP) • ESP transport mode • ESP tunnel mode • Firewall • Internet Key Exchange (IKE) • Internet Security Association and Key Management Protocol (ISAKMP) • IP address spoofing • IP Security (IPSec) • ISAKMP/Oakley • Layer 2 Tunneling Protocol (L2TP) • Packet filter • Point to Point Tunneling Protocol (PPTP) • Proxy server • Screening filter • Screening router • Security Association (SA) • Source routing attacks • Stateful packet filter • Tiny fragment attacks • Tunnel mode • Virtual Private Networks (VPN)

SUMMARY

- Firewalls are specialized routers, which filter unwanted content.
- A firewall can be configured to only allow specific traffic, while getting rid of unwanted traffic.
- A firewall can be of two types: packet filter and application gateway.
- A packet filter examines every packet for suspicious/banned content (e.g., a packet containing some specific words) and allows or stops it.
- An application gateway does not worry about the contents of the packet too much. Instead, it focusses on the application layer protocol in use. For example, it can allow all HTTP traffic and SMTP traffic, but ban FTP traffic.
- Usually, a combination of a packet filter and an application gateway is used to ensure both protocol layer security, as well as packet layer security.
- A special type of firewall called proxy server or circuit gateway can be used to improve the security even further. Here, a special server called proxy server is set up as the firewall, which acts as the middle layer between the internal network and the rest of the Internet.
- The proxy server receives outgoing packets from an internal host, and instead of forwarding them to the external server, opens a separate connection with the external server and then sends the packets.
- Thus, with a proxy server, there are two separate connections—one between the internal host and the proxy, and the second between the proxy and the external server.
- Proxy server helps save the internal network details from the external networks.
- The IPSec protocol is used to connect two firewalls at two ends to create a Virtual Private Network (VPN).
- A VPN allows organizations to use the public, free Internet as if it is a private network.
- VPN allows two firewalls at the two ends of its connection to handle encryption, message integrity, etc.
- VPN can work in two modes: transport mode and tunnel mode.
- Transport mode protects an IP datagram, excluding its IP header.
- Tunnel mode protects an IP datagram, including its IP header. Thus, the original sender and the final recipient details also get hidden from the intermediate routers/networks.
- IPSec protocol has two subprotocols: Authentication Header (AH) and Encapsulating Security Payload (ESP).
- AH takes care of the message integrity and authentication details.
- ESP ensures message confidentiality.
- AH and ESP can work either independently, or also together.

MULTIPLE-CHOICE QUESTIONS

1. Firewall works at the __________ layer.
   (a) application (b) transport (c) network (d) data link
2. Application gateway looks at the __________ layer protocols.
   (a) application (b) transport (c) network (d) data link

3. Packet filter looks at the ________ layer protocols.
   (a) application (b) transport (c) network (d) data link
4. A ________ is used to establish two separate connections from the user to the end server.
   (a) packet filter (b) application gateway
   (c) DMZ (d) proxy server
5. VPN makes use of ________.
   (a) Internet (b) leased lines
   (c) wireless networks only (d) LAN
6. In the ________, the original entire IP datagram is encapsulated into another.
   (a) transport mode (b) tunnel mode (c) None of these (d) Both (a) and (b)
7. In the ________, only the TCP segment is encapsulated into another IP datagram.
   (a) transport mode (b) tunnel mode (c) None of these (d) Both (a) and (b)
8. The ________ ensures message authentication/integrity.
   (a) ESP (b) AH (c) ISAKMP (d) SA
9. The ________ ensures message confidentiality.
   (a) ESP (b) AH (c) ISAKMP (d) SA
10. The ________ is used to identify a unique VPN connection.
   (a) ESP (b) AH (c) ISAKMP (d) SA

DETAILED QUESTIONS

1. Explain the concept of a firewall.
2. What are the various types of firewalls? Explain in brief.
3. Discuss packet filters in detail.
4. Explain application gateways.
5. How are proxy servers useful?
6. What is a VPN? How does it work?
7. What is the AH protocol?
8. Explain the ESP protocol.
9. Discuss the idea of SA.
10. Describe the usage of VPN in practical life.

EXERCISES

1. Study at least one firewall product. Document its features.
2. Study the proxy server implementation in at least one college/organization.
3. What is SSL VPN? Study in detail.
4. What does it take to implement VPN? Examine both the client and the server sides.
5. Which VPN products are most popular? Why?

INTRODUCTION TO XML 13

WHAT IS XML?.. 13.1

13.1.1 Communication Incompatibilities

Extensible Markup Language (XML) is perhaps one of the most misunderstood concepts in the area of computers today. In spite of its tremendous all-around success and widespread use, not many people seem to really understand what XML is and where it needs to be used. It is observed that more often than not, XML is used *because someone has decided* or *because someone has been told to use it*. It may seem strange to read this. However, it is not only true, but is quite common. Perhaps the reason behind this apparent confusion and lack of understanding is due to the fact that unlike a programming language (say Java, C++, or ASP.NET) or a DBMS (say Oracle, DB2, or MySQL), it is not very easy to imagine the end use and applications of XML. Unfortunately, many books and other literature on the subject do not aim at clarifying this confusion. They make an attempt to teach the syntax and semantics of XML. However, they do not answer the all-important question of what XML is all about, and why do we need to learn it in the first place!

XML syntax and semantics are well known, but where to use these is usually not clear!

Therefore, let us try to solve this mystery surrounding XML. For this purpose, let us take a simple example from normal life.

Imagine that there are two persons, wishing to communicate with each other. However, the problem is that both of them speak different languages. One of them can only understand and speak in English, while the other understands and can speak only in Hindi. How will they be able to communicate with each other, then? Clearly, we need some sort of intermediary who can translate between these two languages and thus, convey messages to each other. This is quite similar to how interpreters assist political leaders when the leaders do not understand each others' language (let alone the intent of the conversation!). The problem is depicted in Fig. 13.1.

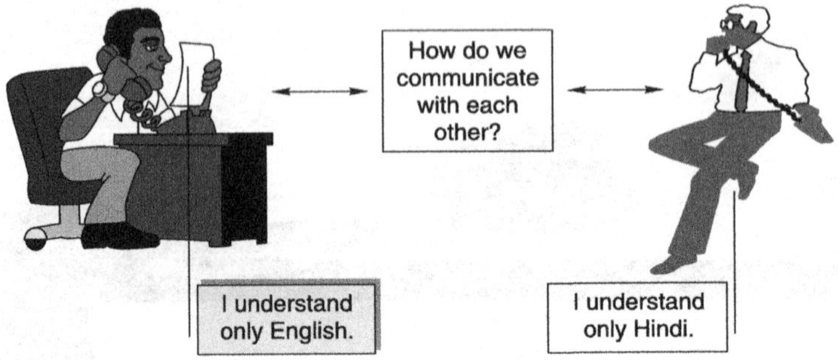

Fig. 13.1 *Problem of incompatibility in human conversations*

We have not answered the all-important question of who this translator is going to be, and how would this translator function. There are two primary approaches to resolve this problem, as follows:

1. When communicating the thoughts of the person who speaks only in English, translate them into Hindi and then pass on the message to the other person who understands only Hindi. The translator would perform an opposite task in the other direction of communication. This approach is shown in Fig. 13.2.

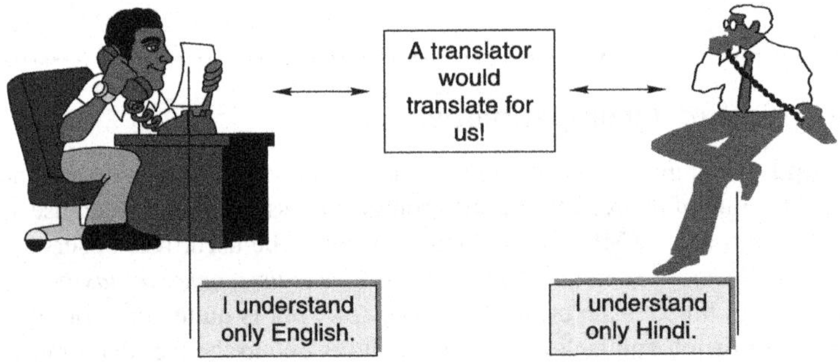

Fig. 13.2 *Approach 1: Use of a translator to solve the problem of incompatibility*

2. Think about a Common Language (let us call this as CL for the sake of brevity) that both the persons should learn. This CL should be universally acceptable, and work for different communicating pairs. That is, even if person *A* is communicating with person *B*, or person *X* with *Y*, or *A* with *Y*, or *T* with *U*; the CL will not change. In this approach, the *translation* needs to happen at the thought process level. That is, the person who is speaking has to speak in the CL itself, and no further translation is necessary, unlike in the previous approach. This is shown in Fig. 13.3. Because the other person understands CL, there is no incompatibility or ambiguity.

Let us now quickly analyze these two approaches. Quite clearly, the first approach provides a *quick-and-dirty* solution. In this case, the communicating parties need not really bother about each others' language. They are free to use their native languages, and the responsibility lies on the translator to correctly communicate thoughts and ideas in the appropriate languages. Therefore, it is the translator, who needs to know multiple (at least two) languages. The second approach is slightly more painful,

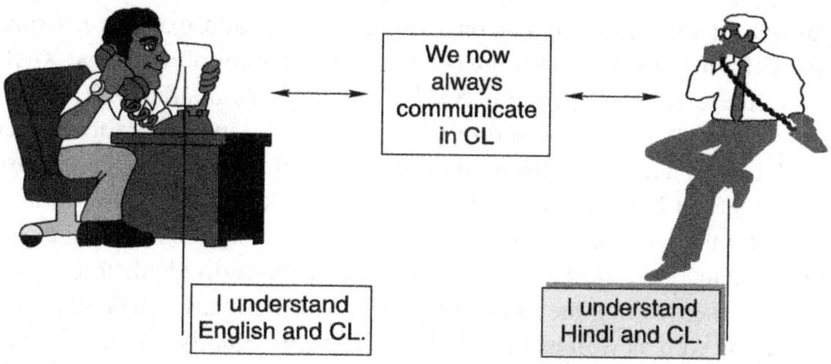

Fig. 13.3 *Approach 2: Making the communicating parties use a Common Language (CL)*

since every communicating party needs to learn a new language (CL). However, in medium-to-long term, this approach is more superior, since the dependence on the translator is no longer there. Also, everyone speaks in and can understand CL.

Therefore, the question really is, are we ready to invest in a solution that is *quick-and-dirty*, but which is not guaranteed to work for all possible situations/persons, or in another one that is a bit annoying to start with, but is bound to pay rich dividends later? If we have time, money, and concurrence from all the communicating parties, we would clearly opt for the second approach. Getting all of them to agree, of course, is not a straightforward job. However, if we somehow succeed in doing that, then the second approach is far better.

Having discussed this background sufficiently well, let us now think as to how this relates to XML and what decisions we are likely to make there.

13.1.2 XML and Application Communication Incompatibilities

Let us relate our discussion so far to XML and see how these concepts are interlinked. Imagine that we have two applications *A* and *B*, possibly on different networks, wanting to communicate with each other. The basic question that arises in this situation, like human conversation, is about the language that they need to use for communication. Of course, we are not just referring to computer languages here, but are instead talking about the overall platform and architecture of these two applications. The situation is depicted in Fig. 13.4.

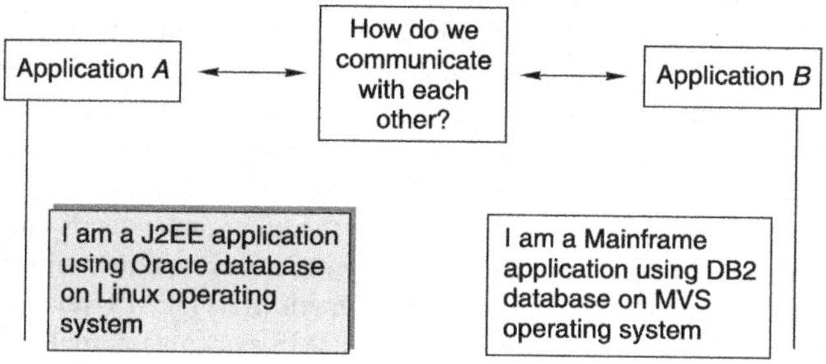

Fig. 13.4 *Problem of incompatibility between applications*

This discussion is quite similar to our earlier discussion about humans wanting to communicate with each other, without worrying about the possible incompatibilities. Let us discuss this in detail.

We know that one of the most popular data representation and exchange formats is **American Standard Code for Information Interchange (ASCII)**. It is commonly said that XML is the ASCII of the present and of the future. Strictly speaking, XML must not be compared with ASCII, because ASCII is merely representation of alphanumeric and other symbolic data in binary form, whereas XML is for other purposes. XML can be used to exchange data across the Internet. XML can be used to create data structures that can be shared between incompatible systems. XML is a common meta-language that will enable data to be transformed from one format to another. It is worth noting that even ASCII was not ambitious to this extent. This would allow organizations and individuals to exchange data over the Internet in a uniform manner. Going one step further, XML need not always be used across the Internet. That is, it can be used for Web as well as non-Web applications equally effectively. This basic concept is illustrated in Fig. 13.5.

XML can be used to exchange data between compatible/incompatible applications in Web/non-Web applications.

Fig. 13.5 *XML as the data exchange mechanism between applications*

Does this sound quite similar to the second approach that we had discussed, with reference to human conversations? We had suggested that everyone should learn a Common Language (CL) and converse in that language. Thus, XML for applications seems to be similar to CL for humans. Let us not jump to this conclusion, however, and reach there step by step.

When we had raised this problem of incompatibility of data formats between applications, the obvious question that arose was as follows. Was data not being exchanged by applications before XML came into picture? Quite clearly, data was being exchanged by applications for several decades now. Since the days of IBM Mainframe applications of the 1960s, varying applications and platforms had needed to *speak* with each other, and they had been able to do so. Then, what is so great about XML? The answer is that XML simplifies this *talking* between two applications, regardless of their purpose, domain, technology, or platform.

XML simplifies the process of data exchange between two or more applications.

Now, the question is, why not use the existing **Database Management System (DBMS)** products such as Oracle, SQL Server, IMS, IDMS, and Informix, etc., for exchanging data over the Internet (and also outside of the Internet)? The reason is incompatibility of various kinds. These DBMS products are extremely popular and provide great data storage and access mechanisms. However, they are not always compatible with each other in terms of sharing or transferring data. Their formats, internal representations, data types, encoding, etc., are different. This creates problems in data exchange. This is similar to a situation when one person understands only English and the other understands only Hindi. English and Hindi by themselves are great languages. However, they are not compatible with each other!

Similarly, for instance, suppose organization *X* uses Oracle as its DBMS (relational) and organization *Y* uses IMS as its DBMS (Hierarchical). Each of these DBMS systems internally represents the data in their own formats as well as by using data structures such as chains, indexes, lists, etc. Now, whenever *X* and *Y* want to exchange any kind of data (say list of products available, last month's sales report, etc.), they would not be able to do this directly, as shown in Fig. 13.6.

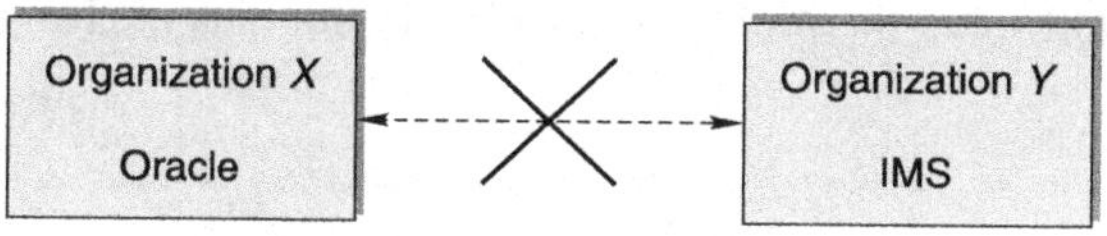

Fig. 13.6 *Incompatible data formats*

Database Management Systems (DBMS) are incompatible with each other, when it comes to data exchange.

If *X* and *Y* want to exchange data, the simple solution would be that they agree on a common data format, and use that format for data exchange. For example, when *X* wants to send an inventory status to *Y*, it would first convert that data from Oracle format into this common format and then send it to *Y*. When *Y* receives this data, it would convert the data from this common format into IMS format, and then its applications can use it. In the simplest case, this common format can be a text file. This is shown in Fig. 13.7.

Fig. 13.7 *Data exchange in a text format*

This approach of exchanging data in the text format seems to be fine. After all, all that is needed is some data transformation programs at both ends, which either read from or write to text format from the native (Oracle/IMS) format. This approach would be very similar to the one used in our translator approach for human conversations. But there are some issues with this approach as well, in addition to what we had discussed earlier in the context of human conversations.

1. For instance, suppose another organization *Z* now wants to do business with *X* and *Y*. Therefore, *X* and *Y* now need to exchange data with *Z* also. Suppose that *Z* is already interacting with other business partners such as *A* and *B*. Now, if *Z* is using a different text format for data exchange with *A* and *B*, its data exchange text formats with *X*/*Y* and *A*/*B* would be different! That is, for exchanging the same data with different business partners, different application programs might be required!
2. Also, suppose that these business partners specify some business rules. For instance, *Z* mandates that a sales order arriving from any of its business partners (i.e., *A*, *B*, *X* or *Y*) must carry at least three items. For this, appropriate logic can be incorporated in the application program at its end to validate this rule, whenever it receives any sales order from one of its business partners. However, can we not apply this business rule before the data is sent by any of the business partners, rather than first accepting the data and then validating it? If different data exchanges among different business partners demand different business rules like this, it might be difficult to apply them in the text format.

Issues such as these resulted in the emergence of a common standard for exchanging business documents—**Electronic Data Interchange (EDI)**. We shall study EDI in detail soon.

EDI is a standard that specifies the formats for different business documents. EDI allows the integration of incompatible data formats by bringing these formats on a common platform—the EDI standard.

Therefore, EDI would solve the problems associated with data exchange in the text format, as shown in Fig. 13.8.

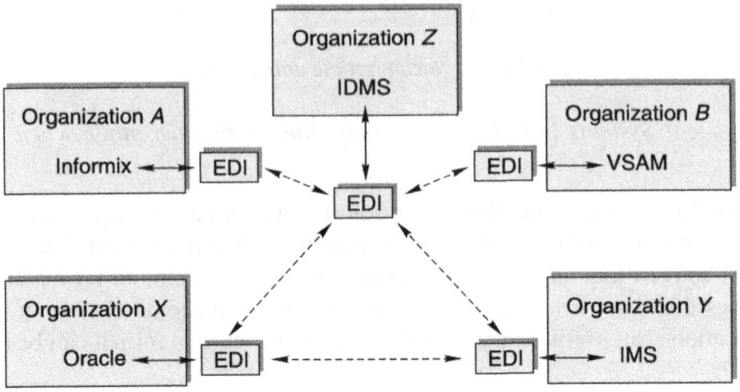

Fig. 13.8 *Using EDI for data exchange*

Now, there was no incompatibility issue. Also, data could be exchanged in a seamless manner as business rules could be built in the EDI standard itself (as we shall study soon). Thus, EDI became the de-facto standard for exchanging business documents. However, this was also not free of issues.

The biggest issue with EDI is cost. EDI solutions are very expensive to implement and maintain. Smaller and medium-sized organizations cannot usually afford this.

Moreover, in the last few years, the idea of using the Internet protocols such as TCP/IP for exchanging business documents started to gain acceptance worldwide. This is because the Internet is a virtually free network, unlike the proprietary EDI networks (called as **Value Added Networks** or **VAN**). Sophisticated hardware and software are not required to a great extent for using the Internet. Since this meant that expensive VAN networks employed by EDI systems had an alternative transport medium, all that was needed was a standard such as EDI. Web-enabling EDI is one such solution. However, that is still in the experimental stage.

In the meanwhile, XML emerged as the data exchange standard over the Internet. That is, the exchange standard was XML and the underlying transport medium was the Internet (i.e., TCP/IP). In the case of EDI, the data exchange standard was EDI and the underlying transport medium was VAN. With some fine-tuning and technology improvements, the underlying transport mechanism for VAN can now be any protocol, such as SNA or even TCP/IP. This means that we can use XML in the place of EDI wherever possible.

This is how XML has become the modern standard for exchanging business documents over the Internet, as shown in Fig. 13.9. Of course, it would be wrong to suggest that XML has replaced all data exchange formats completely, although in this example we have shown such a situation. EDI is still extremely popular. Also, other incompatible formats are still in use. However, it is expected that in a few years, this all will be replaced by XML.

This brings us to an obvious question. What is so great about XML? Why should everyone agree upon and start using XML (similar to our CL in human conversations)? Let us discuss this now.

Think about the book you are holding right now. It was developed almost entirely using Microsoft Word. Whenever we add things such as chapter numbers, section numbers, subsection numbers,

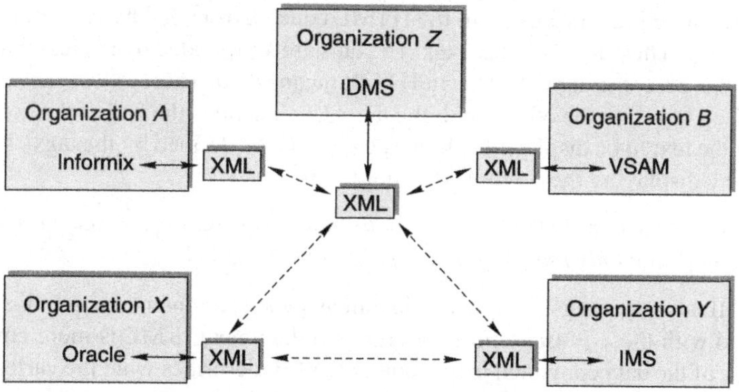

Fig. 13.9 *XML as the data exchange standard*

paragraphs, and so on, Word keeps a track of all such things by formatting them appropriately and retaining the formatting details for ever. Instead of using Word, if we had used XML for creating this book, we would have used a different syntax for creating them. We could have done that quite easily. Now, if a word processor can do what XML is offering us, why do we need XML at all? We have seen the business side of it, but what about cases such as document processing? Well, there is again a problem of data exchange. Different word processors use different styling information. The styling information used by Microsoft Word is completely different from Corel's WordPerfect, which is again different from Sun's StarOffice word processor. We need to convert documents created by using one word processor into another format before they can be used in that other format. In contrast to this, the same XML document can be read by any application without the need for any changes/conversions.

XML VERSUS HTML 13.2

Having understood the basic need for XML, let us now go one step further. Here, we will try to examine what is so unique about XML that it should start becoming the world's leading data exchange mechanism. Also, most of us would know that **Hyper Text Markup Language (HTML)** is used for creating Web pages on the Internet. Can it not be reused instead of creating a new language? Let us examine this question.

As we know, HTML is the de facto language of the Internet. HTML defines a set of **tags** describing how the Web browser should display the contents of a particular document to the end user. For example, it uses tags that indicate that a particular portion of the text is to be made boldface, underlined, small, big, and so on. In addition, we can display lists of values using bullets, or create tables on the screen by using HTML. As an example, Fig. 13.10 shows how a piece of text can be made bold in HTML, and the actual result of this code.

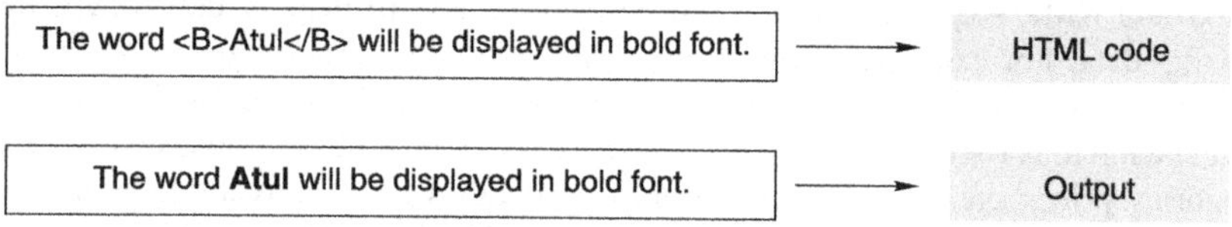

Fig. 13.10 *HTML tags example*

As we can see, there is a word `Atul` in the HTML code, surrounded by two strange pieces of text, namely `<B>` and `</B>`. These are called as tags. The tags are surrounded by the less than (<) and greater than (>) signs. In this case, the tag is *B*. This in HTML means *bold*. Thus, `<B>` means make the text that appears after this tag bold. On the other hand, the tag `</B>` indicates the end of the bold tag. Therefore, the boundaries of the text to be displayed in bold (i.e., `Atul`) are defined by the tags `<B>` and `</B>`. The result shows this by displaying the word *Atul* in bold font.

The similarity between XML and HTML is that both languages use tags to structure documents. This, incidentally, is perhaps the only real similarity between the two!

Although XML also uses tags to organize documents and the contents therein just as HTML does, it is not concerned with these *presentation* features of a document. XML is more concerned with the *meaning* and *rules* of the data contained in a document. XML describes what the various data items in a document mean, rather than describing how to display them. Therefore, whereas HTML is an *information presentation* language, XML is an *information description* language. Thus, conceptually, XML is pretty similar to a data definition language. We shall see how XML achieves this later.

HTML concentrates on the display/presentation of data to the end user, whereas XML deals with the representation of data in documents.

This point is emphasized in Fig. 13.11.

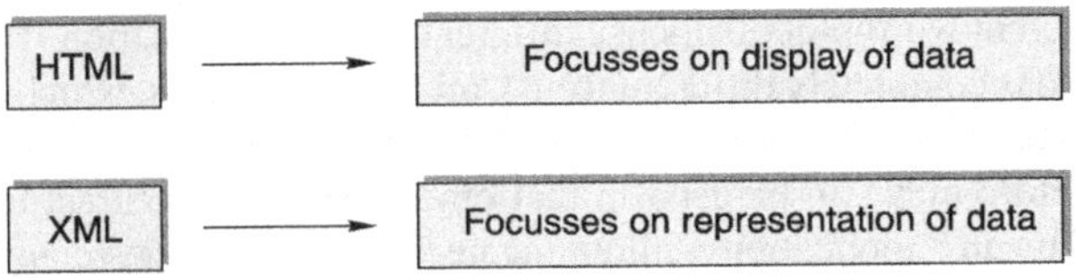

Fig. 13.11 *Basic difference between HTML and XML*

It is necessary to understand why HTML is not sufficient for conducting electronic business on the Internet, and how XML can solve the problems associated with HTML in this regard. As we know, the basic purpose of HTML is to allow presentation of documents that can be interpreted and displayed by a Web browser. However, electronic business applications have other demands such as processing, rearranging, storing, forwarding, exchanging, encrypting, and signing these documents. The data values on an HTML page usually originate from databases or files. The databases or files store not only data items, but also store the inter-relationships between them. However, when using HTML, it is difficult to express or represent these relationships of data items. Therefore, during the transfer of information from the databases to HTML, this information about data is lost. This is because HTML is purely designed for displaying the data values in the desired format. Therefore, if organizations want to exchange business documents in the HTML format, it would serve little purpose, because the HTML format would convey nothing about the meaning of the data. It would convey more details about its formatting.

This is where XML steps in. Rather than describing how to display data, XML describes the meaning of that data. For example, suppose we want to create a Web page describing the products that we sell. The responsibility of making the Web pages attractive by using catchy colours, fonts, and images would be left to HTML. However, the basic data about the products themselves (such as product names, categories, prices, etc.) would be stored in some databases and converted into the form of XML files (also called XML documents). HTML would present this data to the user's browser. This concept is illustrated in Fig. 13.12.

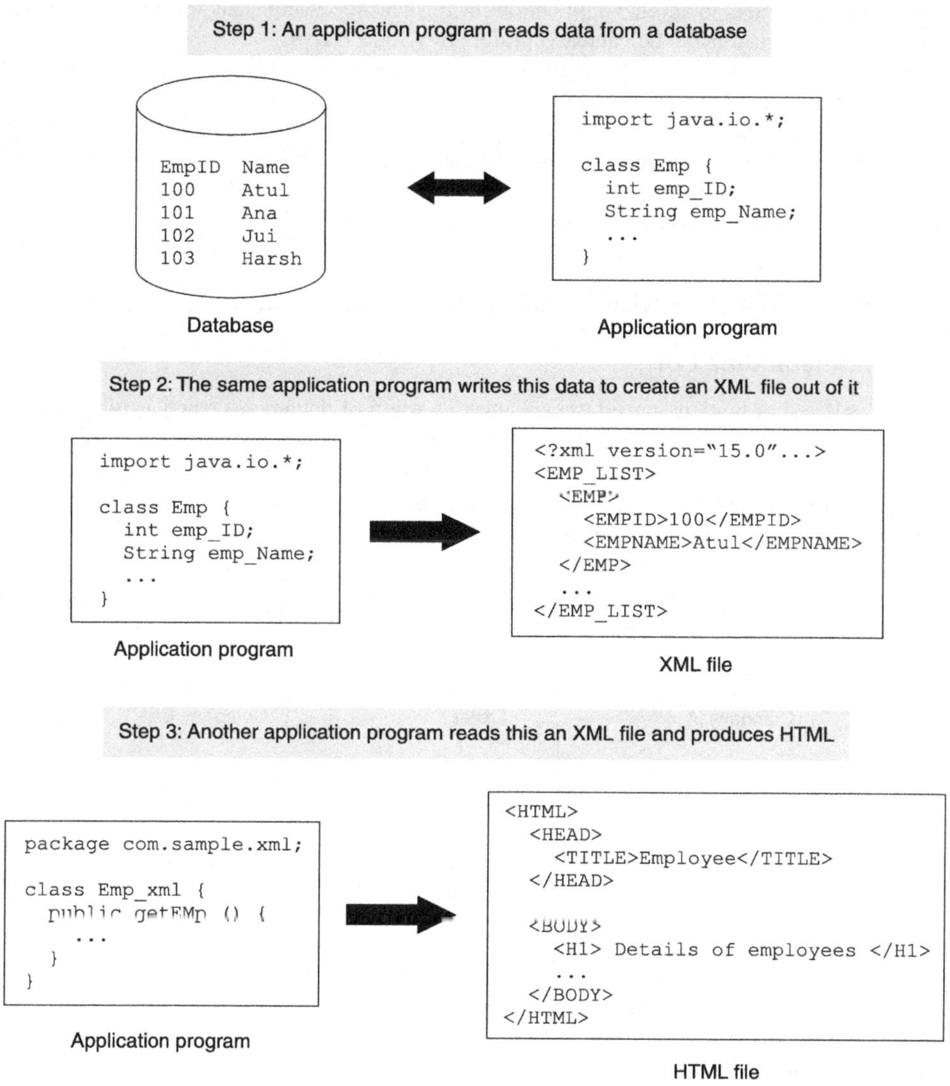

Fig. 13.12 *The role of HTML and XML*

One question needs to be answered here. Why should we transform the data from the database first into XML and then into HTML? Why do we not directly read the data from the database using our application program and create an HTML file out of it? What is the advantage that we are getting by converting the data from the database into XML form as an intermediate step before transforming it into HTML? The reasons for this are many. Once we study technologies such as **XML Stylesheet Language (XSL)**, **Cascading Style Sheets (CSS)**, and **XML parsing**, these things would become clear. For now, it should suffice to remember that an intermediate step of XML helps in areas such as making the final output media independent (i.e., it can finally be displayed as an HTML page, or as a PDF document, etc.), and it can also be sent to another application for further processing. This would not be possible if we transform the data read from the database straightaway into HTML.

The surprising point about all this is that XML implements an idea that is not revolutionary at all. The fact that data should be exchanged in the form of documents (e.g., product catalogs, invoices, purchase orders, contracts, etc.) is not new by any means. Organizations are already familiar with and have been using document exchange procedures. As mentioned previously, EDI was one of them, which has existed for more than a couple of decades. Then what is wrong with EDI, and how is XML slowly replacing it? Let us examine this question now with an overview of EDI.

ELECTRONIC DATA INTERCHANGE (EDI).. 13.3

13.3.1 Understanding EDI

When businesses sell or buy, they need to exchange a variety of documents, such as purchase orders, sales orders, letters of credit, etc. Each company has its own formats for all these documents. The format specifies how various items such as product code, description, quantity, rate, amounts, discounts, etc., will look like, and what their sizes are. Interestingly, when company *A* sends a Purchase Order (PO) to company *B*, company *B* creates a Sales Order (SO) from it. Because the format of *B*'s SO differs from that of the PO of *A*, not only in terms of product codes, etc. but also units of measures, the sizes of various data items, etc. Therefore, company *B* has to re-enter its sales order in its computer system to carry out the further follow-up. This problem is illustrated in Fig. 13.13.

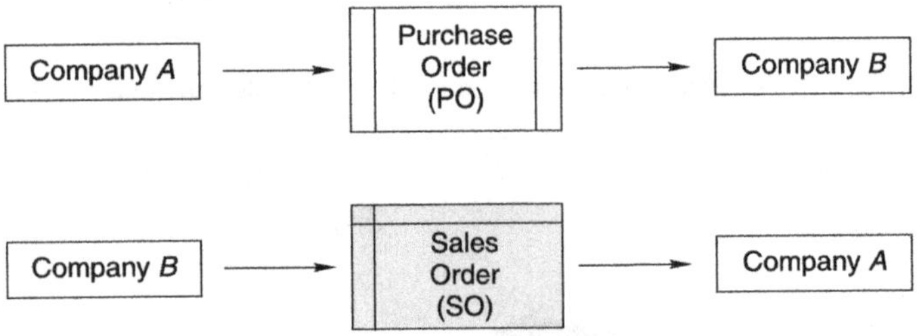

Fig. 13.13 *Problem of incompatible data formats and too many documents*

How nice it would be, if *A*'s PO is sent electronically, and if it automatically gets converted as *B*'s SO, and gets entered into *B*'s SO processing system with very little human intervention? EDI was born precisely with this aim.

Electronic Data Interchange (EDI) is the exchange of business documents such as purchase orders, invoices, etc., in an electronic format. This exchange happens, like email messages, in a few seconds and does not involve any human intervention or any paper.

EDI has been around since the 1960s and is used mostly by large corporations to conduct business with their suppliers and their customers over secure networks. Until very recently, EDI was the primary means of conducting electronic business. However, very high costs have prohibited EDI to be used by smaller organizations. These days, **Business-to-Business (B2B)** kind of electronic commerce transactions that are conducted over the Internet are also getting equally popular, which again can use EDI when it comes to exchanging any business documents. The other category of e-commerce, called **Business-to-Consumer (B2C)**, is not that much related to EDI. Anyway. EDI is a form of communication system that allows business applications in different organizations to exchange information automatically to process a business transaction.

The relationships between the parties involved in EDI transactions are predefined (e.g., trading partners, customers and suppliers of an organization). Most importantly, EDI transactions have traditionally been conducted over privately set-up networks called **Value Added Networks (VAN)** (unlike the e-commerce mode, which is over the public Internet). This explains the higher costs of EDI.

A VAN is a communications network that provides additional applications/functionality to the top of basic network infrastructure.

A network with e-mail application installed on all its subscribers allowing the email facility is one such example. Another example is EDI in which the VAN exchanges EDI messages among the trading partners. It also provides other services such as interfacing with other VANs, and supporting a number of transmission protocols and communication mechanisms. This allows organizations to exchange business documents such as purchase orders, invoices and payment instructions in a secure and automated manner. The basic idea behind EDI is shown in Fig. 13.14.

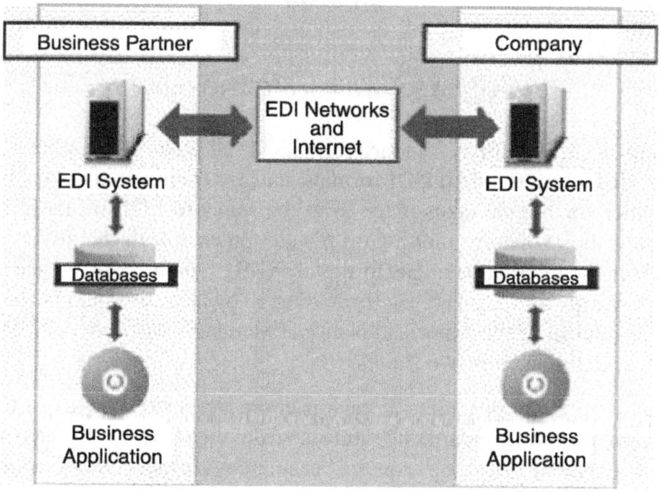

Fig. 13.14 *The basic concept behind EDI*

As we can see, the diagram defines various organizations in the form of business partners and their EDI systems, interconnected by the EDI network and the Internet. The point is that EDI is much more than a data format/representation, unlike XML. There is no concept of an *XML network*. XML is only the common format for data exchange. EDI, on the other hand, not only attempts at unifying the data exchange formats, it also provides the backbone network that is essential for this data exchange.

13.3.2 An Overview of EDI

Let us have a broad-level overview of an EDI system, before we discuss the details. Typically, an EDI service provider maintains a VAN and establishes **mailboxes** for each business partner involved in EDI. The provider stores and forwards EDI messages between these partners. The main aspect here is standardization.

All parties involved in EDI transactions must use an agreed set of document layout standards, so that the same document looks exactly similar no matter who has created it, in terms of the overall layout and format.

All such business forms are then transmitted over the VAN as messages similar to emails. Figure 13.15 shows the overall flow.

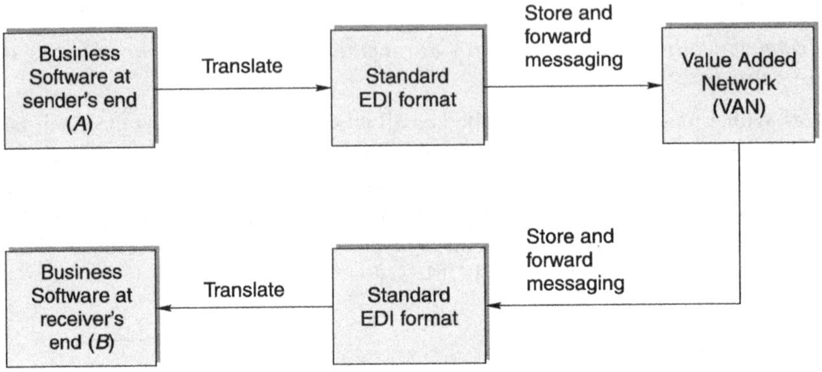

Fig. 13.15 *Overview of EDI software*

As the figure conveys, EDI defines standard formats for all types of documents. Firstly, sender *A*'s documents are converted to the standard EDI formats, and are transmitted over a VAN to the receiver *B*. At this point, another conversion takes place from the standard EDI format to *B*'s internal format, as defined by the application software running on *B*'s computer. Recall that this is quite similar to the conversion of data from the internal database format to XML, which we had discussed earlier.

The document standards for EDI were firstly developed by large business houses during the 1970s, and are now under the control of the American National Standards Institute (ANSI).

As we have noted, EDI demands two things.

1. One is a set of software programs at each user/partner's site to convert the documents from their own formats to the standard ones and also from the standard formats to their own formats, which they understand. These are required because any partner could send or receive documents at different times.
2. Secondly, EDI also demands a network connection between the two companies that want to exchange business documents with each other. This need translates into the trading partners having a dedicated leased line between them, or a connection to a VAN. Since this is very expensive, it is not feasible for many small and medium-sized organizations, which are the trading partners of the bigger corporations. However, because many large organizations, which can easily deploy EDI, demand that their vendors also have EDI setup, small and medium-sized organizations sometimes have no choice but to use EDI rather than lose a big customer.

13.3.3 Advantages of EDI

Having understood where and how EDI systems can be beneficial, let us summarize the advantages offered by EDI systems.

1. Reduced lead-time from placing an order to actually receiving goods.
2. Substantial decrease in the number of errors, otherwise due to manual data entry and paperwork.
3. Reduction in overall processing costs.
4. Availability of information all the time.
5. Provision for planning the future activities in a better and more organized manner.
6. Building long-term relationships between trading partners.

13.3.4 EDI and the Internet

So far, we have focussed our attention on the EDI systems that require a dedicated network connection between the trading partners, called as a VAN. Although this works fine in the large business houses, its high costs make it difficult to implement it for a relatively smaller organization. At times, these costs of setting up and maintaining a VAN can be simply beyond the reach of smaller organizations.

The arrival of the Internet has given everybody in the world a very cheap and simple way to potentially connect to every other computer in the world. Naturally, the idea of *Web-enabling* EDI has emerged in the last few years. Simply put, this means that the EDI systems could be connected to the Internet, so that the trading partners who cannot afford the high costs of VAN services, can simply use the Internet to connect to their bigger partners for conducting EDI transactions.

Of course, this concept has the biggest practical problem of potential lack of security. As we know, the basic aim of setting up a dedicated VAN, or using the services of a VAN provider, is to ensure that the business transactions between two trading partners are totally secure and reliable. This is possible because the VANs are private networks between two partners.

However, the fundamental feature of the Internet is that it is open to every potential computer user in the world, who possesses a Web browser and the basic connectivity features such as a dial-up account. In other words, the Internet was not created with an aim of securely exchanging business information. That has come only as an afterthought, and not as a carefully built-in feature. Stories of online credit card information being tapped and misused still go around. Therefore, the basic purpose of EDI contradicts that of the Internet. In this situation, if the two have to co-exist, there must be a guarantee that we can exchange information securely using the Internet.

Thankfully, with the emergence of technologies such as encryption mechanisms and digital signatures, this is more or less assured these days. Of course, this is still not as safe as having a VAN connection between the trading partners. But surely, this is the closest that the Internet can go to, with the current technology. Therefore, connecting EDI systems to the Internet is certainly a possibility, and some organizations are doing that.

The technology for combining EDI with the Internet can be done by adding a browser-based interface to the VAN networks. Existing users continue to have the usual EDI interface. Neither set of users is aware that depending on whether they are on a VAN or the Internet, a different set of forms (either XML or HTML) is sent to them by the VAN provider. The VAN provider, as shown in Fig. 13.16, does this behind the scene.

As the figure shows, the VAN provider is responsible for translating EDI documents into HTML forms, when presenting data to the Internet users. Similarly, the VAN provider translates HTML forms and data entered by the Internet users into EDI standard forms such as ANSI ASC X12. Neither the Internet users nor the EDI users are aware of this translation process. Thus, the VAN provider performs a dual role here—that of a VAN provider as usual, and the additional role of a Web server.

As we have noted, the actual document interchange can be done using the XML standard. Since the EDI approach of standardizing and exchanging business documents using a hierarchical structure

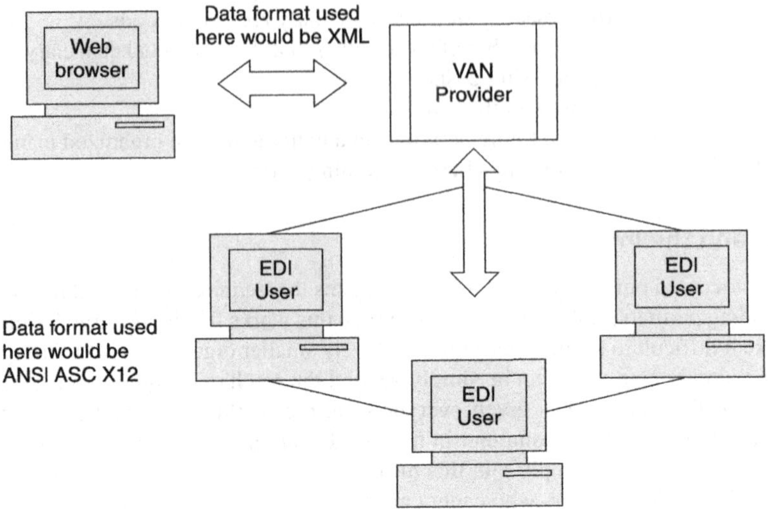

Fig. 13.16 *EDI and the Internet*

such as ASC X12 is extremely close to the way XML documents are organized, the future directions taken for brining EDI and the Internet closer would be by converting all standard EDI documents to their equivalent XML formats. This is the current trend in the business industry at the moment. The basic technology would be VAN on one side, and the use of standard browser-based Internet interface on the other. The former would continue to work with EDI standards such as ASC X12, whereas the latter would employ XML standards.

XML TERMINOLOGY 13.4

We have discussed the origins, need, and relevance of XML. Now let us dig a bit deeper into the XML terminology that we need to be familiar with. The simplest way to do this is to actually take a look at an XML document and then study its various parts. We will use the XML file shown in Fig. 13.17 for our discussion.

```
<?xml version="1.0"?>
<?xml-stylesheet type="text/xsl" href="books_list.xsl"?>

<BOOKS>
  <BOOK pubyear="1929">
    <BOOK_TITLE>Look Homeward, Angel</BOOK_TITLE>
    <AUTHOR>Wolfe, Thomas</AUTHOR>
  </BOOK>
  <BOOK pubyear="1973">
    <BOOK_TITLE>Gravity's Rainbow</BOOK_TITLE>
    <AUTHOR>Pynchon, Thomas</AUTHOR>
  </BOOK>
  <BOOK pubyear="1977">
```

(Contd.)

Fig. 13.17 *Contd...*

```
    <BOOK_TITLE>Cards as Weapons</BOOK_TITLE>
    <AUTHOR>Jay, Ricky</AUTHOR>
  </BOOK>
  <BOOK pubyear="2001">
    <BOOK_TITLE>Computer Networks</BOOK_TITLE>
    <AUTHOR>Tanenbaum, Andrew</AUTHOR>
  </BOOK>
</BOOKS>
```

Fig. 13.17 *Sample XML document*

Every XML file has an extension of .XML. Let us call the above file as *books.xml*. As we can see, the file seems to contain information organized in a hierarchical manner, with some unfamiliar symbols. Let us understand this example step by step. In the process, we will start getting familiar with the XML syntax and terminology.

Figure 13.18 shows a short pictorial explanation of this XML document. A detailed explanation is provided in Table 13.1.

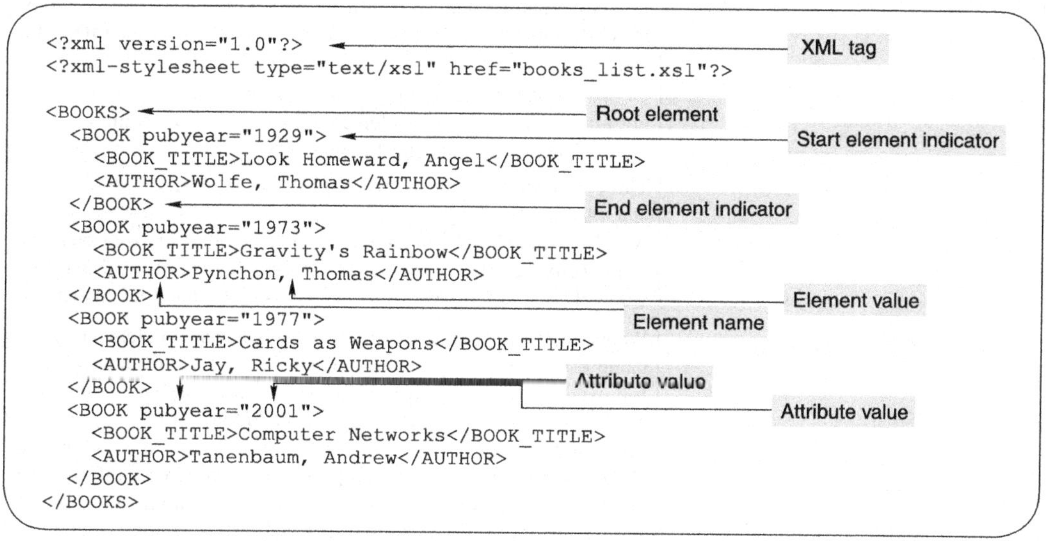

Fig. 13.18 *Terminology in XML—High level overview*

As we can notice, some of the key terms that have been introduced here are, XML tag, element (composed of element name and element value), attribute (composed of attribute name and attribute value), and root element. Some of the other terms are start element indicator and end element indicator. Let us now understand their meanings.

Table 13.1 *XML example described*

Contents of the XML file	*Description*
`<?xml version="1.0"?>`	This line identifies that this is an XML document. Every XML document must begin with this line. Note that the text is delimited inside the opening tag <? and the closing tag ?>. We shall soon see that, in general, XML contents are delimited inside the symbol pair < and >. However, some special keywords, including the *xml* declaration shown here, have a slightly different symbol pair (i.e., <? and >). Regardless, there is always an opening symbol, and a closing symbol for every line in an XML file.

`<?xml-stylesheet`
`type="text/xsl"`
`href="books_list.xsl"?>`
	Note that this line also comes with the symbol pair <? and ?>. This is a style sheet declaration, which we shall ignore for the moment. This has no direct relevance to the content of the XML document. We will discuss this concept later in the book. However, for now, the point to note is that apart from the *xml* declaration, an XML file can also contain other declarations, such as the one shown here.

`<BOOKS>`	This line implicitly indicates the start of the actual contents in the XML file. Note that the word `BOOKS` is delimited by the symbols < and >. In XML, this whole text (i.e., `<BOOKS>`) is called as an **element** or a **tag**. Thus, an element or a tag in XML consists of the following parts: < is the start indicator for an element. `BOOKS` is the name of the element (`BOOKS` is just an example). > is the end indicator for an element. Thus, some of the other element names are `<BOOK>`, `<BOOK_TITLE>`, and `<AUTHOR>`. Also, the first element in an XML file is called as the **root element** or the **root tag**. Thus, `<BOOKS>` is the root element of this XML file. Quite clearly, every XML file must have exactly one root element.
`<BOOK pubyear="1929">`	We should now be able to realize that this is also an element by the name `BOOK`. Like the previous element, there is a start indicator (<), followed by an element name `(BOOK)`, followed by some other text `(pubyear="1929")`, ending with the end indicator (>). The *other text*, i.e., `pubyear="1929"` is called as an **attribute** in XML. An attribute serves the purpose of providing more information about an element. For example, here, the attribute informs us that the book being described was published in 1929. Attribute declarations consist of two portions, the **attribute name** and the **attribute value**. In this case, we have: pubyear as the attribute name and 1929 as the attribute value

`<BOOK_TITLE>Look`
Homeward,
`Angel</BOOK_TITLE>`
	This is another element declaration. The name of the element is `BOOK_TITLE`, enclosed, as before, inside the start indicator (<) and the end indicator (>). However, this declaration of `<BOOK_TITLE>` is followed by some other text, namely `Look Homeward, Angel </BOOK_TITLE>`. What is this text about?

(Contd.)

Table 13.1 *Contd...*

Contents of the XML file	*Description*
	`Look Homeward, Angel` is the element value. </BOOK_TITLE> indicates the end of the element declaration. Now, this may sound confusing and raises the following issues. 1. Why did we not have the end of the element declaration for the previous elements (i.e., for <BOOKS> and <BOOK>)? Well, every element in an XML file must have an end element declaration. That is, <BOOKS> and <BOOK> elements also have their corresponding end element declarations. Look for the </BOOKS> and </BOOK> elements in the XML document. The only question then remains is, why do they not immediately follow the element declarations, i.e., why are there a number of other things between <BOOKS> and </BOOKS>, and between <BOOK> and </BOOK>? This is exactly where the point of arranging information in a hierarchical manner comes into picture. That is, we wish to include all our book details inside the <BOOKS> and </BOOKS> tags. Within this, we want each individual book to be described under its own <BOOK> and </BOOK> tags. This is a hierarchy of information, and it can be described by using this technique of including all contents under the <BOOKS> and </BOOKS> tags, and an individual book inside the <BOOK> and </BOOK> tags. 2. Why did the previous element (i.e., <BOOK>) not have an element value, whereas this one has? Well, elements may or may not have any element value. The previous two elements did not have any value, but this one has. 3. What about attributes? The previous element (i.e., <BOOK>) had an attribute called as `pubyear` with an attribute value of `1929`. Well, like element values, attributes (and therefore, even attribute values) are also optional. The previous element had an attribute, but the current element does not. This is perfectly acceptable.
<AUTHOR>Wolfe, Thomas</AUTHOR>	This element should be clearly understood by us without any explanation. It is simply the second subelement under the first <BOOK> element. It does have an element value, but does not have any attribute. There is nothing special about this declaration.
</BOOK>	This declaration indicates the end of the first <BOOK> element. Thus, whatever follows would *not* be a part of the <BOOK> element now. Instead, it would be a part of the <BOOKS> element. Incidentally, what would be a part of the <BOOK> element? Quite clearly, whatever falls within the range of the <BOOK> and </BOOK> elements, would be part of above. That is, in this case, it would consist of the two tags shown below: <BOOK_TITLE>Look Homeward, Angel <BOOK_TITLE> <AUTHOR>Wolfe, Thomas</AUTHOR>
Remaining tags	We will not describe the `remaining tags`/elements, since they are quite similar to what we have discussed here.

At this stage, we should be quite familiar with the basic XML terminology. In case we are not, it is suggested that we re-read the example and its description until it is clear. This is because the rest of the discussion assumes that we have a good understanding of these terms.

The following exercises will refresh what we have learnt so far.

Exercise 1 Create an XML document template to describe the result of students in an examination. The description should include the student's roll number, name, three subject names and marks, total marks, percentage, and result.

Solution (a) This can be done in more than one ways. The following is one such possible way.

```
<?xml version="1.0">
<exam_result>
   <roll_number> … </roll_number>
   <student_name> … </student_name>
   <subject_1>
      <subject_1_name> … </subject_1_name>
      <subject_1_marks> … </subject_1_marks>
   </subject_1>
   <subject_2>
      <subject_2_name> … </subject_2_name>
      <subject_2_marks> … </subject_2_marks>
   </subject_2>
   <subject_3>
      <subject_3_name> … </subject_3_name>
      <subject_3_marks> … </subject_3_marks>
   </subject_3>
   <total_marks> … </total_marks>
   <percentage> … </percentage>
   <result> … </result>
</exam_result>
```

Note that Solution 1(a) provides an elegant way of providing a template (i.e., structure) for constructing an XML message to store examination results. This could have been done in another manner, as shown in Solution 1(b).

(b) This solution offers another way to describe the XML message for examination results. It does not break down the hierarchy to the lowest possible level. That is, the information about subjects and the marks therein are at the same level, which is not a great approach.

```
<?xml version="1.0">
<exam_result>
   <roll_number> … </roll_number>
   <student_name> … </student_name>
   <subject_1_name> … </subject_1_name>
   <subject_1_marks> … </subject_1_marks>
   <subject_2_name> … </subject_2_name>
   <subject_2_marks> … </subject_2_marks>
   <subject_3_name> … </subject_3_name>
   <subject_3_marks> … </subject_3_marks>
   <total_marks> … </total_marks>
   <percentage> … </percentage>
   <result> … </result>
</exam_result>
```

Notice that we have got rid of the elements that start and end the description of a particular subject, i.e., tags such as `<subject_1>` and `</subject_1>`, etc. It is generally not advisable.

Let us now have an exercise to recap the XML terminologies that we had studied earlier.

Exercise 2 With reference to Solution 1(a), describe the various XML terms found there.

Solution The XML terminology with reference to Solution 1(a) is as follows.

Sr No	XML term	Example
1	XML document indicator	`<?xml version="1.0">`
2	Root element	`<exam_result>`
3	Element	`<roll_number> … </roll_number>`
4	Element name	`<roll_number>`
5	Element end indicator	`</roll_number>`

Note that our example does not have any attributes.

To understand the concepts learned so far better, let us consider a few more XML examples as shown in the exercises below.

Exercise 3 Suppose we want to store information regarding employees in the following format in XML. Show such a file with one example:

Employee ID	Numeric	5 positions
Employee Name	Alphanumeric	30 positions
Employee Department	Alphanumeric	2 positions
Role	Alphanumeric	20 positions
Manager	Alphanumeric	30 positions

Solution

```
<?xml version="1.0"?>
<EMPLOYEES>
    <EMPLOYEE>
        <EMP_ID>9662</EMP_ID>
        <EMP_NAME>Atul Kahate</EMP_ID>
        <EMP_DEPT>PS</EMP_DEPT>
        <ROLE>Project Manager</ROLE>
        <MANAGER>S Ketharaman</MANAGER>
    </EMPLOYEE>

</EMPLOYEES>
```

Exercise 4 Suppose our banking application allows the user to perform an online funds transfer. This application generates an XML message, which needs to be sent to the database for actual updates. Create such a sample message, containing the following details:

Transaction reference number	Numeric	10 positions
From account	Numeric	12 positions
To account	Numeric	12 positions
Amount	Numeric	5 positions (No fractions are allowed)
Date and time	Numeric	Timestamp field

Solution

```
<?xml version="1.0"?>
<FUNDS_TRANSFER>
    <TRN>9101216130</TRN>
```

```
    <FROM_ACCT>003901000649</FROM_ACCT>
    <TO_ACCT>003901000716</TO_ACCT>
    <AMOUNT>10000</AMOUNT>
    <TIMESTAMP>11.09.2005:04.05.00</TIMESTAMP>
</FUNDS_TRANSFER>
```

As we can see, XML can be used in a variety of situations to represent any kind of data. It need not be restricted to a particular domain, technology, or application. It can be used universally.

We will study a lot more about the various aspects of XML and its terminologies now.

INTRODUCTION TO DTD 13.5

Consider an XML document that we intend to write for capturing bank account information. We would like to see data such as the account number, account holder's name, opening balance, type of account, etc., as the fields for which we want to capture information. However, at the same time, we also wish to ensure that this XML document does not contain any other irrelevant information For instance, we would like to make sure that our XML document does not contain information about students, books, projects, or data not needed.

In short, we need easy mechanisms for validating an XML document. For example, we should be able to specify and validate, which elements, attributes, etc., are allowed in an XML document.

The idea is shown in Fig. 13.19.

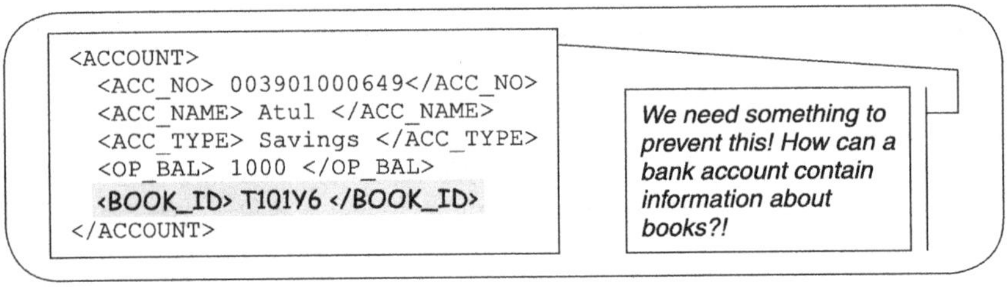

Fig. 13.19 *The need for validating contents of an XML document*

This is where a **Document Type Definition (DTD)** comes to the rescue!

A DTD allows us to validate the contents of an XML document.

For example, a DTD will allow us to specify that a book XML document can contain exactly one book name and at the most two author names.

A DTD is usually a file with an extension of *DTD*, although this extension is optional. Technically, a DTD file need not have any extension. We can specify the relationship between an XML document and a DTD. That is, we can mention that for a given XML file, we want to use a given DTD file. Also, we specify the rules that we want to apply in that DTD file. Once this linkage is established, the DTD file checks the contents of the XML document with reference to these rules automatically whenever we attempt to make use of the XML document. This concept is shown in Fig. 13.20.

Imagine a situation where we do not have anything such as a DTD. Yet, let us imagine that we want to apply certain rules. How can we accomplish this? Well, there is no simple solution here. The programs that use the XML document will need to perform all these validations before they can make use of the contents of the XML document. Of course, it is not impossible. However, it would need to

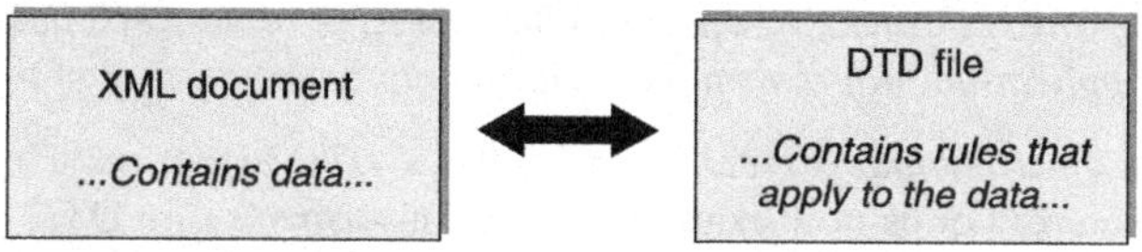

Fig. 13.20 *Relationship between an XML document and a DTD file*

be performed by *every* program, which wants to use this XML document for any purposes. Otherwise, there is no guarantee that the XML document contains bad data! This situation is depicted in Fig. 13.21.

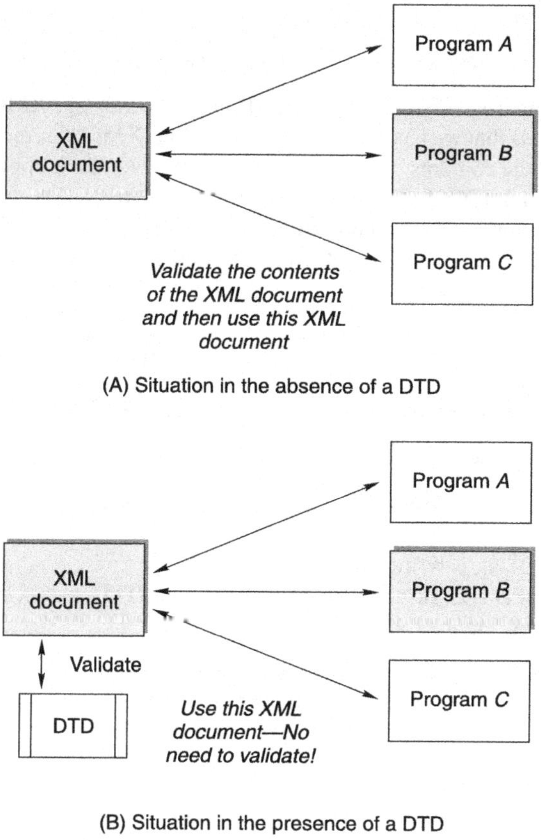

Fig. 13.21 *Situation in the absence/presence of a DTD*

As we can see, a DTD will free application programs from the worry of validating the contents of an XML document. It will take this responsibility on itself. Therefore, the portion of validation is concentrated in just once place—inside the DTD. All other *parties* interested in the contents of an XML document are free to concentrate on what they want to do, i.e., to make use of the XML document the way they want and process it, as appropriate. On the other hand, the DTD would be busy validating the contents of the XML document on behalf of any program or application.

DTD helps us in specifying the rules for validating the contents of an XML document at once place, thereby allowing the application programs to concentrate on the processing of the XML document.

We have mentioned earlier that a DTD is a file with a DTD extension. The contents of this file are purely textual in nature. Let us now examine the various aspects of a DTD and how they help in validating the contents of an XML document.

DOCUMENT TYPE DECLARATION 13.6

An XML document contains a reference to a DTD file. This is similar to, for example, how a *C* program would include references to various header files, or a Java program would include packages.

A `DOCTYPE` *declaration in an XML document specifies that we want to include a reference to a DTD file.*

Whenever any program (usually called as an XML parser) reads our XML document containing a `DOCTYPE` tag, it understands that we have defined a DTD for our XML document. Therefore, it attempts to also load and interpret the contents of the DTD file. In other words, it applies the rules specified in the DTD to the contents of our XML document for verifying them.

The `DOCTYPE` declaration stands for a **document type declaration**. Conceptually, this is illustrated in Fig. 13.22. Note that we are ignoring syntactical correctness for the moment, just for the sake of understanding.

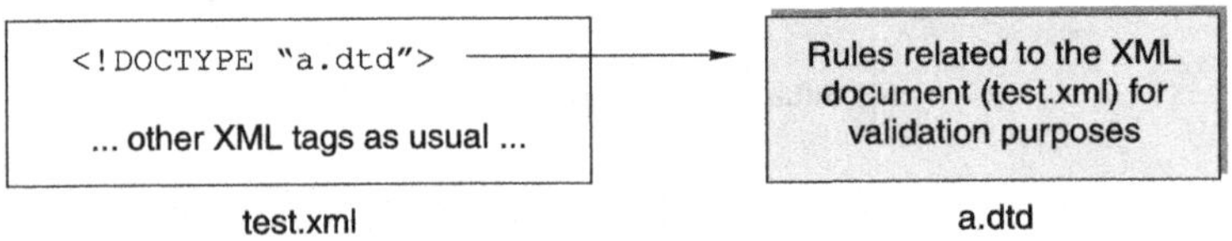

Fig. 13.22 *Using the DOCTYPE tag*

Note that the `DOCTYPE` tag is written as `<!DOCTYPE ...>`.

There are two types of DTDs, **internal DTD** and **external DTD**, also respectively called **internal subset** and **external subset**. Figure 13.23 shows this.

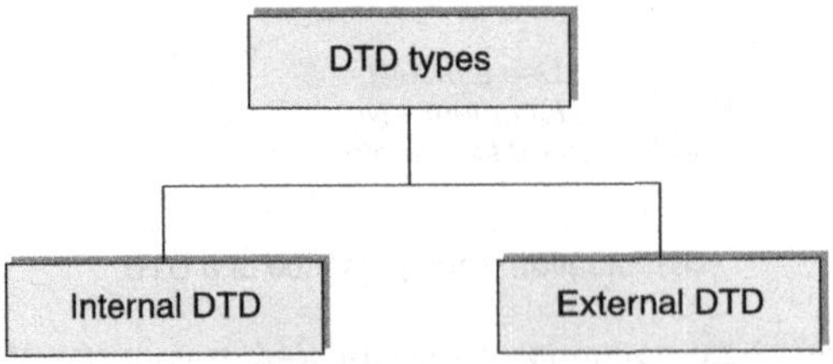

Fig. 13.23 *Classification of DTD*

The two types differ from each other purely on the basis of where they are defined.

An *internal subset* means that the contents of the DTD are inside an XML document itself. On the other hand, an *external subset* means that an XML document has a reference to another file, which we call as *external subset*.

Let us take a simple example. Suppose we want to define an XML document containing a book name as the only element. We also wish to write a corresponding DTD, which will define the template or rule book for our XML document. Then we have two situations: the DTD can be internal or external. Let us call our XML document as *book.xml*, and our external DTD as *book.dtd*. Note that when the DTD is internal, there is no need to provide a separate name for the DTD (since the contents of the DTD are inside the contents of the XML document anyway). But when the DTD is external, we must provide a name to this DTD file.

We take a look at the internal and the external DTD, as shown in Fig. 13.24.

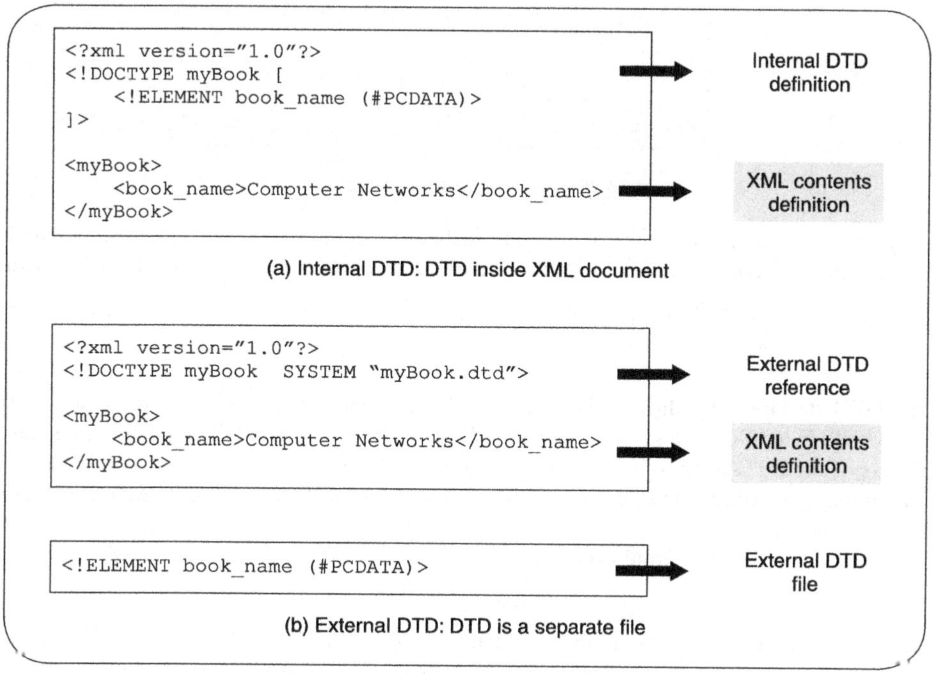

Fig. 13.24 *Internal and external DTD examples*

As we can see, when a DTD is internal, we embed the contents of the DTD inside the XML document, as shown in case (a). However, when a DTD is external, we simply provide a reference to the DTD inside our XML document, as shown in case (b). The actual DTD file has a separate existence of its own. Of course, we have not yet described the syntax completely, which we shall do very soon.

When should we use an internal DTD, and when should we use an external DTD? For simple situations, internal DTDs work well. However, external DTDs help us in two ways.

1. External DTDs allow us to define a DTD once, and then refer to it from any number of XML documents. Thus, they are reusable. Also, if we need to make any changes to the contents of the DTD, the change needs to be made just once (to the DTD file).
2. External DTDs reduce the size of the XML documents, since the XML documents now contain just a reference to the DTD, rather than the actual contents of the DTD.

Another keyword we need to remember in the context of internal DTDs.

*An XML document can be declared as **standalone**, if it does not depend on an external DTD.*

The keyword standalone is used along with the XML opening tag, as shown in Fig. 13.25.

```
<?xml version = "1.0" standalone = "yes"?>

<!DOCTYPE employee [
  <! ELEMENT emp_name        (#PCDATA)>
  <! ELEMENT salary          (#PCDATA)>
]>

<employee>
  <emp_name>Sachin Tendulkar</emp_name>
  <salary>infinite</salary>
</employee>
```

Fig. 13.25 *Use of the standalone keyword*

Let us now understand the syntax of the DTD declaration or reference, i.e., regardless of whether the DTD is internal or external. We know that the internal DTD declaration looks like this in our example:

```
<!DOCTYPE myBook [
   <!ELEMENT book_name (#PCDATA)>
]>
```

This DTD declaration indicates that our XML document will contain a root element called as `myBook`, which, in turn, contains an element called `book_name`. We will talk more about it soon. Also, the contents of the DTD need to be wrapped inside square brackets. This informs the XML parser to know the start and the end of the DTD syntax, and also to help it differentiate between the DTD contents and the XML contents.

On the other hand, the external DTD reference looks like this:

```
<!DOCTYPE myBook  SYSTEM "myBook.dtd">
```

This does not give us any idea about the actual contents of the DTD file, since the DTD is external.

Let us now worry about the `DOCTYPE` syntax. In general, the basic syntax for the `DOCTYPE` line is as shown in Fig. 13.26.

```
<!DOCTYPE root element name ...>
```

Fig. 13.26 *DOCTYPE **basic syntax***

Let us understand what it means.

1. The `DOCTYPE` keyword indicates that this is either an internal declaration of a DTD, or a reference to an external DTD.
2. Regardless of whether it is internal or external, this is followed by the name of the root element in the XML document.
3. This is followed by the actual contents of the DTD (if the DTD is internal), or by the name of the DTD file (if it is an external DTD). This is currently shown with dots (...).

Therefore, we can now enhance our DOCTYPE declaration, as shown in Fig. 13.27.

```
<!DOCTYPE myBook [
    <!ELEMENT book_name (#PCDATA)>
]>
```

Internal DTD: DTD Contents follow the DOCTYPE declaration

```
<!DOCTYPE myBook SYSTEM "myBook.dtd">
```

External DTD: There is just a reference to the DTD file (the actual DTD is not shown here)

Fig. 13.27 *Internal versus external DTD: The actual difference*

ELEMENT TYPE DECLARATION 13.7

We know that elements are the backbone of any XML document. If we want to associate a DTD with an XML document, we need to declare all the elements that we would like to see in the XML document, also in the DTD. This should be quite obvious to understand. After all, a DTD is a template or rule book for an XML document. An element is declared in a DTD by using the **element type declarations** (ELEMENT tag). For example, we can declare an element called as *book_name*, we can use the following declaration:

```
<!ELEMENT book_name (#PCDATA)>
```

As we can see, *book_name* is the name of the element, and its data type is *PCDATA*. We will discuss these aspects soon. The XML jargon calls an element name as *generic identifier*. The data type is called as *content specification.*

The element name must be unique within a DTD.

Let us consider an example. Suppose that we want to store just the name of a book in our XML document. Figure 13.28 shows a sample XML document and the corresponding DTD that specifies the rules for this XML document. Note that we are using an external DTD. We have added line numbers simply for the sake of understanding the example easily by providing references during our discussion. The actual XML document and DTD will never have line numbers.

```
XML document (book.xml)
1. <?xml version="1.0"?>

2. <!-- This XML document refers to book.dtd -->
3. <!DOCTYPE myBook SYSTEM "book.dtd">

4. <myBook>
5. <book_name>Computer Networks</book_name>
6. </myBook>

DTD file (book.dtd)
1. <!ELEMENT myBook (book_name)>
2. <!ELEMENT book_name (#PCDATA)>
```

Fig. 13.28 *Book XML document and external DTD declaration*

Let us understand this example line by line.
Understanding the XML document (*book.xml*)

1. Line 1 indicates that this is an XML document.
2. Line 2 is a comment.
3. Line 3 declares a document type reference. It indicates that our XML document makes use of an external DTD. The name of this external DTD is *book.dtd*. Also, the root element of our XML document is an element called as `myBook`.
4. Lines 4–6 define the actual contents of our XML document. These consist of an element called as `book_name`.

Understanding the DTD (*book.dtd*)

1. Line 1 is an element type reference. It indicates that the root element of the XML document that this DTD will be used to verify, will have a name `myBook`. This root element (`myBook`) contains one sub-element called as `book_name`.
2. Line 2 states that the element `book_name` can contain parsed character data.

13.7.1 Specifying Sequences, Occurrences and Choices

So far, we have discussed examples where the DTD contained just one element inside the root element. Real life examples are often far more complex than this.

1. Sequence The first question is how we add more element type declarations to a DTD. For example, suppose that our book DTD needs to contain the book name and author name. For this, we simply need to add a comma between these two element type declarations. For example:

```
<!ELEMENT myBook (book_name, author)>
```

This declaration specifies that our XML document should contain exactly one book name, followed by exactly one author name. Any number of book name-author pairs can exist.

Figure 13.29 shows an example of specifying the address book.

```
<!ELEMENT address (street, region, postal-code, locality, country)>
<!ELEMENT street          (#PCDATA)>
<!ELEMENT region          (#PCDATA)>
<!ELEMENT postal-code     (#PCDATA)>
<!ELEMENT locality        (#PCDATA)>
<!ELEMENT country         (#PCDATA)>
```

Fig. 13.29 *Defining sequence of elements*

As we can see, our address book contains subelements, such as *street*, *region*, *postal code*, *locality*, and *country*. Each of these subelements is defined as a parsed character data field. Of course, we can extend the concept of sub-elements further. That is, we can, for example, break down the *street* subelement into *street number* and *street name*. This is shown in Fig. 13.30.

```
<!ELEMENT address (street, region, postal-code, locality, country)>
<!ELEMENT street (street_number, street_name)>
<!ELEMENT street_number   (#PCDATA)>
```

(Contd.)

Fig. 13.30 *Contd...*

```
<!ELEMENT street_name      (#PCDATA)>
<!ELEMENT region           (#PCDATA)>
<!ELEMENT postal-code      (#PCDATA)>
<!ELEMENT locality         (#PCDATA)>
<!ELEMENT country          (#PCDATA)>
```

Fig. 13.30 *Defining sub-sub-elements within sub-elements*

2. Choices Choices can be specified by using the pipe (|) character.

This allows us to specify options of the type *A or B*. For example, we can specify that the result of an examination can be that the student has passed or failed (but not both), as follows:

```
<!ELEMENT result (pass | fail)>
```

Figure 13.31 shows a complete example. To a guest, we want to offer tea or coffee, but not both!

```
<!ELEMENT guest (name, purpose, beverage)>
<!ELEMENT name         (#PCDATA)>
<!ELEMENT purpose      (#PCDATA)>
<!ELEMENT beverage     tea | cofee>
```

Fig. 13.31 *Specifying choices*

3. Occurrences *The number of occurrences, or the frequency, of an element can be specified by using the plus* (+), *asterisk* (*), *or question mark* (?) *characters.*

If we do not use any of the occurrence symbol (i.e., +, *, *or* ?), *then the element can occur only once. That is, the default frequency of an element is 1.*

The significance of these characters is tabulated in Table 13.2.

Table 13.2 *Specifying frequency of elements*

Character	*Meaning*
+	The element can occur *one or more times.*
*	The element can occur *zero or more times.*
?	The element can occur *zero or one times.*

The plus sign (+) *indicates that the element must occur at least once. The maximum frequency is infinite.*

For example, we can specify that a book must contain one or more chapters as follows.

```
<!ELEMENT book  (chapter+) >
```

We can use the same concept to apply to a group of subelements. For example, suppose that we want to specify that a book must contain a title, followed by at least one chapter and at least one author, we can use this declaration.

```
<!ELEMENT book  (title, (chapter, author) + )>
```

A sample XML document conforming to this DTD declaration is shown in Fig. 13.32.

```
<book>
  <title>New to XML?</title>

  <chapter>Basics of XML</chapter>
  <author>Jui Kahate</author>

  <chapter>Advanced XML</chapter>
  <author>Harsh Kahate</author>
</book>
```

Fig. 13.32 *Specifying frequency of a group of elements*

Of course, the grouping of subelements for the purpose of specifying frequency is not restricted to the plus sign `(+)`. *It can be done equally well for the asterisk* `(*)` *or question mark* `(?)` *symbols.*

The asterisk symbol `(*)` *specifies that the element may or may not occur. If it is used, it can repeat any number if times.*

Figure 13.33 shows two examples of the possibilities that are allowed.

```
<!ELEMENT organization (employee*)>
```

DTD

```
<organization>
    <employee>Ram</employee>
    <employee>Radhika</employee>
    <employee>Sachin</employee>
</organization>
```

```
<organization>
</organization>
```

Corresponding XML contents

Fig. 13.33 *Using an asterisk to define frequency*

As we can see, our DTD specifies that the XML document can depict zero or more employees in an organization. One sample XML document has three employees, the other has none. Both are allowed.

On the other hand, if we replace the asterisk `(*)` with a plus sign `(+)`, the situation changes. We must now have at least one employee. Therefore, the empty organization case (i.e., an organization containing no employees) is now ruled out. Figure 13.34 shows this.

Finally, a question mark `(?)` *indicates that the element cannot occur at all or can occur exactly once.*

A nation can have only one president. This is indicated by the following declaration.

```
<!ELEMENT nation (president?) >
```

At times, of course, the nation may be without a president temporarily. However, at no point can a nation have more than one president. Figure 13.35 shows these possibilities.

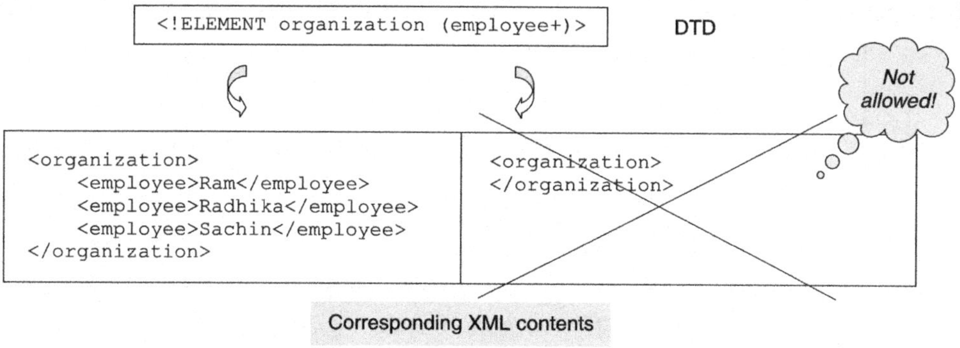

Fig. 13.34 *Using a plus sign to define frequency*

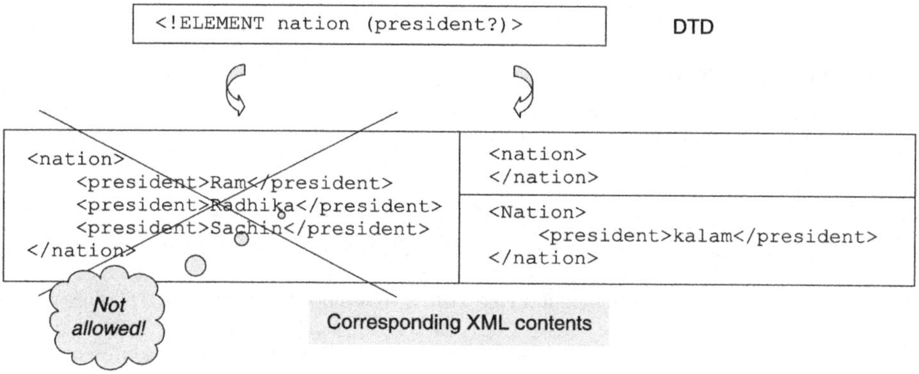

Fig. 13.35 *Using a question mark to define frequency*

ATTRIBUTE DECLARATION 13.8

Elements describe markup of an XML document. Attributes provide more details about the elements. An element can have 0 or more attributes. For example, an employee XML document can contain elements to depict the employee number, name, designation, and salary. The designation element, in turn, can have a manager attribute that indicates the manager for that employee.

*The keyword **ATTLIST** describes the attribute(s) for an element.*

Figure 13.36 shows an XML document containing an inline DTD. We can see that the element contains an attribute.

```
<?xml version ="15.0" ?>

<!DOCTYPE email [
 <!ELEMENT   email        (message) >
 <!ELEMENT   message      (#PCDATA)>
```

(Contd.)

Fig. 13.36 *Contd...*

```
  <!ATTLIST   message     from         CDATA #REQUIRED>
  <!ATTLIST   message     to           CDATA #REQUIRED>
  <!ATTLIST   message     subject      CDATA #REQUIRED>
]>

<email>
  <message from = "jui" to = "harshu" subject = "where are you?">
                It is time to have food!
  </message>
</email>
```

Fig. 13.36 *Declaring attributes in a DTD*

We can see that the *message* element has three attributes: *from, to,* and *subject.* All the three attributes have a data type of CDATA (which stands for *character data*), and a `#REQUIRED` keyword. The `#REQUIRED` keyword indicates that this attribute must be a part of the element.

LIMITATIONS OF DTDs 13.9

In spite of their several advantages, DTDs suffer from a number of limitations. Table 13.3 summarizes them.

Table 13.3 *Limitations of DTDs*

Limitation	*Explanation*
Non-XML syntax	Although DTDs do have the angled bracket syntax (e.g., `<!ELEMENT ...>`), this is quite different from the basic XML syntax. For example, a DTD does not have the standard `<?xml version ...?>` tag, etc. More specifically, a DTD file is not a valid XML document. This means duplication of validating efforts; one logic for XML, another for DTD.
One DTD per XML	We cannot use multiple DTDs to validate one XML document. We can include only one DTD reference inside an XML document. Although parameter entities make things slightly more flexible, their syntax is quite cryptic.
Weak data typing	DTD defines very basic data types. For real-life applications that demand more fine-grained and specific data types, this is not sufficient in many situations.
No inheritance	DTDs are not *object-oriented* in the sense that they do not allow the designer to create some data types and extend them as desired.
Overriding a DTD	An internal DTD can override an external DTD. (This is perhaps DTD's idea of inheritance!). This allows certain flexibility, but often also creates a lot of confusion and leads to clumsy designs.
No DOM support	We shall study later that the **Document Object Model (DOM)** technology is used to parse, read, and edit XML documents. It cannot be used for DTDs, though.

INTRODUCTION TO SCHEMA 13.10

We have studied the concept of a Document Type Definition (DTD) in detail. We know that a DTD is used for validating the contents of an XML document. DTD is undoubtedly a very important feature of the XML technology. However, there are a number of areas in which DTDs are weak. The main argument against DTDs is that their syntax is not like that of XML documents. Therefore, the people working with DTDs have to learn new syntax to work with DTDs. Furthermore, this leads to problems, such as, we cannot search for information inside DTDs, we cannot display their contents in the form of HTML, etc.

*A **schema** is an alternative to DTD.*

It is expected that schemas would eventually completely replace most (but not all) features of DTDs. DTDs are easier to write and provide support for some features (e.g., entities) better. However, schemas are much richer in terms of their capabilities and extensibility. A schema document is a separate document, just like a DTD. However, the syntax of a schema is like the syntax of an XML document. Therefore, we can state:

The main difference between a DTD and a schema is that the syntax of a DTD is different from that of XML. However, the syntax of a schema is the same as that of XML.

In other words, a schema document is an XML document.

For example, we declare an element in a DTD by using the syntax `<!ELEMENT>`. This is clearly not legal in XML. We cannot begin an element declaration with an exclamation mark, as happens in the case of a DTD.

We can use a very simple, yet powerful example to illustrate the difference between using a DTD and using a schema. Suppose that we want to represent the marks of a student in an XML document. For this purpose, we want to add an element called *Marks* to our root element *Student*. We will declare this element as of type *PCDATA* in our DTD file. This will ensure that the parser checks for the existence of the *Marks* element in the XML document. However, can it ensure that marks are numeric? Clearly, no! We cannot control what contents the element *Marks* can have. These contents can very well be alphabetic or alphanumeric! This is shown in Fig. 13.37.

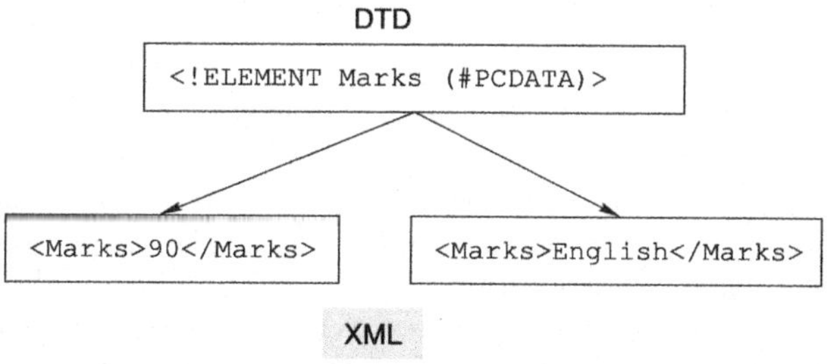

Fig. 13.37 *Use of PCDATA does not control data type*

As we can see, the usage of *PCDATA* in the declaration of an element does not stop us from entering alphabetic data in a *Marks* element. In other words, we cannot specify exactly what should our elements contain. This is quite clearly not desirable at all.

In the case of a schema, we can very well specify that our element should only contain numeric data. Moreover, we can control many other aspects of the contents of elements, which is not possible in the case of DTDs. We use similar terminology for checking the correctness of XML documents in the case of a schema (as in the case of DTDs). An XML document that conforms to the rules of a schema is called as a *valid* XML document. Otherwise, it is called *invalid*.

It is interesting to note that we can associate a DTD as well as a schema with an XML document.

Let us now take a look at a simple schema. Consider an XML document which contains a greeting message. Let us write a corresponding schema for it. Figure 13.38 shows the details.

```
<?xml version = "1.0" ?>
<MESSAGE xmlns:xsi="http://www.w3.org/2001/XMLSchema-instance"
xsi:noNamespaceSchemaLocation="message.xsd">

 Hello World!
</MESSAGE>
```

XML document: message.xml

```
<?xml version = "1.0" ?>
<xsd:schema xmlns:xsd = "http://www.w3org/2001/XMLSchema">
 <xsd:element name = "MESSAGE" type = "xsd:string"/>
</xsd:schema>
```

Schema: message.xsd

Fig. 13.38 *Example of XML document and corresponding schema*

We will notice several new syntactical details in the XML document and the schema file. Let us, therefore, understand this step by step.

First and foremost, an XML schema is defined in a separate file. This file has the extension *xsd*. In our example, the schema file is named *message.xsd*.

The following declaration in our XML document indicates that we want to associate this schema with our XML document:

```
<MESSAGE xmlns:xsi="http://www.w3.org/2001/XMLSchema-instance"
xsi:noNamespaceSchemaLocation="message.xsd">
```

Let us dissect this statement.

1. The word *MESSAGE* indicates the root element of our XML document. There is nothing unusual about it.
2. The declaration *xmlns:xsi="http://www.w3.org/2001/XMLSchema-instance"* is an attribute. It defines a namespace prefix and a namespace URI. The namespace prefix is *xmlns*. The namespace URI is *http://www.w3.org/2001/XMLSchema-instance*. The namespace prefix can change. The namespace URI must be written exactly as shown. The namespace URI specifies a particular instance of the schema specifications to which our XML document is adhering.
3. The declaration `xsi:noNamespaceSchemaLocation="message.xsd"` specifies a particular schema file which we want to associate with our XML document. In this case, we are stating that our XML document wants to refer to a schema file whose name is `message.xsd`.

This is followed by the actual contents of our XML document. In this case, the contents are nothing but the contents of our root element.

These explanations are depicted in Fig. 13.39.

```
<?xml version = "1.0" ?>
```

This is normal XML declaration. There is nothing unusual or unique about this..

(Contd.)

Fig. 13.39 *Contd...*

```
<MESSAGE xmlns:xsi="http://www.w3.org/2001/XMLSchema-instance"
 xsi:noNamespaceSchemaLocation="message.xsd">

  MESSAGE: This is the root element.
  xmlns is the XML schema reference for our schema.
  xsi:noNamespaceSchemaLocation provides a pointer to our
  schema. In this case, it is message.xsd.

  Hello World!
</MESSAGE>

  This is also nothing unusual. We simply specify the contents of our root element,
  and then signify the end of the root element (and hence that of the XML document).
```

Fig. 13.39 *Understanding our XML document*

It is now time to understand our schema (i.e., `message.xsd`).

Note that the schema file is an XML file with an extension of *xsd*. That is, like any XML document, it begins with an `<?xml ...?>` declaration.

The following lines specify that this is a schema file, and not an ordinary XML document. They also contain the actual contents of the schema. Let us first reproduce them:

```
<xsd:schema xmlns:xsd = "http://www.w3org/2001/XMLSchema">
   <xsd:element name = "MESSAGE" type = "xsd:string"/>
</xsd:schema>
```

Let us understand this step by step.

1. The declaration `<xsd:schema xmlns:xsd = "http://www.w3org/2001/XMLSchema">` indicates that this is a schema, because its root element is named *schema*. It has a namespace prefix of *xsd*. The namespace URI is *http://www.w3org/2001/XMLSchema*. This means that our schema declarations conform to the schema standards specified on the site *http://www.w3org/2001/XMLSchema*, and that we can use a namespace prefix of *xsd* to refer to them in our schema file.
2. The declaration `<xsd:element name = "MESSAGE" type = "xsd:string"/>` specifies that we want to use an element called as *MESSAGE* in our XML document. The type of this element is *string*. Also, we are using the namespace prefix *xsd*. Recall that this namespace prefix was associated with a namespace URI *http://www.w3org/2001/XMLSchema* in our earlier statement.
3. The line `</xsd:schema>` specifies the end of the schema.

   These explanations are depicted in Fig. 13.40.

```
<?xml version = "1.0" ?>

  This is normal XML declaration. There is nothing unusual or
  unique about this.
```

(Contd.)

Fig. 13.40 *Contd...*

```
<xsd:schema xmlns:xsd = "http://www.w3org/2001/XMLSchema">

    xsd:schema indicates that this is a schema definition. xsd
    is the namespace prefix. It is associated with an actual
    namespace URI http://www.w3org/2001/XMLSchema.

<xsd:element name = "MESSAGE" type = "xsd:string"/>

    This declares that our XML document will have the root
    element named MESSAGE of type string.

</xsd:schema>

    This signifies the end of our schema file.
```

Fig. 13.40 *Understanding our XML schema*

Based on this discussion, let us have a small exercise.

COMPLEX TYPES 13.11

13.11.1 Basics of Simple and Complex Types

Elements in schema can be divided into two categories: **simple** and **complex**. This is shown in Fig. 13.41.

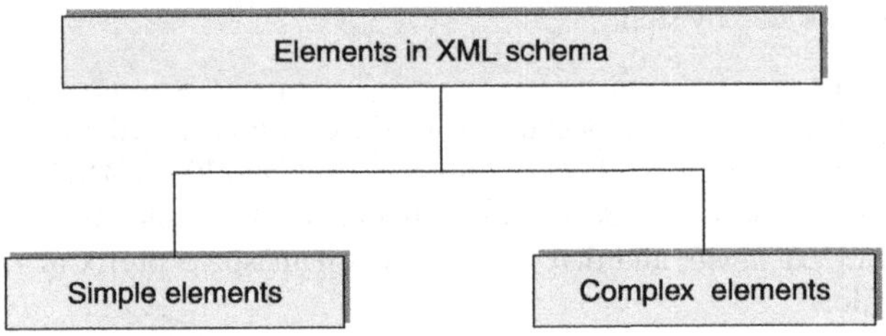

Fig. 13.41 *Classification of elements in XML schemas*

Let us understand the difference between the two types of elements in schema.

1. Simple elements Simple elements can contain only text. They cannot have subelements or attributes. The text that they can contain, however, can be of various data types such as strings, numbers, dates, etc.

2. Complex elements Complex elements, on the other hand, can contain subelements, attributes, etc. Many times, they are made up of one or more simple element. This is shown in Fig. 13.42.

Let us now consider an example. Suppose we want to capture student information in the form of the student's roll number, name, marks, and result. Then we can have all these individual blocks of information as simple elements. Then we will have a complex element in the form of the root element.

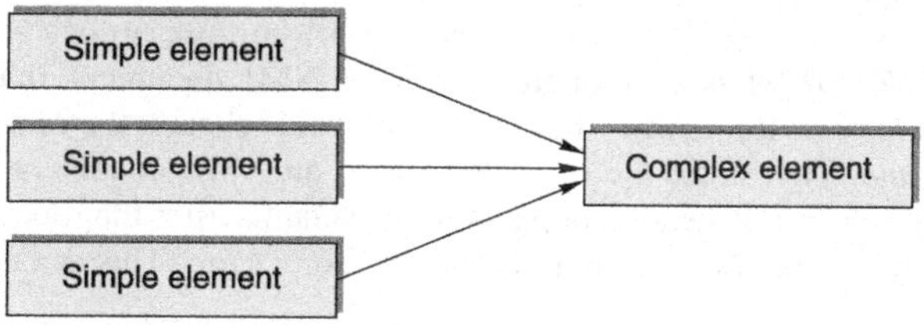

Fig. 13.42 *Complex element is made up of simple elements*

This complex element will encapsulate these individual simple elements. Figure 13.43 shows the resulting XML document, first.

```
<?xml version = "1.0"?>
<STUDENT xmlns:xsi="http://www.w3.org/2001/XMLSchema-instance"
  xsi:noNamespaceSchemaLocation="student.xsd">
 <ROLL_NUMBER> 100 </ROLL_NUMBER>
 <NAME> Pallavi Joshi </NAME>
 <MARKS> 80 </MARKS>
 <RESULT> Distinction </RESULT>
</STUDENT>
```

Fig. 13.43 *XML document for Student example*

Let us now immediately take a look at the corresponding schema file. Figure 13.44 shows this file.

```
<?xml version = "1.0"?>
<xsd:schema xmlns:xsd = "http://www.w3org/2001/XMLSchema">
 <xsd:element name = „STUDENT" type = "StudentType"/>

 <xsd:complexType name = "StudentType">
  <xsd:sequence>
   <xsd:element name = "ROLL_NUMBER"  type = "xsd:string"/>
   <xsd:element name = "NAME"         type = "xsd:string"/>
   <xsd:element name = "MARKS"        type = "xsd:integer"/>
   <xsd:element name = "RESULT"       type = "xsd:string"/>
  </xsd:sequence>
 </xsd:complexType>

</xsd:schema>
```

Fig. 13.44 *Schema for Student example*

Let us understand our schema.

1. `<xsd:schema xmlns:xsd = "http://www.w3org/2001/XMLSchema">`
   We know that the root element of the schema is a reserved keyword called *schema*. Here also, same is the case. The namespace prefix *xsd* maps to the namespace URI *http://www.w3.org/2001/XMLSchema*, as before. In general, this will be true for any schema that we write.

2. `<xsd:element name = "STUDENT" type = "StudentType"/>`
This declares *STUDENT* as the root element of our XML document. In the schema, it is called the *top-level element*. Remember that in the case of a schema, the root element is always the keyword *schema*. Therefore, the root element in an XML document is not the root of the corresponding schema. Instead, it appears in the schema after the root element *schema*.
The `STUDENT` element is declared of *type* `StudentType`. This is a user-defined type.

Conceptually, a user-defined type is similar to a structure in C/C++ or a class in Java (without the methods). It allows us to create our own custom types.

In other words, the schema specification allows us to create our own custom data types. For example, we can create our own types for storing information about employees, departments, songs, friends, sports games, and so on. We recognize this as a user-defined type because it does not have our namespace prefix *xsd*. Remember that all the standard data types provided by the XML schema specifications reside at the namespace *http://www.w3.org/2001/XMLSchema*, which we have prefixed as *xsd* in the earlier statement.
3. `<xsd:complexType name = "StudentType">`
Now that we have declared our own type, we must explain what it represents and contains. That is exactly what we are doing here. This statement indicates that we have used `StudentType` as a `type` earlier, and now we want to explain what it means. Also, note that we use a keyword *complexType* to designate that `StudentType` is a complex element. This is similar to stating `struct StudentType` or `class StudentType` in C++/Java.
4. `<xsd:sequence>`
Schemas allow us to force a sequence of simple elements within a complex element. We can specify that a particular complex element must contain one or more simple elements in a strict sequence. Thus, if the complex element is *A*, containing two simple elements *B* and *C*, we can mandate that *C* must follow *B* inside *A*. In other words, the XML document must have:
```
<A>
    <B> ... </B>
    <C>... </C>
</A>
```
This is accomplished by the *sequence* keyword.
5. `<xsd:element name = "ROLL_NUMBER" type = "xsd:string"/>`
This declaration specifies that the first simple element inside our complex element is `ROLL_NUMBER`, of type string. After this, we have `NAME`, `MARKS`, and `RESULT` as three more simple elements following `ROLL_NUMBER`. We will not discuss them. We will simply observe for now that `ROLL_NUMBER` has a different data type: an integer. We will discuss this in detail subsequently.
We will also not discuss the closure of the `sequence`, `ComplexType`, and `schema` tags.

EXTENSIBLE STYLESHEET LANGUAGE TRANSFORMATIONS (XSLT).......13.12

We have had an overview of XSL earlier. We have also studied the XPath technology in detail. These two together are sufficient for us to now start discussing XSLT.

We know that XSL consists of two parts: XSL Transformation Language (XSLT) and XSL Formatting Objects (XSL-FO). In this section, we would cover XSLT in detail.

XSLT is used to transform one XML document from one form to another. XSLT uses XPath to perform a matching of nodes for performing these transformations.

The result of applying XSLT to an XML document could be another XML, HTML, text, or any other document. The idea is shown in Fig. 13.45.

Fig. 13.45 *XSLT basics*

From a technology perspective, we need to remember that XSLT code is also written inside an XML file, with an extension of *.xsl*. In other words, XSLT is a different kind of XML file. Also, in order to work with XSLT, we need to make use of what is called an **XSLT processor**. The XSLT processor is conceptually an XSLT interpreter. That is, it would read an XSL file as source, and interpret its contents to show its effects. Several companies provide XSLT processors. Some of the more popular ones at the time of writing this are Xalan from Apache, and MS-XML from Microsoft. These parsers are programming-language specific. Therefore, the Xalan parser from Apache, for example, would be different for Java and C++.

In the following sections, we take a look at the various features in XSLT.

13.12.1 Templates

An XSLT document is an XSLT document, which has the following:

1. A root element called **style sheet**
2. A file extension of *.xsl*

The syntax of XSLT, i.e., what is allowed in XSLT and what is not, is specified in an XML namespace, whose URL is *http://www.w3.org/1999/XSL/Transform*. Therefore, we need to include this namespace in an XSLT document.

In general, an XSLT document reads the original XML document (called the **source tree**) and transforms it into a target document (called the **result tree**). The result tree, of course, may or may not be XML. The concept is shown in Fig. 13.46.

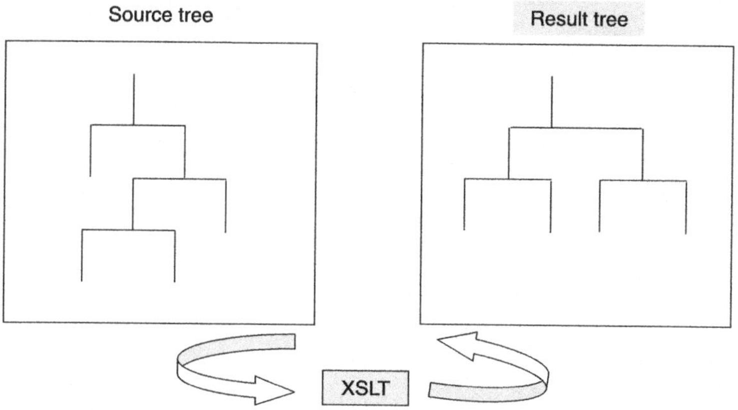

Fig. 13.46 *XSLT transformations using tree concept*

Let us now consider a simple example where we can use XSLT. Suppose that we have a simple XML file that contains a name. Now suppose that we want to apply an XSLT style sheet to it, so that the XML document gets displayed as an HTML document, with the name getting outputted in bold. How would we achieve this? We would need to do several things, as listed below:

1. In our XML document, we would need to specify that we want to make use of a specific XSLT document (just as we need to mention the name of a DTD or schema, when we use one, inside our source XML document).
2. Our XSLT document (i.e., the XSLT style sheet) would contain appropriate rules to display the contents of the above XML document in the HTML format. One of the things our XSLT document needs to do is to display the name in bold.
3. To view the outcome, we need to open our source XML document in a Web browser. The Web browser would apply the XSLT style sheet to the XML document, and show us the output in the desired HTML format.

Let us start with the source XML file. We have deliberately kept it quite simple. As we can see in Fig. 13.47, the XML document contains two elements: a root element by the name *myPerson*, which, in turn, contains the actual name of the person inside a subelement called `personName`. Note that it has reference to a style sheet named `one.xsl`.

```
<?xml version = "1.0" ?>

<?xml:stylesheet type = "text/xsl" href = "one.xsl"?>

<myPerson>
 <personName>Sachin Tendulkar</personName>
</myPerson>
```

Fig. 13.47 *Source XML document (one.xml)*

Figure 13.48 shows the corresponding XSLT document, which would convert our XML document into HTML format.

```
<xsl:stylesheet version = "1.0" xmlns:xsl = "http://www/w3.org/1999/XSL/Transform">

 <xsl:template match = "myPerson">
  <html>
   <body>
    <b> <xsl:value-of select = "personName"/> </b>
   </body>
 </html>
  </xsl:template>

 </xsl:stylesheet>
```

Fig. 13.48 *XSLT document (one.xsl)*

The resulting output is shown in Fig. 13.49.

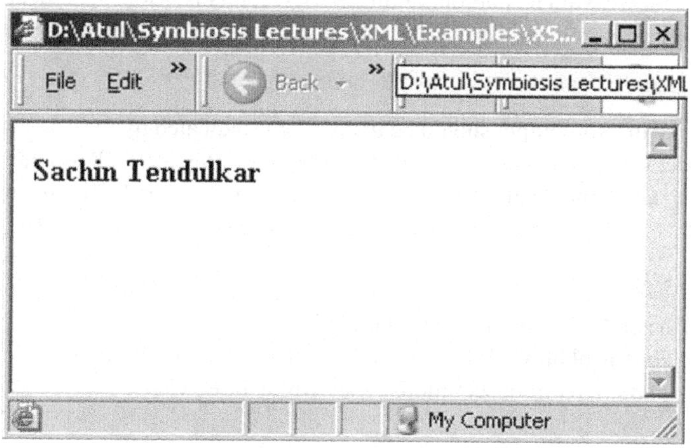

Fig. 13.49 *Resulting output*

Let us now understand how we have achieved this.

Understanding changes done to the source XML file (one.xml)

Let us first see what changes we have done to our source XML document. We have simply added the following line to it:

```
<?xml:stylesheet type = “text/xsl” href = “one.xsl”?>
```

This statement indicates that we want our XML document to be processed by an XSLT style sheet contained in a file named *one.xsl*. Because we have not specified any directory path, it is assumed that the XSLT style sheet is present in the same directory as of the source XML file.

Understanding the XSLT style sheet file (one.xsl)

Now, let us understand the meaning and purpose of the XSLT style sheet file.

The first line declares the fact that this document is an XSLT style sheet.

```
<xsl:stylesheet version = “1.0” xmlns:xsl = “http://www/w3.org/1999/XSL/
Transform”>
```

The keyword *stylesheet* indicates that this is a style sheet. The namespace for the XSLT specifications is then provided.

```
<xsl:template match = “myPerson”>
```

This line indicates a **template** element. It uses the attribute **match** to specify the condition. After match, we can specify any valid XPath expression. In the current example, in plain English, this would read as follows:

If an element by the name *myPerson* is found …

That is, we are trying to go through our XML document (i.e., *one.xml*) to see if we can locate an element named *myPerson* there. If we do find a match, we want to perform some action, which we shall discuss next.

```
<html>
      <body>
```

This is clearly plain HTML. Therefore, what we are saying is that if we find a `myPerson` element in our XML document, we want to start outputting HTML contents. More specifically, we want to start with the `<html>` and `<body>` tags. Obviously, this has nothing to do with the XSLT technology.

```
<b> <xsl:value-of select = "personName"/> </b>
```

Now, we indicate that our output should be in bold font (indicated by the `<b>` tag). This is followed by some XSLT code: `<xsl:value-of select = "personName"/>`. This code says that we want to *select* the *value of* an element called as `personName`, located in our XML document. After this, we close the bold tag.

```
</xsl:template>
```

This indicates the end of our template declaration.

The remaining code is plain HTML.

Thus, we can summarize our observations as shown in Table 13.4.

Table 13.4 *Purpose of basic template tags*

Syntax	*Purpose*
`<xsl:template match = xyz>`	Search for a matching tag named *xyz* in our XML document.
`<xsl:value-of select = pqr>`	Display the value of all tags named *pqr* at this place.

Let us study a few more examples to understand XSLT templates better.

Problem Consider the following XML document:

```
<?xml version = "1.0" ?>
<CATALOG>
   <BOOK>
      <TITLE>Computer Networks</TITLE>
      <AUTHORS>
         <AUTHOR>Andrew Tanenbaum</AUTHOR>
      </AUTHORS>
      <PUBYEAR>2003</PUBYEAR>
      <PRICE>250</PRICE>
   </BOOK>

   <BOOK>
      <TITLE>Web Technologies</TITLE >
      <AUTHORS>
         <AUTHOR>Achyut Godbole</AUTHOR>
         <AUTHOR>Atul Kahate</AUTHOR>
      </AUTHORS>
      <PUBYEAR>2002</PUBYEAR>
      <PRICE>250</PRICE>
   </BOOK>
</CATALOG>
```

Write an XSLT code to only retrieve the book titles and their prices.

Solution We want to do the following here:

1. Search for a `BOOK` tag in our XML document.
2. Whenever found, display the contents of the TITLE and PRICE tags.

The corresponding syntaxes for these will be:

1. Search for a `BOOK` tag in our XML document.
   `<xsl:template match="BOOK">`
2. Whenever found, display the contents of the `TITLE` and `PRICE` tags.
   Name: `<xsl:value-of select="TITLE"/> Price: <xsl:value-of select="PRICE"/>`

Therefore, our XSLT style sheet would contain the following:

```
<xsl:stylesheet version="1.0" xmlns:xsl="http://www.w3.org/1999/XSL/
Transform">
 <xsl:template match="BOOK">
 Book Name: <xsl:value-of select="TITLE"/> Price:<xsl:value-of select="PRICE"/>
 </xsl:template>
</xsl:stylesheet>
```

The final XML document and the corresponding XSLT style sheet are shown in Fig. 13.50.

XML document (two.xml)

```
<?xml version = "1.0" ?>
<?xml:stylesheet type = "text/xsl" href = "two.xsl"?>

<CATALOG>
 <BOOK>
  <TITLE>Computer Networks</TITLE>
  <AUTHORS>
   <AUTHOR>Andrew Tanenbaum</AUTHOR>
  </AUTHORS>
  <PUBYEAR>2003</PUBYEAR>
  <PRICE>250</PRICE>
 </BOOK>

<BOOK>
  <TITLE>Web Technologies</TITLE>
  <AUTHORS>
   <AUTHOR>Achyut Godbole</AUTHOR>
   <AUTHOR>Atul Kahate</AUTHOR>
  </AUTHORS>
  <PUBYEAR>2002</PUBYEAR>
 <PRICE>250</PRICE>
 </BOOK>
</CATALOG>
```

XSLT style sheet (two.xsl)

```
<xsl:stylesheet version="1.0" xmlns:xsl="http://www.w3.org/1999/XSL/Transform">
 <xsl:template match="BOOK">
  Book Name: <xsl:value-of select="TITLE"/> Price:  <xsl:value-of select="PRICE"/>
 </xsl:template>
   </xsl:stylesheet>
```

Fig. 13.50 *Book example*

The resulting output is shown in Fig. 13.51.

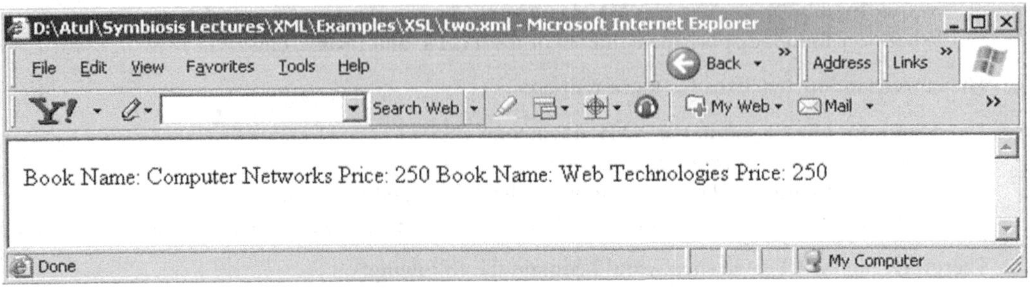

Fig. 13.51 *Output of Book example*

An interesting question at this stage is, can we specify multiple search conditions in an XSLT style sheet? That is, suppose that in the above example, we first want to display book titles with their prices. Later, as an independent activity, we want to display the titles with the authors' names and the years when published. Is this possible?

It is perfectly possible, and the way it works is depicted in Fig. 13.52. Here, we have shown the generic manner in which XSLT processes an XML document (the *source tree*) to produce the desired output (the *resulttree*).

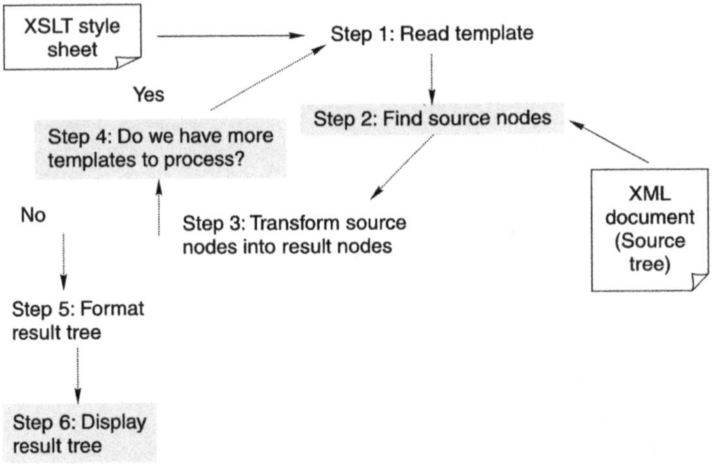

Fig. 13.52 *XSLT processing overview*

As we can see, XSLT technology keeps looking for possible template matches on elements/tags in the source XML document. As and when it finds a match, XSLT outputs it as specified by the user. This also means that there can be multiple independent template matches (i.e., search conditions) in the same XSLT style sheet.

Let us consider a few more examples to understand this.

Problem Consider the following XML document, titled emp.xml:

```
<?xml version="1.0"?>
<?xml-stylesheet type="text/xsl" href="emp.xsl"?>
<EMP_INFO>
   <EMPLOYEE>
      <EMP_NAME empID="9662">
         <FIRST>Sachin</FIRST>
         <LAST>Tendulkar</LAST>
      </EMP_NAME>
   </EMPLOYEE>
</EMP_INFO>
```

Write an emp.xsl file mentioned above, which would:

(a) *Display a heading **Emp Name:**, followed by the employee's name.*
(b) *Display the employee number below this, in a smaller font.*

Solution

Step 1 We need to extract the values of the tags `FIRST` and `LAST`, and display them along with the text EmpName: as an HTML heading. For extracting the `FIRST` and `LAST` tags, we need the following XSLT code:

```
<xsl:value-of select="EMPLOYEE/EMP_NAME/FIRST"/>
<xsl:value-of select="EMPLOYEE/EMP_NAME/LAST"/>
```

Step 2 After this, we need to extract the value of the attribute empID and display it below this. For this purpose, we need the following XSLT code:

```
<xsl:value-of select="EMPLOYEE/EMP_NAME/@empID"/>
```

Along with these XSLT syntaxes, we need to ensure that we have the right HTML code for formatting the output. This simply means that we need to embed the `FIRST` and `LAST` tags inside an HTML heading, say H1; and the emp ID inside another heading, say H3. The resulting code for the XSLT style sheet is as follows:

```
<xsl:stylesheet version="1.0" xmlns:xsl="http://www.w3.org/1999/XSL/Transform">
  <xsl:template match="EMP_INFO">
    <html>
      <head><title>Emp Info!</title></head>
        <body>
          <h1>Emp Name: <xsl:value-of select="EMPLOYEE/EMP_NAME/FIRST"/>
                        <xsl:value-of select="EMPLOYEE/EMP_NAME/LAST"/> </h1>
          <h3> <xsl:value-of select="EMPLOYEE/EMP_NAME/@empID"/></h3>
        </body>
      </html>
</xsl:template>
</xsl:stylesheet>
```

Figure 13.53 shows the original XML document in the browser, without applying the style sheet, and Fig. 13.54 shows the version when the style sheet is applied.

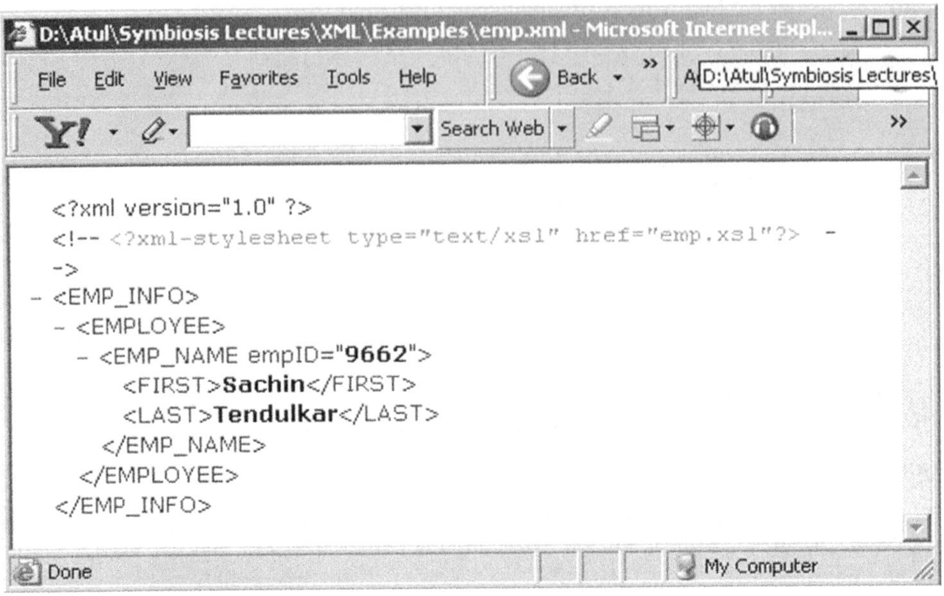

Fig. 13.53 *Original XML document without applying the style sheet*

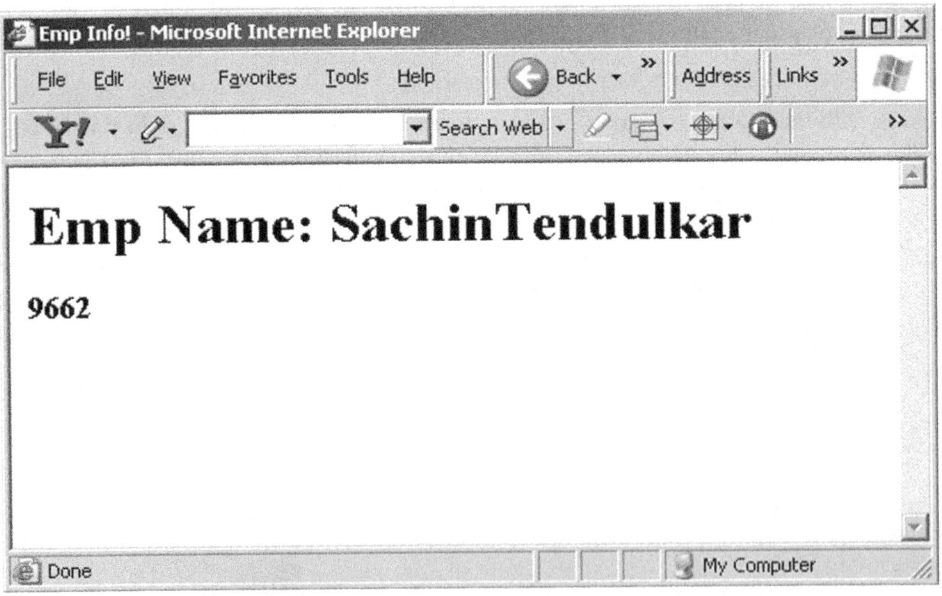

Fig. 13.54 *XML document after applying the style sheet*

Problem Consider the following XML document, titled `history.xml`:

```
<?xml version="1.0"?>
<?xml-stylesheet type="text/xsl" href="history.xsl"?>

<subject>
   <info>History of India</info>
</subject>
```

Write history.xsl file mentioned above, which would:

(a) *Display a heading **XSL Demo**.*
(b) *Display the contents of the info tag on the next line.*

Solution We will not describe the whole style sheet this time, since how to write its contents should be obvious by now. The result is shown below.

```
<xsl:stylesheet version="1.0" xmlns:xsl="http://www.w3.org/1999/XSL/Transform">
   <xsl:template match="subject">
      <html>
         <head><title>Hello World</title></head>
         <body>
            <h1> XSL demo</h1>
            <h3> <xsl:value-of select="info"/> </h3>
         </body>
      </html>
   </xsl:template>
</xsl:stylesheet>
```

Figures 13.55 and 13.56 show the original (without style sheet) and the formatted (with style sheet) outputs in the browser.

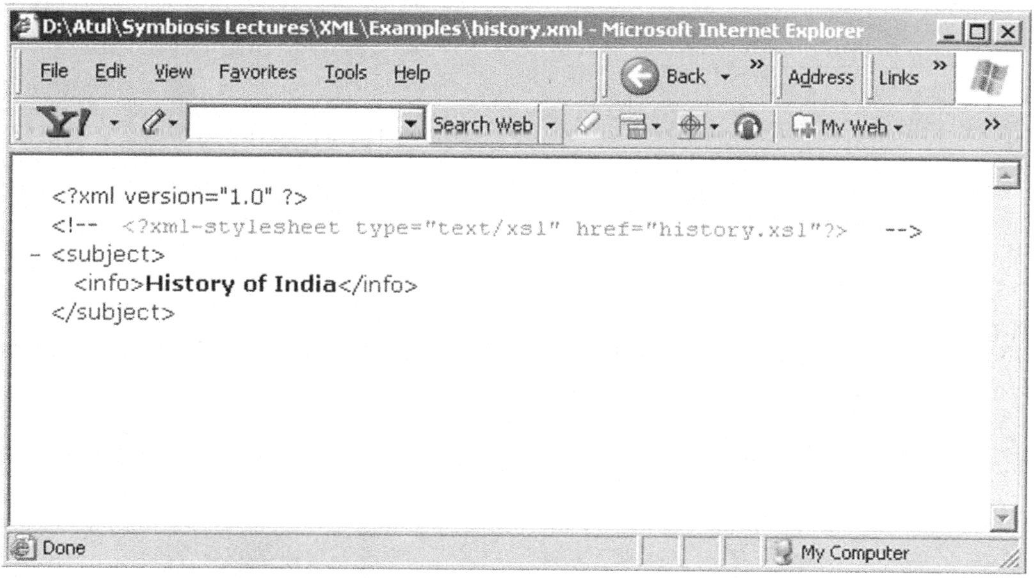

Fig. 13.55 *Original XML document without applying the style sheet*

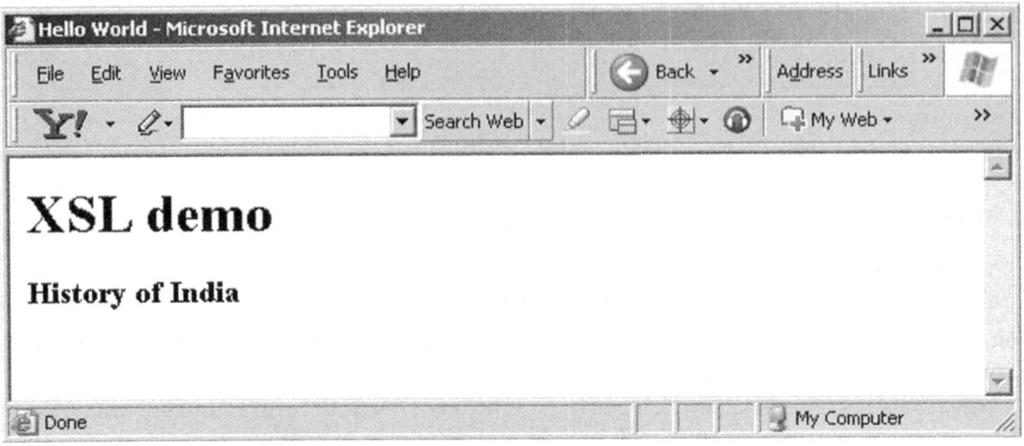

Fig. 13.56 *XML document after applying the style sheet*

Problem Consider the following XML document, titled portfolio.xml:

```
<?xml version=”1.0"?>
<?xml-stylesheet type=”text/xsl” href=”portfolio.xsl”?>
<portfolio>
    <stock exchange=”nyse”>
        <name>zacx corp</name>
        <symbol>ZCXM</symbol>
        <price>28.875</price>
    </stock>
    <stock exchange=”nasdaq”>
        <name>zaffymat inc</name>
        <symbol>ZFFX</symbol>
        <price>92.250</price>
    </stock>
    <stock exchange=”nasdaq”>
        <name>zysmergy inc</name>
        <symbol>ZYSZ</symbol>
        <price>20.313</price>
    </stock>
</portfolio>
```

Write a portfolio.xsl file mentioned above, which would display the stock symbols followed by the price.

Solution We will not describe the whole style sheet this time, since how to write its contents should be obvious by now. The result is shown below.

```
<?xml version=’1.0'?>
<xsl:stylesheet version=”1.0" xmlns:xsl=”http://www.w3.org/1999/XSL/Transform”>
    <xsl:template match=”stock”>
        Symbol: <xsl:value-of select=”symbol” />,
        Price: <xsl:value-of select=”price” />
        </br>
    </xsl:template>
</xsl:stylesheet>
```

Figures 13.57 and 13.58 show the original (without style sheet) and the formatted (with style sheet) outputs in the browser.

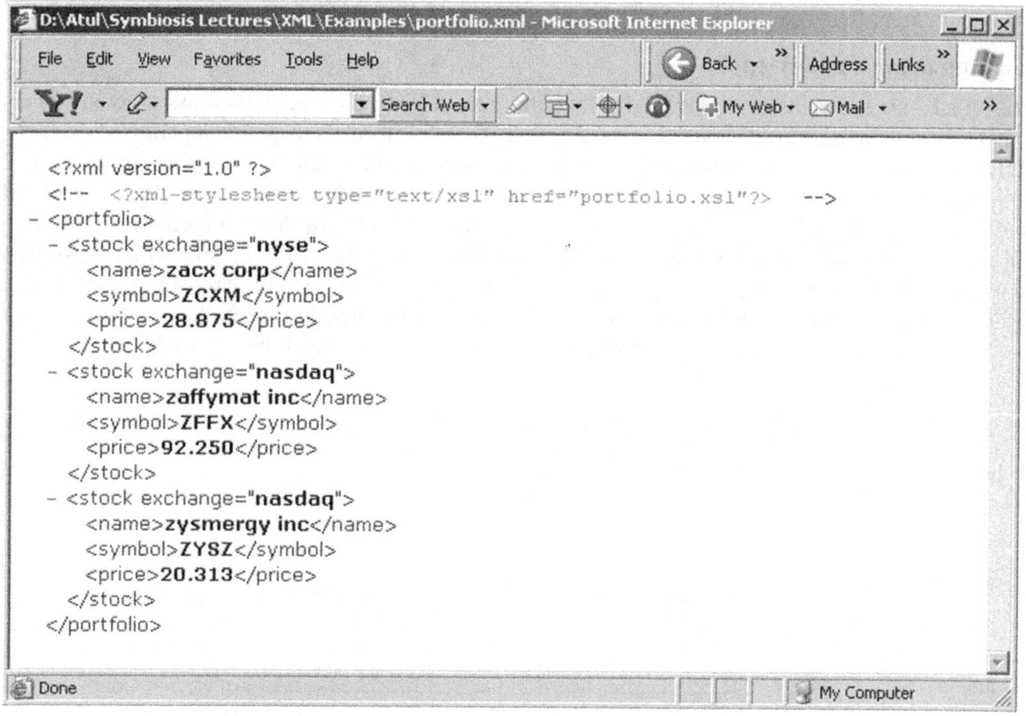

Fig. 13.57 *Original XML document without applying the style sheet*

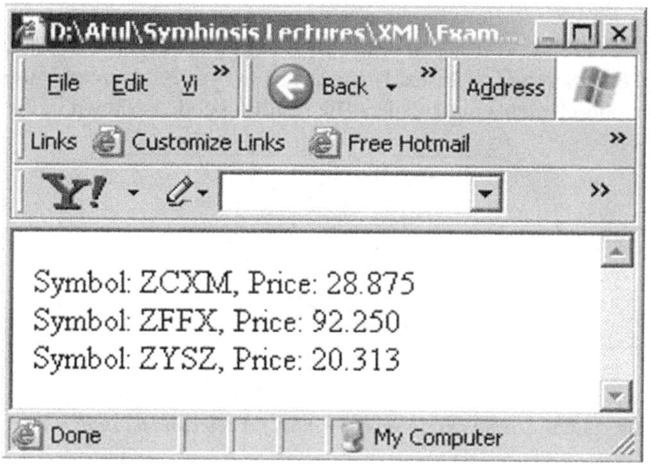

Fig. 13.58 *XML document after applying the style sheet*

13.12.2 Looping and Sorting

In this section, we shall look at two important XSLT constructs: iterating through a list of items by using the <xsl:for-each> syntax, and then sorting information by using the <xsl:sort> syntax.

Looping using <xsl:for-each>

The XSLT <xsl:for-each> syntax is used to loop through an XML document. It allows us to embed one template inside another. In other words, it can act as an alternative to an <xsl:apply-templates> syntax. This can be slightly confusing to understand. Therefore, we illustrate this with the help of a simple example.

Suppose that we want to work with an XML document containing book details. At the first level, we want to go through the BOOK element. This element can, in turn, have a number of CHAPTER subelements. We know that if we now want to iterate through all the CHAPTER subelements, we need to use an <xsl:apply-templates select = "CHAPTER"/> syntax. This causes the XSLT to find a match on every chapter element, and apply the style sheet as later defined in the <xsl:template match = "CHAPTER"> syntax. The corresponding sample code is shown in Fig. 13.59.

```
<xsl:stylesheet …>
  <xsl:template match = "BOOK">
   …
   <xsl:apply-templates select = "CHAPTER"/>
    …
  </xsl:template>

  <xsl:template match = "CHAPTER"> ◄──┘
   …
  </xsl:template>
</xsl:stylesheet>
```

Fig. 13.59 *Using <xsl:apply-templates> syntax for selecting all sub-elements*

It is worth repeating that this syntax causes the XSLT to loop over all the CHAPTER subelements of the BOOK element.

Now let us re-write the code by using an <xsl:for-each> construct. Here, we eliminate the nesting which was used in the earlier syntax. Instead, the <xsl:for-each> syntax causes the XSLT to loop over all the CHAPTER sub-elements one by one. The resulting code is shown in Fig. 13.60.

```
<xsl:stylesheet …>
  <xsl:template match = "BOOK">
   …
    <xsl:for-each select = "CHAPTER">
         …
    </xsl:for-each>
  </xsl:template>

</xsl:stylesheet>
```

Fig. 13.60 *Using <xsl:for-each> syntax for selecting all sub-elements*

Quite clearly, the <xsl:for-each> syntax is very close to the traditional programming languages. It achieves the same result as the earlier <xsl:apply-templates> syntax. So, an obvious question is, which of these syntaxes should be used? There is no clear answer. It all depends on an individual's style preferences and comfort levels.

Let us consider a complete example to illustrate the usage of the <xsl:for-each> syntax. Consider an XML document containing a list of customers, as shown in Fig. 13.61.

```
<?xml version="1.0"?>
<?xml-stylesheet type="text/xsl" href="foreach.xsl" ?>
<customers>
 <customer>
  <name>Mahesh Katare</name>
  <address>Eve's Plaza, Bangalore</address>
  <state>Karnataka</state>
  <phone>(80) 3247890</phone>
 </customer>
 <customer>
  <name>Naren Limaye</name>
  <address>Shanti Apartments, Thane</address>
  <state>Maharashtra</state>
  <phone>(22) 82791810</phone>
 </customer>
 <customer>
  <name>Uday Bhalerao</name>
  <address>Kothrud, Pune</address>
  <state>Maharashtra</state>
  <phone>(20) 25530834</phone>
 </customer>
 <customer>
  <name>Amol Kavthekar</name>
  <address>Station Road, Solapur</address>
  <state>Maharashtra</state>
  <phone>(217) 2729345</phone>
 </customer>
 <customer>
  <name>Meghraj Mane</name>
  <address>Connuaght Place, Delhi</address>
  <state>Delhi</state>
  <phone>(11) 57814091</phone>
 </customer>
 <customer>
  <name>Sameer Joshi</name>
  <address>Gullapetti, Hyderabad</address>
  <state>Andhra Pradesh</state>
  <phone>93717-90911</phone>
 </customer>
</customers>
```

Fig. 13.61 *XML document containing a list of customers (foreach.xml)*

Now, suppose that we want to display the names, addresses, and phone numbers of the customers in the form of a table. The simplest way to do this is to read the contents of our XML document, and display the required fields inside an HTML table. For this purpose, we can make use of the <xsl:for-each> syntax as shown in Fig. 13.62.

```
<?xml version="1.0"?>
<xsl:stylesheet version="1.0"
  xmlns:xsl="http://www.w3.org/1999/XSL/Transform">

 <xsl:template match="/">
  <HTML>
   <BODY>
   <TABLE border = "2">
    <xsl:for-each select="customers/customer">
     <TR>
      <TD><xsl:value-of select="name" /></TD>
      <TD><xsl:value-of select="address" /></TD>
      <TD><xsl:value-of select="phone" /></TD>
     </TR>
    </xsl:for-each>
   </TABLE>
  </BODY>
 </HTML>
</xsl:template>

</xsl:stylesheet>
```

Fig. 13.62 *XSLT document for tabulating customer data*

The logic of this XSLT can be explained in simple terms as shown in Fig. 13.63.

```
1. Read the XML document.
2. Create an HTML table structure for the output.
3. For each customer sub-element in the customers element:
   (a) Display the values of the name, address, and phone elements in a row of the
       HTML table.
4. Next.
```

Fig. 13.63 *Understanding the <xsl:for-each> syntax*

The resulting output is shown in Fig. 13.64.

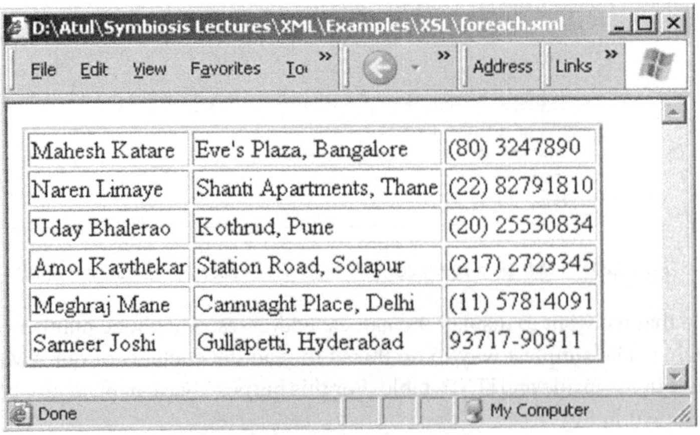

Fig. 13.64 *Resulting output*

Instead of this code, we could have, very well, used the standard code that does not use <xsl:for-each> syntax. This XSLT is shown in Fig. 13.65.

```
<?xml version="1.0"?>
<xsl:stylesheet version="1.0" xmlns:xsl="http://www.w3.org/1999/XSL/Transform">
 <xsl:template match="/">
  <HTML>
   <BODY>
    <TABLE border="2">
     <xsl:apply-templates/>
    </TABLE>
   </BODY>
  </HTML>
 </xsl:template>
 <xsl:template match="customers/customer">
  <TR>
   <TD>
    <xsl:value-of select="name"/>
   </TD>
   <TD>
    <xsl:value-of select="address"/>
   </TD>
   <TD>
    <xsl:value-of select="phone"/>
   </TD>
  </TR>
 </xsl:template>
</xsl:stylesheet>
```

Fig. 13.65 *XSLT document for tabulating customer data without using <xsl:for-each>*

It is needless to say that this XSLT would also produce the same output as produced by the <xsl:for-each> syntax. We will not show that output once again.

BASICS OF PARSING 13.13

13.13.1 What is Parsing?

The term **parsing** should not be new to the students and practitioners of information technology.

We know that there are compilers of programming language, which translate one programming language into an executable language (or something similar). For example, a *C* compiler translates a *C* program (called *object program*) into an executable language version (called *object program*). These compilers use the concept of parsing quite heavily. For example, we say that such compilers *parse an expression* when they convert a mathematical expression such as $a = b + c;$ from *C* language to the corresponding executable code. So, what do we exactly mean? We mean that a compiler reads, interprets, and translates *C* into another language. More importantly, it knows how to do this job of translation, based on certain rules. For example, with reference to our earlier expression, the compiler knows that it must have exactly one variable before the = sign, and an expression after it, etc. Thus, certain rules are set, and the compiler is programmed to verify and interpret those rules. We cannot write the same expression in *C* as $b + c = a$; because the compiler is not programmed to handle this. Thus, we can define parsing in the context of compilation process as follows:

Parsing is the process of reading and validating a program written in one format and converting it into the desired format.

Of course, this is a limited definition of parsing, when applied to compilers. Now, let us extend this concept to XML. We know that an XML document is organized as a hierarchical structure, similar to a tree. Furthermore, we know that we can have *well-formed* and *valid* XML documents. Thus, if we have something equivalent to a compiler for XML that can read, validate, and optionally convert XML, we have a parser for XML. Thus, we can define the concept of a parser for XML now.

Parsing of XML is the process of reading and validating an XML document and converting it into the desired format. The program that does this job is called a ***parser****.*

This concept is shown in Fig. 13.66.

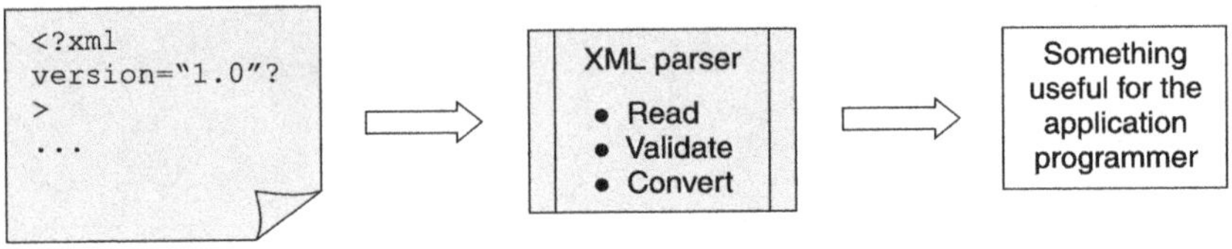

Fig. 13.66 *Concept of XML parsing*

Let us now understand what a parser would need to do to make something useful for the application programmer. Clearly, an XML file is something that exists on the disk. So, the parser has to first of all bring it from the disk into the main memory. More importantly, the parser has to make this *in memory* representation of an XML file available to the programmer in a form that the programmer is comfortable with.

Today's programming world is full of classes and objects. Today's popular programming languages such as Java, C++, and C# are object-oriented in nature. Naturally, the programmer would live to see an XML file in memory also as an object. This is exactly what a parser does. A parser reads a file from the disk, converts it into an in-memory object and hands it over to the programmer. The programmer's responsibility is then to take this object and manipulate it the way she wants. For example, the programmer may want to display the values of certain elements, add some attributes, count the total number of elements, and so on. This concept is shown in Fig. 13.67.

This should clarify the role of a parser. Often, application programmers are confused in terms of where parser starts and where it ends. We need to remember that the parser simply assists us in reading an XML file as an object.

Now an obvious question is, why do we need such a parser? Why can we ourselves not do the job of a parser? For example, if we disregard XML for a minute and think about an ordinary situation where we need to read, say, an *employee* file from the disk and produce a report out of it, do we use any parser? Of course, we do not. We simply instruct our application program to read the contents of a file. But wait a minute. How do we instruct our program to do so? We know how the file is structured and rely on the programming environment to provide us the contents of the file. For example, in C# or Java, we can instruct our application program to read the next *n* bytes from the disk, which we can treat as a record (or the fields of a record). In a more programmer-friendly language such as COBOL, we need not even worry about asking the application program to read a certain number of bytes from the disk, etc. We can simply ask it to read *the next record*, and the program knows what we mean.

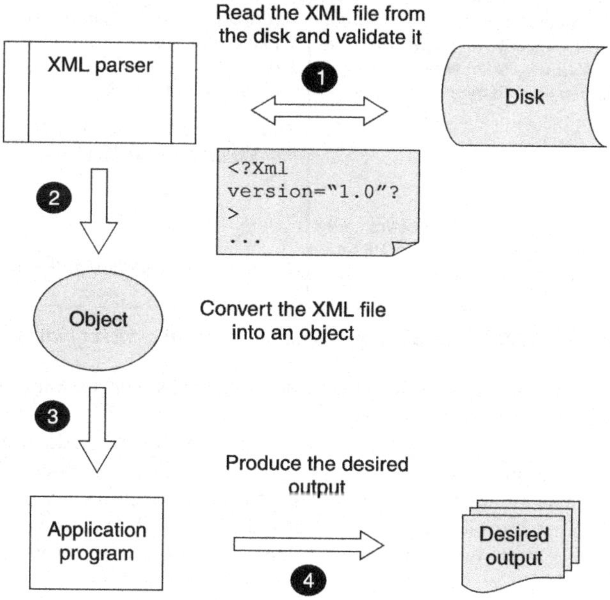

Fig. 13.67 *The parsing process*

Let us come back to XML. Which of the approaches should we use now? Should we ask our application program to *read the next n bytes* every time, or say something like *read the next element*? If we go via the *n bytes* approach, we need to know how many bytes to read every time. Also, remember that apart from just *reading next n bytes,* we also need to know where an element begins, where it ends, whether all its attributes are declared properly, whether the corresponding end element tag for this element is properly defined, whether all subelements (if any) are correctly defined, and so on! Moreover, we also need to validate these *next n bytes* against an appropriate section of a DTD or schema file, if one is defined. Clearly, we are getting into the job of writing something similar to a compiler ourselves! How nice it would be, instead, if we can just say in the COBOL style of programming, *read the next record.* Now whether that means reading the next 10 bytes or 10,000 bytes, ensuring *logic* and *validity*, etc., need not be handled by us! Remember that we need to deal with hundreds of XML file. In each of our application programs, we do not want to write our own logic of doing all these things ourselves. It would leave us with humungous amount of work even before we can convert an XML file into an object. Not only that, it would be quite cumbersome and error-prone.

Therefore, we rely on an XML parser to take care of all these things on our behalf, and give us an XML file as an object, provided all the validations are also successful.

If we do not have XML parsers, we would need logic to read, validate, and transform every XML file ourselves, which is a very difficult task.

13.13.2 Parsing Approaches

Suppose that someone younger in your family has returned from playing a cricket match. He is very excited about it, and wants to describe what happened in the match. He can describe it in two ways, as shown in Fig. 13.68.

"We won the toss and were elected to bat. Our opening pair was Sachin and Viru. They gave us an opening partnership of 100 when Viru was dismissed. It was the 16th over. Sachin was batting beautifully as usual. ... ... Thus, while chasing 301 runs to win in 50 overs, they were dismissed for 275 and we won the match by 25 runs. Sachin was declared the man of the match."	*"We won today! We had batted first and made 300. While chasing this target, they were dismissed for 275, thus giving us a victory by 25 runs. Sachin was declared the man of the match. The way it started was that Sachin and Viru opened the innings and added 100 for the first wicket. ... ... This is what happened in the match today, and thus we won."*

Fig. 13.68 *Two ways of describing events of a cricket match*

Now we will leave this example for a minute and come back to it in some time after establishing its relevance to the current technical discussion.

There is tremendous confusion about the various ways in which XML documents can be processed inside a Java program. The problem is that several technologies have emerged, and there has been insufficient clarity in terms of which technology is useful for what purposes. Several terms have been in use for many years, most prominently SAX, DOM, JAXP, JDOM, Xerces, dom4j, and TrAX. Let us first try to make sense of them before we actually embark on the study of working with XML inside Java programs.

We have noted earlier that the job of an XML parser is to read an XML document from the disk, and present it to a Java program in the form of an object. With this central theme in mind, we need to know that over several years, many ways were developed to achieve this objective. That is what has caused the confusion, as mentioned earlier. Let us demystify this situation now.

When an XML document is to be presented to a Java program as an object, there are two main possibilities.

1. Present the document in bits and pieces, as and when we encounter certain sections or portions of the document.
2. Present the entire document tree at one go. This means that the Java program has to then think of this document tree as one object, and manipulate it the way it wants.

We have discussed this concept in the context of the description of a cricket match earlier. We can either describe the match as it happened, event by event; or first describe the overall highlights and then get into specific details. For example, consider an XML document as shown in Fig. 13.69.

```
<?xml version="1.0"?>

<employees>
  <employee>
    <name>Umesh</name>
    <department>EDIReader</department>
    <teamsize>11</teamsize>
  </employee>
  <employee>
    <name>Pallavi</name>
    <department>XSLT</department>
    <teamsize>12</teamsize>
  </employee>
</employees>
```

Fig. 13.69 *Sample XML document*

Now, we can look at this XML structure in two ways.

1. Go through the XML structure item by item (e.g., to start with, the line `<?xml version="1.0"?>`, followed by the element `<employees>`, and so on).
2. Read the entire XML document in the memory as an object, and parse its contents as per the needs.

Technically, the first approach is called **Simple API for XML (SAX)**, whereas the latter is known as **Document Object Model (DOM)**.

We now take a look at the two approaches diagrammatically. More specifically, they tell us how the same XML document is processed differently by these two different approaches. Refer to Fig. 13.70.

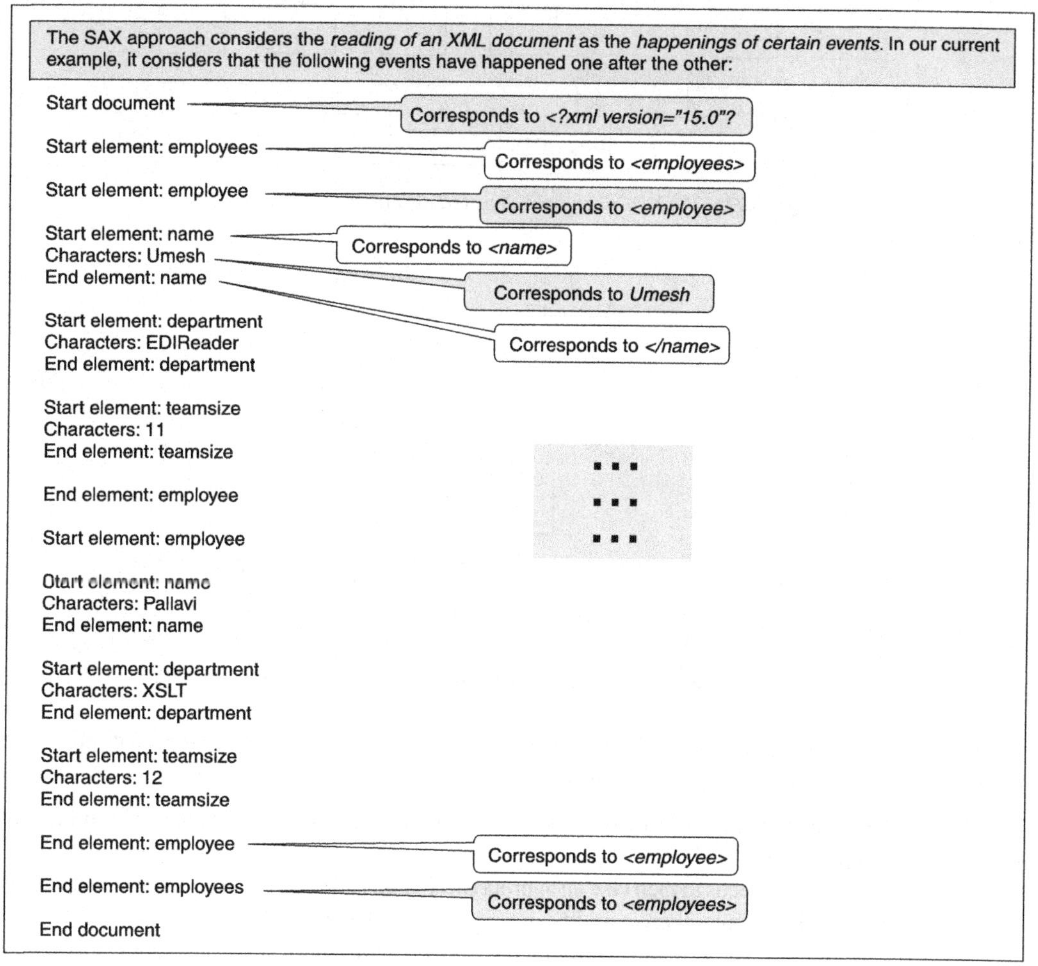

Fig. 13.70 *SAX approach for our XML example*

It is also important to know the sequence of elements as seen by XSLT. If we have an XML document visualized as a tree-like structure as shown in Fig. 13.71, then the sequence of elements considered for parsing by XSLT would be as shown in Fig. 13.72.

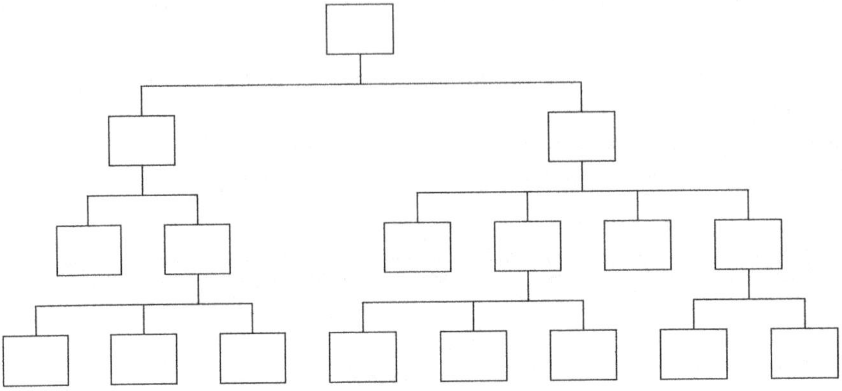

Fig. 13.71 *An XML document depicted as a tree-like structure*

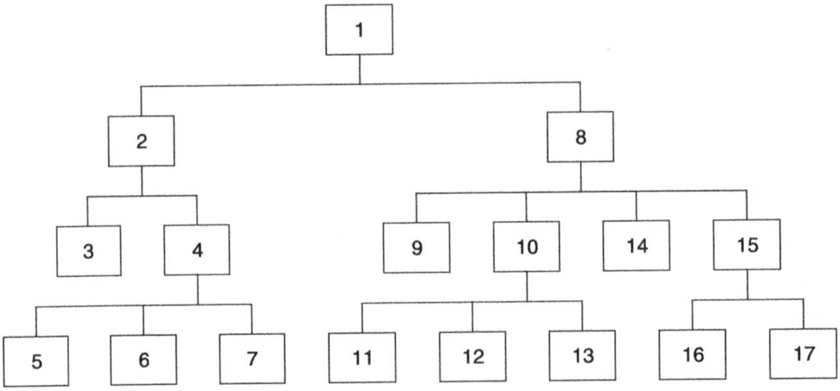

Fig. 13.72 *SAX view of looking at a tree-like structure*

In general, we can equate the SAX approach to our example of the step-by-step description of a cricket match. The SAX approach works on an *event model*. This works as follows:

1. The SAX parser keeps track of various events, and whenever an event is detected, it informs our Java program.
2. Our Java program needs to then take an appropriate action, based on the requirements of handling that event. For example, there could be an event *Start element* as shown in the diagram.
3. Our Java program needs to constantly monitor such events, and take an appropriate action.
4. Control comes back to SAX parser, and Steps (1) and (2) repeat.

This is shown in Fig. 13.73.

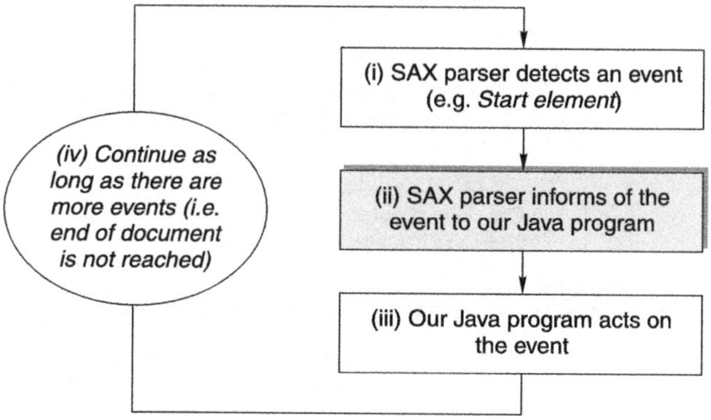

Fig. 13.73 *SAX approach explained further*

In general, we can equate the DOM approach to our example of the overall description of a cricket match. This works as follows:

1. The DOM approach parses through the whole XML document at one go. It creates an in-memory tree-like structure of our XML document, the way it is depicted in Fig. 13.74.

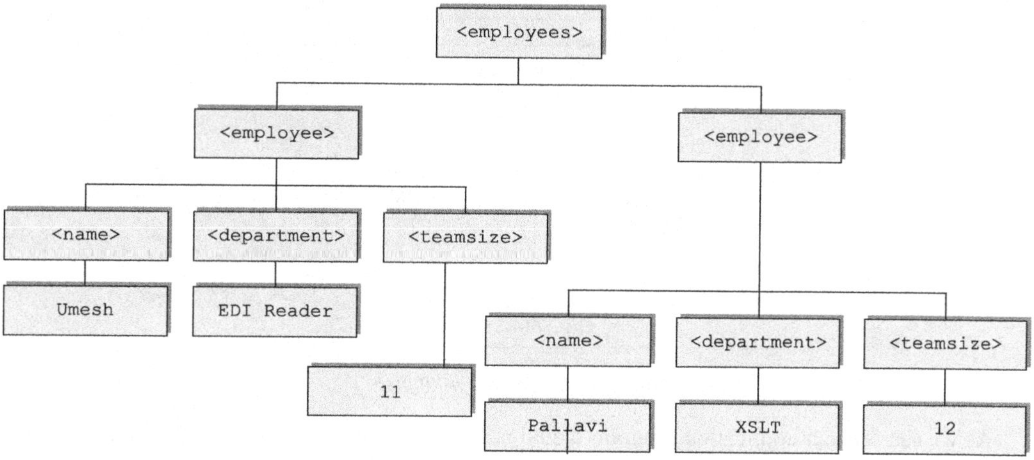

Fig. 13.74 *DOM approach for our XML example*

2. This tree-like structure is handed over to our Java program at one go, once it is ready. No events get fired unlike what happens in SAX.
3. The Java program then takes over the control and deals with the tree the way it wants, without actively interfacing with the parser on an event-by-event basis. Thus, there is no concept of something such as *Start element*, *Characters*, *End element*, etc. This is shown in Fig. 13.75.

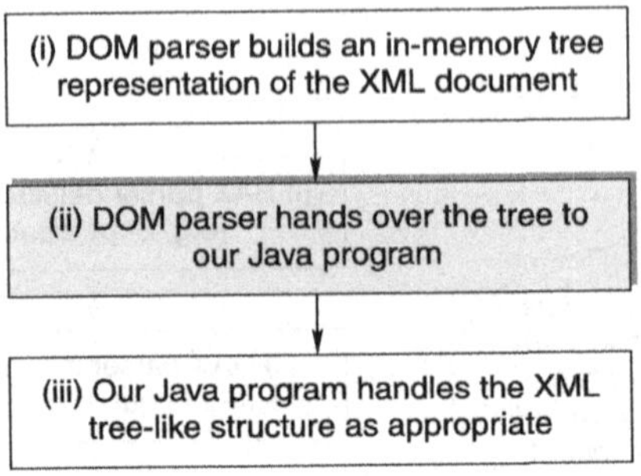

Fig. 13.75 DOM approach explained further

JAXP 13.14

The **Java API for XML Processing (JAXP)** is a Sun standard API which allows us to validate, parse, and transform XML with the help of several other APIs. It is very important to clarify that JAXP itself is not a parser API. Instead, we should consider JAXP as an abstraction layer over the actual parser APIs. That is, JAXP is nor at all a replacement for SAX or DOM. Instead, it is a layer above them. This concept is shown in Fig. 13.76.

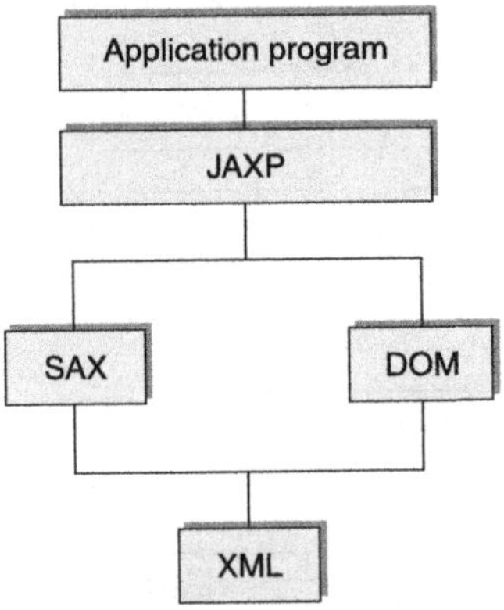

Fig. 13.76 Where JAXP fits

As we can see, our application program would need to interface with JAXP. JAXP, in turn, would interface with SAX or DOM, as appropriate.

JAXP is not a new means for parsing XML. It does not also add to SAX or DOM. Instead, JAXP allows us to work with SAX and DOM more easily and consistently. We must remember that without SAX, DOM, or another parser API (such as JDOM or dom4j), we cannot parse an XML document. We need to remember this.

SAX, DOM, JDOM and dom4j parse XML. JAXP provides a way to invoke and use such a parser, but does not parse an XML document itself.

At this juncture, we need to clarify that even JDOM and dom4j sit on top of other parser APIs. Although both APIs provide us a different approach for parsing XML as compared to SAX and DOM, they use SAX internally. In any case JDOM and dom4j are not popular as standards, and hence we would not discuss them. Instead, we would concentrate on JAXP, which is a standard.

13.14.1 Sun's JAXP

A lot of confusion about JAXP arises because of the way Sun's version of it has been interpreted. When the idea of JAXP was born, the concept was very clear. JAXP was going to be an abstraction layer API that would interface with an actual parser API, as illustrated earlier. However, this was not going to be sufficient for developers, since they needed an actual parser API as well, so as to try out and work with JAXP. Otherwise, they would only have the abstract API of JAXP, which would not do any parsing itself. How would a developer then try it out?

To deal with this issue, when Sun released JAXP initially, it included the JAXP API (i.e., the abstract layer) and a parser API (called as *Crimson*) as well. Now, JAXP comes with Apache Xerces parser, instead. Thus, the actual JAXP implementation in real life slightly modified our earlier diagram, as shown in Fig. 13.77.

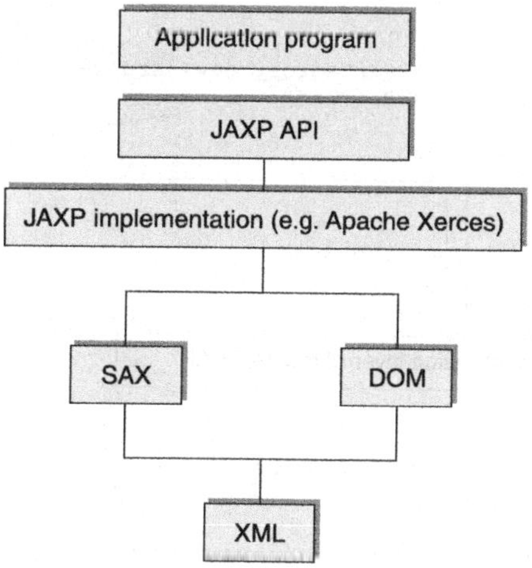

Fig. 13.77 *Understanding where JAXP fits—modified*

Let us now understand how this works as the coding level.

Whenever we write an application program to deal with XML documents, we need to work with JAXP. It should be clear by now. How should our application program work with JAXP?

1. Clearly, looking at the modified diagram, our application program would interface with the abstraction layer of JAXP API.
2. This abstraction layer of the JAXP API, in turn, interfaces with the actual implementation of JAXP (such as Apache Xerces). This allows our application program to be completely independent of the JAXP implementation. Tomorrow, if we replace the JAXP implementation with some other parser, our application program would remain unchanged.
3. The JAXP implementation (e.g., Apache Xerces) would then perform parsing of the XML document by using SAX or DOM, as appropriate to our given situation. Of course, whether to use SAX or DOM must be decided and declared in our application program.

To facilitate this, Sun's JAXP API first expects us to declare (a) which parser implementation we want to use (e.g., Apache Xerces), and (b) whether we want to use SAX or DOM as the parsing approach.

We have discussed that the aim is to keep our application program independent of the actual parser implementation or instance. In other words, we should be expected to code our application program in exactly the same manner, regardless of which parser implementation is used. Conceptually, this is facilitated by talking to the abstraction layer of the JAXP API. This is achieved by using the **design pattern** of **abstract factory**. The subject of *design patterns* is separate in itself, and is not in the scope of the current discussion. Design patterns allow us to simplify our application design by conforming to certain norms. There are many *design patterns*, of which one is *abstract factory*. However, we can illustrate conceptually how the *abstract factory* works, as shown in Fig. 13.78 in the context of JAXP.

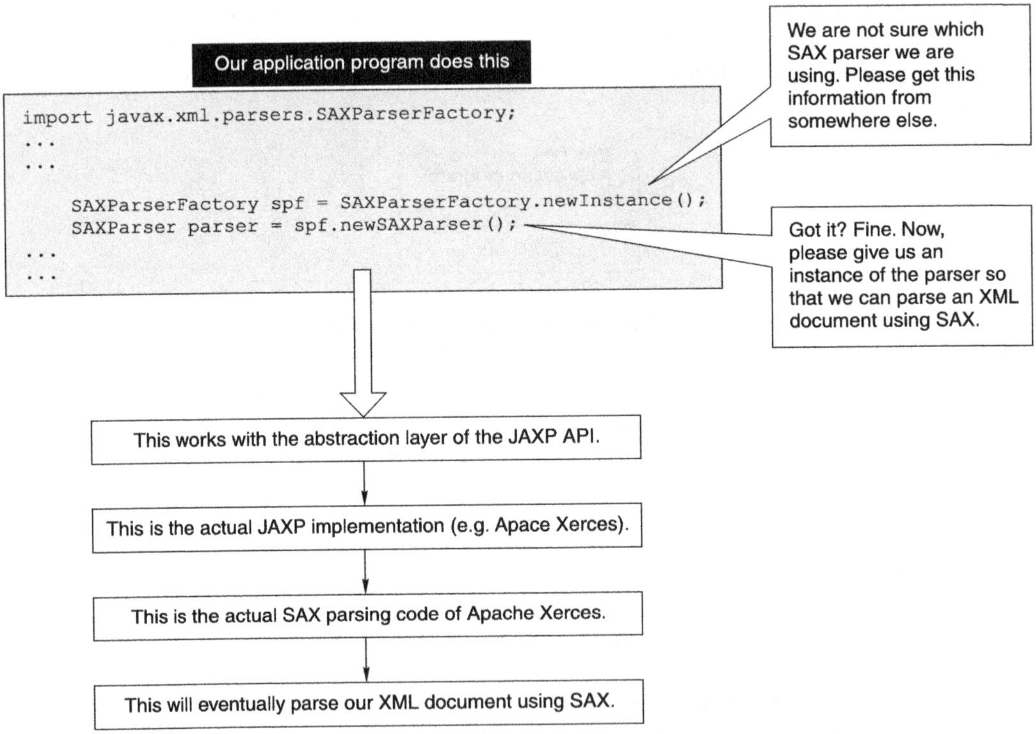

Fig. 13.78 *How to work with JAXP at the code level—Basic concepts*

Let us understand this in more detail.

```
import javax.xml.parsers.SAXParserFactory;
```

This *import* statement makes the SAX parser factory package defined in JAXP available to our application program. As we had mentioned earlier, an abstract factory design pattern allows us to create an instance of a class without worrying about the implementation details. In other words, we do not know at this stage whether we want to eventually create an instance of the Apache Xerces parser, or any other parser. This hiding of unwanted details from our code, so that it will work with any parser implementation, is what abstract factory gives us.

```
SAXParserFactory spf = SAXParserFactory.newInstance ();
```

This line tells us that we want to create *some* instance of the SAX parser factory, and assign it to an object named *spf*. This statement tells JAXP that we are interested in using SAX later in the program. But at this stage, we simply want to create an instance of *some* SAX parser. But then *which* SAX parser? Is it the Apache Xerces version of SAX, or something else? This is hidden from the application programmer in a beautiful manner. Whether to use Apache Xerces or any other implementation of the parser is defined in various ways, but away from the code (to make it implementation-independent). For example, this property can be defined in a Java system property named `javax.xml.parsers.SAXParserFactory`, etc. There, we can set the value of this property to Apache Xerces, or the parser name that we are using. This is how the abstract layer of the JAXP API knows which implementation of JAXP should be used.

```
SAXParser parser = spf.newSAXParser ();
```

Now that we have specified that we want to use a certain implementation of SAX as outlined above, we want to create an instance of that implementation. This instance can be used to work with the XML document we want to parse, as we shall study later. Think about this instance as similar to how a file pointer or file handle works with a file, or how a record set works with a relational database table.

Of course, this example showed the basic concepts of starting to work with SAX in JAXP. These remain more or less the same for DOM, as we shall study later. What will change are the package names, class names, etc. Regardless of that, we can summarize the conceptual approach of working with JAXP as shown in Fig. 13.79.

1. Create an instance of the appropriate JAXP factory (SAX or DOM).
2. The factory will refer to some properties file to know which implementation (e.g., Apache Xerces) of the JAXP parser to invoke.
3. Get an instance of the implemented parser (SAX or DOM as implemented by Apache Xerces or another implementation, as defined in the properties file above).

Fig. 13.79 *Initial steps in using JAXP*

Now it should be quite clear how JAXP makes our application program independent of the parser implementation. In other words, our application program talks to the abstraction layer of JAXP, and in our properties file, we specify which JAXP implementation this abstract layer should be linked with.

13.14.2 Actual Parsing

Once the above steps are performed, the program is ready to parse the XML documents. In other words, the program can either respond to events as and when they occur (i.e., the SAX approach), or ask the parser to build the document in the memory as a tree-like structure, and then call various methods to query the tree-like structure (i.e., the DOM approach).

Our aim here is not to learn the details of how the parsing code works. However, for the sake of completeness, Fig. 13.80 shows a SAX example, and Fig. 13.81 shows a DOM example.

```
import java.io.IOException;
import java.lang.*;
```

(Contd.)

Fig. 13.80 *Contd...*

```
import javax.xml.parsers.SAXParser;
import javax.xml.parsers.SAXParserFactory;
import org.xml.sax.Attributes;
import org.xml.sax.Locator;
import org.xml.sax.SAXException;
import org.xml.sax.SAXNotRecognizedException;
import org.xml.sax.SAXNotSupportedException;
import org.xml.sax.SAXParseException;
import org.xml.sax.XMLReader;
import org.xml.sax.ext.LexicalHandler;
import org.xml.sax.helpers.DefaultHandler;
import org.xml.sax.helpers.ParserAdapter;
import org.xml.sax.helpers.XMLReaderFactory;

public class BookCount extends DefaultHandler{

 private int count = 0;

 public void startDocument() throws SAXException  {
  System.out.println("Start document ...");
 }

 public void startElement(String uri, String local, String raw,
   Attributes attrs) throws SAXException {

  int year = 0;
  String attrValue;

  System.out.println ("Current element = " + raw);

  if (raw.equals ("book")) {
   count++;
  }
 }

 public void endDocument() throws SAXException  {
  System.out.println("The total number of books = " + count);
 }

 public static void main (String[] args) throws Exception {
  BookCount handler = new BookCount ();

  try {
   SAXParserFactory spf = SAXParserFactory.newInstance ();
   SAXParser parser = spf.newSAXParser ();
   parser.parse ("book.xml", handler);
  }
  catch (SAXException e) {
   System.err.println(e.getMessage());
  }
 }
}
```

Fig. 13.80 *SAX example using JAXP*

```
import org.w3c.dom.*;
import javax.xml.parsers.*;
import org.xml.sax.*;

public class DOMExample2 {

 public static void main (String[] args) {

  NodeList elements;
  String elementName = "cd";

  try {
   DocumentBuilderFactory factory = DocumentBuilderFactory.newInstance ();
   DocumentBuilder builder = factory.newDocumentBuilder ();
   Document document = builder.parse ("cdcatalog.xml");
   Element root = document.getDocumentElement ();

   System.out.println ("In main ... XML file openend successfully ...");

   elements = document.getElementsByTagName(elementName);

   // is there anything to do?
   if (elements == null) {
    return;
   }

   // print all elements
   int elementCount = elements.getLength();
   System.out.println ("Count = " + elementCount);

   for (int i = 0; i < elementCount; i++) {
    Element element = (Element) elements.item(i);
    System.out.println ("Element Name    = " + element.getNodeName());
    System.out.println ("Element Type    = " + element.getNodeType());
    System.out.println ("Element Value   = " + element.getNodeValue());
    System.out.println ("Has attributes = " + element.hasAttributes());
   }
  }
  catch (ParserConfigurationException e1) {
   System.out.println ("Exception: " + e1);
  }
  catch (SAXException e2) {
   System.out.println ("Exception: " + e2);
  }
  catch (DOMException e2) {
   System.out.println ("Exception: " + e2);
  }
  catch (java.io.IOException e3) {
   System.out.println ("Exception: " + e3);
  }
 }
}
```

Fig. 13.81 *DOM example using JAXP*

Key Terms

Abstract factory • American Standard Code for Information Interchange (ASCII) • Attribute • Attribute • Business-to-Business (B2B) • Business-to-Consumer (B2C) • Cascading Style Sheets (CSS) • Design pattern • Document Object Model (DOM) • Document Type Definition (DTD) • Electronic Data Interchange (EDI) • Electronic Data Interchange (EDI) • Element • Extensible Markup Language (XML) • External DTD • Hyper Text Markup Language (HTML) • Internal DTD • Java API for XML Processing (JAXP) • Result tree • Root element • Schema • Simple API for XML (SAX) • Source tree • Tag • Value Added Networks (VAN) • XML parsing • XML Stylesheet Language (XSL) • XML Stylesheet Language Transformations (XSLT) • XPath

SUMMARY

- The Extensible Markup Language (XML) can be used to exchange data across the Web.
- XML can be used to create data structures that can be shared between incompatible systems.
- XML is a common meta-language that enables data to be transformed from one format to another.
- An extremely useful feature of XML is the idea that documents describe themselves—a concept called metadata.
- The point to note is that if the tags and attributes are well-designed and descriptive, both humans and machines can read and use the information contained in the XML document.
- An XML parser is an interface that allows a developer to manipulate XML documents.
- In an XML document, an element is a group of tags as well as data. Elements can contain character data, child elements, or a mixture of both. In addition, they can have attributes.
- The process of describing what a valid XML document would consist of, and look like, is called creating a Document Type Definition (DTD).
- A DTD can be internal (i.e., combined with the XML content) or external (i.e., separate from the XML content).
- An XML schema is similar in concept to a DTD.
- Like a DTD, a schema is used to describe the data elements, attributes and their relationships of an XML document.
- Schema, unlike a DTD, is an XML document itself (but with a separate extension of *.xsd*).
- Schema has many powerful features as compared to DTD. For instance, schema supports a number of data types, flexible rules, very specific validations, and clean syntax.
- The Simple API for XML (SAX) parser approach considers an XML document to be composed of many elements and deals with it one element at a time. Therefore, this is an incremental, step-wise sequential process.
- Unlike SAX, the Document Object Model (DOM) approach treats an XML document as a tree-like hierarchical structure. It then parses this tree-like structure at once, in entirety. Here, unlike the SAX approach, the data from the XML document can be accessed randomly in any order.
- Sun Microsystems has provided the Java API for XML Processing (JAXP), which allows a Java programmer to work with XML documents.
- JAXP allows a programmer to read/modify/create an XML document using either SAX or DOM. A new approach called StAX can also be used.
- The Extensible Stylesheet Language Transformations (XSLT) specifies how to transform an XML document into another format (e.g., HTML, text).
- XSLT solves the problem of how to format an XML document at the time of display. XSL deals with two main aspects, (a) how to transform XML documents into (HTML) format, and (b) how to conditionally format XML documents.

MULTIPLE-CHOICE QUESTIONS

1. XML is a ________ standard.
   (a) data representation (b) user interface
   (c) database (d) display
2. An element can be defined in a DTD by using the ________ keyword.
   (a) TAG (b) NEW (c) DATA (d) ELEMENT
3. An XML document can have a DTD declaration by using the ________ keyword.
   (a) DOCTYPE (b) DTD (c) DOCUMENT (d) DESIGN
4. The data type used most extensively in DTDs is ________.
   (a) `#INTEGER` (b) `#PCDATA` (c) `#STRING` (d) `#CHAR`
5. Choices in DTD can be specified by using the ________ symbol.
   (a) | (b) OR (c) || (d) ALTERNATIVE
6. In XSLT, the ________ tag should be used to retrieve and display the value of an element in the output.
   (a) `<xsl:display>` (b) `<xsl:output>`
   (c) `<xsl:value-of select>` (d) `<xsl:select>`
7. An element in schema that has a sub-element or an attribute automatically becomes a ______ element.
   (a) simple (b) composite (c) multiple (d) complex
8. In XSLT, the ________ tag should be used to retrieve and display the value of an element in the output.
   (a) `<xsl:display>` (b) `<xsl:output>`
   (c) `<xsl:value-of select>` (d) `<xsl:select>`
9. In the ________ approach, elements in an XML document are accessed in a sequential manner.
   (a) SAX (b) DOM (c) JAXP (d) complex
10. The Java programming language supports XML by way of the ________ technology.
    (a) JAXR (b) JAXM (c) JAXP (d) JAR

DETAILED QUESTIONS

1. Explain the need for XML in detail.
2. What is EDI? How does it work?
3. What are the strengths of XML technology?
4. What are DTDs? How do they work?
5. Explain the differences between external and internal DTDs.
6. What are XML schemas? How are they better than DTDs?
7. Explain the XSLT technology with an example.
8. Discuss the idea of JAXP.
9. Contrast between SAX and DOM.
10. Elaborate on the practical situations where we would use either SAX or DOM.

EXERCISES

1. Study the real-life examples where XML is used. For example, study how the SWIFT payment messaging standard has moved to XML-based messaging.
2. Investigate the support for XML in .NET.
3. Study the concept of middleware and see how XML is used in all messaging applications based on middleware technologies.
4. What are the different languages based on XML (e.g., BPEL)? Study at least one of them.
5. Which are the situations where XML should not be used in the messaging applications? Why?

CLOUD COMPUTING 14

INTRODUCTION

Imagine your PC and all of your mobile devices being in sync—all the time. Through which you are able to access all of your personal data at any given moment. You can organize and mine your data from any online source. Imagine being able to share that data—photos, movies, contacts, e-mail, documents, etc.—with your friends, family, and co-workers in an instant. This is Personal Cloud Computing promises to deliver you. Whether you realize it or not, you're already using cloud-based services. Pretty much everyone with a computer has been. Gmail, Hotmail, Yahoo! Mail, Google Docs are prime examples; we just don't think of those services in those terms. When you want to access your email you open your Web browser, go to the email client, and log in. The most important part of the equation is having Internet access. Your email is not housed on your physical computer; you access it through an Internet connection, and you can access it anywhere. If you are on a trip, at work, or down the street getting coffee, you can check your email as long as you have access to the Internet. Your email is different than software installed on your computer, such as a word processing program. When you create a document using word processing software, that document stays on the device you used to make it unless you physically move it. An email client is similar to how cloud computing works. Except instead of accessing just your email, you can choose what information you have access to within the cloud.

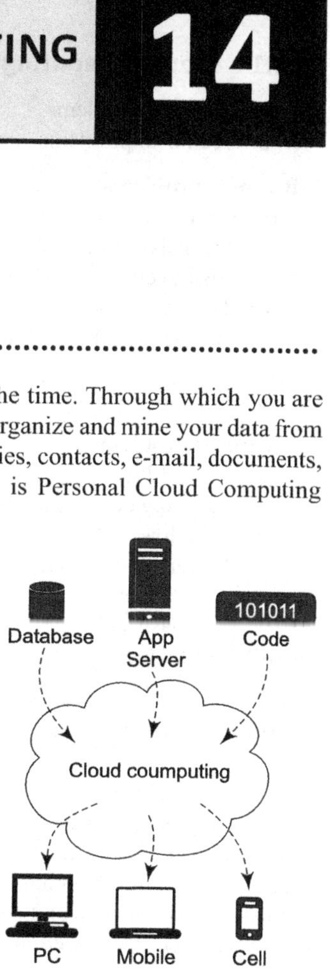

Fig.14.1 *Cloud computing*

WHAT IS CLOUD COMPUTING? 14.1

As per the National Institute of Standard and Technology (NIST), "Cloud computing is a model for enabling convenient, on-demand network access to a shared pool of configurable computing resources (e.g., networks, servers, storage, applications, and services) that can be rapidly provisioned and released with minimal management effort or service provider interaction."

Cloud computing is a general term for anything that involves delivering hosted services over the Internet. It is a subscription-based service where you can obtain networked storage space and computer resources. It can be an application or infrastructure on Internet. It gives illusion of infinite computing resources available on demand for end user which he can use to solve any problem for a short-term period.

14.1.1 Cloud Computing Tries to Address Two Problems

1. Business problems
2. Technical problems

1. Business problems

(a) Cost:
Inconsistent peak loads
Visible cost

(b) Time to market
During transition of platform/ vendor

(c) Risk

(d) Peer pressure

2. Technical problems

(a) Availability
Ensuring costs time, money and effort

(b) Peak loads
Understanding and defining peak load based on usage profile

(c) Lead times
Purchase and readiness of infrastructure

(d) Deployment

HISTORY OF CLOUD COMPUTING 14.2

The concept of cloud computing is related to Internet. The concept of Internet was born in the 1960s from the ideas of pioneers like J.C.R. Licklider (instrumental in the development of ARPANET) envisioning computation in the form of a global network and John McCarthy (who coined the term "artificial intelligence") framing computation as a public utility. Some of the first uses included the processing of financial transactions and census data. Based on a concept first published in 1967, ARPANET was developed under the direction of the U.S. Advanced Research Projects Agency (ARPA). In 1969, the idea became a modest reality with the interconnection of four university computers. The initial purpose was to communicate with and share computer resources among mainly scientific users at the connected institutions. ARPANET took advantage of the new idea of sending information in small units called packets that could be routed on different paths and reconstructed at their destination. The ARPANET in particular led to the development of protocols for inter-networking, where multiple separate networks could be joined together into a network of networks. In the 1980s, ARPANET was handed over to a separate new military network, the Defense Data Network, and NSFNet, a network of scientific and academic computers funded by the National Science Foundation and in 1986 when NSFNET provided access to supercomputer sites in the United States from research and education organizations. In the late 1980 and 1990 many Commercial Internet Service Providers (ISP) emerged to provide services. Then in 1990 ARPANET was decommissioned. The Internet was commercialized in 1995 when NSFNET was decommissioned, removing the last restrictions on the use of the Internet to carry commercial traffic.

The term "**cloud computing**" was most probably derived from the diagrams of clouds used to represent the Internet in textbooks. The concept was derived from telecommunications companies who made a radical shift from point-to-point data circuits to Virtual Private Network (VPN) services in the 1990s. By optimizing resource utilization through load balancing, they could get their work done more efficiently and inexpensively. In these earliest stages, the term "cloud" was used to represent the computing space between the provider and the end user. In 1997, Professor Ramnath Chellapa of Emory University and the University of South California defined cloud computing as the new "computing paradigm where the boundaries of computing will be determined by economic rationale rather than technical limits alone." What we now commonly refer to as cloud computing is the result of an evolution of the widespread adoption of virtualization, service-oriented architecture, autonomic, and utility computing.

During the second half of the 1990s, companies began to gain a better understanding of cloud computing and its usefulness in providing superior solutions and services to customers while drastically improving internal efficiencies. In 1999, Salesforce.com became one of the first major movers in the cloud arena, pioneering the concept of delivering enterprise-level applications to end users via the Internet. The application could be accessed by any customer with Internet access and companies were able to purchase the service on a cost-effective on-demand basis. The next development was Amazon Web Services in 2002, which provided a suite of cloud-based services including storage, computation and even human intelligence through the Amazon Mechanical Turk. Amazon was the first major organization to modernize its data centres, which were utilizing only about 10% of their capacity at any given time. Amazon realized that the new cloud computing infrastructure model could allow them to use their existing capacity with much greater efficiency. Meanwhile, Google had become a key player in the Internet commerce marketplace.

14.2.1 Important Milestones in Cloud Computing Platform

1. The introduction of Google Docs in 2006 really brought cloud computing to the forefront of public consciousness.
2. In 2006 Amazon also introduces Elastic Compute cloud (EC2) as a commercial Web service that allowed small companies and individuals to rent computers on which to run their own computer applications.
3. Technical collaboration in 2007 between Google, IBM and a number of universities across the United States.
4. In 2008, introduction of Eucalyptus, the first open source AWS API compatible platform for deploying private clouds, followed by OpenNebula, the first open source software for deploying private and hybrid clouds.
5. 2009 saw Microsoft's entry into cloud computing with the launch of Windows Azure in November.

GRID COMPUTING AND CLOUD COMPUTING 14.3

Grid computing is often confused with cloud computing. Grid computing is a form of distributed computing that implements a virtual supercomputer made up of a cluster of networked or Internetworked computers acting in unison to perform very large tasks. Many cloud computing deployments today are powered by grid computing implementations and are billed like utilities, but cloud computing can and should be seen as an evolved next step away from the grid utility model. There is an ever-growing list of providers that have successfully used cloud architectures with little or no centralized infrastructure or billing systems, such as the peer-to-peer network BitTorrent.

TYPES OF APPLICATION OR SOFTWARE HOSTING 14.4

1. On – Premises In this case we have our own machine, connectivity, software ,etc. We are the who have complete control and responsibility of it. But we need to investment heavily in infrastructure as we need to look after every single detail.

2. Hosted In this case, we have rented machines, connectivity and softwares. As we have not the who owns it, we have lesser control and fewer responsibility as compare to previous one. Our expenditure is very limited in this case. We need to pay for fix capacity even when we are not using it.

3. Cloud Cloud is shared and multitenant environment. Here we have pools of computing resources irrespective of infrastructure. We can use these resources as per requirement of our system. This environment provides elasticity on expenditure as we need to pay only when we use it.

CLOUD COMPUTING DEPLOYMENT MODELS 14.5

1. Private cloud A private cloud is a proprietary network or a data center that supplies hosted services to a limited number of people. It operates for that particular organization only. It could be either owned by an organization or it can be used as a third party solution.

2. Public cloud A public cloud sells services to anyone on the Internet. It provides services to general public or large industrial group. It's type of service provided by an organization selling cloud services. Currently, Amazon Web Services is the largest public cloud provider. These services are offered on pay per use model or for free.

3. Community cloud A community cloud shares infrastructure with various organizations. It supports a specific community having shared concern. It can be fully owned or acts as a third party service. Expenditure are shared by very few users than public cloud.

4. Hybrid cloud A hybrid cloud is a collection of two or more clouds which are connected together and offers benefits of multiple deployment models. It is bound together by standardized or proprietary technology. It provides data and application portability.

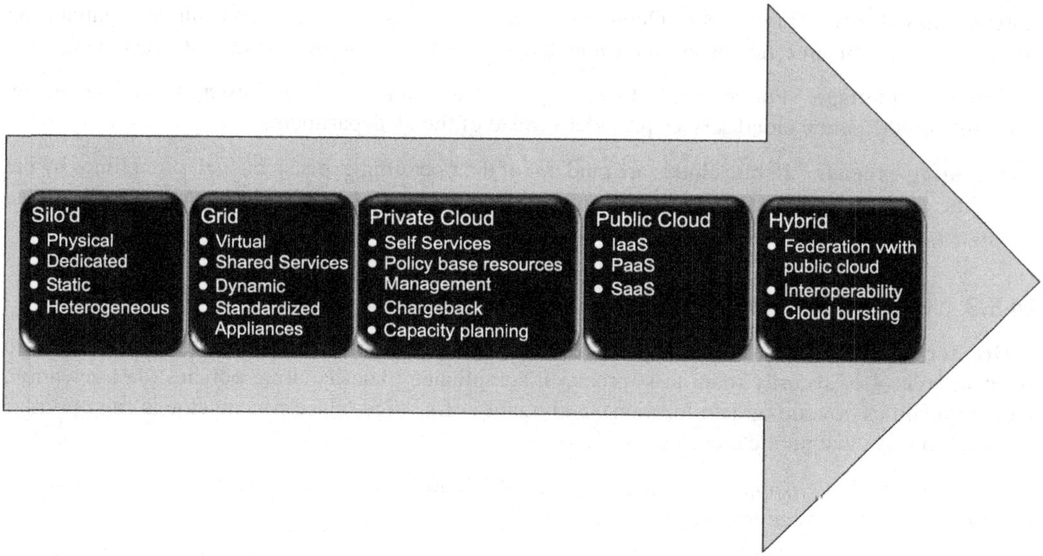

Fig.14.2 *Cloud computing deployment model evolution*

14.5.1 Comparing Public and Private Clouds

The two basic models of public and private clouds have a number of compelling business benefits, some of which are common to both public and private, while others are only for one or the other.

Benefits common to both public and private clouds include:

1. High efficiency Because both public and private clouds are based on a grid computing and virtualization, both offer high efficiency and high utilization due to the sharing of pooled resources, enabling better workload balancing across multiple applications.

2. High availability Another benefit of being based on grid computing is that applications can take advantage of a high availability architecture that minimizes or eliminates planned and unplanned downtime, improving user service levels and business continuity.

3. Elastic scalability Grid computing also provides public and private clouds with elastic scalability, the ability to add and remove computing capacity on demand. This is a significant advantage for applications with highly variable workload or unpredictable growth, or for temporary applications.

4. Fast deployment Because both public and private clouds can provide self-service access to a shared pool of computing resources, and because the software and hardware components are standard, re-usable and shared, application deployment is greatly accelerated.

14.5.2 Some Benefits are Unique to Public Cloud Computing

1. Low upfront costs Public clouds are faster and cheaper to get started, so they provide users with a low barrier to entry because there is no need to procure, install and configure hardware.

2. Economies of scale Large public clouds enjoy economies of scale in terms of equipment purchasing power and management efficiencies, and some may pass a portion of the savings onto customers.

3. Simpler to manage Public clouds do not require IT to manage and administer, update, patch, etc. Users rely on the public cloud service provider instead of the IT department.

4. Operating expense Public clouds are paid out of the operating expense budget, often times by the users' line of business, not the IT department. Capital expense is avoided, which can be an advantage in some organizations.

14.5.3 Other Benefits are Unique to Private Cloud Computing

1. Greater control of security, compliance and quality of service Private clouds enable IT to maintain control of security (data loss, privacy), compliance (data handling policies, data retention, audit, regulations governing data location), and quality of service (since private clouds can optimize networks in ways that public clouds do not allow).

2. Easier integration Applications running in private clouds are easier to integrate with other in-house applications, such as identity management systems.

3. Lower total costs Private clouds may be cheaper over the long term to public clouds, since it essentially owns versus renting. According to several analyses, the breakeven period is between two and three years.

4. Capital expense and operating expense Private clouds are funded by a combination of capital expense (with depreciation) and operating expense.

CLOUD COMPUTING SERVICE MODEL 14.6

Cloud computing providers use various models to provide their services. Three fundamental models are Infrastructure as a Service (IaaS), Platform as a Service (PaaS), and Software as a Service (SaaS). Out of them IaaS is the most basic and each above model abstracts from the details of the lower models.

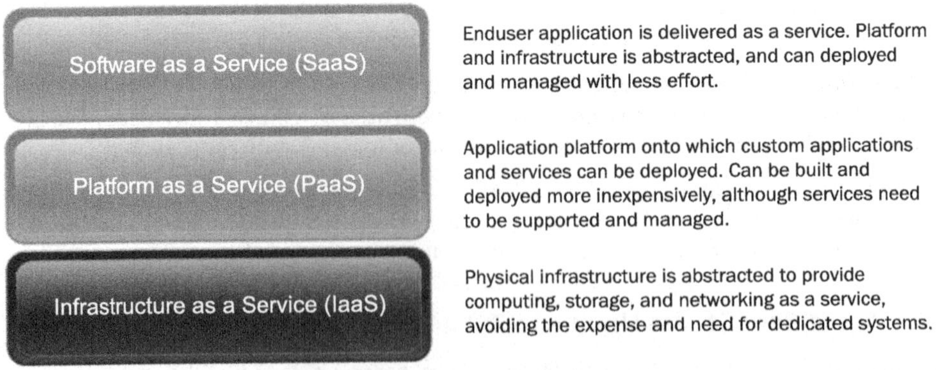

Fig. 14.3 *Cloud computing service model*

1. Infrastructure as a Service (IaaS) Infrastructure as a Service is a provision model in which an organization outsources the equipment used to support operations, including storage, hardware, servers and networking components. IaaS is centered around a model of service delivery that provisions a predefined, standardized infrastructure specifically optimized for the customer's applications. The service provider owns the equipment and is responsible for housing, running and maintaining it. The client typically pays on a per-use basis. End user cannot control or manage the underlying cloud infrastructure. Consumer has control over operating systems, storage, deployed applications and limited control of networking components.

IaaS providers implementations typically include the following layered components:

(a) Utility computing service and billing model
(b) Automation of administrative tasks
(c) Computer hardware
(d) Dynamic scaling
(e) Desktop virtualization
(f) Policy-based services
(g) Internet connectivity

Infrastructure as a service is sometimes referred to as Hardware as a Service (HaaS).

Amazon EC2, Rackspace cloud, Windows Azure Virtual Machines, Google compute engine are some of the examples of **IaaS.**

Companies prefer IaaS because

(a) The billing is on hourly or monthly basis. You pay only for the resources your actually consume. This is unlike the traditional services where you pay a fixed amount even if you do not use the resources, or do not have enough clients to consume the preconfigured resources. In cloud computing, i.e., **IaaS**, you pay less if you have a lower customer base and vice versa.
(b) It includes features like **Elastic Load Balancing.** This feature auto-distributes an application's incoming traffic across multiple instances (virtual computers).

2. Platform as a Service (Paas) Platform as a Service (PaaS) is a way to rent hardware, operating systems, storage and network capacity over the Internet. The service delivery model allows the customer to rent virtualized servers and associated services for running existing applications or developing and testing new ones. This gives capability to customer to deploy onto the cloud infrastructure using programming languages and tools supported by the provider. The PaaS model makes all of the facilities required to support the complete life cycle of building and delivering Web applications and services entirely available from the Internet.

Unlike the IaaS model, where developers may create a specific operating system instance with home-grown applications running, PaaS developers are concerned only with Web-based development and generally do not care what operating system is used. PaaS services allow users to focus on innovation rather than complex infrastructure. Initial and ongoing costs can be reduced by the use of infrastructure services from a single vendor rather than maintaining multiple hardware facilities that often perform duplicate functions or suffer from incompatibility problems. Overall expenses can also be minimized by unification of programming development efforts.

Organizations can redirect a significant portion of their budgets to creating applications that provide real business value instead of worrying about all the infrastructure issues in a roll-your-own delivery model. On the downside, PaaS involves some risk of "lock-in" if offerings require proprietary service interfaces or development languages. Another potential pitfall is that the flexibility of offerings may not meet the needs of some users whose requirements rapidly evolve.

Google App Engine, Microsoft Windows Azure, SalesForce.com, OrangeScape are best examples of PaaS. The USP of these platforms is that they can be used by business analysts (non-developers) as well.

3. Software as a Service (SaaS) Software as a Service (SaaS) is a software distribution model in which applications are hosted by a vendor or service provider and made available to customers over a network, usually the Internet. It provides capability to use the provider's applications running on a cloud infrastructure.

SaaS is becoming an increasingly prevalent delivery model as underlying technologies that support Web services and Service-Oriented Architecture (SOA) mature and new developmental approaches, such as Ajax, become popular. Meanwhile, broadband service has become increasingly available to support user access from more areas around the world. SaaS is also often associated with a pay-as-you-go subscription licensing model.

SaaS is closely related to the ASP (Application Service Provider) and on demand computing software delivery models. IDC identifies two slightly different delivery models for SaaS. The hosted application management model is similar to an Application Service Provider (ASP) model. Here, an ASP hosts commercially available software for customers and delivers it over the Internet. The other model is a software on demand model where the provider gives customers Network-based access to a single copy of an application created specifically for SaaS distribution.

SaaS is most often implemented to provide business software functionality to enterprise customers at a low cost while allowing those customers to obtain the same benefits of commercially licensed, internally operated software without the associated complexity of installation, management, support, licensing, and high initial cost. Many types of software are well suited to the SaaS model (e.g., accounting, customer relationship management, email software, human resources, IT security, IT service management, video conferencing, Web analytics, Web content management).

The distinction between SaaS and earlier applications delivered over the Internet is that SaaS solutions were developed specifically to work within a Web browser. The architecture of SaaS-based applications is specifically designed to support many concurrent users (multitenancy) at once. This is a big difference from the traditional client/server or Application Service Provider (ASP)-based solutions that cater to a contained audience.

Benefits of the SaaS model include:

(a) Easier administration
(b) Automatic updates and patch management
(c) Compatibility All users will have the same version of software
(d) Easier collaboration, for the same reason
(e) Global accessibility

SaaS major examples includes Sales Force (CRM), Google apps, Microsoft Office 365, Quickbooks Online, Paypal, Limelight Video Platform.

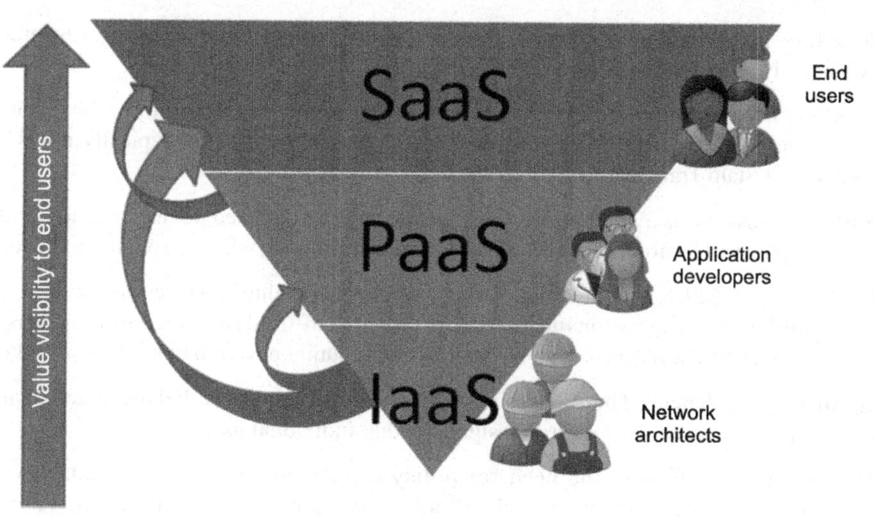

Fig.14.4 *Difference between SaaS, PaaS, IaaS with respect to visibility to end user*

CHARACTERISTICS OF CLOUD COMPUTING 14.7

1. Elasticity The basic value proposition of cloud computing is to pay as you go, and to pay for what you use. This implies that an application can expand and contract on demand, across all its tiers (presentation layer, services, database, security). This also implies that application components can grow independently from each other. So if you need more storage for your database, you should be able to grow that tier without affecting, reconfiguring or changing the other tiers. Basically, cloud applications behave like a sponge; when you add water to a sponge, it grows in size; in the application world, the more customers you add, the more it grows.

Pure IaaS providers will provide certain benefits, specifically in terms of operating costs, but an IaaS provider will not help you in making your applications elastic; neither will virtual machines. The smallest elasticity unit of an IaaS provider and a virtual machine environment is a server (physical or virtual). While adding servers in a datacenter helps in achieving scale, it is hardly enough. The application has yet to use this hardware. If the process of adding computing resources is not transparent to the application, the application is not elastic.

2. On-demand usage Computer services such as email, applications, network or server service can be provided without requiring human interaction with each service provider. This feature is listed by the The National Institute of Standards and Technology (NIST) as a characteristic of cloud computing. Cloud service providers providing on demand self-services includes Amazon Web Services (AWS), Microsoft, Google, IBM and Salesforce.com. New York Times and NASDAQ are examples of companies using AWS (NIST).

The cloud computing self-service requirement prompts infrastructure vendors to create cloud computing templates, which are obtained from cloud service catalogues. The template contains predefined configurations which is used to by consumers to set up their cloud services. The templates or blueprints contains technical information necessary to build ready-to-use clouds. The templates also include predefined Web service, the operating system, the database, security configurations and load balancing.

3. Agility It improves with users ability to re-provision technological infrastructure resources. rapidly and inexpensively re-provision technological infrastructure resources.

4. Application Programming Interface (API) It provides accessibility to software that enables machines to communicate with cloud software. Cloud computing systems typically use REST-based (Representational State Transfer) APIs.

5. Ubiquitous access It is available through standard Internet-enabled devices. Customer don't need to be present at physical location of cloud. She can access it from anywhere through internet connection.

6. Cost It reduces CAPEX by converting into operational expenditure. The customer does not need to purchase or build complete infrastructure as its been provided by third party organization. Customers are charged fees based on their usage of a combination of computing power, bandwidth use and/or storage.

7. Location independence The processing and storage demands are balanced across a common infrastructure with no particular resource assigned to any individual user.

8. Multi-tenacity It refers to the need for policy-driven enforcement, segmentation, isolation, governance, service levels, and chargeback/billing models for different consumer constituencies. It refers to single instance of the software serving multiple client organizations.

Customers might utilize a public cloud provider's service offerings or actually be from the same organization, such as different business units rather than distinct organizational entities, but would still share infrastructure.

9. Reliability Cloud computing improves reliability of service. cloud service providers and cloud customers take advantage of architectural opportunities for mitigating the risks. Elasticity and high availability makes it more suitable for business continuity and disaster recovery.

10. Availability The fact of the matter is that making applications highly available is hard. It requires highly specialized tools and trained staff. On top of it, it is expensive. Many companies are required to run multiple data centers due to high availability requirements. In some organizations, some data centers are simply on standby, waiting to be used in a case of a failover. Other organizations are able to achieve a certain level of success with active/active data centers, in which all available data centers serve incoming user requests.

To a certain degree, certain IaaS provides can assist with complex disaster recovery planning and setting up data centers that can achieve successful failover. However, the burden is still on the corporation to manage and maintain such an environment, including regular hardware and software upgrades. Cloud computing, on the other hand, removes most of the disaster recovery requirements by hiding many of the underlying complexities.

11. Security Cloud provides improved security as centralized data and more security focused resources but there are still many issues related to security issues related with cloud computing. There are some issue faced by cloud service providers while some by customers who are using these services. Service provider must look after issues about infrastructure and client's data security. Customer's must ensure proper security measures which are taken to protect their important data.

12. Measurability Cloud computing resource usage can be measured, controlled, and reported providing transparency for both the provider and consumer of the utilised service. Cloud computing services use a metering capability which enables to control and optimise resource use. This implies that just like air time, electricity or municipality water IT services are charged per usage metrics – **pay per use**.

The more you utilise the higher the bill. Just as utility companies sell power to subscribers, and telephone companies sell voice and data services, IT services such as network security management, data center hosting or even departmental billing can now be easily delivered as a contractual service.

13. Maintainability Cloud Computing Applications are easy to maintain cloud because they do not need to install on every system. They are centrally located and can be handled from different places.

BENEFITS OF CLOUD COMPUTING 14.8

The following are some of the possible benefits for those who offer cloud computing-based services and applications:

1. Cost savings Companies can reduce their capital expenditures and use operational expenditures for increasing their computing capabilities. This is a lower barrier to entry and also requires fewer in-house IT resources to provide system support.

2. Scalability/Flexibility Companies can start with a small deployment and grow to a large deployment fairly rapidly, and then scale back if necessary. Also, the flexibility of cloud computing allows companies to use extra resources at peak times, enabling them to satisfy consumer demands.

3. Reliability Services using multiple redundant sites can support business continuity and disaster recovery.

4. Maintenance Cloud service providers do the system maintenance, and access it through APIs that do not require application installations onto PCs, thus further reducing maintenance requirements.

5. Mobile accessible Mobile workers have increased productivity due to systems accessible in an infrastructure available from anywhere.

CHALLENGES IN CLOUD COMPUTING 14.9

The following are some of the notable challenges associated with cloud computing, and although some of these may cause a slowdown when delivering more services in the cloud, most also can provide opportunities, if resolved with due care and attention in the planning stages.

1. Security and privacy Perhaps two of the more "hot button" issues surrounding cloud computing relate to storing and securing data, and monitoring the use of the cloud by the service providers. These issues are generally attributed to slowing the deployment of cloud services. These challenges can be addressed, for example, by storing the information internal to the organization, but allowing it to be used in the cloud. For this to occur, though, the security mechanisms between organization and the cloud need to be robust and a hybrid cloud could support such a deployment.

2. Lack of standards Clouds have documented interfaces; however, no standards are associated with these, and thus it is unlikely that most clouds will be interoperable. The Open Grid Forum is developing an Open Cloud Computing Interface to resolve this issue and the Open Cloud Consortium is working on cloud computing standards and practices. The findings of these groups will need to mature, but it is not known whether they will address the needs of the people deploying the services and the specific interfaces these services need. However, keeping up to date on the latest standards as they evolve will allow them to be leveraged, if applicable.

3. Continuously evolving User requirements are continuously evolving, as are the requirements for interfaces, networking, and storage. This means that a "cloud," especially a public one, does not remain static and is also continuously evolving.

4. Compliance concerns The Sarbanes-Oxley Act (SOX) in the US and Data Protection Directives in the EU are just two among many compliance issues affecting cloud computing, based on the type of data and application for which the cloud is being used. The EU has a legislative backing for data protection across all member states, but in the US data protection is different and can vary from state to state. As with security and privacy mentioned previously, these typically result in hybrid cloud deployment with one cloud storing the data internal to the organization.

COMMUNICATIONS IN THE CLOUD.. 14.10

For service developers, making services available in the cloud depends on the type of service and the device(s) being used to access it. The process maybe as simple as a user clicking on the required Web page, or could involve an application using:

14.10.1 Using the Communications Services

When in the cloud, communications services can extend their capabilities, or stand alone as service offerings, or provide new interactivity capabilities to current services. Cloud-based communications services enable businesses to embed communications capabilities into business applications, such as Enterprise Resource Planning (ERP) and Customer Relationship Management (CRM) systems. For "on the move" business people, these can be accessed through a Smartphone, supporting increased productivity while away from the office.

These services are over and above the support of service deployments of VoIP systems, collaboration systems, and conferencing systems for both voice and video. They can be accessed from any location and linked into current services to extend their capabilities, as well as stand alone as service offerings.

In terms of social networking, using cloud-based communications provides click-to-call capabilities from social networking sites, access to instant messaging systems and video communications, broadening the interlinking of people within the social circle.

14.10.2 Accessing Through Web APIs

Accessing communications capabilities in a cloud-based environment is achieved through APIs, primarily Web 2.0 RESTful APIs, allowing application development outside the cloud to take advantage of the communication infrastructure within it.

These APIs open up a range of communications possibilities for cloud-based services, only limited by the media and signaling capabilities within the cloud. Today's media services allow for communications and management of voice and video across a complex range of codecs and transport types. By using the Web APIs, these complexities can be simplified and the media can be delivered to the remote device more easily. APIs also enable communication of other services, providing new opportunities and helping to drive Average Revenue Per User (ARPU) and attachment rates.

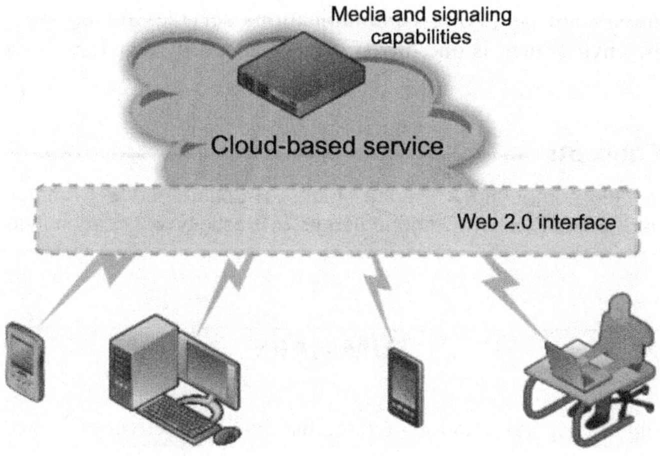

Fig.14.5 *Web 2.0 interfaces to the cloud*

14.10.3 Media Server Control Interfaces

When building communications capabilities into the "core of the cloud," where they will be accessed by another service, the Web 2.0 APIs can be used, as well as a combination of SIP or VoiceXML and the standard media controlling APIs such as MSML, MSCML, and JSR309. The combinations provide different capability sets, but with MediaCTRL being developed in the Internet Engineering Task Force (IETF), it is expected that MediaCTRL will supersede MSML and MSCML and have an upsurge in availability and more developments after it is ratified. JSR309 is a notable choice for those seeking Java development, as it provides the Java interface to media control.

Figure 14.5 is an example of accessing services in the cloud through Web 2.0 and media control interface APIs.

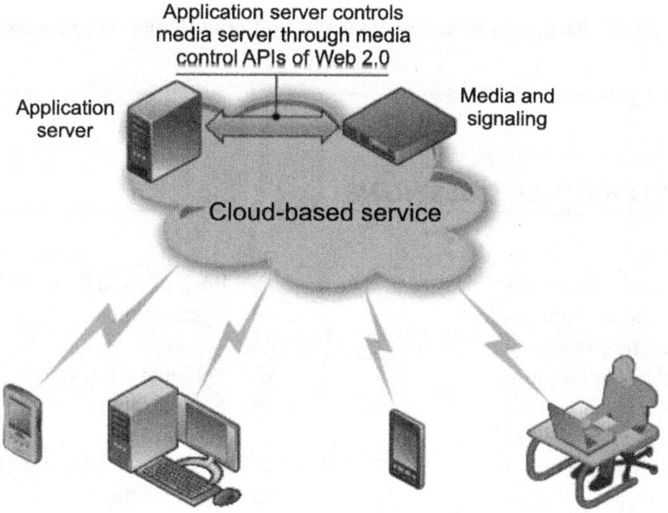

Fig.14.5 *Communication between cloud and end users*

Whether businesses are deploying communications services for access from outside of or within the cloud, the environment is one that supports the speedy development and rollout of these capabilities.

Key Terms and Concepts

ARPANet • VPN • Grid computing • Private cloud • Public cloud • Community cloud • Hybrid cloud • IaaS • PaaS • SaaS • On-Demand usage • Elasticity • Location independence

SUMMARY

- Cloud computing is a general term for anything that involves delivering hosted services over the Internet.
- Cloud computing tries to address two problems, business problems and technical problems.
- In 1997, Professor Ramnath Chellapa defined cloud computing as the new computing paradigm where the boundaries of computing will be determined by economic rationale rather than technical limits alone.
- In 1999, Salesforce.com became one of the first major movers in the cloud arena.
- In Infrastructure as a Service (IaaS),physical infrastructure is abstracted to provide computing, storage and networking as service.
- Platform as a Service (PaaS) is a way to rent hardware, operating systems, storage and network capacity over the Internet.
- In Software as a Service (SaaS), end-user application is delivered as a service, platform and infrastructure are abstract and can deployed and managed with less efforts.
- Elasticity, on-Demand usage, location independence, measurability, availability are key features of cloud computing.
- Security, lack of standard, continuously evolving and compliance are key challenges in cloud computing.

MULTIPLE-CHOICE QUESTIONS

1. Cloud computing tries to address ____________ and ____________ problems.
   (a) logical and technical　　(b) business and technical
   (c) infrastructure and logical　　(d) None of these
2. Grid computing is a form of ____________.
   (a) distributed computing　　(b) personal computing
   (c) cloud computing　　(d) None of these
3. A public cloud sells services to ____________.
   (a) to government　　(b) to anyone on the Internet
   (c) to proprietary network　　(d) None of these

4. Infrastructure as a Service is a provision model in which an organization outsources ____________________.
   (a) equipment used to support operations (b) operating system
   (c) Both (a) and (b) (d) None of these
5. In cloud service model PaaS is based on _______.
   (a) SaaS (b) IaaS (c) TaaS (d) None of these
6. The term VPN expands to ______________.
   (a) Viral Private Network (b) Virtual Public Network
   (c) Virtual Private Network (d) None of these
7. The term API refers to ________.
   (a) Application Programmable Interface (b) Application Programming Interface
   (c) Application Programming Interconnect (d) None of these
8. This implies that an application can expand and contract on demand, across all its tiers.
   (a) on-demand usage (b) elasticity
   (c) agility (d) None of these
9. Amazon EC2 is example of ______________.
   (a) IaaS (b) PaaS (c) SaaS (d) None of these
10. _____________ is a software distribution model in which applications are hosted by a vendor or service provider and made available to customers over a network.
    (a) SaaS (b) IaaS (c) PaaS (d) None of these
11. In 1997, Professor Ramnath Chellapa defined _____________ as the new computing paradigm where the boundaries of computing will be determined by economic rationale rather than technical limits alone.
    (a) grid computing (b) cloud computing (c) cluster computing (d) None of these

DETAILED QUESTIONS

1. What is cloud computing? Explain briefly.
2. What are characteristics of cloud computing?
3. Explain public and private clouds.
4. What are deployment models of cloud computing?
5. Explain in brief various service models of cloud computing.
6. Distinguish briefly between IaaS(Infrastructure as a Service) and SaaS (Software as a Service).
7. Explain benefits of cloud computing.
8. Explain challenges in cloud computing.
9. Explain communication in cloud computing.

15 CREATING GOOD WEB PAGES

INTRODUCTION 15.1

Web designers like to think of a Web site similar to that of a home. Just as a home has a floor, walls, windows, doors, and so many other areas that need a very careful planning and design, so does a Web site. Designed poorly, it can be very unnerving. Hence, the first step in designing a good Web site, like in the case of designing a home, is to create a blueprint of the Web site. This would create a very concrete and solid framework for the Web site. We would exactly know how strong the foundation is, before proceeding with the subsequent steps. The idea is to break the contents of a Web site into smaller blocks or chunks, and then arranging those blocks in a suitable hierarchy, always thinking where they fit the best. This also creates a good relationship between the blocks, and makes them organized in a very logical fashion. Many times, a block of information maps to a Web page. Hence, creating a blueprint helps us organize these discrete Web pages together in a logical manner to create a Web site out of them.

A sample blueprint containing the hierarchical arrangement of the various blocks that make up the Web site is shown in Fig. 15.1.

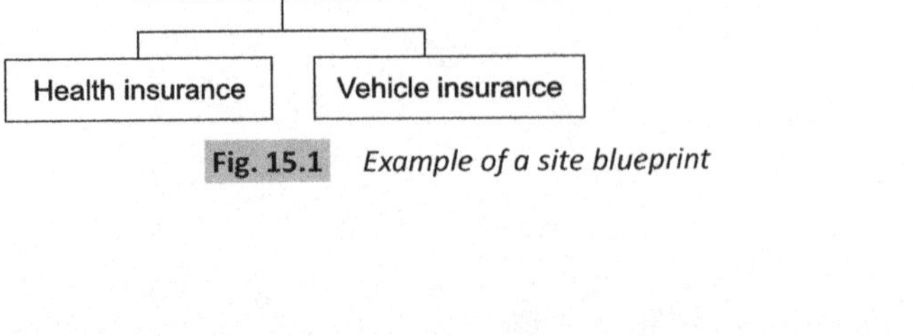

Fig. 15.1 *Example of a site blueprint*

Many times, this sort of blueprint can be derived based on the information provided by the users of the site. For example, in our case, the investment advisory company that has provided the information could have led us to create the blueprint of the site in this manner. However, we should also keep in mind that not all users would be very clear about what they want. Hence, the blueprint could take time to evolve, and could also be very sketchy to start with. However, it would evolve slowly once we speak with the concerned users. Hence, it is important to start with something and also take feedback from the users.

TOP LEVEL NAVIGATION 15.2

The next question is how we want our site to look like in terms of its top level navigation. What we mean by this is the decision about what sort of format/structure we want the top level menu to use. Should we use tabs, menu bars, buttons, plain text links, or some combination of vertical menus, etc.? Various sites choose options that suit them the best, but to understand them better, we have depicted them in Fig. 15.2.

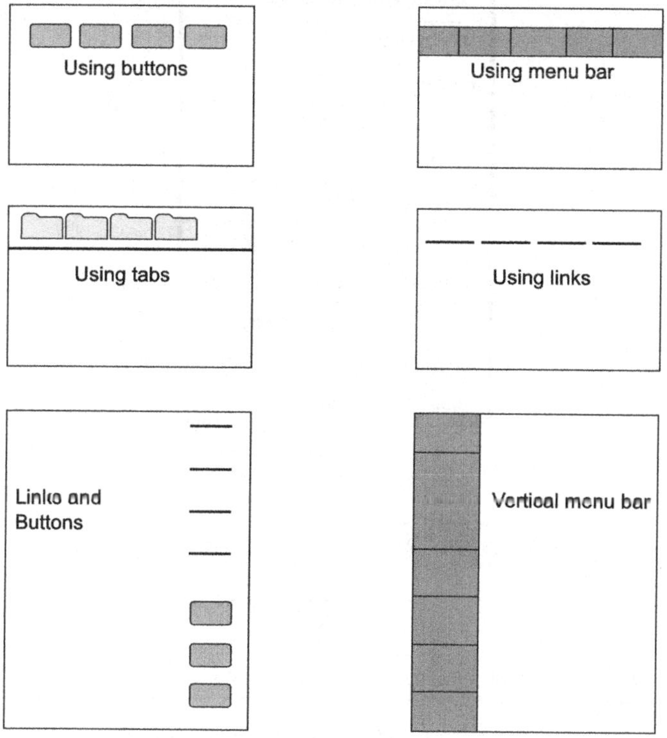

Fig. 15.2 *Various options for top level design*

Here are some examples from real-life sites to illustrate the above approaches, as shown in Fig. 15.3.

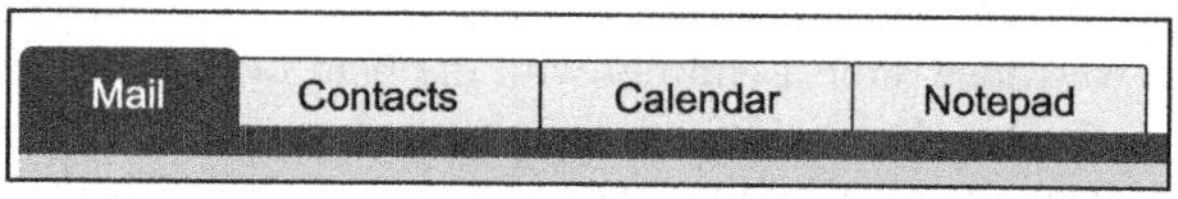

(a) Yahoo using the menu bar

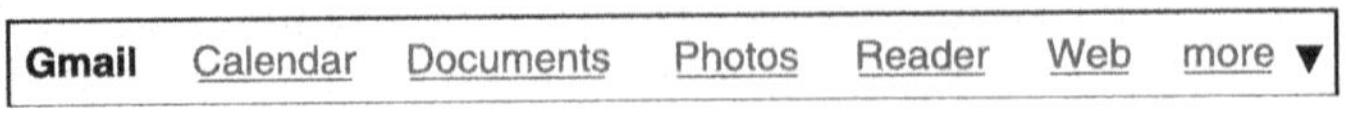

(b) Gmail using links

(c) Gmail also using buttons

(d) Amazon using vertical menu bar

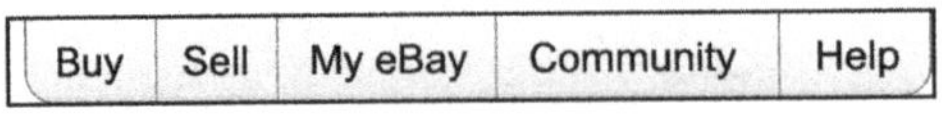

(e) eBay using buttons

(f) Tabs on Indiaplaza.in

Fig. 15.3

Top level navigation allows users of the site know where they are with respect to the overall site. In the earlier days, this was done almost entirely with the help of the vertical menus (the way it is done on the Amazon.com site). Now, things have changed, and many sites use horizontal tabs, horizontal buttons, vertical tabs, vertical buttons, etc., to save space and also give the site a more modern look.

CREATING SAMPLE LAYOUTS.. 15.3

Once the basic blueprint and the top level navigation details are decided, we can come up with a number of sample layouts that possibly depict the overall structure of the Web site on each page. While there are several approaches for achieving this, we shall use some of the most common approaches here. Figure 15.4 shows the various possibilities.

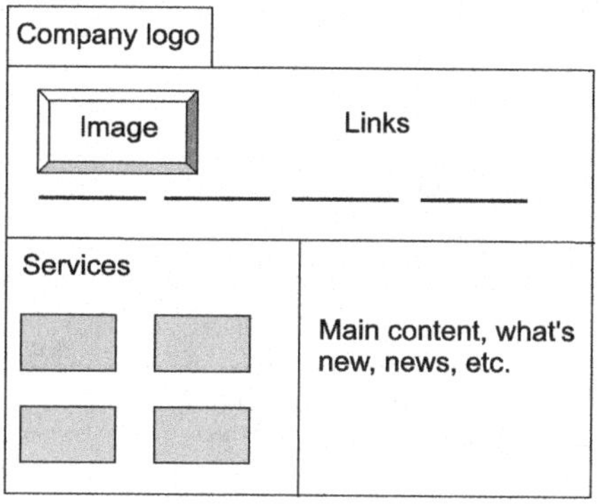

(a) Layout 1 – Traditional and simple

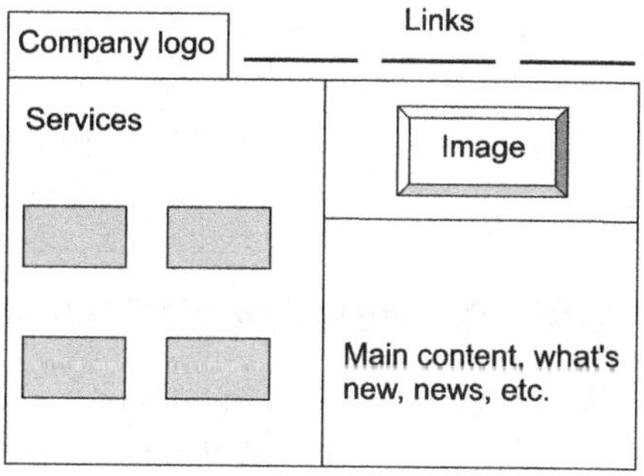

(b) Layout 2 – Has reorganized image and links

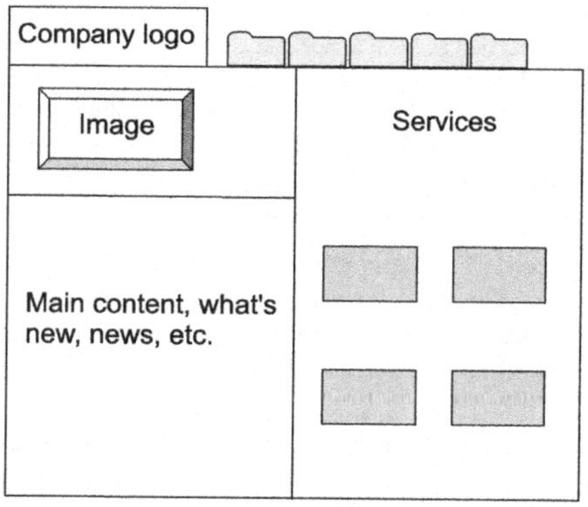

(c) Layout 3 – Use of tabs instead of links, moving Services to the right

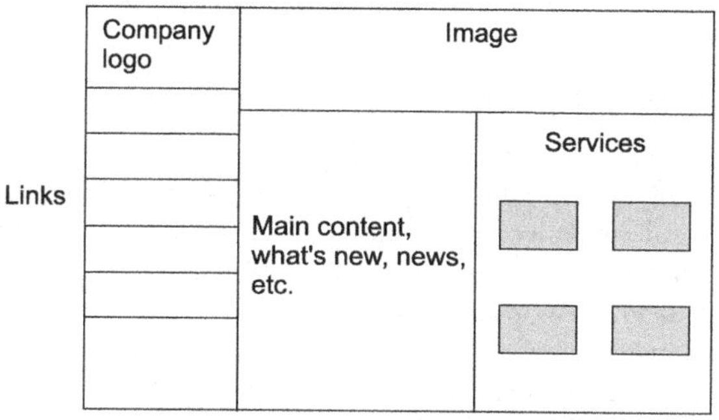

(d) Layout 4 – Three-column design

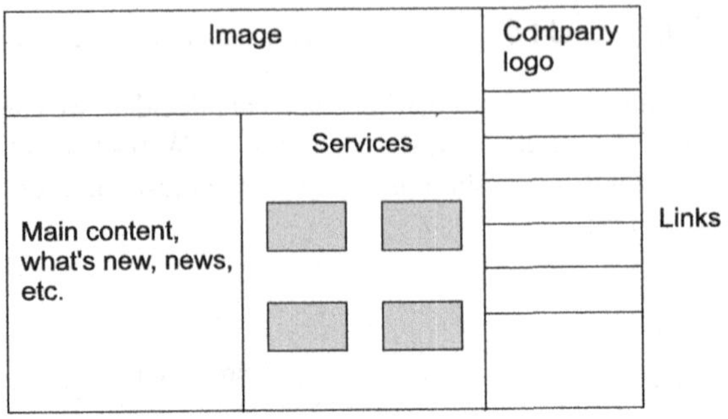

(e) Layout 5 – Three-column design with the menu shifted to the right

Fig. 15.4

METAPHOR, THEME, AND STORYBOARD 15.4

When designing Web pages, the designer needs to think about three aspects to start with, namely **metaphor**, **theme**, and **storyboard**. Let us understand these concepts now, as shown in Table 15.1.

Table 15.1 *Metaphor, theme, and storyboard*

Concept	*Brief description*
Metaphor	The metaphor, also called as visual metaphor is the thought behind the contents of the site and which visual elements need to be used in the site to take care of them. For example, if the site is for general investments and finance advisory, images of calculators, pension-related pictures, depictions of home/personal/health insurance, etc., may help. Also, the colors, fonts, overall site structure need to be thought out accordingly.
Theme	Theme takes the concept of metaphor further, and ensures that the site has the right look-and-feel for the right kind of audience. For example, if the site is meant for selling children's toys, then it should be catchy, attractive, full of colors and bold. On the contrary, if this is a site meant for health-related advices, then the site should be pleasant and should provide visual comfort to the people who are most likely trying to find some solutions to their health-related problems.
Storyboard	Storyboard is the visualization of the design of a Web site. It provides clues regarding how the color combinations on the site look like, how is the navigation appearing, and whether the overall content is appearing to be pleasant for a common user's eyes. A novel idea suggested by some is to take a screen shot of an empty browser screen, print it, and then draw the storyboard on it by hand. That gives a good understanding of how it would eventually look like in the browser without actually coding a single line.

How do we decide the metaphor and theme? We can come out with a list of things we think should go into the site. Then, we can follow some simple steps:

1. While there are many ways to do this, perhaps the best and simplest way this can be achieved is to make use of Adobe Kuler (http://kuler.adobe.com). This site provides a great option for people to try out and save various color schemes. What's more, this can even be exported into design tools such as Photoshop and InDesign.
2. Use elements that match the currently selected theme to create a visual impact.
3. Design the layout based on the content. For example, create new columns only if necessary.

Figure 15.5 shows the various parts of a Web page thus created.

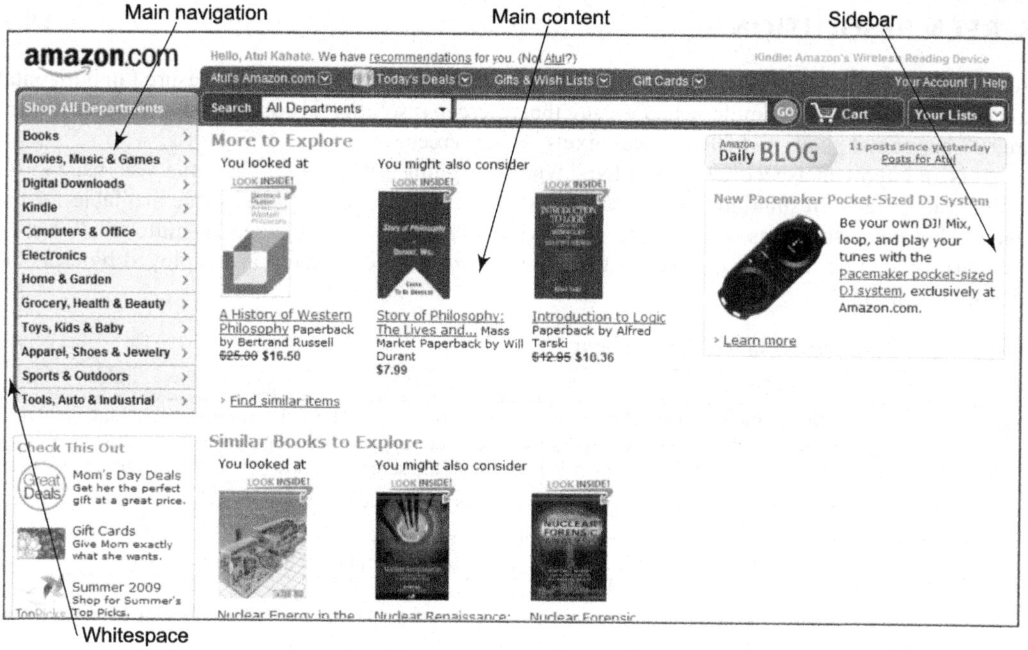

Fig. 15.5 *(a) Main parts of a sample Web page*

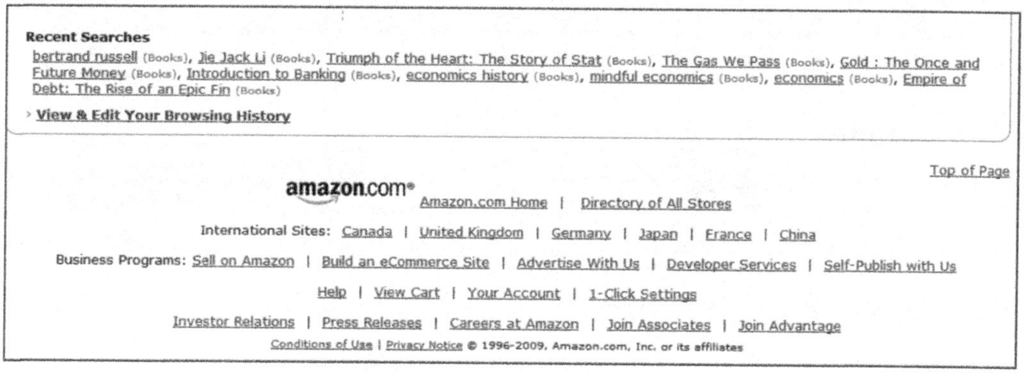

Fig. 15.5 *(b) Footer of the Web page*

Let us summarize these parts of a Web page now.

1. **Main navigation** Specifies links to the other parts of the Web site.
2. **Main content** This is the actual content of the current Web page.
3. **Sidebar** The sidebar is used for specifying links and other secondary content.
4. **Whitespace** This is used to differentiate between elements and shift the user's view to the main content of the page.
5. **Footer** The footer is a very good position to specify the various copyright/legal terms. It can also be used to provide other useful links.

SCREEN RESOLUTION 15.5

Screen resolution is the number of pixels (picture elements) on the screen. It is measured in horizontal and vertical pixels. For example, when we say that a screen resolution is 800 × 480 we mean that there are 800 horizontal pixels and 600 vertical pixels on the screen.

It is an important aspect to be considered when designing a Web page. The same Web page looks different in different resolutions. In general, higher the resolution more is the space available for the content, but that also means that the size of individual characters on the screen is quite small. Let us summarize the characteristics of three of the most common screen resolutions employed by users, as shown in Table 15.2.

Table 15.2 *Characteristics of screen resolutions*

Resolution	*Characteristics*
800 × 600	This is one of the very smallest resolutions used by people. Here, the number of characters on the screen is the smallest. Hence, everything on the screen appears to be bigger than normal. Many times, the layout designer by the designer is larger than the screen window when this resolution is used.
1024 × 768	This is a commonly used resolution. The text is quite readable and not too big as well.
1280 × 800	This is a very high resolution, and is not very commonly used. The number of characters is very low here. Reading text is very easy, but then too little amount of text fits on the screen!

Let us look at all the three resolutions with the help of a sample screen as shown in Figs. 15.6, 15.7, and 15.8.

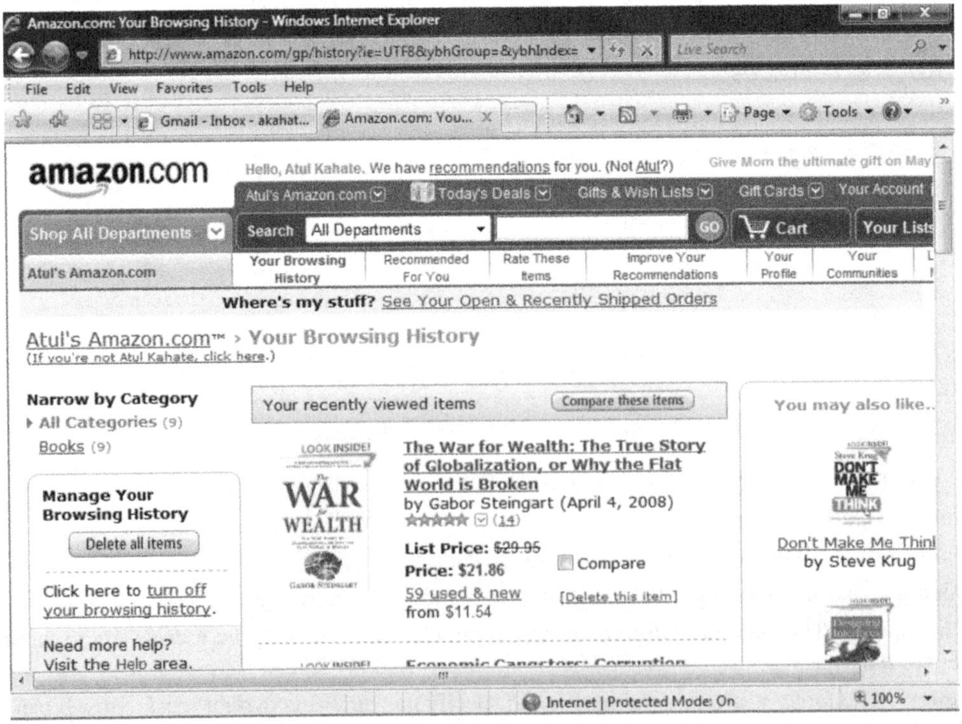

Fig. 15.6 *Resolution of 800 × 60*

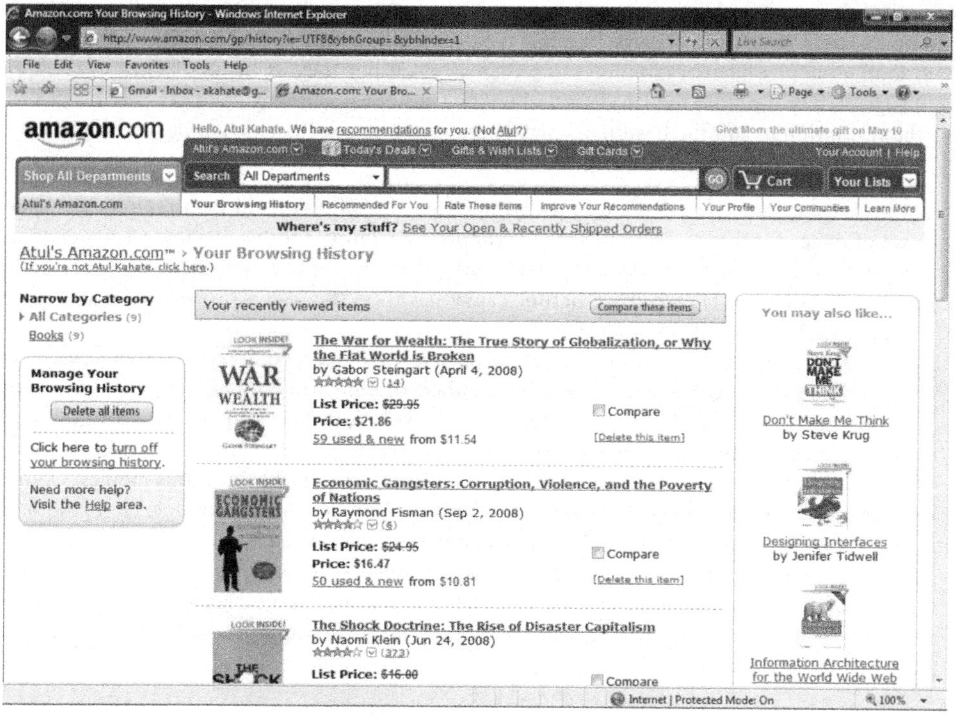

Fig. 15.7 *Resolution of 1024 × 768*

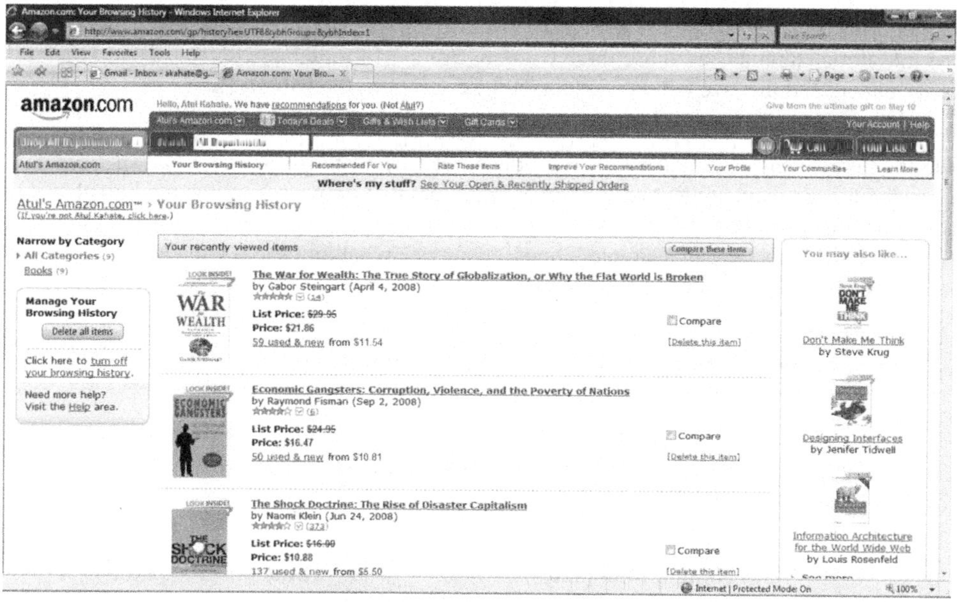

Fig. 15.8 *Resolution of 1280 × 800*

On many sites, we would see a message stating "Site best viewed in 1024 × 768". This is Greek and Latin to many users. They do not care what this means. All they want is that the site be visible and that it should look good in whatever monitor and screen size settings they are using. Hence, it is important for the designer to ensure that the site is tested on a variety of resolutions, and not rely on the user to change the resolution to suit the designer's art! There are some mechanisms to deal with this problem on a technical front, as mentioned below:

1. Use JavaScript to detect the user's current screen resolution, and then redirect the user to a set of pages for that resolution. This would provide ability for the designer to create pages for a number of common resolutions, and flexibly use any one of them depending on the user's screen resolution. However, sometimes JavaScript on the user's browser does not function; and in such cases, this method fails.
2. Instead of using JavaScript to redirect the user so as to use a completely different set of pages according to the user's screen resolution, another solution is to use JavaScript to load a CSS that is in accordance with the user's current screen resolution. This allows the creation of just one set of pages, which can be rendered with multiple style sheets (i.e., one CSS file per resolution, but not one HTML file per resolution). Again, if JavaScript is disabled, this method would fail.
3. Create a single set of pages that works well with various screen resolutions. Here, the smallest resolution that most users would work with needs to be selected as the base. Once this decision is made, screens with higher resolutions would be displayed properly. Screens with resolutions even smaller than our selected smallest resolution would be displayed with scroll bars. The advantages here are that coding and designing efforts are minimized, and there is no reliance on JavaScript at all.

3-COLUMN LAYOUT 15.6

Most modern Web sites are designed to have a **3-column layout**. This means that the screen is vertically divided into three columns and those three columns are used for adding contents as appropriate. But before we understand this, we will take a look at the concept of the **golden ratio**.

The principle of golden ratio for a given case can be applied as follows:

"Divide the number of horizontal pixels (i.e., the screen width in pixels) by 1.62. That gives us the space needed for the main content on the screen. Subtract that number from the total pixel size to get the space remaining for the sidebar."

Let us simplify this with an example. Suppose that we are talking about a screen having resolution 800 × 600. Then let us compute the golden ratio.

← **Horizontal width of the screen is 800 pixels** →

1. Divide 800 by 1.62 to get 494 (rounded). This in pixels is the space for our main content.
2. Compute 800 – 494 = 306. This in pixels is the space for our sidebar.

The results are shown below:

Main content (494 pixels)	**Sidebar (304 pixels)**

However, some people find this technique cumbersome. In such a case, a simpler technique exists. Here, we can divide the screen vertically and horizontally into three areas each in such a way that we have 1/3rd of the overall available space allocated to each of the areas. This creates a grid-like structure as shown in Fig. 15.9, and also gives us the desired 3-column layout.

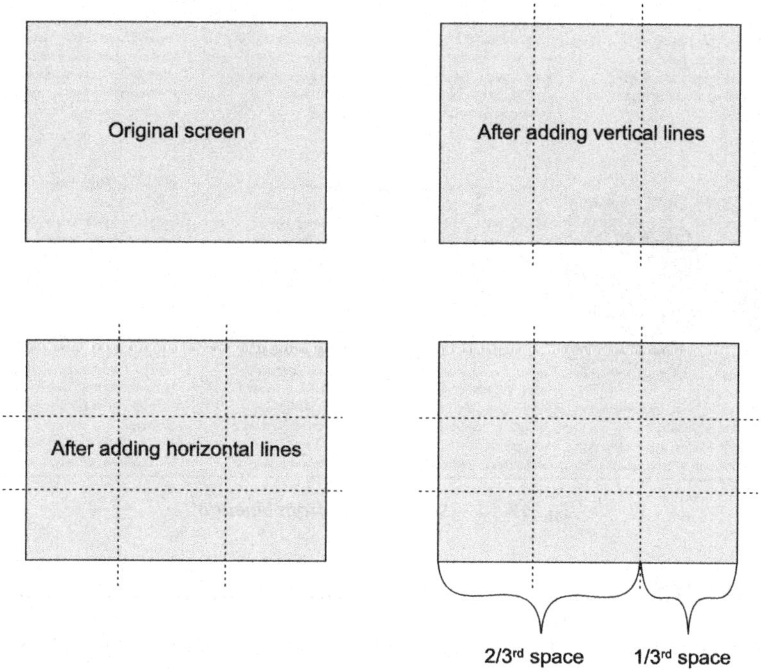

Fig. 15.9 *Creating a 3-column layout without using the golden ratio*

USING FRAMEWORKS 15.7

Designing good Web pages need not be very difficult these days. Several good tools exist. One such tool can be downloaded from http://blueprintcss.org/. This site provides a readymade grid that we can use as the basis for making modifications as needed to create Web pages of our choice. More than the basic grid layout, blueprint also provides features for creating and styling various form elements (such as text boxes, buttons, etc.) and error/status messages. This makes it a complete framework. It is also very flexible to use.

For example, out of the box, it provides the necessary code for displaying a page containing the multi-layout column with headings, page sections, footers, etc. We need not code everything from scratch. A sample page that comes by default with this tool is shown in Fig. 15.10.

We shall discuss some more details of how to use this framework when we discuss the technicalities of usability in a separate chapter.

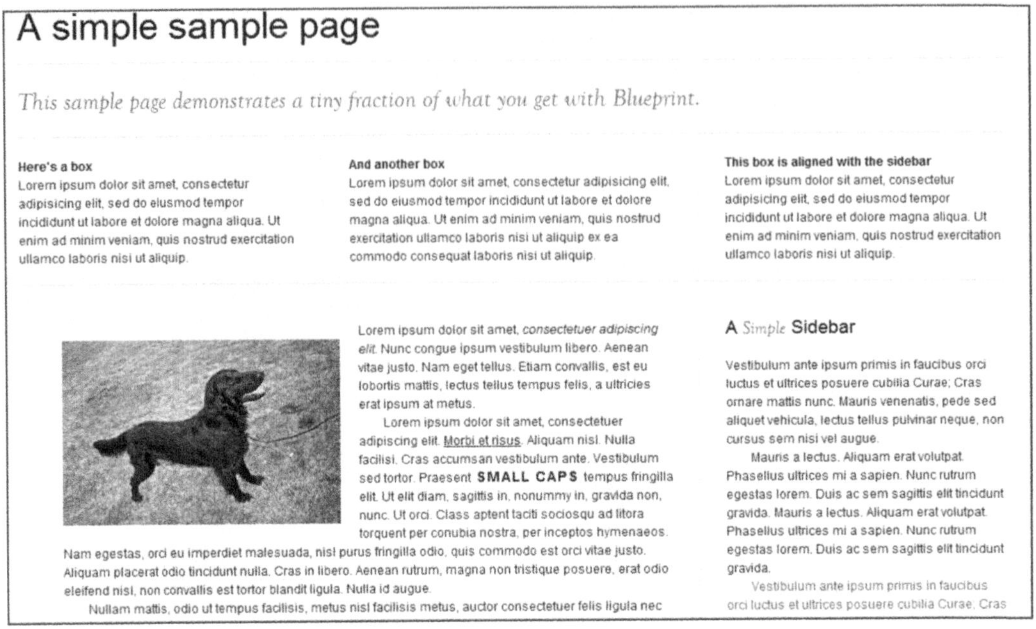

Fig. 15.10 *Sample page from blueprint*

USING GRAPHICS 15.8

Many times, designers are puzzled when it comes to using graphics in Web pages. Should graphics be used at all? If yes, how much of graphics is necessary and even tolerable? Do graphics add to the beauty of the Web page? Does it make it slow? Does it annoy the user?

When designed effectively, graphics can help users work with Web pages better. In other words, they make information processing more enjoyable for the user. As an example, the usage of colors allows the user to mentally separate areas of information and provide attention to specific areas of the Web page in the desired manner, instead of all the information being cluttered together. An image can be a very powerful and most economical way of expressing complex concepts (instead of long text).

Let us answer some of these questions with a few simple guidelines.

1. Do not use heavy graphics when the intention of the page is to allow the user to complete a transaction. This is because in such cases, it is more important for the user to complete the transaction more quickly in the least possible amount of time. Heavy graphics can make it slow.
2. If using graphics is necessary for whatever reasons, use small images. In general, it is recommended that an individual image should not be of size that exceeds 5 Kb. Total size of all the images on a page should be limited to about 25 Kb.
3. Even though Internet connections are much faster these days with the advent of broadband, there are still people who may be using dial-up connections. Also, there are users who use their mobile phone for Internet access. For these users, downloading graphics is just out of question.

Hence, if graphics have to be used, the site should also provide a "text only" option in addition to the graphics version.

4. Using too many colors makes a page look very clumsy. At the most four colors are recommended.
5. If the user is being led to a Web page that has heavy graphics, it is a good practice to warn the user in advance.
6. In terms of size, GIF images are smaller as compared to JPEG, and as such should be used wherever possible. But when more minute details need to be captured, we need to use JPEG images.
7. If a part of an image is clickable, it should be made obvious to the user (maybe by making it look like a button).

USABILITY FOR THE HANDHELD DEVICES 15.9

These days, more and more users are turning to mobile phones and other handheld devices for accessing the Internet. They range from very ineffective displays (1.5" × 2.5" in size and 160 × 160 pixels) to quite powerful ones (6.5" × 3.5" in size and 800 × 400 pixels). More and more people are likely to use the Internet by using the ever-improving mobile phones.

The original Internet usage of handheld devices was limited to checking latest stock prices, news, travel and entertainment information, flight schedules, and shopping. However, now that both the devices themselves and the communication speed between the Internet and the device are dramatically improving, mobile phones soon would be able to do almost everything that a conventional desktop user can do. Figure 15.11 shows a couple of samples.

Fig. 15.11 *Internet access using mobile phones*

Consequently, designers need to keep in mind the needs of the mobile users as well.

The most important area in which the mobile devices differ from the fixed-location PC-like devices is the aspect of *context*. That is, because a mobile device is on the move, there are several points that need to be kept in mind, namely the infrastructure, application, location, and physical contexts.

1. Infrastructure context The changes in the underlying infrastructure cause user experience to vary from time to time. For examples, signals fade and again become string, calls drop, and so on. This should be reflected in the interaction with the user via the user interface of the mobile device.

2. Application context Users may want to have the frequently used commands/choices/options placed in such a way that they are more easily selectable. This means that the users should be allowed to personalize the user interface according to their choice. It should not be kept constant. For instance, the user should be allowed to choose the preferred home page apart from making choices about the font, color, choices, graphics, etc.

3. Location context The present location of a mobile phone is quite significant. This is because depending on the location, personalized content or services can be offered. For example, if a person is traveling from Delhi to Rajasthan and accesses a news site, the site can perhaps start displaying news and weather information about Delhi and Rajasthan.

4. Physical context The user interface should allow the user to work effectively even when environmental and other issues such as lighting, noise, moving vehicles, etc., cause disturbances. For example, instead of a video, should audio be used?

In general, following points need to be considered when designing user interfaces for mobile phones:

1. Allow the user to easily change the text size for adjusting it varying lighting and other conditions.
2. Provide buttons for features/functions that are accessed more frequently.
3. Allow flexibility for the users to make changes to the look and feel the way they want. Aspects related to the various contexts discussed earlier should be kept in mind for this purpose.
4. Consider providing audio inputs for users who are not able to view the output on the screen while driving or moving, etc.
5. Frequently used options should be displayed on the first screen. Do not expect the user to toggle and scroll continuously using very difficult to operate keys.
6. Allow the user to access and navigate Web pages in more than one way.
7. Consider accepting voice commands for navigation, such as *previous*, *next*, *up*, *down*, etc.
8. The links or URLs should be as small as possible.
9. Do not expect the user to type a lot of input. Minimize data entry requirements.
10. Have the text and background sufficiently contrasted.
11. Design with the aspects of access speed and interaction speed in mind.
12. Functionality comes first, more so in mobile phones. Hence, other user interface related aspects can be toned down if needed.
13. Use language that is familiar to the user. Use meaningful words for links, etc.
14. Screen layout should be consistent across pages.
15. Hierarchical organization of importance is a must, considering the very small screen space.
16. Avoid blinking text. It is very irritating in general, and more so, on mobile phones.
17. Whenever using tables, ensure the rows and columns have appropriate labels/headings.

CREATING MULTILINGUAL WEB SITES 15.10

When a Web site is multilingual, it offers the same textual content to users in different languages. This content can be some pages on the Web site, or the entire Web site. Sometimes, multilinguality is achieved by providing the same text in multiple languages on a single Web page. In other words, the same page would have content in English, German, and Japanese languages, for example. But often this is quite clumsy and impractical. As a result, separate Web pages need to be created to have contents in different languages for the same text. Thus, the text in every different language is held in a separate file on the server, and has its uniquely associated URL.

Sometimes, the user can make the choice of language simply by selecting the language option in the Web browser. However, many times this scheme does not work or is not enough, and as a result, the Web page must provide explicit links for the user to select the language of choice. For example, the Web site should offer a very clear option for the user to move from say German language to English language. Here is a good example, taken from an article written by Jukka Korpela, as shown in Fig. 15.12.

de (Deutsch) *Techniken für mehrsprachige Web-Sites*

en (English) *Techniques for multilingual Web sites*

sv (svenska) *Tekniker för mångspråkiga Webbsajter*

Fig. 15.12 *Example of allowing the user to choose preferred language*

Where these links should be placed is a debatable point. There are three options, as outlined in Table 15.3.

Table 15.3 *Placement of the language option link*

Place	*Advantages*	*Disadvantages*
Top right	Helps in making the language menu a separate menu that is clearly visible and noticeable.	Search engines or indexing robots may interpret this content as a part of their entries incorrectly.
After a heading	Resolves the indexing problem that was mentioned earlier.	This is not easy to understand and can easily confuse the user.
Bottom of the page	Minimizes possible disturbances caused to normal reading.	The link may not be noticed by the users at all. The users may miss it entirely and they may think that the site does not provide multilingual support.

In general, the top right option is preferred.

Whenever the user's browser sends the request for a Web page to the server, it sends a header named *Accept-Language*, which signifies the languages acceptable to the user and their characteristics. For example, consider the following header:

```
Accept-Language: jp;q=1, en;q=0.2
```

This indicates to the server that the browser is expecting the server to send output in Japanese or English, in the specified order. That is, if Japanese output cannot be produced, then the server should send English output.

There are two common techniques used for naming the various language versions of the same file:

1. The URL path of the file indicates a subdirectory or separate part to indicate different languages. For example:
   http://mywebsite.com/en/firstpage.html (This would be the English version)
   http://mywebsite.com/jp/firstpage.html (This would be the Japanese version)
2. The actual file name file indicates the usage of different languages. For example:
   http://mywebsite.com/firstpage-en.html (This would be the English version)
   http://mywebsite.com/firstpage-jp.html (This would be the Japanese version)

In the first case, different language pages are organized in different subdirectories such as *en* and *jp*. In the second case, all pages, in spite of the language differences, are kept in the same directory. The difference is indicated by the suffix attached to the end of the file name, before the extension of *html*.

We can use some simple guidelines for making multilingual Web sites work in an error-free manner, as listed below:

1. Make use of the Unicode standard Unicode is the ultimate solution to the problems of different character representations and languages, which provides a unique number for every character in every language that we know of, and therefore, has the capacity to accommodate every possible character in all the scripts that exist in the world. The Unicode standard has been adopted by industry leaders such as Microsoft, HP, IBM, Oracle, Sun, and Sybase, etc. All operating systems support Unicode. On many Web pages, we would see a line at the top looking quite similar to this:

```
<meta http-equiv="Content-Type" content="text/html; charset=utf-8">
```

This is where we specify that our Web page wants to make use of Unicode (indicated by *charset=utf-8*). If the Web page is created using plain ASCII, it cannot handle languages other than English.

2. Understanding the issues with a particular language Most languages that we know of expect the content and therefore, the user input also to flow from left to right. Common examples are English, German, Hindi, etc. However, a few languages such as Arabic, Persian, and Hebrew expect that the content should flow from right to left. In such cases, the Web page should allow the user to type in the contents from right to left, instead of the usual left to right order.

3. Entry page If a Web site provides support for two or more languages, the entry page can ask the user to select the preferred language. This can avoid a lot of later confusions.

4. Database-driven Web sites If the Web site expects the user to enter information that is likely to go into the database, more care needs to be taken; since several database-related issues can come up. A detailed discussion of this topic is not in the scope of the current text. But the designer should make a note of this and ensure that this is addressed well.

5. Search engines Multilingual Web sites are tough to optimize for search engines. Google does this well, but not all search engines have that capability.

6. Domain name The domain name of a site should be in English. Although now domain names can possibly also be in other languages, until we have sufficient clarity on that issue, it is safe to have domain names in plain English only.

There are other issues about multilingual Web sites as well. It is not just about supporting multiple languages. For example, in some languages, the thousand separator is a dot instead of a comma. Thus, we would have the following situation sometimes to depict the number 10000:

10,000	In English
10.000	In German

Date and time formats is another headache. Most countries use the DD/MM/YY format, but America and some other countries use MM/DD/YY. Some others have YY/MM/DD.

XHTML AND WEB BROWSER COMPATIBILITY ISSUES 15.11

XHTML stands for **EXtensible Hyper Text Markup Language**. It is a combination of HTML and XML. It is expected to replace HTML slowly but surely. Syntax-wise it is identical to HTML but addresses the poor coding standards of HTML. XHTML mandates strict adherence to coding rules. XHTML is a W3C recommendation and all the new browsers support XHTML. Also, the issue with browser incompatibilities is effectively dealt with by XHTML. This is because all browsers are expected to adhere to the XHTML standard, unlike what has happened with HTML.

There are three main parts in an XHTML documents:

1. DOCTYPE
2. Head
3. Body

An XHTML example is shown in Fig. 15.13.

```
<!DOCTYPE html PUBLIC "-//W3C//DTD XHTML 1.0 Strict//EN"
                  "http://www.w3.org/TR/xhtml1/DTD/xhtml1-strict.dtd">
<html xmlns="http://www.w3.org/1999/xhtml">
  <head>
    <title> Sample XHTML</title>
  </head>
  <body>
    <p> This is a sample XHTML file. </p>
  </body>
</html>
```

Fig. 15.13 *XHTML example*

XHTML document types

There are three Document Type Definition (DTD) *validation types,* which describe the allowed syntax and grammar in an XHTML document.

1. Strict

```
<!DOCTYPE html
PUBLIC "-//W3C//DTD XHTML 1.0 Strict//EN"
"http://www.w3.org/TR/xhtml1/DTD/xhtml1-strict.dtd">
```

Fig. 15.14 *Strict XHTML document*

The XHTML strict document type separates the HTML tags and their presentation-related specifications by using Cascading Style Sheet (CSS). For example, the font type and size for a text tag would be specified in a separate CSS file.

2. Transitional

```
<!DOCTYPE html
PUBLIC "-//W3C//DTD XHTML 1.0 Transitional//EN"
"http://www.w3.org/TR/xhtml1/DTD/xhtml1-transitional.dtd">
```

Fig. 15.15 *Transitional XHTML document*

If we are using older version of browsers that do not recognize CSS or in case of transformation from HTML to XHTML where presentation part is included in HTML then we can give preference to transitional DOCTYPE.

3. Frameset

```
<!DOCTYPE html
PUBLIC "-//W3C//DTD XHTML 1.0 Frameset//EN"
"http://www.w3.org/TR/xhtml1/DTD/xhtml1-frameset.dtd">
```

Fig. 15.16 *Frameset XHTML document*

This is simply XHTML 1.0 transitional with added elements to support HTML frame-related tags, namely <frameset>, <frame>, and <noframes>.

Benefits of XHTML

1. Syntax checking There are so many Web pages containing *bad* HTML. The main reason behind this is that the HTML language rules are not implemented strictly by the Web browsers. Figure 15.17 shows an example of *bad* HTML, but this page will surely work well in all kinds of browsers and will produce the specified output.

```
<html>
  <head>
    <title>HTML Sample</title>
  <body>
    <h1>HTML Sample
    <p> Hello
    <br>
    <h2> How are you?
  </body>
```

Fig. 15.17 *Bad HTML*

The strictness of XHTML is useful in today's world where there are so many channels in use such as browsers, mobile phones, PDAs, etc.

2. Extensibility XML documents are required to be well-formed (elements nesting properly). Under HTML, the addition of a new group of elements requires alteration of the entire DTD which leads to wait for next HTML version. In a XML-based DTD, the new set of elements has to be internally consistent and well-formed which can be added to an existing DTD. This greatly eases the development and integration of new collections of elements.

3. Portability By being strict about well-formed tags, XHTML requires less processing power and less complicated algorithms to render. This means that XHTML can be displayed by devices with less processing power, such as mobile phones.

Major Differences Between HTML and XHTML

1. Elements must be in lowercase in XHTML (optional in HTML)
Invalid Syntax:

```
<BODY>
<p> Invalid Syntax </p>
</BODY>
```

Fig. 15.18 *Invalid HTML syntax*

Valid Syntax:

```
<body>
<p> Valid Syntax</p>
</body>
```

Fig. 15.19 *Valid HTML syntax*

2. Elements must be paired with a closing tag in XHTML (optional in HTML)
Invalid Syntax:

```
<br>
<hr>
<img src="pic1.jpg>
```

Fig. 15.20 *Invalid HTML syntax*

Valid Syntax:

```
<br />
<hr />
<img src="pic1.jpg />
```

Fig. 15.21 *Valid HTML syntax*

3. Elements must be properly nested in XHTML (optional in HTML)
In HTML, element's closure sequence can be improper, like this:

```
<b><i>Sample Code</b></i>
```

Fig. 15.22 *Invalid HTML syntax*

In XHTML, element's closure sequence should be proper, like this:

```
<b><i> Sample Code </i></b>
```

Fig. 15.23 *Invalid HTML syntax*

4. Structure must be separated from content For example, the <p> tag is a content tag (paragraph) so we cannot include a table inside it for example, because a table is a format construct. We can, however, put the <p> tag inside <td> </td> tags with no problem because the content goes in the construct, not the other way around.

5. XHTML documents must have one root element All XHTML elements must be nested within the <html> root element. Nested elements can have subelements correctly nested in parent element.

```
<html>
<head> ... </head>
<body> ... </body>
</html>
```

Fig. 15.24 *Root element and nesting*

The W3C Markup Validation Service

The Markup Validator is a free service by W3C that helps check the validity of Web documents, hosted at the URL http://validator.w3.org/#validate_by_input. Examples below show a valid and invalid XHTML document.

Valid XHTML

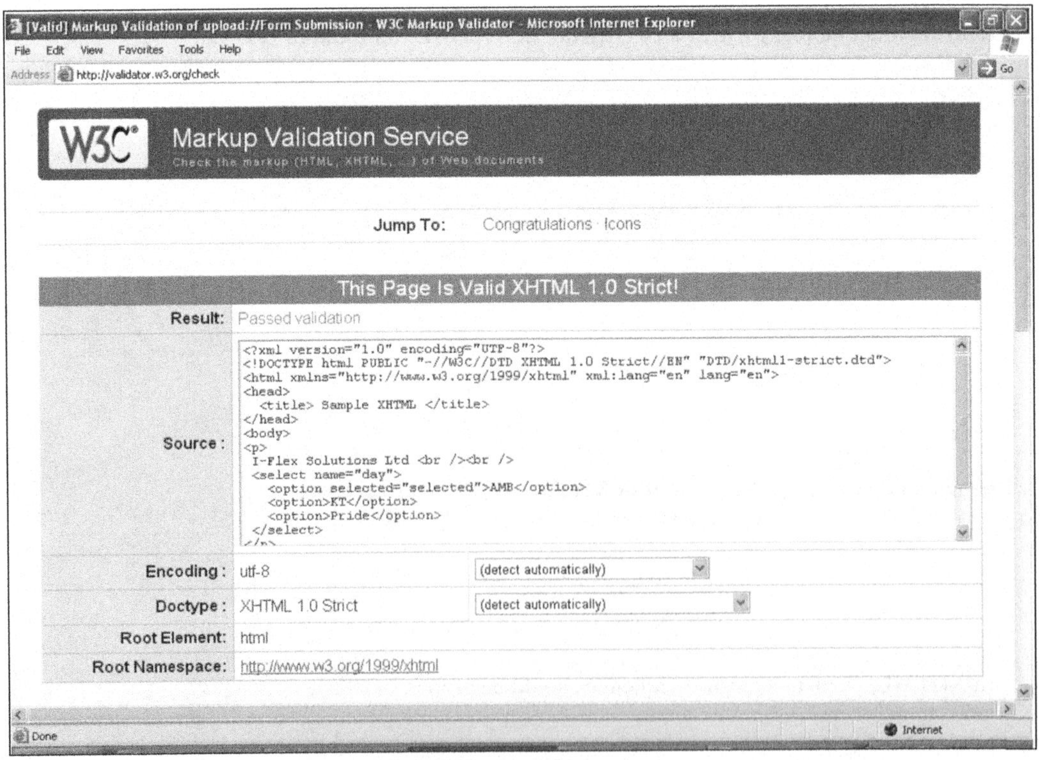

Fig. 15.25 *Valid HTML syntax*

Invalid XHTML (which is valid HTML)

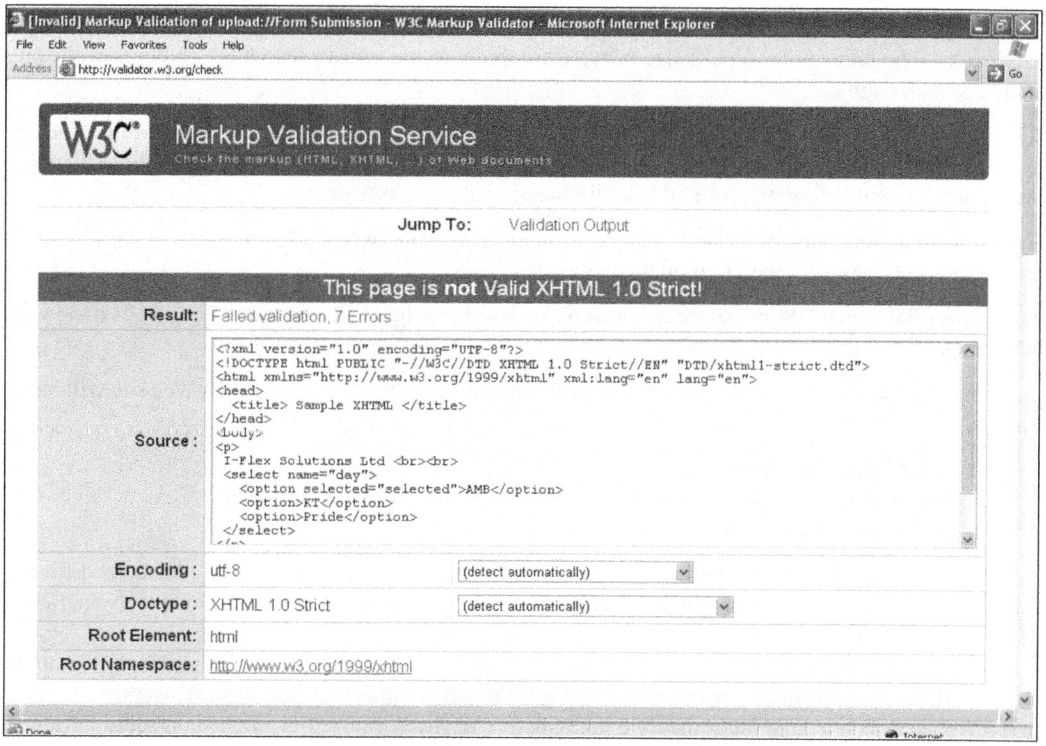

Fig. 15.26 *Invalid HTML syntax*

DESIGNING THE HOME PAGE 15.12

The home page is obviously the most important part of any Web site. This is the page that conveys a very specific message about the site to the user. It also helps set a trend. It sets the user's perception and also the expectations. If the home page experience is not good, perhaps the user would just not visit any other page on the site. Hence, it is important to create a professional and sound home page. This would ensure that the user's attention is captured and kept.

A number of areas are covered by the home page, as listed below:

1. Identity and purpose The home page conveys the information about why does the site exist, and what is its purpose. In other words, the home should clearly try to distinguish the site with other sites of similar/different nature. The fact that the user should be visiting this site and not some other site should come out very clearly with reasoning.

2. Structure The overall structure or hierarchy of the site should come out very clearly on the home page. This should be in terms of the site's contents, organization, and key features.

3. Frequently updated/fresh content For the user to feel that the contents of the site are not outdated, they should be updated frequently. Some recent developments or news need to be appropriately highlighted. Also, this is not a one-off event, and needs to be handled at regular time intervals.

4. Search The home page should also provide an option to the user to search the contents of the site using a search engine.

5. Registration If the site expects the user to register, then there needs to be a registration panel on the home page. Also, for users that have already registered, there should be a facility to log in by using the regular authentication mechanism (usually the user id and password).

6. Promotions and teasers The home page should catch the user's attention with some attractive promotions and teasers, depending on the nature of the site.

7. Commercial space Some space needs to be reserved for showing advertisements, deals done with other sites/companies, etc.

In general, the home page needs to answer some basic questions that any visitor of a Web site will have, such as:

1. What is this site all about?
2. Why should I be visiting this site, and not some other site?
3. What does this site have for me?

If the design is good, answering these questions in an easy and quick manner should not be difficult. It is easy for a visitor to get frustrated and lose interest in the site altogether, if the visitor's experience of the home page is not good.

Often, users start going through a Web site from its home page. Hence, the importance of a home page need not be specifically mentioned anyway. Also, it is observed that even if users start going into a Web site with a page other than the home page (maybe because they clicked on some URL and directly entered the internal portion of the site or because they were searching for some information, and the search took them to such an internal page), eventually more often than not, they do visit the home page. This makes the home page of a site really key. The attention it gets as compared to the other pages on the site is really very high. As such, from a usability point of view, its significance must also be considered very high.

GOOD HOME PAGE DESIGN GUIDELINES 15.13

Derek Powazek has provided a list of guidelines for creating good home pages. We shall discuss some of those principles here. He has put his theory in the form of goals behind creating a home page, which are tabulated in Table 15.4.

Table 15.4 *List of good home page design goals*

Goal number	*Description*
1	Answer the question, *What is this place?*
2	Don't get in the repeat visitor's way.
3	Show what's new.
4	Provide consistent, reliable global navigation.

Let us now discuss these goals.

1. Goal 1 – Answer the question, What is this place? This is said to be the most important goal of a home page. If we leave a doubt in the user's mind as to why she is on our home page after going through it, we have lost the battle already! When the user visits a new site, this is the first question that the user has. Why has the user landed or is even going through this site? The home page should provide a very clear, unambiguous answer to this question. Otherwise, the user would be confused, would not know the purpose of staying on the site, and just quit.

The text should identify the nature and purpose of the site. This should be kept brief. For those interested in knowing more, an additional page or site tour can be created and a link from the home page can be provided. This will ensure that the introduction of the site is neither too long nor too brief. Also, only interested users would have an opportunity to get into more details.

Figure 15.27 shows an example.

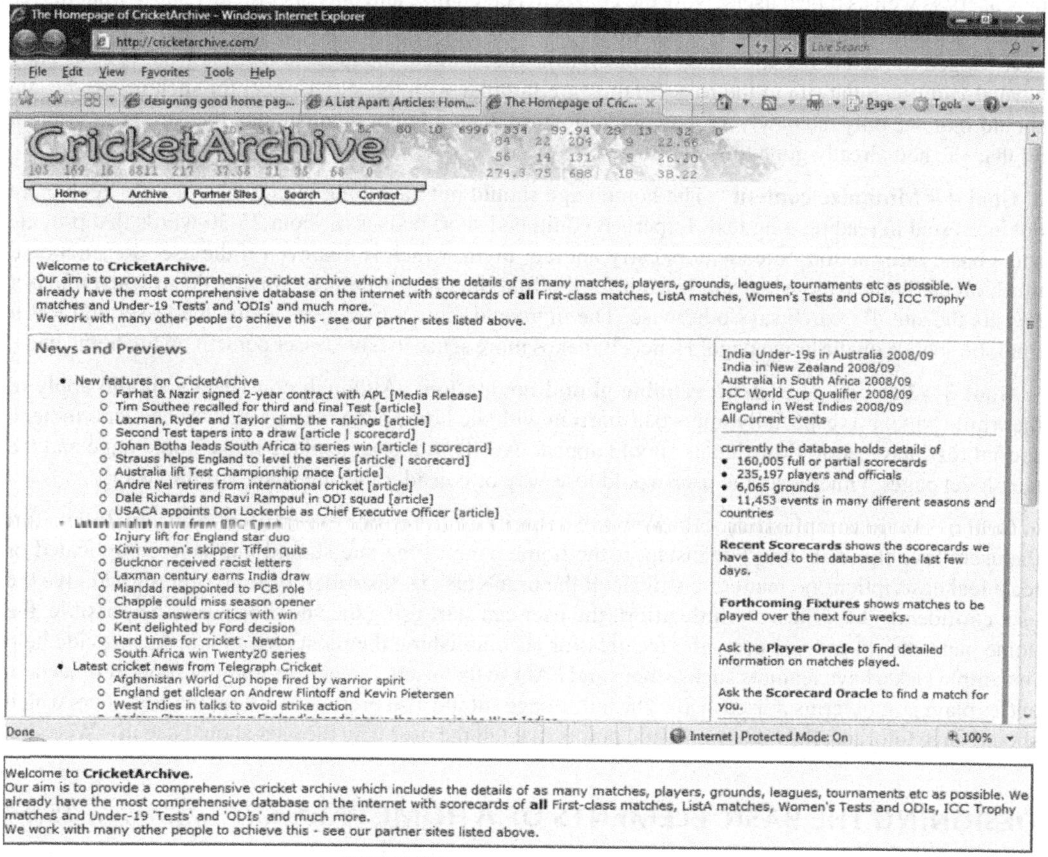

Fig. 15.27 *Example of welcome text*

2. Goal 2 – Do not get in the repeat visitor's way The second goal contradicts the first one, but only for users who are familiar with the site. If a user has already visited a site and is revisiting, chances are that she is not interested in the introduction to the site. It can be safely presumed that the user knows enough about the site as she is revisiting. However, just in case, a link can be provided for the user to still access the introductory information. But the user should be provided a more detailed and internal view of the site, since by logging on, the user would have identified herself.

Interestingly, a simple trick to accomplish both goals 1 and 2, a simple technique is to make a part of the home page changing or dynamic. If a user is visiting the site for the first time, the basic introductory information can be presented. However, if the site recognizes that this is a repeat visitor, the dynamic part should take over and display information having recognized the user as a repeat user. Not only should the user be recognized as a *general repeat visitor*, but also as a *specific repeat visitor*. We shall shortly discuss this point in more detail.

Some sites (e.g., Flickr) take an extreme, and show a completely different page depending on whether the user has logged in or otherwise. It may not work for all sites, though.

3. Goal 3 – Show what is new If goals 1 and 2 are met, it means that we have already taken care of new users as well as repeat users. Now the goal is to personalize and only specifically show what makes sense to a given user, not in the overall generic sense. Or the other way of saying it is that for users who have logged in (and hence identified themselves), what matters the most to them is what is new. They have already seen the site in the past. So they are familiar with the site. Hence, for such users, the site should indicate only the newly added content/feature. It should not mandate that the user goes through all that she had already gone through earlier.

4. Goal 4 – Minimize content The home page should not have long paragraphs of text. People are not interested in reading long text. Experts recommend short texts, say about 25-30 words that provide some basic information. Site creators carry another myth, which is that even if the user does not read much on the home page when she visits it for the first time they would eventually do so when the user revisits the site. Research says otherwise. The more and more a user visits a site, the lesser and lesser time she spends on the home page! Hence, it makes more sense to have lesser content on the home page.

5. Goal 5 – Provide consistent, reliable global navigation Although consistency should apply to the whole page, it is especially important starting with the home page. Things such as headers, footers, special text, navigation flow details should appear exactly at the same place in the home page and the next level pages. Otherwise, the user would lose way or consider the site shabby right away!

6. Goal 6 – Avoid complexities If a Web site helps its users become expert users with very little effort the users love the Web site. For instance, the home page of the site should not have complicated or technical descriptions no matter how difficult the user's task is. Instead, the home page should give the user confidence that with very little effort, the user can start using the site. For this to be possible, the home page should provide users the features for accomplishing the most common tasks, provide help for simple tasks, have features such as blog and FAQ so that users can get community support if needed, and explain jargon/terms if used at all. The home page should also provide a link for the beginners which should have tutorials, flow diagrams, and points that tell the user why the user should use this Web site.

DESIGNING THE BASIC ELEMENTS OF A HOME PAGE...................... 15.14

Tagline and blurb

Two important aspects of a home page are **tagline** and **blurb**. Let us understand them in brief.

1. Tagline The tagline is an additional line of text added next to the logo of a site. For example, the famous online video sharing site *YouTube* has the tagline *Broadcast yourself*.

Some interesting taglines are shown in Fig. 15.28.

Fig. 15.28 *Examples of taglines*

Several recommendations are given for coming up with a tagline, as listed below:

(a) Short and sweet A tagline should not be more than 6-8 words, according to many usability experts. It should be short, sharp, and memorable. It needs to be clear, informative, and attractive. Examples of such catchy and yet informative taglines are: *Finding books just got easier* (www.abebooks.com), Unmissable Weekly Articles for Bloggers (http://nortxeast.com), Copywriting tips for online marketing success (http://www.copyblogger.com), etc. Some of the confusing ones are And you are done (www.amazon.com – discontinued now), Me music. Its mine. (www.sonicnet.com).

(b) Mission statement A good mission statement about the site is a great help, since it can become the tagline, or the tagline can be carved out from it. But the mission statement needs to indicate vision and creativity also. For instance, just saying that the mission is to "become the largest online bookseller" is not very attractive at all!

(c) Identify the keywords Select a few keywords that describe the business or activity of the company or the Web site the best. Why should people be concerned about it? This should be reflected in these keywords. Try out different permutations and combinations of these keywords/phrases to ensure that the tagline is neither too fancy, nor does it convey something very vague.

(d) Clarity and information Good taglines are very clear and informative. Examples are shown in Fig. 15.29.

Fig. 15.29 *Good tagline example*

In other words, a tagline should not be vague.

(e) General/specific taglines Taglines should not be too generic in nature. Otherwise, the uniqueness in the tagline is lost. Just conveying some good, positive message is not enough for a tagline. It has to also distinguish between a general message and a very specific powerful targeted message.

(f) Tagline length A tagline should neither be too short or too long.

However, there are also a number of very successful Web sites that do not have a tagline at all! Experts suggest that even they would actually benefit by having a tagline. But they are now so well established that their success is anyway guaranteed, with or without a tagline. Some examples are shown in Fig. 15.30.

Fig. 15.30 *Some very successful Web sites that do not have a tagline*

2. Blurb **Blurb** is a short description of the site that the user can view prominently to understand the main purpose of the site. Text in a blurb should not scroll. An example of blurb along with the tagline is shown in Fig. 15.31.

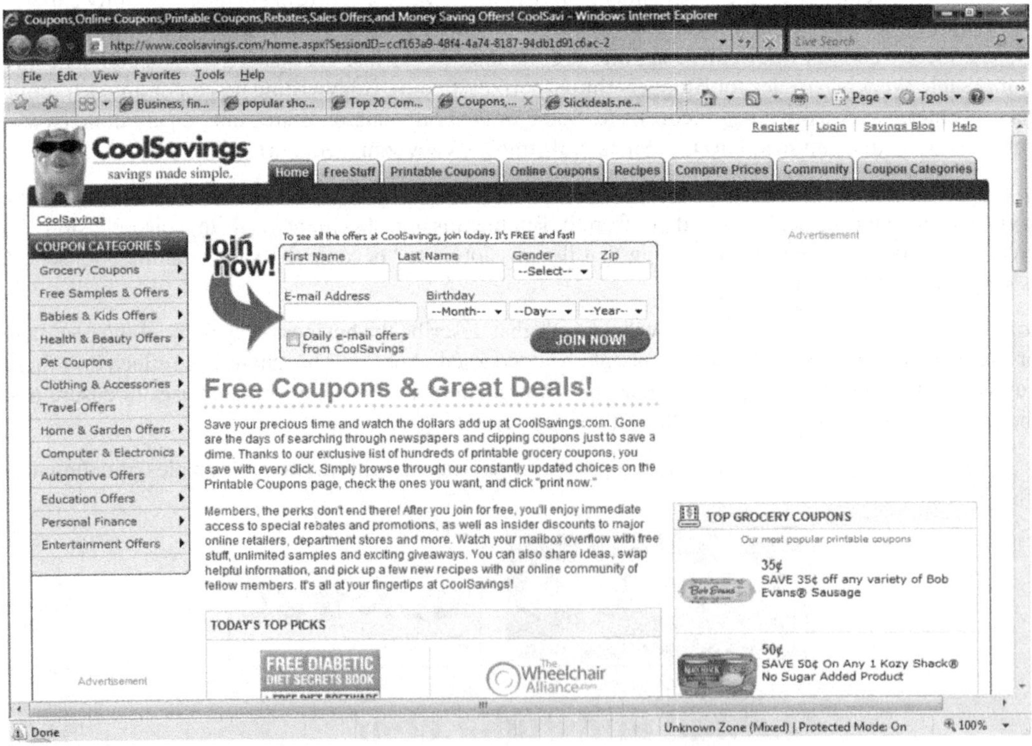

(Contd.)

Fig. 15.31 *Contd...*

Save your precious time and watch the dollars add up at CoolSavings.com. Gone are the days of searching through newspapers and clipping coupons just to save a dime. Thanks to our exclusive list of hundreds of printable grocery coupons, you save with every click. Simply browse through our constantly updated choices on the Printable Coupons page, check the ones you want, and click "print now."

Members, the perks don't end there! After you join for free, you'll enjoy immediate access to special rebates and promotions, as well as insider discounts to major online retailers, department stores and more. Watch your mailbox overflow with free stuff, unlimited samples and exciting giveaways. You can also share ideas, swap helpful information, and pick up a few new recipes with our online community of fellow members. It's all at your fingertips at CoolSavings!

The blurb

Fig. 15.31 *Tagline and blurb*

Like the tagline, even the blurb has started disappearing from several sites these days.

It is also recommended that the blurb should not be the mission statement of the organization or the site. It should convey the purpose of the site in crisp terms. If it is too long, users would not bother reading it. Hence, it should be short, understandable, and catchy.

(a) Page title The page title is one of the most ignored but very useful elements of a home page. It should state the company name, followed by a brief idea about the Web site. Remember that whatever you write here is going to be looked at by the search engines for indexing your Web site. When people search for information, it is the value of this title that is most likely to appear in the user's search results. Hence, it should be as meaningful as possible. Also, the *bookmark* feature in most Web browsers is going to store this text in the browser's list of bookmarks for a user. Hence, we should make the text as easy to remember and refer to the user as possible.

Many titles are written in all lowercase or all uppercase. Instead, they should be written in the proper Title Case (e.g., MNN | My News Network).

How long should a title be? The W3C recommends that it should not exceed 64 characters. Hence, we should attempt to restrict ourselves to this limit.

Some people like to add different characters to make their page titles look different. There is nothing wrong in this approach, as long as it is not overdone or not done with wrong characters. Some examples are shown in Fig. 15.32.

```
((( MyBank)))
: : : Your Shopping Site : : :
* * * Your Online Newspaper * * *
| XYZ Company Limited |
$ PQR Mutual Fund $
» TTT Insurance «
¤ Web Development Inc ¤
```

Fig. 15.32 *Adding some special characters to the page title*

Most search engines correctly display the special symbols such as copyright (©), trademark (™), and registered trademark (®). To add these to the page title, we can refer to Table 15.5.

Table 15.5 *Adding special symbols to the page title*

Symbol	*How to add it*
©	©
™	™
®	®

3. Main tasks The home page should list the most important tasks that the users are likely to be interested in. The number of such tasks should not be too small or too long. These tasks should have very clear headings and boundaries. Two more tasks should not overlap. Otherwise this will surely cause the users to get confused about the various options available, and which one to choose from them.

4. Search box The home page should have a search box that allows the user to search for information on the site. Also, we should make sure that the length of the search text box is sufficiently large for the user to see the complete search query to be visible (about 25-30 characters, as recommended by some experts).

5. Disappearing content On many sites, we see some content, like it; and decide to revisit the site. When we come back though, that content disappears and something else appears in the place. When we attempt to search for the disappeared content, we just cannot find it! Hence, links to such *disappearing home page content* should be provided to the users, in case they are interested in reading it again.

6. Glimpses of actual content Instead of just listing the contents available on the site, it is much better to show some glimpses of those contents. This gives the user a feel of how the actual contents look like, what is their format, etc. It also tells the user that the site is updated regularly (provided the contents are badly outdated, in which case, it would create a completely negative impression!). Instead of keeping the home page very abstract and general, such specific examples help entice the user to the actual content.

7. Make links meaningful When the user takes a look at the links on the home page, they should be very meaningful and clear. They should also be different from each other. Otherwise, the user would tend to get confused, thinking they all (or some of them) look similar. On a few sites, all links start with the company/site name, which makes it very difficult for the user to distinguish between them. Instead, if the purpose and catchiness of the link is conveyed in crisp terms (e.g., instead of saying *ABC Search* just *Search* is enough!), the user is more likely to grasp the contents of the links and that of the site very quickly.

8. Avoid overemphasis Many times, we think that overemphasizing content would make it catchy. For example, if we add a different layout or format to the content, we think it looks very different, and therefore, the user would not miss it. Quite contrary to this belief, as pointed out by Jacob Nielsen, a user thinks of such content as an advertisement (since it looks quite different from the rest of the content), and ignores it! Figure 15.33 shows such a Web page.

Fig. 15.33 *Overemphasizing some content*

We would think that the US population figure, displayed in big bold letters on the right side of the page would be seen by all the users immediately. In other words, this information simply cannot be missed out! However, Nielsen points out that according to a study, 86% of the users could not recognize this information at all! What was the reason? As mentioned, a large user population thought of this area as an advertisement. However, those users who did not think of this as an advertisement did actually look at the specified area (because it had catchy formatting) only to vaguely look at it and ignore it!

9. Home page size Not all users have displays that can work with fix-sized screens. Hence, it is always a good idea to design pages that have flexible size. In other words, we should allow the user to resize the window without distorting the contents on the screen. Otherwise the home page is not very usable.

10. Distinguish between visited and unvisited links Users like to know if they have already visited a link to avoid repetition only to discover it a while later. There is an easy trick to do so. We can use different colours for links that the user has already visited, and those that the user has not. This is a very simple yet useful feature that takes away a lot of user irritation.

11. Using graphics effectively Many sites show graphics (e.g., pictures and images) that have no direct relation with the content, or then they are abstract. Instead, it is recommended to use images that are very relevant and close to the topic. An example is showing the photograph of a very common person instead of a model in a story.

Key Terms

Application context • Blurb • 3-column layout • Footer • Golden ratio • Infrastructure context • Location context • Main content • Main navigation • Metaphor • Mission statement • Multilingual site • Physical context • Resolution • Sidebar • Storyboard • Tagline • Theme • Unicode • Whitespace • EXtensible Hyper Text Markup Language (XHTML)

SUMMARY

- Blueprint of a site is a high-level view of the overall structure and hierarchy of the site.
- Top level navigation allows us to decide how the top level menu of a Web site should look like and work (e.g., should we have links, buttons, etc., and where should they be displayed)?
- A good way to proceed with the design is to create a sample layout that shows the likely look-and-feel of a general Web page on the site.
- Metaphor is the thought behind the contents of the Web site.
- Theme provides the look-and-feel details of a Web site.
- Storyboard is the visualization of the design of a Web site.
- Screen resolution tells us how much of display space is available for a Web page, and how it would look to the user. An appropriate resolution helps the user to view the Web page in the desired size/layout.
- These days, most Web sites use what is called a 3-column layout, which divides the screen space into three vertical columns with each column containing appropriate contents.
- Readymade frameworks are available for creating Web sites now.
- Usability for handheld devices is a very important issue in the modern world full of mobile phones and other handheld devices.
- Since Web sites are created and accessed across geographical boundaries, it is important to create multilingual Web sites.
- HTML will give way to a new language called EXtensible Hyper Text Markup Language (XHTML) in the near future. This would impose a number of rules and restrictions on the loose syntax of HTML.
- The home page is the most important part of a Web site.
- There are several good home page design guidelines.
- The tagline is an additional line of text added next to the logo of a site.
- Blurb is a short description of the site that the user can view prominently to understand the main purpose of the site.

MULTIPLE-CHOICE QUESTIONS

1. What is the structure/format of the menus of a Web site at the entry point called?
   (a) Top-level navigation (b) Highest navigation
   (c) Entry point (d) First navigation
2. What is the concept of ideas behind the contents and visual elements of a site called?
   (a) Wizard (b) Metaphor (c) Guide (d) Art
3. We use this to specify the various links and other secondary content on a Web page.
   (a) Toolbar (b) Margin (c) Padding (d) Sidebar
4. Which screen resolution is most commonly used?
   (a) 980 × 760 (b) 1024 × 750 (c) 999 × 768 (d) 1024 × 768
5. How many colors at the most are recommended to be used on a single Web page?
   (a) 4 (b) 3 (c) 2 (d) 1

6. Which HTTP header is significant in conveying that the browser supports the specified languages?
   (a) Accept-Text (b) Accept-Language
   (c) Accept-Content (d) Accept-Following
7. What are the three important parts of an XHTML page?
   (a) Head, body, margin (b) Head, title, body
   (c) DOCTYPE, head, body (d) Table, header, footer
8. If our Web browser does not support CSS or transformation from HTML to XHTML, what DOCTYPE should we specify?
   (a) Permanent (b) Semi-permanent (c) Temporary (d) Transitional
9. What should be the first and foremost goal of a good home page design?
   (a) Answer the question, "what is this place?"
   (b) Answer the question, "why are we here?"
   (c) Answer the question, "where do we go from here?"
   (d) Answer the question, "what brought us here?"
10. What is a short and rightly worded description of a Web site called?
    (a) keyword (b) Tagline (c) Punchline (d) Buzzword

DETAILED QUESTIONS

1. What are the main areas covered by a home page?
2. What is a tagline? Give some good examples.
3. Explain blurb with some examples.
4. What are the main elements of a home page?
5. Outline good home page design guidelines.
6. What do we mean by blueprint of a site? How is it relevant?
7. Discuss the idea of golden ratio.
8. Write a note on metaphor, storyboard, and theme.
9. Explain how and why screen resolution is important from usability perspective.
10. What is a 3-column layout?

APPENDIX

WEB 2.0 ....

Introduction

Web 2.0 refers to second-generation of Web based communities and hosted services, such as social networking, sites, **wikis** (*Online information system that can be edited by any visitor) and* ***folksonomies*** *(user generated classification used to categorize and retrieve Web content)*—that facilitate collaboration and sharing between users.

Web 2.0 indicates improved form of the World Wide Web. Technologies such as **Weblogs (*Blogs*), social bookmarking, wikis, podcasts** (a digital media file or a series of such files, that is distributed over the Internet using syndication feeds for playback on portable media players and personal computers), **RSS feeds** (and other forms of many-to-many publishing), **social software, Web APIs, Web standards and online Web services** imply a significant change in Web usage.

Web 2.0 can also refer to one or more of the following:

1. It enables the communication between incapable information system and sources of content and functionality.
2. It facilitates generating and distributing Web content itself, characterized by open communication, decentralization of authority, and freedom to share and re-use.
3. It provides enhanced organization and categorization of content, emphasizing on deep linking (making a hyperlink that points to a specific page or image on another Website, instead of that Website's main or home page).

Key Principles and Characteristic of Web 2.0

Web 2.0 means more than design element like glossy buttons, large colorful fonts and "wet-floor" effect. Any Web 2.0 Web site may exhibits some basic common properties. The may include:

1. The Web as a platform—delivering (and allowing users to use) applications entirely through a browser.
2. Data—the driving force.
3. Architecture of participation—The system which facilitate user to add his contribution.
4. A rich, interactive, user-friendly interface base on AJAX.
5. Lightweight business models (Keeping it simple) enabled by content and service combination.
6. The end of the software release cycle ("the perpetual beta").
7. Software above the level of a single device.
8. Some kind of social-networking aspect.

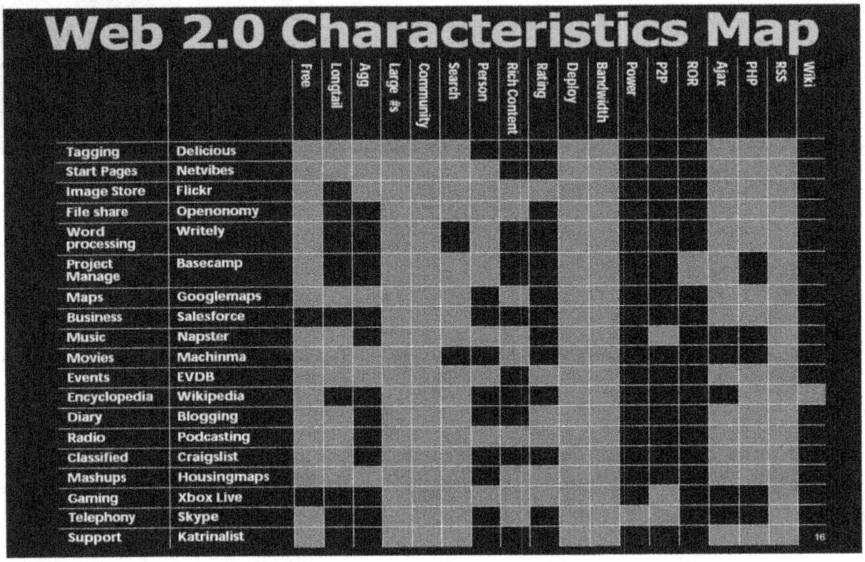

Technical Innovations Associated with Web 2.0

The following lists of technical innovations have set the foundation for Web 2.0:

1. Web-based applications and desktops:
   (a) Richer user-experience—AJAX, Web Office.
   (b) Several browser-based "operating systems" or online desktops, WebEx, meta.
2. Rich Internet applications with use of AJAX, Adobe Flash, Flex and OpenLaszlo to improve user experience
3. Server-side software
4. Client-side software
5. XML and RSS (Really Simple Syndication—also known as "Web syndication")
6. Specialized protocols (FOAF & XFN for social networking)
7. Web protocols (REST and SOAP)

In one way or the other "Web 2.0" is formed on principles demonstrated by success stories of Web 1.0 and interesting new applications.

Web 2.0 Core Principles

The Web as a Platform

The Web is considered as platform rather than as an information medium. Google pioneered this concept and began a native Web application delivering a "service at no cost" to the customers. Overture (Now Yahoo!) and Google also figured out how to enable ad placement on virtually any Web page. Similarly, eBay enables transactions between single individuals, acting as an automated intermediary. Other Web 2.0 success stories demonstrate this same behavior of making innovative use of data.

Collective Intelligence

An essential part of Web 2.0 is harnessing collective intelligence, turning the Web into a kind of global brain. Rather than collecting data one should use the data to one's own advantage, like Google page rank. It allowed users to rank the page when they use the search and this information is then fed back to get more relevant results. Companies like Nike are using people to get new design ideas through blogs. Some financial companies are using blogs to understand needs of people and are creating products like loans on the terms favorable to the users.

The Architecture of Participation

Web 2.0 companies set inclusive defaults for aggregating user data and building value as a side-effect of ordinary use of the application. The architecture of the Internet, and the World Wide Web, as well as of open source software projects like Linux, Apache, and Perl, is such that users build collective value as an automatic by-product. Each of these projects has a small core, well-defined extension mechanisms, and an approach that lets any well-behaved component be added by anyone.

Data Management

Every significant Internet application to date has been backed by a specialized database: Google's Web crawl, Yahoo!'s directory (and Web crawl), Amazon's database of products etc. Database management is a core competency of Web 2.0 companies, so much so that we have sometimes referred to these applications as "infoware" rather than merely software.

End of the Software Release Cycle—the Perpetual BETA

Operations must become a core competency. Software will cease to perform unless it is maintained on a daily basis. Users must be treated as co-developers, in a reflection of open source development practices (even if the software in question is unlikely to be released under an open source license.) The open source dictum, "release early and release often" in fact has morphed into an even more radical position, "the perpetual beta," in which the product is developed in the open, with new features slipstreamed in on a monthly, weekly or even daily basis.

Lightweight Programming Models

Support lightweight programming models that allow for loosely coupled systems. Simple Web services, like RSS and REST-based Web services, are syndicating data outwards. Design for "hackability". Web 2.0 will provide opportunities for companies to beat the competition by getting better at harnessing and integrating services provided by others.

Software above the Level of a Single Device

One other feature of Web 2.0 that deserves mention is the fact that it's no longer limited to the PC platform but has extended to devices like Hand held PC, mobiles, digital music and storage devices like iTunes and TiVo. These are not Web applications per se, but they leverage the power of the Web platform, making it a seamless, almost invisible part of their infrastructure.

Web 2.0 in Financial Services industry

More and more financial services institutions will use Web 2.0 concepts and technologies both internally and externally to make their services and applications richer and more compelling to users. The following could be some of the Web 2.0 uses in financial industry:

1. Improved Web interfaces that mimic the real-time responsiveness of desktop applications within a browser window.
2. Improved communication between people via social-networking technologies.
3. Improved communication between separate software applications.
4. Financial services applications like Social lending, in which borrowers and lenders come together without the involvement of a bank, could benefit from Web 2.0.
5. Information and knowledge gathered from people's blogs to identify target markets, create project teams and discover unvoiced conclusions.
6. Intuitive page building—user should see on the home page what she often visits.
7. Rather than hosting on single costly machines, software can be hosted on multiple redundant cost effective machines like in the case of Google and Yahoo.
8. Use Mashup technology to build a complex site rather that go for a big-bang solution.
9. Easier integration with help of Rich Internet applications (RIA) and Use technologies like SOA that complement the RIA.
10. Intellectual content development via Collective intelligence.
11. Use blogs to give executives an informal channel for employee and customer discussions.
12. RSS feeds to funnel news and data into system and other data subscribers also the subscriber can customize the information according to their own preferences.
13. Capture user's trail on the Web site to understand users behavior and needs from Web site and improve on them.
14. Extend the interface to mobile and other devices.

Glossary

1. **Web syndication** A form of syndication in which a section of a website is made available for other sites to use (RSS).
2. **Syndication** A group of individuals or organizations combined or making a joint effort to undertake some specific duty or carry out specific transactions or negotiations.
3. **Social bookmarking** A way for Internet users to store, classify, share and search Internet bookmarks.
4. **Blog (Web log)** A website where entries are written in chronological order and displayed in reverse chronological order.
5. **REST** REST is a simple interface that transmits domain-specific data over HTTP without an additional messaging layer such as SOAP or session tracking via HTTP cookies.
6. **RSS** A family of Web feed formats used to publish frequently updated content such as blog entries, news headlines or podcasts. An RSS document, which is called a "feed," "Web feed," or "channel," contains either a summary of content from an associated Web site or the full text.
7. **Social software** Softwares that enable people to rendezvous, connect or collaborate through computer-mediated communication (IM, Chat, Forums,Weblogs/Blogs, Wikis, Collaborative real time editor (Google Docs) and prediction Markets.

What is RSS?

RSS (Really simply syndication) is one of the formats used in publishing latest contents such as blogs, news headlines or podcasts on Internet Web sites.

RSS is

1. an easy way to distribute latest news
2. a lightweight XML format, and
3. used to improve traffic.

An RSS document is called **"feed"**, **"Web feed"** or **"channel"**. This document contains summary of the actual content. This document is in XML format and there are various links available in the document. When user clicks on a particular link, the corresponding Web page is displayed in the browser.

All the major Web sites such as Google News, BBC, CNN, and NDTV, provide the feature of RSS feeds. Interested users can subscribe to these feeds by using RSS reader so that they can receive updated content from such Web sites.

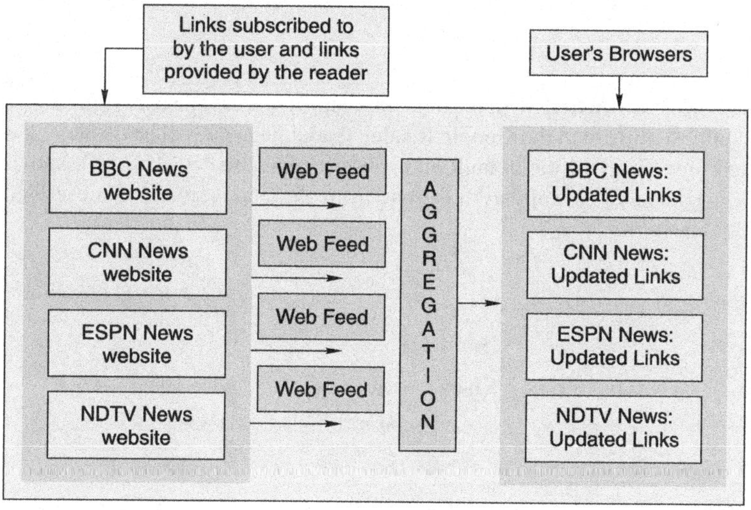

Web feed and RSS Aggregators

Web feed means providing the latest content to the subscribed users. Web feed is provided by Web sites. Web feed is also regularly updated summary content. A Web feed is a document which contains web links. A user has to subscribe to a particular Website's feed by using feed reader. There can be many Web feeds across various Web servers during the particular time period. The feed can be downloaded using the Web sites or the programs that syndicate from the feed. All the web feeds can be collected using **Aggregator** or **news readers**.

RSS feed format is based on XML and it is not easily understandable by humans. Hence, to interpret the RSS contents "news reader" or "aggregator" programs are used. A user needs to subscribe to an aggregator. For example, Google Reader is an aggregator provided by Google and Yahoo News is provided by Yahoo. Google Reader provides news from various top news sites such as BBC news, ESPN and Google news, etc. Apart from these, a user can subscribe to any other sites as well. The aggregator or reader checks continuously or after certain time interval, as defined by the user for new contents and downloads them from that site. Thus, the user can have all the updated links from various Web sites in one single window of the browser. Clearly, this is "pulling" of information by the end users.

Feeder programs can be Web-based (accessed as a Web Service) or client-based (desktop-based). If feeders download multimedia data, this kind of RSS data is called a **podcast**.

Web Syndication

Web syndication is a method/process where some part of the Website is made available to the other Websites to use. It is a process in which Web feeds are made available so that others can get recently added material on the Web site, such as news. Thus, Web syndication helps both the Web sites by providing the information and displaying that information. Web syndication helps in exchanging the information in automated and structured format and it reduces the time also.

RSS can be treated as a mini database which contains headlines and description about the latest updates on the Web site.

RSS Example

1. A real life example is shown here with the help of Google Reader. The user signs in to Google Reader. After successfully signing in to the Google Reader, the home page will be displayed, which will have all the updated links from all the default and subscribed Web sites. This will show the latest Web feeds that are updated and consolidation is done from all default sites and subscribed links with the help of Web syndication.

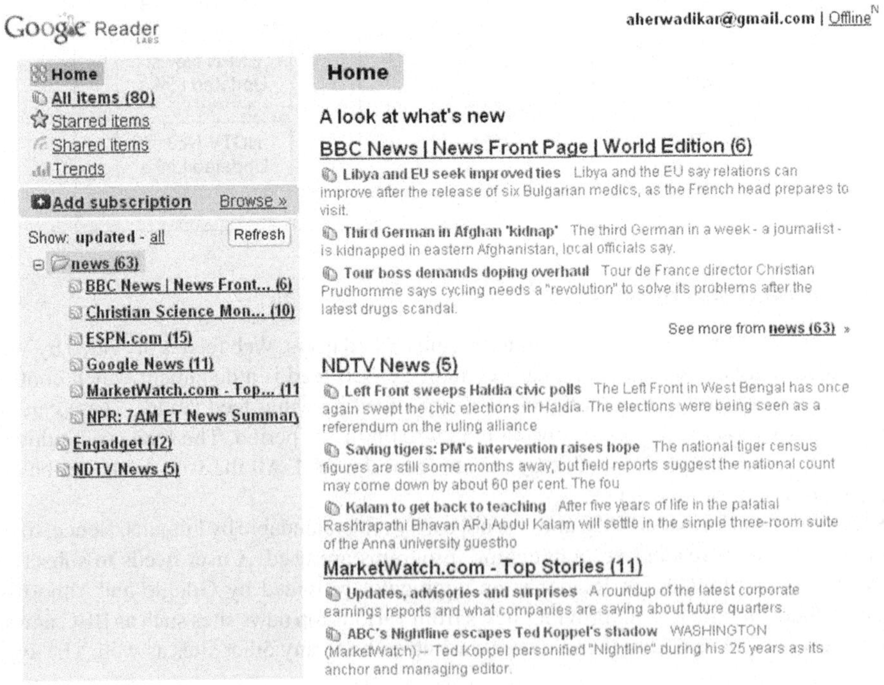

2. If the user clicks on any URL above, an appropriate screen will be displayed.

3. From here, the user can go to the actual contents.

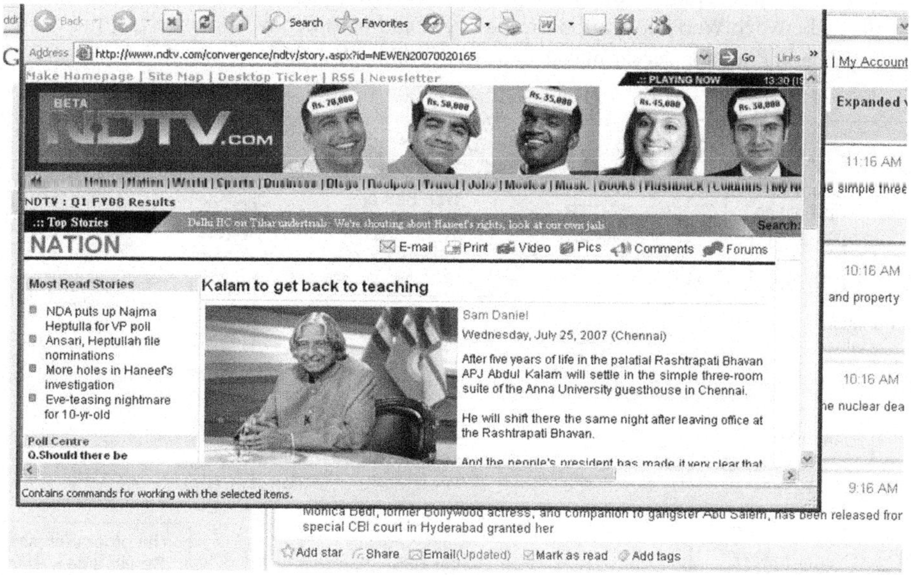

MASHUP

Mashup—Overview

Mashup is a Web application that integrates data from more than one source or Web sites. Contents used in mashup generally come from other sources or third party using public interfaces or APIs provided by that source. These interfaces/APIs are exposed in the form of Web Services.

In simple terms, a Web site that uses data, services and functionality from another Web site is called Mashup. However, simply linking of to another Web site through an HTML hyperlink can not be called Mashup.

There are various services provided by Web sites that generate different type of contents. Mashup means integrating services and contents from multiple Web sites. User can see this information on the screen but does not have the knowledge about the source of the particular information. Integration of the services and content in a smooth fashion happens in the background.

Usage of Mashup is increasing at extremely high rate. Majority of mashup are using map services such as those provided by Yahoo Maps and Google Maps. Although Mashup is being heavily used in map services, they are not limited to the map services only.

Mashup styles

There are two mashup styles: Server side mashup and Client side mashup.

Server-side mashup

In server-side mashup, the integration of services and contents happens at server side. Here, the server acts as a proxy between Web application on the client and on other Web sites. Here, the client makes requests to the server and the server makes calls to the other Web site.

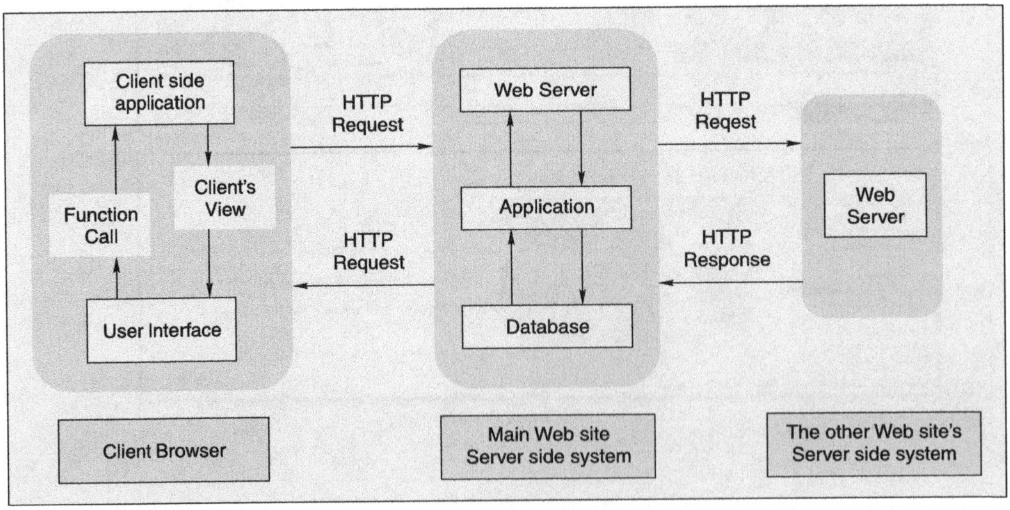

The above diagram can be explained as follows:

1. The client makes a request to server of its Web site. The request could be an AJaX request in the form of an XmlHttpRequest object.
2. The request is received by the Web component (such as a Java servlet). The request is processed by a Java class, which called a **proxy class**.
3. The proxy class opens the connection to the other web site that provides the information.
4. The mashup site receives the request and processes and returns response to the proxy class.
5. The proxy class receives the response and converts into proper data format.
6. The Web component delivers the data to the client and client receives the response.
7. Finally, the client's page is updated.

The benefits of this approach are as follows:

1. Proxy is used as buffer between the client and the other Web site.
2. In this style, only required data can be sent to the client and in small chunks.
3. Transformation of data and manipulation of data is possible before sending it to the client.
4. Security can be handled in a more efficient manner.

It suffers from the following possible issues:

1. Using server side mashup can result into significant delay since the request goes to Web sever of the main Web site and then to the other Web site. The same happens with the response also.
2. The proper security measure should be in place to protect server side proxy from unauthorized use.

Client-side mashup

In client-side mashup, the services and the content are integrated at client side. Here, the client mashup directly interacts with other Web site's data.

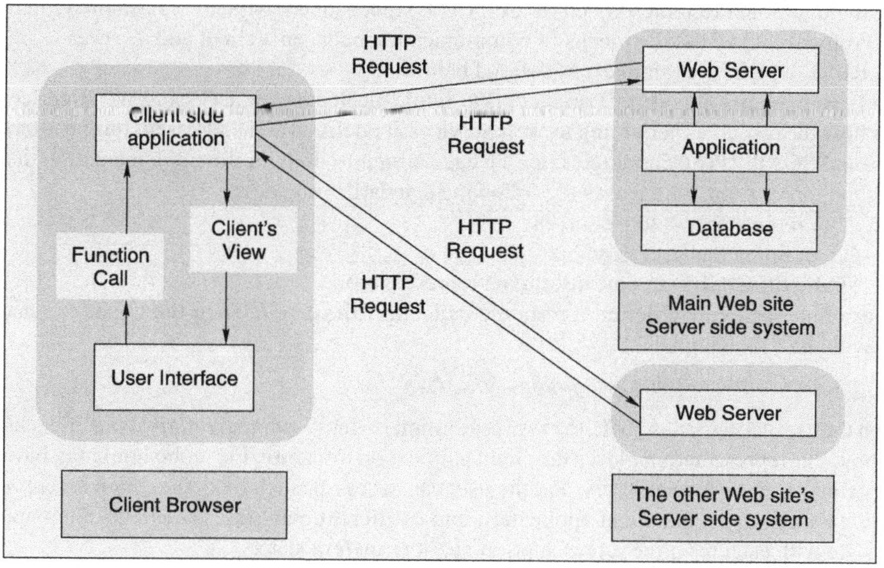

The above diagram can be explained as follows:

1. Browser makes the request for the Web page on its Web site.
2. In response to the request made by the client, the Web server of the main Web site returns some data.
3. This data is encoded by the client and the address of the other Web site is retrieved.
4. The connection to the other Web site is made and required data is retrieved.
5. Finally, client's view is refreshed.

Following are the advantages of this approach:

1. No server side Web component is required.
2. Performance wise, client side mashup is better; since response and request go directly from browser to the mashup server and back.
3. It also reduces the load of the server since the server side proxy is not responsible for processing of the request and response.

Following are the issues in this approach:

1. No buffer is provided.
2. Sometimes, other Web site return large data and it is difficult to handle this much of data at the client side.
3. No transformation of the data and data manipulation happens before the data is sent to the client.
4. Handling security requirements are difficult at the client.

REST PROTOCOL..

What is REST?

Today, Web Services can be written in two ways:

1. Using the traditional Remote Procedure Call (RPC) mechanism, which uses Simple Object Access Protocol (SOAP) as the means of communication between a client and a server.
2. Using REST, which is far simpler; as defined below.

REST (Representation State Transfer) is a simple mechanism of accessing Web Services. REST describes how the resources pertaining to Web Services are defined and addressed. It is an alternative to the traditional SOAP/RPC technologies. REST has nothing to do with the implementation details and which technology is used. REST uses the following standards/protocols:

1. HTTP—For remote access to resources
2. URL—For defining end access points
3. XML/HTML/JPEG/GIF—As means of data representation

For example, i-flex may define a resource called as "flexcube". Then the client can access this resource with the following URL:

http://www.iflexsoltions.com/products/flexcube

When the user accesses this URL, the **representation** of this resource is returned (i.e., flexcube.html). At this point, this representation places the client application in a **state**. Flexcube.html may have several other hyperlinks (i.e., *representations*) and the user can access all such links (i.e., *representations*). The new representation places the client application into a different/new state. Thus, the client application changes state with each resource representation i.e., it **transfers** state.

Combining these keywords (*representation*, *state*, and *transfer*), we have the acronym REST.

REST Features

1. **Statelessness** The basic highlight of the REST philosophy is the **statelessness** approach. To overcome the drawbacks of the stateless HTTP protocol, we know that developers need to provide for session management in their applications. For instance, they need to use session objects, cookies, URL rewriting, etc. However, REST goes back to the traditional stateless approach. This means that each request from the client to the server goes with all the details to understand the request and cannot depend on the any stored on past information.
   Therefore, it should be clear that the application interacts with the resource just by knowing two things: (i) the identifier of the resource, and (ii) the action required. Other things such as the past information of that client or intermediaries (i.e., the session state information) are not needed. Application designers need to keep this in consideration.
2. **Support for only HTTP methods** How can a Web Services client access a Web Service? If it is an RPC/SOAP kind of Web Service, the client can call methods on the objects exposed as Web Services [e.g., *account.transfer (100);*]. In contrast, with REST, we can only use HTTP-based methods such as GET, POST, DELETE, etc.
   In an RPC, an application is made up of remotely accessible objects and each object has different methods which can be invoked as and when required. The client needs to be aware of identity of the object before trying to accesses these methods, so that client can locate the objects in the first place. In REST, the client can interact with the resources and navigate using hyperlinks without the knowledge of the resources.

RESTful Web Service Example

Web Services based on the REST approach are called as **RESTful Web Services**.

Let us look at an example of creating Web Services from the REST perspective.

ABC Publications has deployed some Web Services to enable its customer to do the following:

1. Get the list of available books
2. Get detailed information about a book
3. Submit a purchase order (PO)

Get the list of books

The appropriate Web Service would make available resource to the book list resource. For example client would use this URL to get the book list:

http://www.abcpublications.com/books

If the client submits this URL, the XML document containing a list of all the books would be returned the client. The implementation of this Web Service is completely transparent to the client and ABC Publication Co. can modify the underlying implementation of this resource without impacting clients.

```
<?xml version="1.0"?>
<Books>
  <Book Id="00123" xlink:href=http://www.abcpublications.com/books/00123"></Book>
  <Book Id="00124" xlink:href=http://www.abcpublications.com/books/00124"></Book>
  <Book Id="00125" xlink:href=http://www.abcpublications.com/books/00125"></Book>
</Books>
```

As we can see, every book entry has a link to get the detailed information about that book. This is a key feature of REST.

Get detailed information about the book

The Web Service makes available a URL for each book. For example, to view the details of the book *00123*, this would the URL:

http://www.abcpublications.com/book/00123

The following would be the document received by the client after submitting the above request.

```
<?xml version="1.0"?>
<Book>
   <Book-Id >00123</Book-Id>
   <Name>Information Technology></Name>
   <Description> This book is useful to understand the concepts of IT</Description>
   <Details xlink:href:=http://www.abcpublication.com/books/00123/details"></Details>
   <Price>200.00</price>
</Book>
```

Again, there is a link to see the detailed description about the book. Each response document allows the client to drill down to get more detailed information.

Submit a purchase order

In this situation, Web services makes available to submit the purchase order to the customer. The client creates the PO in required format let's say XML and submit that XML (using HTTP POST method).

The PO service would take that XML and do the necessary processing and additionally it will provide URL to the client so that client and edit that PO in the future.

```
<?xml version="1.0"?>
<Purchase_Order>
   <Book-Id >00123</Book-Id>
   <Customer-Id>ABC</Customer-Id>
   <Order-Ref>2007-08-30-A567</Order-Ref>
</Purchase_Order>
```

REST VS SOAP

SOAP and *REST* are two main techniques to work with Web Services. In this article, we will compare their pros and cons. But before that, let us quickly recap the basic concepts in Web Services.

A Web Service is a software service provided by a server (implemented as a program) and can be used by a client. In other words, Web Services allow different providers and consumers to speak with each other over a network; irrespective of the technologies, operating systems, etc. Earlier, ***Remote Procedure Call (RPC)*** techniques were in use and technologies such as DCOM, RMI, CORBA, or plain RPC were used for this purpose. There are some important buzzwords in web services:

1. **WSDL (Web Service Description Language)** An XML document which provides the description about the Web Service.
2. **UDDI (Universal Discovery Description and Integration)** The registry of the Web Services and user/client can take the help of this to find out different Web Services.
3. **SOAP and REST** We shall examine these now.

What is SOAP?

SOAP stands for ***Simple Object Access Protocol***. SOAP uses XML format to exchange data. It can also be considered as a free-form message format based on XML standards. An XML message encapsulated inside a SOAP envelope (which contains header and footer to identify each message uniquely) travels on top of the HTTP protocol. Usage of XML makes SOAP platform and language independent.

To access any resource using SOAP, the client needs to call that particular service. For example, when a client wants to check the balance in her bank account, the client would send a SOAP request to and receive a SOAP response from the Web Service.

SOAPRequent

```
<Envelope>
  <GetBalanceRequest>
        <AcctNo>00712343902</AcctNo>
  </GetBalanceRequest>
</Envelope>
```

SOAP Response

```
<Envelope>
  <GetBalanceRequest>
        <AcctNo>00712343902</AcctNo>
  </GetBalanceRequest>
</Envelope>
```

What is REST?

REST stands for ***Representational State transfer***. It is an architecture used for describing the Internet and to access it as well. It is much simpler way than traditional RPC/SOAP to access the Web Services. It does not use any new standard for accessing Web Services. It relies on the traditional HTTP, URL, HTML, XML, and GIF, etc. It is light weight and reduces the burden from the server. It is stateless in nature and needs to make use of information pieces such as cookies, URL rewriting, etc. Naturally, it does not maintain the session state automatically.

According to the REST style, each resource can be identified by a unique URI (Universal Resource Identification) and it can be accessed by the Web Service. Standard HTTP interface is used in the form of methods such as GET, POST, PUT, and DELETE. According to the principle of REST, each resource should be classified based on its usage. Also a good URI should be assigned to that resource.

The following samples should help us understand the differences between SOAP and REST:

RESTful Example: Online Book Purchase

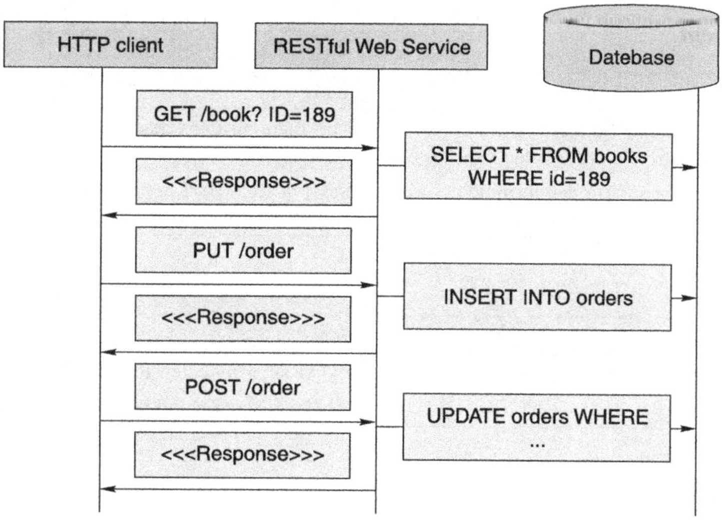

SOAP Example: Online Book Purchase

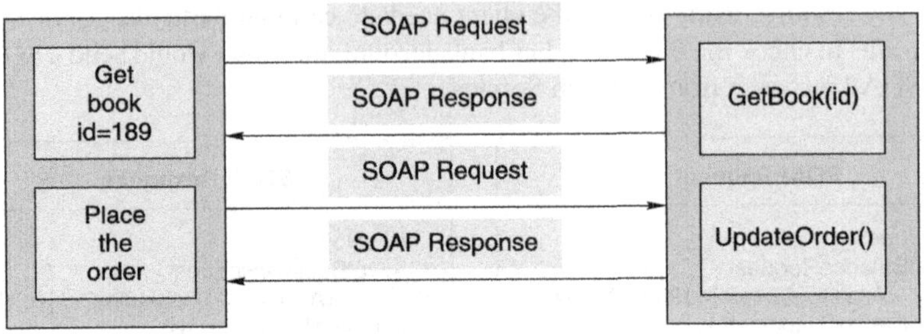

Technology Comparison

REST	*SOAP*
Uses the existing infrastructure such as HTTP, URL and XML/HTML,GIF, etc.	Uses the existing infrastructure and additionally SOAP standards.
A unique URL identifies one resource.	Generic interfaces are used to group and identify many resources together.
Focus is on performance.	Focus is on integration of distributed applications.

Protocol Comparison

REST	*SOAP*
Request is URI and the result is XML.	Request is SOAP and response is also SOAP.
HTTP is application layer protocol.	HTTP is more like a transport protocol.
Synchronous in nature.	Supports both synchronous and asynchronous operations.

State Management

REST	*SOAP*
Stateless—each request to the server must contain all the necessary information to process the request.	May maintain conversion state across multiple message exchanges.
Cookies, URL rewriting and Hidden form fields have to be explicitly used for session management.	Session Headers can be added to the SOAP envelope itself to maintain session.

Security

REST	*SOAP*
Security is handled by HTTP/HTTPS.	SOAP security extensions are defined by WS-Security.
SSL 1.0 is used.	XML encryption and XML Signature can be used.

Design

REST	*SOAP*
Identify the resources that can be exposed as services.	Define Services and operations into WSDL document.
Define URL address to the resources.	Define data model for the messages exchanged by the service.
Distinguish the resource based on GET, PUT, POST and DELETE methods.	Choose appropriate transport protocol, security and transactional polices.
Implement and deploy on Web server	Implement and deploy on Web Services container.

XHTML—THE NEW HTML STANDARD

Introduction

XHTML stands for ***EXtensible HyperText Markup Language***. It is a combination of HTML and XML. It is expected to replace HTML slowly but surely. Syntax-wise it is Identical to HTML but addresses the poor coding standards of HTML. XHTML mandates strict adherence to coding rules. XHTML is a W3C recommendation and all the new browsers support XHTML.

There are three main parts in an XHTML documents:

1. *DOCTYPE*
2. *head*
3. *body*

An XHTML example is shown below.

```
<!DOCTYPE html PUBLIC "-//W3C//DTD XHTML 1.0 Strict//EN"
                       "http://www.w3.org/TR/xhtml1/DTD/xhtml1-strict.dtd">
<html xmlns="http://www.w3.org/1999/xhtml">
   <head>
      <title> Sample XHTML</title>
   </head>
   <body>
      <p> This is a sample XHTML file. </p>
   </body>
</html>
```

XHTML Document Types

There are three Document Type Definition (DTD) *validation types*, which describe the allowed syntax and grammar in an XHTML document.

1. Strict

```
<!DOCTYPE html
PUBLIC "-//W3C//DTD XHTML 1.0 Strict//EN"
"http://www.w3.org/TR/xhtml1/DTD/xhtml1-strict.dtd">
```

The XHTML Strict document type separates the HTML tags and their presentation-related specifications by using Cascading Style Sheet (CSS). For example, the font type and size for a text tag would be specified in a separate CSS file.

2. Transitional

```
<!DOCTYPE html
PUBLIC "-//W3C//DTD XHTML 1.0 Transitional//EN"
"http://www.w3.org/TR/xhtml1/DTD/xhtml1-transitional.dtd">
```

If we are using older version of browsers that do not recognize CSS or in case of transformation from HTML to XHTML where presentation part is included in HTML then you can give preference to Transitional DOCTYPE.

3. Frameset

```
<!DOCTYPE html
PUBLIC "-//W3C//DTD XHTML 1.0 Frameset//EN"
"http://www.w3.org/TR/xhtml1/DTD/xhtml1-frameset.dtd">
```

This is simply XHTML 1.0 transitional with added elements to support HTML frame-related tags, namely <frameset>, <frame>, and <noframes>.

Benefits of XHTML

Syntax Checking

There are so many Web pages containing *bad* HTML. The main reason behind this is that the HTML language rules are not implemented strictly by the Web browsers. Following is an example of *bad* HTML, but this page will surely work well in all kinds of browsers and will produce the specified output.

```
<html>
   <head>
      <title>HTML Sample</title>
   <body>
      <h1>HTML Sample
      <p> Hello
      <br>
      <h2> How are you?
   </body>
```

The strictness of XHTML is useful in today's world where there are so many channels in use such as browsers, mobile phones, PDAs, etc.

Extensibility

XML documents are required to be well-formed (elements nesting properly). Under HTML, the addition of a new group of elements requires alteration of the entire DTD which leads to wait for next HTML version. In an XML-based DTD, the new set of elements has to be internally consistent and well-formed which can be added to an existing DTD. This greatly eases the development and integration of new collections of elements.

Portability

By being strict about well-formed tags, XHTML requires less processing power and less complicated algorithms to render. This means that XHTML can be displayed by devices with less processing power, such as mobile phones.

Major Differences Between HTML and XHTML

1. Elements must be in lowercase in XHTML (optional in HTML)

Invalid Syntax:

```
<BODY>
<p> Invalid Syntax </p>
</BODY>
```

Valid Syntax:

```
<body>
<p> Valid Syntax</p>
</body>
```

2. Elements must be paired with a closing tag in XHTML (optional in HTML)

Invalid Syntax:

```
<br>
<hr>
<img src="pic1.jpg>
```

Valid Syntax:

```
<br />
<hr />
<img src="pic1.jpg />
```

3. Elements must be properly nested in XHTML (optional in HTML)

In HTML, element's closure sequence can be improper, like this:

```
<b><i>Sample Code</b></i>
```

In XHTML, element's closure sequence should be proper, like this:

```
<b><i> Sample Code </i></b>
```

4. Structure must be separated from content

For example, the <p> tag is a content tag (paragraph) so we cannot include a table inside it for example, because a table is a format construct. We can, however, put the <p> tag inside <td> </td> tags with no problem because the content goes in the construct, not the other way around.

5. XHTML documents must have one root element

All XHTML elements must be nested within the <html> root element. Nested elements can have sub elements correctly nested in parent element.

```
<html>
<head> ... </head>
<body> ... </body>
</html>
```

W3C Markup Validation Service

The Markup Validator is a free service by W3C that helps check the validity of Web documents, hosted at the URL ***http://validator.w3.org/#validate_by_input***. Examples below show a valid and invalid XHTML document.

Valid XHTML

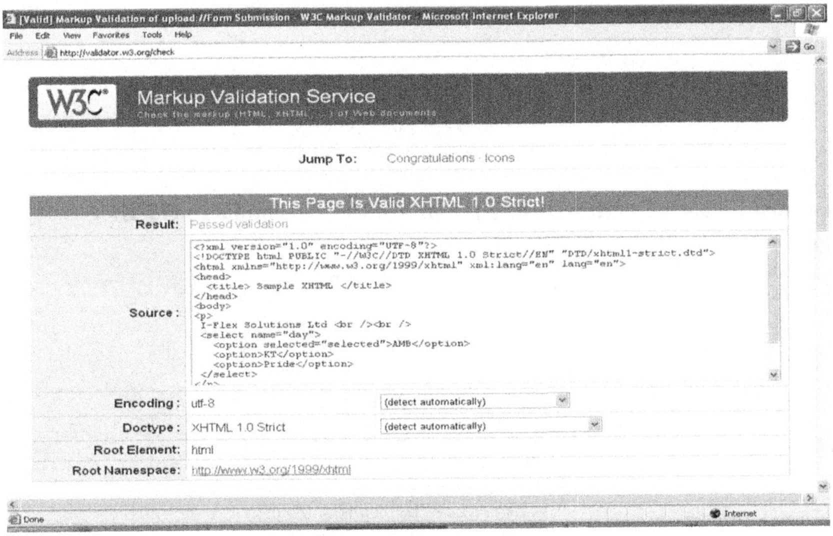

Invalid XHTML (which is Valid HTML)

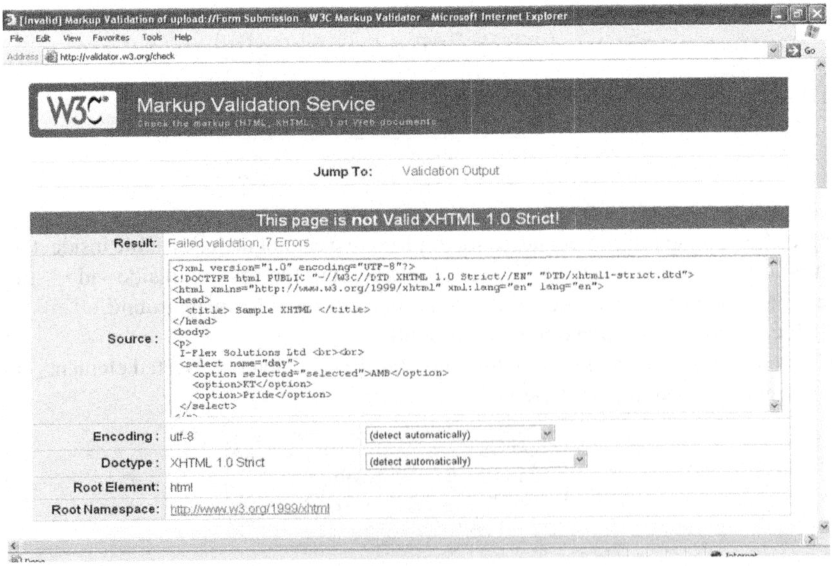

INDEX

Made in the USA
Monee, IL
05 November 2026

67815689R00334